DATE DUE

			PRINTED IN U.S.A.

Children's
Literature
Review

Guide to Gale Literary Criticism Series

When you need to review criticism of literary works, these are the Gale series to use:

If the author's death date is:	You should turn to:
After Dec. 31, 1959 (or author is still living)	**CONTEMPORARY LITERARY CRITICISM** for example: Jorge Luis Borges, Anthony Burgess, William Faulkner, Mary Gordon, Ernest Hemingway, Iris Murdoch
1900 through 1959	**TWENTIETH-CENTURY LITERARY CRITICISM** for example: Willa Cather, F. Scott Fitzgerald, Henry James, Mark Twain, Virginia Woolf
1800 through 1899	**NINETEENTH-CENTURY LITERATURE CRITICISM** for example: Fyodor Dostoevsky, Nathaniel Hawthorne, George Sand, William Wordsworth
1400 through 1799	**LITERATURE CRITICISM FROM 1400 TO 1800** (excluding Shakespeare) for example: Anne Bradstreet, Daniel Defoe, Alexander Pope, François Rabelais, Jonathan Swift, Phillis Wheatley
	SHAKESPEAREAN CRITICISM Shakespeare's plays and poetry
Antiquity through 1399	**CLASSICAL AND MEDIEVAL LITERATURE CRITICISM** for example: Dante, Homer, Plato, Sophocles, Vergil, the Beowulf Poet

Gale also publishes related criticism series:

CHILDREN'S LITERATURE REVIEW

This series covers authors of all eras who have written for the preschool through high school audience.

SHORT STORY CRITICISM

This series covers the major short fiction writers of all nationalities and periods of literary history.

POETRY CRITICISM

This series covers poets of all nationalities and periods of literary history.

DRAMA CRITICISM

This series covers playwrights of all nationalities and periods of literary history.

BLACK LITERATURE CRITICISM

This three-volume series presents criticism of works by major black writers of the past two hundred years.

volume 28

Children's Literature Review

Excerpts from Reviews,
Criticism, and Commentary
on Books for Children
and Young People

Gerard J. Senick
Editor

Sharon R. Gunton
Associate Editor

 **Gale Research Inc.** • *DETROIT* • *WASHINGTON, D.C.* • *LONDON*

STAFF

Gerard J. Senick, *Editor*

Sharon R. Gunton, *Associate Editor*

Jeanne A. Gough, *Permissions & Production Manager*
Linda M. Pugliese, *Production Supervisor*
Paul Lewon, Maureen A. Puhl, Camille Robinson, Jennifer VanSickle, *Editorial Associates*
Donna Craft, Rosita D'Souza, Sheila Walencewicz, *Editorial Assistants*

Sandra C. Davis, *Permissions Supervisor (Text)*
Maria Franklin, Josephine M. Keene, Michele M. Lonoconus, Denise M. Singleton,
Kimberly F. Smilay, *Permissions Associates*
Brandy Johnson, Shelly Rakcozy, Shalice Shah, *Permissions Assistants*

Margaret A. Chamberlain, *Permissions Supervisor (Pictures)*
Pamela A. Hayes, *Permissions Associate*
Amy Lynn Emrich, Karla Kulkis, Nancy Rattenbury, Keith Reed, *Permissions Assistants*

Victoria B. Cariappa, *Research Manager*
Maureen Richards, *Research Supervisor*
Mary Beth McElmeel, Tamara C. Nott, *Editorial Associates*
Andrea B. Ghorai, Daniel J. Jankowski, Julie K. Kazmarin, Robert S. Lazich,
Julie A. Synkonis, *Editorial Assistants*

Mary Beth Trimper, *Production Director*
Mary Winterhalter, *Production Assistant*

Cynthia Baldwin, *Art Director*
Arthur Chartow, *Cover Design*
Nicholas Jakubiak, C. J. Jonik, Yolanda Y. Latham, *Keyliners*

Library of Congress Catalog Card Number 76-643301
ISBN 0-8103-5701-1
ISSN 0362-4145

Printed in the United States of America

Published simultaneously in the United Kingdom
by Gale Research International Limited
(An affiliated company of Gale Research Inc.)

10 9 8 7 6 5 4 3 2 1

Contents

Preface

Children's literature has evolved into both a respected branch of creative writing and a successful industry. Currently, books for young readers are considered the most popular segment of publishing, while criticism of juvenile literature is instrumental in recording the literary or artistic development of the creators of children's books as well as the trends and controversies that result from changing values or attitudes about young people and their literature. Designed to provide a permanent, accessible record of this ongoing scholarship, *Children's Literature Review* (*CLR*) presents parents, teachers, and librarians—those responsible for bringing children and books together—with the opportunity to make informed choices when selecting reading materials for the young. In addition, *CLR* provides researchers of children's literature with easy access to a wide variety of critical information from English-language sources in the field. Users will find balanced overviews of the careers of the authors and illustrators of the books that children and young adults are reading; these entries, which contain excerpts from published criticism in books and periodicals, assist users by sparking ideas for papers and assignments and suggesting supplementary and classroom reading. Ann L. Kalkhoff, president and editor of *Children's Book Review Service Inc.*, writes that "*CLR* has filled a gap in the field of children's books, and it is one series that will never lose its validity or importance."

Scope of the Series

Each volume of *CLR* profiles the careers of a selection of authors and illustrators of books for children from preschool through high school. Author lists in each volume reflect these elements:

- an international scope.

- approximately fifteen authors of all eras.

- a variety of genres covered by children's literature: picture books, fiction, nonfiction, poetry, folklore, and drama.

Although earlier volumes of *CLR* emphasized critical material published after 1960, successive volumes have expanded their coverage to encompass important criticism written before 1960. Since many of the authors included in *CLR* are living and continue to write, their entries are updated periodically. Future volumes will supplement the entries of selected authors covered in earlier volumes as well as include criticism on the works of authors new to the series.

Organization of This Book

An author section consists of the following elements: author heading, author portrait, author introduction, excerpts of criticism (each followed by a bibliographical citation), and illustrations, when available.

- The **author heading** consists of the author's name followed by birth and death dates. The portion of the name outside the parentheses denotes the form under which the author is most frequently published. If the majority of the author's works for children were written under a pseudonym, the pseudonym will be listed in the author heading and the real name given on the first line of the author introduction. Also located at the beginning of the introduction are any other pseudonyms used by the author in writing for children and any name variations, including transliterated forms for authors whose languages use nonroman alphabets. Uncertainty as to a birth or death date is indicated by question marks.

- An **author portrait** is included when available.

- The **author introduction** contains information designed to introduce an author to *CLR* users by presenting an overview of the author's themes and styles, occasional biographical facts that relate to the author's literary career or critical responses to the author's works, and information about major awards and prizes the author has received. Introductions also list a group of representative titles for which the author or illustrator being profiled is best known; this section, which begins with the words "major works include," follows the genre line of the introduction. Where applicable, introductions conclude with references to additional entries in biographical and critical reference series published by Gale Research Inc. These sources include past volumes of *CLR* as well as *Authors & Artists for Young Adults, Classical and Medieval Literature Criticism, Contempo-*

rary Authors, Contemporary Authors Autobiography Series, Contemporary Authors Bibliographical Series, Contemporary Literary Criticism, Dictionary of Literary Biography, Drama Criticism, Nineteenth-Century Literature Criticism, Poetry Criticism, Short Story Criticism, Something about the Author, Something about the Author Autobiography Series, Twentieth-Century Literary Criticism, and *Yesterday's Authors of Books for Children.*

- **Criticism** is located in three sections: **author's commentary** (when available), **general commentary** (when available), and **title commentary** (in which commentary on specific titles appears). Centered headings introduce each section, in which criticism is arranged chronologically. Titles by authors being profiled are highlighted in boldface type within the text for easier access by readers.

The **author's commentary** presents background material written by the author or by an interviewer. This commentary may cover a specific work or several works. Author's commentary on more than one work appears after the author introduction, while commentary on an individual book follows the title entry heading.

The **general commentary** consists of critical excerpts that consider more than one work by the author or illustrator being profiled. General commentary is preceded by the critic's name in boldface type or, in the case of unsigned criticism, by the title of the journal. Occasionally, *CLR* features entries that emphasize general criticism on the overall career of an author or illustrator. When appropriate, a selection of reviews is included to supplement the general commentary.

The **title commentary** begins with title entry headings, which precede the criticism on a title and cite publication information on the work being reviewed. Title headings list the title of the work as it appeared in its first English-language edition. The first English-language publication date of each work is listed in parentheses following the title. Differing U.S. and British titles follow the publication date within the parentheses.

Entries in each title commentary section consist of critical excerpts on the author's individual works, arranged chronologically by publication date. The entries generally contain two to six reviews per title, depending on the stature of the book and the amount of criticism it has generated. The editors select titles that reflect the entire scope of the author's literary contribution, covering each genre and subject. An effort is made to reprint criticism that represents the full range of each title's reception—from the year of its initial publication to current assessments. Thus, the reader is provided with a record of the author's critical history. Publication information (such as publisher names and book prices) and parenthetical numerical references (such as footnotes or page and line references to specific editions of works) have been deleted at the editor's discretion to provide smoother reading of the text.

- Selected excerpts are preceded by **explanatory notes,** which provide information on the critic or work of criticism to enhance the reader's understanding of the excerpt.

- A complete **bibliographical citation** designed to facilitate the location of the original book or article follows each piece of criticism.

- Numerous **illustrations** are featured in *CLR.* For entries on illustrators, an effort has been made to include illustrations that reflect the characteristics discussed in the criticism. Entries on major authors who do not illustrate their own works may also include photographs and other illustrative material pertinent to the authors' careers.

Special Features

Entries on authors who are also illustrators will occasionally feature commentary on selected works illustrated but not written by the author being profiled. These works are strongly associated with the illustrator and have received critical acclaim for their art. By including critical comment on works of this type, the editors wish to provide a more complete representation of the author's total career. Criticism on these works has been chosen to stress artistic, rather than literary, contributions. Title entry headings for works illustrated by the author being profiled are arranged chronologically within the entry by date of publication and include notes identifying the author of the illustrated work. In order to provide easier access for users, all titles illustrated by the subject of the entry will be boldfaced.

CLR also includes entries on prominent illustrators who have contributed to the field of children's literature. These entries are designed to represent the development of the illustrator as an artist rather than as a literary stylist. The illustrator's section is organized like that of an author, with two exceptions: the introduction presents an overview of the illustrator's styles and techniques rather than outlining his or her literary background, and the commentary written by the illustrator on his or her works is called "illustrator's commentary" rather than "author's commentary." Title entry headings are followed by explanatory notes identifying the author of the illustrated work. All titles of books containing illustrations by the artist being profiled as well as individual illustrations from these books are highlighted in boldface type.

Other Features

• The **acknowledgments,** which immediately follow the preface, list the sources from which material has been reprinted in the volume. It does not, however, list every book or periodical consulted for the volume.

• The **cumulative index to authors** lists all of the authors who have appeared in *CLR* with cross-references to the various literary criticism series and the biographical and autobiographical series published by Gale Research Inc. A full listing of the series titles appears on the first page of the indexes of this volume.

• The **cumulative nationality index** lists authors alphabetically under their respective nationalities. Author names are followed by the volume number(s) in which they appear. Authors who have changed citizenship or whose current citizenship is not reflected in biographical sources appear under both their original nationality and that of their current residence.

• The **cumulative title index** lists titles covered in *CLR* followed by the volume and page number where criticism begins.

A Note to the Reader

CLR is one of several critical reference sources in the Literature Criticism Series published by Gale Research Inc. When writing papers, students who quote directly from any volume in the Literature Criticism Series may use the following general forms to footnote reprinted criticism. The first example pertains to material drawn from periodicals, the second to material reprinted from books.

[1] T. S. Eliot, "John Donne," *The Nation and the Athenaeum,* 33 (9 June 1923), 321-32; excerpted and reprinted in *Literature Criticism from 1400 to 1800,* Vol. 10, ed. James E. Person, Jr. (Detroit: Gale Research, 1989), pp. 28-9.

[1] Henry Brooke, *Leslie Brooke and Johnny Crow* (Frederick Warne, 1982); excerpted and reprinted in *Children's Literature Review,* Vol. 20, ed. Gerard J. Senick (Detroit: Gale Research, 1990), p. 47.

Suggestions Are Welcome

In response to various suggestions, several features have been added to *CLR* since the series began, including author entries on retellers of traditional literature as well as those who have been the first to record oral tales and other folklore; entries on prominent illustrators featuring commentary on their styles and techniques; entries on authors whose works are considered controversial; occasional entries devoted to criticism on a single work or a series of works by a major author; sections in author introductions that list major works by the author or illustrator being profiled; explanatory notes that provide information on the critic or work of criticism to enhance the usefulness of the excerpt; more extensive illustrative material, such as holographs of manuscript pages and photographs of people and places pertinent to the authors' careers; a cumulative nationality index for easy access to authors by nationality; and occasional guest essays written specifically for *CLR* by prominent critics on subjects of their choice.

Readers who wish to suggest authors to appear in future volumes, or who have other suggestions, are cordially invited to write the editor.

Acknowledgments

The editors wish to thank the copyright holders of the excerpts included in this volume, the permissions managers of many book and magazine publishing companies for assisting us in securing reprint rights, and Anthony Bogucki for assistance with copyright research. We are also grateful to the staffs of the Detroit Public Library, the Library of Congress, the University of Detroit Library, Wayne State University Purdy/Kresge Library Complex, and the University of Michigan Libraries for making their resources available to us. Following is a list of the copyright holders who granted us permission to reprint material in this volume of **CLR.** Every effort has been made to trace copyright, but if omissions have been made, please let us know.

COPYRIGHTED EXCERPTS IN *CLR,* VOLUME 28, WERE REPRINTED FROM THE FOLLOWING PE-RIODICALS:

The ALAN Review, v. 18, Spring, 1991; v. 19, Fall, 1991; v. 19, Winter, 1992. All reprinted by permission of the publisher.—*Algol,* n. 21, November, 1973 for "Dreams Must Explain Themselves" by Ursula K. Le Guin. Copyright © 1973 by the author. All rights reserved. Reprinted by permission of the author and the author's agent, Virginia Kidd.—*Appraisal: Science Books for Young People,* v. 16, Winter, 1983; v. 21, Spring, 1988; v. 23, Fall, 1990. Copyright © 1983, 1988, 1990 by the Children's Science Book Review Committee. All reprinted by permission of the publisher.—*Best Sellers,* v. 41, May, 1981; v. 42, December, 1982; v. 44, September, 1984. Copyright © 1981, 1982, 1984 Helen Dwight Reid Educational Foundation. All reprinted by permission of the publisher.—*Book Week—New York Herald Tribune,* November 10, 1963; January 26, 1964; April 17, 1966. © 1963, 1964, 1966, New York Herald Tribune Inc. All rights reserved. All reprinted by permission.—*Book World—The Washington Post,* May 19, 1974; December 7, 1986; February 25, 1990; May 13, 1990; v. XXI, March 10, 1991. © 1974, 1986, 1990, 1991, *The Washington Post.* All reprinted with permission of the publisher.—*Bookbird,* v. XIV, December 15, 1976; n. 1, March 15, 1984. Both reprinted by permission of the publisher.—*Booklist,* v. 73, February 15, 1977; v. 73, April 15, 1977; v. 73, July 15, 1977; v. 74, October 1, 1977; v. 74, March 15, 1978; v. 74, June 15, 1978; v. 74, July 1, 1978; v. 75, October 15, 1978; v. 76, September 1, 1979; v. 76, January 1, 1980; v. 76, February 15, 1980; v. 76, June 15, 1980; v. 77, November 1, 1980; v. 77, December 15, 1980; v. 77, February 15, 1981; v. 78, April 15, 1982; v. 78, June 15, 1982; v. 79, October 1, 1982; v. 79, June 15, 1983; v. 80, September 1, 1983; v. 80, March 1, 1984; v. 80, May 15, 1984; v. 80, August, 1984; v. 81, October 15, 1984; v. 81, December 15, 1984; v. 81, February 1, 1985; v. 81, August, 1985; v. 82, September 1, 1985; v. 83, September 15, 1986; v. 84, October 1, 1987; v. 84, November 1, 1987; v. 84, February 1, 1988; v. 85, November 1, 1988; v. 85, March 15, 1989; v. 85, April 1, 1989; v. 85, May 1, 1989; v. 85, August, 1989; v. 86, November 15, 1989; v. 86, December 15, 1989; v. 86, March 1, 1990; v. 86, April 1, 1990; v. 87, September 1, 1990; v. 87, October 15, 1990; v. 87, November 1, 1990; v. 87, November 13, 1990; v. 87, January 15, 1991; v. 87, March 15, 1991; v. 87, April 1, 1991; v. 87, April 15, 1991. Copyright © 1977, 1978, 1979, 1980, 1981, 1982, 1983, 1984, 1985, 1986, 1987, 1988, 1989, 1990, 1991 by the American Library Association. All reprinted by permission of the publisher.—*The Booklist,* v. 71, July 1, 1975. Copyright © 1975 by the American Library Association. Reprinted by permission of the publisher.—*Books and Bookmen,* n. 357, July, 1985 for "High Flyers and Dragon Slayers" by Mary Cadogan. © copyright the author 1985. Reprinted by permission of the publisher.—*Books for Keeps,* n. 39, July, 1986; n 49, March, 1988; n. 70, September, 1991; n. 71, November, 1991. © School Bookshop Association 1986, 1988, 1991. All reprinted by permission of the publisher.—*Books for Young People,* v. 1, October, 1987 for "Annabel and Goldie Go to the Sea, Josephine Goes to School" by Susan Perren; v. 2, December, 1988 for "Quebec Illustrators' Welcome Invasion" by Peter Carver. All rights reserved. Both reprinted by permission of the publisher and the respective authors.—*Books for Your Children,* v. 10, September, 1975; v. 15, Autumn-Winter, 1980; v. 19, Summer, 1984; v. 21 Spring, 1986. © *Books for Your Children* 1975, 1980, 1984, 1986. All reprinted by permission of the publisher.—*Books in Canada,* v. XX, April, 1991.—*British Book News,* Winter, 1980. © *British Book News,* 1980. Courtesy of *British Book News.*—*British Book News,* Children's Supplement, Spring, 1981; Autumn, 1982. © *British Book News,* 1981, 1982. Both courtesy of *British Book News.*—*British Book News Children's Books,* March, 1986; June, 1986. © The British Council, 1986. Both reprinted by permission of the publisher.—*Bulletin of the Center for Children's Books,* v. XVI, June, 1963; v. XVII, December, 1963; v. 27, April, 1974; v. 28, October, 1974; v. 29, November, 1975; v. 31, September, 1977; v. 32, April, 1979; v. 33, April, 1980; v. 33, June, 1980; v. 34, July-August, 1981; v. 35, July-August, 1982; v. 36, September, 1982; v. 36, January, 1983; v. 36, February, 1983; v. 36, April, 1983; v. 36, May, 1983; v. 38 January, 1985; v. 38, February, 1985; v. 38, June, 1985; v. 39 December, 1985; v. 39, April, 1986; v. 39, July-August, 1986; v. 40, April, 1987; v. 41, September, 1987; v. 41, October, 1987; v. 41, March, 1988; v. 42, September, 1988; v. 42, October, 1988; v. 42, April, 1989; v. 42, May, 1989; v. 42, July-August, 1989; v. 43, September, 1989; v. 43, October, 1989; v. 43, November, 1989; v. 43, June, 1990; v. 43, July-August, 1990; v.

COPYRIGHTED EXCERPTS IN *CLR,* VOLUME 28, WERE REPRINTED FROM THE FOLLOWING BOOKS:

and Sexism Resource Center for Educators, 1976. Copyright © 1976 by the Council on Interracial Books for Children, Inc. All rights reserved. Reprinted by permission of the publisher.—Inglis, Fred. From *The Promise of Happiness: Value and Meaning in Children's Fiction.* Cambridge University Press, 1981. © Cambridge University Press 1981. Reprinted with the permission of the publisher.—Jones, Cornelia and Olivia R. Way. From an interview in *British Children's Authors: Interviews at Home.* American Library Association, 1976. Copyright © 1976 by the American Library Association. All rights reserved. Reprinted by permission of the publisher.—Landsberg, Michele. From *Reading for the Love of It: Best Books for Young Readers.* Prentice Hall Press, 1987. Copyright © 1986, 1987 by Psammead Associates Ltd. All rights reserved. Published in Canada as *Michele Landsburg's Guide to Children's Books.* Penguin Books, 1986. Copyright © Michele Landsberg, 1985. Used by permission of Prentice Hall/A Division of Simon & Schuster, Inc., New York, NY 10023. In Canada by Penguin Books Canada Limited.—Massee, May. From *Illustrators of Children's Books, 1744-1945.* Edited by Bertha E. Mahony, Louise Payson Latimer, and Beulah Folmsbee, eds. Horn Book, 1947. Copyright 1947, renewed 1974, by The Horn Book, Inc. All rights reserved. Reprinted by permission of the publisher, 14 Beacon St., Boston, MA 02108.—Molson, Francis J. From "The Earthsea Trilogy: Ethical Fantasy for Children," in *Ursula K. Le Guin: Voyager to Inner Lands and to Outer Space.* Edited by Joe De Bolt. Kennikat Press, 1979. Copyright © 1979 by Kennikat Press Corp. All rights reserved. Reprinted by permission of the author.—Moss, Elaine. From *Picture Books for Young People 9-13.* Second edition. The Thimble Press, 1985. Copyright © 1981, 1985 Elaine Moss. Reprinted by permission of the publisher.—Patteson, Richard F. From "Le Guin's Earthsea Trilogy: The Psychology of Fantasy," in *The Scope of the Fantastic-Culture, Biography, Themes, Children's Literature.* Edited by Robert A. Collins and Howard D. Pearce. Greenwood Press, 1985. Copyright © 1985 by The Thomas Burnett Swann Fund. All rights reserved. Reprinted by permission of Greenwood Publishing Group, Inc., Westport, CT.—Peterson, Linda Kauffman. From "The Cadecott Medal and Honor Books, 1938-1981," in *Newbery and Caldecott Medal and Honor Books: An Annotated Bibliography.* By Linda Kauffman Peterson and Marilyn Leathers Solt. G. K. Hall & Co., 1982. Copyright © 1982 by Marilyn Solt and Linda Peterson. Reprinted by permission of Linda Kauffman Peterson.—Sadker, Myra Pollack and David Miller Sadker. From *Now Upon a Time: A Contemporary View of Children's Literature.* Harper & Row, Publishers, 1977. Copyright © 1977 by Myra Pollack Sadker and David Miller Sadker. All rights reserved. Reprinted by permission of HarperCollins Publishers, Inc.—Sebesta, Sam Leaton and William J. Iverson. From *Literature for Thursday's Child.* Science Research Associates, 1975. © 1975, Science Research Associates, Inc. All rights reserved. Reprinted by permission of the authors.—Slusser, George Edgar. From *The Farthest Shores of Ursula K. Le Guin.* R. Reginald, The Borgo Press, 1976. Copyright © 1976 by George Edgar Slusser. All rights reserved. Reprinted by permission of the publisher.—Smith, Lillian H. From *The Unreluctant Years: A Critical Approach to Children's Literature.* American Library Association, 1953. Copyright 1953, renewed 1981, by the American Library Association. All rights reserved. Reprinted by permission of the publisher.—Swinfen, Ann. From *In Defence of Fantasy: A Study of the Genre in English and American Literature since 1945.* Routledge & Kegan Paul, 1984. © Ann Swinfen 1984. Reprinted by permission of the publisher.—Thompson, Judith, and Gloria Woodard. From "Black Perspective in Books for children," in *The Black American in Books for Children: Readings in Racism.* Edited by Donnarae MacCann and Gloria Woodard. The Scarecrow Press, Inc., 1972. Copyright 1972 by Donnarae MacCann and Gloria Woodard. Reprinted by permission of the publisher.—Townsend, John Rowe. From *Written for Children: An Outline of English-Language Children's Literature.* Third revised edition. J. B. Lippincott, 1987, Penguin Books, 1987. Copyright © 1965, 1974, 1983, 1987 by John Rowe Townsend. All rights reserved. Reprinted by permission of the author.—Trease, Geoffrey. From *Tales Out of School.* Second edition. Heinemann Educational Books Ltd., 1964. Second edition © Geoffrey Trease 1964. Reprinted by permission of the author.—Wood, Susan. From "Discovering Worlds: The Fiction of Ursula K. Le Guin," in *Voices for the Future: Essays on Major Science Writers, Vol. 2.* Edited by Thomas D. Clareson. Bowling Green University Popular Press, 1979. Copyright © 1979 by Bowling Green State University Popular Press. Reprinted by permission of the publisher.

PERMISSION TO REPRODUCE ILLUSTRATIONS APPEARING IN *CLR*, VOLUME 28, WAS RECEIVED FROM THE FOLLOWING SOURCES:

Illustration by Jeannie Baker from her *Where the Forest Meets the Sea.* Copyright © 1987 by Jeannie Baker. Reprinted by permission of Greenwillow Books, a division of William Morrow & Company, Inc./ Illustration by Jeannie Baker from her *Home in the Sky.* Copyright © 1984 by Jeannie Baker. Reprinted by permission of Greenwillow Books, a division of William Morrow and Company, Inc./ Illustration by Val Biro from his *Gumdrop: The Adventures of a Vintage Car.* Follett Publishing Company, 1967. Copyright © 1966 by Val Biro. Reprinted by permission of Brockhampton Press Ltd./ Illustration by Val Biro from his *The Honest Thief: A Hungarian Folktale.* Holiday House, Inc., 1973. Copyright © 1972 by Val Biro. Reprinted by permission of Holiday House, Inc./ Illustration by Lois Ehlert from her *Color Zoo.* Copyright © 1989 by Lois Ehlert. Reprinted by permission of HarperCollins Publishers./ Illustration by Lois Ehlert from her *Eating the Alphabet: Fruits and Vegetables From A to Z.* Copyright © 1989 by Lois Ehlert. Reprinted by permission of Harcourt Brace Jovanovich, Inc./ Illustration by Margorie Flack from *Taktuk, an Arctic Boy,* by Helen Lomen and Marjorie Flack. Doubleday, 1928. Copyright © 1928 by Doubleday, a division of Bantam Doubleday Dell Publishing Group, Inc. Used by permission of Doubleday, a division of Bantam Doubleday Dell Publishing Group, Inc./ Illustration by Marjorie Flack from her *Angus and the Ducks.* Copyright © 1930 by Doubleday, a division of Bantam Doubleday Dell Publishing Group, Inc. Used by permission of Doubleday, a division of Bantam Doubleday Dell Publishing Group, Inc./ Illustration by Kurt

Wiese from *The Story about Ping,* by Marjorie Flack and Kurt Wiese. Copyright © 1933 by Marjorie Flack and Kurt Wiese, renewed © 1961 by Hilma L. Barnum and Kurt Wiese. Reprinted by permission of Penguin USA./ Illustration by Marjorie Flack from her *The Restless Robin.* Copyright © 1937 by Marjorie Flack Larsson. Reprinted by permission of Houghton Mifflin Company./ Illustration by Ruth Robbins from *A Wizard of Earthsea,* by Ursula K. Le Guin. Bantam Books, 1975. Copyright © 1968 by Ursula K. Le Guin for story, by Ruth Robbins for drawings. Reprinted by permission of Atheneum Publishers, an imprint of Macmillan Publishing Company./ Illustration by Gail Garraty from *The Tombs of Atuan,* by Ursula K. Le Guin. Atheneum, 1971. Copyright © 1971 by Ursula K. Le Guin. Reprinted by permission of Atheneum, and imprint of Macmillan Publishing Company./ Illustration by Gail Garraty from *The Farthest Shore,* by Ursula K. Le Guin. Atheneum, 1972. Text copyright © 1972 by Ursula K. Le Guin. Reprinted by permission of Atheneum Publishers, an imprint of Macmillan Publishing Company./ Map by Margaret Chodos-Irvine from *Tehanu: The Last Book of Earthsea,* by Ursula K. Le Guin. Atheneum, 1990. Map copyright © 1990 by Margaret Chodos-Irvine. Reprinted by permission of Atheneum Publishers, an imprint of Macmillan Publishing Company./ Illustration by Stéphane Poulin from his *Ah! Belle cite!/A Beautiful City ABC.* Copyright © 1985 by Stéphane Poulin. Reprinted by permission of Tundra Books, Inc./ Illustration by Stéphane Poulin from his *Have You Seen Josephine?* Copyright © 1986 by Stéphane Poulin. Reprinted by permission of Tundra Books, Inc.

PHOTOGRAPHS AND ILLUSTRATIONS APPEARING IN *CLR,* VOLUME 28, WERE RECEIVED FROM THE FOLLOWING SOURCES:

AP/Wide World Photos: **p. 1;** Courtesy of Brent Ashabranner: **pp. 4, 8, 13;** Photograph by R.N. Khanna: **p. 6;** Photograph by Jennifer Ashabranner: **p. 11;** Courtesy of Eve Bunting: **p. 41;** Photograph by Lark Gilmer, courtesy of Oxford University Press: **p. 83;** Courtesy of Chris Crutcher: **p. 98;** Photograph by Lillian Schultz, courtesy of HarperCollins Publishers: **p. 109;** Photograph by Mina Turner: **p. 116;** Photograph by Marian Wood Kolisch: **p. 144;** Photograph by Wes Guderian: **p. 179;** Photograph by Ruth Furman, courtesy of Louis Furman: **p. 200.**

Children's
Literature
Review

Brent K(enneth) Ashabranner

1921-

American author of nonfiction, fiction, and picture books, and reteller.

Major works include *Morning Star, Black Sun: The Northern Cheyenne Indians and America's Energy Crisis* (1982); *To Live in Two Worlds: American Indian Youth Today* (1984); *Dark Harvest: Migrant Farmworkers in America* (1985); *Always to Remember: The Story of the Vietnam Veterans Memorial* (1988); *The Times of My Life: A Memoir* (1990).

The creator of informational books on intercultural subjects for readers in the middle grades through high school as well as fiction with a similar base, Ashabranner is respected as a socially conscious writer of warmth and technical skill who provides his audience with outstanding portraits of national and international minorities and other ethnic groups. He combines case histories and personal events with well-researched facts and background information to address crises that affect the lives of Africans, Arabs, Jews, and South American Indians as well as Native Americans, immigrants, refugees, and migrants in the United States. Writing his books in a compassionate, empathic manner which stresses the humanity of these individuals and their right to dignity and justice, Ashabranner presents straightforward accounts of how society manipulates and maltreats people. Although his works include instances of violence, prejudice, poverty, illiteracy, and alcoholism, Ashabranner emphasizes the courage of the individuals he profiles as they attempt to retain their cultural and personal identities. Ashabranner presents the personal side of social and political issues through interviews he conducts with his subjects, a feature which is often acknowledged as especially effective and involving; in addition, each work includes historical information, current facts and statistics, and personal notes. Written in a lively yet unobtrusive prose style, the books are often noted for their timeliness and the value of their messages as well as for the enrichment and emotional awareness they provide for young readers. *Kirkus Reviews* calls Ashabranner "a talented, compassionate man who has consistently used his gifts to make the world a better place," while critic Roger Sutton says that "no current events writer for young people does a better job than Ashabranner in providing an enlightening balance of solid information, pertinent anecdote, and thoughtful opinions."

As a young boy growing up in Oklahoma, a setting on which he draws for several of his works on Native Americans, Ashabranner was inspired to travel to exotic places by the works of such authors as Richard Halliburton, Rudyard Kipling, Christopher Wren, and Edgar Rice Burroughs. After serving as an instructor of English at the university level, Ashabranner went to Ethiopia with the Point Four program, where he worked as an educational materials advisor; he also served in this capacity in Libya

and Nigeria, where he started the first Peace Corps program. Ashabranner was involved with the Peace Corps from its inception and helped to create a number of its programs; he also served as director of its largest program in India from 1964 to 1966. Before he left the Peace Corps in 1969, Ashabranner had become its deputy director. Ashabranner continued to work abroad for various agencies until 1980, when he became a full-time writer. His earliest books for young people were written during the late 1950s and early 1960s with Russell Davis, a good friend with whom Ashabranner had worked in several countries. Their first collaboration, *The Lion's Whiskers* (1959), a collection of Ethiopian folktales, was prompted by the stories heard by the team as they travelled throughout the country preparing school textbooks for the Ethiopian Ministry of Education. Ashabranner and Davis also collaborated on such works as a biography of Chief Joseph, the Chief of the Nez Percé tribe, and a story about a boy who befriends a Native American man. After he became a full-time writer, Ashabranner developed his documentary approach to history in works that are often noted as unique in the genre of juvenile nonfiction. In addressing his subjects, Ashabranner often focuses on the young people who are intimately involved with the issues he describes; for example, in *Children of the Maya: A Guatemalan Indian Odyssey* (1986), he recounts how Mayan children and their parents were forced to flee to Mexico and the United States when the Guatemalan army destroyed over four hundred Indian villages. Ashabranner is the author of works on the United States Census, Arlington National Cemetary, and the Vietnam Veterans Memorial in addition to his books on individuals and ethnic groups; he has also written his autobiography, a picture book about a squirrel who wants to live in the zoo, and several books for adults, including a history of the first ten years of the Peace Corps and a college English textbook. Ashabranner has recently begun to collaborate with his daughters Melissa and Jennifer, Melissa as a writer and Jennifer as a photographer; black-and-white photographs by Paul Conklin grace several of Ashabranner's works and are often praised for contributing to their overall effectiveness. *Morning Star, Black Sun* won the Carter G. Woodson Book Award, National Council for the Social Studies, in 1983, a prize also received by *To Live in Two Worlds* in 1985 and *Dark Harvest* in 1986; the latter was also named a *Boston Globe-Horn Book* honor book in 1986. *Children of the Maya* won a Christopher Award and was named a *School Library Journal* Best Book of the Year and a Jane Addams Children's Book Award honor book in 1987. Several of Ashabranner's works have been named notable children's trade books in the field of social studies and American Library Association notable books.

(See also *Something about the Author,* Vol. 1; *Authors and Artists for Young Adults,* Vol. 6; *Contemporary Authors New Revised Edition,* Vols. 10, 27; and *Contemporary Authors,* Vols. 7-8, rev. ed.)

AUTHOR'S COMMENTARY

I have never had any doubt that the books I read as a boy influenced the direction of my life, including my life as a writer. I grew up in a small Oklahoma town, but I was fascinated by books about foreign countries. I devoured Kipling, practically memorized *Beau Geste,* and lived every moment of the wonderful overseas adventures Richard Halliburton described in travel books, the titles of which I have long since forgotten. For an afternoon of lugging boxes around, I was once offered any book on the shelves by the owner of the tiny local bookstore. I remember that I picked Alec Waugh's *Hot Countries.* Waugh was a bit much for a thirteen-year-old Oklahoma boy, but I had sweated for the book, and I read it.

I cannot prove that this exotic reading diet was responsible for my having lived and worked much of my adult life in Ethiopia, Libya, Nigeria, India, the Philippines, and Indonesia; but I strongly suspect that Kipling, Wren, Halliburton, and a few other mesmerizing writers about Africa and Asia—including Pearl Buck—made my initial decision to work in foreign assistance programs much easier than it otherwise would have been.

Most of my books for children and young adults, beginning with *The Lion's Whiskers* in 1959, have been about cross-cultural encounters or have explored cultures other than my own. The things I felt I was learning about under-

standing other cultures and about people of different cultures trying to understand each other seemed worth sharing with young readers. Since returning to the United States to live, I have concentrated on nonfiction and have written mostly about minorities, including Native Americans, and the growing ethnic groups in America. My years of living and working overseas have helped me to understand better their hopes, desires, frustrations, and fears.

When I describe the refugee boy in **Into a Strange Land** who spent sleepless nights preparing to make his first classroom talk in English and then, standing before his classmates, found that nothing but Vietnamese would come out of his mouth, I have at least some firsthand sense of what he felt.

Not much more than ten years ago, as a Ford Foundation staff member in Indonesia, I made my first visit to a village on the island of Bali. I knew that I would be welcomed with a speech by the headman, and I had spent a considerable amount of time the night before rehearsing my reply in Indonesian. The word for *headman* in Indonesian is *kepala,* and it so happens that the word for coconut is *kelapa,* just a reversal of two syllables. It was, of course, inevitable that I should begin my words of thanks by addressing the headman as *kelapa.* Now, when you go into a Balinese village and begin by calling the revered leader of the people a coconut, you are not off to a good start. I do know what it is like to try to function in a strange culture, and I do know what the Vietnamese boy was going through.

Most of my books for upper elementary, junior high, and high school students deal with complex cross-cultural issues and problems: the changing nature of U.S. immigration in **The New Americans,** the desire of young American Indians to succeed in the dominant white culture while retaining their tribal heritage in **To Live in Two Worlds,** the plight of Hispanic migrant farm workers in **Dark Harvest,** a genocidal threat to Guatemalan Indians in **Children of the Maya,** the melding of cultures along our frontier with Mexico in **The Vanishing Border.**

Occasionally an adult will express to me some astonishment and—usually tactful—skepticism that young readers can understand or would be interested in such subjects. A few years ago I wrote a book called **Morning Star, Black Sun,** which is about the fight of the Northern Cheyenne Indians to save their Montana reservation from power companies. About a year after the book's publication, I was invited by the Atlantic-Richfield Company, ARCO, to take part in a workshop intended to give some cultural sensitivity to ARCO staff members who were going to carry out oil exploration on the Northern Cheyenne reservation.

I flew to Denver and had a lively discussion with the group, based on **Morning Star, Black Sun,** which I think everyone had read. At some point I mentioned that the book had been written for students in about grade six and up. I had assumed that everyone knew that, but immediately one of the participants said, a bit dejectedly, "I had been congratulating myself because I understood everything in the book. Now I learn it was written for children." Then he asked, a note of polite doubt in his voice, "Did you really write that for children?" I assured him that I had, and I said, "I learned a long time ago that if I can explain something so that children understand it, most adults can understand it, too." I went on to explain that a writer who hopes to make a complex subject clear to young readers must understand it so well that he knows what he can leave out without distorting, oversimplifying, or reducing the subject to an insipid pap. He must then find a clear and straightforward organization for his material; this structure may take him almost as long to locate as the actual writing takes. Such a selection of material, such a presentation, I said, will benefit adult readers as much as it does young ones. Franklyn Branley once remarked that it is only when he must explain a subject to children that he realizes he doesn't understand it at all.

I believe subjects that involve cross-cultural issues and problems can be made interesting to readers of all ages because they deal with conflict on all levels—conflict between people, conflict with a strange environment, conflicting desires within a person. The latter may be the hardest of all to resolve. The poverty-stricken Cheyenne Indian in **Morning Star, Black Sun** must decide between a great deal of money and the destruction of the sacred land of his ancestors. The Korean immigrant in **The New Americans** sees the educational opportunities in America for her children but longs for the familiar traditions, the loved ones, the language of her homeland.

Last year I met with a sixth-grade class in Arlington, Virginia; afterward one of the students came up to tell me that he had read **The New Americans** all the way through and had understood it all. I told him that there was scarcely anything more complimentary he could say to a writer, certainly, to this writer. "I liked the stories about people best," he said, "but all that other stuff was okay, too."

I confess to having been a bit awed by the casual way he lumped together "all that other stuff," which happened to be some immigration history, law, and politics; demographic projections; and speculations about America as a pluralistic society. I had tried to integrate that information smoothly and succinctly into the text, but the student had put his finger squarely on the best way, probably the only way, to make the subjects I write about interesting to my youthful audience. I write stories about people—and not stories of people I have read about or heard about but people I have talked with in their homes, at work, or wherever they may be. There is no other way.

I collected material about refugees for two years before I found my method, in **Into a Strange Land,** of telling the story through the voices of refugee children who have been set adrift in the world alone, without parents or loved ones. I have indications from all over the country that young readers can hear those voices. (pp. 749-52)

Paul Conklin's photographs illustrate most of my recent books. Good illustrations are essential to most young readers' nonfiction today. Properly done, they expand the text and contribute to a more interesting, more readable, more informative book. In Paul I have a master who sets the very highest standards for himself. We first met almost thirty years ago when I was starting the Peace Corps pro-gram in Nigeria, and Paul was an adventurous young free-lance photographer learning to make a living with his camera. Later he joined the Peace Corps as a staff photographer and visited me in India when I was directing the Peace Corps program there. Paul and I care about the same things. Usually we develop a book idea together, and we always travel together while we collect material, sharing every experience. When the time comes for me to lock myself in my study and write, I have Paul's wonderful black-and-white pictures to help keep mood and memory alive.

Since leaving the Ford Foundation in 1980, I have spent most of my time writing books for young readers. I love the work I do, and there have been few disappointments. Perhaps the only regret I have is that it is difficult to stay in touch with most of the people I write about. Our paths seldom cross again, and these people do not write many letters. But occasionally I do get some feedback, and usually it is heart-warming. When Paul and I were gathering material for **The Vanishing Border,** we had a chance to visit a migrant farmworker family who had appeared in **Dark Harvest** and who were then in their winter home in Texas. In the tiny living room of their house was a small table on which lay the copy of **Dark Harvest** we had sent them. The wife said, "Our friends"—she meant their migrant farmworker friends—"still come to look at the book. They can't believe people like us could be in a book." I did receive a letter from a young girl who had spent her entire life in migrant camps; she gave me a box number in Florida where I could send a copy of the book, and I did. Her letter, in its entirety, said, "Thank you for the book. What you wrote is true. I like the part about me best." **Dark Harvest** received the Carter G. Woodson Book Award and was a Boston Globe-Horn Book Honor Book, and I am proud of those awards. But I am at least as proud of that letter from the migrant farmworker girl in Florida.

No matter what social issues or problems my books may deal with, I have one overriding hope for each of them: that the people I write about will emerge as human beings who have lives that are real and valuable and who have a right to a decent life. If I can get that truth across, young readers will hear it and know what I am talking about. (pp. 753-54)

> *Brent Ashabranner, "Did You Really Write That for Children?" in* The Horn Book Magazine, *Vol. LXIV, No. 6, November-December, 1988, pp. 749-54.*

TITLE COMMENTARY

The Lion's Whiskers: Tales of High Africa   (with Russell Davis, 1959)

As a general rule I prefer my folk-tales straight. *The Lion's Whiskers* however is more than a book of folk-tales; it is a study of Ethiopia and its inhabitants, using the tales current today to illustrate the characteristics of each tribe. It shows how in a remote country like this, where traditions live naturally, the art of story-telling flourishes. There are some fascinating examples of folk-tales in the

Ashabranner and his older brother Gerard circa 1925.

making, notably in the story of the man who, at thirty, went to school after a fifteen-year-long walk.

For the collector and the story-teller there are some original treasures here, as well as some interesting variants on tales in Grimm and other European collections. I recommend as additions to anyone's repertoire **"The Wise Judge,"** a gloriously funny tale about two deaf litigants and a deaf and half-blind judge, a nice story about native roguery called **"The Gold-lined Donkey,"** and a long classical story of courage, cowardice and wit **"The Brave Prince."**

The authors, two American educationalists who worked in the Ethiopian Ministry of Education on the preparation of school text-books, became interested in the tales they heard, and travelled throughout the country listening, arguing and recording.

They have set down the stories in a pointed, oral form which seems authentic, and have added comments which one would think ought to seem intrusive but in fact are not. They are indeed the kind of comments which a good tale would draw from a native audience.

Altogether a most unusual addition to the literature of folk-lore. (pp. 278-79)

> *A review of "The Lion's Whiskers," in* The Junior Bookshelf, *Vol. 23, No. 5, November, 1959, pp. 278-79.*

The Choctaw Code (with Russell G. Davis, 1961)

A story, barely skirting sentimentality, as it relates the adventures of Tom Baxter, newly arrived in Indian Territory (now Oklahoma). He forms a strong friendship with an adult Choctaw, condemned to die by tribal law. Tom's efforts to save his friend and his gradual acceptance of the Choctaw moral code present a penetrating picture of a boy growing up. While there are such stock characters as the "good" Indian and the obviously evil villains, there is enough authentic background and suspense to hold the interest.

> *Ruby W. Ewing, in a review of "The Choctaw Code," in* Junior Libraries, *Vol. 7, No. 9, May, 1961, p. 44.*

A strong and moving book about a man with deep ethical convictions. Unusual in setting and in its unity of construction, this is the story of the friendship between a white boy of fifteen and an Indian man, Jim. Jim was sentenced to die; by the Choctaw mores, he refused to accept the pardon he knew he could have obtained. Jim had a year of freedom, and he spent much of it giving to young Tom Baxter all of the training as a woodsman and hunter that he could. No happy ending here to weaken the character that has been built up; Jim shows his young friend a model of honor and of courage in addition to the material evidences of his friendship. Excellent characterization, a sympathetic and dignified treatment of the Choctaw nation and its problems.

> *Zena Sutherland, in a review of "The Choctaw Code," in* Bulletin of the Center for Children's Books, *Vol. XV, No. 9, May, 1962, p. 140.*

Chief Joseph, War Chief of the Nez Percé (with Russell Davis, 1962)

Portrayal of the sensitive but stalwart Chief Joseph of the Nez Percés begins with the war years with General Howard and the tribe's final defeat and surrender. Passages on battle preparation and action are skillfully woven in with the stoicism and introspection of Chief Joseph. Less heavily documented and not as broad in historical coverage as Shannon Garst's biography of 1953, this book has greater vividness and a stronger sense of reality as well as depth of character. Well written. Recommended for general purchase.

> *Lois Anderson, in a review of "Chief Joseph: War Chief of the Nez Percé," in* Library Journal, *Vol. LXXXVII, June 15, 1962, p. 2414.*

Books about Indians—factual, fictional, or confusingly mixed—continue to be written and published so relentlessly that the appearance of one that is noteworthy in content or style must be quickly heralded lest it get lost in the flood. In *Chief Joseph* the experienced and able team of Davis and Ashabranner have found a noble subject; and the facts they present bear out their conviction that this was a great man as well as a great Indian. Chief Joseph, in spite of extreme provocation from settlers, miners, and the United States Government, stood firmly for peace with the white man until, in 1877, he was ordered to remove his tribe from ancestral land in Washington Territory to a hated reservation. Joseph and his people refused. Women, children, babies, and old people, protected by three hundred warriors, then began an 1800-mile search for a safe and free home. The final surrender of the pitiful remnant, trapped in a bitter snowstorm by vastly superior army forces, is unforgettable. So, too, are Chief Joseph's courage, tactical skill, and abiding concern for his people. The authors add a caustic finale—the surrender terms promised a return to Washington, to a reservation, not to freedom. This promise was immediately broken, the Nez Percé being sent instead to the alien climate of Oklahoma.

> *Margaret Warren Brown, in a review of "Chief Joseph, War Chief of the Nez Percé," in* The Horn Book Magazine, *Vol. XXXVIII, No. 4, August, 1962, p. 381.*

The authors succeed admirably in being sympathetic without being sentimental, and in evoking mood and atmosphere. Joseph is a strong and consistent character, dignified and thoughtful, but the chief impact of the book is in the colorful and moving picture of the whole Nez Percé tribe.

> *Zena Sutherland, in a review of "Chief Joseph: War Chief of the Nez Percé," in* Bulletin of the Center for Children's Books, *Vol. XVI, No. 10, June, 1963, p. 158.*

Land in the Sun: The Story of West Africa (with Russell Davis, 1963)

[This] is a slender book but it gives readers from 11 on through the early high-school years an excellent survey of the new nations in West Africa. Children will be drawn to it by the orange, blue and yellow gaiety of the many pictures [by Robert William Hinds] depicting city, farm and forest. The text does not belie the illustrations for it tells in language that seems natural and simple—but not simplified—of the 17 lands and 60 million people of West Africa—Ghana, Guinea, Cameroun, Togoland, Dahomy and Nigeria and the older nations like Liberia. The whole area is treated together rather than broken into political fragments. The lives of the people are described through their activities: the production of cocoa, herding, trading, agriculture or hunting. An excellent introductory book emphasizing the great variety of life from tribal to a modern industrialized society as well as the colorful details of "magic and mystery in the bush."

> *"An Armchair Safari," in* Book Week—New York Herald Tribune, *November 10, 1963, p. 18.*

This is a once-over-lightly story of West Africa where 16 countries have gained independence within the last few years. The authors tell their story for 8's on up and do not attempt to cover each country separately. Instead, they survey the whole area showing us what these countries have in common and what is unique here and there. As a rule, West Africans are industrious and independent people and this part of Africa is producing bustling cities,

growing industries and all the problems that go along with both. But much of West Africa is still "bush" and here magic, ancient customs and pagan religions still hold sway. There is a wealth of information in these few pages and it is simply told with a never-flagging interest. And the authors admirably succeed in communicating that one thing which West Africans have in common with people everywhere—the desire to be free men.

> *M. J. T., in a review of "Land in the Sun," in* The Christian Science Monitor, *January 2, 1964, p. 7.*

Strangers in Africa (with Russell Davis, 1963)

Wes and Paul are entomologists who have come to Nigeria to work for a year on the problem of the tsetse fly. Most of the people they meet accept casually the fact that these two, one a white American and one a Negro, can be friends; they themselves are aware that it will not be as easy in the States, but are determined that they shall stay friends. Wes woos and wins the daughter of the project head; Paul has ambivalent feelings about Africa and about his role as an American Negro in Nigeria. The book doesn't quite come off. The writing style is adequate, the background details are interesting, the characters are all quite believable, but the story doesn't coalesce. The love story seems extraneous, there is a plethora of information about trypanosomiasis, and the impact of Africa on Paul is only superficially explored.

> *Zena Sutherland, in a review of "Strangers in Africa," in* Bulletin of the Center for Children's Books, *Vol. XVII, No. 4, December, 1963, p. 56.*

Morning Star, Black Sun: The Northern Cheyenne Indians and America's Energy Crisis (1982)

The author provides a history of the Cheyenne Indians of the North (another group, in an amicable separation, had gone south) and of their confrontation with white settlers and soldiers, as background to a discussion of the contemporary challenge to tribal life. Assigned to a Montana reservation, the Cheyenne have lived in peace if not great prosperity for almost a century. It was discovered that coal lay beneath the reservation land. The Cheyenne experience with the heavy hand of the Bureau of Indian Affairs (originally called the Indian Bureau) had made them justifiably dubious about outside management of tribal concerns; now the threat was that the one thing the Cheyenne held most dear, the land on which they live, might go (via large-tract leases) to the coal mining companies which had not offered equitable royalty revenue to the owners. Particularly vexatious had been the prospect that instead of shipping coal, the companies would set up generating plants and transmit electrical power—a process that would contribute to pollution at the sites. This would also have brought even more workers into the reservation area, inevitably changing the peaceful Cheyenne way of life. In 1973, learning some of the facts behind the offers, the tribal council petitioned the Bureau to cancel all leases. Thus began a long legal battle, into which the Environmental Protection Agency entered, to avert the "black sun" of the title and to annul the leases; this happened in 1980. A final chapter describes the lives of the Cheyenne today, an interesting but poorly placed section of the book. An index gives access to the text, which is a bit dry but competent in style, and is based on research that has resulted in a detailed, informative, and well-organized book. (pp. 1-2)

> *Zena Sutherland, in a review of "Morning Star, Black Sun: The Northern Cheyenne Indians and America's Energy Crisis," in Bulletin of the Center for Children's Books, Vol. 36, No. 1, September, 1982, pp. 1-2.*

The book provides a clear account of the struggle of the Northern Cheyenne Indians over the past hundred years to save their homeland and to protect their culture. The author outlines the complex social organization of the tribe, discusses its religious beliefs, and relates the legend of a prophet who foretold the extinction of the Cheyenne at the hands of a white people. . . . By tracing Cheyenne history from the days of the Indian wars, the book shows how the Northern Cheyenne are still very close to their tragic past; and by referring to individual members of the tribe and including their thoughts and observations, the author personalizes his account of a people determined to maintain the spirit and traditions of their ancestors.

Ashabranner and Peace Corps director Jack Vaughn in India in 1965.

> *Kate M. Flanagan, in a review of "Morning Star, Black Sun: The Northern Cheyenne Indians and America's Energy Crisis," in The Horn Book Magazine, Vol. LVIII, No. 5, October, 1982, p. 528.*

The report is buoyed by the author's obvious sympathy with the Cheyenne people and by numerous quotes from individuals involved in the struggle. The human-interest quotient is high, as is the book's status as one of the very few titles that deals with contemporary issues of native American peoples.

> *Denise M. Wilms, in a review of "Morning Star, Black Sun: The Northern Cheyenne Indians and America's Energy Crisis," in Booklist, Vol. 79, No. 3, October 1, 1982, p. 200.*

The New Americans: Changing Patterns in U.S. Immigration (1983)

Stories from the lives of recent US immigrants—featuring the 80 percent who now come from Asia and Latin America—with a brief introductory reprise of US immigration history and a brief concluding discussion of current immigration issues. Though Ashabranner's writing is bland, it is simple and clear; though he frequently straddles the fence (almost inevitably, on illegal immigration), he does fairly indicate the conflicting positions. And his individual stories do add up to a representative, if mostly upbeat, sampling. There is the large Vietnamese-family-by-marriage of American civilian worker Frank Brown, airlifted out in 1975 and now—thanks to the subsequent boat-escape of father-in-law Hai—ensconced one-and-all in Ocean Spring, Miss. Also among the Vietnamese: the Royal Laotian Classical Dance Troupe, reconstituted (via a Thai refugee camp) in Nashville; the several hundred Cambodians—"uneducated," "gentle," "hard-working"—sheltered by Oklahoma City's Catholic Refugee Resettlement Program; and—for a glimpse of the darker side—testimony of homesickness ("most refugees would return . . . ") and word of the Gulf Coast fishing troubles. The Koreans are shown to be seeking education for their children (some dubious, unsourced statistics here, however); the Arabs, education for themselves. The Filipino husband-and-wife exemplify America's traditional lure for the venturesome. From Latin America and the Caribbean come: a Los Angeles processor of Mexican foods (*re* the Hispanic market and way-of-life); an El Paso mechanic and his border-straddling family (epitomizing the incongruities of immigration policy); diverse Haitians, driven here "by fear, poverty, the hope of a better life or all three" (who raise the problem of defining a refugee); a member of the 1980 Cuban boat-lift (who occasions a positive, air-cleaning update on that episode); and a Jamaican doing very well indeed in Washington, D.C. (suggesting, not erroneously, that Jamaicans have what it takes). Material on the scanty immigration from Africa challenges the three current bases-of-choice—family unification, job skill, political or religious persecution—and also raises the brain-drain issue; apropos of Europe, the position of the Russian Jews is mentioned and a Czech refugee appears. In the last chapter, demographer Leon Bouvier explains the implications of current trends ("a Multicultural Society") and Ashabranner describes the pending Simpson-Mazzoli Bill, designed chiefly to deal with the illegal-immigrant problem. Judith Bentley's *American Immigration Today* (1981) offers a considerably more developed discussion of the groups and the issues, and even the second, contemporary half of Lydia Anderson's *Immigration* (1981) has more social-science-type material. But Ashabranner's personalized, feature approach covers a lot of ground in an undemanding fashion.

> *A review of "The New Americans: Changing Patterns in U. S. Immigration," in* Kirkus Reviews, *Vol. LI, No. 12, June 15, 1983, p. 667.*

Combining personal stories with information on the effect of immigration on America and on the immigrants' native countries, the author briefly covers the history of immigration in America, making comparisons to present day immigration and forecasting the future. Some of the stories are patronizing and condescending, as when Sr. Anne describes the Cambodian immigrants she helped resettle as "gentle people": even though they lived through the slaughter of hundreds of thousands by the Khmer Rouge, "Some were depressed . . . but they were never angry. . . . They always smiled." There are many other books on immigrants which are better, such as "The Dream of America" series (Creative Education, 1983) and "Coming to America" series (Delacorte, 1980).

> *Sandy Parks Boettcher, in a review of "The New Americans: Changing Patterns in U.S. Immigration," in* School Library Journal, *Vol. 29, No. 10, August, 1983, p. 72.*

In another highly successful collaboration the author and the photographer [Paul Conklin] of **Morning Star, Black Sun** have created a colorful, well-documented picture of immigration in the United States. . . . What distinguishes the work is its emphasis on case histories: Much of the text consists of conversations with former Ethiopians, Mexicans, Cubans, and other immigrants and refugees. Not only do these individual testimonies reflect a diversity of experience, but—combined with an assortment of sharply-focused photographs—they add vividness and drama to the book. An excellent study of the people who " 'enrich our lives, and . . . enrich our vision.' "

> *Karen Jameyson, in a review of "The New Americans," in* The Horn Book Magazine, *Vol. LIX, No. 6, December, 1983, p. 723.*

To Live in Two Worlds: American Indian Youth Today (1984)

The author of **Morning Star, Black Sun: The Northern Cheyenne Indian and America's Energy Crisis** again provides a sensitive and penetrating look at today's American Indians, specifically, those of high school or college age and those getting started in a career. To find out how young Indian men and women feel about the future, Ashabranner and his photographer-colleague traveled around the U.S. interviewing reservation and urban Indians. Though Ashabranner acknowledges that many native

Americans are still disadvantaged by poverty, inappropriate education, language difficulties, and a heritage of failure, he chooses to focus on the positive. . . . Personalized not only by the comments and stories of individuals but also by the perceptive black-and-white photographs [by Paul Conklin], the treatment highlights the struggles of individuals and tribes to retain their Indian identity while striving for success in a dominant non-Indian culture that has a history of trying to wipe out Indian tradition and assimilate Indians into the white culture. This has broad human-interest appeal combined with definite curriculum-related value. (pp. 1604-05)

> *Sally Estes, in a review of "To Live in Two Worlds: American Indian Youth Today," in* Booklist, *Vol. 80, No. 22, August, 1984, pp. 1604-05.*

Young people reading these brief accounts will gain an emotional awareness not possible from sociology or history texts. Readers will appreciate the efforts made by these young adults to seize the opportunities offered and then to return and help others in their tribes. The Navajo Academy in New Mexico typifies this effort with its high standards of math and science and studies of the Navajo history, language, philosophy and culture. The old saying "every picture tells a story" is very evident in the photographs that illustrate this book. The lives, dreams and hopes of these young Indians shine through and enliven the written words. The primary value of this book will be as a supplementary text for U.S. history students and for all those who wish to enrich their understanding of the problems of today's Native Americans.

> *Joyce Baker, in a review of "To Live in Two Worlds: American Indian Youth Today," in* School Library Journal, *Vol. 30, No. 10, August, 1984, p. 80.*

Ray Apodoca, a Tigua Indian, comments, " 'The overwhelming majority of Americans couldn't tell you anything about modern Indians and certainly nothing about their problems.' " With statistics, life histories, photographs, and interviews, the volume attacks this ignorance and attests to the presence, the plight, and the progress of one of America's fastest growing ethnic groups. Without ignoring the dark side of Indian life—the highest unemployment, the lowest average income, and the highest arrest and conviction rate of any minority group—the proficient author-photographer team stresses the strengths and successes of individuals and their altruistic institutions and agencies. . . . In the informative, up-to-date book, the difficulties of trying to straddle two cultures and garner the best of each are vividly related; for instance, a Navajo scholarship student moves from the fire in her grandparents' one-room hogan to her dormitory room at a posh Eastern preparatory school and worries over losing her Indian identity. And a prison inmate recounts a common experience, "drifting back and forth between the reservation where there was nothing to do and the town where I didn't feel like I belonged."

> *Nancy C. Hammond, in a review of "To Live in Two Worlds: American Indian Youth*

Today," in The Horn Book Magazine, *Vol. LX, No. 5, September-October, 1984, p. 604.*

Gavriel and Jemal: Two Boys of Jerusalem (British edition as *Two Boys of Jerusalem,* **1984**)

With objectivity and simplicity, Ashabranner explores the diversity of life in the Arab and Jewish sectors of the Old City of Jerusalem. Gavriel, a 12-year-old Israeli Jew, lives with his large family in the Jewish Quarter of the Old City. His Arab counterpart is 14-year-old Jemal, a Palestinian whose family has inhabited the same house in Jerusalem's Arab Quarter for five generations. Both boys come from loving homes in which religion plays a major role. Separated as they are by their ethnic and historical differences, they live strikingly parallel lives. Ashabranner's deft exploration of each boy's weekly routine, coupled with Conklin's large black-and-white photos, clearly depict the diversity of Jerusalem and contrast the two great civilizations that coexist in this most sacred of historic cities. Foreign and religious terms are explained. The lesson here is quite clear: the harmony and love apparent in the homes of these boys can and must filter into the relationship between Arab and Jew for the success of peace in Israel and the world. A one-of-a-kind book that will be an excellent introduction for young people to a very important problem facing today's world. (pp. 70, 72)

> *Susan Scheps, in a review of "Gavriel and Jemal: Two Boys of Jerusalem," in* School Library Journal, *Vol. 31, No. 5, January, 1985, pp. 70, 72.*

So near and yet so far apart; the cliché nonetheless is an apt description of the circumstances of these two Jerusalem boys—one a Jew, the other a Palestinian Arab—who live within blocks of each other in Jerusalem's Old City, yet whose lives are worlds apart. . . . [As] Ashabranner states in his conclusion, these boys and other children like them are the key to the future, for if the conflict between their two peoples is ever to be solved, "it is they and other young Palestinians and Israelis like them who someday must solve it." The profiles of both young people are carefully neutral, a tactic that makes the quiet conclusion intensely logical, yet laden with a sense of futility. A sharp portrait of great human interest, this will engage both independent readers and students seeking background on this Middle Eastern hot spot.

> *Denise M. Wilms, in a review of "Gavriel and Jemal: Two Boys of Jerusalem," in* Booklist, *Vol. 81, No. 11, February 1, 1985, p. 785.*

Gavriel is an Israeli Jew and Jemal is a Palestinian Arab. Both live in the city of Jerusalem but Gavriel has a nation behind him while Jemal feels he has no true homeland. The two boys have never met, yet the possibility of peace in the Middle East will clearly lie in their hands in the future. For this reason the book is impressive for its implied message. It is impressive too for the careful enumeration of details which should make it possible for young readers to follow each boy through the day; mealtimes and food, religious practices and school matters, family backgrounds are all clearly described. . . . The quietly honest,

Ashabranner being sworn in as deputy director of the Peace Corps by Vice President Hubert Humphrey, 1967.

unostentatious text is extended in photographs showing the boys at home, in the street, at school or at prayer, naturally and memorably. The whole book speaks of the certainty and strong feeling of those who made it.

> *Margery Fisher, in a review of "Two Boys of Jerusalem," in* Growing Point, *Vol. 26, No. 1, May, 1987, p. 4811.*

Dark Harvest: Migrant Farmworkers in America (1985)

Ashabranner, who has written several fine intercultural studies . . . , again combines dramatic human stories with general information in a highly readable account. From Texas, Florida, and California—the three great reservoirs of migrant (mainly Hispanic) labor—to New York and Maryland, he observes and interviews migrant farmworkers at work, on the road, and at home: families, single men, officials, crew leaders. A tragic picture emerges of backbreaking work for poor pay under wretched working and living conditions; high rates of disease, injury, and pesticide poisoning; and widespread child labor, interrupted education, and a massive high school dropout rate. A theme running throughout is that the illegal aliens and legal foreign guest-workers are exploited victims, who also deprive Americans of jobs and keep wages low. Although Ashabranner makes it clear that accurate facts and figures are difficult to find, his sources should be more fully documented: it is not enough to cite "an article in the *New York Times*" or "a 1982 study." But the power of the book lies in the immediacy of the personal reporting and the oral histories that show hardworking people trapped in a cruel system as they follow the crops and long for a home.

> *Hazel Rochman, in a review of "Dark Harvest: Migrant Farmworkers in America," in* Booklist, *Vol. 82, No. 1, September 1, 1985, p. 49.*

An outstanding combination of coherent narrative and [Paul Conklin's] sensitive photography will take readers into the fields with migrant workers who, in many cases, tell their own stories of what life is like following the crops. Using information based on research and interviews, Ashabranner presents facts with a personal sense of involvement that lends urgency to descriptions of children housed and fed below poverty standards, shatters some myths about lazy migrant workers, and yet gives a clear outline of the labor, routes, ethnic groups, agribusiness corporations, and educational/legal problems involved. The black and white photos are expressive and well-composed, a few parent-child portraits classic in the Dorothea Lange tradition. This team, which collaborated on *The New Americans: Changing Patterns in U.S. Immigration,* has an ability to project the people behind the data. Readers will learn to care about these subjects and recognize the strong family traditions they nurture in the face of a devastating system. (pp. 61-2)

> *A review of "Dark Harvest: Migrant Workers in America," in* Bulletin of the Center for Children's Books, *Vol. 39, No. 4, December, 1985, pp. 61-2.*

Poignant testimony to the backbreaking labor and to the often desperate poverty of migrant workers emerges in a telling portrayal of those who live almost unseen among us and yet pick, sort, and ship the fruits and vegetables we choose at our grocery stores with barely a second thought. The author attempts an objective picture but reveals his sympathies for those who must "go on the season" year after year and for the hardships they and their children endure. Mexican, Haitians, blacks, and other groups are among those who pursue this meager means of existence, and we see their lives through interviews with representative families and reflected in the drawn features, but often gallant smiles, on their faces in the fine black-and-white photographs. The writing style is narrative and informative. Statistics are cited but do not overburden the text. The bondage of poverty and exploitation is treated directly, with a matter-of-fact presentation which permits readers to form their own opinions and with a few success stories to mitigate the misery stemming from financial need and lack of education. The author has brought to our attention the plight of a hardworking and nearly voiceless group who need our support and protection. (pp. 215-16)

> *Ethel R. Twichell, in a review of "Dark Harvest: Migrant Farmworkers in America," in* The Horn Book Magazine, *Vol. LXII, No. 2, March-April, 1986, pp. 215-16.*

Dark Harvest is an excellent introductory survey of migrant labor in America. Ashabranner's journalistic skills border on professional ethnography, and Conklin's black-and-white photographs alone are worth the price of the book. . . . This sturdy, clothbound book belongs in every high-school and undergraduate library on the social studies shelf. Although it was never meant to be a definitive academic study, **Dark Harvest** is a readable, moving account of migrant life styles told by the workers themselves to a sensitive reporter and magnified by the lens of an equally sensitive photographer.

> *Morris Simon, in a review of "Dark Harvest: Migrant Farmworkers in America," in* Science Books & Films, *Vol. 21, No. 5, May-June, 1986, p. 302.*

Children of the Maya: A Guatemalan Indian Odyssey (1986)

Children of the Maya is a somewhat misleading title for this book, since it covers the plight of Guatemalan refugees of Mayan descent, who escaped the death squads of the Guatemalan army. The hardships and horrors they endured are vividly recounted through first-person narratives. Their recollections are often gruesome: Luis Garcia tells of finding his father's decapitated body in a ditch; Antonio Guerra remembers the sights and sounds of the army's massacre of his neighbors and the burning of his village. Accompanying black-and-white photos [by Paul Conklin] illustrate the stark contrast between the primitive camps in Mexico where the refugees took temporary shelter and the modest but clean apartments of Indiantown, Fla., where they now live. The author also discusses the problems of adjusting to life in America and the lasting impressions of terror left on the children's psyches. A preface gives a helpful overview of Mayan culture and history. These stories are important, and should acquaint children with the crisis facing the Guatemalan people, whose plight is underpublicized.

> *A review of "Children of the Maya," in* Publishers Weekly, *Vol. 229, No. 17, April 25, 1986, p. 86.*

The most intensely focused and moving of all the reportage in [the series on U.S. minorities by Ashabranner and photographer Paul Conklin] provides brief background on the political dynamics behind the genocide of Mayan Indians at the hands of the Guatemalan army. Most of the book is devoted to the stories told by survivors of village massacres, their escapes, experiences as refugees through Mexico and across the border, and their resettlement in Indiantown, Florida, a population center for black, Hispanic, and native American migrant workers. Both the narrative and the photography are informal but clear; as a history and current events resource, this gives not only information but also a sense of immediate involvement in a situation too close and too tragic to be ignored.

> *A review of "Children of the Maya: A Guatemalan Indian Odyssey," in* Bulletin of the Center for Children's Books, *Vol. 39, No. 11, July-August, 1986, p. 202.*

"And most of all we wanted to see the children again," says Brent Ashabranner as he explains why he and photographer Paul Conklin returned to Indiantown, Florida, the site for and impetus of this fine book. The photographs of the children and their parents fill the book with haunting faces as the text chronicles the flight of the Mayas from their native Guatemala, where the national army destroyed over four hundred Indian villages and killed over thirty thousand Mayas. . . . As in his earlier books, [Ashabranner] uses sections of direct narrative. The style is very effective in transmitting the experiences of these quiet, hard working people. Connections between the contemporary Mayan and the ancient Mayan civilization are traced, and references to the ancient ways appear in the narratives. The photographs underline the text, although for protection none of the Mayas are identified. Ashabranner has once again written a thought provoking book about human beings in distress and about those who are trying to help. Bibliography and index.

> *Elizabeth S. Watson, in a review of "Children of the Maya: A Guatemalan Indian Odyssey," in* The Horn Book Magazine, *Vol. LXII, No. 5, September-October, 1986, p. 606.*

While the book is interesting and the individual accounts captivating, the overall presentation is weakened by a pervasive tendency to romanticize and overempathize with the situations of the refugees. This same tendency is extended to the brief, very outdated section on the ancient Maya that contains a number of dubious assertions and folk wisdom that serve to emphasize further the Indians' "fall from paradise." Despite these shortcomings, the book presents all the intricacies of the refugee situation and attempts to raise the question of its effect on the refugee children. Since the intended audience is juvenile, the book would serve to raise general awareness of the Guatemalan situation and introduce the larger problems of refugees, immigration, and culture change. The illustrations are excellent, even though some are obviously posed, and they provide a useful visual element to the text. The book is recommended, particularly for younger readers, and should engender interest and thought about the plight of the world's refugees. (pp. 175-76)

> *William O. Autry, Jr., in a review of "Children of the Maya: A Guatemalan Indian Odyssey," in* Science Books & Films, *Vol. 22, No. 3, January-February, 1987, pp. 175-76.*

Into a Strange Land: Unaccompanied Refugee Youth in America **(with Melissa Ashabranner, 1987)**

An easily read account of the plight of unaccompanied refugee youth in America. The saga unfolds from the secreting of a child onto a boat after a very high price for passage is paid, to arriving at a camp to await placement and transport to a free country. The drama and emotional upheaval continue after the child arrives in America and is placed in foster care. High expectations and the traumatic loss of family, country, culture, and language make adjustment most difficult and often results in deep depression. Interviews with foster parents, child welfare case workers, officials, but most importantly, the refugee minors themselves, provide the basis for this book about courage and love. Most of the subjects are from Southeast Asia, but some refugees from Africa and other continents are included. The various cases and interviews help readers to develop an appreciation for the trauma and apprehension faced by these individuals as well as those of the foster parents. . . . This book provides new subject matter for junior high school students and should be of general interest to any community that is assimilating a refugee or immigrant population. It would pair nicely with Jack Bennett's novel *The Voyage of the Lucky Dragon* (Prentice-Hall, 1982).

> *Sue Geren Diehl, in a review of "Into a Strange Land: Unaccompanied Refugee Youth in*

America," in School Library Journal, *Vol. 33, No. 10, June-July, 1987, p. 103.*

Like previous Ashabranner books that document a minority experience in America through the lives and voices of its adolescent members, this conveys both information and humanity. . . . What comes through most clearly is courage: of the parents, sending their children to a hoped-for better life; of the foster parents, bridging an enormous cultural gap; and of the young people themselves. Most poignant are the stories of Amerasian children fathered by American soldiers: " 'I'm always watching on the streets. Maybe that way someday I'll see him. His face will be my face.' " Index and bibliography. (pp. 1-2)

> *Roger Sutton, in a review of "Into a Strange Land," in* Bulletin of the Center for Children's Books, *Vol. 41, No. 1, September, 1987, pp. 1-2.*

Starting with the story of Tran, a Vietnamese refugee teenager whose father, with absolutely no preliminary announcement, put him on a boat for freedom, and ending with a bibliography of books and reports on unaccompanied refugee minors in the United States, the authors describe the trials of this particularly needy group of refugees, primarily those from Asia, but also from Latin America. Interspersed with pictures of the refugee minors, not only right after rescue and in refugee camps, but also with American foster families, the text is as warm and personal as enlightening since it is sprinkled with interviews and anecdotes of their experiences. . . . To anyone who has not followed the international refugee situation closely, this book is a revelation and very upsetting. It is heartwarming to read that most of these kids are surviving well here and leading productive working and academic lives. Given the absence of fictional accounts of their experiences, this book fills an enormous gap in documenting their struggles in print and raising awareness among the rest of us. Unfortunately this format is not conducive to YA pickup appeal, but the first chapter is so utterly mesmerizing that good booktalkers should be able to attract readers. It should definitely be available in libraries where there are large numbers of new immigrant populations as a means of possibly helping new and established American kids understand each other better. It gives pause to all of us who take being a U.S. citizen for granted. (pp. 183-84)

> *Mary K. Chelton, in a review of "Into a Strange Land," in* Voice of Youth Advocates, *Vol. 10, No. 4, October, 1987, pp. 183-84.*

The Vanishing Border: A Photographic Journey along Our Frontier with Mexico **(1987)**

Author and photographer have made several trips to the U. S.-Mexican border over the years. Here they recreate a 2,000 mile journey from west to east, from the Pacific Ocean to the Gulf of Mexico. Their main focus is life on the U. S. side of the border and, more specifically, some of the problems with labor and immigration. While it would be virtually impossible to cover every issue and every aspect in one volume, Ashabranner has done an admirable job of distilling the essence of life in the various

Ashabranner with a group of students at the Vietnam Veterans Memorial, Washington, D.C.

regions along our southern frontier. He writes in a lively style that is sure to capture readers' interest, offering personal experiences supported by facts and statistics. Emminently readable, Ashabranner's verbal portrait is greatly enhanced by [Paul] Conklin's black-and-white photographs.

> *Dennis C. Tucker, in a review of "The Vanishing Border: A Photographic Journey along Our Frontier with Mexico," in* School Library Journal, *Vol. 34, No. 6, February, 1988, p. 87.*

In their usual informal documentary style, combining photographs, interviews, commentary, and history, Ashabranner and photographer Conklin focus on what they have touched on in some of their earlier photo essays—life in the 2,000-mile U.S.-Mexico border country. . . . The general tone is upbeat, but the book does not evade the huge, complex problems: the desperate poverty that drives thousands to risk illegal entry; the U.S.-owned border factories that provide jobs, but at pitifully low wages; the smuggling in both directions. . . . Though the colloquial tone is occasionally overdone—one place "fairly drips with history"—the humane text and photos bring immediacy to abstract issues by showing not only individual border people in all their variety but also the connections that

barbed wire cannot sever. No notes; bibliography of books, articles, and reports; index.

> *Hazel Rochman, in a review of "The Vanishing Border: A Photographic Journey along Our Frontier with Mexico," in* Booklist, *Vol. 84, No. 11, February 1, 1988, p. 921.*

Ashabranner's investigative journey is recorded in a text that is sympathetic and lucid, based on many interviews on both sides of the border. He points out how interdependent the neighboring areas are, especially in the establishment of U.S.-owned assembly plants in Mexican border cities, in the sharing of conservation or irrigation schemes, in the back-and-forth flow of tourist, family, or business crossovers. The book is marred occasionally by florid passages, but is informative and detailed, is given variety by cited interviews, and is enhanced by the many well-placed photographs.

> *Zena Sutherland, in a review of "The Vanishing Border: A Photographic Journey along Our Frontier with Mexico," in* Bulletin of the Center for Children's Books, *Vol. 41, No. 7, March, 1988, p. 130.*

Always to Remember: The Story of the Vietnam Veterans Memorial (1988)

No current events writer for young people does a better job than Ashabranner in providing an enlightening balance of solid information, pertinent anecdote, and thoughtful opinion. Beginning with a concise (and fair) chapter on the Vietnam War, the author then recounts the hard work of Jan Scruggs, the vet who began the Vietnam Veterans Memorial Fund, and Maya Lin, the 21-year-old architecture student who won the contest to design the monument. While there is plenty in this book to bring tears, Ashabranner is unobtrusive, allowing the veterans, families, and the memorial to speak for themselves, and his own message that war "is about sacrifice and sorrow, not about glory and reward" is quietly woven in. Although the book lacks pictures that convey a sense of the sculpture as a whole (an aerial view would have been helpful), Jennifer Ashabranner's photographs capture the details of flowers and fatigues left along the base of the monument wall but, as the architect intended, viewers will find their attentions primarily caught by the endless rows of names.

> *Roger Sutton, in a review of "Always to Remember: The Story of the Vietnam Veterans Memorial," in* Bulletin of the Center for Children's Books, *Vol. 42, No. 1, September, 1988, p. 2.*

In this slender volume, readers discover the how and why of the building of the National Vietnam Veterans Memorial in Washington, D.C. . . . This is a story of history, of political pandering and grandstanding, and probably most importantly, of conflict resolution and healing. The description in the final chapters of the variety of visitors to the memorial and their displays of grief and reverence are stirring regardless of one's view of the war itself. The vital statistics of the physical memorial are given in an appendix, but the real meaning of the memorial is captured in the retelling of its improbable history and the depiction of its compelling and awe-inspiring presence. Well positioned black-and-white photographs add depth and interest. Like the memorial itself, *Always to Remember* will inspire contemplation and reflection among its readers. (pp. 165-66)

> *Steve Matthews, in a review of "Always to Remember: The Story of the Vietnam Veterans Memorial," in* School Library Journal, *Vol. 35, No. 2, October, 1988, pp. 165-66.*

Ashabranner does an outstanding job of providing a historical explanation as to why the wall was built. . . . [He] also writes about people's reactions to the wall when they visit it. The feelings which he describes are moving. I feel teenagers in the 1980s will readily be able to relate to these feelings since their lives have been directly affected by their fathers' and mothers' experiences from that era. In a sense, this book shows how the healing process for the nation is taking place, and as Ashabranner states, "It will make us remember that war . . . is about sacrifice and sorrow, not about glory and reward." The script is written simply and will appeal to anyone with an interest in the Vietnam War. I highly recommend this book.

> *Laura L. Lent, in a review of "Always to Remember: The Story of the Vietnam Veterans Memorial," in* Voice of Youth Advocates, *Vol. 11, No. 6, February, 1989, p. 297.*

Born to the Land: An American Portrait (1989)

Though less a portrait of Luna County, New Mexico, and its county seat—Deming—than a series of portraits of some of its more successful ranch and farm families, this nonetheless gives a good sense of what it might be like to live in this unique, relatively unfamiliar region.

After a brief historical introduction, the author devotes the book's longest section to ranch life, especially on the hard-working, multigenerational Nunn family's 130,000 acres—not enough to make them wealthy in this arid country: Joe Bill Nunn and his wife couldn't afford a washing machine till after their children were out of diapers. Still, it's clearly satisfying labor in beautiful surroundings. Nearby, farmers like Frank Smyer—whose great-grandfather homesteaded here—stay afloat by introducing new crops: chiles, peacans. A final chapter describes Deming and mentions Luna County's ethnic diversity (50% Hispanic, "the backbone of [the] work force," but accorded only a page here).

As in their other collaborations . . . , [Paul] Conklin's searching portraits, candid photos, and telling landscapes (all in black and white) contribute a great deal to the information. An interesting, authentic picture of a tough, valuable slice of American life.

> *A review of "Born to the Land: An American Portrait," in* Kirkus Reviews, *Vol. LVII, No. 5, March 1, 1989, p. 374.*

Focusing on the Nunn family, whom the author previously interviewed in *The Vanishing Border,* Ashabranner examines the contemporary situation of ranchers, and, to a lesser extent, farmers, in southwestern New Mexico. While the empathy that the author and illustrator consistently demonstrate with their subjects is usually a strong aspect of their books, here the fellow-feeling falls into an idyllic, adulatory tone—Ashabranner usually asks tougher questions than the ones posed here. Scant attention is paid to the Mexican-American inhabitants of Luna County—it is not until the end of the book that we are told Hispanics constitute half the county population. The ranchers never mention their Hispanic neighbors or employees, and the book glides over problems of ethnic relations. Although Ashabranner is usually better at providing social and political context (as in *The Vanishing Border* or *Dark Harvest*), his (and Conklin's) gift for detail serves them well when describing the actual work of a ranch: branding, corralling, selling cattle, and always praying for rain.

> *Roger Sutton, in a review of "Born to the Land: An American Portrait," in* Bulletin of the Center for Children's Books, *Vol. 42, No. 9, May, 1989, p. 216.*

"It is not a lucrative business and it is awfully hard work." With such a sentiment so universally expressed by the folks from Luna County, New Mexico, one might well ask, "Just why *do* people stay in farming and ranching?" The answer to this mystery unfolds gently through probing interviews and revealing photographs. Spiced with anecdotes and local color, the prose is friendly and highly readable: " 'They say,' [Smokey] said to us once, 'that if you wear out a pair of boots in this country, you will never leave.' But then he couldn't resist adding, 'Of course, if you stay that long, you won't have enough money to leave.' " Ashabranner weaves several dramatic subplots into the skillfully written prose: the ever-present threat of drought; the interplay of the generations; the effect of history and chance on the present; and the impact of geography on an area's development. The balanced selection of interviewees presents a complete portrait of a community: young and old, men and women, minorities, newcomers and old-timers. The clear black-and-white photographs complement the text perfectly. Throughout the book, readers meet many people, each unique, yet all similar in their tenacious love of the land and willingness to struggle to make a living from it. There is much to be learned and enjoyed in this short piece of fine nonfiction. (pp. 143-44)

> *Lee Bock, in a review of "Born to the Land: An American Portrait," in* School Library Journal, *Vol. 35, No. 12, August, 1989, pp. 143-44.*

I'm in the Zoo, Too! (1989)

Addressing children's curiosity about animals that live in the zoo without being part of it, Ashabranner tells how Burl the Squirrel asks what the zoo animals have that he doesn't. Panda says she's cute; Peacock mentions his beautiful tail; Gorilla ruefully admits that, though he's really shy and gentle, "You have to frighten people." But when

Ashabranner at his desk.

Burl moves into an empty cage and gets locked in, he discovers the true difference: zoo animals can't get out. [Illustrator Janet] Stevens' popular, comic style is appropriate to the story; her expressive animals look as though they can speak, as in fact they do. In a couple of scenes, the enclosures for some of the fiercer animals look disconcertingly inadequate, but that's a minor flaw in an unusual, entertaining story.

> *A review of "I'm in the Zoo, Too!" in* Kirkus Reviews, *Vol. LVII, No. 15, August 15, 1989, p. 1241.*

In a contemporary version of Aesop's *The Dog and the Wolf,* Burl the squirrel decides it would be more interesting to be a zoo exhibit than just a squirrel living in the zoo park. He canvasses several of the animals to find out how to qualify as a zoo resident, but getting locked in an empty cage turns out to be more than he bargained for. He returns to his family, deciding that although he will visit from time to time, living in the zoo is not as desirable as he had thought. Stevens' familiar humorous illustrations, with her characters occasionally bulging out of their frames, succeed better than the text. Washes of bright color are supported in close-up by black line drawing. Human characters are a nice mix of ages, sexes, and races; and animal characters, except when communicating with each other, are more realistically portrayed than in Stevens' earlier work, in keeping with their realistic setting. Ashabranner's story, too, has touches of humor, as when Burl identifies himself proudly as not just any old generic squirrel, but as an *Eastern Gray Squirrel.* The "grass is greener" theme and the reassuring return home are scaled to younger readers, but the premise is awkwardly stated and therefore confusing. There are other thin spots too—if the squirrel family can see what the monkeys are eating, why can't they see Burl locked in the nearby cage? Stevens' fans will enjoy this picture book, but because of its weak story line, it's not a first purchase. (pp. 220, 222)

> *Barbara Hutcheson, in a review of "I'm in the Zoo, Too!" in* School Library Journal, *Vol. 35, No. 13, September, 1989, pp. 220, 222.*

People Who Make a Difference (1989)

Ashabranner and Conklin's latest has a simple and worthy theme: "This is a book about heroes." The fourteen people interviewed here demonstrate a wide variety of concerns, but all share an unwavering commitment to their chosen causes. While the adulatory tone throughout the book is, perhaps, inevitable, the accounts rise above the encomium to become interesting as well as inspiring. Mary Joan Willard trains capuchin monkeys to assist quadraplegics; Frank Trejo teaches karate to handicapped children; Beverly Thomas is the principal of an inner-city high school in Detroit that sends its graduates on to Ivy League colleges. Like these heroes, the rest of the subjects—some young people themselves—seem to have been chosen not only as worthy role models, but as people whose accomplishments will have a special meaning for young adults. A welcome balance to the teen-magazine most-admired polls that always seem to put Michael J. Fox at the top of the list.

Roger Sutton, in a review of "People Who Make a Difference," in Bulletin of the Center for Children's Books, *Vol. 43, No. 2, October, 1989, p. 27.*

Mr. Ashabranner invites the reader along as he and Paul Conklin interview a collection of very special people who have a common commitment to making life better in their communities, for themselves and for their families. . . . Wonderful as a focal point for discussion, the book will be useful in social studies class and can be easily sold in a book talk. Readers cannot help but be inspired and spurred on to emulate these ordinary citizens who have chosen the extraordinary. Bibliography and index.

Elizabeth S. Watson, in a review of "People Who Make a Difference," in The Horn Book Magazine, *Vol. LXVI, No. 2, March-April, 1990, p. 218.*

Counting America: The Story of the United States Census (with Melissa Ashabranner, 1989)

The Ashabranners' examination of a crucial governmental operation, which will take center stage during the upcoming 1990 census, is informed with historical perspective and contemporary anecdote. The authors explain how census data are collected, collated, and used, including a cogent explanation of congressional apportionment. Readers will enjoy the stories of dogged enumerators trying to track everybody down even in circumstances such as the Mount Saint Helens eruption in 1980. Sensitive social and political questions about undercounting and illegal immigrants are fairly discussed; unfortunately, the authors do not discuss the increasing privatization and cost of census information. Photographs clearly chronologize the refinements in census automation; glossary, bibliography, and index are included.

Roger Sutton, in a review of "Counting America: The Story of the United States Census," in Bulletin of the Center for Children's Books, *Vol. 43, No. 3, November, 1989, p. 50.*

Basic literature on this topic has been largely confined to the publications of the Census Bureau itself, so this source represents new material for this grade range. Black-and-white contemporary and historical photographs along with samples of census questionnaires complement the clear, engaging writing style. This title should find a ready audience as the bicentennial anniversary of the census is observed in 1990. Provision of a glossary, bibliography, and index also ensure continued use as a reference tool beyond next year.

Nancy E. Curran, in a review of "Counting America: The Story of the United States Census," in School Library Journal, *Vol. 35, No. 16, December, 1989, p. 104.*

One of the best features of this volume is the sharp black and white illustrations on nearly every page. They visually confirm what the text states—that the decennial census is a vast undertaking of great importance to government and business in the United States. Photographs show census enumerators calling on homes or finding the homeless. Census employees are pictured at work reviewing stacks of completed census forms, inspecting microfilm, and using an automated map system. Historic prints and photographs provide a visual history of the different systems of tabulating results.

In light of the problems encountered in completing the 1990 census, the reader will appreciate the Ashabranners' points about historical mistrust of census takers, the difficulty of getting people to pick out census forms from piles of junk mail, and efforts to find 'invisible' people. Since publication of the book was timed to coincide with preparation for the 1990 census rather than its completion, supplementary reading will be necessary to finish the story of the difficulties in carrying out the 1990 census and the new information which will be compiled from the results.

Unfortunately, the 1990 census is referred to in the future tense throughout, giving the false impression that the book is already out of date. One other minor complaint is that the book omits mention of how censuses from 1790 to 1920 are used for research in family history. Librarians who have not already bought a copy should submit an order now for this excellent presentation of information on a timely topic. (pp. 8-9)

Susan Hamilton, in a review of "Counting America," in Appraisal: Children's Science Books, *Vol. 23, No. 3, Fall, 1990, pp. 8-9.*

Crazy about German Shepherds (1990)

This picture of a rough and tumble life with four German shepherds (plus puppies) must have been a refreshing assignment for Ashabranner *père et fille.* Raising dogs in Virginia's Blue Ridge mountains, Peggy O'Callaghan has just the life she aimed for: "a rural place with enough room to raise German shepherds, a place close enough to affluent centers for me to build a grooming business, teach classes in obedience training, and, in time, raise and sell puppies." The text is by Peggy as told to the author, and it has an appealing combination of facts about shepherds, information about training and grooming, and—most important for kids—lots of dog anecdotes, including two first-rate snake stories: "As I carefully lowered the flashlight, Zoe suddenly rushed toward me, snarling ferociously. I looked down and there, only a few inches from my hand, was another copperhead, coiled and ready to strike." Vocational portraits are rarely as comprehensive or as involving as this one, which will convince both dog-lovers and -haters that they made the right decision. The many photos [by Jennifer Ashabranner] are of varying quality: some clear and informative, others fuzzy or gray and poorly placed in relation to the text. An index and suggested reading list are included.

Roger Sutton, in a review of "Crazy about German Shepherds," in Bulletin of the Center for Children's Books, *Vol. 44, No. 1, September, 1990, p. 2.*

Through a first-person narrative, Peggy O'Callaghan describes her life raising and working with German shepherds. The restrained, low-key style includes anecdotes about many dogs over several years. This is not a "how to" in any sense, although O'Callaghan discusses many aspects of dog care and psychology as she tells readers about how she set up her breeding kennel and grooming business. It is more about a woman's dream, of what she wanted from life, and how she made that dream come true through unremitting hard work and sacrifice. Her story is about personal happiness and dedication; the dogs are simply a vehicle. (pp. 125-26)

> *Carole B. Kirkpatrick, in a review of "Crazy about German Shepherds," in* School Library Journal, *Vol. 36, No. 12, December, 1990, pp. 125-26.*

The Times of My Life: A Memoir (1990)

Ashabranner's own story lacks the emotional impact and candor of his many fine nonfiction books for young people. It's hard to believe that this earnest autobiography with its avuncular tone is by the writer of such stunning books as **Always to Remember.** Not that Ashabranner hasn't lived through interesting times, from his Depression childhood and his World War II navy experience to his years as a top administrator in the Peace Corps. But unlike Meltzer in *Starting from Home,* Ashabranner gives us too little insight into how external events affected him personally. When he does let down his guard—for example, about his motives in going to war or to underdeveloped Africa—he shows an honest tangle of duty and self-interest ("More than anything else, it was a feeling of not wanting to be left out"). Readers will like his anecdotal account of what he did in the Peace Corps, abroad and at home, especially if his **Moment of Truth: The First Ten Years of the Peace Corps** (1971) is unavailable in the library. Bibliography, photos, index.

> *Hazel Rochman, in a review of "The Times of My Life: A Memoir," in* Booklist, *Vol. 87, No. 6, November 15, 1990, p. 611.*

Ashabranner is a fine storyteller, and what he chooses to tell is always interesting; he includes some wonderful anecdotes, especially from his Peace Corps years (e.g., one volunteer, bitten by a venomous snake, seized the opportunity to demonstrate the proper treatment to his class), and illuminates historical events from his personal vantage point. Meanwhile, he paints an engaging, modest picture of a talented, compassionate man who has consistently used his gifts to make the world a better place. Like Meltzer's *Starting from Home* (1988), a memorable self-portrait. (pp. 1597-98)

> *A review of "The Times of My Life: A Memoir," in* Kirkus Reviews, *Vol. LVIII, No. 22, November 15, 1990, pp. 1597-98.*

As the author recounts his childhood and adult life, a picture emerges of a good and caring human being. The portrait is not surprising to anyone who has read Ashabranner's nonfiction for young people, in which he tells human stories with compassion and concern. A man who has unconsciously lived his life in the mode of one of his own subjects, so as to "make a difference," he tells his story in a straightforward account whose impact is the greater because it doesn't try to impress. Whether recounting his experiences in World War II, the Point Four program, the Peace Corps, or the Ford Foundation, the author's values are clear. Through his eyes and experiences, today's young people will learn a great deal about developing principles and convictions—ones different, perhaps, from those that are popularly held—and then basing one's life decisions on those principles and convictions. The very best of biography for children expands their knowledge and gives them new ideas to ponder; Brent Ashabranner has provided just such ideas in his memoir.

> *Elizabeth S. Watson, in a review of "The Times of My Life: A Memoir," in* The Horn Book Magazine, *Vol. LXVII, No. 1, January-February, 1991, p. 81.*

A Grateful Nation: The Story of Arlington National Cemetery (1990)

A gentle, intelligent portrait of the Virginia site that has become a national shrine where members of the armed services are honored with dignified tradition and carefully honed ritual.

Surveying the cemetery's history, Ashabranner enlivens his story with telling facts. The property came to Robert E. Lee through his wife, Washington's step-great-granddaughter; it was confiscated, through a legal ruse, during the Civil War (in 1883, the Supreme Court awarded Lee's son $150,000 compensation). A cemetery was urgently needed for the Union dead, but burying them around the Lees' home was also an act of vengeance. Later, Confederate soldiers were also buried at Arlington; at first they were denied flowers, but even that symbolic retribution was revoked after a strong wind redistributed blossoms during the night after the first Memorial Day, in 1868, suggesting reconciliation as a better policy.

Ashabranner interviews people at Arlington (a sergeant who plays taps at funerals, men who train the horses, a landscaper, a guard at the Tomb of the Unknown Soldier) and depicts its daily and annual events and ceremony. [Jennifer Ashabranner's] b&w photos nicely complement the text, dramatizing the range of events that occur there. Well-crafted nonfiction that gives insight into how a well-established institution evolves through the interaction of history and more personal events. (pp. 1667-68)

> *A review of "A Grateful Nation: The Story of Arlington National Cemetery," in* Kirkus Reviews, *Vol. LVIII, No. 23, December 1, 1990, pp. 1667-68.*

[To] many Americans, perhaps, the cemetery at Arlington means above all a plain slate tablet set before a wavering flame in a field of granite stones: the grave of John F. Kennedy.

In this meditative and unsentimental portrait of the cemetery, Brent Ashabranner does devote a chapter to its most famous grave, recalling the poignant story of how Kennedy had looked out over the rows of headstones from the portico of Arlington House on a visit earlier in 1963 and remarked, "It's so beautiful, I could stay here forever."

But Ashabranner, author of many award-winning children's books on historical and social issues, also sets the cemetery in a much wider context. He writes about its bitter Civil War origins. . . .

He also writes about the Tomb of the Unknown Soldier, to him the spiritual heart of the place, and what it means to the men of the U.S. 3rd Infantry who do guard duty there. He talks to some of the many people who serve at Arlington, from the superintendent to the soldiers who provide escorts and the buglers who play taps at military funerals to horticulturists and gravediggers, all with a part to play in the ironically peaceful and ordered burial ceremony that takes place here on average 15 times a day.

> *Elizabeth Ward, in a review of "A Grateful Nation: The Story of Arlington National Cemetery," in* Book World—The Washington Post, *Vol. XXI, No. 10, March 10, 1991, p. 8.*

Pertinent facts that an encyclopedia entry would contain are here, but *A Grateful Nation* goes far beyond that. Ashabranner, an accomplished nonfiction author for young readers, brings soul to his moving account of our most famous national cemetery. In his excellent depictive and anecdotal style, Ashabranner describes many aspects of the shrine: its origins, famous people interred there, the Tomb of the Unknown Soldier, President Kennedy's funeral, and Memorial Day ceremonies. While illustrating the solemn ambience and natural beauty of this historic site, the author also imparts a sense of the industriousness behind the scenes. He introduces staff members and describes their various jobs dealing with funerals, special ceremonies, and care of the grounds.

> *Jackie Cronin, in a review of "A Grateful Nation: The Story of Arlington National Cemetery," in* The ALAN Review, *Vol. 18, No. 3, Spring, 1991, p. 31.*

An Ancient Heritage: The Arab-American Minority (1991)

A fascinating picture of this large but little-known group (between two and three million). Cogently summarizing Arab-American history, Ashabranner describes a steady "trickle" of Arabs to the US from the late 19th century until 1924, when non-European immigration was severely limited. Characteristically, Arabs began as peddlers and later opened small stores; readily absorbed by the mainstream, their children often became professionals. The establishment of Israel began a second wave that included many Palestinians, whose plight Ashabranner presents with well-founded sympathy. The bulk of the book consists of positive anecdotal portraits (beautifully supported by [Paul] Conklin's b&w photos), based on interviews and

featuring hard-working achievers like researchers, artists, and businessmen. A gas-station owner and out-of-work automotive worker are exceptions here; the author is deliberately countering negative stereotypes, and his examples and explicit discussion of the problem are especially telling. A bit one-sided, but still a valuable survey. Bibliography; index.

> *A review of "An Ancient Heritage: The Arab-American Minority," in* Kirkus Reviews, *Vol. LIX, No. 5, March 1, 1991, p. 305.*

Ashabranner and Conklin, who have worked together on such excellent ethno-cultural photo-essays as **The Vanishing Border,** demonstrate their usual empathy for their subjects, a warming combination of personal involvement and unobtrusive background research. The book shows what's special about Arab-American culture: what various groups left behind in the strife-torn Middle East ("I left a country that once was beautiful and part of me will always be sad"); why they came here; why they stay; and how they live—students, teachers, shopkeepers, artists, doctors, etc., from Boston and Detroit to Portland and New Orleans. At the same time, readers will see how Arab Americans are like all immigrant groups: the differences among generations; the need to live in two cultures; for some, the memory of pain and dream of return, even while they work hard and enjoy their good fortune in America. Especially important in a time of war and bigotry, this enjoyable introduction to a unique ethnic minority demonstrates its rich contribution to our national culture.

> *Hazel Rochman, in a review of "An Ancient Heritage: The Arab-American Minority," in* Booklist, *Vol. 87, No. 14, March 15, 1991, p. 1462.*

Believing that people often dismiss—or even hate—what they don't know or understand, social science writer Ashabranner formulates a sturdy response to the defamation that Arab-Americans often endure. One immigrant points out that Americans don't realize Arabs came here to escape hatred and violence. Placing particular emphasis on how cultural traits came about from the harsh desert environment, the profiles stress close Arab family ties, a driving work ethic and emphasis on education. From this, youngsters can conclude Arab-Americans are more like themselves and other immigrant groups than they are dissimilar. The author reports that most Arab-Americans here feel Jews have turned American opinion against them; one is quoted as saying, "Arab Americans bear the burden of the Israeli-Arab conflict." (Readers will have to look elsewhere for Israel's point of view on the longstanding Palestinian issue.) Impressive photos complement an informative, timely introduction.

> *A review of "An Ancient Heritage: The Arab-American Minority," in* Publishers Weekly, *Vol. 238, No. 14, March 22, 1991, p. 81.*

Jeannie Baker

1950-

English-born Australian author and illustrator of picture books.

Major works include *Grandmother* (1978), *Home in the Sky* (1984), *Where the Forest Meets the Sea* (1987), *Window* (1991).

Considered one of Australia's most gifted contemporary creators of juvenile literature, Baker is respected as an original and inventive artist whose unique vision and distinctive technique has expanded the boundaries of the picture book genre. The author of thought-provoking works which reflect her observations of both human nature and the natural world, Baker usually features environmental subjects and the warm relationships between small children and older adults in her books. Underscoring her works, which are usually set in Australia, is Baker's attempt to raise the consciousness of her readers regarding the environment; for example, on the last page of *Where the Forest Meets the Sea,* a picture book set in a tropical forest in North Queensland which is perhaps her most popular title, Baker includes an explanation of the dangers currently facing the forest. Her interest in the environment also influences Baker's work as an illustrator: calling her technique "relief collage," she combines natural materials such as wood, clay, sand, and hair with paper, cloth, string and other items—both acquired and handmade—to create textured pieces which have tactile and spatial dimensions. Lauded for the beauty, craftsmanship, sophistication, and realism of her art as well as for its stunningly evocative qualities, Baker is often praised as a designer; author and critic Elaine Moss, for whom Baker provided the pictures for *Polar* (1975), the story of an inventive white teddy bear, notes that "collage pictures of extraordinary quality and detail lift this artist's work into a class on its own."

Baker began her career as a writer and illustrator for children with *Grandfather* (1977) and *Grandmother,* picture books in which a small girl shares activities with her grandparents at work and at home; the latter story, in which Baker depicts the older character as a sculptor and craftswoman whose works are displayed in her home, is especially well received. With *Millicent* (1980), a story inspired by the milieu of Sydney's Hyde Park, Baker describes the solitary thoughts of an elderly bag lady who walks through the park to feed the pigeons while a variety of activities takes place around her. With *One Hungry Spider* (1982) and *Home in the Sky,* Baker introduces animals as protagonists: in *One Hungry Spider,* she presents information about spiders, their prey, and their predators in a narrative that also serves as a counting book, while in *Home in the Sky* she uses a Manhattan setting to outline how a white homing pigeon, who escapes from his elderly owner and is found in a subway by a young boy, safely returns home. Baker's concern for nature is especially strong

in *When the Forest Meets the Sea* and *Window.* In the former, a boy and his father explore the Daintree Wilderness, a tropical forest that borders the Great Barrier Reef. Seeing its wildlife, the boy imagines prehistoric creatures and the aborigines who have lived there as well as the future possibilities of the forest being littered or cleared for high-rise apartments. In *Window,* which is Baker's only wordless book, a mother holding her newborn son gazes out of the window of their Australian home at the lushness of the landscape; in subsequent pages, Baker shows the changes to the area over a twenty-year period. As a parallel to the thirteen scenes depicting the development of the land from farming community to suburb and city, she outlines the growth of the baby boy, Sam, who in the last frames has married and moved to a new house in the country; in the final scene, Sam holds his own newborn son and looks out at a sign that says "House Blocks for Sale." *Home in the Sky* was commended for the Australian Picture Book of the Year in 1985, while *Where the Forest Meets the Sea* was the recipient of the Earthworm Award in 1988 and was selected as an honor book by the IBBY committee in the same year. Baker's art has been exhibited frequently in both Australia and England and is represented in the permanent collections of both the Australian National

Gallery and the Dromkeen Museum of Children's Literature.

(See also *Something about the Author,* Vol. 23, and *Contemporary Authors,* Vols. 97-100.)

AUTHOR'S COMMENTARY

[Jeannie Baker] must be one of the world's finest exponents of the art of collage.

I have been intrigued by and have admired Jeannie's work ever since I saw the original collage constructions for *Grandmother* hanging at "Dromkeen", and above our bed at home hangs a framed, signed print blown up from the opening spread of her book *Home in the Sky.* A flock of pigeons wheel across the sky behind the turrets of the Woolworth Tower in New York. To me it symbolizes the energy and the elegance which characterize all of Jeannie Baker's work. No other print that I have ever seen is as three-dimensional or as tactile. In my imagination I have climbed that tower many times. I have reached out and have felt the fluttering of pigeons. In the book itself I want to touch and feel the stone lace-work of the balustrades and on another page I want to stroke the pigeon nestling on Mike's shoulder. Mike's coat and hat, the fuzz on his face, the tough, sculptured skin of his neck, nose and cheek bones and the pigeon itself make up a gradation of textures more sensory than any photograph could capture, and they combine to form a powerful but tender image that goes straight to the heart.

While Jeannie was a student at Brighton College of Art in England she developed her personal idea of "grandfatherliness" through a simple text which she extended by images in collage. "My characters are always based on real people," she admitted, "but are composites. And I find old faces interesting and beautiful. Young faces don't work in quite the same way—but, then, children aren't afraid of old faces, indeed they relate and warm to old people." So *Grandfather* and her later book *Grandmother* are essentially studies of elderly people and of places (the setting for *Grandfather* is as English as football pools, that for *Grandmother* is pure Tasmanian) seen through a child's eyes and perceptions. They are also Jeannie playing around with ideas; exploring herself. (p. 20)

Her aim, she told me, was to explore sensory experiences; to share her appreciation of everyday things and their characteristics; to convey feelings rather than to produce a traditional narrative; to create images of relationships. Her books evolve through word and drawings. "The words," she says, "have to be carefully placed like the words of a poem. I work and re-work the text until I get it as right as I can." Then she develops the drawings into collage constructs which are photographed to make the plates for her books.

In 1982 Jeannie, with the assistance of the Crafts Board of the Australia Council, had a studio in New York. She spent days walking the streets, jotting down ideas [for *Home in the Sky*] as she responded to the vibrancy of the city. At the same time she was learning about herself—a true journey of exploration, symbolized perhaps by Mike's homing pigeons which he keeps in the heart of the most cityish of all cities.

Scenes for the story were constructed from an array of materials: leaves, grass, pigeon feathers, cloth, clay, hair, scraps of paper and newsprint, litter—whatever suited her purpose. The leaves and grass were preserved in a variety of chemicals including glycerine to preserve the flexibility of the vegetation, then sprayed with oil paint to give a permanent colour. From these materials she constructed and sculptured scenes which were then photographed ready for production. (pp. 20-1)

I asked Jeannie if she were essentially a city person and she said "Yes". But she feels that city dwellers and most Australians have lost touch with the land. So in 1984 she went to Cairns and took off for two months by herself with her camera and sketch book into the wilderness between the Daintree River and Bloomfield. If her slender build suggests fragility, that is an illusion. Carrying a tent and supplies and a sheet of plastic for sleeping out; warned to take a gun to ward off wild pigs, drug growers and snakes that don't even live in the forest, Jeannie set off on another and very different journey of self discovery and development. The pages of *Where the Forest Meets the Sea* trace that journey, in which not only Australians but all spiritual people will join as in a pilgrimage. This time, and rightly so, the story is told in the first person by a young boy. His father is present at the beginning and near the end (and again the quiet strength of age is wonderfully expressed) but the boy journeys alone into the forest. As he follows the creek we enter a primeval world and go with him to experience the majesty, mystery and meaning of the forest. Before the boy leaves the beach, once in the forest, and again when he comes out of the forest a double image is superimposed photographically on the scene to give a time perspective. The forest itself is frozen in time and is so powerfully represented that I could feel it, smell it, and hear its sounds and silences.

The actual collages which will form a Travelling Exhibition from March 1988 to January 1989 are breathtaking. I asked Jeannie if she used tweezers to place the tiny fish cutouts of blue sweet wrapping and she said, "No, I only use my fingers." The sand is real, but painted over to get the exact colour for reproduction, the foliage and other materials Jeannie collected on her second sojourn in the wilderness. I don't think any book has ever given me a stronger sense of place and therefore, paradoxically, a greater sense of universality. . . .

If *Millicent* is an image of the earth-bound city dweller and *Home in the Sky* is a symbol of how man can soar above his man-made environment, *Where the Forest Meets the Sea* confirms the value to man of elemental things and the enduring pattern of nature itself—although the final image of the book carries an urgent warning which we neglect at our peril.

I asked Jeannie Baker about the origins of her preoccupation with shape, colour and texture. "As long as I can remember I was fascinated with peeling plaster on an old wall. I could see the natural effects of erosion: the cracks, the frayed edges. I could see beauty in a rusting tin on a tip. I have always thought deeply about materials."

To obtain the effect she wants, this meticulous artist will change and refine her work over and over again. There are four or five lay-out versions of the last page of her latest book, she tells me.

Such artistry and craft, such integrity, are a gift she offers the reader and the viewer. (p. 21)

> *Maurice Saxby, "Know the Author/Illustrator: Jeannie Baker," in* Magpies, *Vol. 3, No. 1, March, 1988, pp. 20-1.*

TITLE COMMENTARY

Grandfather (1977)

Grandfather, which depends for its best effects on collage, is perhaps just a little too clever. Grandfather runs a junk shop and the little girl is allowed to help. Nothing much happens. The drawing is scaled down to the same uneventful level. Small children will find many things to identify here, but they may feel just a little cheated by this sophisticated naivety.

> *M. Crouch, in a review of "Grandfather," in* The Junior Bookshelf, *Vol. 41, No. 5, October, 1977, p. 272.*

This is the very intimate story of a little girl's day spent in her grandfather's junk shop. The first-person narration has immense charm and authenticity. One feels very close to the inner as well as the outer life of the child as she dresses up in old-fashioned garments or secretly picks paint off the window frame to explore the colours underneath. The pictures are done in collage using materials ranging from old photographs to knitted fabric; they can be a special source of interest to children wishing to attempt similar work themselves. (pp. 230, 233)

> *Aidan Warlow, in a review of "Grandfather," in* The School Librarian, *Vol. 26, No. 3, September, 1978, pp. 230, 233.*

Grandmother (1978)

Carefully selected objects and scenes create a mood of affection and aesthetic pleasure in which a small girl and her grandmother (who is bent and wrinkled but lively and concerned) enjoy a day together in a house deep in a tangled garden, full of *objets trouvés* (stones, feathers) and of Grandmother's own creations (cat figurines, gnarled wood carvings of deities among the bushes). Montage and photography are brilliantly used to back up and develop the short, artless sentences in which a child expresses a unique and mutually rewarding relationship.

> *Margery Fisher, in a review of "Grandmother," in* Growing Point, *Vol. 17, No. 2, July, 1978, p. 3368.*

Grandmother's house is a homey one indeed, and Baker's textured collages give the impression of "real" nubby carpet, weathered wood, and crinkly leather chair. You might expect the three bears to pop into that empty parlor, but instead we have a little girl (in a similarly textured knit sweater) visiting grandmother. The two walk among stone statues in a jungle-like garden; they feed the birds and take Grandmother's wash from the line; they drink chocolate and tea and start to knit a "scarf of rainbows." (This last, of course, brings several balls of colored yarn into the picture.) "I love my grandmother," reads the last sentence—the falsest note of all, as Baker's tricky pictures call such attention to the artifice that the intrusion of human emotion seems bizarre.

> *A review of "Grandmother," in* Kirkus Reviews, *Vol. XLVII, No. 7, April 1, 1979, p. 384.*

Of Jeannie Baker's three outstanding picture books about the relationship of old and young, *Grandfather* and *Millicent* are out of print . . . but *Grandmother* lives on. In it a girl visits her lonely old grandmother who is, despite gnarled hands and rheumatic knees, still a craftswoman. Once a sculptor, she now makes patchwork quilts, and after a walk in her jungly garden she teaches her granddaughter to knit. Collage pictures of extraordinary quality and detail lift this artist's work into a class on its own.

> *Elaine Moss, in a review of "Grandmother," in her* Picture Books for Young People 9-13, *second edition, The Thimble Press, 1985, p. 28.*

Millicent (1980)

Walking through the park to feed the pigeons, an old lady wearing a baggy sweater and carrying a shopping bag is thinking her private thoughts while all around her other people go about their business of talking, playing, sunbathing, taking pictures or sleeping on the grass. The author/artist's highly realistic photo-collage pictures use clay, cardboard and paint as well as real hair, straw, feathers, cloth, wood and leaves and grass to form the people, birds, animals, benches, statues, fountains and the park and city street settings. The pictures are quiet in tone but with odd twists of humor here and there and a wealth of telling detail, including a sprinkling of graffiti and a broken umbrella hung over the outstretched arm of a statue; the other people in the scenes look as if they, too, have their own stories to tell. But Millicent's story, such as it is, doesn't offer much for picture-book age children unacquainted with the sociological phenomenon of shopping bag ladies. (pp. 57-8)

> *Karen Ritter, in a review of "Millicent," in* School Library Journal, *Vol. 27, No. 3, November, 1980, pp. 57-8.*

[*Millicent*] will hold child and adult suspended in wonder. To say that Millicent, the park, the people there, the pigeons the old lady comes to feed, are collage pictures made from feathers, leaves, tiny hand knitted jerseys, small clay people, suggests something cosy and cuddly. Quite otherwise. This is a book of brilliant design and quite extraordinary vision—and with its humaneness I reckon it's a masterpiece.

> *Leila Berg, "Matters of Life and Death," in*

The Times Educational Supplement, *No. 3545, June 8, 1984, p. 50.*

One Hungry Spider   (1982)

In the world of counting books, Eric Carle's *The Hungry Caterpillar* is hard to follow. Jeannie Baker has tried with **One Hungry Spider.** "One hungry spider spun a web between two branches. Three birds flew by . . . ". The pictures are photographs of stuffed insects set against an increasingly dilapidated web and a few twigs. It is not easy to make this type of ingredient look interesting and the author hasn't.

Lucy Micklethwait, "One to Ten and Beyond," in The Times Literary Supplement, No. 4146, September 17, 1982, p. 1003.

An oversize book uses a mixed-media collage to show numbers from one to ten, tell a story, and give some information about spiders, and does it very nicely. There is a double-page spread for each digit, and a sentence or two on each verso page. "One hungry spider / spun a web between two branches / Three birds flew close by, the spider kept still, she did not want them to see her / Four grasshoppers came jumping along . . . " At the end, the spider eats her old web and builds a new one, and an appended section gives more information about the spider in the book, Orbweb Eriophora. The illustrations and text are carefully integrated in a functional and attractive counting book.

Zena Sutherland, in a review of "One Hungry Spider," in Bulletin of the Center for Children's Books, Vol. 36, No. 5, January, 1983, p. 82.

This is more than the usual counting book, for although numbers do appear in progression, there is also a continuous sequence of events and information. Children can see which insects escape the spider and which the spider declines to eat, can distinguish between its prey and its predators, and can meet as an extra the unusual orb-spider. Montage lifts the book from the ordinary too, with a web beautifully rendered in thread, preserved or textured leaves and embroidered insects. Bold colours and subtle shapes make the lesson a fascinating one.

Margery Fisher, in a review of "One Hungry Spider," in Growing Point, Vol. 21, No. 5, January, 1983, p. 4018.

Home in the Sky   (1984)

The tactile and spatial and atmospheric reality of these "collage constructions" of Manhattan rooftops and streetfronts will wow youngsters, and anyone else who sees them. The Central Park trees are constructed of real leaves; the buildings are modeled in relief. But this is more than skillful model-making, or clever miniaturization; it's more than three-dimensional illusionism too—though there's bound to be much exclaiming along those lines. Baker, an English-born resident of Australia, combines photographic vision, a still-life painter's sense of composi-

From Home in the Sky, *written and illustrated by Jeannie Baker.*

tion and color relations, and a goldsmith's delicate, expressive detailing. But the object of all her attention is, first, "an abandoned, burned-out building" where a man named Mike keeps pigeons; the subject is what happens when one pigeon, Light, flies away instead of coming home. Light soars over Central Park; he loses food to the street pigeons; "his wings become heavy" in the rain. Then he flies through an open doorway, into a subway car—"where a boy picks him up, holding him firmly so he will feel safe." The first miraculous illustration is the rooftop where Mike's pigeons take off, the brown- and gray-toned roof-scape stretching to the grayed Manhattan skyline on the horizon. The second miraculous illustration is its antithesis, the subway car—where without jokiness (or Cabbage Patch mushiness) we see New York's motley people individualized in fabric and paper and clay. The boy takes Light home; "his mother explains that the band around Light's leg means that he belongs to someone"; and Light, released, flies back to Mike by "instinct." (A spectacular camera-angle up between skyscrapers.) The next morning the boy eyes a flock of wheeling pigeons, "sure he sees a white pigeon among them." The matter does suit the manner; though the verisimilitude of the constructions works against any story, this one is elemental and integral enough to pretty well hold its own. The reason: there's as much that's magical as literal in the pictures. (pp. J-86-J-87)

A review of "Home in the Sky," in Kirkus Reviews, *Juvenile Issue, Vol. LII, Nos. 18-21, November 1, 1984, pp. J-86-J-87.*

Jeannie Baker, a British artist now living in Australia, recently came to New York to cast a cold eye on its tenements, subways, Fifth Avenue, Central Park. In [this] book she has hung her sequence of handsome, sometimes engrossing views of the city on a fragile narrative string. Her art speaks for itself but the text of *Home in the Sky* can hardly be called a story.

An old man named Mike raises homing pigeons, and one day one of them, a one-legged bird of brilliant white plumage named Light, strays from the flock. After a couple of mishaps, he is befriended by "the boy" and then released to return to Mike. That is it. The prose is serviceable at best. ("He flies through an open doorway. The doors close behind him. He is in a train.") There is really nothing in the events or in the language for a child to think twice about.

The illustrations are another matter entirely. Miss Baker has constructed her superreal cityscapes from bits of cloth, paper, wood, clay, string and other mundane materials, then painted these ingenious collages, sometimes mixing sand with her pigment. The results (while not the manner) suggest what the author Elizabeth Cleaver has done in her children's books, but are not as abstract; they are also reminiscent of Red Grooms's sculptures, but lack his humor. The introduction of real feathers for feathers, real grass for grass, real human hair for human hair seems to be cheating a bit. . . . Still, Miss Baker makes stunning use of the double-page spread. Her work as a picture book artist will be worth waiting for as she develops something to say.

Michael Patrick Hearn, in a review of "Home in the Sky," in The New York Times Book Review, *December 30, 1984, p. 19.*

The story is slight and strung together; the strength of the book lies in the meticulously created (and then photographed) three-dimensional collage-constructions which colorfully detail the busy city-scape: litter, graffiti, washlines, roller skaters, baby strollers and the facades of numerous buildings form a visually pleasing and intriguing jumble. Everything from plaster to branches and twigs to fabric to chicken wire seems to have gone into this exacting recreation of the New York scene. Translating these laboriously created works of art into photographs and binding them together, however, does not necessarily make a successful picture book. Children will enjoy the initial viewing for its novelty and variety, but the text will not draw them back for a second look. (pp. 62-3)

Kristi Thomas Beavin, in a review of "Home in the Sky," in School Library Journal, *Vol. 31, No. 5, January, 1985, pp. 62-3.*

Home in the Sky has extraordinary illustrations, collages created out of fabric, clay objects, grasses, etc. It's obvious Baker spent a great deal of time creating these collages, but for all the painstaking details of the art, the realism is one-sided. A Central Park scene, for instance, shows people of color dancing to large portable radios or in other non-productive stances. In another scene that depicts people of color in stereotypical ways, one Black woman carries a shopping bag on her head, another wears multicolored rollers in her hair, three young males sit on the curb, while another group stands on the street doing nothing.

I don't doubt that the artist saw such scenes but she must have seen others of a more positive nature as well. What a shame so much effort went into such a limited picture of urban life. (pp. 8-9)

Emily Leinster, in a review of "Home in the Sky," in Interracial Books for Children Bulletin, *Vol. 17, No. 1, 1986, pp. 8-9.*

Where the Forest Meets the Sea   (1987)

From Australia, a picture book illustrated with photographs of relief collages, ingeniously constructed from many materials (including clay and preserved natural materials such as leaves, sand, and shells) to create a realistic, tactile effect.

The story is simple: a boy and his father explore a seaside tropical forest (Australia's Daintree Rainforest), the boy seeing present-day wildlife, imagining animals and aborigines of the past, and finally wondering whether a return visit will find this primeval area intact or overrun by development. The imaginary forms—whether of prehistoric creatures or the future's threatened litter—are intriguingly transparent and evanescent in contrast to the present's vivid solidity. Unusual and beautiful, this serves well its admitted purpose of provoking thought on the vexed question of preservation of natural areas; Baker's young narrator has well conveyed their majesty and wonder.

A review of "Where the Forest Meets the Sea," in Kirkus Reviews, *Vol. LVI, No. 6, March 15, 1988, p. 449.*

A careful blend of realism and imaginary situations is created skilfully by superimposing pictures within scenes, as well as by hiding creatures and people for young readers to find. The art work thus becomes a reflection of the text, both blending together. In past books, Baker's collages have overshadowed the text, but in this case, both work together to take the reader through a series of real and imaginary experiences in the rainforest. Jeannie Baker visited the Daintree Rainforest many times to collect samples of vegetation and to capture the visual impressions she needed which have given this book such an impressive authenticity. She took four years to complete this book, which is really a story, a work of art and a statement about the importance of our environment, notably the Daintree which is under threat from our encroaching civilisation. Indeed, the story ends with the boy pondering *But will the forest still be here when we come back?*

This book has wide appeal for all ages. The context of the story and the high quality of the art work readily qualify it for inclusion in school libraries and as a meaningful book at home. (pp. 26-7)

Julie Long, in a review of "Where the Forest

Meets the Sea," in Reading Time, *Vol. 32, No. 3, 1988, pp. 26-7.*

Some picture books are stunning; some are compelling; some are truly innovative in technique and design. Rarely are all three elements equally balanced as they are in this remarkable fresh variation on an ecological theme. The plot is simple; the theme is not, for it concerns the preservation of rapidly diminishing untamed lands. . . . The illustrations, which translate the text into an extraordinary visual experience, are exciting as individual works of art yet do not violate the basic requirements of the picture-story concept. They are relief collages "constructed from a multitude of materials, including modeling clay, papers, textured materials, preserved natural materials, and paints." Integrated by the artist's vision, the collages create three-dimensional effects on two-dimensional pages, drawing the reader into each scene as willing observer and explorer. Past and present merge as the forms of long vanished animals and children can be discerned in textured forms of trees and vines, scaly shapes of rocks and sand, or skeletal twigs along the creek. The final double-page spread—depicting the initial scene overlaid with the shadowy detritus of a resort development—is a powerful statement which conveys the message without preaching. An uncanny and unforgettable experience, the book represents a truly notable achievement in the picture-book genre, breaking new ground, adding new dimensions. (pp. 475-76)

> *Mary M. Burns, in a review of "Where the Forest Meets the Sea," in* The Horn Book Magazine, *Vol. LXIV, No. 4, July-August, 1988, pp. 475-76.*

A real feast for the eye (though, to my eye, the collage works less well for the human figures). The minimal text is a letdown by comparison, with no natural rhythm. In fact, the illustrations could stand alone without any text. When the boy wanders into the forest, pretending 'it is a hundred million years ago', the author provides herself with a convenient device for superimposing extinct primitive creatures from the past. I feel very uneasy that this is the only instance of Aboriginals in the text. This is an honest attempt to air the issue of the rain forests, but I do find the final image, which spells out the message hinted at throughout the book, rather crude. I would have preferred a more subtle ending, leaving it to the reader to think about why the rain forest is under threat. What will children make of it, I wonder? They will pore over the illustrations and enjoy spotting the half-hidden creatures. I doubt that young children will gain much else from the book but it will make a useful contribution in a junior classroom for a topic theme on environmental issues.

> *Angela Redfern, in a review of "Where the Forest Meets the Sea," in* The School Librarian, *Vol. 36, No. 4, November, 1988, p. 139.*

The excellent illustrations, made of relief collages, continually remind the reader of the great age of the forest, the prehistoric animal and plant life that once existed there, and the visions of the past that a youngster can experience while wandering among the trees. The book does not focus on making scientific discoveries but on imparting a sense of the importance of maintaining this forest, the largest original rain forest in Australia. The language is simple and easy to understand by 1st and 2nd graders, but the subtle message may elude them. Teachers will have to help youngsters learn the lesson, which is conveyed by illustrations rather than the text. For general awareness of our responsibility to maintain all natural resources, this book is excellent. No adult could read it without grasping the impact of the message, and no child will hear the book discussed without sensing the importance of preserving such forests.

> *Martha Sanders, in a review of "Where the Forest Meets the Sea," in* Science Books & Films, *Vol. 24, No. 3, January-February, 1989, p. 164.*

Window (1991)

A mother, holding her newborn son, gazes out the window of his room at lush vegetation, tropical birds, a pond, a kangaroo. Ten double-page illustrations following show the development—during a 20-year period—of the area outside the window. As Sam (the baby) grows older, the land is cleared, a road is built, then a farm. A housing development goes up, then takes over a hill that was once green with lush growth. Development becomes suburb, then city, complete with billboards, high-rises, noise pollution, litter, and overpopulation. Sam marries and moves to a new house in the country, where the final window scene shows him, holding his baby, staring at a sign announcing, "House Blocks For Sale." Words are unnecessary, as Baker's carefully rendered collage scenes explicitly detail the situation. Varying symbolic objects on Sam's windowsill (and the cracking and peeling of paint on the wall) add to the book's message. Baker's meticulous collages, formed from natural materials, clay, fabric, and real hair, are so detailed that they require many viewings. A final, short author's note explains the inspiration for the book: ". . . by understanding and changing the way we personally affect the environment, we can make a difference." This unusual, exceptionally well-crafted picture book might be a good way to begin.

> *Susan Scheps, in a review of "Window," in* School Library Journal, *Vol. 37, No. 3, March, 1991, p. 166.*

Baker's latest plea for the environment, like Van Allsburg's *Just a Dream* (1990), is explicit: 12 views through the same framing window detail what happens during a single generation as ugly urban life crowds out a wilderness vista. The first picture's infant becomes a boy who litters and traps wild creatures; his toys evolve from plastic dinosaurs to rockets. In the 13th picture, he and his baby are looking out a new window on another forest where "house blocks" are already for sale.

This talented Australian's collages of natural and other materials are especially suited to these beautifully evocative illustrations, in which the many carefully chosen details build a realistic picture of civilization's sorry progress. There's contagious concern here, and a great deal to

On the bank of the creek, the vines and creepers
try to hold me back.
I push through. Now the forest is easy to walk in.

From Where the Forest Meets the Sea, *written and illustrated by Jeannie Baker.*

ponder and discuss—even more powerful because the message is visual: a brief, last-page note is the only text.

A review of "Window," in Kirkus Reviews, *Vol. LIX, No. 5, March 1, 1991, p. 315.*

The book does not accuse but it is a multilayered approach to problems of ecology, human geography and time. Baker has produced a magnificent book with brightly coloured collage that must appeal to viewers of all ages. Whereas **Where the forest meets the sea** treats the problems of our vanishing rainforests **Window** deals with urban spread. As with her previous production **Window** is likely to become a cult book with teachers and librarians. Not to be missed.

Howard George, in a review of "Window," in Reading Time, *Vol. 35, No. 2, 1991, p. 13.*

It has been said that the only constant in our lives today is change. For children that change is most manifest in the alterations to the environment in which they live. A house going up on a long-vacant block, an old tree felled, a new street, ever changing gardens, painting of premises. But here, in Jeannie Baker's long-awaited new book, the changes are much more than the slight, intermittent alterations many adults will recall that occurred to the neighbourhood of their youth. For here is the rampant urban growth of modern times. A growth caused by that charac-

teristic Australian urge to flee suburbia to settle out in the bush, in open areas. Witness the spectacular growth of "rural residential" living on the outskirts of nearly every town and city in Australia. Through the upstairs window of a small house, Jeannie Baker observes 24 years of change in a fixed setting that could be part of any major Australian city. . . . The detail of the pictures invites very close scrutiny for there are myriad manifestations of change and growth; the reader will find this book a fresh and enjoyable browse many times. Much of the change is striking, obvious, and predictable. But there are subtle signs; the window—its sill and architrave—is a clever device. Occasional birthday cards propped upon the sill provide a measure of time. Initially insects crawl around the window; later in the absence of bush we see no more. The native birds outside give way to toy birds dangling from the window.

Baker's tremendous craftsmanship and acuity of observation creates a complete picture of change, best exemplified in the very subtle deterioration of the easily overlooked minimal interior. The sill wood dries and shrinks creating striations in the paint, the wallpaper pulls slightly away from the architrave, a crack spreads in the wallpaper, the wood joints spread a little.

The boy's development, too, is interesting and easily observable. From teddybears by the window, to a frog in a bottle, to a football trophy, to McDonald's litter. We see the little fellow in a Superman outfit, walking to school, building a treehouse, shanghaiing doves, patting his ageing cat by the window at night, repairing a motorbike, and, newly-wed, moving out.

We have all watched with considerable interest the development of Jeannie Baker's unique art over her past seven books up to that tour-de-force, **Where the Forest Meets the Sea,** and have probably wondered what will she do next. Therein lies a problem in our reception of her work—the reader tends to be awed by the artistry and industry of her constructions such that the story is easily forgotten. There are some striking, new effects in **Window** and some little details do lack her customary finesse with this difficult medium; however, here we are not distracted from the story. The pictures are the story—a powerfully evocative depiction that will remain with the reader long after the reading.

Kevin Steinberger, in a review of "Window,"
in Magpies, *Vol. 6, No. 2, May, 1991, p. 4.*

Val Biro

1921-

(Real name Balint Stephen Biro) Hungarian-born English author and illustrator of picture books, reteller, and editor.

Major works include the "Gumdrop" series, *Hungarian Folk-Tales* (1981), *Fables from Aesop* (1983), *The Pied Piper of Hamelin* (1985), *The Donkey That Sneezed* (1986).

Biro is a popular author and artist who is best known for the approximately fifty picture books he has created about his car Gumdrop, a 1926 Austin Heavy Twelve-Four, Clifton Model. In these humorous works, which are often praised for their spirited, amusing qualities as well as for their successful blend of fantasy and fact, Biro takes Gumdrop on a series of fast-paced adventures with his kindly owner Mr. Oldcastle—a characterization of Biro himself—that often incorporate encounters with thieves, exciting chase scenes, and suprising twists of plot; throughout the series, Biro introduces such characters as Mr. Oldcastle's nephew Dan and the faithful cocker spaniel Horace, who was Biro's own pet, as well as other animals and vehicles with which Gumdrop comes into contact. Biro is also well regarded for his retellings of traditional tales from Hungary and England; in addition, he is the reteller of stories by such authors as Aesop and Hans Christian Andersen, is the creator of a controversial prose version of *The Pied Piper of Hamelin,* and has collected and illustrated a volume of nursery rhymes. In his first book, *Gumdrop: The Adventures of a Vintage Car* (1966), Biro describes how Gumdrop is acquired and restored; subsequent books, which often end with Gumdrop being rewarded or honored, depict the exploits of the vintage car in both real and imaginary settings. For example, in *Gumdrop Goes to London* (1971) Gumdrop drives to London to appear on television and stops a group of robbers by blocking their escape route, while in *Gumdrop's Magic Journey* (1984) Gumdrop goes on a tour through Storyland and meets such characters as Pinocchio, the Seven Dwarves, and Mr. Toad from Kenneth Grahame's *The Wind in the Willows,* who steals Gumdrop to replace another stolen car he has taken. The Gumdrop series is often celebrated for its freshness and fun as well as for Biro's characterization of Gumdrop, which he humanizes but does not anthropomorphize. The books also reflect Biro's obvious affection for his vehicle; "[The] joy of driving Gumdrop," he has written, "[is] only exceeded by that of writing about him." Acknowledged for his integration of text and picture as well as for the accuracy of his details, Biro writes his stories about Gumdrop in succinct, economical language and illustrates them with bright watercolors and cartoonlike pen drawings; several of the books also include endpapers that depicts the engineering of the cars and trucks that appear in them. In his retellings and nursery stories, Biro provides comic illustrations that often incorporate historical backgrounds.

Biro has had a passion for automobiles since boyhood. Born in Hungary, he came to England to study art in London; after graduation, he worked as a publisher's assistant and as a fireman while freelancing as an artist, working in such mediums as oils and wood engraving. Before entering the field of children's literature, he worked as an advertising artist and art director, and became well known for designing book jackets for a variety of adult trade books. Biro is the illustrator of works by such authors as Shakespeare, John Bunyan, Noel Coward, C. S. Forester, and Raphael Sabatini as well as several volumes of nonfiction; he also provided illustrations for the magazine *Radio Times* for twenty-one years. His first contributions to juvenile literature were illustrations for books by such authors as H. E. Todd, Dora Thatcher, and Elizabeth Goudge; he later provided pictures for works by such writers as E. W. Hildick, Enid Blyton, L. Frank Baum, and Kenneth Grahame. In 1961, Biro bought Gumdrop from a car salesman in Oxford: "[This] Austin," he writes, "changed my life." He began the series after receiving a commission to write and illustrate a story about Gumdrop and has since incorporated many of his experiences from driving the car into his stories. Asked by a publisher to retell his favorite Hungarian folktales, Biro wrote *Hungarian Folk-Tales*

from memories of the stories he heard as a child; his literary style in this work emphasizes the origin of the stories as oral tales, a format which he retains in his other collections and individual tales in order to make them accessible for contemporary children. Biro received a mixed reception for his reworking of *The Pied Piper of Hamelin;* some observers note that changing the familiar poetic version by Robert Browning to more colloquial prose and revising the ending to one where the Piper returns the children of Hamelin to their parents destroys the mystery and beauty of the original source. However, Biro is usually considered a skillful author and artist whose works have definite appeal for young readers. Critic Margery Fisher has noted, "For helping a child to get into a picture you can't go wrong with the Gumdrop books. . . . These books are brilliant in their mixture of humor and technicality and the texts are models of succinct simplicity. . . . ," while reviewer G. L. Hughes adds that "[The] characters seem to leap out of the pages and into the hearts of children."

(See also *Something about the Author,* Vol. 1; *Something about the Author Autobiography Series,* Vol. 13; *Contemporary Authors New Revision Series,* Vol. 11; and *Contemporary Authors,* Vols. 25-28, rev. ed.)

AUTHOR'S COMMENTARY

I generally take it as axiomatic that whatever happens to one's life, good or bad, it is usually one's own fault. (p. 14)

So I've learnt to look for the fault not in my stars, but in myself. And yet, on the other side of the coin, there is that evasive and mysterious event, the Happy Accident. You can be engaged on a painting, the dog can jog your elbow and you make a splash: and that splash will be the making of your picture. (Whether you exploit such accidents later, on purpose, is your own affair, but that dog has taught you something that day.) Or, you may be going to Oxford in order to look at a secondhand car that you are interested in, (as I did about 14 years ago), when you come upon a wayside garage in the country, see a 'for sale' notice on an ancient vehicle in the forecourt, fall for it, examine it a little, love it even more, haggle briefly for it and so become the dazed owner of a 1926 Austin Heavy 12/4 and christen it Gumdrop. Had it not been for that chance meeting with the car, there would have been no Happy Accident to start me off as the author, six years later, of the Gumdrop books. That was eight years ago, and there are now seven Gumdrops and the eighth is coming along nicely. So thank Heaven for the Happy Accident—even if you have to work on it a little afterwards. And if the thing doesn't work out, well, again, it must be your fault.

The fact that I can drive around in the central character of my books—and that I do my own illustrations for them—makes the circumstance in which these books come about a little different. I will not say that the stories write themselves (though what author won't confess that every now and then the tale takes a slightly different turn from the one intended) but writing about a real car is different from writing about, say, a dinosaur. You must imagine your dinosaur from nose to tail, and invent stories *for him.* But you have your car from radiator to taillamp

in solid reality, and stories happen to *him.* Well, it is at any rate unlikely that if you go around in a vintage car with a brass radiator and a curly horn for 14 years, *something* interesting shouldn't happen on the way. And it is also unlikely, if you write stories, that these interesting incidents shouldn't find their way into them. How you organise them into a convincing tale is again your affair, but at any rate there is your subject, solid and tangible in the garage; there are the interesting incidents ('accidents' in this instance would be the wrong word to use) when you drive out; and there is your next story—or at any rate some ingredients which you can work into one. At least you can be sure that you will write with conviction and affection, for the reality of the car is convincing enough, and you love it.

To illustrate my own stories is a luxury. Usually when I illustrate someone else's story—and in fact that is my main work still—I find myself moaning about the non-pictorial nature of some passages, just at a junction when from a production point of view a drawing is required: and nothing pictorially interesting happens. There may be a conversation, and you've shown the protagonists two pages back already; but on they go, saying probably the most amusing or exciting things, but physically doing nothing. Or there may be a flashback in the story and important as that is, you can't illustrate it because it would confuse the pictorial sequence of the book. These are occupational hazards, and the very ones which I can circumvent in my own stories. In fact, I can write—and I do write—pictorially. My own story can feed my own pictures. When I find that the pictorial possibilities of one scene have been exhausted, on I go to the next. And that one, I know, must be different in every respect from the one before (because that is one of the chief requirements of a picture book) so that I, the artist, can tell myself, the author, how to proceed with the story. So the Gumdrop books go on. One day a little boy saw the real Gumdrop parked in a London street with me in the driver's seat. He looked at me and enquired: "Are you Gumdrop?" It was a shrewd guess, and I answered "Yes." To be truthful I should have added "but not entirely." Because I do not live by Gumdrop alone. Nor indeed by the many other children's books I illustrate, much as I enjoy doing them. (There are no moans from me when the author of a book I am doing happens to have the same turn of mind as I have, and who can give me all the visual fodder I need. Such a one is E. W. Hildick with his brilliant McGurk Mysteries, or H. E. Todd with Bobby Brewster. I had enormous fun with his *Sick Cow* last year, and I am enjoying his *George, The Fire Engine* at the moment.)

No, there are things for grown-ups also, and I am grateful: an illustrator needs to use all his muscles. Occasionally, indeed, his stomach ones in particular—not so much when I decorated Robert Carrier's enormous 'Cookery Course' with hundreds of vegetable and food pictures, but especially when The Good Food Guide sent me to visit a number of top restaurants to sketch their owners or chefs. (pp. 14-15)

At other times I need to become a countryman, especially when I illustrate the yearly collection of essays by

J. H. B. Peel; or do a book on shooting by Daniel Green, or one on fishing by D. Macer-Wright. Yet again, I become a student of history, when I decorate the numerous books by Jean Plaidy on virtually all the Royal Houses of England—we are doing the Plantagenets at the moment, having already been forward in time with the Georges and Queen Victoria. And then there are bookjackets, of which I do a great many in between all the books. This is a subject all to itself, and it brings all the muscles into use; rather like those of the Players in Hamlet, who, according to Polonius, are required to perform either 'for tragedy, comedy, history . . . ' or in 'tragical-comical-historical pastoral' plays, 'scene individable, or poem unlimited'.

It happens, or at least it happened earlier this year, that I am asked to do something I've not attempted before: to paint a mural some 25 feet long in half a morning. It was at the Ilkley Literary Festival, and I found myself confronted with that huge expanse, supplied with tins of emulsion paint, and flanked by some dozen children all armed with paintbrushes, rearing to go. So off we went: I sketched the outlines and they filled in the colour. A happy morning, and I hope that Ilkley won't mind putting up with the result. And the subject of the mural? Why, Gumdrop, of course. (p. 15)

Val Biro, "'Gumdrop' and Val Biro," in Books for Your Children, *Vol. 10, No. 4, September, 1975, pp. 14-15.*

GENERAL COMMENTARY

Margery Fisher

[Gumdrop is] an Austin Clifton Heavy Twelve-Four, made in 1926 and the property of the artist Val Biro. . . . For the first of [his picture books about Gumdrop, Biro] contrived an artful reason for describing the vintage car. It is stolen from its owner, a certain Mr Oldcastle, at a time when, reluctantly deciding to sell it, he has removed horn, speedometer, clock and other accessories to sell separately. The inefficient thieves crash the car in the town and Gumdrop loses more parts; headlamps are picked up in the ruins of the greengrocer's outside display, the engine and battery are appropriated to run a cement mixer, the wheels are commandeered by a gypsy for his caravan. The now derelict car, bought by an enthusiast, is furbished up and by patience and happy chance the lost parts are restored.

With theft as a recurring theme—for the car is usually being stolen or helping its owner to catch thieves—the books would be congenial to children even without the lively character lent to Gumdrop. Unusually, this does not depend on any fantasizing of the vintage car's shape (indeed, accuracy in every visual detail is an essential part of the success of the books); nor is Gumdrop given the power of speech or thought. Simply, the reader catches from

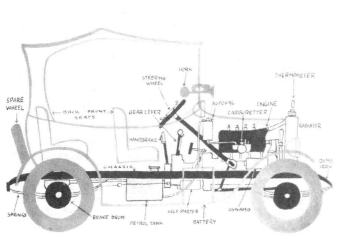

This is a cross-section of Gumdrop. He is an Austin Clifton Twelve-Four, and was made in 1926. His engine has a capacity of 1,600 cc. and he is 13 ft. 6 in. long. On the opposite page is a picture of the view from the driving seat, showing the instruments and the pedals. Underneath is the engine which the police found so useful!

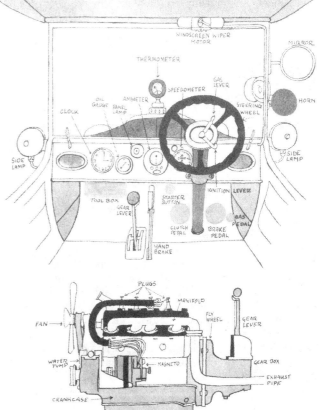

From Gumdrop: The Adventures of a Vintage Car, *written and illustrated by Val Biro.*

those who meet Gumdrop, from Mr Oldcastle and Bill McArran to mayors, garage hands, children and crooks, the habit of apostrophizing the resourceful vehicle as 'him', and a personage he certainly is.

> *Margery Fisher, "Who's Who in Children's Books: Gumdrop," in her* Who's Who in Children's Books: A Treasury of the Familiar Characters of Childhood, *Holt, Rinehart and Winston, 1975, p. 132.*

Margery Fisher

Gumdrop the vintage car fits far better than one might expect into a small format; Val Biro's skill in composition sees to that. Each page [of **Gumdrop and Horace, Gumdrop and the Steamroller, Gumdrop Posts a Letter,** and **Gumdrop Races a Train**] has its measure of action, even of drama. Scenes show Gumdrop and the train confronting one another at a level-crossing; the blue car sinks gracefully into a ditch to avoid a steam-roller; Horace the dog stampedes through the market; these and other happenings are shown in pictures with detail and movement working together. Val Biro draws his people in an off-natural style but manages to suggest personality, not only in Mr. Oldcastle, with his drooping whiskers and permanently puzzled eyebrows, but also in the minor characters encountered day by day—a stout, bovine crane-driver, for instance, in **Gumdrop posts a letter,** or enraged shoppers in **Gumdrop and Horace,** each one a recognisable social type. The craftsmanship on these little books is superb.

> *Margery Fisher, in a review of "Gumdrop and Horace" and others, in* Growing Point, *Vol. 21, No. 3, September, 1982, p. 3951.*

Kathleen Brachmann

Gumdrop, a vintage automobile and the title character in several of Biro's earlier books, returns in six new adventures [**Gumdrop and the Secret Switches, Gumdrop Finds a Friend, Gumdrop Finds a Ghost, Gumdrop Gets His Wings, Gumdrop Has a Birthday, Gumdrop in Double Trouble**]. However, despite his prominence in the titles, Gumdrop is more of a backdrop than the hero; that role clearly belongs to Gumdrop's owner, Mr. Oldcastle, ably assisted (and sometimes hindered) by his black cocker spaniel, Horace. Mr. Oldcastle first encounters Horace in . . . **Finds a Friend,** when the little dog helps his new owner capture a pair of smugglers. Horace again plays a major role in . . . **Secret Switches** when he discovers switches which enable Gumdrop to float on water and fly through the air. The faithful spaniel is temporarily replaced by Mr. Oldcastle's grandson, Dan, when the two of them visit a supposedly haunted castle in . . . **Finds a Ghost.** A lesson in highway safety is the theme of . . . **Gets His Wings,** in which Gumdrop becomes not only the best but the best-looking car on the road. Gumdrop's 50th birthday is celebrated in . . . **Has a Birthday** as Mr. Oldcastle's neighbors bring presents and Horace helps himself to more than his share of birthday cake. In . . . **Double Trouble,** the entire village (plus a bull named Balthazar) chase an autoparts thief. There is an annoying emphasis on the various auto parts and their maintenance throughout; for example, in . . . **Finds a Friend,** an entire page is

spent in a step-by-step description of how Mr. Oldcastle changes Gumdrop's tire. Most children won't be interested in the mechanics involved. Terms for various auto parts (magneto, flywheel) may be incomprehensible to youngsters as well as their parents and teachers, and the British background and terms may require some explanation. Certain words throughout the stories (veritable, recompense, knowledgeably) may be beyond the reading abilities of the suggested age group, making this series more appropriate for telling aloud. The bright water color illustrations are both amusing and appealing and impart a lightly humorous feeling overall, greatly enhancing the text. There are no sinister or unfriendly overtones here—even the villains appear cheerfully incompetent rather than truly evil. The plots are thin, with a minimum of suspense, but this won't deter young listeners who will undoubtedly be cheering for Mr. Oldcastle, Horace and Gumdrop. (pp. 157-58)

> *Kathleen Brachmann, in a review of "Gumdrop and the Secret Switches" and others, in* School Library Journal, *Vol. 29, No. 7, March, 1983, pp. 157-58.*

Pam Harwood

Born in Budapest, Hungary in 1921, Val Biro was the younger of two children. He and his sister, Lilla, and their parents lived 'in a big flat overlooking the Houses of Parliament . . . the law courts and, glory of glories, a fire station'. With an eye for detail that was going to be so effective later on in his life, he 'watched the firemen for hours as they polished every bit' of their equipment—a fascination that was to emerge again in war-torn Britain. Val, newly finished from art school, found that as an 'enemy alien' he was banned from joining the armed forces but the ambulance service or the National Fire Service were open to him. There was no question in his mind—'before long I was kitted out with helmet, uniform, boots and an axe'. So began a wartime double life of publisher's assistant during the day and fireman on most nights.

When not fireman watching, the young Val drew cartoons even in his earliest school days. His first drawing was published in an Hungarian national newspaper when he was 17. A talent for catching funny, facial expressions brought him unwanted attention from one of his school masters who predicted he would go far, but not in his lessons! How could they have realised the truth amid the political uncertainties of that 1939 summer so long ago? These may have contributed to Mr Biro senior's decision to send his son to London to further his studies in art. To our enduring pleasure he stayed.

At the Central School of Art in London, Val found there was more to art than funny faces. Experimentation in many media left him feeling that wood-engraving was his first love. It still is. Oils were also rewarding to use but time-consuming when working 'against a commission and up to a deadline, which is always yesterday, so in the end it came down to watercolour . . . with gouache and other things'. Enjoying the contrasting opacity and transparency, Val has adapted his style to many things. 'At one time in the sixties I must have designed more dust jackets in a year than any other artist,' he says. 'Each author needed to be differentiated from the others and the subsequent change in artistic style each time became a sort of game. What to use now—1, 2, 3, or 4?' I began to wonder what the real Biro style was—and never really found out—but, as I suspected, 'Gumdrop is very, very near to me'.

Looking back at some of the recent Gumdrops—*Gumdrop For Ever, Gumdrop and the Elephant* and *Gumdrop and the Secret Switches*—I've become increasingly sensitive to the 'sharper image and brighter colours' that he feels are needed in picture books for children. As we were talking, I found myself distracted by the assembled sheets of his latest partly finished commission. Casually propped up at the back of the desk were pictures that had the uncomplicated harmony in their arrangement artists can achieve: the no-matter-where-they-put-it-it's-going-to-look-wonderful syndrome. The new book is about dinosaurs. They glow beguilingly with an intensity of colour that's irresistible. This is going to be 'a sideways book because it requires wide, prehistoric landscapes. I've never done an oblong book before . . . I really am enjoying this one.' It was then that I began to realise the enthusiasm and joy that went into each and every picture.

Val took the pictures down and as we went from one to another the dinosaur world began to peel back layer by layer. The pencil sketches with their spontaneity and freshness are faithfully copied to capture and freeze the moment ready to have life-giving colour applied. The story unfolded through the images and visual action. There were 'little ancillary dinosaurs who pop up on each page, each one silently commenting on the action'. My response, I found, was exactly that of the children. Looking closer, there they were, peeking around trees, hiding in bushes or behind the huge legs of the main characters. The facial expressions reveal their true thoughts. Was I hearing Val's words correctly when he maintained that 'animals are only humans in disguise'? But here, with each one doing its own animal thing, there was no anthropomorphic change, no one had 'made them talk' but it was only too evident that they could certainly speak quite clearly. The secondary plot was there for the children 'to discover for themselves' while the main story bounced along quite happily in the text. The technicalities of wet-on-wet, goache or sub-plots were forgotten in the enchantment that Val Biro wove around his pictures.

The text and the pictures integrated perfectly and I wondered aloud how close the rapport was between author and artist. Val told me of the close collaboration that had flourished between himself and H E Todd, who died a couple of years ago. 'He would often show me his text before he would send it to the publishers, then he encouraged me to make any suggestions for improving it before it became a picture book.' This rare co-operation produced 14 books in all and is certainly a time which has left many rich memories he still treasures with affection.

Eventually we got around to talking about Gumdrop. I'd been waiting for the moment like the last cherry in a cake. In fact 'I'll show you Gumdrop before you go' was a surprise! I realised I was beginning to catch the magic when I answered as promptly as a seven-year-old, 'Oh lovely, yes please!' Val saw him for the first time in 1961 at an old-fashioned corner garage in Hardwick when he was on the way to view another car in Oxford. The name came from an unconscious remark by his wife. 'A stroke of genius, really' he acknowledges. The stroke of genius stuck. High in personality and low on top speed—'40 miles per hour is a comfortable top'—Gumdrop is an Austin Clifton Healey 12/4 and was around for four years before, accidentally almost, he turned the first corner to becoming a legend. It is a 'he' by the way. After lunch with a publisher when Gumdrop had been the subject of what Biro suspects might have been a rather one-sided conversation, 'because once you have a car like that you can't stop talking about it', the casual question arose 'Why don't you go and write a story about this car?' This question 'changed my direction'. The drive home was spent planning the outline of the first story: *Gumdrop, the Adventures of a Vintage Car.* Feverish writing occupied the next two days or so, this and the early sketches were sent off and promptly accepted, then a contract was in the post. Gumdrop was born!

The apparent ease of this astonished me, having been led to believe in school days by fervent teachers of Eng. Lit. that the best stories were born only of suffering, starving and the penury of attic habitation. 'Mind you it was because the publisher asked for it', Val says. Now, about 38 stories and 25 years later, his appeal endures and thrives. There's a new Gumdrop this year and another for next year is being pondered. The story doesn't always happen easily, though, I was assured. Often it comes when other things are going on, 'cleaning my teeth or something'. The initial conception happens very suddenly. 'It literally strikes your head.' Those of us old enough to remember the earliest Gumdrops will have noticed the subtle changes that have come about with the passage of time. Val Biro acknowledged easily that 'Mr Oldcastle has changed too. Mr Oldcastle, let's face it, is me, because you can't write about a man who is roughly your age without him becoming you. It's more convincing if you think it's yourself.' Some of the other characters are real, too, although this doesn't always happen. Bernie Denton in *Gumdrop For Ever* is a family friend who appears in the book, along with his children, complete of course with his re-built yellow Renault 'Reggie'. He's very proud to be in the book; so, no doubt, is Reggie. After all, he did win the race.

Other real-life episodes in Gumdrop's long history pop up in the books too—the day a modern Jaguar ran into the back of Gumdrop at a zebra crossing demolishing the radiator grille of the Jaguar but leaving Gumdrop unscathed, for instance. Austin Clifton Healey 12/4s, it seems, are a strong breed and well able to resist unwelcome advances from brash newcomers. The episode in the book is blamed upon the ever present Horace who 'lurched against the handbrake in his clumsy way'. They collaborate to persuade Oldcastle that selling Gumdrop must be the worst idea he's ever had. For most readers it's unthinkable that Gumdrop and Oldcastle should be parted. In reality, the affinity is strong too and this is only partly because Val's had Gumdrop so long. 'Gumdrop is so considerate I hardly ever break down unless I'm almost home or very near a telephone box.'

The latest Biro is **Rub-a-Dub-Dub; Val Biro's 77 Favourite Nursery Rhymes,** the publication of which is timed for his 70th birthday. 'It's a book I've wanted to do for 20 years perhaps.' Originally starting life as a smaller collection of 20 rhymes, it has had a long period of gestation, changing radically in the process. A change of publisher and an expansion in content has given us the 64 pages of rhymes, some of which are 'great ones' and many of which are 'the subtle ones which demonstrate the joy of language and sheer fun'. Confessing to be on the mouse's side anyway, I found **'Six Little Mice'** terrifying with the huge cat's face crowding the tiny mouse-sized window. The hickory-dickory clock in the book I noticed was ticking away in the corner of Val's study.

The chiming of this reminded me that my visit to Val's world was drawing to a close. Our short walk down the winding garden path led me face to face with Gumdrop gleaming 'bluely' in the garage, spotless and ready for a journey to London the next day. It was to be an early start for Gumdrop and Val so reluctantly I knew that I'd have to go. I must admit, though, I've never felt more like thumbing a lift. (pp. 16-17)

> *Pam Harwood, "Authograph No. 70: Val Biro," in* Books for Keeps, *No. 70, September, 1991, pp. 16-17.*

TITLE COMMENTARY

Gumdrop: The Story of a Vintage Car   (1966)

Of this group of English picture-books [which also includes *The Canal Trip* by Joan Cass, *The Green Children* by Kevin Crossley-Holland, and *Noah's Journey* by George MacBeth], Biro's seems most sure of success, not just for its intrinsic merits, which are many, but because it should sell to the great army of adult enthusiasts for old cars. Among children it is likely to appeal most to those who are normally too old to bother with picture-books. Gumdrop, a real car belonging to Biro . . . falls upon hard times and is gradually reduced to a battered shell, of use only as a home for a tramp. In this sad state he is seen by an enthusiast who gradually tracks down his original components. The conclusion is most satisfying. This is an excellent story very well told, with fine economy and a nice feeling for words. The pictures are in a broader, bolder style than that associated with this artist's work in line. They should give a great deal of pleasure. (pp. 302-03)

> *A review of "Gumdrop," in* The Junior Bookshelf, *Vol. 30, No. 5, October, 1966, pp. 302-03.*

The adventures of a vintage car are described with blithe humour and accurate detail which commend the book particularly to small boys and their fathers. The story is a model of good planning. First the car loses all its parts through various mishaps, then, one by one, they are found and restored so that Gumdrop wins first prize at the rally. This is a real car, and its specifications are shown in a neat engineering drawing on the end-papers as a solid accom-

paniment to the near-fantasy of the story and the oddity of smooth-coloured, sharp drawings.

> *Margery Fisher, in a review of "Gumdrop," in* Growing Point, *Vol. 5, No. 5, November, 1966, p. 801.*

No vintage car should have to suffer the indignity of being called **Gumdrop.** What nonsensical whimsy. Gumdrop's somewhat arbitrary adventures are told by Val Biro in illustrator's prose and pleasantly ironic but rather too static drawings. (p. 627)

> *Kevin Crossley-Holland, "In the Picture," in* The Spectator, *Vol. 217, No. 7220, November 11, 1966, pp. 627-28.*

[Gumdrop is] a vintage car which is gradually dismantled by different people who find uses for its component parts, until it becomes the immobilized, one could say debased, home for a tramp. Halfway through the book the tide turns, and a loving enthusiast reassembles Gumdrop with all its original trappings and equipment; a process of integration, no doubt, in an easily assimilated form. [A] pleasing story . . .

> *A review of "Gumdrop," in* The Times Literary Supplement, *No. 3378, November 24, 1966, p. 1083.*

The demise of an Austin (English) car, called Gumdrop, and its subsequent rejuvenation will be enjoyed by a wide range of boys and girls. The vocabulary is too difficult for most primary-grade children, but the story is effectively told in clever color pictures. Some boys in the fifth grade will be entertained by this book in spite of its large print and picturebook format because of the fast-moving plot and humorous illustrations and a double-page spread showing a detailed cross-section diagram of the car.

> *Flossie Perkins, in a review of "Gumdrop: The Adventures of a Vintage Car," in* School Library Journal, *Vol. 14, No. 6, February, 1968, p. 67.*

Gumdrop and the Farmer's Friend   (1967)

Introduced in the end-papers to an Austin Clifton 1926 and a Fowler Traction Engine of 1903, we see how each helps the other in a crisis—the last one involving an exciting chase after thieves who have stowed Gumdrop the vintage car in a lorry. This congenial frolic is illustrated in clear bright colours with dash and humour, and a commendable accuracy of detail. Fathers or sons, there is pleasure here for both.

> *Margery Fisher, in a review of "Gumdrop and the Farmer's Friend," in* Growing Point, *Vol. 6, No. 6, December, 1967, p. 1034.*

It is good to have [Gumdrop] back for another story of his adventures. Going about his lawful business, Gumdrop gets into serious difficulties and is twice rescued by the Farmer's Friend, a 1903 single cylinder 6 h.p. Fowler traction engine—a character worthy to share the pages with Gumdrop. This is an attractive story and it is accompa-

The King and Queen were sitting at dinner next day. The cook had just placed a great dish in front of them when a hand reached in through the window toward the dish. "That's Michael!" yelled the King in triumph. "Yo-ho-ho! We shall catch him now!"

From The Honest Thief: A Hungarian Folktale, *written and illustrated by Val Biro.*

nied by an excellent set of illustrations—the colour, the scenes, the people, and, emphatically, their expressions. There is a quiet humour in the telling, and even more in the illustrations. Long live Gumdrop!

> *A review of "Gumdrop and the Farmer's Friend," in* The Junior Bookshelf, *Vol. 32, No. 1, February, 1968, p. 28.*

A good-natured, entertaining sequel to the first story about Gumdrop. . . . The illustrations and much of the language are typically British (the text refers to gas while a diagram label refers to a petrol tank), but the color and animation of the cartoon-like drawings, the unusual names, and the story—telling of the Farmer's Friend . . . , its rescues of a first stuck, then stolen, Gumdrop and Gumdrop's reciprocal aid—should please all young car lovers. (pp. 283-84)

> *Florence E. Sellers, in a review of "Gumdrop and the Farmer's Friend," in* School Library Journal, *Vol. 15, No. 5, January, 1969, pp. 55-6.*

Gumdrop on the Move (1969)

The fourth adventure of that delightful vintage car, Gumdrop who is so well known to so many young children from the earlier books and Television. They will not be disappointed with his latest quest to find an owner who will really appreciate him. He is not smart enough for Mr. Banger, nor fast enough for Archibald Gridline, nor strong enough for Bodger Prescott, but for Mr. Josiah Oldcastle he was just right.

Val Biro's bold, colourful pictures are full of vigour and no detail is too small to be included. Children up to 8 or 9 will wish to have this book for their own, whether they are vintage car fans or not. It is witty and amusing, gay and colourful and reads aloud very well. A book to place high on the list for presents.

> *A review of "Gumdrop on the Move," in* The Junior Bookshelf, *Vol. 33, No. 6, December, 1969, p. 360.*

For helping a child to get into a picture you can't go wrong with the Gumdrop books. ***Gumdrop on the move*** calls for loving attention; what could be more congenial than the fate of a car gradually stripped of horn, lamps, mudguard, doors, till nothing but a shell is left and then, through sundry coincidences, part by part put together again. These books are brilliant in their mixture of humour and technicality and the texts are models of succinct simplicity which puts them within reach of an intelligent listener as young as three.

> *Margery Fisher, in a review of "Gumdrop on the Move," in* Growing Point, *Vol. 8, No. 8, March, 1970, p. 1481.*

This latest in the adventures of a 1926 Austin will undoubtedly be welcomed by readers of Gumdrop's previous experiences. . . . The colorful, detailed comic illustrations add zest to this humorous story that will be especially enjoyed by young car-minded readers.

> *Eleanor Glaser, in a review of "Gumdrop on the Move," in* School Library Journal, *Vol. 18, No. 5, January, 1971, p. 40.*

Gumdrop Goes to London   (1971)

In his latest adventure Gumdrop, the vintage motor car, is asked to appear on television in the great city. As they pass the Tower of London a beefeater thumbs a lift from them. At St. Paul's Cathedral a policeman jumps on board, urging them to give chase to some bank robbers. Outside the Law Courts a man in a wig . . . And so it goes on. Really quite an exciting way to see London with the balance between sights and chase neatly preserved.

> *Jeff Jackson, in a review of "Gumdrop Goes to London," in* Children's Book Review, *Vol. I, No. 5, October, 1971, p. 155.*

It is not necessary to be familiar with the Gumdrop series to enjoy this book; it is a sheer delight on its own. From the Beefeater with his partisan which he cannot take on the bus to the Judge knocked over on a zebra crossing and the players of the Philharmonic Orchestra the characters seem to leap out of the pages and into the hearts of children. Gumdrop is real, the tales about him are fantasy but the end result is a book with a difference which cannot fail to please young children, parents and teachers. (pp. 359-60)

> *G. L. Hughes, in a review of "Gumdrop Goes to London," in* The Junior Bookshelf, *Vol. 35, No. 6, December, 1971, pp. 359-60.*

Buckingham Palace and Westminster Abbey provide a colorful backdrop for this slick cops-and-robbers chase through London. . . . Although there are many farcical elements, the story is implausible and not really funny. (pp. 51-2)

> *Virginia Lee Gleason, in a review of "Gumdrop Goes to London," in* School Library Journal, *Vol. 19, No. 8, April, 1973, pp. 51-2.*

The Honest Thief: A Hungarian Folktale   (1972)

Val Biro's **The Honest Thief** comes from the author's native Hungary and tells the story of young Michael, whose wisdom and ability are so farfamed that the king himself begins to worry. Honest Michael's wisdom triumphs over all the king's tricky schemes to outwit and destroy him, and eventually it is the trickster who is ruined by his own jealousy. The story is both funny and eventful, and Mr Biro's colourful illustrations, with their seventeenth-century setting, add to the excitement.

> *A review of "The Honest Thief," in* The Times Literary Supplement, *No. 3692, December 8, 1972, p. 1498.*

Biro's trick is to make his hero an honest peasant lad and a clever swindler at the same time for it is the king himself (jealous of Michael's high reputation) who orders him to steal the royal treasures: "If you fail the task I set, I shall put an end to you, but if you succeed, you can have what you stole and in addition all my treasure, for I stole that myself long ago." But each time that Michael manages a near impossible feat of thievery the king sets him an even harder task. There is no more hint of why Michael doesn't question the king for breaking his word than there is of why after meeting five such challenges he finally announces: "I performed the tasks, Your Majesty, and I have come to claim the rewards you promised." But never mind; those broadly gesticulating fairy tale pictures should be an indication that you're not expected to look too closely—and Michael's coups are clever enough for a quick run through.

> *A review of "The Honest Thief," in* Kirkus Reviews, *Vol. XLI, No. 6, March 15, 1973, p. 311.*

The stratagem of theft that is no theft does, somewhat remotely, fit the story's theme, and the prince's essential virtue is emphasised by his smooth, handsome face, which contrasts with the grotesque, shaggy look of corrupt courtiers and selfish old king. The pictures are lively but the alternating pages of colour seem garish and the total effect of the book is laboured and restless.

> *Margery Fisher, in a review of "The Honest Thief," in* Growing Point, *Vol. 12, No. 1, May, 1973, p. 2173.*

The smoothly written story brings the hero through five (instead of the usual three) tasks to the expected conclusion of winning the princess and kingdom. However, the illustrations fail to capture the spirit of the tale: the full-color paintings are reminiscent of calendar art, while the more humorously detailed black-and-white drawings are slightly better. This could be used as a read-aloud, but it would be only an additional title for folklore collections.

> *Patricia McCue Marwell, in a review of "The Honest Thief: A Hungarian Folktale," in* Library Journal, *Vol. 98, No. 13, July, 1973, p. 2184.*

Gumdrop Finds a Friend   (1973)

On holiday in Cornwall, Mr. Oldcastle in his vintage car is accidentally mixed up with smugglers who have rashly chosen Gumdrop's boot as a temporary hiding-place for their loot. A stray spaniel narrowly escaping death under Gumdrop's wheels becomes the "friend" who helps to bring the villains to justice. The story is little more than a pretext for the clear colour and lively practical details of the pictures which present far more vividly Gumdrop's latest adventure.

> *Margery Fisher, in a review of "Gumdrop Finds a Friend," in* Growing Point, *Vol. 12, No. 6, December, 1973, p. 2301.*

Gumdrop, that indefatigable Austin Clifton Heavy

Twelve-Four vintage 1926 car, is at it again. This time he and his owner, Mr. Oldcastle, become involved with a gang of nasty smugglers who, having hidden their loot in Gumdrop, accuse Mr. Oldcastle of being the smuggler in the first place! Naturally Gumdrop, with the aid of Horace the dog, a newcomer to the series, and Mr. Oldcastle, ensures that right will out and collects a large reward as well. This book has lost none of the appeal of the earlier five in the series. If anything it is an improvement because the story line is stronger, and Gumdrop really is an old friend who will be welcomed by every child. (p. 377)

> *G. L. Hughes, in a review of "Gumdrop Finds a Friend," in* The Junior Bookshelf, *Vol. 37, No. 6, December, 1973, pp. 376-77.*

Gumdrop on the Brighton Run   (1976)

When Gumdrop is declared ineligible for the Brighton run of veteran cars, Mr. Oldcastle decides to drive there anyway by back roads but by a series of chances he eventually wins for his 1926 car the title "Honorary Veteran Car Extraordinary". Dogs, cars, trucks, a thief and a 'bus with defective brakes, all add to the fun of yet another spirited picture-book in which vehicular accuracy is matched with a mild degree of facetiousness in the treatment of faces.

> *Margery Fisher, in a review of "Gumdrop on the Brighton Run," in* Growing Point, *Vol. 15, No. 7, January, 1977, p. 3051.*

Gumdrop, the vintage car, has a habit of getting into all sorts of adventures and his latest one is, perhaps, the best of the lot. . . . The illustrations in this eighth title in the Gumdrop series are as appealing and amusing as ever, and the story is a worthy successor to the previous seven. (pp. 76-7)

> *G. L. Hughes, in a review of "Gumdrop on the Brighton Run," in* The Junior Bookshelf, *Vol. 41, No. 2, April, 1977, pp. 76-7.*

Gumdrop Posts a Letter   (1976); Gumdrop and the Steamroller   (1976)

In the "Stepping Stones" series, [**Gumdrop Posts a Letter** is] a story exploiting the popular image of Gumdrop the vintage car in an anecdote demonstrating a few combinations of letters (cane, plain, lane; better, letter, matter, and so on). Mr. Oldcastle's chase after a post van ends in a neat twist, and text and pictures alike have a friendly, persuasive air.

> *Margery Fisher, in a review of "Gumdrop Posts a Letter," in* Growing Point, *Vol. 15, No. 8, March, 1977, p. 3072.*

Val Biro's **Gumdrop and the Steamroller** and **Gumdrop Posts a Letter** are two British imports about Mr. Oldcastle's trustworthy old car, illustrated by the author in brightly colored, exaggerative cartoon-style drawings. In **Gumdrop Posts a Letter**, Mr. Oldcastle just misses the postman's last pickup. Eager to get a birthday card to his grandson on time, he hops into his old car and chases after the mail truck. When he finally catches up with it, he discovers he has driven all the way to his grandson's home so he stops for a visit. A tame adventure and British word usage, e.g., "posts" instead of "mails" will be alien to this age group. A . . . **Steamroller** blocks Mr. Oldcastle's path on his way home for lunch and accidentally pushes Gumdrop into a ditch. A group of hardy workmen tow it out and are invited home to lunch in appreciation. The semi-rhyming singsong dialogue is stilted and again the Briticisms (e.g., "This is rum, by gum!") will confuse beginning readers.

> *Judith S. Kroneck, in a review of "Gumdrop Posts a Letter" and "Gumdrop and the Steamroller," in* School Library Journal, *Vol. 23, No. 9, May, 1977, p. 76.*

Gumdrop Has a Birthday   (1977)

Tomorrow Gumdrop, the vintage car, will be fifty, so Mr. Oldcastle and puppy Horace decide to buy a birthday cake. The neighbours have errands, too. Stan wants a belt, the baker requires some tasty nuts, old Mrs. Wood needs strong thread, Mr. Dyer's boots have to be replaced. On the journey Gumdrop's tyre bursts, the nuts to fix the spare wheel roll down a drain, the old car's fan belt breaks and its hood tears. Next day, the neighbours visit Gumdrop, bringing birthday gifts: a new fan belt from Stan, metal nuts from the baker, thread for mending the hood from Mrs. Wood and tyres from Mr. Dyer, but only Horace knows where the birthday cake has gone!

Val Biro's colourful drawings remain ample, humorous and filled with affection for his own elderly Austin. This is not a particularly strong story but the book is, as usual, pleasant and lighthearted.

> *R. Baines, in a review of "Gumdrop Has a Birthday," in* The Junior Bookshelf, *Vol. 42, No. 2, April, 1978, p. 79.*

Gumdrop Gets His Wings   (1979)

In Gumdrop's new adventure the usual technical information is extended by a social moral introduced by the road-signs on the end-papers. Tyre, lamp, front wing, clock and horn bulb suffer in minor accidents which give Mr. Oldcastle the chance to explain the Highway Code to incautious kids, dogs and drivers; his reward, the necessary repairs and the silver symbol he has coveted for so long. The message is lightly conveyed in an energetic text full of spirited dialogue and in amiably off-realistic, suavely coloured pictures. (pp. 3551-52)

> *Margery Fisher, in a review of "Gumdrop Gets His Wings," in* Growing Point, *Vol. 18, No. 2, July, 1979, pp. 3551-52.*

Gumdrop Finds a Ghost   (1980)

In his thirteenth 'Gumdrop' book Val Biro handles a spooky theme with his usual skill. This time Mr Oldcastle and grandson Dan are off to Mildew Manor on a ghost hunt. How Gumdrop runs away and leads them to a totally unexpected 'ghost' is a satisfyingly complete story with a surprising twist. The art-work is a real joy and the leafy vistas of Mildew Manor caused cries of delight. After so many books one might expect Gumdrop to creak a little. Val Biro, both as story-teller and artist, is better than ever.

> *Ann Pilling, in a review of "Gumdrop Finds a Ghost," in* Books for Your Children, *Vol. 15, No. 4, Autumn-Winter, 1980, p. 41.*

Each of Val Biro's delightful illustrations is a masterpiece of the cartoonist's art. Add colour, subtly used, and an amusing and lively text, and the result is a book which will be treasured and enjoyed by boys of all ages, and a lot of girls too. (pp. 280-81)

> *A. Thatcher, in a review of "Gumdrop Finds a Ghost," in* The Junior Bookshelf, *Vol. 44, No. 6, December, 1980, pp. 280-81.*

Hungarian Folk-Tales   (1981)

Val Biro, much loved for his *Gumdrop* books, has turned to the country of his birth for his **Hungarian Folk-Tales.** He has got the matter-of-factness right in these stories that are by turns fantastic (including one about a castle that spins like a top balanced on a cockerel's leg, and another about a castle that flies) and droll. His rollicky style, though, varies little from story to story, and is often an unhappy hybrid of the conventional and slangy (" . . . and if I don't speak the truth you can take me to the clink.") He is no conjuror with atmospherics and, for all the richness of the material at his disposal, this is a rather poor addition to the generally dependable Oxford *Myths and Legends* series.

> *Kevin Crossley-Holland, "Where Ice and Fire Fused," in* The Times Educational Supplement, *No. 3389, June 5, 1981, p. 40.*

Biro left his native Hungary more than forty years ago but his memory, jogged by the classic collections of Grandpierre and Illyes, is good and he retells the stories of his childhood with evident delight. He is still not quite at ease in colloquial English. His versions are a compromise between the 'literary' manner of the old folk-tale collections and today's fashion for the cadences of the spoken word. Oral storytellers who use this as a source book will need to make some adjustments and abridgements, but the stories are, in essence, delightful. Hungary in the nineteenth century, with its peasant culture, its vast gulf between rich and poor, its large-scale illiteracy, was a classic breeding ground for folk tale; it offered treasures as rich as those which the Grimms discovered in rural Germany. Some of the themes are closely related to those of Grimm, but they have their characteristic Magyar twists and atmosphere. Humour predominates in Biro's collection, especially the fun which comes from the defeat of villainy by guile. There are some admirable peasant rogues, and cunning and resourceful discharged soldiers. (pp. 230, 233)

> *Marcus Crouch, in a review of "Hungarian Folk Tales," in* The School Librarian, *Vol. 29, No. 3, September, 1981, pp. 230, 233.*

[**Hungarian Folk Tales**] is merry from the outset, with crisp, colloquial sentences and fast-paced narrative full of recognizable folk-tale elements. The fireside-telling tone of the delivery suits the subject-matter well and the "word-of-mouth" tradition which Val Biro acknowledges in his introduction, together with his two major sources, is given further credence by his quiet dedication of the book to the memory of his mother. However, a larger typesize might have made the book more attractive and accessible to children, as would a greater use of diagonal spreads to enliven double-pages. As it stands, the book may well attract adults who want to read it aloud rather than children who want to read it for themselves.

> *Josephine Karavasil, "Cosmic Tales," in* The Times Literary Supplement, *No. 4094, September 18, 1981, p. 1068.*

These tales in Biro's collection contain motifs similar enough to those of the more familiar western European stories to be accessible and yet different enough to be uniquely rewarding. **"King Greenbeard,"** for example, begins with a new formula, "Beyond the seven kingdoms, and further still, where the short-tailed piglets grub, there lived, once upon a time, a greenbearded king." And in **"The Thieving Goblins"** and **"The Honest Thief,"** handsome young princes are promised (as princes always are) the hand of a princess and half a kingdom if they can perform a series of tasks. Cleverness and kindness are among the heroic virtues which give shape to the folk-dream of being strong and in control rather than weak and oppressed. In addition to the heroic tales, Biro has included some trickster tales. In them, the heroes are not really admirable, but their quickness of mind and their triumphs over the foolish and pompous are themselves rewarding. The pen-and-ink drawings are cartoon-like, centering on characters and minimizing background (as folk tales themselves do), but filled with action and energy (as the tales themselves are). In all, this is a firstrate collection in which the tales, the retellings and the illustrations all work together well.

> *Katharyn F. Crabbe, in a review of "Hungarian Folk-Tales," in* School Library Journal, *Vol. 29, No. 8, April, 1983, p. 109.*

Gumdrop and the Secret Switches   (1981)

After picnicking on a sunny day Mr Oldcastle and his dog Horace are relaxing in Gumdrop . . . preparatory to visiting a vintage car race.

Horace's inquisitive nose reveals a switch marked POT-BARC concealed behind the ammeter. Mr Oldcastle realises that this means Pull Out To Beat Any Racing Car, and sets off to join the race. After their totally unexpected victory it is necessary for Gumdrop to beat a hasty retreat, pursued by irate racing drivers. Fortunately Horace discovers two more secret switches, POTSORAL and POT-FLAB. Final disaster threatens when the car runs out of petrol in mid air, but then Mr Oldcastle—wakes up.

Gumdrop is marvellous, and Val Biro's writings and drawings are always infused with love for his elderly vehi-

Biro at his desk, 1981.

cle. Still, there is no denying that "it was only a dream" is the oldest cheat in any book and never fails to be disappointing disillusionment.

> *R. Baines, in a review of "Gumdrop and the Secret Switches," in* The Junior Bookshelf, *Vol. 45, No. 5, October, 1981, p. 185.*

The Magic Doctor (1982)

A lively retelling of a folk tale in which a shoemaker pretends to be a doctor, although he can neither read nor write. At first his pretence brings him fame and prosperity and a reputation for wisdom, even though he prescribes the same remedy for every ailment on a prescription no one can read. When he is really put to the test, only his native wit saves him from death. However, he has learnt his lesson and returns to his cottage and the skill he really knows.

An old and familiar story is presented here anew with humour and skill. Every page is alive with colour and character, not least that of the 'hero', so naive and yet with a homely wit and kindness. A picture book of this calibre can be enjoyed again and again, for each page is full of comical detail.

> *E. Colwell, in a review of "The Magic Doctor," in* The Junior Bookshelf, *Vol. 46, No. 5, October, 1982, p. 179.*

Fables from Aesop (1983)

Val Biro is one of those illustrators children find irresistible because his drawing is detailed, fresh and humorous. He has recently taken a break from Gumdrop and H. E. Todd's wonderful stories to retell six well-known fables in very simple, picture-caption sequences. All the best devices are used—narrative style akin to oral form which trips lightly off the tongue, balloon speech, and a perfect match between text and illustration. One of the disadvantages of simplified traditional stories is that the original detail gets lost along the way, but this has been overcome by printing complete 'Read-Aloud' versions of the stories in the accompanying booklet. Not only do these versions read aloud extremely well, but the text in the children's books has been incorporated and printed in 'bold' so that if listeners have their picture books in front of them they can follow the story, matching the key sentences to what they hear. Given sensitive and careful use, everything is here to provide a story-based introduction to reading. What more could we ask?

> *Cliff Moon, in a review of "Fables from Aesop," in* The School Librarian, *Vol. 31, No. 2, June, 1983, p. 133.*

These books are nice to handle, I like the illustrations and the text is short enough for children to read it by heart. The language is direct and clear, with just enough repetition to help the less-able readers. Personally, I've always found Aesop's morals a little on the priggish side, but an exception must be made for the dénouement of **The Goose That Laid the Golden Egg,** which is a winner. " 'This goose must be full of gold,' said the man 'let us see'. So they cut the goose open. But the goose was full of goose." If only you could see the picture.

> *Mary Jane Drummond, "Stiggy," in* The Times Educational Supplement, *No. 3496, July 1, 1983, p. 44.*

Gumdrop at Sea   (1983)

Mr. Josiah Oldcastle, kind as ever, transports the Bumblebee family to the seaside in Gumdrop . . . after their car breaks down. The extra weight ruins Gumdrop's engine; Josiah fears a long search for another but Horace the dog finds a replacement.

Val Biro's jaunty illustrations follow these popular characters through another series of mishaps: there is plenty of noise—honking and woofing, clanging and banging—and, somewhat predictably, Josiah and the Bumblebees fall out of their boat into the sea. It is all good fun and certain to delight devotees of the earlier Gumdrop sagas.

> *G. Bott, in a review of "Gumdrop at Sea," in* The Junior Bookshelf, *Vol. 47, No. 6, December, 1983, p. 233.*

Gumdrop's Magic Journey   (1984)

When Mr. Oldcastle filled up with petrol at Merlin's Garage in the wood he was hardly prepared for a tour through Storyland but he and his small passenger took encounters with the White Knight, the Seven Dwarfs, Pinocchio and other beings calmly enough, though when Toad stole Gumdrop to replace the Darraq he was driving (also stolen, naturally) they suffered some anxiety until they found the miscreant in the clutches of the rural police. Dan's disappointment when the magic journey ended was assuaged when he found that Merlin had left a pile of the relevant books for him. A pleasantly amusing way to lead children to certain classics—though I must confess I prefer the vintage car when he is enjoying adventures at only one remove and not two from reality. (p. 4346)

> *Margery Fisher, in a review of "Gumdrop's Magic Journey," in* Growing Point, *Vol. 23, No. 4, November, 1984, pp. 4345-46.*

I hope there are still readers ready to respond to . . . the temptation to discover earlier children's books generously offered by Val Biro in **Gumdrop's Magic Journey** when his classic car finds itself in the land where such stories are at home.

> *Audrey Laski, "Pyrotechnics and Passion," in* The Times Educational Supplement, *No. 3669, October 24, 1986, p. 24.*

Gumdrop Goes Fishing; Gumdrop Has a Tummy Ache; Gumdrop Is the Best Car; Gumdrop on the Farm   (1984)

Like the trains of Sodor [in the books of W. V. Awdry], Gumdrop the vintage car is a strongly conceived character. He is less of an individual, perhaps, than the irascible tank-engine James or his giggling, grumbling coaches, and he has no visual contrivance for a 'face', but he is treated by his devoted owner Mr. Oldcastle as an individual, perhaps most of all as a surrogate child. In **Gumdrop has a tummy ache,** for example, mechanical defects are interpreted in human terms (like the Rev. Awdry's trains, who suffer abdominal pains from overheating or a block in a water tank). As with Awdry, Val Biro balances fancy and fact. The garage proprietor's diagnosis is fanciful:

> He has a moderately upset tummy, a slight cold in the horn, a touch of temperature, a little stiffness in his joints and flatulence in his front tyre. And of course the measles.

The measles are in fact spots of mud and the other ailments are sorted out in a perfectly practical way:

> The garage doctor and his assistants were gentle and kind. They began their work, with spanners and wrenches, grease guns and oil cans, chargers and wires and hoses and pumps. It was all quite painless and Gumdrop began to feel a lot better.

The vintage car's reactions are as simply and directly humanised in **Gumdrop on the Farm** and **Gumdrop goes Fishing,** while the theme of the triumphing underdog, expressed in the recurrent defence of Gumdrop's old-fashioned mechanism, is predominant in **Gumdrop is the Best Car.** As with the Awdry engine-stories, illustration accounts for much of the popularity of the Gumdrop tales; mildly grotesque, sharply coloured and racily expressive, the pictures bind car and people in comic situations which lightly reflect the bond, so readily satirised, between humans and their cars. (p. 4361)

> *Margery Fisher, in a review of "Gumdrop Is the Best Car" and others, in* Growing Point, *Vol. 23, No. 5, January, 1985, pp. 4360-61.*

The Pied Piper of Hamelin   (1985)

Biro has the gusto for the rich meatiness of the old story, and he clearly is familiar with and fond of Teutonic architecture and costume. His Hamelin leaps out of the page in all its noisy, smelly vitality. It seems a pity to waste all this on his own fairly feeble prose version of the story, complete with happy ending. Browning's words would have made it a much longer book, but surely an infinitely better one.

M. Crouch, in a review of "The Pied Piper of Hamelin," in The Junior Bookshelf, *Vol. 49, No. 4, August, 1985, p. 171.*

In any retelling Browning's rampageous words are inevitably lost: in this recasting we have a new ending to the poem as well, in which the Mayor is thrown into the Weser by the angry townsfolk and the Piper, duly paid, brings back their children. The cartoon-style of the illustrations does equal disfavour to the poem and to the legend; the grotesqueness of the pictures, active though they are, and the graceless, laconic text, allow nothing of the mystery and symbolism which underlie the patter of rats and the discomfort of housewives.

Margery Fisher, in a review of "The Pied Piper of Hamelin," in Growing Point, *Vol. 24, No. 3, September, 1985, p. 4502.*

I am aware that Robert Browning did not create the Pied Piper story, that it is a 'famous legend' and that it is therefore in the public domain, which means that monkeys can make a monkey of it. But what monkeys must not do is keep the Browning version by their side, batting the verse on the head with coconuts, knocking it lifeless. For example:

Rats!
They fought the dogs and killed the cats,
And bit the babies in the cradles,
And ate the cheeses out of the vats,
And licked the soup from the cooks' own ladles,
Split open the kegs of salted sprats,
Made nests inside men's Sunday hats,
And even spoiled the women's chats
By drowning their speaking
With shrieking and squeaking
In fifty different sharps and flats.

RATS! Hamelin was absolutely full of rats. They chased the people. They fought the dogs and cats. They bit the children. They ate all the cheese and they licked up the soup. They gnawed people's clothes and crawled into their hats. (Biro)

Into the street the Piper stept,
Smiling first a little smile,
As if he knew what magic slept
In his quiet pipe the while;
Then, like a musical adept,
To blow the pipe his lips he wrinkled,
And green and blue his sharp eyes twinkled,
Like a candle-flame where salt is sprinkled;
And ere three shrill notes the pipe uttered,
You heard as if an army muttered;
And the muttering grew to a grumbling;
And the grumbling grew to a mighty rumbling;
And out of the houses the rats came tumbling.

So the Pied Piper walked out into the Market Square, followed by the awestruck Mayor and Corporation. He began to play his pipe, and at the first notes of his magical tune the strangest thing happened. The rats of Hamelin came scampering out. Every one of them! From houses and shops, from cellars and roofs they came, dancing to the tune of the piping Pied Piper. (Biro)

Now I am sure that those responsible for the crime that is Val Biro's *Pied Piper of Hamelin* (the illustrations are passable in a Disney world) believe they are bringing culture to the masses—but in fact, like the Book Marketing Council in another context, they are selling the children short. What child, they may ask, can understand readily 'So Willy, let you and me be wipers / Of scores out with all men—especially pipers!' Certainly I, as an eight-year-old, hadn't a clue what it meant. But I know now.

I remember my first Pied Piper, the full Browning text printed for classroom use with outline pictures 'for the pupil to colour in'. 'His queer gay coat from heel to head / Was half of yellow and half of red' ('It was a tall thin stranger in red and yellow' says Biro.) 'Brown rats, black rats, grey rats, tawny rats.' What a gift! And how lovingly I chalked in those pictures. I made many more pictures in my mind than those provided by the artist, however. And I remember *The Pied Piper of Hamelin* for something else: for the poetry, for the strangeness, for the larger-than-life characters—and for the disturbing ending that still haunts me. I have remembered it over the years as much for what I didn't understand as for what I did. Where there is a mystery, the reader returns.

Val Biro has removed the mystery and turned the story into a jolly tale. Gone are the elements of treachery, of suffering, of nemesis that have ensured the survival of the Pied Piper of Hamelin as a legend since, some think, the Children's Crusade in the thirteenth century. Biro's Mayor and Corporation are drowned in the (unnamed) river—their Beano-type comeuppance; the Piper then gets paid, the children come back, the 'lovely town of Hamelin became a happy town at last'. Significantly, there is no lame boy in Biro's version because there would be no place for him in happy-town Hamelin.

What is important, in young people's reading, is that they should come across a great deal of literature that, at some point in their lives, they will return to and understand better, even return to for an enlightenment they had recognized as being there but had not been ready fully to absorb. If 'difficult' text (Browning's 'Pied Piper' is encrusted with a fair number of barnacles) is emasculated as in the Biro version, if text itself is pushed into the wings as in the Best Books for Babies campaign, the rising generation stands in danger of losing literature as a lifelong friend.

And, Book Marketing Council promoters please note, the book trade will be the loser. (pp. 136-38)

Elaine Moss, "Selling the Children Short," in Signal, *No. 48, September, 1985, pp. 135-38.*

This large-sized picture book version of the famous legend is recommended only to those who don't mind having their folk literature mutilated. Biro's colorful, cartoonish illustrations portray the town's rat problems with great humor amid attractive medieval settings. His children dance joyfully behind the Piper, unlike Kate Greenaway's (Warne), who seem to be in a trance and floating on air. The narration is more vivid and descriptive than other prose versions in print, with a Piper who speaks in rather good rhyme, although there is one lapse in style. But the text is much superior to Donna Diamond's *Pied Piper of*

Hamlin (Holiday, 1981) and to Tony Ross' (Lothrop, 1978), which has enjoyable, messy, exaggerated pictures but a much shortened text with some anachronistic embellishments. It is unfortunate, therefore, that Biro creates a new ending for the legend: the mayor and council are washed away down the river, and the enchanted children are immediately returned to their parents by the Piper. This unauthentic touch lessens the power of the legend and trivializes it. (pp. 148-49)

> *Ronald Van de Voorde, in a review of "The Pied Piper of Hamelin," in* School Library Journal, *Vol. 32, No. 2, October, 1985, pp. 148-49.*

For the life of me, I cannot see the purpose of this book. It does for the *Pied Piper* what Enid Blyton does for the Bible, and I can't understand what persuaded Val Biro, whom I generally admire, to undertake it. I'm against the conversion of poetry into prose, even when it is done for the sake—usually specious—of greater accessibility; but when the verse is as straightforward as Browning's in this work, it seems both redundant and unwise. As a child, I didn't recall the poetic form in any conscious way, other than that it seemed a story which needed to be read aloud, and it's significant that children learn it by heart with great pleasure and ease. What has happened to Browning's:

> Rats!
> They fought the dogs and kill'd the cats,
> And bit the babies in their cradles.?

It is now: 'Rats! Hamelin was absolutely full of rats'; and the Piper's first magical appearance has lost:

> His queer long coat from heel to head
> Was half of yellow and half of red

and is now 'a tall thin stranger in red and yellow'. Will it do? No, by no means. I recommend teachers to find the edition of Browning's original with the Harold Jones illustrations. The book under review did me a service. I went back to the Jones edition and the magic worked all over again.

> *Gabrielle Maunder, in a review of "The Pied Piper of Hamelin," in* The School Librarian, *Vol. 34, No. 1, March, 1986, p. 44.*

Gumdrop and the Monster　(1985)

The long-running adventures of this much-loved car include some subtle social comment. See the Edinburgh Festival picture. The American dialectal forms are less easy to read than the Scots, but the monster is a pleasant surprise.

> *A review of "Gumdrop and the Monster," in*

Biro and Gumdrop in 1991.

The School Librarian, *Vol. 33, No. 4, December, 1985, p. 325.*

The Hobyahs (1985)

This illustrated retelling of an old tale by Joseph Jacobs doesn't work. A little old man; a little old woman; a little girl, Lucy; and her little dog Turpie live in a little old house. When Turpie barks in the night to scare off the wild Hobyahs who want to put little Lucy in their sack, his barking annoys the little old people, so he is sold to a farmer. The Hobyahs return, pop Lucy into their sack, and hang the sack (with Lucy peeking out) on the wall of their cottage. Little dog Turpie frees Lucy by biting a hole in the sack and hides in it himself. He bites off the Hobyahs' "wild brave tails," and they run away, never to be seen again. The text is boring; the color illustrations are too saccharine. There are too many other good adaptions of folk tales to warrant buying this one.

Barbara Peklo Serling, in a review of "The Hobyahs," in School Library Journal, *Vol. 33, No. 2, October, 1986, p. 156.*

The Donkey That Sneezed (1986)

Val Biro can always be relied upon to bring vitality to an old tale. **The Donkey That Sneezed** is a typical teutonic fairy-tale, in which three brothers are sent out to earn their keep. Two are tricked out of their reward by a wicked innkeeper but the third turns the tables on him. The family then enjoy prosperity thanks to a table that produces food, a donkey that sneezes gold and a stick that beats crooks. The illustrations are vigorous, bright and fun. The story has already stood the test of time and here it is confidently retold in simple language. The book will give pleasure to parents and children alike.

Valerie Caless, in a review of "The Donkey That Sneezed," in British Book News Children's Books, *June, 1986, p. 12.*

'Umbrella Books' designed for early reading practice have a picture-book format and a brief text full of judicious repetitions. This one has also the advantage of a folk-tale basis, the familiar tale of the three fortune-seeking brothers, the magic tablecloth and the greedy innkeeper. Cheerfully ugly cartoon-illustrations set a traditional rustic background where men wear tattered clothes and display huge red noses; a jokey book which should carry beginner-readers along on its energetic course.

Margery Fisher, in a review of "The Donkey That Sneezed," in Growing Point, *Vol. 25, No. 3, September, 1986, p. 4688.*

The familiar story, "The Table, the Ass and the Stick," is rewritten as the equivalent of a beginning reader. The choppy, crudely written text has little of the style or the humor of the Grimm version in Wanda Gag's *More Tales from Grimm* (Coward, 1947; o.p.) or the Jacobs' variant in *English Fairy Tales* (Dover, 1898). What humor the book does have comes from the cartoonish illustrations. They are pen-and-ink drawings with color washes and

have a certain gruff vitality. They do not, however, make up for the mediocrity of the text.

Ellen Loughran, in a review of "The Donkey That Sneezed," in School Library Journal, *Vol. 33, No. 4, December, 1986, p. 79.*

Gumdrop and the Dinosaur (1988)

In this episode of Gumdrop's adventurous life, he travels, with Dan and Dan's grandfather, to prehistoric times, helped by a miracle computer wired to his battery. Sixty-five million years back they find a friend in a Triceratops (Topsy for short) whose skeleton they have met already in the local museum. An unfortunate meeting with a Tyrannosaur is nearly fatal for Gumdrop but ends in the extinction of the Tyrannosaur instead. Gumdrop is made an Honorary Dinosaur before he and his friends return to the present.

Dinosaurs are popular with young children who recite their formidable names with apparent ease. No doubt this latest story with its many coloured, slightly comical, illustrations of amiable dinosaurs and the faithful old car, will be popular as always. (pp. 156-57)

E. Colwell, in a review of "Gumdrop and the Dinosaur," in The Junior Bookshelf, *Vol. 53, No. 4, August, 1989, pp. 156-57.*

Jack and the Beanstalk (1989)

A sprightly retelling of the traditional tale from Jacobs, including an unaltered version of the "Fee-fi-fo-fum . . . " refrain. A wide-eyed, innocent Jack becomes more wily in the illustrations as well as in the text as he progresses from a young boy trading a cow for magic beans to a clever rogue who can outwit an ogre. Here, he makes three trips before the requisite happily-ever-after ending—one for gold, one for the hen, and lastly for the golden harp that sings. The ogre is fierce but not frightening. He first appears on the first version in tears, presumably after being tricked by Jack on one occasion. The cartoonlike illustrations are full of action and the characters are expressive. Endpapers are filled with a lush beanstalk motif to help set the mood. Not as stylized as Cauley's version (Putnam, 1983) or as comic as Galdone's interpretation (Clarion, 1982), Biro's offering is a solid, basic addition to fairy-tale collections.

Micki S. Nevett, in a review of "Jack and the Beanstalk," in School Library Journal, *Vol. 36, No. 8, August, 1990, p. 136.*

Val Biro's comic illustrations will make your students laugh as they listen to this familiar tale. The ogre, warty and snaggletoothed, is more funny than frightening.

Lee Galda, in a review of "Jack and the Beanstalk," in The Reading Teacher, *Vol. 44, No. 2, October, 1990, p. 146.*

Gumdrop and the Pirates   (1989)

Another jolly story in the thoroughly reliable 'Gumdrop' series. This one, about how Dan, Mr Oldcastle and Gumdrop help an extremely inefficient pirate regain his treasure, is enhanced by some wonderfully comic drawings in true Val Biro style. Silly, but entertaining and well-told, this would be ideal for the rather older reluctant reader as well as for reading aloud or for young fluent readers to enjoy alone.

> *L. W., in a review of "Gumdrop and the Pirates," in* Books for Keeps, *No. 71, November, 1991, p. 7.*

Miranda's Umbrella   (1990)

Biro must qualify as a veteran now . . . , but he keeps his freshness of approach and his skill in blending words and pictures. Miranda, a self-composed six-year-old, has an unusual birthday present, a multi-coloured umbrella. It has strange functions, serving as a parachute when needed and also leading Miranda into some alarming situations with a large and hungry giant and an equally unpleasant witch. The adventures last only one day after which the umbrella loses its powers. Not the most original of stories, but it serves very well as the basis of the artist's bold and dramatic pictures which command the page, taking attention from his rather naively written text. Nicely scarey. (pp. 265-66)

> *M. Crouch, in a review of "Miranda's Umbrella," in* The Junior Bookshelf, *Vol. 54, No. 6, December, 1990, pp. 265-66.*

The story is a familiar one, and the ending is hardly a surprise, but Biro's title does have charm in its humorous watercolor illustrations. The giant is fierce and the witch wicked, yet both show their softer sides as well. However, the text is wordy and does not offer the succinct prose of Sendak's *Where the Wild Things Are* (Harper, 1988).

> *Nancy Menaldi-Scanlan, in a review of "Miranda's Umbrella," in* School Library Journal, *Vol. 37, No. 2, February, 1991, p. 67.*

The Three Little Pigs   (1990)

These piglets are so pinkly innocent and this wolf leers and slavers so confidently, and with such teeth, that the traditional story loses none of its power. Val Biro retells and illustrates this version for very young children, 3 years and older. The front cover leaves them in no doubt that a malignant wolf has enormously more strength than the three little fellers who set out to seek their fortunes. Then the early pages—where the three houses get built—encourage young readers to spot where the spying wolf is hidden. You could say at this stage that the reader's anxiety is likely to be outweighed by the sense of his or her own cleverness in detecting where the wolf is and what he intends to do.

When the first two pigs' houses are blown to smithereens by the huffing and puffing, there is no doubt about the pigs' fate. The wolf eats them up. (They deserve it don't they?) So it is a relief and satisfaction, in the last ten pages of story, to see this self-serving murderer foiled by foresight, determination, a calm spirit and quick-footed intelligence—and then killed and boiled away.

This is a well executed version. I will be reading it to our granddaughter when she is 3 or 4 if her mother lets me.

> *Don Pemberton, in a review of "The Three Little Pigs," in* Magpies, *Vol. 6, No. 2, May, 1991, p. 25.*

With over 30 editions of this perennial favorite currently in print, an illustrator must make any new attempt so unique as to divert attention from the others. Unfortunately, such is not the case with this British import. Unlike James Marshall and Tony Ross, whose highly individualized brands of humor and illustrative style mark their versions as true stand-outs, Biro has added nothing significant to his retelling, either textually or visually, to warrant purchase of this book over any other equally inoffensive and lackluster version. The roly-poly pigs, depicted as innocent rubes, fall to the Disney side of the barnyard. However, bravo to Biro for adhering to tradition in that the pesky wolf is destroyed rather than merely scared away, as has been the case in more "gentle" renderings. Biro's most singular contribution to this centuries-old title is the *Where's Waldo?* touch of hiding the wolf in every picture (a not-too-subtle prompt is provided on the back cover for the less observant). Nothing sets it apart—buy multiple copies of Galdone, Marshall, and others while you still can.

> *Dorothy Houlihan, in a review of "The Three Little Pigs," in* School Library Journal, *Vol. 37, No. 9, September, 1991, p. 226.*

Rub-a-Dub-Dub: Val Biro's 77 Favorite Nursery Rhymes (1991)

Quantity is a selling point for this collection of traditional rhymes. All the familiar standards are here with a table of contents to help readers locate their own favorites. One or two of Biro's humorous, richly colored cartoons illustrate each rhyme. However, two or three entries have been jumbled together on some pages, and it's difficult at first glance to tell which drawings go with which rhymes. An optional purchase.

> *Judith Gloyer, in a review of "Rub-a-Dub-Dub: Val Biro's 77 Favorite Nursery Rhymes," in* School Library Journal, *Vol. 38, No. 2, February, 1992, p. 81.*

Eve Bunting

1928-

(Born Ann Evelyn Bolton; has also written as Evelyn Bolton and A. E. Bunting) Irish-born American author of fiction, nonfiction, and picture books.

Major works include *One More Flight* (1976), *The Empty Window* (1980), *The Sea World Book of Whales* (1980), *Surrogate Sister* (1981), *The Happy Funeral* (1982), *Face at the Edge of the World* (1985), *The Wednesday Surprise* (1989), *The Wall* (1990).

A prolific and popular author who has written more than one hundred books for preschoolers, primary graders, middle graders, and young adults, Bunting is respected as a skillful writer who addresses a variety of subjects and themes in works considered both entertaining and thought-provoking. Praised as a masterful storyteller whose books reflect her sensitivity, insight, and understanding of children and of what appeals to them, she is often acknowledged for successfully treating difficult issues with compassion and humor in works which range in effect from thrilling to moving. Bunting is the creator of mysteries, fantasies, romances, ghost stories, horse stories, informational books, and picture books—some of which are written in verse—as well as realistic fiction, science fiction, and historical fiction. Many of her works, which are often published as series, are recognized as being among the most substantial in their respective genres and are often noted as the first books on their subjects. In her fiction, she creates protagonists of a variety of ages and backgrounds: her main characters are from such nationalities as Japanese, Chinese-American, Inuit, Puerto Rican, Hawaiian-Irish, and Northern Irish as well as black and white American, and she also includes characters who are abused, homeless, and disabled in her works. Bunting is also acknowledged for the timeliness of her subjects: her books include such issues as surrogate parenthood, teenage suicide, prostitution, and IRA terrorism. An environmentalist whose books often stress respect for nature and the hope for harmony between humans and the natural world, Bunting takes a light but firm approach to her themes. She writes about the feelings of her protagonists, especially as these boys and girls attempt to adjust to such situations as death and loss, divorce, stepparents, and personal fears. Bunting often places her characters in difficult situations which require them to use their ethical judgment, and her works clearly show the negative consequences of making improper choices; for example, several of her books include tragedies resulting from peer pressure and irresponsibility. Through their experiences, her characters become more self-confident and learn to accept life as it is. Underscoring her works is Bunting's philosophy of the importance of love, trust, and peace with each other and with nature. "Each of us," she has said, "has a choice of what we do with our lives. . . . I hope the children make the right choice, whatever it is, and in my books I try to help them make it."

Born in Northern Ireland, a setting that figures in several of her books, Bunting started her writing career at the age of forty-three after enrolling in a course entitled "Writing for Publication"; she has since taught courses of this type at the university level and at writer's conferences. Bunting is perhaps best known for her realistic fiction, mysteries, and picture books about holidays as well as for introducing science fiction to readers in the early grades. She has often received accolades for such works as *One More Flight,* a novel for middle and upper elementary graders about how Dobby, a troubled eleven-year-old who has escaped from the Residential Treatment Center where he has lived most of his life, learns about the meaning of freedom from nineteen-year-old Timmer, a boy who cares for injured birds; *The Wednesday Surprise,* a story for primary graders which describes how small Anna teaches her grandmother to read; and *The Wall,* a picture book about the journey of a young boy who goes to the Vietnam War Memorial to find the name of his grandfather on the wall. In her nonfiction for middle graders, Bunting characteristically writes about sea creatures—sharks, whales, and squids—in works that address the evolution, physical characteristics, and habits of her subjects while including interesting background information about them. Writing her fiction in a clear, lyrical style, Bunting is commended for the solid characterizations and accurate dialogue of her books as well as for the liveliness of their pace. Although her works are accused of lacking depth and of being overly formulaic, Bunting is usually considered a writer of quality. Critic Eric A. Kimmel calls Bunting "the consummate professional," adding that "[as] a master of the craft of writing she is probably the best in the juvenile field." *One More Flight* won the Golden Kite Award and was named both an Outstanding Social Science Book for Children and an Outstanding Science Book for Children in 1976, while *The Wednesday Surprise* was named a Jane Addams Children's Book Award honor book in 1990. In 1984 Bunting received a PEN Special Achievement Award for her contributions to children's literature. She has also received several children's choice awards and regional awards from her home state of California.

(See also *Something about the Author,* Vol. 18; *Authors and Artists for Young Adults,* Vol. 5; *Contemporary Authors New Revision Series,* Vols. 5, 19; and *Contemporary Authors,* Vols. 53-56.)

AUTHOR'S COMMENTARY

I was meeting friends for lunch last week. One of them had bought several of my books and brought them for me to autograph. I was a little late and when I arrived I could see they were amused about something. My friend, Elizabeth, explained.

"We were admiring your books," she said. "And we discovered one was for very young children, one for middle-sized and one for older children. And then we discovered that your picture on the cover looks slightly different for each book." She showed me.

"In this one you're really smiling and fun-loving. In this, sweet and grandmotherly. In this . . .wow! The ultimate Valley Girl! Are these the three faces of Eve?" I laughed with them.

I had not deliberately portrayed myself differently for the three age levels of books, but that was the way it had turned out. And when I came home and thought about it, I realized that yes, I do change personalities, depending on the age of the child for whom the book is intended. Since I've written a lot of books, ranging from a preschool, wordless picture book through all the in-betweens to young adult novels, I guess I've changed my mental sophistication level rather often in the past decade. I should be at least schizoid by now.

A children's book writer who tackles all age levels in about equal numbers is relatively rare . . . and in high demand as a speaker in schools. ("We usually have someone to speak to the kindergartners, Mrs. Bunting, and someone for the older kids. But since you do *all* grades . . .") It's like having three authors for the nuisance value of one!

There are other advantages to producing a mixed bag. When a good idea comes along it never has to be dismissed as too young or too old to fit in the age level for which I

write. If it's *that* good I won't rest till I write about it; maybe not in this book, or the next one, but certainly in the one after that.

I was in Detroit at a teachers' conference a while back. At lunch time I talked with a librarian who happened to be in line with me at the one and only cafeteria in the conference center. During our conversation, she told me about a meeting she had just attended where the speaker described a "sleepover" in the school library that he'd organized for the kids in his elementary school reading club. I instantly got that special tingle that means an idea virus is taking hold. Soon, as she told me about his talk in more detail, the lights began flashing and Bingo! It took me a whole year before I was able to begin *Sixth Grade Sleepover* . . . , but the idea didn't go to waste.

That project was a particularly refreshing one for me. I had just completed a YA novel in which the protagonist's best friend commits suicide. The book had been grim to do . . . unrelenting, the kind that gets between you and sleep. Since it was also a rather adult mystery, there were all those intricate puzzle pieces to fit neatly together. When I finished *Face at the Edge of the World* I had the satisfaction of having written something difficult but that I considered worthwhile. But what a pleasure and relaxation it was to romp my way through *Sixth Grade Sleepover,* which, although it has its serious moments, is mostly fun all the way. It was satisfaction of a totally different kind that you can only experience by writing different kinds of books.

When I drive the freeway from my home in Pasadena to Los Angeles I pass a cluster of deserted old houses, set higgledy-piggledy on an empty lot. I'd examine them as closely as I dared, driving at fifty-five m.p.h. through the always unbelievable traffic. Even that kind of examination convinced me that those wonderful, abandoned Gothic houses would make a great setting for a book. One day I found the right turn-off and studied them at closer range.

They sat locked away behind a high wire fence, relics of a more gracious time. I learned that this was a restoration project. It would take years, and lots of work, money, and love to bring the houses back to the way they once were. I walked around the perimeter of the fence and knew I would write about it.

"There's a young couple who live in there," a lady told me. "They're the caretakers." She shivered. "Think how spooky it must be at night." Yes indeed!

I had my idea. The book would have to be young adult. And wasn't I lucky? I just happen to write for young adults. *The Haunting of Safekeep* was published by Harper and Row in 1985.

There are, of course, some disadvantages to being a jack of all trades author. For Norma Fox Mazer there is instant name recognition. "Norma Fox Mazer? Sure! She's that very good young adult writer." Or maybe "Arnold Lobel, who does those wonderful picture books." There is an age level association. You are a specialist of sorts, not a general practitioner, and that's nice. But being a general practitioner is nice too. You have a great, wide range of children for readers. You get notes, laboriously printed on lined paper, half of the sentences sliding off the page, or you get professional-looking letters, run off on a word processor. (pp. 132-34)

When I speak to writers at conferences I often suggest that they try moving out of their usual and most comfortable age level and into something different. Often the name tags at these conferences have colored dots on them. Each different color indicates if the author writes for the picture book crowd, middle graders, junior highers or young adults. I ask them to check their dots. Most of the name tags have only one, but many could indeed have more than that.

"Wouldn't it be more fun to be a rainbow?" I ask.

"How? I can only write for . . ."

"Have you tried?"

There is no special secret to writing for all age levels. You climb inside the head and the heart of the young person in your story. You think like that child. You feel like that child. You are that child.

If you're five today and you're writing about little mice searching in the meadow for the perfect Mother's Day gift, you're doing a picture book.

If you're thirteen and you're dreading the kissing games at your birthday party because you don't know how to kiss, and that real cute boy you like a lot is going to be there, then you're writing for the middle graders.

If you're eighteen and your boyfriend is asking you to move into his apartment and share the rent and a whole lot more, you're definitely in the young adult genre.

Changing your age level from week to week may be a little disconcerting for those you live with. But I guarantee they'll never be bored. You won't either. (p. 134)

> Eve Bunting, "Slightly Schizoid but Never Boring: Writing for Children of All Ages," in Top of the News, *Vol. 42, No. 2, Winter, 1986, pp. 132-34.*

GENERAL COMMENTARY

Allen Raymond

Eve Bunting's books span the childhood spectrum, from kindergarten picture books to young adult novels. They tackle difficult subjects like teenage suicide, and lighter topics like what happens when two bears, "Mr. and Mrs. Bear," before they settle down for a long winter's nap, set their alarm clock for February 14. They want to celebrate their first Valentine's Day together. (p. 39)

Bunting books are upbeat and morally straight. "I'd never have a kid messing with drugs or messing with sex," she says. "In my books my kids are always tempted, because I think that's life. But whatever the tempting situation, kids will find a message, well-hidden I hope, that says, 'better not.'"

"Each of us has a choice of what we do with our lives,"

she continued. "I hope the children make the right choice, whatever it is, and in my books I try to help them make it."

Reviewers generally praise Bunting books. Whether it is due to the clarity and liveliness of the dialogue, to the real-life situations in which the author puts her characters, or whether it is the moral approach to difficult choices, there is something about her books which brings praise from reviewers for *The New York Times, Publisher's Weekly, ALA Booklist* and a host of magazines and newspapers throughout the country. . . .

Her newest book, *Sixth-Grade Sleepover* was published this September. It's the story of a sixth grade reading club which is planning to hold a sleepover in the cafeteria. But Janey is afraid of the dark and Rosie is only reading at a kindergarten level. Eve Bunting handles the problem, the embarrassments and the hurts with compassion, understanding and, when needed, humor.

Eve Bunting's style can be almost lyrical, as in *Demetrius and the Golden Goblet,* a picture book beautifully illustrated by Michael Hague. Savor this passage, as the prince who is the hero of the story sits on a cliff overlooking his beloved ocean: "Sometimes, when the prince sat on his cliff top, fog would creep across the ocean, gathering her great gray skirts about her. Or a storm cloud would hang like a black blister over the waiting sea. There were other times when the blueness was all a-shimmer, when every fish had its own color, and fingers of green weed waved to him, beckoned to him."

But she can change her style, talk like kids talk. In *Jane Martin, Dog Detective* dialogue carries the day as Jane, for 25¢ a day, finds lost or stolen dogs.

Throughout her books lives are guided by The Golden Rule, "do unto others as you would have them do unto you." There is nothing overt, no preaching. Eve Bunting simply means to score a few points with her readers, perhaps redirect a few lives. The popularity of her books seems to indicate that kids get the message. (p. 40)

> Allen Raymond, "Eve Bunting: From Ireland with Love," in Early Years, *Vol. 17, No. 2, October, 1986, pp. 39-40.*

TITLE COMMENTARY

The Once-a-Year Day (1974)

The once-a-year day is like Christmas, Easter and all other holidays rolled into one for the Eskimo children in a remote part of Alaska. That's the day when barges arrive, bringing supplies to last the tribe until the next year and Annie, a 13-year-old, can't wait for the unloading. The girl is irritated by her orphaned cousin, Emma, who has been taken in by Annie's family and who is sulky, dull and slow—not at all the bright companion Annie had longed for. Annie has saved up for a treasure—a single orange— and Emma's reaction to her cousin's offer to share the treat promises a better future and the joys of friendship. This is an endearing story, raised from slightness by Ms.

Bunting's sensitive telling and [W. T.] Mars's revealing pictures.

> *A review of "The Once-a-Year Day," in* Publishers Weekly, *Vol. 205, No. 21, May 27, 1974, p. 64.*

The story is brief, adequately written and nicely illustrated, and while it has the universal qualities of jealousy and generosity, it is weakened by the two facts that Annie's understanding comes so quickly and that she didn't seem to understand earlier that a recently bereaved child would be disoriented and unhappy.

> *Zena Sutherland, in a review of "The Once-a-Year Day," in* Bulletin of the Center for Children's Books, *Vol. 28, No. 2, October, 1974, p. 25.*

High Tide for Labrador   (as A. E. Bunting, 1975)

Newfoundlander Jimmy Donovan, thirteen, resents the solicitude of Big Simon, the new friend of Jimmy's widowed mother who has also signed him onto his own fishing ship, the *Kathleen II.* But when Jimmy, in an attempt to prove his mettle and stake an advantageous spot for the ship, secretly takes the anchored ship's dory on a hazardous night mission, it is Big Simon who leaps ice flows to rescue him from exposure. The two of them then set the lines that Jimmy had come out for, saving the voyage for the *Kathleen II* and convincing Jimmy of Big Simon's worthiness as a possible stepdad. A boys' magazine type of adventure story, with crude characterization and a rudimentary plot but a passable recreation of the harsh northern locale.

> *A review of "High Tide for Labrador," in* Kirkus Reviews, *Vol. XLIII, No. 9, May 1, 1975, p. 511.*

Although this sea story borders on cliché, it keeps up a fast pace and has some compensating elements of originality. . . . Jimmy's hostility toward the suitor, Big Simon, and his immature desires to live up to his dead father's image reach a climax when he tries a risky solo venture in the ice-filled waters off Labrador. His rescue by Simon brings him a new understanding of the older man, and the two miraculously pull off the mission in spite of Jimmy's earlier blunder. Bunting's mission, on the other hand, is barely saved by some good sea scenes and "getting inside" Jimmy's head during moments of high tension.

> *A review of "High Tide for Labrador," in* The Booklist, *Vol. 71, No. 21, July 1, 1975, p. 1126.*

A well-written thriller that grips readers with suspense and action. . . . Although the ending is too sweet and tidy and there is an unnecessary antagonist to Jimmy in the form of a bullying deck hand, the story remains realistic and enthralling.

> *Hayden Atwood, in a review of "High Tide for Labrador," in* School Library Journal, *Vol. 22, No. 1, September, 1975, p. 98.*

The Day of the Dinosaurs; Death of a Dinosaur; The Dinosaur Trap; Escape from Tyrannosaurus   (1975)

The four entries in the Dinosaur Machine series provide motivational material for the middle grades. In the first, *The Day of the Dinosaurs,* Joe Lopez gets a chance to apply his knowledge of prehistoric creatures when, during a museum field trip, he and two friends accidentally move a hidden lever and are whisked back 150 million years. Joe, Carmen, and Riley find themselves in a world where the air is hot and damp, plant life is unfamiliar, and brontosauri shake the earth. In spite of dangers they vow to return, and do in the next three books (each summarizes previous action but the books are better read in sequence). Characterization is shallow but the pace is fast and suspense quickly built.

> *Gail Kish, in a review of "The Day of the Dinosaurs" and others, in* School Library Journal, *Vol. 22, No. 5, January, 1976, p. 44.*

Dream Dancer; Goodbye, Charlie; Lady's Girl; Ride When You're Ready; Stable of Fear; The Wild Horses   (as Evelyn Bolton, 1975)

Six short, colorfully illustrated stories about girls and horses that might be useful for high interest, low level reading and special education classes. *Dream Dancer* parallels the plight of a young girl's grandfather who is forced to retire, and an old horse forgotten on parade day. Caroline not only manages to win back her grandfather's job, but also becomes the hit of the parade when Dream Dancer steps to the music as he once did in the circus.

In *Goodbye, Charlie,* Ellen must face the loss of the family's horse, now too small for her and her sister, and accept a new horse in Charlie's place.

Another correlation is drawn in *Lady's Girl* between Jenny, whose mother is in the hospital, and the new foal of a dead mare. With much care, the orphaned foal survives, and Jenny's father finally decides not to send Jenny away during her mother's absence.

When Pat enters her first gymkhana show in *Ride When You're Ready,* she is overweight and lacks self-confidence. An error in judgment causes her disqualification from her first competition, but the experience prepares her for the next meet.

In *Stable of Fear,* Jill is back exercising thoroughbred race horses after a bad kick for which she was hospitalized. She must overcome her fear of horses to keep her job and does when she leads the frightened animals to safety during a freak fire.

Her family's concern over *The Wild Horses,* sold at auction in New Mexico leads Maria to bid for a horse, only to set it free again.

Although not noted for literary or artistic quality, this series is appropriate for the third to fifth grade transitional readers and also for older students reading on this level. As a whole, the stories are of more interest to girls; but read individually, they might be enjoyed by boys, too.

Ronna Dishnica, in a review of "Dream Dancer" and others, in School Library Journal, *Vol. 22, No. 1, September, 1978, p. 97.*

One More Flight (1976)

A chronic runaway from foster homes and from the Center where he's spent most of his eleven years, Dobby is lucky enough on his latest flight to be picked up by nineteen-year-old Timmer who lives in a barn and takes care of injured birds for the Audubon Society. To Dobby's disappointment, Timmer sends him back to the Home; but meanwhile the two become friends, and Dobby learns something he can apply to his own situation as he comes to understand why Timmer won't release the birds until they're "ready." The parallels are too transparently contrived to be as effective as they should be, tho Bunting does do better with the textures of Dobby's sojourn than with the outline. One more diluted *Dorp Dead?*

A review of "One More Flight," in Kirkus Reviews, *Vol. XLIV, No. 6, March 15, 1976, p. 321.*

Bunting's understated delivery saves this from becoming too heavy-handed, and realistic black-and-white illustrations [by Diane de Groat] aptly reflect the mood of the story, but this will still only appeal to introspective readers.

Gale K. Shonkwiler, in a review of "One More Flight," in School Library Journal, *Vol. 22, No. 9, May, 1976, p. 57.*

Eve Bunting is the author of more than twenty-five books for children; this one is smoothly constructed, truthful without being dangerous, realistic without being painful. The pictures are nice too, soft chalky pencil blurred at the edges like the story itself. It is a well made plastic toy. (p. 335)

Dorothy Nimmo, in a review of "One More Flight," in The School Librarian, *Vol. 24, No. 4, December, 1976, pp. 334-35.*

Appropriately, in such a story, the main characters are highly individualistic. Dobby is stubborn, quick to anger but easily hurt; the reader shares his memories, fears, and wishful, poignant fantasies. Timmer, gentle but remote, is unusual in his lifestyle and in his dedication to his work; he provides a balance as he gropes to help Dobby accept his own situation. He is aided by Miss Bee, the spunky old woman who owns Timmer's barn. The three come to life in a warm, well-crafted story that avoids simple solutions and conventional characters while making a strong plea about the plight of captive wild birds.

Christine McDonnell, in a review of "One More Flight," in The Horn Book Magazine, *Vol. LIII, No. 2, April, 1977, p. 158.*

[This is an] outstanding story of the search for freedom. . . . The story is completely satisfying and never dull, when Dobby has his chance to protect the birds from the night prowler when Trimmer is injured, you are wholly convinced of his sincerity. Not a book to mask emotions or to shirk from the harsh realities of nature as it affects both human and animal life, but a look at a wide world where nothing is wholly good nor anyone wholly bad.

J. Russell, in a review of "One More Flight," in The Junior Bookshelf, *Vol. 41, No. 2, April, 1977, p. 85.*

Blacksmith at Blueridge (1976)

Extremely self-conscious and anxious to escape the memory of the accident that left her facially scarred, Mel Grant breaks ties with her family and strikes out on her own. Armed with blacksmith's credentials, she applies for a job with the prestigious Blueridge Stables and, due in part to the urging of champion rider Dee-Dee Chalmers, is hired. With the help of the stable's attractive head blacksmith, Mel begins to regain her confidence; but when Dee-Dee's mother accuses her of causing the Chalmers' horse to cripple, she tries to run from the problem. Only after Mel discovers that Dee-Dee, prompted by fear of competitive riding, had crippled her own horse, does she realize that hiding from problems is never the answer for anyone. Familiar teenage problems handled in a nonpatronizing, easy-to-read manner. . . .

A review of "Blacksmith at Blueridge," in Booklist, *Vol. 74, No. 3, October 1, 1977, p. 283.*

As far as this reviewer is concerned, this Double Action Library 1 collection, to which these two titles [**Blacksmith at Blueridge** and *Narc One Going Down* by Chet Cunningham] belong, is absolutely what high/low books should be all about. For anyone planning a junor and/or senior high school reading lab. they are a must—carefully controlled vocabulary on about a third-grade reading level, great plots that appeal to the 12-to-16 year old, terrific photographic illustrations, and all this without a hint of condescension. And they do not date; I have used them for five years now, across a range of students from differing socioeconomic groups, and the appeal is as strong as it ever was.

Blacksmith at Blueridge is about Melissa (Mel,) whose face was scarred in a car accident. On the insurance proceeds she sends herself to blacksmith school, because she has always liked working around horses, and also outfits a truck from which she can work. She applies for a job at Blueridge Stables and gets a two-week trial over the objections of Paddy, the main blacksmith. How Mel eventually overcomes Paddy's objections and gets the job permanently, grows to feel less self-conscious about her scar and learns to accept herself and cope with her feelings rather than running away from them are all nicely developed in the framework of the story. I like the way Mel grows as a person. There's a budding romance, too. Highly recommended for girls 12 to 16.

Marguerite Leighton, in a review of "Blacksmith at Blueridge," in The High/Low Report, *Vol. 2, No. 6, February, 1981, p. 6.*

Winter's Coming (1977)

"The sky is full of ducks flying south. The whistling swans are leaving too. By day and by night we hear the beating of their wings, but they leave no trace behind them in the blue emptiness . . . . Grandma says it will be cold this winter." Piece by piece, the signs of a hard winter appear as the family makes its preparations accordingly. The child narrator catches little moments in time and terse commentary by the family, concluding with the proper child-summation: "I hope it comes soon." A sense of wonder at the happenings of nature and at man's possible harmony with his surroundings emerges through this poetic, yet largely concrete, piece of writing. Bunting, moreover, flourishes within the confines rather than struggling against a limited vocabulary and sentence structure. [Howard] Knotts' black-and-white illustrations, though they lack the text's elegance as well as its deeper meanings, have fine-lined country charm.

> *Judith Goldberger, in a review of "Winter's Coming," in* Booklist, *Vol. 73, No. 12, February 15, 1977, p. 900.*

An even-toned catalog of the preparations for winter observed by a small boy and girl around their farm. . . . Not resonant enough to be memorable, this does strike a quiet, expectant note, and though Knotts' scratchy, cross-hatched, winter-gray drawings lack the poetry of his illustrations for Barnstone's *A Day in the Country* (1971), they do their share to maintain the tone.

> *A review of "Winter Is Coming," in* Kirkus Reviews, *Vol. XLV, No. 8, April 15, 1977, p. 424.*

The story avoids the beginning reader trap of starting each sentence in the same way, and the specific signals of a hard winter ahead will be enlightening to many urban and suburban children ("The hornets have built their paper nests high in the eaves so they will be out of the deep snow. The caterpillars are furrier this year.") A cozy, pleasant choice.

> *A review of "Winter Is Coming," in* School Library Journal, *Vol. 23, No. 9, May, 1977, p. 74.*

The Big Cheese (1977)

Thin, prim Tillie is a proverb-spouting organizer who bakes bread and is tight enough to save the crumbs to make crumb cake on Sunday. Bee, on the other hand, is a looser, easy-going sort who thinks it would be nice to go to the village for a treat once in a while. The precisely plotted life Tillie has set up for them undergoes a change when she takes a huge cheese off a farmer's hands after his wagon has broken down. To stave off mice they acquire a cat; once the mice depart, the cat is in danger of starving, so they take on a cow. The cow needs grass, so they buy a meadow. Now overstocked with milk and butter, they offer to give it away, and folks come by with smiles and goods to exchange. When the cheese runs out, it's a problem for compulsive Tillie to justify her new living standard until she hits on the obvious solution—make more cheese.

Bunting's sly personality sketch bounces vitally along as Tillie's comic dilemma is underscored by the insistent logic of her waste-not-want-not code. It's a neat trick Bunting has worked; though Bee's easy-going ways are never fully asserted, Tillie's arrival at the same conclusion via her own circuitous route makes a telling comment on live-and-let-live peacemaking. (pp. 1263-64)

> *Denise M. Wilms, in a review of "The Big Cheese," in* Booklist, *Vol. 73. No. 16, April 15, 1977, pp. 1263-64.*

There's some appeal in the cumulation, and some humor in the final decision, but it's a bit contrived, and the author has substituted comic typing for characterization; Miss Bee is irrevocably silly-sweet and Miss Tillie adamantly practical, speaking almost entirely in old saws and clichés.

> *Zena Sutherland, in a review of "The Big Cheese," in* Bulletin of the Center for Children's Books, *Vol. 31, No. 1, September, 1977, p. 8.*

Ghost of Summer (1977)

The author of over 30 fine novels for young people tops herself in her latest publication. The novel is set in ravaged northern Ireland. Besides its value as suspenseful entertainment, the story is a subtle plea for peace and tolerance. At 15, Irish-American Kevin arrives to spend his vacation with his grandfather, Reverend Hugh Garvin, rector of the Protestant church in Trallagh, and his gentle housekeeper, Miss Lillian. Bat (short for Bridget Anne Tierney) is another guest at the house and a likable girl Kevin's age. Because the boy and girl search together for a treasure buried a century earlier by a notorious thief, they get into the crossfire between battling Protestants and Catholics. But they are not in deadly danger until they are trapped by a truly evil criminal who lusts after the fortune and whose unmasking is a stunning blow.

> *A review of "Ghost of Summer," in* Publishers Weekly, *Vol. 211, No. 24, June 13, 1977, p. 107.*

[This story] functions as both an intelligent mystery-adventure and a thoughtful portrait of young people in contemporary rural Ireland. The tale's outcome, which plays fairly to all sides tangled in a burgeoning conflict, nicely satisfies both the mystery's plot needs and character development.

> *Denise M. Wilms, in a review of "Ghost of Summer," in* Booklist, *Vol. 73, No. 22, July 15, 1977, p. 1726.*

Magic and the Night River (1978)

A low-keyed, cross-cultural visit with Japanese Yoshi, who goes out each night on his grandfather's fishing boat but must give half their catch to Kano, who owns all the boats. Yoshi is worried because Kano threatens to take the boat away from his aging grandfather, whose catch has fallen off; he also hates Kano for the way he handles his cormorants, as Yoshi and his grandfather are kind and appreciative of theirs. But that night on the water a sort of traffic jam entangles everyone's cormorant lines, and Grandfather's gentleness pays off when he frees his birds to get them clear of the mess, and they unexpectedly return to him, bearing fish. Heartened by Kano's awe-struck response, Yoshi anticipates "many more nights" on the river, for though "[grandfather's] strength grows less every day, my strength grows greater." Aided by [Allen] Say's charming, softly lit illustrations, Bunting gives children a pleasantly personalized glimpse of the old fishing practices—ringed cormorants, wood-burning lanterns, exploitative owner; as a story, it is thin and conventional.

> *A review of "Magic and the Night River," in* Kirkus Reviews, *Vol. XLVI, No. 5, March 1, 1978, p. 243.*

Bunting's writing is smooth, and the closeness of Yoshi with his grandfather is carefully drawn; the resulting warmth plus the dignity that emanates from the protagonists themselves help reduce the artificiality of the contrived finish. Though a traditional story pattern governs the action, the strong satisfaction it generates will appeal to younger readers. (p. 1186)

> *Denise M. Wilms, in a review of "Magic and the Night River," in* Booklist, *Vol. 74, No. 14, March 15, 1978, pp. 1185-86.*

The Haunting of Kildoran Abbey (1978)

Kildoran Abbey is where seven orphaned, starving children meet secretly during the scourging year of 1847 in Ireland. The potato famine and callous landlords have decimated the native population. Sir James Blunt earns the hatred of the survivors by confiscating their meager belongings, evicting them and destroying their poor cottages. At the Abbey, the twins Columb and Finn plot with the other orphans, including a daring girl named Ryan. They raid Blunt's storehouse and distribute the loot to the hungry townspeople. The rebels get support from a British boy and his conscientious father who bring them the grand news that Blunt has been called to account for his crimes, at last. Bunting's tense, exciting drama is rewarding as a novel and as an addition to the record of historic events left unmentioned for too long in children's books.

> *A review of "The Haunting of Kildoran Abbey," in* Publishers Weekly, *Vol. 213, No. 21, May 22, 1978, p. 233.*

Set against the harsh backdrop of the 1847 Irish potato famine, Bunting's story is one of wholehearted historical adventure. . . . A thin supernatural thread runs through the story in the form of Witch's spontaneous future visions and, less acceptably, in the fortuitous entry at one point of Kildoran Abbey's alleged ghosts. There is also contrivance at hand in the escapes and a bit of didacticism in bids for Irish-English tolerance. However, the pace is fast and the characters and their underdog status emotionally appealing in this light, satisfactory escape fare.

> *Denise M. Wilms, in a review of "The Haunt-*

ing of Kildoran Abbey," in Booklist, *Vol. 74, No. 21, July 1, 1978, p. 1677.*

Bunting is obviously drawing a parallel between history and today's English-Irish troubles, especially in the relationship between Columb and Christopher. But her message is not belabored and the descriptions of the famine are moving and honest. Characterizations are interesting, action is fast, and the touch of the supernatural adds spice.

> *Nancy Berkowitz, in a review of "The Haunting of Kildoran Abbey," in* School Library Journal, *Vol. 25, No. 1, September, 1978, p. 154.*

Fifteen; For Always; The Girl in the Painting; Just Like Everyone Else; Maggie the Freak; Nobody Knows but Me; Oh, Rick!; A Part of the Dream; Survival Camp!; Two Different Girls (1978)

The bittersweet growing experiences of teenage love and like are explored in [the Young Romance books, a] series for reluctant readers. The stories are brief, with only four illustrations per book, and concern a variety of plausible situations and personalities. Although somewhat formularized, the books retain credibility through relatively solid characterization, lively writing style, and depth of content. There is also a degree of racial, sexual, and class balance, including several titles with ethnic characters and a romance told by a boy. In spite of heavy black typeface, the series has obvious appeal and meets minimum literary standards; a winner for readers and book-pushers alike.

> *Judith Goldberger, in a review of "Fifteen" and others, in* Booklist, *Vol. 74, No. 20, June 15, 1978, pp. 1620-21.*

Billed as a series exploring boy-girl relationships, these selections are uniformly trite and superficial. The young people who are supposed to be enticed by the familiar situations and large type will be put off by the formulaic plotting and moralizing that undercut the stories.

On her 15th birthday, Jordan [the protagonist of **Fifteen**] makes a fool of herself at sophisticated Clay's party while trying to impress handsome Neil who still thinks of her as a little girl. Jordan defers to Neil's dictum that "anything worthwhile is worth waiting for" and decides, at **Fifteen,** to wait for him. New girl Carla's art talent wins her popular Troy as a date for the Fall Dance in **The Girl In the Painting.** In two of the better stories, *Shelby* leaves boyfriend Brian (to whom she has sworn eternal love) for a month-long skateboarding competition and realizes that 16 is too young to decide **For Always.** When Eric meets Maeve, who has come from Ireland to spend a summer with his California family, he learns that peer pressure can be cruel and that there is no intrinsic value in being **Just Like Everyone Else. Maggie the Freak** is an athlete who deliberately loses the shot put to Tod because "boys don't like girls to be good at . . . cars, and sports." But Todd's admiration for her mechanical skills when she fixes his car gives her permission to excel at her "unfeminine" pursuits. In **Nobody Knows But Me,** Ellen admits that her idol, Leo, is a dumb jock and chooses smart, reliable George.

Beth's 10 days at a weight-loss clinic, undergone in the hopes of making *. . . Rick* notice her, motivates her to take more control of her life, even if all of her self-improvement goals are aimed at getting other people's approval. When Lisa goes on vacation with her newly divorced mother she ignores nice Tony Westridge for seductive, fickle Carlos who works at the hotel. Then she understands that his flirting was all *A Part of the Dream* furnished for girls who cherish passionate vacation rendezvous. Mimi's parents send her to *Survival Camp* to develop independence and resourcefulness, which she supposedly does by staying with an injured friend and sending for help. She also wins a nod from Brad Taylor, and suddenly the world "had a new pink glow." Donna overcomes her shyness—and possibly gets a date for the prom—when she helps an injured dog in the only story featuring Black protagonists, *Two Different Girls.* The message throughout is clear: girls derive their feelings of self-worth and are accepted by the "in-crowd" only by being attractive to boys. There is indeed a need for good teenage romances; but this series, marred by poor writing and a badly designed format, only manages to reaffirm sexist stereotypes and offer leaden insights. (pp. 130-31)

> *Cyrisse Jaffee, in a review of "Fifteen" and others, in* School Library Journal, *Vol. 25, No. 1, September, 1978, pp. 130-31.*

Day of the Earthlings; The Followers; The Island of One; The Mask; The Mirror Planet; The Robot People; The Space People; The Undersea People   (1978)

This uneven series ["Creative Science Fiction"] is problematical but nevertheless carries punch: Bunting's style is smooth and energetic, the genre is popular, the youthful characters are convincing, and action is plentiful. Perhaps these factors outweigh some contrivances and logistical stumbling blocks in the plotting, at least in terms of overall appeal and readability. Subjects range from the supernatural to futuristic science fiction and almost pure fantasy. The stories are brief and the format, with the exception of young covers, should draw middle and upper graders who lack the motivation to read longer works.

> *Judith Goldberger, in a review of "Day of the Earthlings" and others, in* Booklist, *Vol. 75, No. 4, October 15, 1978, p. 389.*

A series of short science fiction aimed at the high interest, low vocabulary fourth-fifth grade market. The stories themselves are competently written, following the rules now set up for hi-lo efforts—short sentences, short paragraphs, little description, direct narrative, etc. Each uses a fairly common sci fi theme and involves readers in a basic moral dilemma (overcoming fear, learning to trust strangers, protecting loved ones, keeping faith with a scientist-father, etc.). The flaw in this series is in the packaging—thin, "easybook" format with garish, unappealing covers which shriek baby-book to older children. Thin, difficult-to-read print (large yes, clear no) with chapter headings on a slant and no illustrations damn the material for both young and older children.

> *Sara Miller, in a review of "Day of the Earth-*

lings" and others, in School Library Journal, *Vol. 25, No. 5, January, 1979, p. 51.*

The Big Red Barn   (1979)

A tenuous construct, barely a story, with none of the usual aids or lures for a beginning reader. The first-person narrator sets up the situation in disconnected offhand remarks about the family's beloved big red barn; sister Susie's pet goat, a rooster, a barn owl, and a nest of kangaroo rats (denizens of the barn); his new, resented stepmother and "the hayloft where I went when Mom died." Then, without warning, the barn burns down—and the question becomes whether its shiny aluminum replacement can actually take the old barn's place. The narrator resists; but, says wise Grandpa, "The new barn has to make its own place. It will if we give it a chance." That's a sidelong reference to stepmother Emma, seen in affectionate consort with Susie on the page before (and in the picture [by Howard Knotts] opposite); but the inference is both too fragile and too facile to make this diffuse mood-piece into a satisfactory story—even if it *weren't* an easy reader.

> *A review of "The Big Red Barn," in* Kirkus Reviews, *Vol. XLVII, No. 10, May 15, 1979, p. 574.*

A boy coping with his mother's death and the advent of a stepmother seems heavy stuff for an easy reader. The author tries to draw a parallel to a beloved old red barn which burns down and is replaced by a new aluminum one. Fortunately, Bunting does not belabor the analogy, a bit unsettling because of the facile equation of people with buildings. Soft pencil sketches are more soothing and blessedly less complex than the disturbing text.

> *Kathy Coffey, in a review of "The Big Red Barn," in* School Library Journal, *Vol. 26, No. 1, September, 1979, p. 104.*

The Cloverdale Switch   (1979)

As Bunting's brooding SF novel grows more intricate and tense, the weird truth begins to show itself. The author provides not only extraordinary entertainment but also situations about lifelike characters that induce readers to think carefully about moral issues.

> *A review of "The Cloverdale Switch," in* Publishers Weekly, *Vol. 216, No. 12, September 17, 1979, p. 146.*

The Cloverdale Switch is a spirited rewrite of two of the oldest clichés in science fiction: 1) Mysterious aliens are kidnapping human beings and replacing them with almost-perfect replicas; and 2) the aliens' purpose is to study, in hopes of eventually emulating, the unique ability to feel emotion. The story is set in a believable small town; the aliens' scheme is uncovered by a likable young boy and his slightly wacky grandfather, who conduct their sleuthing operations with intelligence, courage and good humor. The only problem with this book is its lack of originality; readers who are unfamiliar with "Star Trek" and its many precursors and imitators (if any such innocents exist) should find it enthralling.

> *Gerald Jonas, in a review of "The Cloverdale Switch," in* The New York Times Book Review, *December 30, 1979, p. 19.*

In a science fantasy that is a smooth blend of fantasy and realism, Bunting has structured a convincing, fast-paced story that has logic within the parameters she has set for her characters.

> *Zena Sutherland, in a review of "The Cloverdale Switch," in* Bulletin of the Center for Children's Books, *Vol. 33, No. 8, April, 1980, p. 147.*

The Sea World Book of Sharks (1979)

This appealing and much-researched text is crammed full of information most children's books on sharks overlook: the ancient history of these "living fossils," their place in the ecosystem, how and where they swim and hunt. Also included is information about their keen senses, mating, attacks on humans, experiments with sharks, and other interesting material about these feared and little-understood creatures.

> *George Barr, in a review of "The Sea World Book of Sharks," in* Children's Book Review Service, *Vol. 8, No. 6, February, 1980, p. 55.*

This is Sea World's first title in a new series that will no doubt be a big seller in their gift shops. Its format presents wide columns of text on coated paper. . . . Basic details about sharks are given the once-over: the evolution of the shark; their physical makeup; how they stay afloat, mate, and bear their young; and how the difficult research on this little-understood fish is accomplished. Ten specific kinds of sharks are described in terms of their relative size, eating habits and distinctive physical characteristics. Regretfully, several common failings of shark books are present—a focus on teeth; the stated or implied motivational attributes of sharks, hunger and savagery; inadequate explanations of sensory mechanisms; and a lack of relevant diagrams and maps. Throughout, Bunting attempts to provide a balanced portrayal of the shark; but for every sober statement made—" . . . sharks don't kill humans for fun, or because they hate us . . ."—an emotional one is uttered: "From the moment of birth they are . . . savage."

> *Cheryl Toth, in a review of "The Sea World Book of Sharks," in* School Library Journal, *Vol. 27, No. 2, October, 1980, p. 142.*

This is an excellent book on sharks for young readers. The writing is usually clear and succinct, although youthful jargon does creep in. The book is organized in seven chapters that briefly deal with the evolution of sharks, their major characteristics, how they are studied, their senses and reproduction, some selected life histories and their future. . . . If a criticism is to be made, it is that this book emphasizes the dangerous natures of some sharks at the expense of their useful qualities—such as their use for food

and leather. **The Sea World Book of Sharks** is noteworthy for the accuracy of the information it imparts. Most juvenile books on this subject are replete with bad information. The few inaccuracies in this book, however, are slight and do not detract from its overall excellence. (pp. 155-56)

> *Sanford A. Moss, in a review of "The Sea World Book of Sharks," in* Science Books & Films, *Vol. 16, No. 3, January-February, 1981, pp. 155-56.*

Yesterday's Island (1979)

Kama's Irish father was banished from Milanao by Mrs. Sommers, whose family had owned both island and islanders for generations. His islander mother chose to accompany the "unsettling" Timothy Sullivan into exile. While Leolani died when he was four, Kama's father lived long years enough to instill in his son a hatred of Mrs. Sommers and a deep need for revenge. Now, with adoption imminent, 12-year-old Kama runs away and sells his mother's star-shell lei to buy a boat to reach Milanao and kill Mrs. Sommers. A stray cat accompanies him, and when the decrepit boat sinks, Kama is forced to beat the panicked creature away before it claws him. The cat's drowning stays Kama's hand at the moment of murder. Death, he has learned, is final. His subsequent destruction of the family flag strikes a stronger blow at Mrs. Sommers, telling her she and her island are one with forgotten Yesterday. Purged, Kama faces his future. As in most hi/lo's, character development falls by the wayside with a resounding thud, and the plot consists of much direct action with a minimum of logical interference. As hi/lo's go, a medium/lo.

> *Patricia Manning, in a review of "Yesterday's Island," in* School Library Journal, *Vol. 26, No. 6, February, 1980, p. 52.*

The story's portrayal of complicated emotions is burdened by some overly deliberate exposition. On the other hand, Kama's presence and inner turmoil are strongly apparent. This is sometimes labored, but absorbing nonetheless, and graced with a strong, natural sense of the Hawaiian setting.

> *Denise M. Wilms, in a review of "Yesterday's Island," in* Booklist, *Vol. 76, No. 12, February 15, 1980, p. 832.*

Blackbird Singing (1980)

Despite the title, blackbirds, grackles, and starlings are not much in the singing department; and neither is this tale much in the fiction realm. Take about a million blackbirds that settle in the maple trees of a farm in Ohio, a father/farmer who wants to get rid of the birds because they're eating his corn, a vegetarian mother who opposes killing anything, a boy who starts stuttering—apparently because of his parents' conflict, and a stutters doctor who has a letch for the kid's father. Shake these together, and what do you get? Very little; but the boy gets histoplasmosis from bird droppings. "Th-th-that's it, folks." If it weren't for Fred Johnson, the family's black cat so fat he can only ogle the birds, the story would be a complete washout.

George Gleason, in a review of "Blackbird Singing," in School Library Journal, *Vol. 26, No. 7, March, 1980, p. 138.*

There's a compromise solution (cutting down a grove of trees, which Mom also loves, so that the birds won't return to nest there) and Marcus, who comes down with histoplasmosis (from bird droppings) resigns himself to the fact that the world is imperfect but that he can cope with it. Although the story is burdened by the message, it makes an impact because of the depth and sensitivity of Bunting's exploration of a child's conflicting emotions; seen believably from Marcus' unhappy point of view, the double conflict of loyalty to each of his parents and ambivalence about principles, the dilemma has wider implications (and, perhaps, applications) for readers than the issue in the story.

Zena Sutherland, in a review of "Blackbird Singing," in Bulletin of the Center for Children's Books, *Vol. 33, No. 10, June, 1980, p. 186.*

Eve Bunting keeps us turning the pages of *Blackbird Singing.* She brings economy and tension to her telling of Marcus's bad summer—the summer when clouds of blackbirds settled in the trees of his family's farm, ravaged the corn crop, brought disease in their droppings and increased the tension in his parents' troubled marriage. Ultimately, though, the book leaves us feeling let down and manipulated. Marcus ends up in the benevolent therapist's office, his hope for the future resting on his willingness to resign himself to the sorry condition of things; we feel we've taken a crash course in How Kids Can Cope, with divorce, stuttering and women's rights as some of the lecture topics.

Through pat psychological awakenings and the dubious consolation that others are suffering, too, . . . Eve Bunting's hero is taught to consider [his] losses as part of the inevitable disillusionment that passes, these days, for growing up. This isn't growth; this is erosion.

Kathleen Leverich, in a review of "Blackbird Singing," in The New York Times Book Review, *September 28, 1980, p. 34.*

Terrible Things (1980)

A wolf in a rabbit coat, this political allegory should get no place on juvenile shelves, no matter how fuzzy-wuzzy the pictures [by Stephen Gammell]. One by one, the critters living in a certain forest clearing are snatched up by the *Terrible Things.* First, this formless force of evil comes "for every creature with feathers on its back." The frogs, squirrels, porcupines, rabbits, and fish all quickly demonstrate their lack of feathers and then rationalize the situation with: "Those birds were always too noisy," and "There's more room in the trees now." When Little Rabbit asks "What's wrong with feathers?", he's silenced with "Just be glad it wasn't us they wanted." And life goes on

"almost as before" until the Terrible Things come back—and come back—and come back, until only the White Rabbits are left. Of course they get it too—all except Little Rabbit who is smart enough to hide. He goes off to warn other forest creatures and sadly thinks: ". . . if only we creatures had stuck together, it could have been different." Hardly! The Terrible Things as pictured here are just too supernatural and titanic a force to overcome with a few more animals. Purposely kept vague in the drawings (why? to scare less—or more?), the threat won't be easy for children to recognize, disarm and dismiss, which makes this uncontrolled, unresolved nightmare fodder. The terror of the wild-eyed animals is pretty graphic, though, as they are snatched up by swirling tentacles of a shadowy blob with suggestions of claws and ferocious faces. What's the point? Granted life may be like this for too many people around the world, but the five to eight year olds are not going to be able to do anything about it.

Marilyn R. Singer, in a review of "Terrible Things," in School Library Journal, *Vol. 26, No. 8, April, 1980, p. 91.*

An earnest fable that is too ponderous and too shadowy to be effective. . . . "If only we creatures had stuck together, it would have been different," says Little Rabbit sadly, making Bunting's point clear but not its application. Who or what are the Terrible Things in a small child's world? (Their own answer might be parents and teachers.) And how can children gang up against them? Kids will probably be able to parrot the lesson, but without a lot of pulling and prodding, will they relate to it? And if so, how?

A review of "Terrible Things," in Kirkus Reviews, *Vol. XLVIII, No. 10, May 15, 1980, p. 641.*

The overt symbolism in Bunting's tragedy may be considered too strong for children but it teaches an essential lesson. . . . Little Rabbit hides under a stone and escapes, to race off to another clearing in hopes of finding wildlings who will heed his warning that they should *stick together.*

A review of "Terrible Things," in Publishers Weekly, *Vol. 217, No. 20, May 23, 1980, p. 77.*

St. Patrick's Day in the Morning (1980)

Somewhere in Ireland, on Saint Patrick's day in the morning, Jamie wakes up early, resenting that he's too small to walk in the parade. So he dons his mother's raincoat, his father's hat, and his brother's green sash, takes another brother's flute, and with his dog Nell marches about in his own parade. Along the way Hobble the Hen Man gives him an egg, Mrs. Simms at the sweet shop (open early, it seems) gives him some ginger ale and a wee flag, he enjoys his drink on the parade's-end platform set up for the day's festivities, and then heads home with proud thoughts of the music he's played. Other small children might enjoy sharing underdog Jamie's secret, while sharing at the same time the author's pointed skepticism as to the beauty of his music. But they are unlikely to see the outing as much of a lark. Bunting tries too hard for color and imagery without supplying any narrative structure or incidents. . . .

> *A review of "St. Patrick's Day in the Morning," in* Kirkus Reviews, *Vol. XLVIII, No. 8, April 15, 1980, p. 510.*

The Robot Birthday   (1980)

The title may lure fantasy fans, but they'll not be disappointed to learn that Bunting bases her story in reality. A perfectly plausible robot—run by a remote control device and made verbal by dint of a tape recorder in its back—is presented to twins Pam and Kerry by their recently divorced mother. She and her electronics students have created Robot, whose talents help to ease the twins' transition to a new neighborhood and family. Robot fascinates newfound friends, breaking the ice at Pam and Kerry's birthday party. He also manages to intimidate a group of bullies who have taken over the playground. Later, Robot acts as a signal when the twins and their mother discover a washed-out bridge during a storm. The family dynamics and attendant problem solving are handled delicately and with insight. This is a somewhat longer beginning reader with a story that has appeal for a broad age range.

> *Judith Goldberger, in a review of "The Robot Birthday," in* Booklist, *Vol. 76, No. 20, June 15, 1980, p. 1540.*

Mom makes the robot as a birthday gift for twins Pam and Kerry shortly after she's divorced and they've moved to a new house. ("Mom's smart.") . . . Despite [Marie] De John's dreary one-color pictures, there is laugh potential in the sight of the playground bad gang sticking out their tongues and growling in compliance with the robot's orders. (The robot is playing back an exercise program taped by the twins' sitter.) Otherwise, pretty flat.

> *A review of "The Robot Birthday," in* Kirkus Reviews, *Vol. XLVIII, No. 13, July 1, 1980, p. 835.*

The stories [in each chapter] are exciting, well and simply told, and quite believable. Second graders can enjoy this book on their own and older children will not find it babyish. The illustrations in blue wash show very real children and adults and a robot that could be built with today's technology. This is one of the best efforts so far at easy reading with a science fiction appeal.

> *Carolyn Caywood, in a review of "The Robot Birthday," in* School Library Journal, *Vol. 27, No. 1, September, 1980, p. 56.*

The Empty Window   (1980)

Told by a boy whose close friend Joe is dying, this story gives poignancy and thrust to feelings children may have about death. C. G.'s determination to catch a wild parrot for Joe is a mystery even to himself. Nonetheless, he does so with the help of his younger brother and at considerable physical risk. Having avoided Joe for the length of his illness, C. G. suddenly finds himself in his friend's room,

confronting his own fear and guilt. Joe, though weak-looking, is still the "same old Joe"; C. G. realizes he has wanted to catch the parrot not because Joe has obsessively watched these birds from his window, but to keep Joe company in place of C. G. Joe asks to have the parrot set free, for it is the bird's freedom that fascinates him, and the boys' friendship is renewed at what becomes their last meeting. Bunting's writing is quietly original, sensitive, and child-oriented. (pp. 402-03)

> *Judith Goldberger, in a review of "The Empty Window," in* Booklist, *Vol. 77, No. 5, November 1, 1980, pp. 402-03.*

In a slim volume of picture-book dimensions is a seventh-grader's story of catching a wild parrot for a dying friend—a mismatch that would doom the book even if it were worthier than it is. C.G.'s brief narrative, however, is all problem, portent, and patent symbolism. . . . Though dread of the dying is natural enough, nothing else here is. . . .

> *A review of "The Empty Window," in* Kirkus Reviews, *Vol. XLIX, No. 2, January 15, 1981, p. 75.*

This book is difficult to categorize—it's too long for a picture book, and the age of the main character is about 10 or 11, but it has the appearance of a picture book rather than a story for older readers (the CIP classifies it as "fiction"). Moe's *Pickles and Prunes* (McGraw, 1976) and Lowry's *A Summer To Die* (Houghton, 1977) have the same theme of fear and guilt over the physical changes in a dying child, but are for much older readers. Most other books on death for this age level involve either a pet or an elderly person, making this one unique as well as sensitively written. . . .

> *Karen Ritter, in a review of "The Empty Window," in* School Library Journal, *Vol. 27, No. 6, February, 1981, pp. 62-3.*

The Sea World Book of Whales   (1980)

Beginning with a description of whales' evolution, the text then details their physical characteristics and habits. Comments on the mating, birth, and care of the babies lead to a focus on nonbiological matters such as the whaling industry, the work of Sea World in San Diego, scientific studies on whales, and the story of the Gigi experiment (more completely covered in Coerr's *Gigi: A Baby Whale Borrowed for Science and Returned to the Sea*). Bunting's scope is comprehensive, though marred at times by a chatty style and overuse of exclamatory statements: "plankton [is] absolutely delicious . . . and such large helpings!"

> *Barbara Elleman, in a review of "The Sea World Book of Whales," in* Booklist, *Vol. 77, No. 8, December 15, 1980, p. 571.*

Like several other good books on whales for the same audience, this surveys the various species of toothed and baleen whales and discusses evolution, physical characteristics, behavior and the history of whaling and touches briefly on conservation. Bunting's admiration for the animal seems genuine and not excessive; her style is slightly jocular and journalistic with minimal use of scientific terminology. . . . A bibliography of diverse sources is nearly lost in being placed on the back of the last index page. The book is an attractive and interesting complement to such titles as John A. Barbour's *In the Wake of the Whale* (Macmillan, 1969), Helen Hoke and Valerie Pitt's *Whales* (Watts, 1973) and Ada and Frank Graham's *Whale Watch* (Delacorte, 1978), which each make a strong contribution on this ever popular subject.

> *Margaret Bush, in a review of "The Sea World Book of Whales," in* School Library Journal, *Vol. 27, No. 6, February, 1981, p. 63.*

The Skate Patrol (1980)

James and Milton, two roller-skating friends, find their wheels are not wanted anywhere. Shooed away from park, sidewalk, and parking lot, they decide to concentrate on tailing an odd park bench-sitter they've decided is the notorious Creep Thief, who has been robbing old women. The skate patrol, as the boys call themselves, is sharp—almost too sharp—as James and Milt discover in the breathless climax of this brief, fast-paced story. Bunting handles both action and dialogue with ease; a well-worn plot idea with a roller skater's twist added to it won't wear down reader's attention spans. For primary-graders who want something longer than beginning-to-read books and for reluctant middle-graders, here is light, brisk material.

> *Judith Goldberger, in a review of "The Skate Patrol," in* Booklist, *Vol. 77, No. 12, February 15, 1981, p. 813.*

The Waiting Game (1981)

It's a sorry fact that big egos and athletes with above average talent often travel together. The humor of any athlete proclaiming himself the greatest begins and ends with Muhammed Ali.

Of the three main characters in this sports tale, two are egocentric. Griff is easy to ignore because he really doesn't say or do much. Unfortunately, the same can't be said for Luther, who drags the reader through his episodes.

When he is not awarded a football scholarship to Ohio State, Luther cannot believe, and he wouldn't have others believe, that he just isn't a good enough player. So he tells everyone that he turned his Ohio State offer down in order to play at the local junior college with the third main character, Dan, a deaf friend whom Luther helped with signals while playing football in high school. He eventually owns up to the truth in a non-convincing way, and it just isn't enough. We leave our sorry hero tearing up a football scholarship offer from a "semi-big time college," not wanting anyone, including himself, to know he isn't big time material.

Both Griff and Luther are to be pitied. Their main concerns are themselves and football. They have a lot to learn, but through the course of this story, they learn nothing.

Dan is a cardboard excuse for an admirable character. He can and should be more human than the others but the author portrays him as a big, dumb lunk.

In short, Eve Bunting has written a very narrow story with very narrow characters, even for young readers. There are enough twists in the plot to make the book marketable. However, any notion that **The Waiting Game** is really about friendship would be extremely pretentious. At best, it is about a conceited high school jock who survives his own self-arrogance without learning anything from the battle.

> *Mike Klodnicki, in a review of "The Waiting Game," in* Best Sellers, *Vol. 41, No. 2, May, 1981, p. 78.*

This simply written story has an undeveloped potential for an exploration of friendship values; as it is written, it touches on the intricacy of rivalry and loyalty only superficially, with Dan a minor shadow figure until the end, and with Luther going through several shifts in attitude in one day, to create an abrupt and not very convincing ending. Because of the ages of the three boys, the simplicity of the writing style and the vocabulary, the large print, and the subject, this should be useful for slow readers in senior high school.

> *Zena Sutherland, in a review of "The Waiting Game," in* Bulletin of the Center for Children's Books, *Vol. 34, No. 11, July-August, 1981, p. 208.*

The Spook Birds (1981)

The Spook Birds—a case full of stuffed birds—used to be kept at Larry's late grandfather's club but, since the club is being torn down, his grandmother has brought them home. Larry finds out that the birds were stuffed ten years ago by the late Bill Bedder, an ex-scientist with odd ideas. Larry senses something strange about the birds: eyes open and close, and one night he hears whistling in the dining room. While inspecting the inside of the case, Larry finds what seems to be a refrigeration system. At the end the birds come to life and fly away. One gets the feeling that Eve Bunting wasn't sure what to do with her story. **The Spook Birds** certainly has an original idea for a plot, but the ending is confusing and the mystery unsatisfying overall.

> *Drew Stevenson, in a review of "The Spook Birds," in* School Library Journal, *Vol. 28, No. 4, December, 1981, p. 80.*

The Giant Squid (1981)

Perhaps Bunting has written a more specialized book than is usual for high-low readers, but the subject is no less mysterious and attractive for that. Favoring accounts of sightings of and run-ins with the "monster of the deep" (both rumored and documented), Bunting spends little time on anatomical descriptions, though her style is not sensationalized. . . . Only the cover gives the book a young appearance; with luck, interested browsers will look inside for more.

> *Judith Goldberger, in a review of "The Giant Squid," in* Booklist, *Vol. 78, No. 16, April 15, 1982, p. 1099.*

Only a very few people have actually seen a giant squid, though body parts turn up from time to time in the stomachs of whales. Bunting recounts various recorded accounts of giant squid encounters, intersperses some descriptions of physiology, and speculates on probable behavior and research value to man. The text does not have a well-developed theme or focus and becomes repetitive. . . . Squid have not been well treated in children's books, and the far more interesting title for most children is an adult book—*Octopus and Squid: The Soft Intelligence* (Doubleday, 1973) by Jacques Cousteau and Philippe Diolé. Gladys Conklin's *The Octopus and Other Cephalopods* (Holiday, 1977) is serviceable.

> *Margaret Bush, in a review of "The Giant Squid," in* School Library Journal, *Vol. 28, No. 10, August, 1982, p. 111.*

The cover of this book and its table of contents promises so much! Unfortunately, the writing is dull, choppy, and often inconsistent in mode or tense. Clear differentiation between fact and hearsay is too frequently lacking. . . . The biology presented is very confusing to say the least. The reader is often left in the dark as to where or when an incident takes place. The book is a great misfavor to the mysterious, exciting, and even elegant squid. It is even more so to the reader.

> *Dottie Wendt, in a review of "The Giant Squid," in* Science Books & Films, *Vol. 18, No. 1, September-October, 1982, p. 33.*

The Great White Shark   (1982)

To complement a subject with obvious appeal and the power to frighten and fascinate, Bunting writes dramatically. A quantity of accounts of a grim nature are included, along with sections on the filming of *Jaws* and on protecting oneself in the water. Smoothly written and fast paced, the book will no doubt be eaten up by reluctant readers.

> *Judith Goldberger, in a review of "The Great White Shark," in* Booklist, *Vol. 78, No. 20, June 15, 1982, p. 1371.*

"The great white shark is one of the most terrifying creatures in today's world—and one of the most wonderful." Using such epithets as Big Whitey, The Mad Shark of New Jersey and The Great White Death, Bunting focuses on the terrifying savagery of the great white shark as a man-killer. She cites several alleged cases of attacks on humans, some historical and some more current, and makes scattered comments about the filming of *Jaws*. She does not cite sources nor does she provide much specific information about actual frequency or location of white shark attacks or sightings other than the several episodes described. She sketches some of the history of the species and

includes a bit of information about physical characteristics. . . . The book is slim in format and content. The treatment of the subject is not nearly as dramatic as the author implies it will be, but it does tend to perpetuate the mythology associated with the shark rather than supply information or build understanding of this intriguing animal's behavior.

> *Margaret Bush, in a review of "The Great White Shark," in* School Library Journal, *Vol. 29, No. 3, November, 1982, p. 78.*

The first question librarians might ask about this book is, "Do we really need another book about sharks?" If the answer is yes, the second question should be, "Do we need one that uses photos from the movie, *Jaws,* to emphasize the terror sharks can cause?"

This book has too many surmises, "The shark may think the human is a juicy seal or sea lion" for it to be of any use as a serious study of sharks, and it is too filled with gruesome stories about actual shark attacks, underlined and emphasized with photographs from several horror movies, for it to be considered seriously as educational fare for children.

There are several good parts, of course, such as innovative tagging of sharks for study, but all in all this is not Bunting's best effort and is best left on the publisher's shelf. (pp. 15-16)

> *Norma Bagnall, in a review of "The Great White Shark," in* Appraisal: Science Books for Young People, *Vol. 16, No. 1, Winter, 1983, pp. 15-16.*

The Happy Funeral   (1982)

[The story] is told by Laura, who goes with her sister and parents to the funeral home in Chinatown where Grandfather lies in an open casket. How can it be, as Mom has prophesied, a "happy funeral?" Not until it is all over does Laura realize that what Mom meant was that after a long and happy life, an old person may not be unhappy at the prospect of death—but that does not mean that it is a happy funeral for the bereaved. The story is written in a direct style, nicely maintaining the viewpoint of a child and dealing candidly with the facts of death; it gives information about ceremonial customs of a Chinese-American community with grave simplicity.

> *Zena Sutherland, in a review of "The Happy Funeral," in* Bulletin of the Center for Children's Books, *Vol. 35, No. 11, July-August, 1982, p. 203.*

The rightness of death for the deceased, the painfulness for the survivors—conveyed with exceptional directness in the context of an unfamiliar culture. The reader will immediately wonder, with small narrator Laura, how Grandfather can have a "happy funeral"; as older sister May-May protests, "It's like saying a sad party. Or hot snow. It doesn't make sense." But as the Chinese-American leavetaking unfolds, each custom falls into meaningful place. At the funeral parlor, relatives lay gifts in the casket. Mom's is food "for Grandfather's journey": soy beans, lichee nuts, and, at Laura's suggestion, chocolate chip cookies. Play money, burned, "will be real when it turns into smoke and rises to the spirit world." May-May and Laura have drawn pictures to alight—Laura of Chang, "a dog my grandfather had when he was a boy." (When Chang turns to flame, Laura cries—first, ashamedly, for Chang; then for Grandfather himself.) The funeral brings speeches, recollections, tears; the funeral procession is a fanfare: two cars of flowers, with Grandfather's picture atop the first; a marching, tootling band. ("You'd never guess it was hymns, all jazzed up like this!") But at the cemetery: "Tears are running down Mom's face." The band stops playing. And at the graveside, Laura links her Grandfather's smiling visage with her mother's baffling words. "She never said it was happy for us to have him go." The light-fingered, gray-toned pencil-and-wash drawings [by Vo-Dinh Mai] display the same combination of sensitivity, economy, and finesse.

> *A review of "The Happy Funeral," in* Kirkus Reviews, *Vol. L, No. 15, August 1, 1982, p. 867.*

Whether the funeral of Laura's grandfather is a happy one is up to readers to decide (when someone is very old and has lived a good life, is he *really* happy to go, as Laura's mother claims?). But the story is sensitively, thoughtfully and lovingly written. And the fact that the protagonists are a Chinese-American family opens a cultural window for those unfamiliar with Oriental funerary customs, although the feelings of loss and sadness at the departure of a loved one are obviously universal.

> *Michael Cart, in a review of "The Happy Funeral," in* School Library Journal, *Vol. 29, No. 3, November, 1982, p. 65.*

The Ghosts of Departure Point (1982)

It's hard to reconcile the Eve Bunting of, say, *The Happy Funeral* with the author of crude teenage suspensers like *The Waiting Game* and this. Vicki West and Ted Clark, two of the 13 victims of auto accidents at Departure Point, meet as ghosts and fall in love. ("It was almost as good as being alive," says narrator Vicki.) Both are haunting the site, they realize, because they were to blame for the accidents they were in and for the death of others. But if they atone for their guilt—the way fellow-ghost Rebecca does for the unrelated accident-death of her son—their ghostly existences will end and they'll lose each other. So: should they or should they not try to prevent further accidents at Departure Point? And suppose the town decides *independently* to straighten the hazardous road: "Maybe we'll be off the hook, because we at least tried." Apart from the conundrums (and an ingenious balloon-stunt), altogether flat—and tacky even so.

> *A review of "The Ghosts of Departure Point," in* Kirkus Reviews, *Vol. L, No. 19, October 1, 1982, p. 1109.*

This is a story about ghosts told by a ghost and that premise is, for this reader, a problem from beginning to end. (p. 363)

The plot and ghost-narrator device perhaps could sustain a whimsical short story, but are too flimsy for this longer novel. The book flirts with some serious social problems—drunk driving, speed and joyriding—which are killing and maiming young people at alarming rates, but in this setting they take on trivial proportions.

Though not a pivotal reading experience, *The Ghosts of Departure Point* can serve as light entertainment for avid young readers. (p. 364)

> *Kathleen D'Angelo, in a review of "The Ghosts of Departure Point," in* Best Sellers, *Vol. 42, No. 9, December, 1982, pp. 363-64.*

At a time when the art of ghost story writing has assumed the trappings of trite formula production, it's refreshing to note the publication of a very different kind of ghost story, in which the protagonists are not victims or discoverers of ghosts, but are themselves spirits drawn to the scene of their deaths.

Bunting's first-person story reveals the inside ghostly life of Vicki West, a teen cheerleader who, as a victim of a car accident, experiences guilt over her part in causing the accident to occur. Add an equally-guilt-stricken ghostly companion, a variety of theories about guilt, purgatory, and divine retribution, and the efforts of the ghosts to correct their faults despite their fears of oblivion as a heavenly reward, a fast-paced, intriguing plot develops which will attract and intellectually stimulate young adults interested in supernatural fiction. Bunting's writing is logical and tight; the premise unusual enough to warrant adult attention, as well.

> *Diane C. Donovan, in a review of "Ghosts of Departure Point," in* Voice of Youth Advocates, *Vol. 5, No. 5, December, 1982, p. 30.*

The Skate Patrol and the Mystery Writer (1982)

With their octogenarian neighbor as top-floor lookout for their apartment, James and Milton (on rollerskates) watch to see who is painting signs on the walls of their apartment building. At first they suspect the new girl in the building, Erica, who's irritated them because she uses their pet slang expression and skates as well as they do; then they get up early one morning to catch the suspect after they have a clue about a reversed letter in one of the graffiti. This is not Bunting at her best: the structure is slight, the suspense and the deduction minimal, and the writing style pedestrian. . . . Almost any mystery has some appeal for primary grades readers; this is believable but slight.

> *Zena Sutherland, in a review of "The Skate Patrol and the Mystery Writer," in* Bulletin of the Center for Children's Books, *Vol. 36, No. 6, February, 1983, p. 103.*

For those who enjoyed *The Skate Patrol* this is another rolling crime stomper for James and Milton, skaters extant. Someone is defacing their apartment building with red paint. James' mother, the building manager, is tired of paying to have the building repainted so James and Milton set out to catch the villain red-handed. Young readers will delight in the villain being apprehended because he makes his *S*'s backwards. . . . In this book, the Skate Patrol accepts another member, a girl, who most likely will appear in future adventures.

> *Candice Morris, in a review of "The Skate Patrol and the Mystery Writer," in* School Library Journal, *Vol. 29, No. 7, March, 1983, p. 158.*

The Valentine Bears   (1983)

For just one moment, lightning almost strikes: Mrs. Bear, settling in for the winter, set the alarm early—for February 14—so she and Mr. Bear could, for once, celebrate Valentine's Day. But when she rises, goes out in the unaccustomed cold, and prepares a Valentine breakfast for Mr. Bear, he won't be awakened and he won't get up. So what does this loving, Valentine-proferring spouse do? She goes for a can of ice water—whereupon Mr. Bear springs up and hugs her and says it was all a joke, he even had a present (chocolate-covered ants) tucked away and waiting. Now if she had let him go back to sleep, that would have been true love. A banal conceit. . . .

> *A review of "The Valentine Bears," in* Kirkus Reviews, *Vol. LI, No. 5, January 15, 1983, p. 59.*

This has the appeals of an animal story and a holiday popular with children, but it's slight in structure; the writing style is adequate if not impressive; the illustrations [by Jan Brett] are a bit repetitive, but nicely textured and composed.

> *Zena Sutherland, in a review of "The Valentine Bears," in* Bulletin of the Center for Children's Books, *Vol. 36, No. 8, April, 1983, p. 144.*

There is very little action here, but the illustrations and the gentle story are lovingly detailed. A nice addition to the list of valentine stories, of which there are never enough.

> *Brenda Durrin Maloney, in a review of "The Valentine Bears," in* School Library Journal, *Vol. 30, No. 1, September, 1983, p. 103.*

Karen Kepplewhite Is the World's Best Kisser   (1983)

Karen Kepplewhite isn't at all convinced that she's the world's best kisser. But she and her closest friend Janet are immersed in the book *How to Kiss like an Expert* ("If you want to nibble on his ear, go right ahead") in anticipation of Karen's upcoming birthday party, at which she has reluctantly agreed to feature kissing games. The plot line is pleasantly predictable: after countless "was-my-face-red" embarrassments, Karen discovers that the boy she's attracted to is as unsophisticated as she is, and that maybe that's okay when you're only in the seventh grade. Several well-rounded characterizations (Karen's sensible grandmother, affection-starved Janet) give the story more sub-

stance than the conventional preteen romance, and the breezy first-person narrative has a realistic flair. (pp. 79-80)

> *Karen Stang Hanley, in a review of "Karen Kepplewhite Is the World's Best Kisser," in* Booklist, *Vol. 80, No. 1, September 1, 1983, pp. 79-80.*

When you're almost 13, learning to kiss is serious business. Karen and Janet, the delightfully authentic characters of Bunting's latest novel, embark on their learning experience with utmost diligence. . . . Bunting has a good handle on the jargon of the group and easily depicts the modern preteen. The novel is clever and amusing and Bunting accurately portrays the shyness and uncertainty young adolescents experience.

> *Valerie A. Guarini, in a review of "Karen Kepplewhite Is the World's Best Kisser," in* School Library Journal, *Vol. 30, No. 4, December, 1983, p. 64.*

The Man Who Could Call Down Owls   (1984)

An owl is a whisper of midnight wings, a shadow across the moon, a dark mystery not to be imprisoned. Yet the essence and power of these elusive creatures are captured by Eve Bunting in this beautiful and evocative tale of the man who could call down owls.

Each evening, the man who could call down owls would go into the woods followed by a few villagers and the boy Con. He would raise his willow wand, "And the owls came. They came swooping on noiseless wings. To perch on his shoulders. To perch on his wand. To gather on branches closest to where he stood. Always, the owls came." By day, the owl man cared for owls that were injured or ill and Con would watch him and learn. "When an owl is sick and frightened you must hold it firmly. Then it can't hurt itself or you. Always remember that," the owl man said.

One night, a stranger appeared. He watched the owl man and was envious of his power. The next night, the stranger appeared in the woods wearing the owl man's cloak and carrying his willow wand. Con asked the stranger how he had gotten the owl man's cloak and wand but when Con saw the great snowy owl suddenly emerge from the woods, Con knew "that the owl was the man and the man the owl, and that the man who could call down owls would never return." The stranger raised the willow wand and the owls came, led by the snowy owl. They attacked and tore at the stranger and drove him off into the woods. Then, peacefully, the owls turned and came to Con just as they had come to the owl man before.

Eve Bunting has a simple, poetic style that lends beauty and poignancy to her tale. These same qualities are also reflected in Charles Mikolaycak's dramatic, shaded pencil drawings. Together, story and pictures make a book that is, like the owl, lovely and mysterious, wonderful and memorable.

> *Anne D. Jordan, in a review of "The Man Who*

Could Call Down Owls," in The New York Times Book Review, *February 19, 1984, p. 29.*

This is a beautifully told and illustrated book, a haunting story of good and evil and love of nature. . . . The moral is absorbed rather than forced, and children will feel both extreme sadness when the old man dies and joy when Con receives his special tribute. This is a sensitive story well illustrated with eerie pencil drawings that bring it to life. Although older children will enjoy reading this story, it will reach a wider and more appreciative audience if read aloud.

> *Deanna J. McDaniel, in a review of "The Man Who Could Call Down Owls," in* School Library Journal, *Vol. 30, No. 10, August, 1984, p. 57.*

Clancy's Coat   (1984)

The tried-and-true theme of friendship gone awry works wonderfully well with an Irish shine put on it. When Tippitt the tailor's cow, Bridget, gets loose and ruins Clancy's garden, the friendship of the two men is destroyed as well. One blustery day, Clancy turns up at Tippitt's door, but only because his coat needs mending, something the tailor hesitantly agrees to do. Week after week, Clancy keeps coming back for his coat, but there's always some hitch. Either the coat is being used to cover a broken window, or the hen has appropriated it as a place to lay her eggs. The delay is not all bad, however. Clancy's visits to check on the state of his coat bring the tailor and the farmer closer together; by the time spring arrives, the friendship is repaired, even though the coat still isn't. Bunting's appealing story is illustrated by [Lorinda Bryan] Cauley's cheery drawings, some in color, others in black and white. The strong message about working out differences, combined with the humorous vitality of the pictures, makes this a piece of substance as well as fun.

> *Ilene Cooper, in a review of "Clancy's Coat," in* Booklist, *Vol. 80, No. 13, March 1, 1984, p. 966.*

Without resorting to stereotypical expressions the author has captured the sense of metaphor and the lilting cadence of Irish speech. Despite the brevity of the text the two old curmudgeons are skillfully developed through dialogue and action and become appealing characters with distinctive personalities. The same robust down-to-earth quality is extended in vigorous but finely detailed illustrations, half of which are in full color, and the combination is as irresistibly optimistic as an Irish spring. A fine choice for St. Patrick's Day programs.

> *Mary M. Burns, in a review of "Clancy's Coat," in* The Horn Book Magazine, *Vol. LX, No. 2, April, 1984, p. 181.*

The language of this warm and satisfying story has an Irish lilt to it, and the excellence of the text is equalled by the strength of the expressive illustrations. Alternating soft black-and-white and color pictures contain details that catch the humor of the situation and reflect the warmth of cozy farm life. They also convey the tenderness

present in the story, as the two men move closer and closer to a reconciliation. Love has seldom been expressed more happily than in Cauley's depiction of Tippitt covering his cow, Bridget, with Clancy's coat.

> *Anne L. Okie, in a review of "Clancy's Coat," in* School Library Journal, *Vol. 30, No. 8, April, 1984, p. 99.*

Monkey in the Middle   (1984)

No folk-tale inevitability, only the merest figment of Eastern imagination—but an amusing bit of buffoonery. . . . Neighbors Mohammed and Hashim, once friends, are now coconut-picking rivals—"since Mohammed got his monkey and Hashim got his bicycle." The monkey picks Mohammed's coconuts, while Hashim toils; but the bicycle carries Hashim's coconuts, while Mohammed and the monkey trudge. Then the monkey revolts, plays sick—and sympathetic Hashim ("I have nothing against the monkey, only the monkey's master") carries the monkey, and Mohammed, to the doctor on his bicycle. (Mohammed: "I would take nothing from you for myself, but this I will accept on behalf of my monkey.") While they're all at the doctor's, Hashim's bicycle is stolen. The monkey's acrobatics then draw an appreciative crowd; he presents their coins to Hashim—"in return," Mohammed explains, "for the loss of your bicycle"; and as the two head home, carrying the monkey in the middle, they seal a bargain to go partners. Amiable and nimble, if featherweight.

> *A review of "Monkey in the Middle," in* Kirkus Reviews, *Juvenile Issue, Vol. LII, Nos. 6-9, May 1, 1984, p. J-29.*

A story with a gentle moral, exotic setting and humorous illustrations, **Monkey in the Middle** is reminiscent of a folk tale, but it was actually inspired by a Malaysian newspaper article. . . . The story is appealing, if not wildly exciting, and would fit neatly into a library program or classroom discussion about envy, friendship or foreign settings. Most children will prefer the latter part of the story, which describes the monkey's antics, more than the first part, which concentrates on the enmity of the men. . . . Certainly not a "must have," but a useful addition to picture book collections.

> *Beatrice F. Stein, in a review of "Monkey in the Middle," in* School Library Journal, *Vol. 31, No. 3, November, 1984, p. 104.*

If I Asked You, Would You Stay?   (1984)

It's with trepidation that Crow brings the half-conscious girl he's rescued back to Sasha's beachfront room above the old carousel, and his uneasiness lingers despite Valentine's promise that she will leave in a few days. As far as Crow is concerned, Valentine is not only unhappy and confused, but she's also unattractive, self-willed, and a threat to Sasha's secret hideaway and the safe haven it provides. But more disturbing to Crow yet are the bewildering feelings he begins to have about the girl—feelings that endanger the defenses he's erected to keep himself safe from the hurt that personal attachments have brought him in the past. A simply written, high-interest problem novel/romance, featuring convincing characters, good pacing, and a male protagonist. It should attract reluctant readers of both sexes.

> *Stephanie Zvirin, in a review of "If I Asked You, Would You Stay?" in* Booklist, *Vol. 80, No. 18, May 15, 1984, p. 1340.*

Yes, yes—you will have no trouble staying with this teenage novel about two young people trying to get their lives back on the right track. Each has a background that has made him suspicious and leery of people. . . . References to sexual child abuse, exploitation and teenage sexuality are subtle and tastefully presented, but with strong attention to the damage such experiences do to the human spirit. . . .

It has been a long time since we've met two such appealing teenagers in a book. Both Crow and Valentine are decent, honorable people with a keen moral sense. They are lonely but not necessarily loners, and together they piece together their lives, each taking a different but familiar road back as the book ends. This title is an excellent choice for both boys and girls. Books like this are long overdue. It is a realistic, romantic novel with a message. And it avoids the pitfall of the trashy novel for the young—a genre new upon the scene.

> *Patricia A. Morgans, in a review of "If I Asked You, Would You Stay?" in* Best Sellers, *Vol. 44, No. 6, September, 1984, p. 231.*

The story, covering only a few days, is of drifting loners coping with the consequences of both their circumstances and their decisions about those circumstances. The characters are believably drawn, and the story's events are alternately suspenseful and touching. The bonds developed between Crow and Valentine are well-forged, and so their eventual separation seems anticlimactic and lacking in the strong emotionality that each brings to the story. While easy to read, the introspective character study and smaller type size set this one apart from others in this series for reluctant readers.

> *Catherine vanSonnenberg, in a review of "If I Asked You, Would You Stay?" in* School Library Journal, *Vol. 31, No. 1, September, 1984, p. 126.*

Someone Is Hiding on Alcatraz Island (1984)

Seeking revenge because 14-year-old Danny saved a woman being mugged by Priest's younger brother, Priest and his gang, the Outlaws, follow Danny to Alcatraz Island. Thinking he'll outwit them, Danny remains behind after the last excursion boat leaves for San Francisco—and to his horror discovers that they have stayed, too. Biddy, a young woman ranger on guard for the night, also falls victim to the Outlaws' treachery, and both she and Danny find themselves locked in the old abandoned prison cells. Fearing for their lives, the two tap their physical and mental skills and eventually obtain release, triggering Danny's comment that being a hero is "maybe being afraid, and

doing what you have to do anyway." Bunting builds suspense and sustains it with brisk dialogue and taut scenes. Characters aren't given much depth, and the ending is fairly predictable, but the swiftly unfolding events are sure to keep kids turning pages. The story's content, simple style, and fast pace also target this as a good selection for reluctant readers.

> *Barbara Elleman, in a review of "Someone Is Hiding on Alcatraz Island," in* Booklist, *Vol. 81, No. 4, October 15, 1984, p. 303.*

[The plot development of this book] is an example of award-winner Bunting's enviable skill. Her new novel moves swiftly, creating white-knuckle suspense and an unfudged denouement. Everyone acts and reacts according to his and her established character. No one switches abruptly to a different persona for the sake of a "happy" ending.

> *A review of "Someone Is Hiding on Alcatraz Island," in* Publishers Weekly, *Vol. 226, No. 16, October 19, 1984, p. 47.*

The narrator, Danny, is fourteen, short and slight and understandably afraid of the four tough bullies who call themselves the Outlaws and who are pursuing him along the San Francisco waterfront. . . . This is a taut and tough story, and it maintains suspense impressively, incorporating strong characterization and dialogue, both of which are deliberately unpleasant. (p. 81)

> *Zena Sutherland, in a review of "Someone Is Hiding on Alcatraz Island," in* Bulletin of the Center for Children's Books, *Vol. 38, No. 5, January, 1985, pp. 80-1.*

Jane Martin, Dog Detective (1984)

Business is booming for **Jane Martin, Dog Detective,** as she solves three mysteries while charging only 25¢ a day. In the first, Jane knows that the stolen dog can bark his age and uses this trick to find him. In the second, she proves that it is an owl, and not two dogs named Mutt and Spot, who is chasing Mrs. Nelson's cat up a tree every night. And finally, Jane uses the fact that the missing dog loves ice cream to track him to an ice cream truck. [Amy] Schwartz's line drawings have the detail and humor to make these appealing stories even more appealing, while Bunting's text proves that stories need not be long to be clever.

> *Drew Stevenson, in a review of "Jane Martin, Dog Detective," in* School Library Journal, *Vol. 31, No. 4, December, 1984, p. 98.*

[This easy-reading story] looks like a picture book but has a lengthy text written somewhat like a primer. Use of short, direct sentences will help beginning readers but does give a choppy feel to the trio of tales, which see Jane methodically track down two missing pets and absolve another of guilt in a cat-treeing problem.

> *Denise M. Wilms, in a review of "Jane Martin, Dog Detective," in* Booklist, *Vol. 81, No. 8, December 15, 1984, p. 586.*

Although the drawings here have more softness and textural variety, they are like Lenski's work in the stiffness of the little figures. The text is a bit on the stiff side, also, in three episodes in which Jane successfully pursues three cases. . . . Despite the weakness in style, the book should appeal because of the animal connection and because of the successful and logical detective efforts of the dedicated dog detective.

> *Zena Sutherland, in a review of "Jane Martin, Dog Detective," in* Bulletin of the Center for Children's Books, *Vol. 38, No. 6, February, 1985, p. 101.*

Surrogate Sister (1984)

"I guess Mom was in the Rent-a-Womb business, if you wanted to be real nasty about it." Cassie's mother has been artificially inseminated to provide a child for an anonymous couple, and Cassie is having none of it. Gossip breaks out at school when Cassie and Mom are interviewed in the paper; graffiti appears on a blackboard: "CASSIE DEDRICK'S MOTHER DOES IT FOR MONEY." While in many ways this is a standard problem novel (about a problem you never figured was a problem before), Bunting weaves some interesting strands among the issues of sex, abortion, pregnancy and love. There are Mom and her pregnancy, wild yet lonely cousin Deenie and her abortions (and she is a bit of a stereotype), and Cassie herself, deciding whether to sleep with her boyfriend or not. She doesn't. The romance between Cassie and boyfriend Sam is very real; other aspects, such as Cassie tracking down the childless couple, are forced and unbelievable. Still, this moves right along and, well, it is a first.

> *Roger D. Sutton, in a review of "Surrogate Sister," in* School Library Journal, *Vol. 31, No. 5, January, 1985, p. 82.*

Surrogate Sister deals with a range of choices women have about their bodies and their sex life. It is written with taste and humor, and presents the conflicts realistically. (p. 47)

A nice contrast to the teen romance, better than Mazer's *Up in Seth's Room,* and Blume's *Forever.* A good basis for discussion of sex issues, written with taste and no cause for censorship. (p. 48)

> *Ruth Cline, in a review of "Surrogate Sister," in* Voice of Youth Advocates, *Vol. 8, No. 1, April, 1985, pp. 47-8.*

The author has done a fine job of showing a teenager's reaction to this nontraditional situation. Cassie's thoughts and feelings and her relationship with her mother (a good example of a healthy single-parent family) and with Sam all ring true. I was also impressed with how Cassie's perceptions as an artist permeate her point of view.

There is a problem, however, in the portrayal of a minor character, Jay, who is a model in Cassie's life drawing class. While the author never states that Jay is gay, I was not comfortable with the number of tired old stereotypes Jay conforms to.

I was also confused by the cover art, in which Cassie looks Asian or Asian American. Although Cassie describes herself as having olive skin (as opposed to her mother's "wonderful creamy skin"), everyone in the book is white.

Despite these flaws, **Surrogate Sister** is definitely a cut above the typical young adult "problem novel." The characters are realistic, the dialogue is smooth, and, despite a few far-fetched coincidences, the plot is believable. (pp. 36-7)

> *Christine Jenkins, in a review of "Surrogate Sister," in* Interracial Books for Children Bulletin, *Vol. 16, Nos. 5 & 6, 1985, pp. 36-7.*

The Haunting of SafeKeep (1985)

Surrounded by civilization but enclosed by a fence, SafeKeep, a collection of old, empty Victorian buildings in San Diego, has a disturbing, isolated aura about it. When they see an ad for a live-in caretaker's position that requires a couple, Sara, a college freshman, and Devlin strike up an awkward friendship to get hired. From the very beginning, Sara senses something is wrong. She sees a mysterious figure appearing and disappearing near the church and gradually unravels the tragic story behind *The Haunting of SafeKeep.* The ghosts of North Star Church are laid to rest, as are the ghosts of Sara's own haunted past. Although SafeKeep is an original and appropriately eerie setting for a ghost story, the plot is more haunting than chilling. As the plot unfolds, readers will feel sadness rather than fear, a sadness not alleviated by the bittersweet ending. Although Sara and Devlin's troubled home lives lack a sharp focus, Bunting has still skillfully brought together haunted lives, past and present in conflict and resolve. (pp. 110-11)

> *Drew Stevenson, in a review of "The Haunting of SafeKeep," in* School Library Journal, *Vol. 31, No. 9, May, 1985, pp. 110-11.*

[There] is a haunted aspect to SafeKeep that is an obdurately discrete element of fantasy in the realism of the summer job and the inevitable falling in love. It adds the element of the occult, but that element never quite fuses with the story, unfortunately. Otherwise, the situation, the relationship between Dev and Sara, and their discovery that there are different kinds of loves that need to be given and received, all form a coherent pattern.

> *Zena Sutherland, in a review of "The Haunting of SafeKeep," in* Bulletin of the Center for Children's Books, *Vol. 38, No. 10, June, 1985, p. 181.*

The suspense here is skillfully built, both about the mystery itself and about Sara and Dev's impending romance and personal secrets. The solutions are a trifle anticlimactic considering the buildup; however, the characters are well-drawn and likable and the story is well-paced and engrossing. Will appeal to romance readers as well as mystery fans.

Alice F. Stern, in a review of "The Haunting of SafeKeep," in Voice of Youth Advocates, *Vol. 8, No. 3, August, 1985, p. 183.*

Face at the Edge of the World (1985)

The suicide of his long-time best friend, Charlie, a gifted, black high school senior, stuns Jed, who begins to recall how preoccupied Charlie had seemed recently, but Jed himself had been too busy with his girlfriend, Annie, and thoughts (frequently lustful) of her to zero in on Charlie's feelings. A peculiar statement from a freshman "doper," a cryptic note left to Jed by Charlie, and the strange attitude of Charlie's white girlfriend strengthen Jed's determination to find out why Charlie hanged himself. He's unable to talk again to the "doper," who turns up dead of an overdose (accident or suicide?), and Charlie's girl is definitely hiding something. Only when he locates the hidden message and burden that Charlie left for him does Jed learn the full story of Charlie's last traumatic month of life. This is at once a moving portrayal of grief, love, and friendship and a taut suspense story in which Jed finds out as much about himself as he does about what happened to Charlie. The narrative is leavened by enough humor to avoid being maudlin; characterizations, including that of Charlie, are sufficiently realized to make readers care about them; and the whole is uncluttered and satisfying.

Sally Estes, in a review of "Face at the Edge of the World," in Booklist, *Vol. 81, No. 22, August, 1985, p. 1656.*

Bunting's newest novel is a disappointment. . . . Personalities of the characters are wooden and not well developed, eliciting little sympathy from readers. Jed's futile search for answers about Charlie's death takes up most of the story, and the explanation coming at the novel's conclusion is pat and too easy. A novel about a serious subject that lacks tension and impact.

Nancy E. Black, in a review of "Face at the Edge of the World," in School Library Journal, *Vol. 32, No. 4, December, 1985, p. 98.*

Recipient of a college scholarship and a promising young black writer, Charlie Curtis shocks the small community of Oceanside, California, by committing suicide shortly before graduation. No one is more bewildered than his best friend, Jed Lennox, who believes that he and Charlie shared their innermost thoughts and worries. . . . As described by Jed, the quest [to discover the reason for the suicide] leads him through complex patterns of human behavior, hidden emotions, and questions of ethical judgments—for Charlie is not the only casualty among the Oceanside students. The Edge of the World—the popular name for an isolated promontory high above the town dump—is the link which connects all the lives and deaths. As the pieces fall into place, like a giant jigsaw puzzle, the motives become clear as well as the pervasive feelings of disillusionment and alienation among the young people involved: Idris, addict, died from a bad lot of dope from the local high school pusher; Charlie found her at the Edge of the World but was persuaded to keep quiet by Dominique, whose wealthy and prejudiced father would not

have allowed her to date a member of the black community. Later, regretting his decision, Charlie returned to the site, found the body missing, and unearthed evidence indicating that she stumbled over the cliff. Unaware that the dope dealer disposed of the body, he assumed that his negligence killed her. Jed, forced to face his own inadequacies as well as his friend's death, discovers that there are no easy, facile solutions and that "death doesn't hand out second chances." The staccato style suggests agitation just as expressions such as "for sure" suggest current teenage argot. The viewpoint is that of a seventeen-year-old in whose experience adults, for the most part, seem unable or unwilling to understand the pressures on the average adolescent: their "hormones on the rampage," escape from reality proffered by drugs, peace alluringly promised by suicide. Suspenseful and stark, the story deals realistically with the lifestyle of many young people today; it is a revealing look, not pleasant, explicit but not sensational. (pp. 61-2)

Mary M. Burns, in a review of "Face at the Edge of the World," in The Horn Book Magazine, *Vol. LXII, No. 1, January-February, 1986, pp. 61-2.*

Janet Hamm Needs a Date for the Dance (1986)

This companion volume to **Karen Kepplewhite Is the World's Best Kisser** takes another breezy look at preteen life.

Seventh-grader Janet panics when she discovers that her two best friends have dates to her school's year-end dance. Nothing could be more humiliating than to go to the dance dateless and land in the "dog pen." Janet invents an "older man" to accompany her, and tries unsuccessfully to get her brother's best friend to fill the role. At the last minute she is saved from embarrassment when Rolf, the new boy in town, accepts her invitation. And when Rolf becomes the star of the evening with his drum performance, Janet basks happily in reflected glory. Meanwhile, Janet's mother passes through a crisis of her own, as phone calls to an answering-machine Adonis encourage her back into circulation after a post-divorce slump.

Not much is new here in the way of plot, but middle readers will latch on to this lighthearted book. The writing is smooth and the characters appealing.

A review of "Janet Hamm Needs a Date for the Dance," in Kirkus Reviews, *Vol. LIV, No. 3, February 1, 1986, p. 208.*

The Mother's Day Mice (1986)

Three little mice tiptoe out into the early morning to find presents for their sleeping mother. One finds a ripe strawberry, the second a dandelion fluff ball; the smallest mouse hopes to get some honeysuckle but is prevented by the proximity of a ferocious cat. Waiting in vain, Little Mouse gives up the thought of honeysuckle because he has a wonderful idea: he composes a poem. They scamper home, there is a tender scene of gift-giving, and they all join in saying the poem of Little Mouse together. The strongest part of the story is the sharing among the mice brothers, and the story should be useful for Mother's Day reading-aloud in preschool groups, but it's slight and a bit sugary.

> *A review of "The Mother's Day Mice," in* Bulletin of the Center for Children's Books, *Vol. 39, No. 8, April, 1986, p. 143.*

A part of the Bunting/Brett holiday picture book series, the painless, if obvious, story of what three mice give their mother on her day. (p. 633)

Sharp dialogue distinguishes one mouse from the other and adds an edge to an otherwise saccharine plot. [Jan] Brett's illustrations crowd frames with detail, some of it eccentric (mice dressed like Russian peasants?), most of it effective. In all, a warmly utilitarian holiday book. (p. 634)

> *A review of "The Mother's Day Mice," in* Kirkus Reviews, *Vol. LIV, No. 8, April 15, 1986, pp. 633-34.*

Sixth-Grade Sleepover (1986)

Book lovers young and old will appreciate a story in which reading is something kids are eager to do. Two clever teachers have devised a sixth-grade reading club, the Rabbits (Read-A-Book; Bring-It-To-School), which kids aspire to join. As a special treat the Rabbits are having a "sleepover" in the school cafeteria, but as much as Janey wants to go, she's afraid she can't because of her secret problem—she's scared of the dark. She knows the reason: an irresponsible baby-sitter locked her in a closet several times as punishment, but neither that awareness nor some counseling has helped her deal with her fears. Will the prospect of a whole night near the groovy Blake Conway be enough of an inducement to sleep in the dark? Although this is somewhat contrived, Bunting does her story justice by not offering easy answers. Her characters are amusingly realistic and the dialogue is crisp. Best of all, of course, is a whole book in which people love to read and are the envy of those who don't. Also, librarians and teachers may pick up a few tips for giving reading its deserved status in their own schools.

> *Ilene Cooper, in a review of "Sixth-Grade Sleepover," in* Booklist, *Vol. 83, No. 2, September 15, 1986, p. 126.*

What's not to like about a book that features a sixth-grade reading club planning and carrying out a sleepover in the school cafeteria? That's the basic story, but there is much more to it. Janey, an avid and excellent reader, is terribly afraid of the dark. Her parents, a wise, loving, and understanding pair, have made appropriate accommodations at home, but she isn't sure she can make it through the night at school. Rosie, a new, rather odd classmate, lugs around big books—but has her own fear—that her classmates will find out that she can't read. How the girls face and deal with their fears makes a satisfying denouement to a story which, while light on the surface, deals with very real and important issues. Sure to appeal to fans of Johanna Hurwitz and Betty Miles. (pp. 71-2)

> *Li Stark, in a review of "Sixth-Grade Sleepover," in* School Library Journal, *Vol. 33, No. 5, January, 1987, pp. 71-2.*

Scary, Scary Halloween (1986)

Little goblins will love this beautiful book, for it captures the essence of Halloween in its striking illustrations [by Jan Brett] and simple rhythmic verse. Narrating this story is a mother cat crouched under a porch, swallowed up by the darkness all except for her big green eyes. And what sights they see! A parade of eerie creatures come up the jack-o-lantern-lined path. A skeleton so white it glimmers in the moonlight. A ghost with sunken eyes. Three little sets of green eyes pop open at the sound of creature feet on the stairs above. "Will he find us here, below?" the little kittens ask of their mother. "Shh, my love, I cannot know." But when the trick or treating is over and all the scary figures gone, the cats come out of hiding and resume their nightly routine, romping and prowling in the darkness until they will take cover again next Halloween.

> *Bonita Brodt, "Rotten Ralph Is No Treat on Halloween," in* Chicago Tribune—Books, *October 26, 1986, p. 3.*

Ghostly tree trunks suggest a proscenium arch that defines the narrator's field of vision in this handsomely illustrated Halloween poem. The reader can make the telling as scary as the audience can stand. The lines flow rhythmically, each ending with the word *Halloween,* and form a skipping cadence that is wonderful for story hour. . . . From sunset on the half-title page to moon's wane at the end, the author and illustrator have created a satisfyingly scary Halloween night for the three- to five-year-old set.

> *Elizabeth S. Watson, in a review of "Scary, Scary Halloween," in* The Horn Book Magazine, *Vol. LXII, No. 6, November-December, 1986, p. 752.*

A Halloween offering that is sure to be snatched up year-round by children on the prowl for scary books. The rhymes are full of repetitions that give the text the quality of a chant. . . . Bunting's strong verbs and Brett's clean, clear line drawings and vivid palette bring a devil, skeleton, ghost, etc., to life, and the effect is exciting but not in the least sinister or fear-inspiring. (Bunting's language does become a bit turgid at points, however.) The creatures are a troupe of spirited trick-or-treaters, but this is not known by the mother cat who tells story. Nor are readers aware of the identity of the narrator at the beginning. But as the parade progresses, and three more little eyes appear in the dark, readers begin to get a sense of those eyes warily watching the spectacle from a safe distance. Brett creates skillful shifts in visual perspective and effectively interprets the book's final turnabout: the tiny eyes, mere points of light, clustered under a house, are hidden so long as the trick-or-treaters are about. But when all is quiet, they suddenly blossom into cats that form their own parade and claim Halloween, just as the rising golden harvest moon at the book's beginning blossoms into a milky moon above them. Carefully planned and executed, illustrations and text nicely unified, this is well designed for group use and a fine introduction to Halloween story programs.

Susan Powers, in a review of "Scary, Scary Halloween," in School Library Journal, *Vol. 33, No. 4, December, 1986, p. 81.*

Ghost's Hour, Spook's Hour   (1987)

Near midnight on a windy night in late autumn, a small boy awakens. Not only are the nighttime sounds frightening to him and his dog, but the lights aren't working and his parents aren't in their bedroom. He confronts creaks and howling (both his and the dog's) before he finds his parents, who are sleeping downstairs, and who comfort him. Bunting masterfully paces her story, with each fear of the child climaxing in his discovery of the basis for the sound. The images that frighten the narrator will also make young readers and listeners feel shivery, but in each case, the rational explanation will reassure them. The narrator's range of emotions—being scared but trying not to show it, transferring his feelings to his dog, and his overwhelming relief at finding his father—is marvelously portrayed in the text through small details. Bunting also provides a range of sensory details that make the boy's experiences readily identifiable. . . . A book that provides the perfect blend of chills and comfort.

David Gale, in a review of "Ghost's Hour, Spook's Hour," in School Library Journal, *Vol. 34, No. 1, September, 1987, p. 160.*

A prize for Halloween but cathartic for any night of the year, this is a powerful evocation of childhood fears. . . . Bunting is proficient at the spare narrative and sound effects that accumulate for such a realistic depiction here. It is [Donald] Carrick's watercolor paintings, however, that galvanize the text into action. The vivid contrasts of light and dark, along with sudden shifts of shape, color, perspective, build tension, catch the breath, and keep the eye moving. Satisfying as story, art, and empathy.

Betsy Hearne, in a review of "Ghost's Hour, Spook's Hour," in Bulletin of the Center for Children's Books, *Vol. 41, No. 2, October, 1987, p. 23.*

Making it till morning with your dignity intact is the subject of two new picture books for children. **Ghost's Hour, Spook's Hour** and [Harriet Ziefert's] *I Won't Go to Bed!* Both tell of small boys who are awake in the house when the clock strikes midnight. Only a staircase away from parental comfort, each boy makes a long journey of it, gaining fortitude as the night wears on. Though the subject matter is similar, these books are as different in mood as "The Cabinet of Dr. Caligari" and "E.T."

While **Ghost's Hour, Spook's Hour** is filled with enough ghastly special effects to furnish an amusement park fun house, it fails to give children's fears any real weight. By contrast, *I Won't Go to Bed!* achieves a far more disquieting impact with fewer props.

Ghost's Hour, Spook's Hour bursts at the seams with every cliché of the classic horror tale—howling wind,

shapeless blobs moving out of the darkness, mysteriously empty beds and a grandfather clock whose tick sounds like artillery fire. Yet underneath the Gothic trappings, it takes a sentimental view of the night terrors that we all must master.

When Jake awakens and is unable to light his bedside lamp, he stumbles down the hall to his parents' room and finds them missing from their beds. . . . The family is reunited in the living room, and by the buttery glow of candlelight his parents clear everything up: how the wind knocked out the lights, and a noisily banging tree branch sent them downstairs to sleep on the couch. Jake allows that Biff had been pretty scared by the whole thing, but once he climbs onto the couch with Mom and Dad his worries apparently are over. More than they ever seem to in real life, parents' rational explanations do the trick.

Ann Banks, in a review of "Ghost's Hour, Spook's Hour," in The New York Times Book Review, *November 15, 1987, p. 36.*

Will You Be My Posslq?   (1987)

When UCLA sophomore Kyle Pendleton asks Jamie McLaughlin to share living quarters, he maintains that he has strictly economic motives in mind. Jamie is hesitant because her sister's pregnancy led to an early marriage. But Kyle proves to be an ideal posslq (person of opposite sex sharing living quarters), and Jamie begins to hope the relationship will blossom into more. She's reluctant to tell him that she had cancer three years ago, although she's been pronounced cured, because she's afraid that he'll reject her as a previous boyfriend did. Jamie experiences a complex welter of emotions as a result of the disease, from the nightmarish fear that it will recur to a renewed appreciation of the joys of being alive. When their affection grows, Jamie convinces Kyle to retreat to separate living quarters so that the relationship can flourish. Jamie's grappling with her previous bout with cancer adds depth to both plot and characterizations, making this more than just another boy-meets-girl story. Her fresh narrative aptly conveys the awkwardness and anxiety of the artificial posslq situation. Coupled with Norma Fox Mazer's *Someone to Love* (Delacorte, 1983), this could provoke lively discussions about the care and feeding of male-female relationships.

Merilyn S. Burrington, in a review of "Will You Be My Posslq?" in School Library Journal, *Vol. 34, No. 2, October, 1987, p. 137.*

Bunting makes a good case to support Jamie's reluctance to tell Kyle about her illness and provides further perspective on the emotional consequences of cancer through Jamie's relationship with a dying friend. Her juxtaposition of Jamie's living circumstances with her sisters' situations (Phoebe is afraid that marriage will trap her; Tig faces sexual intimacy at 14) is obvious, but Jamie's opting for traditional morality is not stridently set, and its underpinnings are credibly rendered. A grade 5 reading level makes this suitable also as high/low material.

Stephanie Zvirin, in a review of "Will You Be

My Posslq?" in Booklist, *Vol. 84, No. 3, October 1, 1987, p. 253.*

Jamie's experience with cancer adds another dimension to the story. While the romantic tension and conflicting feelings are used to develop the plot, the theme of the book goes much deeper. Bunting accurately captures the emotions, thought processes, and reactions of a "cured" cancer patient and uses them to make Jamie's decision an affirmation of hope for the future rather than simply a lightweight romance with a moralistic ending.

Marlene M. Kuhn, in a review of "Will You Be My Posslq?" in Voice of Youth Advocates, *Vol. 11, No. 1, April, 1988, p. 21.*

A Sudden Silence   (1988)

Jesse Harmon's struggle to cope with the death of his younger brother, Bry, in a hit-and-run accident is complicated by his sense of guilt for having failed to prevent the accident and by his relationship with Bry's girl, Chloe.

Jesse had been close to Bry, a talented 16-year-old whose deafness contributed to his death. Trying to deal with their grief, Jesse and Chloe collaborate in a search for the killer; working together, they feel a mutual attraction. Bunting skillfully creates suspense through an elusive witness (a local wino) and a false lead (a young drunk who can't remember whether he killed Bry). When the clues lead inexorably to Chloe's alcoholic mother, Jesse finds himself forced, with her acquiescence, to hurt Chloe by making the truth public.

Despite the suspenseful pacing, Bunting handles Jesse and Chloe's relationship with sensitivity. By including several minor characters whose alcoholism is pivotal to the plot, she emphasizes the tragedy that alcohol can inflict on innocent bystanders and other family members.

A review of "A Sudden Silence," in Kirkus Reviews, *Vol. LVI, No. 7, April 1, 1988, p. 535.*

A thought-provoking portrayal of the hit-and-run death of a deaf teenager. Bry Harmon . . . could not hear the rush of the car or the warning shout of his brother Jesse. It is Jesse who narrates the story, recounting his terrible feelings of guilt and his teaming-up with Bry's friend, Chloe Eichler, to find the guilty driver. Jesse finds himself attracted to Chloe, which compounds his troubled feelings. This predictable development is one of several aspects contributing to a sense of formula fiction. The contrasts between the Harmon and Eichler families tend to be stereotypical oppositions of the working class and well-to-do. The Harmons live in a trailer park, have inner resources in facing their problems, and are bolstered in their grief by neighbors and family. Though the wealthy Eichlers are seen only sporadically, their lives seem marked by materialism and strain. The story is well crafted and credible in its configuration of events, people, and emotions. . . . There is a sobering emphasis on alcohol abuse woven into the story's resolution, with several characters having serious drinking problems. To the great credit of the author the theme is persuasively conveyed through realistic observation in a moving story, which reveals both human caring and the painful consequences of irresponsible actions. (pp. 499-500)

Margaret A. Bush, in a review of "A Sudden Silence," in The Horn Book Magazine, *Vol. LXIV, No. 4, July-August, 1988, pp. 499-500.*

First published in U.S.A., Eve Bunting's elegantly written novel for young people sets an emotive tone from the first sentence. "It was Saturday 20th June at 11.30 p.m. when my brother, Bry, was killed." Thus we move directly into a highly contemporary tale of loss, search and love. The writer's story-line is strong and her sense of place accurate and true. She sets the novel in Nowhere, U.S.A. and while there are plenty of 'local' references (Clambake Point, Pasadena, White Sands) the overall feel is of a universal location. The American life-style as depicted similarly offers interest without being parochial.

The dialogue is casual yet genuine. The rather sombre tone, properly reflecting Bry's death at the hands of a hit-and-run driver, is effective without ever becoming morose. An absorbing and affecting read, and without doubt the novelist proves her high-level capability as a story-teller.

Wes Magee, in a review of "A Sudden Silence," in The Junior Bookshelf, *Vol. 53, No. 5, October, 1989, p. 235.*

How Many Days to America? A Thanksgiving Story (1988)

A moving fictional presentation of the perilous voyage of a group of Caribbean refugees to this country.

When the soldiers come, the narrator and his little sister hide under the bed, but they can see the soldiers' muddy boots. When they're gone, Father says, "We must leave right now . . . Because we do not think the way they think." Leaving behind their most cherished possessions, the little family boards a small, crowded fishing boat with other refugees. The motor fails; men from their own country shoot at them; traveling under sail, they find their food and water running out, and people are ill. Thieves arrive by boat to take the little they have; on one shore, soldiers give them fruit but will not let them land. At last, on Thanksgiving Day, the refugees arrive in America, giving thanks for being free and safe at last—and believing that they can stay.

[Beth] Peck's beautiful full-color, double-spread illustrations capture the dignity and humanity of these humble folk, the somber night sky, and the sweep of the sea. A fine companion to Barbara Cohen's *Molly's Pilgrim* for broadening the Thanksgiving message—and a compassionate depiction of the plight of many of our recent would-be immigrants.

A review of "How Many Days to America? A Thanksgiving Story," in Kirkus Reviews, *Vol. LVI, No. 15, August 1, 1988, p. 1146.*

Bunting's simple tale focuses on the hardships of the journey and on the American ideals of freedom and safety. She wisely leaves aside the issues of politics in the homeland or in this country. Her prose is poetically spare, as her runaways move "silently along the secret streets." . . . Other titles on this subject that are equally valuable are Barbara Cohen's *Molly's Pilgrim* (1983) and *Gooseberries to Oranges* (1982, both Lothrop). A poignant story and a thought-provoking discussion starter.

> *Ruth Semrau, in a review of "How Many Days to America? A Thanksgiving Story," in* School Library Journal, *Vol. 35, No. 2, October, 1988, p. 115.*

When read as a realistic story, the contrivances and the unexplained appearance of some soldiers are bothersome—and the question of illegal entry also arises. However, viewed as a symbolic tale of oppressed people seeking liberty, the story, clothed in contemporary dress, echoes the voyages made by many through the years in search of liberty. Peck's deepened chalk colors and misty backgrounds bolster the fragile facial expressions and fearful body postures, lending suspense and believability to the saga. A discussion starter on several levels. (pp. 479-80)

> *Barbara Elleman, in a review of "How Many Days to America? A Thanksgiving Story," in* Booklist, *Vol. 85, No. 5, November 1, 1988, pp. 479-80.*

Is Anybody There?   (1988)

Thirteen-year-old Marcus has been a resourceful latchkey kid since he was eight, when his father died. Now Marcus believes that someone has been coming into the house where he and his mother live: his housekey is taken, food seems to be missing, Mom's alarm clock is gone. Marcus is convinced the intruder is Nick, the handsome boarder who lives in the upstairs apartment, and who seems to be developing a romance with Mom. The mystery and problem novel aspects of the novel are well integrated, and Marcus' suspicious treatment of Nick changes gradually and plausibly. While the mystery is more puzzling than suspenseful, and the denouement improbable, the ending is emotionally satisfying.

> *Roger Sutton, in a review of "Is Anybody There?" in* Bulletin of the Center for Children's Books, *Vol. 42, No. 2, October, 1988, p. 28.*

This well-crafted, high interest/low reading level novel promises—and delivers—a first-rate story. Bunting's characterizations are strong and believable, and her attention to detail, like the descriptions of Michael's home-built bike and school friends, makes the book thoroughly satisfying.

> *A review of "Is Anybody There?" in* Publishers Weekly, *Vol. 234, No. 16, October 14, 1988, p. 77.*

While the mystery takes center stage, two subplots involve Marcus' concern about his widowed mother's growing relationship with Nick, the man who lives upstairs, and Anjelica, a girl in his class who is interested in him. Characters are well drawn, particularly the mother and Nick, both of whom are well-meaning, caring people who obvi-

ously like and respect kids. Bunting does an admirable job of showing how time drags while Marcus waits in the empty house, as well as of developing Marcus' conflicting feelings about Nick and Anjelica. With its easy sentence structure and vocabulary and attention-getting first chapter, this is likely to have appeal to reluctant readers as well as non-demanding mystery fans.

> *Trev Jones, in a review of "Is Anybody There?" in* School Library Journal, *Vol. 35, No. 4, December, 1988, p. 102.*

The Wednesday Surprise   (1989)

Grandma and narrator Anna are planning a wonderful surprise for Dad's birthday. While Mom works late on Wednesdays, Grandma comes over with a mysterious, heavy sack so that they can work together. Dad, who drives a truck, comes home just in time for the big day, bringing gifts for his family—a smooth pebble from the desert for Anna's rock collection, a bunch of wild flowers he picked for Mom. These simple gifts are received with real appreciation, but the best is yet to come: Anna, who at seven has just learned to read, has also taught Grandma to read well enough so that she reads *The Velveteen Rabbit* aloud after the birthday cake.

Bunting includes just the right details to bring this nice family to three-dimensional life. . . . A heartwarming, inspiring story; readers may well find that when his mother's accomplishment brings tears of joy to Dad's eyes, there are tears in theirs as well.

> *A review of "The Wednesday Surprise," in* Kirkus Reviews, *Vol. LVII, No. 2, January 15, 1989, p. 120.*

With the groundswell of attention on literacy, this book is the perfect manifesto to the cause. . . . The tone is tender, loving, and humorous, with just a nudging, but not didactic, comment about the importance of reading given by grandmother to Anna's older brother. The beauty of a young child sharing her precious gift with an older person and the grandmother's perseverence are noteworthy themes for today's readers. . . . This is an enriching account of new literacy among older Americans that will be enjoyed by all readers.

> *Marianne Pilla, in a review of "The Wednesday Surprise," in* School Library Journal, *Vol. 35, No. 10, June, 1989, p. 84.*

The Ghost Children   (1989)

After their mother dies, Matt, 13, and his sister Abby, 5, come to live with their great-aunt Gerda in a canyon near Los Angeles, bringing little except a portfolio of their mother's paintings.

In front of Aunt Gerda's ramshackle house are spooky, life-sized figures of children—made for Aunt Gerda by her deceased husband—dressed in real clothes, swaying in the wind. Apparently because they are alarmed by the way Aunt Gerda treats the "dolls" like real children, local people are harassing her, hoping to get her to move. Matt tries to discover who has sent anonymous hate notes and vandalized the dolls; to help out financially, he also tries to sell his mother's paintings, and in doing so discovers the dealer who has stolen two of the figures. Amazingly, a patron appears to declare the figures folk art of great value and to relieve the family of financial worries—without depriving Aunt Gerda of her beloved children.

Matt and Abby are believable, their concern for one another both funny and touching. Unfortunately, however, the story's resolution is pat and implausible; and the title here is misleading, since the dolls are not ghostlike enough to create much suspense. For a more intelligent fictional use of senior-citizen-created junk that proves to be valuable as art, see Levin's *The Trouble with Gramary* (1988).

> *A review of "The Ghost Children," in* Kirkus Reviews, *Vol. LVII, No. 6, March 15, 1989, p. 459.*

The creepy premise is well-managed in a believable mystery story, and the children's adjustment to their mother's death provides an emotional subtext as well as the key to the resolution. While the ending is a bit of a letdown, vitiating the power of some of the previous special effects, the ghostly atmosphere is maintained through the conclusion.

> *Roger Sutton, in a review of "The Ghost Children," in* Bulletin of the Center for Children's Books, *Vol. 42, No. 8, April, 1989, p. 189.*

Bunting's story holds lots of appeal—there's mystery, several devious villains, a touch of the supernatural, and a strongly characterized protagonist who is decent without being goody-goody. However, Bunting boxes herself in at the end. The dolls, excellent pieces of folk art, turn out to be worth quite a bit of money. But since the soft-hearted, eccentric woman would never sell her "children," the author arranges for a generous endowment from an art patron so that Gerda, Matt, and Abby can continue to live together. Not a likely happening. Nevertheless, kids caught up in the story won't care.

> *Ilene Cooper, in a review of "The Ghost Children," in* Booklist, *Vol. 85, No. 15, April 1, 1989, p. 1379.*

The Wall (1990)

While there are books for older readers on the Vietnam Veterans War Memorial, notably Ashabranner's *Always to Remember,* this is the first picture book on the subject. In Bunting's brief story, a young boy describes the visit he and his father make to the memorial. They are there to find Grandfather's name; "he was just my age when he was killed," says the little boy's father. The two search out the name and make a rubbing, and when they are through, they place a picture of the boy on the grass beneath the name. [Ronald] Himler's intense, quiet watercolors capture the dignity of the setting as Bunting's story reaches right to the heart of deep emotions. Families who have lost members to the war may be particularly interested in this; it's also an effective preparation for young children who

may be visiting the wall for the first time. A quiet, respectful exposition.

> *Denise Wilms "Vietnam Revisited," in* Booklist, *Vol. 86, No. 15, April 1, 1990, p. 1544.*

This is a book that will need some preamble and discussion to be meaningful to a picture book audience, but it does offer possibilities for children to talk about similar experiences of visiting the wall or to acquire an introduction to the Vietnamese conflict that has affected so many of their families.

> *Betsy Hearne, in a review of "The Wall," in* Bulletin of the Center for Children's Books, *Vol. 43, No. 11, July-August, 1990, p. 261.*

[*The Wall*] does not explain the war; it discusses our loss. It is a gentle book, filled with feeling and sympathy for those who served in Vietnam and for those who still feel their pain. A storybook about a visit to the Vietnam Veterans Memorial in Washington for very young children, it reminds adults of how necessary it is to understand what happened, so that it will not happen again. (p. 49)

> *Walter Dean Myers, "Why Were We in Vietnam, Daddy?" in* The New York Times Book Review, *November 11, 1990, pp. 48-9.*

Such Nice Kids (1990)

This cautionary tale, as tantalizing as a tabloid headline, illustrates the manner in which a single error in judgment can set off an avalanche of mistakes. When Pidge needs to borrow a car for a hot date, he turns to best friends Meek and Jason. Unwillingly, and without his parents' knowledge, Jason lends Pidge the family car. After that, everything goes wrong: Pidge crashes into an expensive sportscar and leaves the scene, and the boys' efforts to cover up the accident plunge them into a maelstrom of criminal activity. The writing is brisk and the plotting convincing enough to enable most readers to overlook the fairly one-dimensional characterizations. Even reluctant readers will be caught up in this fast-paced tale of a deadly chain reaction.

> *A review of "Such Nice Kids," in* Publishers Weekly, *Vol. 237, No. 37, September 14, 1990, p. 126.*

While this didactic short novel makes points about the dangers of passively following another's lead, it reads like a parent's ultimate scare tactic—"See what happens when you borrow my car without asking?" Moreover, there is no real character development. As they do with stagy accident films in driver's ed, readers are likely to shrug this off as just too much to be believed.

> *A review of "Such Nice Kids," in* Kirkus Reviews, *Vol. LVIII, No. 20, October 15, 1990, p. 1453.*

Booktalking may be needed to get YAs past the morose-looking boys on the cover, but the short, cliffhanging chapters should provide ample motivation to keep them turning the pages. Readers will identify with the difficult choices facing these well-differentiated characters and will clearly understand the consequences of making the wrong choices. This book should appeal to less skilled readers above the indicated age range and should provide plenty of discussion if read seriously. (p. 121)

> *Joel Shoemaker, in a review of "Such Nice Kids," in* School Library Journal, *Vol. 36, No. 12, December, 1990, pp. 120-21.*

Our Sixth-Grade Sugar Babies   (1990)

Mrs. Oda challenges her sixth graders with a demanding proposition: each will assume full parental responsibility during an entire week for a baby—a 5lb. sack of sugar baby. Vicki vows to be the best parent in the class and not to cheat in caring for her "Babe." She soon learns, however, that responsibility affects, and is affected by, many circumstances. Two neighbors, senile Mr. Ambrose and a seventh-grade "terrific hunk" who has just moved in across the street, create unanticipated dilemmas for Vicki. The boy's charm causes her to temporarily abandon Babe to Mr. Ambrose's vacant gaze. When both Babe and Mr. Ambrose disappear, Vicki churns with guilt and the desire to cover up her indiscretion. Finally she confesses everything to her mother and faces up to the necessity of also telling her teacher and classmates. The plot elements conclude happily, and Mrs. Oda declares Vicki honest and courageous. The first-person narrative conveys an appropriate sixth-grade perspective and adroit sketches of Vicki and her friends. Her mother is well realized, a single working parent whose response to her daughter is sympathetic and supportive, yet astute in helping Vicki deal with her actions and their consequences. An absorbing and believable story that will set readers thinking.

> *Katharine Bruner, in a review of "Our Sixth-Grade Sugar Babies," in* School Library Journal, *Vol. 36, No. 10, October, 1990, p. 113.*

The delicious drama of sharing a crush on an unattainable love is treated with such wry comedy in this story that the serious issues catch you unawares. . . . The adults are a little too perfect (with none of the complexity of a story by Byars, for example), but they don't preach or spoil the fun, and Vicki's colloquial first-person narrative is never too earnest. She wrestles with moral demons, but she always needs to check that her ears don't show. A great read-aloud. (p. 442)

> *Hazel Rochman, in a review of "Our Sixth-Grade Sugar Babies," in* Booklist, *Vol. 87, No. 4, October 15, 1990, pp. 441-42.*

Responsibility and honesty are major themes here, but Bunting's light touch makes them easily digestible lessons. Parental estrangement (Mom and Dad are divorced) and mother-daughter conflict are both honestly dealt with. Characters are convincingly developed, and Bunting shows a genuine understanding for pre-teen angst.

> *Ruth Ann Smith, in a review of "Our Sixth-Grade Sugar Babies," in* Bulletin of the Center for Children's Books, *Vol. 44, No. 3, November, 1990, p. 55.*

Fly Away Home   (1991)

"My dad and I live in an airport. That's because we don't have a home and the airport is better than the streets. We are careful not to get caught." Thus begins this poignant narrative in the voice of a preschooler. The boy's widower-father leaves him with another homeless family when he goes to his part-time job as a janitor, and searches second-hand newspapers for more work and an apartment they can afford: "After next summer, Dad says, I have to start school"—but how? Meanwhile, in the vast, impersonal space where lucky travelers are welcomed home, the two find some sense of community but treasure their hope of escape to a place of their own. Using quiet browns and blues to suggest the sterile-looking airport and depicting the homeless with undefined faces and averted eyes—which evoke both their own need to be unseen to survive and others' aversion to seeing them—[Ronald] Himler matches Bunting's understated text with gentle sensibility. Like *The Wall*, an outstanding presentation of a serious topic for young children.

> *A review of "Fly Away Home," in* Kirkus Reviews, *Vol. LIX, No. 3, February 1, 1991, p. 172.*

Stories about the poor and outcast child risk being sentimental and preachy. We've had too many earnest socio-novels that harangue young readers with tearful messages.

But from Dickens' *Oliver Twist* (the first great novel in English with a child as protagonist) through some outstanding contemporary children's books (Sachs' *The Bears' House*, Hamilton's *The Planet of Junior Brown*, Holman's *Slake's Limbo*, and Myers' *Scorpions*), the best stories draw you into a world beyond any abstraction of "the poor."

Bunting and Himler's extraordinary picture book *Fly Away Home* begins: "My dad and I live in an airport. That's because we don't have a home and the airport is better than the streets. We are careful not to get caught." The airport as home is a bitterly ironic setting, both in fact and in metaphor. All that the man and boy don't have is emphasized by the power and promise, the space and light and bustling activity, around them. All that makes the airport an exciting place for the temporary traveler—the break from home and routine, the strange hours—intensifies the suffering of those for whom dislocation is permanent.

On the basic level are the physical details of survival: Where do they wash, eat, sleep? How do they keep from getting caught? How will the boy go to school when he's old enough? Himler's soft-textured watercolors have a hard realistic edge, showing the individualized man and boy carefully blending in (their blue jeans and jackets even echo the security guards' uniforms). They have the slightly rumpled, exhausted look of travelers who've had little rest: in fact, they sleep sitting up, in a different place every night (Tonight it's "Alaska Air"). When Dad works weekends, another homeless airport family—grandmother, mother, child—takes care of the boy.

As in Bunting and Himler's *The Wall,* which also focuses

on a father and son, the words and pictures are quiet. In one double-page spread the father and son stand on an escalator ("We stay") while travelers and workers rush by and jets roar in and out. In another aching scene, the isolated boy can hardly bear to watch the warm casual meetings of those who are coming home. Yet he can't express his pain; he mustn't shout or cry. He sees that the airport guards are kind but firm in removing the mentally ill or disorderly—the homeless who've drawn attention to themselves. "Fly United," the posters call, but no gate lets the boy through, and the arching sky is beyond the glass. . . . Does the airport father have to be tall and nice-looking, sad but always loving, never cross? Both books [*Fly Away Home* and Carol Fenner's *Randall's Wall*] are idealized. Yet they don't exploit the suffering; they understate it. In fact, the lesson both boys learn is inescapably harsh; I must be invisible, I must hide who I am; if I'm nobody, I'll be safe. These beautiful, disturbing books deny that anonymity and make us imagine the lives of individuals like ourselves.

> *Hazel Rochman, "Poor, Pure, and Invisible," in* Booklist, *Vol. 87, No. 15, April 1, 1991, p. 1567.*

Andrew and his father (a widower who has a job as a weekend janitor) live at an airport; Andrew, who tells the brief and wistful story, is not yet of school age but is wise enough to understand that if you are homeless, you take care that nothing makes you stand out. . . . Himler's quiet paintings echo the economy and the touching quality of the story, which is all the more effective in depicting the plight of the homeless because it is so low-keyed.

> *Zena Sutherland, in a review of "Fly Away Home," in* Bulletin of the Center for Children's Books, *Vol. 44, No. 9, May, 1991, p. 212.*

The Hideout (1991)

Bunting dispenses information slowly; readers do not find out until the middle of the book just why Andy has run away. This careful plotting overcomes some of the story's more obvious ploys—Andy luckily has a walkie-talkie with him when he's kidnapped, for instance. There's some emotional depth, too, as Andy's confusion about Paul's place in his life eventually turns to understanding. A common family situation becomes an action-filled drama in Bunting's capable hands.

> *Ilene Cooper, in a review of "The Hideout," in* Booklist, *Vol. 87, No. 15, April 1, 1991, p. 1563.*

In a plot device that is becoming familiar, a new stepparent is the reason that a child—here it's 12-year-old Andy, in San Francisco—ventures into the streets, where he discovers that the world is more wicked than anything he has faced at home. Having run away, Andy makes camp in the luxury suite of a nearby hotel, to which he has found a key. He periodically phones his real father, in London, hoping he'll send air fare. But Fred (of the hotel staff) cuts short Andy's plans, horning in on his faked kidnapping and making it all too real. Shortwave radio is the means for Andy's rescue; Paul, the "wicked" stepfather, is forgiven.

Largely contrived, and, though Andy's uneasiness with his mother and Paul's sexuality is clearly compelling, any realistic exploration of his perfectly believable feelings is pushed aside to make room for the hollow, feel-good ending.

> *A review of "The Hideout," in* Kirkus Reviews, *Vol. LIX, No. 7, April 1, 1991, p. 468.*

The novel has elements of Bunting's *Is Anybody There?*, including the illicit use of a key, a hideaway, and a boy too scared to sleep at night, but the overall plot is less plausible. However, the involving first-person narrative and the mounting tension offset the unlikely events. Andy's character—his jealousy of Paul and fear of discovery—is vividly portrayed. Those who like light mysteries should find this easy-to-read, moderately suspenseful story satisfying.

> *Pat Katka, in a review of "The Hideout," in* School Library Journal, *Vol. 37, No. 5, May, 1991, p. 91.*

A Perfect Father's Day (1991)

It's Father's Day, and four-year-old Susie has planned a perfect outing with all the things she knows her dad will like the best. First it's lunch at the fast-food restaurant, followed by feeding the ducks in the park, then playing on the swings, the monkey bars, and the merry-go-round. Dad wants a balloon, of course, as well as a surprise chocolate cake with four candles (one for every year that he's been Susie's dad). And in fact, Susie's right—her dad does think the day is perfect. Bunting's simple, witty text sketches a warm father-daughter relationship and affectionately glances at the four-year-old mind at work. . . . A charming Father's Day offering that would be equally good reading all year long.

> *Leone McDermott, in a review of "A Perfect Father's Day," in* Booklist, *Vol. 87, No. 16, April 15, 1991, p. 1648.*

Night Tree (1991)

Decorating the tree on Christmas Eve is not such an unusual custom, but this Christmas tree is in the woods, where one little boy and his family go each year to decorate it for the animals. Every year the tree is a little bigger, like the two children, but the ornaments are the same: popcorn, apples, tangerines, balls made of millet, honey and sunflower seeds. "We scatter shelled nuts and bread-crumbs and pieces of apple underneath for the little creatures who can't climb very well." With its twin appeals of Christmas generosity and kindness to animals, this is a realistic story that will have young listeners scouting for trees of their own to decorate. Bunting's quiet text and [Ted] Rand's watercolors have just the right nighttime mood, capturing the mystery of the woods where there are "secrets all around us." This family tradition is both cozy and mysterious, and a last doublespread of the animals' Christmas is a tribute to the friendly beasts.

Roger Sutton, in a review of "Night Tree," in Bulletin of the Center for Children's Books, *Vol. 45, No. 2, October, 1991, p. 32.*

Sharing Susan (1991)

Something is seriously wrong at Susan's house—a worry so big that even discussing it with her best friend doesn't help. It turns out she was accidently switched at birth with Marlene. The mix-up was discovered through medical testing after Marlene was hit and killed by a truck. Susan's biological parents now want her to live with them. Susan's family must deal with the loss of their unknown biological daughter and learn to "share" Susan. Straight out of the tabloid headlines, this unconsolable and complex situation is handled with sensitivity and restraint. There are no villains, only believable characters dealing with overwhelming emotions.

Gretchen S. Baldauf, in a review of "Sharing Susan," in Children's Book Review Service, *Vol. 20, No. 4, December, 1991, p. 45.*

Susan's "Big Worry" is that her parents' secretive whispering is a cover-up for an imminent divorce. But the truth turns out to be even worse. Susan was a "switched at birth" baby. . . . The idea of belonging to a totally new set of parents is abhorrent and Susan decides to circumvent any such happening. She feels her own parents are giving her up too easily, and indeed, they do seem remarkably fair and reasonable even though they obviously suffer over the loss of a child they never knew. Bunting is, of course, capitalizing on a recent similar event. Nevertheless, this novel is poignant and filled with enough dilemma and realistic emotion to keep the reader reading. Good middle-grade fare—solid Bunting.

Bette DeBruyne Ammon, in a review of "Sharing Susan," in Voice of Youth Advocates, *Vol. 14, No. 5, December, 1991, p. 306.*

Jumping the Nail (1991)

"Jumping the nail" is the expression used by a group of California teenagers for jumping from a high cliff into the ocean, risking the chance that they will hit rocks rather than water. There have been fatalities, and it is a decade since anyone tried the jump; this story of braggadocio daredevil friends, some of whom have succumbed to peer pressure, is told by one of the adolescents who tries to prevent a friend's participation. Bunting makes Dru's account believable, sustains suspense, and concludes with expectable, almost inevitable tragedy, but—despite the fact that this captures the phenomenon of don't-be-a-chicken conformity—the story is too narrow in scope, too melodramatic in development to be fully effective. (pp. 119-20)

Zena Sutherland, in a review of "Jumping the Nail," in Bulletin of the Center for Children's Books, *Vol. 45, No. 5, January, 1992, pp. 119-20.*

Pauline Clarke

1921-

(Also writes as Helen Clare) English author of fiction, nonfiction, short stories, poetry, and plays.

Major works include the "Five Dolls" series (as Helen Clare), *Merlin's Magic* (as Helen Clare, 1953), *Torolv the Fatherless* (1959), *The Twelve and the Genii* (1962; U. S. edition as *The Return of the Twelves*), *The Two Faces of Silenus* (1972).

Praised as an author of originality and literary skill, Clarke is well known for creating works that blend realism with fantasy or weave historical elements into contemporary life. Lauded for her understanding of children and what appeals to them, she is also acknowledged for her characterization, dialogue, and narrative ability as well as for her excellent historical sense and gift for creating background and atmosphere. Although she has written in a variety of genres for readers in the primary and middle grades, most of Clarke's works are fantasies and realistic or historical fiction that features both human and anthropomorphic characters. She is best known as the author of *The Twelve and the Genii,* the story of how a modern boy discovers the toy soldiers belonging to the Brontë children, and the five books about Elizabeth Small, a young girl who shrinks to a tiny size to enter the world of her toys. In *The Twelve and the Genii,* which was published as *The Return of the Twelves* in the United States, Clarke describes how young Max, who lives in a Yorkshire farmhouse close to the Haworth parsonage that was the childhood home of the Bronte children, finds the twelve Napoleonic wooden soldiers around which Branwell Brontë and his sisters—who dubbed themselves the "genii" or guardian angels of the soldiers—wove the adventures documented in *The History of the Young Men* and other juvenilia. After the soldiers come to life before Max's eyes and place their trust in him as their new "genius," he helps to return them to the parsonage in order to prevent their being sold to an antiquarian. Celebrated for creating a wholly believable story that has as its theme the respect for all individuals no matter what their size, Clarke is lauded for creating a moving and exciting story which is considered a classic example of fantasy. "In this book," critic Marcus Crouch writes, "Pauline Clarke stood tiptoe, reaching upwards to an idea of the highest excellence, and stretching and refining her craft to match it in words, characters, and narrative worthy of so rare a theme," while Margaret Sherwood Libby adds that *The Return of the Twelves* "sets a standard of imaginative excellence." Clarke is often noted for her characterization of the soldiers, giving them striking personalities while retaining their toylike natures; she is also praised for investing her "Five Dolls" series with this same quality. In *Five Dolls in a House* (1953), *Five Dolls and the Monkey* (1956), *Five Dolls in the Snow* (1957), *Five Dolls and Their Friends* (1959), and *Five Dolls and the Duke* (1963), Clarke introduces young readers to Elizabeth Small and her family of

dolls; with the dolls and their friend, a flippant Cockney monkey, Elizabeth enters into amusing adventures that delineate the individual characters of the dolls. Called "miniature novels" by critic Margery Fisher, the stories have also been collected in two omnibus volumes.

A journalist, book reviewer, editor, and lecturer on juvenile literature who has also written short stories and plays for adults, Clarke lived for several years in Norfolk, England, the setting for several of her stories for children. Throughout her career, Clarke has used both her own name and the pseudonym of Helen Clare; as Clare, she created the "Five Dolls" series and such works as *Merlin's Magic,* the story of a treasure hunt that includes historical periods and personages as well as fictional and mythic characters. Clarke is often acknowledged for her historical fiction, which often incorporates real events. For example, in *Torolv the Fatherless* an orphaned nine-year-old Viking boy comes to Saxon England and pledges his loyalty to the Saxons during the Battle of Maldon, while *The Boy in the Erpingham Hood* (1956) provides young readers with an eyewitness account of Agincourt in the time of Henry the Fifth. Clarke notes the relationship between the past and the present in *The Two Faces of Silenus;* in this novel, two children who have accompanied their parents to Italy become involved with the Roman gods Silenus, the satyr who is the son of Pan, and his enemy Medusa when they wish the stone figures alive. The rivals are returned to stone after a battle, but not before both the children and their parents have been affected positively by the influence of Silenus. In addition to her novels and stories, Clarke is the author of a collection of short stories in the folktale tradition; a volume of poetry that includes counting rhymes, ballads, and verse based on old legends; and a book that blends nonfiction with fiction to explain the collective names of a variety of real and imaginary animals. *The Twelve and the Genii* received the Carnegie Medal in 1963, the Lewis Carroll Shelf Award (as *The Return of the Twelves*) in 1965, and the Deutsche Jugendbuchpreis in 1968; it also was placed on the honor list for the Hans Christian Andersen Medal in 1964.

(See also *Something about the Author,* Vol. 3, and *Contemporary Authors,* Vols. 29-31, rev. ed.)

AUTHOR'S COMMENTARY

[The following excerpt is from an interview by Cornelia Jones and Olivia R. Way.]

> Jones and Way: Miss Clarke discusses the Brontë children and the stories they wrote called **The History of the Young Men,** on which she based her book **The Return of the Twelves.**

You have to remember that the games the Brontë children played with their soldiers came before the stories. You must imagine the four of them in the family in Yorkshire: Branwell, the oldest and a boy, Charlotte, Emily, and Ann, getting together in a tiny little room which you can still see if you go to Haworth—a little room above the porch—playing these wonderful games with this set of soldiers. Branwell had had various sets of soldiers before, but these seem to be very special, these Twelves. He had them in 1826 when he was eight years old. He describes how his father bought them for him and how each of the girls chose one for her own. They worked a very special game with these Twelves. They worked out this idea of being their genii, or guardian angels. Each child had a particular soldier that was hers or his. You can imagine them in this little room having very rowdy games, I think. Branwell was the ringleader, with battles and adventures and sea voyages and journeys. They had, in fact, a set of ninepins which they pretended were cannibals, and they would launch these, we can imagine, against the soldiers and have fights between the two. The genii would then swoop down and rescue their own soldiers and look after them. Branwell himself had red hair, and when he came to write the story, he made one of these strange creatures, these genii, have a red halo, and we know that this is what he is referring to—his red hair.

Well, above all you can imagine them making a terrific noise. I'm sure they did. I'm sure they were very much more natural children, as little children, than we sometimes think—this Brontë family. The noise was sometimes terrific. One time Tabby, the cook, who looked after them, called in her nephew from the street because she thought they'd all gone mad.

Branwell made up a special language for his soldiers, and he's said to have done it (I can't remember where I read this, but it is, in fact, stated somewhere) by speaking in bold Yorkshire and holding his nose at the same time. He wrote a rather strange little language for them, too. It was a mixture of English and French with bits of Greek letters in it as well. The children invented this idea of wooden soldiers coming alive again when they got killed because, of course, the soldiers can't be killed off permanently. Well, if you can imagine, all that was going on as they grew from their early years when they were six and seven and eight, until about 1830 when Branwell was twelve, and then I suppose the soldiers were perhaps lost.

The Brontës were getting older, and they had an absorbing interest in writing and began to write down the stories of the soldiers. They brought in all the games they had played and expanded them, made them bigger and more detailed. They wrote them in tiny little books with tiny pens and wee writing (they made it look like printing), I think partly because they had the idea that this was the proper scale for the soldiers and partly, no doubt, to save paper.

Branwell put all the games into the writing. He had imagined that these twelve soldiers had set off to Africa in a ship called *The Invincible,* and they were going to carve themselves out a kingdom amongst the Ashantis in Africa. He tells all this in *The History of the Young Men.* They built towns, twelve towns. They had parliaments. They had constant battles and excitements, visits of the genii in the desert. And when the Twelves, or Young Men, as they called them, got settled, the Brontës even started to write a series of magazines for them. They called them the *Young Men's Magazines,* with poems and stories and articles all about their life in Africa. You can see these whenever you go to the museum in their home in Haworth. These tiny little books are only twice the size of an English penny (3½ inches tall). There are lots more stories other than *The History of the Young Men,* and quite a few are written by Charlotte as well as Branwell. The whole series are called the Angria stories because they called this country Angria instead of Africa. Branwell's are the liveliest stories, and Charlotte's are more romantic. I use Branwell's mostly as background, especially for the characters of the twelve soldiers.

> Jones and Way: Miss Clarke discusses the techniques of writing fantasy. In **The Return of the Twelves** each soldier has a unique personality. Miss Clarke explains how she developed their personalities.

Their characters and their looks are very clearly described by Branwell in all his stories, and I simply tried to develop the outlines and the ideas that he gave. I'd like to read his list of their names and their ages from *The History of the Young Men.* Here it is: "Butter Crashey, captain, age 140 years; Alexander Cheeky, surgeon, age 20 years; Arthur Wellesley, trumpeter, 12; William Edward Parry, trumpeter, 15; Alexander Sneaky, sailor, 17; John Rose, lieutenant, 16; William Bravey, sailor, 27; Edward Gravey, sailor, 17; Stumps, 12, middy (that means midshipman); Monkey, 11, middy; Tracky, 10, middy; Crackey, 5, middy." Charlotte has rather different sailors, but I stuck to Branwell's mainly because he is very good at developing their characters and telling you about them. For instance, he goes on to say, "Crashey, the captain, was a patriarch, full of years and full of wisdom. Cheeky was the most stouthearted man in the ship. A. Sneaky was ingenious, artful, deceitful, but courageous; J. Ross, frank, open, honest, and of a bravery, when in battle, sometimes approaching to madness. W. Bravey was of a character similar to Ross, but his countenance and habits seemed to like to say 'Give us good cheer. Eat, drink, dance, and be merry.' Different from these was the character of Edward Gravey. He was naturally grave and melancholy, and his temper was still further soured by the sneers and laughter which the rest raised against him, but like the rest he was daring and brave. Of the other four midshipmen I need not speak particularly. Suffice it to say that like other middies they were merry, thoughtless, liked sport, and cared not for the future." Well, that's what Branwell says about his soldiers, and he adds a great deal to that throughout the stories.

What I tried to do was simply to develop this and use his ideas. I can give you some examples of this. It was quite easy to make Butter Crashey wise and alert and dignified with this wonderfully dignified, rather Biblical language, and cool and benign because he's very clearly drawn, not at all difficult to follow. Now Gravey is a good character. Branwell makes comic and yet disastrous things happen to Gravey. He always seems to have disasters that are rather funny happening to him. For instance, he's swept overboard with the mast in a sea battle. So, I followed this idea and made rather disastrous comic things always happen to Gravey. I also developed the notion of his being rather melancholy, which is why he is called Gravey, of course. Now, Sneaky was Branwell's own soldier, and he's like his name. He's artful and rather jealous, and he counsels treachery when they are discussing their advances on the Ashantis. He's very cocksure. He actually, in the Parliament, proposes himself as the king. This was easy to follow, too. I made him into a kind of ringleader, a rather envious person and full of himself. Stumps is another rather important character in my book because Max is so fond of him. Stumps in Branwell's stories is constantly dying and being made alive and coming back and disappearing. You never can quite keep track of Stumps, so this is why I let him get lost in the kitchen and also be swept off the raft and drowned, or not quite drowned, in the river. Stumps is a very lovable and solid character in Branwell's stories, and I tried to develop this. These are just some examples of how I've tried to do it with all of them, really. (pp. 66-9)

I did the march back to Haworth from maps and photos and imagination and from memory. I had been there in 1953 and I wrote the book, I suppose, in 1961-62, but I must tell you that the artist [Cecil Leslie] had a part here, too. She wanted very much to go to Haworth to get the feeling of the countryside before she began all the pictures, even though in the English edition she wasn't going to have very much space to draw a countryside. She also wanted to (and felt she must) see Branwell's own paintings and drawings of his soldiers which are in the museum at Haworth. So, while she was at Haworth, she actually walked out that march for me and in one particular she corrected it. When she saw Branwell's drawings, very faded watercolors of the soldiers, she noticed that some of the soldiers were wearing feathers in their caps in his drawings, and they were carrying a flag in a battle. This is why I let them pick out the feathers they found in the straw stack and wear those feathers, and why I gave them a flag.

> Jones and Way: Max's life with his family and his life with the soldiers are so skillfully juxtaposed that at no time does the reader question the reality of either. Miss Clarke discusses how she accomplished this.

This was not difficult exactly, but I had to feel my way. As each new child and finally the one adult, Mr. Howson, was let into the secret, I was conscious of it becoming more and more delicate to keep up the belief in the magic. You have to build up a totally convincing real setting, and then your reader will believe anything. If my characters, Max and the others, are real enough to you when you read the book, then whatever fantastic happenings come to Max will be believed. This sounds a contradiction, but I think it's at the bottom of good fantasy—to make your real setting so real that it grips the reader, and then he will believe what you tell him.

Although I tried to make the whole family real, I never let the parents openly into the secret, you notice, though Mrs. Morley is sympathetic to some strangeness that she feels is going on, and is very sympathetic to Max's feeling for his soldiers. Now, the adult who is let in, Mr. Howson, knows all about the Brontës and is very sympathetic to the whole idea. I don't think I could have kept up the reality if I'd let everyone into full enjoyment of the secret. I let the whole neighborhood get excited when the two little girls said they had seen the soldiers in the corn, but I only told this. I didn't show the grown-ups actually searching at firsthand or discussing it much. You can tell more than you can show in this kind of situation. I think to show the soldiers alive in the museum in public would have been a mistake, perhaps not believable. They had this useful freezing habit to outsiders. They went dead, they froze when they needed to. That is to say that some will see them alive and some won't. Imagination is just this—it's seeing more than your neighbor sees—sometimes. Children have it particularly.

Now the Twelves themselves know that they must freeze at times and they keep to this rule. There's an occasion when Butter is on the mantle shelf, having been brought back and found by the farmer, and the children stand around wondering what will happen. "He and Jane and Philip all stood silently gazing at the patriarch, each thinking the same thing—'What would happen if Crashey, recognizing the genii's voices, should hold up his tiny arms and then bow and smile and speak to them?'" Well, of course, Crashey knows perfectly well that there are outsiders in the room and he does no such thing. It doesn't happen; it doesn't arise. He stays frozen, and this is an important and useful part of keeping the fantasy going.

Then there was the very important question of scale. I never forgot scale. It was never out of my mind. The soldier's-eye view had to be given in detail. It had to be made as real as the human's. You alter the focus, but you alter it accurately all the time from one setting to the other. There is an occasion again when Butter is in the farmer's pocket and he describes how he finds himself in this dark, smelly hammock with what looks like a piece of old sheet which is, of course, a handkerchief, and what looks like a stake as long as himself, which is a nail, and a long coil of rope, which is a piece of string. That is a little example of doing it from a soldier's-eye view, and this has to be done constantly and never to be forgotten.

I built up the liveliness of the toys themselves in various ways. I did it partly by this wonderful difference, this individuality, which Branwell had already given them in looks and characters. Partly, I think, they have life because of their very antiqueness and their old-fashioned talk (both the very dignified Biblical talk of the patriarch, and the rather rowdy, swashbuckling talk of the people like Bravey). It's all old-fashioned. It's something rather individual. Then very importantly, very much a part of their life and their character—which Max himself realizes—is that they had to do things for themselves. When Philip has made a plan to get them back into the museum, he says it's a good plan because they can do it with dignity and they can also do it under their own steam. This is very important to Max, for he'd realized quite early that part of their life depended on their being left to do things by themselves and not being interfered with. He could oversee and suggest but not dictate. The soldiers had undertaken the whole march without consulting him. I think that this is a point which adds to their reality.

I think that you get this sixth sense as to what you can get away with, what the rules are for any particular story, as you write. You get it by being completely absorbed in the story and sure of it yourself. You're there. You're in the pocket with Crashey, and you're in the moonlit yard with Max and Stumps, you're in the museum waiting with Philip. And this is how you alter the focus. There's no other way to do it. You feel your way, like Max imagining what his soldiers are doing as he lies in bed. That chapter is meant to be a parallel about his imagining what goes on. So, it is a very delicate operation with its own rules which you have to feel for.

The *Five Dolls* books, which I wrote under the name of Helen Clare, have their own rules, too. There are no grown-ups in person in those books at all. They are only referred to. They're only talked about, as is Elizabeth's brother Edward. Elizabeth is the little girl who can get small enough to go into her doll's house. All the action takes place amongst toys—toy trains, toy castles, a toy zoo. It's a toy world. The doll's house exists in its own small world and the great real world is always there for Elizabeth to come from and go back to. The real world is talked about, but it doesn't really come into the stories; although, all the things the dolls do are simply what children do in real life. From this point of view the doll books

are sheer realism. The dolls go to weddings, they go to fetes, and they have picnics. They help in the house or the garden, they do the washing, they do the spring cleaning. It is just life from a doll's-eye view. (pp. 69-72)

I think each kind of story has its own kind of satisfaction. Also, they're not so very different. You've got to make a real setting and real characters, whether you're writing fantasy or a real life story. Otherwise, the setting and characters won't stand out, they won't be real at all, or convincing. Imaginative stories are very freeing; they're very releasing to the writer because, in effect, you have this feeling of having a godlike power to make anything happen that you fancy.

I remember once writing a short story, and greatly enjoying it, about an Oriental prince, a schoolboy prince, who went to spend Christmas with one of his school friends in London. The family took him shopping for presents at various big London stores. He arranged a snowstorm in one of the stores, and made the taxi that they were in take off from a traffic jam like a helicopter. In the end, he flew away on the hall carpet, accompanied by the chancellor from his country who had come to fetch him.

Making anything like this happen is tremendous fun. But in practice you find that every situation in a fantasy has its own rules and its own logic, and if the author doesn't keep to them, the story will break down. The story needs to be anchored in good reality to convince any but the very youngest child. I suppose that the very young child's notion of reality is nothing like as rigid as ours. Anyway, the line between fantasy and reality is so cloudy. We all have fantasies—young and old. But realistic stories have another kind of satisfaction. They have the satisfaction of describing the everyday truthfully, yet making it just that much larger than life, to be exciting, inspiring, or harrowing. That is, to make the everyday shine, as it does sometimes in reality, with promise or with warmth or with comedy, or sometimes even with a visionary quality.

In historical stories I get great pleasure and satisfaction from building up a picture of a past time with countless tiny details—social details about clothes and kitchens, and cooking and daily life, and ships and armies and buildings. Of course, you never really know how close your picture is to the real one. You never can know this about earlier times. You can only aim at making it a total and convincing picture, after doing your research as widely as you can. I have written two historical stories. One is called *Torolv the Fatherless,* which is a story about Anglo-Saxons and Vikings, and its climax is the Battle of Maldon on the Essex coast in 991. Its theme is the conflict of loyalties between the boy, Torolv, who comes to England with the Vikings, gets left behind accidently, and is looked after by the Saxons. Then he finds his former lord fighting with his present lord, and he's in a great conflict.

Then I've written another story about the Henry V period called *The Boy with the Erpingham Hood,* which has the Battle of Agincourt in it and various other stirring deeds.

In really fast-moving, realistic stories—such as thrillers, for instance—there is a great satisfaction (though a dreadful headache) in working out a tightly connected plot with all the strands really dovetailing and working together. Really, plot is always the most taxing part of making a story, but in a thriller it's perhaps more difficult than in other kinds of stories that move more slowly. Family stories, for instance, may go from incident to incident rather gently.

Of all my books, I think *Torolv, the Fatherless* is really my favorite. I don't quite know why except that I've always been very devoted to that period of history, and it seems to me to be the most shapely book I've written. I think I almost enjoyed it more than any. But it is difficult to say that because one really enjoys each book as one is doing it, and each book is a different experience, of course. (pp. 72-4)

> *Pauline Clarke, Cornelia Jones and Olivia R. Way, in an interview in* British Children's Authors: Interviews at Home, *by Cornelia Jones and Olivia R. Way, American Library Association, 1976, pp. 65-75.*

GENERAL COMMENTARY

Margery Fisher

The Victorian child took it for granted that his stories would have an improving note and I think our children will end up by doing the same. Certainly the morals in their stories will be more lightly stated and stated with more humour, for when children live cheek by jowl with their parents, authority has to wear a different, less noticeable guise. A story like Pauline Clarke's *The Robin Hooders* strikes the typical note of today. Robert, Serena and Tom, who live in a village, decide to do good deeds; but not because they want to be good. Serena has been re-reading stories of Robin Hood and they think robbing the rich to help the poor would make a good game. They are not under instructions from tracts or parents, and they have to find the path to generosity through mistakes and minor successes, until the major triumph when they discover (by accident) a treasure which helps their dear Miss Laurel to regain her manor house. In a word, they are children learning to behave suitably and with energy in a very mixed world. (p. 45)

In Pauline Clarke's novel of Henry V's times, *The Boy with the Erpingham Hood,* we have, as it were, an eye-witness account, not only of Norwich with its monastic houses, its markets and festivities, but also of Harfleur and Agincourt. The Londoners discuss the war which they can foretell from the piling up of supplies and the building of new ships. The dialogue is colloquial, designed to give an immediate, vivid picture; for instance, in this description of the Norwich wrestlers waiting to perform at Windsor before the King:

> A man in motley leaped out of a tree into the middle of the nervous men, making them jump and curse before they laughed.
>
> 'Scram! Scatter! Pass along from the clearing please! No standing about 'ere, his Grace is to watch some half-baked, rough wrestlers from a

little village called Norridge who will tear each other to pieces with their Norfolk outplay.'

> He laid about him with a blown-up bladder on the end of a stick, hitting whoever was in his way.
>
> 'You fool, we *are* the wrestlers,' William Thweyt snapped. 'From the city of Norwich.'
>
> The fool smiled slyly, he knew this perfectly well. He somersaulted out of the way, making faces at them through his legs each time and tripping over his balloon. They roared with laughter, and felt better.

The battle of Agincourt is dealt with in the same practical vein. We are conscious of the weather, the men's fatigue and hopelessness, the details of strategy, the camp-fire and the tending of weapons. But there is a slight heightening of tension, an echo of Shakespeare's grand manner, to isolate the end of the description of Agincourt . . . .(pp. 227-28)

> *Margery Fisher, "There and Back by Tricycle" and "Truth and Ginger-bread Dragoons," in her* Intent Upon Reading: A Critical Appraisal of Modern Fiction for Children, *Brockhampton Press, 1961, pp. 36-49, 225-50.*

Margery Fisher

Elizabeth Small [in the "Five Dolls" books] gives herself this surname after the day when she began to visit, as landlady, the gabled dolls' house where her five little dolls live. She has always preferred the house when the front door is shut because 'when the dolls were shut in and nobody stared, they did all kinds of things' and not just what she 'made happen herself'. All the same, when one day she looks in at the windows and sees how untidy everything is, she decides it is time she spring-cleaned the dolls' house. 'If you had the sense you was born with, you'd know how to get small, 'stead of only knowing how to get big', remarks the rude monkey who lives on the roof. It seems natural that he should speak to her, for Elizabeth often talks to him, and she is scarcely more surprised to find that she can walk in through the front door (though rather more so when Vanessa mistakes her for the new charlady and only belatedly recognizes her as their landlady).

Once Elizabeth has fulfilled all the requests pressed on her by the dolls—for blankets, a new battery for the lights, real food instead of plaster dishes—she enters with delight into the life of her tenants. Their activities are as familiar and as fragmentary as if they have somehow been snipped off her own life. There are picnics and tea parties, a wedding and a funeral (with Elizabeth as the vicar each time), a train journey through the nursery, an outbreak of measles and an operation, spring cleaning and decorating for Christmas. New scenes develop from the presents her godmother gives her for the dolls' house—a telephone, a parrot in a cage, a baby in a cradle; but most of all Elizabeth enjoys the clashes of temperament inevitable in a household that includes bossy Vanessa (who boasts that she is the daughter of the Duke of Cranberry), giggly Amanda who carries on a reprehensible flirtation with the monkey, and the paying guest, Jacqueline, who never seems to learn any English. Together with Lupin, the youngest doll, who wears nothing but a vest, and the gentle Jane, who writes poetry, the dolls lead a varied life, enlivened now and then by the monkey's interruptions down the chimney or his occasional appearances in disguise (as a sweep and a visiting Duchess, for example). The dolls alternate amusingly between correct behaviour and a total disregard for time and consistency, sharing in the glorious liberty which Elizabeth's imagination has allowed them. (p. 102)

The characters of the Twelve [in *The Twelve and the Genii*] are of course borrowed from *The History of the Young Men*. Butter Crashey the patriarch, with his dignified mode of speech; Stumps, often lost, with 'his round, turnipy head, and his stumpy, rather bandy legs', who has a second identity as Frederick Guelph, Duke of York; the tall, dominating soldier, once a trumpeter, then honoured by Charlotte Brontë as Arthur Wellesley, Duke of Wellington; Gravey the doctor; Parry and Ross the intrepid explorers; the ambivalent Sneaky, 'ingenious, artful, deceitful and courageous'—Pauline Clarke has chosen scenes and episodes so that the personalities lent to the toys by the Brontë children can reveal themselves gradually in action and in speech.

Thus half the characters in her fantasy are derivative—brilliantly so. The other half illustrate an underlying theme, of respect for the individual. The attitude of the Morley children (and of their parents and neighbours) to the Twelve, tells us something about their natures. Max has the right kind of imagination to be chosen as a successor to the Genii; he believes in his games and in the animate lives of the Twelve. He realizes at once that they are people in their own right. He knows that he must not carry them down from the attic to the kitchen, but must give them the means (in this case, string tied along the banister rails) to find a way down for themselves. He never allows his sense of wonder to stop him from being tactful and respectful in his dealings with them. His sister Jane, who finds out by accident that the soldiers can come alive, is gentle and careful with them, and is admitted at once as one of the Genii, but Philip, who is old enough to be aware of the power of money, is accepted less readily. His remorse when he does find out who and what the soldiers are is what one would expect from this thoughtless but honest boy. In a sense the Twelve are a kind of testing point and the three children (as well as the vicar, who is allowed to see the soldiers marching to Haworth and accepts the marvel as a matter of faith) are each revealed in their true light by this magical and totally believable happening. (pp. 222-23)

> *Margery Fisher, "Who's Who in Children's Books: 'Elizabeth Small' and 'Max Morley',"* in her *Who's Who in Children's Books: A Treasury of the Familiar Characters of Childood, Holt, Rinehart and Winston, 1975, pp. 102, 221-23.*

TITLE COMMENTARY

The Pekinese Princess (1948)

In a far distant land, long, long ago, the Pekinese dogs lived in a kingdom of their own. But trouble came to their peaceful land and the Emperor's lovely daughter was carried away by an enemy on the eve of her wedding. Amber Face, with a small band of brave warriors, set out in pursuit of his bride and after many adventures in the true fairy tale manner brought her safely home again. Then the Lord of Heaven translated the whole kingdom to the top of a mountain in the middle of the world. A few Pekes crept out and these are they who now live in the world, returning to their ancient kingdom only in happy dreams. Thus their often sad expressions are due to their longings for their old beloved homes.

This is a charming fantasy, delightfully told, with due regard to the natural characteristics of the animals who take part in it and following the recognised fairy tale tradition.

> *E. R. W., in a review of "The Pekinese Princess,"* in The Junior Bookshelf, *Vol. 12, No. 3, October, 1948, p. 125.*

[*The Pekinese Princess* is] an apt parody of fairy tale. . . .leads his troop on a quest to find and rescue his beloved, Star-in-a-dark-pool. Line drawings with a story-book Chinese flavour [by Cecil Leslie] underline gracefully the point of this civilised little adventure.

> *Margery Fisher, in a review of "The Pekinese Princess,"* in Growing Point, *Vol. 12, No. 6, December, 1973, p. 2296.*

The White Elephant (1952)

Two children, Alistair and Georgina, are taken out for the day by their grown up cousin Nona, and their activities are prefaced by Nona's purchase of a new fur coat. Mysterious pursuers and the finding of valuable jewellery in the pockets of the fur coat lead to an interrupted theatre visit and a chasing and rounding up of thieves. The hackneyed theme is treated with some originality, and although the children are indistinct: Nona is recognisable and Great Aunt Edith an amusing caricature. The style is racy and the story moves with ease but there are moments when the tale becomes trite and unconvincing melodrama. Richard Kennedy's illustrations lend vitality and atmosphere and the whole is a pleasant production. (pp. 274-75)

> *A review of "The White Elephant,"* in The Junior Bookshelf, *Vol. 16, No. 5, December, 1952, pp. 274-75.*

A splendid day's outing in London with their cousin Nona is made even more memorable for Alister and Georgie when they become unwittingly involved in a jewel robbery. The bizarre events which follow are made more exciting and even credible by their accurate geographical setting in London; while Miss Clarke's characters are, as always, life-size. First published in 1952 and well worth reissuing.

> *A review of "The White Elephant,"* in The

Times Literary Supplement, *No. 3351, May 19, 1966, p. 432.*

This is a very welcome new edition of one of the author's earlier works. . . . [It] is a highly entertaining story told in a skilful and stirring way, and although the book is not quite of the quality of the best of her later ones, it is well worth buying.

> *Robert Bell, "The White Elephant," in* The School Librarian and School Library Review, *Vol. 14, No. 3, December, 1966, p. 352.*

Merlin's Magic (as Helen Clare, 1953)

Here is a curious book, but one which shows considerable originality in its plot and some quality in its style. The author has evidently been influenced by Lewis Carroll, E. Nesbit, and perhaps by Elizabeth Goudge, but her book falls short of being a first-class work of the imagination, partly because it is thus derivative, and partly because the central theme—the battle between romance and mechanization—is artificially created. We begin by following the trail of what appears to be an ordinary summer afternoon's treasure hunt, though the mention of a "classical beast of great antiquity" and the fanciful names of some of the children should have prepared us for the flight into the world of fantasy which soon follows. Each child has to follow a clue which leads to the intangible treasures of his own heart and mind, and in each case the search is imperilled by the appearance of an army of robot-like monsters, who, lacking imagination themselves, want to seize it from those so gifted. The contrast between the glories of the days of King Arthur, Elizabeth I or Kubla Khan, and the Wellsian atmosphere created by the robots is too sharp; if each period of history had raised its own peculiar enemies the story would have sounded a truer note. The characters of romance are not always true to their periods, either; no one minds the delightful hippogriff lapsing into Cockney, but to find Queen Morgan Le Fay speaking of people "barging about" or Sir Walter Ralegh (author's spelling) mixing himself up with Edward Lear's Jumblies is a little odd. (pp. 111-12)

> *A review of "Merlin's Magic," in* The Junior Bookshelf, *Vol. 17, No. 3, July, 1953, pp. 111-12.*

Merlin's Magic has so ecstatic a publisher's blurb that one is not impressed, but the book compels by its quality of writing and reach of imagination. Six children set out to find a treasure which is the same for all and yet different for all, and in doing so make excursions into realms of well-loved literature. It is not likely to be a popular book. The author makes great demands on her young readers, but those who can respond will do so thankfully, and reap great reward.

> *P. M. Hostler, in a review of "Merlin's Magic," in* The School Librarian and School Library Review, *Vol. 6, No. 6, December, 1953, p. 424.*

A feast of fantasy. This is a story that junior teachers will welcome, for it has been written to be read aloud to a class of lively young children. The class will wait breathlessly

for the next episode. The book is written with such skill and zest that it seems like a fast-moving film.

It begins with six children going off on a treasure hunt, and what a hunt it turns out to be! Their destinations are as far apart as the bottom of the ocean and the glittering planets. They meet real and mythical heroes, and throughout the book the characters are helped by a fabulous beast, the hippogriff, which might have walked straight out of *Alice in Wonderland.*

Miss Clare certainly knows what the young want, and fortunately she has the ability to write it.

> *D. V. Gulliver, in a review of "Merlin's Magic," in* The School Librarian and School Library Review, *Vol. 11, No. 6, December, 1963, p. 664.*

Five Dolls in a House (as Helen Clare, 1953)

What happens inside when the dolls' house door is shut? Countless little girls must have imagined adventures for their small inhabitants, and in this amusing tale of five dolls, varying from Vanessa the domineering doll with the feathery hat to quiet little Lupin who wears only a blue vest—not forgetting the Cockney monkey who makes rude remarks down the chimney Miss Clare has written a book which invites comparison with Rumer Godden's *The doll's house.* **Five dolls** has more immediate appeal to the child herself, being more simply written and printed in larger type. Miss Clare has brought imagination, skill and humour to the telling of the dolls' adventures, and one can guess that this will be a favourite with seven and eight-year-old girls, in spite of the illustrations [by Cecil Leslie] which oddly appear against bright blue backgrounds. The pull-out plan of the house, however, makes up for this, and adds to the attraction of the book.

> *A review of "Five Dolls in a House," in* The Junior Bookshelf, *Vol. 18, No. 1, January, 1954, p. 12.*

A very charming story on a theme which only a few writers of children's books have used with any real success. In most, the dolls are not characters, but remain merely puppets. Here is a book in which the dolls come alive, and when Elizabeth visits her dolls' house the reader feels she is stepping with her into a living world. The unusual things which happen on these visits are original and full of humour.

> *Betty Brazier, in a review of "Five Dolls in a House," in* The School Librarian and School Library Review, *Vol. 7, No. 1, March, 1954, p. 77.*

The talent that produced the remarkable **The Return of the Twelves** is evident in the dialogue and imaginative details of **Five Dolls in a House**. . . . The illustrations by Aliki show a delightful monkey but unfortunately make the five dolls comic characters lacking any resemblance to real dollhouse dolls, which weakens the impact of an already slender story. The five dolls are carefully individualized, and their activities pleasantly diverting.

Margaret Sherwood Libby, "The Fancy Touch," in Book Week—New York Herald Tribune, *April 17, 1966, p. 16.*

Smith's Hoard (1955; also published as *Hidden Gold* and *The Golden Collar*)

The author makes no hesitant steps at the beginning of this story. She enters at once into the atmosphere of a holiday train journey being made by two young people, and the motion of train and conversation has an echoing and insistent rhythm that is closely felt. But this intimacy is not maintained. The author becomes a little more aloof and a little more crowded out as events push in and the story enters into the category of competent but more prosaic works. There is throughout however, no lack of sustained interest. The pattern is intriguing enough and the intrigue is enriched by the historical and archaeological information which supplies the excuse and inspiration for the invention. An unpleasant antique dealer, a bewildered farm labourer, buried Celtic treasure and four interested young people are the props of the tale, and while one of the young people sometimes appears to be surprisingly clever, he is not unbelievably so. There is an element of ghostly mystery which remains unsolved to the end, and this gives a happy imaginative touch to the otherwise more ordinary turn of events. The chatty style of the first person rides smoothly and easily along and is not used to hide too many faults.

A review of "Smith's Hoard," in The Junior Bookshelf, *Vol. 19, No. 2, March, 1955, p. 85.*

It is still true that, as one father remarks in **Smith's Hoard,** "parents are quite redundant", but this at least puts the youngsters on their mettle, and certainly the four in this book bring a new liveliness to the outworn theme of treasure trove. There is genuine feeling in this story of their resolve to rescue the treasure of the *Iceni*—rings, bracelets and torques—from the fate of the scrap-merchant. Their attractive young leader has "read a bit" about those ancient days and is able to sustain the difficult role of imparting large wads of information on the subject to his companions as they await the thief at night. They and the villagers make the book alive and reflect the life of men of the Iron Age.

P. Hostler, in a review of "Smith's Hoard," in The School Librarian and School Library Review, *Vol. 7, No. 5, July, 1955, p. 355.*

Alister and Georgina Murray, en route to their aunt's home for the summer, meet a suspicious character on the train. He says that he is a dealer in second-hand jewelry, but the object he shows them, Alister tells his sister later, is part of a priceless Celtic torc. The Murrays and two friends make elaborate plans including a concealed lookout and night watches; they suspect that the torc is part of a buried hoard, in which case it is the property of the government. The mystery is solved by the young people and the culprit brought to light. The four children are depicted as being very enterprising; they are also secretive and disobedient, and not always quite truthful. The characters are artificial and the interpolation of stories by Al-

ister about the Iron Age, showing an encyclopedic knowledge, are received by the other children with unbelievable eagerness.

Zena Sutherland, in a review of "Hidden Gold," in Bulletin of the Children's Book Center, *Vol. XI, No. 11, July-August, 1958, p. 119.*

Bel the Giant and Other Stories (as Helen Clare, 1956)

These stories keep close to the folk-tale tradition in a way equalled only by Diana Ross among contemporary writers. This is partly because Miss Clare has studied her sources carefully, but more because she has kept her mind clear of the clutter of urban civilisation, and writes simply and without sophistication. Correct in tone, with humour and personality, they are excellent material for reading aloud or re-telling.

A review of "Bel the Giant, and Other Stories," in The Junior Bookshelf, *Vol. 20, No. 3, July, 1956, p. 123.*

Not all the stories in **Bel the Giant** have equal quality but the best possess the direct simplicity of good story-telling. While some are in the style of the traditional legend, others tell of the everyday world of adventure which means so much to the young reader. Such is **"The Boy Who Ran Away"** which has the repetitive touch of the House That Jack Built. Sincere and neat, the stories are well-suited to reading aloud.

Betty Brazier, in a review of "Bel the Giant and Other Stories," in The School Librarian and School Library Review, *Vol. 8, No. 3, December, 1956, p. 226.*

Five Dolls and the Monkey (as Helen Clare, 1956)

Elizabeth Small is able, by some magic formula, to make herself as small as her dolls and thus to enter her dolls' house and share the adventures of her five dolls and the monkey who lives with them. The author too, in her imagination, has bent low and peeped into this house. Every detail is remembered and the individual personalities of each doll are well known. Yet they are still dolls. Their manner is stiff and wooden enough to be appropriate to their station, while their pursuits and occupations are apt and amusing. The chatter is constant, but beneath the trivial surface is a host of imaginative pictures that will stimulate and delight the young reader. Some of Miss Clare's humour is a little trite and misplaced, but for the most part it is a gay and happy book.

A review of "Five Dolls and the Monkey," in The Junior Bookshelf, *Vol. 20, No. 3, July, 1956, p. 123.*

A mischievous monkey married to a doll, a houseful of dolls with headsful of projects, a British Elizabeth who can be doll-sized or child-sized, all appear in a stilted text which tells cute-cute stories. Like the time the five dolls and Elizabeth went skating on broken glass with cold cream to make them slide, or the time they took up dress-making and the littlest sewed her dress up so the legs went through the armholes and the hem tied at the neck. Each doll has her set phrases and the monkey speaks only Cockney. Preciously contrived and rather dull.

> *A review of "Five Dolls and the Monkey," in* Kirkus Service, *Vol. XXXV, No. 4, March 1, 1967, p. 268.*

Like the first book, **Five Dolls in a House,** each chapter is an imaginative play, complete in itself. To an adult, the stories are virtually a tape recording of a child's imaginings as she invents these slight but typical plays, and they are skillfully done. Whether there is enough action to hold a child's interest is questionable. The British dialogue, despite a glossary, may be a handicap also, and the dolls are rather shadowy in personality even at the end of two books. . . . Although there may be little girls who find the detail and scale of these stories endearing, probably librarians will not find a large audience for this book and should buy it only after consideration of the doll stories already available in the collection.

> *Marguerite M. Murray, in a review of "Five Dolls and the Monkey," in* School Library Journal, *Vol. 13, No. 8, April, 1967, p. 68.*

Five Dolls in the Snow   (as Helen Clare, 1956)

Another minidrama with the five dolls . . . , the parrot, the monkey, and the dollhouse landlady Elizabeth Small (who can turn herself small) in eight episodic adventures. Their genteel British life is always interrupted either by projects—a dancing class, a christening, a garden party—or by Elizabeth's gifts—scraps of wallpaper, a baby of indeterminate sex. The humor is minor malaprop, the pictures are as precious as the plot—creeping cuteness (and two more to come.)

> *A review of "Five Dolls in the Snow," in* Kirkus Service, *Vol. XXXV, No. 15, August 1, 1967, p. 876.*

That unique family of unique characters, whose house is situated on the Small family's property: those delightful dolls, with their monkey, are back in residence. Your reviewer suggests to all doll-lovers that they drop whatever they're doing and rush right over to welcome them back.

> *A review of "Five Dolls in the Snow," in* Publishers Weekly, *Vol. 196, No. 6, August 7, 1967, p. 54.*

The story differs little from others in the series; its slightness and very British idiom make it of dubious value to libraries.

> *Marguerite Murray, in a review of "Five Dolls in the Snow," in* School Library Journal, *Vol. 14, No. 6, February, 1968, p. 76.*

Sandy the Sailor   (1956)

Sandy the Sailor is an account of a small boy's voyage to

New Zealand and back in a sailing clipper. Without ever being prosy, Pauline Clarke manages to give much information on the habits of sailing ships, never forgetting the small boy's way of looking at life. It is most successful.

> *G. Taylor, in a review of "Sandy the Sailor," in* The School Librarian and School Library Review, *Vol. 8, No. 4, March, 1957, p. 313.*

Torolv the Fatherless   (1959)

Torolv, an orphan aged nine, drifts out to sea in an open boat. He is rescued by a Viking whose strength and personality win his admiration. Torolv is accidentally left behind in Saxon England when the Vikings are raiding the coast, but he finds a new master, a Saxon earl. The Danes attack and in the battle of Maldon the bravest of the East Saxon army are killed. Torolv, realising the ruthlessness of his Viking hero, remains loyal to the defeated Saxons.

The story is full of action, there is plenty of fighting and an excellent period background. Torolv's adventures particularly with the colourful Vikings, will appeal to boys. It seems a pity that Torolv is boastful and has a "calculating cleverness in pleasing others," qualities which seem unattractive in a hero.

It is obvious that the author has a detailed knowledge of the Saxon poems of the period and occasionally this makes her style difficult for children, especially as there are many characters in the story, all with unfamiliar names. The child interested in Vikings will, however, enjoy this book and its spirited drawings of the times [by Cecil Leslie]. Torolv himself, unfortunately, looks too young and this may discourage older readers from reading the book.

> *A review of "Torolv the Fatherless," in* The Junior Bookshelf, *Vol. 23, No. 4, October, 1959, p. 216.*

This is a really fine adventure story for children, showing the author's fine historical sense, narrative power and ability to create characters. . . . Life in a Saxon stronghold and the Saxons' preparation for war is excellently drawn.

For those whose historical sense is fired by the story, there is also a translation of the Old English poem on the Battle of Maldon and a historical note on the main characters of the book.

> *R. Bradbury, in a review of "Torolv the Fatherless," in* The School Librarian and School Library Review, *Vol. 9, No. 6, December, 1959, p. 483.*

This is a clever story, a little cerebral but deeply pondered and written with clarity and, in the battle-scene, with passion. The author's starting-point is the famous poem of the Battle of Maldon of which she provides a translation, and much of the story is in the spirit of the poem, with its insistence on courage and integrity and on the need to defend and avenge the Ring-Giver, and its constant reminder that Fate, which haunted the lives of these brave and industrious Anglo-Saxons, would inevitably change and blow away happiness like 'fleet clouds'. There is much tenderness in **Torolv the Fatherless** but little consolation.

Marcus Crouch, "The Abysm of Time: 'Torolv the Fatherless'," in his The Nesbit Tradition: The Children's Novel in England 1945-1970, *Ernest Benn Limited, 1972, p. 79.*

Like Sutcliff, Clarke has the ability to blend historical details so deftly into her narrative that they seem effortless. While the book has many characters and incidents (identified in the author's concluding notes) that are real, they are not wooden insertions but vivid parts of the whole.

> *Zena Sutherland, in a review of "Torolv the Fatherless," in* Bulletin of the Center for Children's Books, *Vol. 32, No. 8, April, 1979, p. 132.*

Seven White Pebbles   (as Helen Clare, 1960)

The Acorn Library represents an interesting idea imperfectly realised. There is a real need for stories which are short enough to offer a reasonably limited objective to children who have just learnt to read and long enough to look like real books. It is desirable that such books should be attractively produced, with a clear large print and good illustrations. On the physical side the Acorn Library is excellent. . . . The stories are less consistently satisfactory.

Helen Clare, in **Seven White Pebbles,** has come nearest to realising the aim of the series. Her story of Polly who is eight and who counts the seven days to her holiday has the right tone, strict regard for the limited experience of the reader, a satisfactory use of language. It seems also a little dull, but not perhaps to eight year-olds.

> *A review of "Seven White Pebbles," in* The Junior Bookshelf, *Vol. 24, No. 3, July, 1960, p. 133.*

The Robin Hooders   (1960)

The use of the first person narrative style leads here to some flurry and obscurity from which, however, there emerge some real and ordinary children behaving in a familiar way. They are a family of four wanting to be modern Robin Hoods and they manage to play this game without having to resort to either stealing or make-believe. The children are natural and lively and the author succeeds in creating an unusual story without detracting from the familiarity of the scene and background. She obviously has a discerning eye and a natural liking for and sympathy with young children and the whole is nourished and sustained by sound values and a healthy vigorous outlook. The climax of the story, when the children are instrumental in finding a valuable manuscript that does indeed help the owner is the only incident that seems a little artificial and mars the reality of the scene. The production and [Cecil Leslie's] illustrations are of a high standard. A happy worthwhile little book.

> *A review of "The Robin Hooders," in* The Junior Bookshelf, *Vol. 24, No. 3, July, 1960, p. 145.*

Keep the Pot Boiling   (1961)

During the first two or three chapters of Pauline Clarke's latest book, however much one likes the four young Carlisles whose father is the vicar of a parish near Camden Town, the reader still feels that the children do belong to a privileged family, and even though the vicar's stipend may be low and therefore Mother has to illustrate books to make ends meet, are the activities of such a family going to interest children with a very different background? Yet as the story goes on this feeling vanishes, because Randolph, Kate, Emma, and Claire are such fundamentally decent children who behave like most other children do—helpful sometimes, hurt sometimes, but because they are basically generous, sensible young people never sulky. They are capable of enormous fun—such as the incident when Kate dresses up as a stranger to her mother's Sewing Circle, and fools all the other people present—and they are capable of concealing their worry when their father is ill. The title of the book refers to a game the children play, and the whole happy family atmosphere will find many devoted admirers. The author draws her characters with superb skill, striking a clear contrast between the carefree Kate, the very sensitive Emma, determined little Claire, and a very sensible elder brother Randolph.

> *A review of "Keep the Pot Boiling," in* The Junior Bookshelf, *Vol. 25, No. 4, October, 1961, p. 218.*

Well written and entertaining, this story of the Carlisle family . . . is very accurately described by its title. It has little real plot but relies for its success on the vitality which the author brings to her description of every-day events at the vicarage: the children themselves, the vicar their father—highly strung and on the verge of a breakdown—their mother, an artist who supplements the family income by her work as an illustrator, and the people of the parish. The traditional lack of money in such a household seems to be a stimulus to imagination and leads the children to find adventure where others would see none, whether raising money for refugees, impersonating a new member of the parish sewing party or tracking their mother to a lunch appointment in the West End.

> *F. P. Parrott, in a review of "Keep the Pot Boiling," in* The School Librarian and School Library Review, *Vol. 10, No. 6, December, 1961, p. 568.*

The Twelve and the Genii   (1962; U. S. edition as *The Return of the Twelves*)

In Pauline Clarke's story the expectation of marvels is linked with the practical good sense of intelligent children. She tells how a small boy finds the Napoleonic wooden soldiers round whom the young Brontës wove *The History of the Young Men*. The author held me completely spellbound in the world where Max, in rapture, watched the patriarch Butter Crashey, the tall Duke, Gravey the melancholy and the rest of the Twelve. For the inherent beauty of style and setting, the poetic nature of the fantasy and the enchanting, comic, miniature quality of the pictures,

The Twelve and the Genii may well be one of the half dozen best children's books of 1962.

Margery Fisher, in a review of "The Twelve and the Genii," in Growing Point, *Vol. 1, No. 2, July, 1962, p. 19.*

All children know that their toys, or some of them, are alive; that dolls freeze into silence as the door opens and that *Boutique Fantasque* is a part of the truth; and here is a book to prove it. One holds one's breath with Max, afraid to disturb the tiny soldiers, drilling so smartly in their shabby uniforms, and one shares his shock of pleasure when Butter Crashey tells him his name—" 'How did you get it?' 'I fell long ago into the butter', said his friend. 'I thought you must have', said Max." This is the ultimate satisfaction, to have toys that not only live but have lives of their own. Here is no suspension of disbelief. Miss Clarke is telling the truth and this is exactly how it happened.

The Twelve and the Genii is true not only in the reading but on reflection afterwards. One can remember Butter Crashey's first jerk into life and the patter like rice falling of those tiny clapping hands, and it is remembering not a fancy but a fact. It is imagined right through. . . .

"Two Forms of Magic: Adventures in An Unseen World," in The Times Literary Supplement, *No. 3169, November 23, 1962, p. 901.*

[The Twelves are] the most remarkable group of characters to be presented to children in a long time. Adults who have been fascinated by the extraordinarily gifted but doomed family of the Reverend Patrick Bronte of Haworth parsonage have met them before in the "Chronicles of Angria," "The History of the Young Men" and other writings of the Bronte children.

Although Max had barely heard of the Brontes, he did not find it odd that the queer old-fashioned soldiers in Napoleonic uniforms should come to life before his eyes. After all, "what he imagined" about things "was really true. In his mind. It was only that these had gone one step further and come alive and he could watch it." And watch he did with a passionate delight (immediately communicated to the reader of any age) as there in his attic the Duke of Wellington, Butter Crashey, Stumps and the other nine drilled, battled (with marbles for cannon balls), reconnoitered, reminisced about Angria and came abruptly to accept him as their protective genie. From them and from judicious questioning of his family and friends he pieced together much of their history and, aided by his sister and older brother, determined to help them to return to Haworth parsonage as they ardently desired in order to avoid being sold as literary curios to an antiquarian from overseas.

And what an odyssey that return march of the valiant Twelves proved to be—every detail inevitable and right. . . .

"Utterly splendid," as an older friend of the Morley children said—a tribute which can be given the book as well as its heroes. No wonder it won the Carnegie prize in England in 1962. Appearing here before 1964 is a fortnight old (though with a 1963 imprint), it sets a standard of imaginative excellence and many other books of the year are likely to achieve.

Margaret Sherwood Libby, "The Long March Home," in Book Week—New York Herald Tribune, *January 26, 1964, p. 14.*

The children's book based on a brilliant and original idea is very rare. Mary Norton found one in *The Borrowers.* For the most part even the finest of writers dedicate their talent to a variant of one of the few basic themes.

In one sense Pauline Clarke's theme in **The Twelve and the Genii** is a basic one, that of the animated inanimate object. In another and a more important one it is marvellously original, one of those ideas so fine and simple that one wonders how it lay so long undiscovered.

One night in 1829 the Reverend Patrick Bronte came home from Leeds bringing—somewhat surprisingly for so notoriously harsh a character—a set of wooden soldiers for Branwell. The Bronte children played with these, and built around them a fabric of wonder and adventure. Would not the playthings of genius gain from their experience a lasting and independent life? That was Pauline Clarke's thesis, which she developed with fine resourcefulness and consistency. (p. 117)

Writers tread the path of fantasy at their peril. This genre, in which the finest children's literature in our language has been cast, demands discipline and a voluntary sacrifice of tautology and sentimentality alike. Miss Clarke's book is a model for the study of this fine art. She allows herself a single improbability, that wooden soldiers can move and talk. Out of this the story grows naturally. There are no easy solutions, no short cuts. The story is slow, but tension is maintained, and increased, with firm control. The story is exciting, amusing, moving, and based solidly on the idea that the work of genius can matter, in a highly personal way, to small children.

There must nearly always be a doubt at the back of the minds of those charged with the award of the Carnegie Medal—is this not merely a good book but also one which represents the author at a little better than his best? No such doubt attaches to **The Twelve and the Genii.** In this book Pauline Clarke stood tip-toe, reaching upwards to an idea of the highest excellence, and stretching and refining her craft to match it with words, characters and narrative worthy of so rare a theme. (pp. 117-18)

Marcus Crouch, "1962: 'The Twelve and the Genii,' by Pauline Clarke," in Chosen for Children: An Account of the Books Which Have Been Awarded the Library Association Carnegie Medal, 1936-1975, *edited by Marcus Crouch and Alec Ellis, third edition, The Library Association, 1977, pp. 117-23.*

An unusual story by Pauline Clarke, **The Twelve and the Genii,** was awarded the Carnegie Medal in 1962, the judges being partly influenced, one suspects, by the 'literary' element in its theme. A small boy, Max, finds the twelve toy soldiers with which the Brontës played as children. The stories which the Brontës invented as they played with these soldiers are, of course, known and these are reenacted by the soldiers for Max and the reader. Though the plot sounds superficial, even meretricious, when summarised baldly like this, the book is very well done and holds attention while it is being read. But its 'other plane' aspects are not completely convincingly handled and there are aspects of it that are teasing and even exasperating to an adult reader. The soldiers themselves, for example: the author says that they are in a museum, but this is apparently not so; and, if they are lost and Max could not possibly have seen them anywhere (nor has he read about them or the adventures the Brontës played out with them) why should the soldiers and their stories suddenly come alive for this particular small boy? This is a tedious response, admittedly, but the fact that it is provoked by the book is a legitimate comment. Children at the right age can, of course, read the book as a straight adventure, without any such teasing doubts, simply as a story about a small boy who finds some soldiers who behave in what seems to children a natural enough way for toy soldiers. But if that is the author's intention the introduction of the Brontës seems unnecessary. (pp. 125-26)

> *Frank Eyre, "Fiction for Children 'The Twelve and the Genii',"* in his British Children's Books in the Twentieth Century, *revised edition, Longman Books, 1979, pp. 125-26.*

The small soldiers in **The Twelve and the Genii** are not strictly Lilliputians, they are the wooden soldiers which inspired the first stories of the Brontë children, rediscovered after more than a hundred years under the floorboards of an attic in a Yorkshire farmhouse. Played with by another sensitive and imaginative boy, they come literally to life for Max as they had done (at least through the activity of an intense imagination) for Branwell Brontë. Some of their adventures curiously repeat those described in *The History of the Young Men* and other Brontë juvenilia, while other adventures are entirely new, under their new Genius, Max.

As he becomes better acquainted with them, Max realizes that he has a strange mental rapport with the soldiers. Thoughts which he has not voiced are spoken by Butter Crashey, the Patriarch of the Twelves, of whom Branwell said: 'Revere this man Crashey, he is entrusted with secrets which you can never know'. By visualizing their actions in his mind, Max can discover what the soldiers have been doing—or is it that by imagining he creates their actions? The alternate 'freezing' and coming to life of the soldiers is another kind of metamorphosis, of wooden toy into sentient being, and touches on one of those deep springs of fantasy, so often sentimentalized and trivialized through overuse, and yet deeply moving in the hands of a master of serious fantasy like Hans Andersen. Pauline Clarke does the notion full justice—the soldiers are quarrelsome, rude, courageous and inventive.

There is something particularly persuasive in the notion that a toy, or a statue, in human or animal form, has a secret life of its own. Above all, in the case of a toy which has been invested with all the attributes of a complex personality by its owner, the assumption of the marvellous in the form of sentient life seems only a small step away from reality. Branwell Brontë's soldiers are a special case of a common phenomenon. All children pretend that favourite toys are alive. Few invest them with the passionate life with which Branwell and his sisters endowed the Twelves. These wooden soldiers were the originals of all the characters who peopled the imaginative worlds devised by the young Brontës, which formed the basis of a quite remarkable series of early literary compositions. For Charlotte, Emily and Anne, this was the training ground for their mature literary talents. For Branwell, the literary achievement stopped here. It is entirely convincing, in Pauline Clarke's novel, that the Twelves, having been made so vibrant with life by the Brontë children, should be awoken from a 'living death' by another boy of vivid imagination and passionate feelings, who has an instinctive sympathy for Branwell, the boy who promised so much, and achieved so little. This use of the marvellous thus opens up a new perspective for the reader, both a sense that anthropomorphic objects, sub-created in man's likeness as man is said to be in God's, may have a secret sentient life, and a sense that an object, a toy, upon which deep human emotional resources have been expended by someone of imaginative genius, may hold within itself some key to that genius and that emotion. (pp. 127-28)

> *Ann Swinfen, "Experience Liberated: 'The Twelve and the Genii',"* in her In Defence of Fantasy: A Study of the Genre in English and American Literature since 1945, *Routledge & Kegan Paul, 1984, pp. 127-28.*

Silver Bells and Cockle Shells (1962)

A pleasant volume of verse touches on many subjects from the joy of the seasons to the whimsy of make-believe characters. Many of the poems are based on old legends, others on holiday customs, but the book as a whole reflects Miss Clarke's many and varied interests. . . . These poems are ideal read-aloud material for third and fourth graders.

> *A review of "Silver Bells and Cockle Shells,"* in Virginia Kirkus' Service, *Vol. XXX, No. 19, October 1, 1962, p. 971.*

The range and imaginative thrust of the poems make us wish that they were written with a surer mastery. As it is, words like "exaltation" and "elusive" are totally out of place, and some of the rhythms are just too subtle for children. The real difficulty, however, is that this book was written for English children and should not have been presented in unaltered form to American youngsters to whom English saints' days are even more of a mystery than fog and tea.

> *William Turner Levy, "Voices That Know How to Say It in Verse,"* in The New York Times Book Review, *Part II, November 11, 1962, p. 3.*

To be successful, juvenile verse must please alike children and the adults who read to them, but this last is easily accomplished—the poems need only sound enough like other ones. Like popular songs, such poems never need break with conventions. Like all writing for children, it's just that they must never condescend or embarrass. And yet most of the poems written for children today seldom even run the risk of inclusion in the repertory, falling somewhere midway between the memorable and the merely benign.

I don't mean this as a harsh judgment on Miss Pauline Clarke's attractive collection. Her book of verses contains a bit of almost everything, from quasi-exotica in the manner of De la Mare to pastiches of folk material—counting rhymes, ballads and the like. The extremely derivative quality of all the poems can't be held too seriously against them, and they avoid falling into the kind of sophisticated archness that has become popular in many children's books of late, particularly those whose jackets describe them as being 'for the young of all ages' or the like (very common in the US). Still, it was a bit startling to come up against quite as strong an echo of a particular early Robert Graves poem as this:

> Where is the moon, o Robin Goodfellow?
> Down in the lake by the willow.
> Who brought her down from the
> heavens, then?
> I brought her down by her golden gown
> To trouble the minds of men.

One may also observe traces of Milne, Eleanor Farjeon and Stevenson here and there. But in general the variety of types of poem is both pleasing and instructive, and if Miss Clarke *were* to find a manner of her own, her poems might be something even more than that.

> *John Hollander, "Verses for Children," in* New Statesman, *Vol. LXV, No. 1679, May 17, 1963, p. 766.*

Five Dolls and the Duke   (as Helen Clare, 1963)

Dolls, to a child, are real people; they have personality, they have character, created for them by the owner. So, to countless children Helen Clare's stories of the Five Dolls must have given untold pleasure. She has the ability to enter into the mind of the child and to re-create the world of the dolls' house so that young readers will readily accept the phantasy which allows Elizabeth Small to step into that miniature world and be one with her family of five and their distinguished visitor the duke. (pp. 559-60)

> *F. P. Parrott, in a review of "Five Dolls and the Duke," in* The School Librarian and School Library Review, *Vol. 11, No. 5, July, 1963, pp. 559-60.*

Crowds of Creatures   (1964)

This is an unusual book which should prove useful on the classroom bookshelf. As its title implies, it deals with the collective names of various creatures. Starting with a pace of asses it works the usual menagerie to a herd of zebras, and finally to eggs which become a peep of chicks. Not all, however, are strictly according to the Oxford or to Webster. When there is no word available the author is more than equal to the moment and provides us with a trample of tigers and a dream of unicorns.

An attractive book with a nice bold type face. The illustrations [by Cecil Leslie] are highly competent within the limitations of two-colour printing. The illustrator would have made this an altogether exciting and memorable book given full colour, which is available on the continent if not here.

Nevertheless, a good buy for sevens to nines.

> *H. Millington, in a review of "Crowds of Creatures," in* The School Librarian and School Library Review, *Vol. 12, No. 3, December, 1964, p. 334.*

The Bonfire Party   (1966)

Two little sisters are getting excited about their bonfire party. Alison (6) is bossy, Jennett (4) is obligingly dependent. Friends are invited and mother makes a guy, christened Salty for his seamanlike appearance. For Alison, Salty is a person; almost too late, she realises he is to be burnt. The resolution of the problem is clever and satisfying—as indeed is the whole book, for an engaging humour does not hide the author's knowledge of how children feel and behave.

> *Margery Fisher, in a review of "The Bonfire Party," in* Growing Point, *Vol. 4, No. 9, April, 1966, p. 688.*

An ideal book for the child who is just beginning to read. The author uses simple but expressive words and skilful repetition in a lively tale of a little girl, who joined in all the fun of preparation for a bonfire party and then rescued the guy at the last moment.

> *F. P. Parrott, in a review of "The Bonfire Party," in* The School Librarian and School Library Review, *Vol. 14, No. 2, July, 1966, p. 253.*

Five Dolls in a House; Five Dolls and Their Friends   (as Helen Clare, 1967)

Five Dolls in a House and *Five Dolls and Their Friends* are omnibus volumes containing reprints of Helen Clare's penetrating and humorous microcosmic adventures of Elizabeth Small and the tenants of her dolls' house. The stories in these delightful volumes belong together and their new presentation, with the original illustrations by Cecil Leslie, is to be welcomed not as a mere reprint but as a bid for establishing the Five Dolls in the stream of outstanding works of English satirical fantasy for children.

> *"Over the Dream Wall," in* The Times Literary Supplement, *No. 3404, May 25, 1967, p. 451.*

Helen Clare's Five Dolls wear very well; there is a perennial joy for a child in imagining she can shrink and visit a dolls' house as Elizabeth does in these lively chronicles. These two volumes contain all five books published between 1953 and 1963. Re-reading them after a little while I found I had forgotten that they are laced with a light irony and that the author has, for all the simplicity of her prose, allowed herself as an adult to enjoy working out just how bossy Vanessa or sophisticated Lupin would respond to a certain domestic disaster or triumph. These are miniature novels, to be enjoyed by children around eight or so with a sense of fun.

> *Margery Fisher, in a review of "Five Dolls in a House" and "Five Dolls and Their Friends,"* in Growing Point, *Vol. 11, No. 7, January, 1973, p. 2083.*

The Two Faces of Silenus (1972)

Pauline Clarke's *The Two Faces of Silenus* has some delights also, but a good deal less humour [than Patricia Wrightson's *An Older Kind of Magic*]; the clumsiness of the title is not entirely overcome in the book. The localized magic is Italian—Roman—but perhaps that is just the trouble: the descriptions of the small Tuscan hill town read like a tourist brochure, if an unusually sensitive and well-written one.

Drusilla and Rufus, accompanying their parents to a conference, succeed in wishing the stone Silenus of the fountain alive; and with the little Italian boy they befriend, and . . . their respective parents, are given in turn their hearts' delight (Rufus, for instance, is made to recognize his potential as a writer, while Drusilla somewhat curiously overcomes her timidity and romps with lions, like Lyca in Blake's "Little Girl Lost"; Miss Clarke makes all the right archetypal noises). At the same time they fall under the evil shadow of Silenus's all-time enemy, the gorgon Medusa. The book culminates in a battle between their rival forces, in which the whole town is involved. It is very effectively done; and yet . . . perhaps Miss Clarke chose the wrong gods; Roman gods always were pale shadows of the Greek ones. At any rate one remembers the twelve Brontë soldiers of *The Twelve and the Genii* as much more essential, elemental presences.

> *"Keeping Magic in Its Place," in* The Times Literary Supplement, *No. 3687, November 3, 1972, p. 1325.*

[*The Two Faces of Silenus* is a] loving evocation of Umbria . . . . [It] starts, literally, with a bang. Rufus and Drusilla Greenwood, exploring a hill-town, throw coins into the fountain of Silenus, make a wish, and—bang, flash, crash—the stone face crumbles and Silenus (oldest Satyr, son of Pan) comes alive. Dru, Rufus, their friend Luigi first experiences panic, then a sense of vast well-being, of never-to-be-forgotten revelation and fulfillment.

Wherever joy in life is, there must evil also be. Medusa personifies this evil—unconvincingly, though. Nothing prepares the reader for her appearance halfway through the book. Now other weaknesses set in: Silenus's songs get a little sententious at times; and the Saturnalia toward the end is too frenetic and chaotic.

But the faults are minor. There is far more to admire and delight in: For instance, woods and wildflowers as bright and delicate as on Roman wall paintings; Rufus and Dru's unprettified brother-sister relationship; Dru and her mother's memorable quarrel; the way the mother and father count as people. And, above all, the author's lively enthusiasm for Roman civilization.

> *Doris Orgel, "Galoomphing along on the Wings of Pegasus," in* The New York Times Book Review, *November 15, 1972, p. 2.*

In *The Return of the Twelves,* the author made a highly successful use of the Brontës as the literary background of the story: in the present book, she relies on a more esoteric background. The past impinges on the present during a four-day visit of the Greenwoods to an Italian town which is drenched in reminders of an ancient era. Based on one of Virgil's eclogues, the story brings to life a fountain-statue of shaggy-haired, wine-loving, pipe-playing Silenus (son of Pan and companion of Bacchus) as well as snake-haired Medusa, who could turn people to stone. The fantasy begins when Rufus and Drusilla make a wish as they throw coins into Silenus' open stone mouth. To Rufus and Drusilla and to Luigi, a local boy, the magical experience of meeting these statues which come to life is full of puzzles—as it must be for the young reader. For seekers of fantasy, however, the unanswered questions will be unimportant, and avid readers will not worry about such unusual comments as Drusilla's "The whole thing reminds me of Comus." The story is ingenious, well-based, and dramatic. A gathering momentum and crisscrossing of events leads to a tremendous climax before all is stone again. Noteworthy are the moments of petrifaction and transformation of the children into animals by Medusa. Although many of the scenes are dependent on a knowledge of classical lore, the atmosphere of the book is charged with intensity. (pp. 594-95)

> *Virginia Haviland, in a review of "The Two Faces of Silenus," in* The Horn Book Magazine, *Vol. XLVIII, No. 6, December, 1972, pp. 594-95.*

This has one of the best opening sentences I have ever read, "The two explorers came to a simultaneous, silent full-stop, looking at an antique stone face". It is all pure fantasy, so fantastic that it could be true. Drusilla and Rufus are staying in a small Italian town where their father is attending a conference of mediaeval historians. As they stare at this stone face over a fountain they wish it alive, and suddenly the god, half man and half horse materialises. From here on he dominates their life and that of Luigi, an Italian boy they meet. Silenus is a happy man and he greatly influences not only the children but also their parents. The plot varies from reality to fantasy as the young people become more deeply involved; Medusa raises her ugly head and tries to turn them all to stone. Eventually Silenus returns to his waterbowl fountain and the book ends on a contented note, all those involved having benefitted deeply from their experience as will have the readers. The query is who will these be? I found I had to concentrate on every line and also that a fairly good knowledge of mythology was necessary to really appreciate the book. I hope twelve to fourteen-year-olds will be encouraged to read it, for it is a beautiful story and should prove an exciting experience for them. (p. 396)

> *J. Murphy, in a review of "The Two Faces of Silenus," in* The Junior Bookshelf, *Vol. 36, No. 6, December, 1972, pp. 395-96.*

Gillian Cross

1945-

English author of fiction.

Major works include *The Iron Way* (1979), *The Dark Behind the Curtain* (1982), *The Demon Headmaster* (1982), *On the Edge* (1984), *Chartbreak* (1986; U. S. edition as *Chartbreaker*), *Wolf* (1991).

One of England's most respected authors for children and young adults, Cross is celebrated as a gifted, versatile, and challenging writer whose works reflect a variety of genres, subjects, and themes and range in effect from chilling to hilarious. She is lauded for addressing many of the standard types of juvenile literature, such as realistic fiction, historical fiction, the school story, the adventure story, the mystery, the comic novel, the Gothic novel, and the psychological thriller in a fresh manner. In addition, she is recognized for her insight into provocative topics and is often acknowledged for creating books that are both suspenseful and thought-provoking. Fast-paced and filled with incident, her novels are noted both for their electrifying quality and their incisive explorations of human behavior. Cross is often praised for her successful interweaving of past and present as well as for her accurate delineation of both historical and contemporary backgrounds. Noted for their social realism, her works include such topics as terrorism, labor strikes, racial tensions, the effects of poverty, and the price of fame. Focusing on young male and female protagonists who are often considered loners or misfits, Cross outlines how the involvement of her characters in the world of adults brings about changes both in themselves and their situations. Through personal crises often involving the inner workings of their families, the protagonists are faced with dilemmas—usually regarding issues of personal freedom—that require them to make moral decisions and to change the way they view their lives; through their experiences, the characters become more self-confident and independent. Cross often weaves dark threads into her books with themes such as hatred, hostility, cowardice, malice, fear, and betrayal; several of her works also contain dealings with the supernatural as well as instances of cruelty, violence, and death. However, the stories often include humor and are noted for introducing young people both to the world of adults and to the sophistication of the adult novel. Called "a master of suspense" by critic Trev Jones, Cross is named by Margery Fisher as a "master in establishing through seemingly ordinary words an atmosphere of danger and disturbance. . . . "

Cross has said, "I like to write for children and young people because then I feel free to write about important things: love, death, moral decisions. . . . " Interested in books and stories since childhood, Cross received degrees in literature and philosophy and worked as a teacher of impaired teenagers as well as at the university level before beginning her career as a writer for children. Her first

book to receive critical attention was *The Iron Way,* a historical novel for young adults set in the period of British railway expansion; in this work, the coming of the railroad to a small Sussex village brings conflict to the lives of twelve-year-old Jem and his sixteen-year-old sister Kate, who become embroiled in the struggle between the villagers and the "navvies," or railroad workers. With the popular *Save Our School* (1981), a humorous story for primary graders, Cross introduces the characters Barny, Spag, and Clipper, who attempt to prevent the closing of their school through a variety of inventive schemes; in *The Mintyglo Kid* (1983), the children learn to manage Spag's spoiled cousin, while in *Swimathon!* (1986), the trio enter a swimming race to raise money for the repair of their school's vandalized minibus. Cross combines the school story with the ghost story in *The Dark Behind the Curtain,* a novel in which a school production of *Sweeney Todd* brings about the return of a group of ghostly children who once suffered under a Fagin-like master; when Colin, who is taking part in the play against his will, notices that his dominating friend Marshall is taking his role as Sweeney Todd too literally, he averts tragedy and helps to set the child spirits to rest. Cross is especially well known as the author of *The Demon Headmaster,* a school story with a humorous twist: in this book for primary graders, young Dinah thwarts the plans of her evil headmaster, who is hypnotizing his students in order to gain control of the country during a school quiz program; in *The Prime Minister's Brain* (1985), Dinah is drawn into another plot by the headmaster, who is now a computer director, to take over the world by brainwashing gifted students who are part of a national computer competition. In the mystery *On the Edge,* terrorist kidnappers try to brainwash the son of a prominent journalist in their plan to destroy the traditional family, while in *Wolf,* the father of fourteen-year-old Casey is a fugitive terrorist who holds her grandmother hostage in her home. In this award-winning novel which critic Brian Slough calls "an outstanding achievement in its genre" and Margaret Meek calls "a splendid, daring book," Casey confronts her father and his wolfish nature when she is sent to London to join her divorced mother, her mother's lover, and his son in a London squat and participates in their theatre-in-schools production of "Wolf." Cross parallels the story with information about the animal species that suggests that human behavior has taken on the negative characteristics which have often been associated with wolves. *Wolf* received the Carnegie Medal in 1991, an award for which *The Dark Behind the Curtain* was highly commended in 1983 and *Chartbreak* was commended in 1986. *The Dark Behind the Curtain* was a runner-up for the Guardian Award in 1983, while *On the Edge* was a runner-up for both the Whitbread Award in 1984 and the Edgar Award in 1986. Several of Cross's books have been named Best Books for Young Adults or Notable Books by the American Library Association in their respective years of publication.

(See also *Something about the Author,* Vol. 38, and *Contemporary Authors,* Vol. 111.)

AUTHOR'S COMMENTARY

I was nearly thirty when I wrote my first book. It seems extraordinary, now, that it took me so long to begin. Even when I was eight or nine, I used to invent titles for novels and write myself glowing reviews in my head. The actual books were beyond me (how did anyone write so many *words*?) but I practised for my future as An Author by writing self-conscious, arty little descriptions—when I could escape from making up cowboy stories to entertain my little brother.

At secondary school, as befitted a Budding Writer, I specialised in English Literature. And how daunting it was. All those metaphors and similes! The characterisation! The symbolism! How did anyone cram all those into a novel and still manage to tell a story?

My own attempts to write became stilted, never progressing beyond Chapter One, and I kept them secret from my friends—amusing them, instead, with an interminable serial story of which they were the heroines. I told it on the train journey home, making it up as I went along.

At University, I was still an Eng. Lit. student, and growing anxious, because it was time to stop Budding and start Writing Seriously. But by now I could hardly get past

Page One of anything I began. The more I studied, the more I understood the importance of every word. The nuances. The patterns of sound. The differences in register. Altering and realtering my own skimpy efforts. I wondered how anyone developed a style like the ones I analysed in my tutorials. It was a relief to forget the whole business and go home in the evening. There was no time to worry about my ambitions while I was playing with my little son, or telling him stories. He liked to hear his favourites over and over again. I particularly remember one I made up about a little blue car. After telling it every evening for a month, I knew the final, polished version by heart.

By the time my daughter was born, I was beginning a research degree, investigating decadent influences on G. K. Chesterton. Fascinating, intricate stuff, involving close analysis of language and literary developments. My own Great Novel had faded into the remote, improbable distance now that I knew how complex writing was. Anyway, I had no time for it with two children to entertain. My storytelling for them had progressed beyond the little blue car. Now I was making them picture books, and we joined a Children's Book Group, discovering a whole flood of marvellous children's books which we read together. It was very relaxing to read for pleasure, without having to dissect every sentence.

Then, one evening when everyone else in the family was out or asleep, I had a rare couple of hours to myself. I settled down with K. M. Peyton's *The Beethoven Medal* and, for the first time for years, I read a book through at a single gulp, utterly absorbed. I can remember coming to the surface at the end, dazed and blinking. As though a door in my mind had opened, I understood, at last, what I had been too stupid to see in years of studying. A novel is a *story*. All the other things—beautiful words, symbolism, imagery—would sneak in if the writer were skilful, but they couldn't be put there consciously, like glacé cherries stuck on top of a trifle. And all the time I was trying to do that, getting more and more pretentious on paper, I had been telling stories aloud, quite happily, whenever I could find an audience. *That was how novels got written.* Almost immediately, I began to write my first real book, and I sailed straight through from start to finish.

It was a very bad book. Quite unpublishable, although it took me a lot of rejection slips to realise it. But once I had finished it I was hooked and I went on and on writing. Finally, five books and three years later, I had something accepted and published, but even if that had never happened I think I would still be scribbling away compulsively, adding to my heap of tatty manuscripts.

And why do I write for *children?* Partly because, like me, they want books where things happen and character and relationships are expressed by actions, but also because I started to write when I stopped trying to be Shakespeare and began to enjoy myself as a storyteller. And children are the best audience in the world. (pp. 15-16)

Gillian Cross, "How I Started Writing for Children," in Books for Your Children, *Vol. 19, No. 2, Summer, 1984, pp. 15-16.*

GENERAL COMMENTARY

Margaret Carter

"I like books where things happen and character and relationships are expressed by actions" Gillian Cross has written and her enjoyment in writing is obvious. She knows that instruction and entertainment are not natural enemies although the varying backgrounds of her stories have obviously not been chosen deliberately to instruct. That they do so is at once incidental and integral to their plot and characterisation.

Plot springs from characterisation, we are always told, but characters are formed by the times we live in, what happens to us and where we live. Abby, Susan and Chris—the central characters in *Revolt at Ratcliffe's Rags*—would not have behaved as they did had they not lived where they did—on the edge of an area of small factories and underpaid labour—nor become involved in the fight for fair wages if the school had not suggested they write a *'project'* on something of local interest. Kate and Jem, in *The Iron Way,* live in Sussex when a man, their father, could be sent to Van Dieman's Land for poaching, and when local feeling was strong enough about the *'foreign'* labourers working on the new railway that tragedies follow their friendship with the Irish itinerant workers.

But a story cannot be a story unless there is change; when the book is closed the end must be different from the beginning—whether to circumstances, happenings or people. In Gillian Cross' stories it is the change in people which is most important and the constant in many of her books is of children—or near-children on the cusp of adolescence and adulthood—caught up into adult worlds and somehow changing those worlds by their actions, sometimes planned, sometimes fortuitous. Jem and Kate in *The Iron Way* provoke tragedy and perhaps cause the death of a friend through innocence and their inability to foresee that goodwill is not simple and can provoke tortuous results: Chris, Susan and Abby begin an adult campaign but cannot cope with its adult results: Paula in *Born of the Sun* observes and sorrows at the failings of adults whom she had thought beyond failure. There is the thread of romance in all Gillian Cross' stories, too: not the boy-meets-girl romance but the romance of change and adventure and *'the dark behind the curtain'* the title of another of her novels dealing with contemporary children engaged in making a stage play who are touched by dark emotional forces from the past: *Born of the Sun* tells of a search for the lost city of the Incas, the city which the last Inca ruler of Peru—Atahualpa—intended to be the last stronghold of his race. With her father, Paula sets out on the journey of exploration, but it is not only physical exploration which results but also emotional and mental and eventually it is only Paula who is privileged to see the ruins of the city and to bring back a small memento of the experience: physically small, that is, for she also brings back a new self.

> *Margaret Carter, "The Work of Gillian Cross," in* Books for Your Children, *Vol. 19, No. 2, Summer, 1984, p. 15.*

TITLE COMMENTARY

The Runaway (1979)

Denny has lost his parents in an accident and lives with Gran, under somewhat neglected circumstances, in a council flat. When Gran is taken ill and has to go into hospital, the immediate prospects for Denny aren't appealing. When the suited 'lady from the Council' arrives, obviously to place Denny in the local children's home, the time for action has arrived. Armed with Gran's £5 rent money and haunted by the apparition of Bouncer Bradley, the area's resident bully, Denny goes 'on the run'. Nachtar Singh, from a totally different environment, proves to be an unlikely ally and friend in his adventures. Contrived and unbelievable in any social realism sense, but taken purely as one-level fiction, it makes a very readable and enjoyable story.

> *B. B., in a review of "The Runaway," in* Books for Keeps, *No. 39, July, 1986, p. 17.*

[*The Runaway* is] a hide-and-seek tale which depends as much on character as on local colour. . . . A community opens up in this book, with racial tensions and financial problems adding an edge to the central problem of a boy fearful of his future, giving an authentic note to a story exciting in action and warm in feeling.

> *Margery Fisher, in a review of "The Runaway," in* Growing Point, *Vol. 25, No. 2, July, 1986, p. 4650.*

The Iron Way (1979)

If you want something . . . realistic about the lives of the 19th-century rural poor, and yet full of a sense of the excitement of the changes brought by the railways, *The Iron Way* by Gillian Cross will do you very well. Indeed Mrs. Cross's book is impressive not just in its own right, but as representative of the extraordinary professionalism of contemporary children's writers. The solidity of the research behind the historical stories, the quality of the writing almost throughout and the ability to ring new changes on familiar themes are very striking.

> *Alan Ryan, "Two at a Time," in* New Statesman, *Vol. 98, No. 2538, November 9, 1979, p. 729.*

The social issues explored in *The Iron Way* suggest rather older readers—eleven upwards—and so does the somewhat more complex plot, in which a country boy, ostensibly the central character, in fact makes little impression beside his elders and their pressing concerns. The true centre of the book, in fact, as suggested by the title, is the projected railway through the Sussex Downs to London, and historical facts are used to demonstrate the situation of the navvies whose wild ways disturb village families with lives barely changed for centuries. Young Jem's mother is dead, his father has been transported to Van Diemen's Land, and his tough sister Kate at sixteen is left to support the family, her life being further complicated by the hostility of her neighbours after she has taken Con O'Flynn as a lodger. The local smith and his associates lay explosives in a tunnel to ensure that the navvies' time contract is broken: Con, intervening, is killed by his own mates as a suspected spy; Kate hopes the railway, by widening people's horizons, will lessen their intolerance. The message is clear and well supported by the successive scenes, but I doubt whether the characters are real enough to make this a true piece of fiction rather than fact/fiction. (pp. 3620-21)

> *Margery Fisher, in a review of "The Iron Way," in* Growing Point, *Vol. 18, No. 5, January, 1980, pp. 3620-21.*

[*The Iron Way* is] a gripping story, with much to say about hostility, friendship, and loyalty. Personalities are sharply defined, mainly through dialogue, and the tension is painfully apparent throughout the course of events. The English dialect may intimidate some readers, but perseverance will be rewarded as the reader is caught up in the suspense.

> *Marilyn Kaye, in a review of "The Iron Way," in* Booklist, *Vol. 76, No. 9, January 1, 1980, p. 666.*

Revolt at Ratcliffe's Rags (1980)

Gillian Cross, the author of **Revolt at Ratcliffe's Rags,** is far less experienced than Bernard Ashley [, whose *Break in the Sun* is also reviewed]. Her style is sometimes clumsy, but her heart, like his, is full of admirable sympathy for loners and underdogs. Her novel **The Iron Way** was a likable story of the railway navvies of the past century. **The Runaway,** an unsophisticated contemporary story which was also published last year, gave no hint of the skill evident in **Revolt at Ratcliffe's Rags.** Like earlier Ashleys, the book is perhaps a little too heavily documented, but there is no doubt that Gillian Cross is now a writer to watch.

She has hit on an excellent theme a Grunwick-type strike among the women workers at a clothing factory which they are investigating for a school project. The three main characters, united only by their teacher's decision that they will work together on the project, are all real children, with the sort of "hurtful carelessness" children so often show even to their friends. All the children have problem parents of one sort and another. Abby is the daughter of "progressive" intellectuals (some nice satire here), Susan's father, embarrassingly, plays golf with the factory owner, and Chris's mother turns out to be a blackleg.

But the particular virtue of the book for me is that it not only tells a good story but admirably fulfils a role too often neglected by children's writers: it helps to fill in the pieces of the jig saw, to make more sense of that extraordinary adult world which touches children whether they like it or not.

> *Ann Thwaite, "Contemporary Fables," in* The Times Literary Supplement, *No. 4034, July 18, 1980, p. 807.*

Revolt at Ratcliffe's Rags presents a latter day Miss Redgrave up to her neck in a Sweat Shop Strike. The boss is yet another fanged Sheriff of Nottingham, stuffed to the eyeballs with Jaguars and moneybags. What saves this story from simply portraying a middle class socialist's view of the world is the shifting tide of convictions and loyalties. Parents goad children in every direction until these children are lost in the torrent which they have helped to undamn. It is a well-worked plot and powerfully told despite the predictable characters. Gillian Cross shows a craftsman's skill, even though her ending is a little self-conscious. Will the workers' cooperative fail after the flags and the trumpets fade?

> *Peter Fanning, "Nasties in the Woodshed," in* The Times Educational Supplement, *No. 3361, November 21, 1980, p. 32.*

It is unusual for a writer with a feel for history as displayed in **The Iron Way** to write also with the sureness of the present day which Mrs Cross displays here. **Revolt at Ratcliffe's Rags** starts with Abby, Susan and Chris undertaking a project to study a local factory. They choose a small clothing factory because Chris's mother works there. In the heat of the moment Abby incites a strike and Susan and Chris are unwillingly drawn in. They are then taken over by the momentum of events and the ending is somewhat predictable, but the fine writing and characterization make that unimportant. Abby, Susan and Chris are individuals, a product of their up-bringing; one trendy, one working-class and one terrifyingly middle-class. They are drawn together by the situation and their differences are what make this story so alive: Abby with the ideals of the young, Susan under-confident but finding the courage to stand up to her parents, and Chris seeing his parents in a new light. This is a challenging novel for ages thirteen and upwards.

> *Janet Fisher, in a review of "Revolt at Ratcliffe's Rags," in* British Book News, *Winter, 1980, p. 715.*

An excellent English novel on a subject unusual in children's books—labor problems and a workers' revolt against high-handed management practices. Susan Grantley, Abby Proctor, and Chris Benton are classmates assigned to do a school project together on factories. A trio of more dissimilar young people would be hard to imagine—neat, obedient Susan with untidy, rebellious, and bright Abby, who are close friends; and Chris, who is detached and quiet—a loner. Struggling to put their project together, Chris reluctantly tells them about the clothing factory where his mother works. When they go to look at it, they realize that conditions are outrageous; the workers, for example, must frequently work overtime without previous notice, or be fired. Abby cannot understand why the workers have not organized, and she proceeds to persuade them to do so while Chris and Susan watch in horror. The undertaking grows, and Abby is surprisingly successful, appearing on TV and organizing a large demonstration; the other two help where they can. But the strike is a failure, for the owner merely closes the factory for good, and Abby drops the cause. Chris and Susan, however, having become more independent, carry on to a modestly hopeful conclusion. The portrayal of most of the characters, even of the minor ones, is outstanding; and the dismal slum scenes are effectively presented.

> *Ann A. Flowers, in a review of "Revolt at Rat-cliffe's Rags," in* The Horn Book Magazine, *Vol. LVI, No. 6, December, 1980, p. 647.*

Save Our School (1981)

Save Our School describes the efforts of a graceless trio, led by an infant Napoleon brilliantly named Barny Gobbo, to prevent the threatened closure of the Bennett Junior School, a "horrid place" until made desirable by its imminent surcease. A variety of ludicrous schemes, culminating in a perilous "sit-in" only lead them into trouble but success comes, of course, from an unexpected direction. Racy, frequently vulgar and abounding in character, Barny, Spag and Clipper—two boys and a girl—are as real and recognizable as the streets among which they live.

> *Anne Carter, "Encouraging Stories," in* The Times Literary Supplement, *No. 4069, March 27, 1981, p. 340.*

It is good to have laughed out loud at a story and **Save Our School** makes the reader do this several times. Barney decides to save his school from closure and involves his friends, Clipper and Spag. His ideas go sadly wrong but all ends well. The scenes of life in an old school building and at the various homes of the three are beautifully drawn and the warmth and humour of the story come spilling over the pages. A welcome read for sevens to elevens and useful with older, less able children as the humour is universal. (pp. 21-2)

> *Janet Fisher, in a review of "Save Our School," in* British Book News, *Children's Supplement, Spring, 1981, pp. 21-2.*

The crusaders in **Save Our School** are energetically and forcefully characterised—Spag, who is clever and spectacled, Clipper, restless, wisecracking and black, and Barny whose nickname of Gobbo, basically a variant of his surname, suits his fat, lackadaisical nature. The given characters hardly develop in the story but they do serve to hold together a series of scenes in which the children man a float for a street demonstration, paint pictures of the school and write propaganda essays. None of their enterprises alters the situation until Barny's mother, finding letters they had written to the newspapers and put aside for lack of confidence, posts them after all, with predictable results. In spite of a cheerful style and plenty of incidental humour, there is hardly enough particularity to make this more than a routine piece of fiction.

> *Margery Fisher, in a review of "Save Our School," in* Growing Point, *Vol. 20, No. 2, July, 1981, p. 3911.*

A Whisper of Lace (1981)

[*A Whisper of Lace*] is not as the title might suggest romantic as well as historical, although it must be said that the heroine does have "over-heated brown eyes" and a "mobile mouth". In fact it is a dashing tale of contraband, ruthless blackmail and escape. The young crippled Daniel and his tomboyish sister, Selina, had always played at being pirates. On the return of one of their elder brothers, the cool, mocking Francis, Selina who is bored and impatient with her life becomes involved in a glamorous real-life smuggling adventure. Only Daniel and his new friend, the sensible servant girl Betty, realize the genuine danger of the escapade, and to them falls the task of saving the day.

The plot is kept moving, but the characters seem to be chosen from a manual of stereotypes, and the inevitable pointers—"unfashionably" flushed cheeks, the "fastidiously" taken pinch of snuff—live only within the safe confines of the cliché.

> *Cara Chanteau, "The Stuff of Fiction," in* The Times Literary Supplement, *No. 4086, July 24, 1981, p. 842.*

This well-told adventure story of earlier days has a touch of Baroness Orczy and Jeffery Farnol, but with a modern and satisfying realism of character. Crippled Dan Merrowby and Betty the rocker, niece of the drunken old family nurse, find themselves at the heart of a smuggling plot masterminded by a ruthless stranger who has a hold on both Francis Merrowby and the sinster Whispering Zak, known to Betty from her earlier days as an exploited Honiton lace-maker. The reader experiences both setting and events almost physically through the writer's vivid sensual descriptions, with their Dickensian metaphors and similes. She knows about the social life of both rich and poor in (presumably) early nineteenth-century Devon, and draws convincingly the emotions of Betty, torn between humanity and indignation at the smuggled Chantilly lace which will ruin native lacemakers, and the impotent Dan trying to save his daredevil sister Selina, who has deserted him for real adventure with Francis.

> *M. Hobbs, in a review of "A Whisper of Lace," in* The Junior Bookshelf, *Vol. 45, No. 5, October, 1981, p. 207.*

Set in the days when smugglers were hanged, this is a story which involves the reader by both vivid characterisation and the unusual twists of the plot. One feels for young Daniel Merrowby, bereft of a companion since his older sister has become a fine lady. She could not play her games without him, and would urge him on, yelling 'Keep up, Morgan, me old shipmate! I can't board this vessel alone!', so that he forgot his lame leg. Accused now of tagging along, he does his best to protect the headstrong Selina from the dangers into which she is straying.

The writing is subtle, and one's view of the characters keeps changing. Francis Merrowby, presented initially as a sweet-tempered contrast to his priggish older brother George (who is not quite what he seems either), shows an unkind edge to his teasing, and is eventually revealed as a shallow and cowardly young man; while the chilling old villain Zachary has at the last considerable stature. My own favourite is Daniel's reluctant helper, the little servant-girl Betty. I was fascinated by the details of lace-making in Honiton, from which she has 'escaped' to help her aunt nurse the Merrowby baby. In spite of all its hardships and humiliations, this is a step up in her world.

The book grips to the end, and is the kind about which one thinks: 'Good, still two more pages. What will happen now?'

> *Rodie Sudbery, in a review of "A Whisper of Lace," in* The School Librarian, *Vol. 29, No. 4, December, 1981, p. 340.*

In *A Whisper of Lace* Gillian Cross brilliantly puts the stagy conventions of costume fiction ("The post-chaise crunched up the sloping gravel", reads the first sentence) at the service of a real sense of history's complexity. The exciting and melodramatic events are scarely credible, but the feelings and conflicts to which they give shape are absolutely convincing. The reader gets the best of both worlds: a thrilling full-blooded adventure, suspenseful and mysterious, and a closely-textured study of character and emotion. . . .

The character of Betty and her perception of the wider implications of Francis and Selina's foolishness, opens the book out in a remarkable and stimulating way. But even without her it would be well worth reading. It is pacy, accessible, and cuttingly precise in its use of realistic detail to prop up its splendidly unrealistic story.

> *Neil Philip, "Blackmail and Old Lace," in* The Times Educational Supplement, *No. 4123, April 9, 1982, p. 29.*

The Dark Behind the Curtain (1982)

In the child's critical vocabulary "scary" ranks high among the accolades. Gillian Cross promises well from her first page, with a schoolboy actor's macabre portrayal of Sweeney Todd—and, let it be said at once, she delivers generously thereafter. The famous melodrama is being rehearsed by Miss Lampeter, a dedicated follower of fashionable theories. She knows all about "total involvement", which she tirelessly and all too successfully demands from her pupils, but she has not the common sense to realize the imprudence of allowing her juvenile demon barber to wield his grandfather's actual cut-throat razor on stage.

This lad, the clever and monstrous Marshall, dominates the class, at once popular, admired and feared, whereas poor Jackus, school misfit and suspected pilferer, is a reluctant participant, foisted upon a hostile cast for strictly remedial and non-artistic reasons. Mysterious occurrences punctuate the rehearsals. Pencils fly through the air, private possessions vanish, rows of library books cascade from their shelves, pots of scene-paint spill and spread across the floor, lunch sandwiches are disgustingly nibbled by unknown teeth. Jackus seems to the other children the obvious culprit. Only the reader knows his innocence, and, as the author piles on the spookiness and suspense— culminating with a naked footprint in the paint—is led to the inescapable conclusion that these are true psychic phenomena. Marshall has become so totally involved, so convincing an incarnation of bygone evil, that he has stirred

up not one poltergeist but a whole pack, the restless spirits of exploited Victorian children.

Gillian Cross has a practised icy hand at producing a delicious frisson. She can curdle the blood and at the same time, paradoxically, send it racing through the veins as the apprehension gathers. Everything is concentrated into a well-wrought plot, a handful of vividly-drawn characters, and a unity of setting, oppressively enclosed. Quite deliberately, one presumes, she is vague about ages, home backgrounds, and even the type of school, apart from a mention of homework and blazers. This, the young reader is meant to feel, with a nervous glance over his shoulder, could be happening anywhere.

> *Geoffrey Trease, "Curdling the Blood," in* The Times Literary Supplement, *No. 4138, July 23, 1982, p. 788.*

[*The Dark Behind the Curtain* is a] chilling story. . . .

The stories of past and present are skilfully interwoven. The pace is fast, the suspense tremendous, the book an outstanding blend of subtlety and excitement. As ghost story and school story alike, this excellent novel will appeal widely to readers over ten.

> *Peter Hollindale, in a review of "The Dark Behind the Curtain," in* British Book News, Children's Supplement, *Autumn, 1982, p. 19.*

The author has already written several books which have been praised, notably *The Iron Way.* Each book has been different in scope and character and this one is no exception.

This is a grim story, suffused by malice, hatred and the betrayal of trust. It makes compulsive reading, however, for the build-up of atmosphere is powerfully contrived. The supernatural presences are somewhat difficult to accept, but the violence and cruelty are there indisputably, an unpleasant reminder of what happens in the real world today.

> *E. Colwell, in a review of "The Dark Behind the Curtain," in* The Junior Bookshelf, *Vol. 46, No. 5, October, 1982, p. 197.*

Gillian Cross uses her power to evoke historical atmosphere (I remember *The Iron Way* with pleasure)— obliquely in this modern, school ghost story. . . . A perceptive, exciting and well-controlled story with memorable characters—enthusiastic drama teacher, understanding headmaster, and powerfully-threatening Marshall. I found it gripping.

> *Dorothy Nimmo, in a review of "The Dark Behind the Curtain," in* The School Librarian, *Vol. 30, No. 4, December, 1982, p. 358.*

The Demon Headmaster (1982)

The Demon Headmaster would, I suppose, qualify as a rattling good yarn, with the overtones of science-fiction to add savour to an old theme. Dinah and her foster brothers are at a school dominated by a strange, green-eyed headmaster who holds most of the school in hypnotic thrall.

Only a handful of pupils resist his spell and at the last minute succeed in thwarting his plans to dominate the country through the television screen during a school quiz programme. The book contains a television compère who specializes in revolting gimmicks and humiliation for his victims. The author carries this caricature to the point of absurdity, although the intended reader would probably not object as much as an adult would. . . . But the school atmosphere is rather well caught and this book will undoubtedly appeal more to children than to their parents.

> *Ann Martin, "Forms of Believability," in* The Times Literary Supplement, *No. 4146, September 17, 1982, p. 1002.*

[How Dinah thwarts the Headmaster's dastardly plot] will delight readers of this fearsome extravaganza. The story moves at a good pace. The preposterous plot unfolds so rapidly that its absurdity is unnoticed. Girls may not take to it so much as boys but uncritical thirteen year olds of either sex will find it highly amusing.

> *D. A. Young, in a review of "The Demon Headmaster," in* The Junior Bookshelf, *Vol. 46, No. 6, December, 1982, p. 229.*

This very British import has plenty of creepy moments. . . . Briticisms abound, but this is so suspenseful that engrossed readers should be able to ignore them. The malevolent mood is well described and hardly needs the black-and-white illustrations [by Gary Rees and Mark Thomas] scattered throughout. (pp. 1336-37)

> *Ilene Cooper, in a review of "The Demon Headmaster," in* Booklist, *Vol. 79, No. 20, June 15, 1983, pp. 1336-37.*

[Though] there are strong elements of humour in *The Demon Headmaster,* it is making important points about independence of mind, about certain kinds of cowardice, and about sibling relationship, through its fantastic tale of a head who hypnotises his whole school (and Tomorrow the World?) until a difficult girl and the boys in whose family she is fostered find a way to defeat him.

> *Audrey Laski, "More Than Readers," in* The Times Educational Supplement, *No. 3656, July 25, 1986, p. 21.*

The Mintyglo Kid (1983)

Denzil—the Mintyglo kid—is left to stay with his cousin while his parents claim their prize cruise. His cousin, Spag, is worried; and his friends Barny and Clipper . . . soon discover why. Denzil has been brought up by his over-indulgent mother to regard 'self-expression' as the ultimate necessity—and his own ideal excuse for the mishaps he revels in causing. This promising theme is executed with a series of escapades that Tyke Tiler and Gowie Corby would enjoy; less characterisation, less plot, less demanding language, but amusing and quick fire none the less, ending with an exciting, last-over-result cricket match.

This book would be useful for encouraging readers who need plenty of comic-strip action to sustain their interest.

The line drawings [by Gareth Floyd]—reminiscent perhaps of Papas—capture the essentials of the plot well; and the Mintyglo kid, far from crushed at the end of the book, is left alive—and kicking . . .

> *Graham Chase, in a review of "The Mintyglo Kid," in* The School Librarian, *Vol. 31, No. 2, June, 1983, p. 139.*

The book is full of very funny exploits, although it sometimes lacks continuity. It maintains throughout, however, a progressive tone. Clipper (black and female) leads a small gang of white boys; ageism—like racism and sexism now rightly recognised and condemned—is niftily countered in the text when an elderly character, who is confined to a wheel-chair, cannily gives Clipper & Co a vital clue to the understanding of Spag's unco-operative cousin.

> *Mary Cadogan, "High Flyers and Dragon Slayers," in* Books and Bookmen, *No. 357, July, 1985, p. 25.*

Born of the Sun (1983)

Fortunate the adolescents who cope with changes in their attitude to parents gradually and painlessly. Gillian Cross poses a situation of extreme crisis, making it believable partly by distancing the scene from the domestically familiar and partly by the strength of her character-drawing. *Born of the Sun* concerns a small private expedition to the Peruvian jungle initiated by explorer Karel Staszic, who through a document found in the Vatican library has been put on the track of the lost city of the Emperor Atahualpa. Only his wife Jean knows that Karel is seriously ill and that this is a desperate last effort in a life of varying success. His 'teenage daughter has to find this out gradually as she sees her father's hysterical energy overcome by physical weakness, his judgment distorted by manic impulses. The gruelling journey over mountains, across a river, through tropical forest, is described in almost brutal detail as the only possible accompaniment to such a crucial experience, and whatever one feels about the final twist of fortune which reverses Karel's illness, Paula's enforced understanding of her parents and of herself is honestly shown as an inevitable welding of sorrow and the lightening of spirit that comes from maturity in sight. Melodramatic and tense action, this is a tale of individuality put to the test.

> *Margery Fisher, in a review of "Born of the Sun," in* Growing Point, *Vol. 22, No. 5, January, 1984, p. 4189.*

While Cross' symbolic reach may occasionally exceed her writer's grasp, *Born of the Sun* is an exciting adventure story which charts not only Paula's journey to the lost city of Atahualpa but also to an implied destination of self-discovery. What Paula learns about herself, her emerging capabilities and her relationships with others will interest and inform the large readership this book will, no doubt, enjoy.

> *Michael Cart, in a review of "Born of the Sun," in* School Library Journal, *Vol. 31, No. 8, April, 1985, p. 96.*

On the Edge (1984)

On the Edge, a title which refers to the mind as well as to the hills. . . .

The "Free People" in *On the Edge* . . . are committed to destroying the nuclear family, which they see as the chief mechanism for maintaining capitalist oppression. Having exploded bombs on crowded beaches, they now take a boy hostage and demand state homes for teenagers and the abolition of parental tax reliefs. But the story is not at all as crude as this may suggest. The kidnapping was unplanned, a hasty response to the discovery by the boy's mother, a journalist, that the gang is preparing to blow up the highest family in the land. The boy is captured to ensure her silence and the demands are a blind. The cause the terrorists are fighting for is thus integral to the plot: this is not just another hostage adventure but a study of why and how far families matter. The mother is in a trap whichever way she turns, while her son is forced by his captors to treat them as parents until he doubts his own identity. Two local families become involved, each with its own tensions and loyalties, and in each another teenager establishes his or her freedom from parental domination. The captive overcomes his self-doubt by remembering things about himself that are his own, including his delight in running, and in the end he becomes independent from both his real and his substitute mothers in a triumphant sprint along the Edge. Despite some unrealistic details, this is an ingenious and stimulating book.

> *Dominic Hibberd, "Family Feelings," in* The Times Literary Supplement, *No. 4270, February 1, 1985, p. 130.*

[*On the Edge*] takes a hackneyed plot and uses it to point to the genuine pressures and dangers of our time in an incisive way that suggests the book belongs in a readership of early or mid-'teens, and to thoughtful readers at that. The 'Edge' of the title is an outcrop on Derbyshire moors where a kidnapped boy, son of investigative journalist Harriet Shakespeare, is submitted to brainwashing by a man and woman who, for differing reasons, belong to a freedom group pledged to destroy traditional family patterns in the interests of revolution. The changing relationship between Tug and his captors is piercingly real to the reader and just as real are the actual events of the story, as Jinny at the farm grows curious about the boy in the neighbouring cottage and gradually discovers who he is. Most important of all, Tug realises as he escapes (and a completely plausible escape it is) just how binding and yet how liberating his feelings for his mother can be. Gillian Cross explores human pressures and problems within the framework of tales of action with increasing strength and commitment, and this new example has enough substance to engage readers well into the 'teens.

> *Margery Fisher, in a review of "On the Edge," in* Growing Point, *Vol. 23, No. 6, March, 1985, p. 4390.*

The terrorist theme made me think of Peter Dickinson's *Seventh Raven.* Not that this one is as clever or as well written, but its immediacy and tension are as great. Gillian Cross keeps you sweating almost to the last page.

This is the story of two young people, very different in background and character and initially separated in space, but brought together by the chance of a terrorist coup. It is also about identity and being true to your own idea. . . . The climax is swift, exciting and not entirely incredible.

Gillian Cross is particularly good with Jinny and her family and the relationships they have established in the village. Tug and his 'parents' are perhaps less convincing, but then they are a much more complex proposition. Doyle and The Woman, who are committed to imposing on the rest of society their own childhood misery and the hatred it has generated, ought to be terribly real as they build up the pressure on Tug, but somehow we don't quite go along with them. It is a near thing, and I am grateful to Gillian Cross for the experience of her book, but it does, I feel, fall just short of greatness; and it is a measure of her ability that we expect her to be great. A powerful novel for all that; it leaves the reader with a feeling of exhaustion and with some fundamental questions waiting to be answered. (pp. 87-8)

> *M. Crouch, in a review of "On the Edge," in* The Junior Bookshelf, *Vol. 49, No. 2, April, 1985, pp. 87-8.*

As the title suggests, Gillian Cross has crafted a tense, compelling adventure-mystery in which the lives of two adolescents move on convergent tracks to a chilling dénouement. Action is concentrated in a ten-day period, matched by the stark sentences which heighten tension through their staccato rhythms. . . . How [Jinny Slattery] unravels the mystery, persuades the authorities of the truth, and penetrates the hide-out are the principal stages of plot development in a stunning psychological thriller. . . . The final scene is a real chiller, as the couple posing as Tug's parents offer the boy a Hobson's choice—and one slim chance for freedom. The cover, showing Tug tracked by a shotgun, is guaranteed to attract readers—who will not be disappointed by the content, for the story is a cut above the ordinary mystery with intriguing characters and a provocative theme.

> *Mary M. Burns, in a review of "On the Edge," in* The Horn Book Magazine, *Vol. LXV, No. 1, July-August, 1985, p. 453.*

The Prime Minister's Brain (1985)

In *The Prime Minister's Brain* the computer-crazy heroine is drawn into a chilling enterprise in which geniuses are brainwashed into gaining control of the country, no less. Gillian Cross is particularly skilful in exploiting the fun to be had from the word-play of computerspeak. Younger readers will enjoy the humour, pace and action; older, more sensitive interpreters will read the gentle message about the dangers in the hypnotic power of the technology.

> *Colin Mills, in a review of "The Prime Minis-*

ter's Brain," in British Book News Children's Books, *March, 1986, p. 30.*

This seems to be the second book about SPLAT (the Society for the Protection of our Lives Against Them), and here again the six members are up against a character called the Demon Headmaster (though he has now become a Computer Director). It would appear from the book's last sentence that further confrontations are planned. They should go down well with readers who like fast-moving, far-fetched stories.

In this one, dozens of children who have proved themselves clever at computer games are incarcerated together and forced to use their abilities in an attempt to break into the Prime Minister's private computer, so that the Demon Headmaster can take over the government of the country (and eventually of the world). Dinah is among the chosen Brains, and the other five members of SPLAT track her through the rubbish chutes of an eerie skyscraper run by robots. The story is a little unconvincing (particularly the part when every child chooses to risk being burned alive rather than let the Demon Headmaster get away with his devilish plans); and I was more aware than I like of the author working hard to differentiate between her characters. My sixteen-year-old tester, however, thought it was the best book she has come across for ages. (pp. 67-8)

> *Rodie Sudbery, in a review of "The Prime Minister's Brain," in* The School Librarian, *Vol. 34, No. 1, March, 1986, pp. 67-8.*

Computer technology is a monster. Like a gigantic octopus it has entangled a whole generation in its tentacles. . . .

The octopus is an apt central motif for Gillian Cross's entertaining new book, **The Prime Minister's Brain.** Once again the six children who form SPLAT (the Society for the Protection of our Lives Against Them) are up against the hypnotic powers of the Demon Headmaster—this time channelled through the waving arms of an octopus which is part of a computer game.

With this, his second outing, the headmaster has become even more demonically ambitious. The computer game is part of a national competition, the winners being invited to his computer-controlled Saracen Tower in London. Once there, they are forced to become a junior brain-bank, connected to a mainframe and ordered to crack the code of the Prime Minister's computer itself. Today 10 Downing Street; tomorrow, the world. The headmaster plans to hypnotize just about everybody and only SPLAT can stop him.

What follows is a light-hearted and engaging battle between Orwellian efficiency and youthful chaos. While computer-regulated meals are served to the young conscripts (each and every portion exactly the same) the SPLAT gang have to fight their way through a talking door, an aggressively automatic store-room and a rubbish chute, all of which live up to their names. The chapters cut between the two groups, between brain and brawn perhaps, with a series of well-managed cliff-hangers building to a genuinely exciting climax.

Gillian Cross launched an idea for an almost limitless series with **The Demon Headmaster,** to which this is a sequel. She has given her new book an intriguing title. And in the headmaster she has created that most compelling of villains; a man motivated not by greed or lust for power but by the simple conviction that his dream of an ordered and efficient world is right.

And yet **The Prime Minister's Brain** doesn't quite live up to the idea. The actual execution is rather childish. The fantasy fails to grip because the author has all too casually dismissed any semblance of reality. The very premise of the book—the arrival of the competitors at Saracen Tower—is so unlikely as to be implausible. Why are none of the children escorted? They aren't even provided with a proper address. And although the breaking of the Prime Minister's code is funny, it happens so quickly and so simply that the effect is too contrived to be truly satisfying.

There is also a distinction to be drawn between childish and childlike. If the overall perception was childlike, it might be easier to give in to the spirit of the thing. But Cross often seems out of sympathy with children as they really are today. Her characters cannot tell fibs without a show of remorse. Let loose in London, they can hardly wait to visit the Science Museum. "We played all sorts of games . . .", one character enthuses, but he's quick to add, ". . . and learnt some things as well." Is this not a little too responsible? It rings as false as some of the oaths used by another young boy: "Thundering hamburgers!" and "What a naughty tarradiddle!" It goes without saying, though, that none of this is likely to concern its intended readership who will enjoy **The Prime Minister's Brain** and look forward to the next, appearance of the Demon Headmaster.

> *Anthony Horowitz, "Tapping the Junior Brain-Bank," in* The Times Literary Supplement, *No. 4328, March 14, 1986, p. 286.*

He's back—and a good thing too. Gillian Cross's Demon Headmaster was far too enjoyable a character for one novel alone, and here he is again this time running an evil empire based on computer games. Those who enjoy such pursuits themselves will find more for them in this engagingly diverting story than most. Those who simply like an exciting, intriguing plot will be equally happy.

> *N. Tucker, in a review of "The Prime Minister's Brain," in* Books for Your Children, *Vol. 21, No. 1, Spring, 1986, p. 17.*

Swimathon! (1986)

Following **Save our School** and **The Mintyglo Kid,** here is a third tale about Spag and Gammy and West Indian Clipper in rivalry with nasty Thrasher and his big brother Tiny, who do everything they can to prevent the three resourceful children from playing their part in a sponsored swimming race to raise money for the repair of the vandalised school minibus. Two of the three pupils are confident of their skill but they find it hard to conceal the fact that Clipper, a crack athlete, in fact can't swim; this awkward fact provides an element of tension in a brisk, jokey story of youthful effort which readers in the early 'teens may find themselves comparing with their own experience of extra-curricular events.

Margery Fisher, in a review of "Swimathon!" in Growing Point, *Vol. 25, No. 4, November, 1986, p. 4716.*

An easy, uncomplicated story, with little depth to plot or character analysis. This is a book for a Middle Junior child to gobble up.

The tale revolves around a vandalised school minibus, and how the pupils resolve to raise money to renovate the vehicle. The three main characters, Clipper, Spag and Barry . . . organise a Swimathon, and their subsequent problems are all linked with this event. How they succeed in demolishing their opponents, in spite of the handicap of Clipper being a non-swimmer, is rather far-fetched, but all's well that ends well.

Nigel Spencer, in a review of "Swimathon!" in Books for Keeps, *No. 49, March, 1988, p. 19.*

Chartbreak   (1986; U. S. edition as *Chartbreaker*)

The technical side of **Chartbreak** should appeal to rock-enthusiasts, even if they are surprised to see how much agonising discipline and dispute goes on behind the scenes before the apparent spontaneity of performance. The first-person narrative should be congenial too, with its rough-edged sentences and crackles of adolescent exuberance—young Janis comments, as slowly she is welded into the group, 'Whatever we did, the songs limped like geriatric crocodiles' and later she rates a sentimental ballad sung by a rival group as 'turgid as old semolina'. A sequence of gigs, auditions and recordings, of venal agents and dodgy promoters, of cold, hungry tours and unexpected moments of luxury, go to make up a story to hold attention, but dominating it is the stormy relationship of Christie, determined to mould the group in his way, and 'Finch', fighting for independence. The raw, jerky style of the narrative, the recurring symbol of the *nunchaku*, the metal sticks and chain which, with Finch's karate gestures, enforce the almost brutal atmosphere of *Kelp's* performances, the terse, matter of fact irony of their lyrics, all contribute to the effect of a book which offers an honest view of one kind of sexual attraction and antagonism and an equally honest, exacting view of the pains which perfectionist performers must suffer if they are to achieve their goal. An old theme which Gillian Cross has brought up to date memorably. (pp. 4759-60)

Margery Fisher, in a review of "Chartbreak," in Growing Point, *Vol. 25, No. 6, March, 1987, pp. 4759-60.*

Into this thoroughly consistent and uncompromising first-person narrative, Cross packs a great deal: bitter satire of rock entrepreneurship; a sympathetic understanding of New Wave Music and of the significance of rock video; and memorable, sharply-etched characters whose names encapsule their personalities. She also breaks up the well-paced narrative with eye-catching devices that help tell the story (rock concert reviews; a love-lorn column; an inter-

view; and an obituary of Finch's mother). An engrossing pathbreaker, bringing the rhythms and rhymes of rock music in the '80s to the young adult novel.

Jack Forman, in a review of "Chartbreaker," in School Library Journal, *Vol. 33, No. 7, April, 1987, p. 108.*

The story is told by Finch herself at the height of the band's fame, as if she were relating the facts for a documentary. It is interspersed with realistic clippings from major rock magazines. It is a hard-hitting story, and successfully avoids the clichés that this type of novel can so easily fall into. The reader is immediately drawn into the plot, and the build-up towards the climax is so powerful that I found myself unable to put it down until I had finished it. A thoroughly enjoyable book with a language and style which will make it very accessible to young people.

Anne Everall, in a review of "Chartbreak," in The School Librarian, *Vol. 35, No. 3, August, 1987, p. 252.*

The contemporary music scene becomes the backdrop for an impelling story of a troubled teen and her metamorphosis from angry, unappreciated schoolgirl into rock star. As insistent as a music video, the story vibrates with emotion, believable because of its central character and narrator, Janis Finch. Cross has prevented her plot from becoming another cliché in the confessional genre by treating it as a lengthy interview, interspersed with commentaries from the popular press. The contrast between the real Janis and "Finch," her stage name and public image, adds tension and creates drama. Basically, her Cinderella story is the reason for the media hype that threatens to overwhelm her. As she sets the record straight, the complex emotions that make her an individual are gradually revealed. . . . Although skillfully foreshadowed, the conclusion has the impact of a surprise ending. Like Bruce Brooks in *Midnight Hour Encores,* Cross has used her knowledge of a particular kind of music to develop a story and a personality. That knowledge adds interest and gives verisimilitude to the narrative, but iconoclastic, vulnerable Finch gives it life. (pp. 614-15)

Mary M. Burns, in a review of "Chartbreaker," in The Horn Book Magazine, *Vol. LXIII, No. 5, September-October, 1987, pp. 614-15.*

Roscoe's Leap   (1987)

A chilling psychological drama from a master of suspense. A young man researching Roscoe's Leap, the 200-year-old home of an eccentric millionaire, upsets the tightly controlled household in which 15-year-old Hannah and 12-year-old Stephen live with their mother. On the other side of the house, whose two wings are built on either side of a waterfall, live mad Great-Uncle Ernest Roscoe, grandson of the original owner; and Doug, his nephew and companion. The atmosphere of the home is tense—conversation is polite, no questions are asked, no voices ever raised. All of this ends when the stranger's research reveals the French Terror, a life-size model of a guillotine that has working parts. It is this guillotine around which the threads of the story are woven. Characters act their roles perfectly, from the mother who is as unbending and rigid as the rock into which the house is built; to tormented Stephen, blocking out some terrifying event from his childhood; and mechanical Hannah, who prefers machines to people, for she can control them. In a breathtaking conclusion, the events of the past become the present, and secrets are unveiled. This is a compelling but difficult story, but it is well worth the effort and thought that it takes. It demands a second reading in order to pick up all that is beneath the surface—the guilt, the hedging, the unraveling of emotional armor with which the characters have protected themselves. All of the pieces of the story, as well as Cross' expert choice of words and language patterns, fit as neatly together as Hannah's beloved machines, leaving no loose ends or extra parts. It is a tragic story, and yet at the end, readers can hope that the pieces of the family will be put back together.

> *Trev Jones, in a review of "Roscoe's Leap," in* School Library Journal, *Vol. 34, No. 3, November, 1987, p. 114.*

Roscoe's Leap—one might as well say it at once—goes well over the top. It begins with beguiling audacity. The Roscoes live in a folly, confidently described by Gillian Cross as it appears in Pevsner: "built in 1879 for Samuel Roscoe, the millionaire sewage contractor", on "an iron framework and the main parts of the structure are of poured and shuttered concrete with dressings of York stone". It rises "in irregular clusters of Neo-Gothic turrets" on two sides of a small but appreciable ravine, spanned by a gallery of glass and cast iron.

In the buildings on one side, Hannah and Stephen live with their mother in an extreme of genteel poverty. Servantless, they eat small meals off Royal Worcester and Crown Derby, wash their glasses in three waters, and restore cutlery to "the plate safe in the butler's pantry". Mother, "small and thin and very, very straight", is given to emotional blackmail.

On the other side of the ravine live Uncle Ernest, a moody, grimy monolith in a wheelchair, and Doug, who appears to be his minder—so docile and placatory, and yet so much given to the heavy breathing of stifled emotion that one braces oneself for fashionable revelations about child-molesting. He turns out, however, to be the children's father, who has not communicated with their mother for eight years, since something very traumatic happened.

Relations across the ravine are therefore pretty tense. Hannah, a forthright girl with a penchant for mending machinery—"nothing was as mind-blowingly beautiful as a machine", is how her thoughts are expressed—realizes that Uncle Ernest pays the boarding-school fees, but often longs for a definitive row, "even if it meant going to ordinary schools and living in some beastly flat".

So far, so unlikely; but one accepts it. Action is initiated by a likeable unwitting innocent called Nick Honeyball, who is researching a thesis on the sewage millionaire and "social mobility". He is instrumental in re-starting the Roscoe collection of mechanical toys, and notably a late

eighteenth-century enactment of the French Revolution, where life-size automata circulate and guillotine themselves.

This releases atrocious memories which Stephen, now twelve, has been suppressing for eight years. Everything becomes, in detail, blurred and difficult to follow—much messing about on mysteriously half-cleared driveways, and searches for missing counter-weights—but is resolved in a climax of high melodrama over the ravine. Stephen becomes brave, and Doug, we gather, is going to have to live happily ever after again with Mother.

Gillian Cross is demonstrably very able; but here she has set herself too many jumps too close together. Her naturally commanding manner does, indeed, increasingly suggest a riding-mistress, alternately bossy and matey, bucketing round an ill-set circuit on a clumsy pony: one may admire her hands, her seat, her turn-out, but one really cannot applaud the performance. Even her bracing prose runs ragged at times (as when Nick, whose question has been received evasively, "was too polite to ask the question again, seeing it had met with such a ravingly enthusiastic response"—this comes of trying to write on both sides of the fence at once, as it were). It is something of a curate's egg of a book, as a result—very good in parts, but much too hard-boiled. The sadly true little story at its heart, about human misunderstanding and pain, needs more space, and time, in which to be developed.

> *Anne Duchêne, "Across the Ravine," in* The Times Literary Supplement, *No. 4416, November 20-26, 1987, p. 1285.*

The Gothicised architecture of two houses standing on opposite sides of a gorge, joined by a glassed-in bridge-conservatory, is no less striking than the working automatons housed in one part of the building, carefully preserved by Great Uncle Ernest as a family trust. *Roscoe's Leap* depends in part on meticulous descriptions of the clockwork animals and the huge, terrifying 'French Terror' which Doug keeps in working order and in part on the relations between this silent man and the woman who lives with her children Hannah and Stephen on the opposite side of the bridge. It is the children who make what seems to them a leap indeed when they meet Nick Honeyball, a student who has chosen Old Roscoe as the subject of a thesis; escorting the inquisitive visitor over the bridge to interview their great uncle in his wheelchair, they initiate a series of events, increasingly alarming and extraordinary, during which the reader gradually discovers how these people are really related and how the impressive Victorian models have affected their lives. The mystery of human emotions is backed by elements just as mysterious—keys lost and found, windows in odd places, dusty cellars and the weird shapes of animals and machines designed by a man of bizarre imagination. Gillian Cross is a past master in establishing through seemingly ordinary words an atmosphere of danger and disturbance and her latest book seems to me her most powerful essay in Gothicised fiction. (pp. 4905-06)

> *Margery Fisher, in a review of "Roscoe's Leap," in* Growing Point, *Vol. 26, No. 5, January, 1988, pp. 4905-06.*

Gillian Cross's elegantly structured, taut, and suspenseful novel is the type of book that entertains while providing deeply satisfying literary nourishment. Her characters are both uniquely individual and, through their vulnerability, their fears, and their capacity for courage, universal: They could be us. . . .

Alternating between Stephen's and Hannah's viewpoints, the narrative compels us to care about both, and once we understand their dilemma, we forgive the parents as well. This thoughtful novel provides insights into the complex interactions of a likeable, interesting family.

> *Susan Patron, in a review of "Roscoe's Leap,"*
> *in* The Five Owls, *Vol. 11, No. 3, January-*
> *February, 1988, p. 45.*

A Map of Nowhere (1988)

Growing-pains . . . afflict Gillian Cross's adolescent hero Nick, who has outgrown the football and dirty pictures that obsess his fourth-year schoolmates, and not yet graduated to the glamorous local gang of motorcycle tearaways that includes his big brother Mick. This in-between stage has been occupied by solitary adventure-games featuring star-warriors and subterranean mazes, which serve as a substitute for the bikers' dangerous version of reality; but their cynical exploitation of his ambitions, for their own criminal ends, soon plunges him into a maze of real problems, where fact and fantasy reflect each other confusingly.

The first conditions of membership oblige him to cultivate a phoney friendship with playground-outcast Joseph Fisher, whose "holy-joe" parents eke out a feckless existence in a bleak marshland grocery-store; and Nick's unpleasant brief, which he accepts under increasing duress, is to case the joint as a target for one of the gang's vicious nocturnal robberies. His detective-work entails participation in the Fisher children's own elaborately disciplined adventure-games, in which the sister Ruth plays a dauntingly macabre Master; but his success as a snoop is undermined by his affection for the family, whose innocence and kindness he finds disarmingly pathetic.

Matters are complicated by the underground subsidence that has condemned the shop, and made the Fishers hanker secretly for a well-insured disaster, such as robbery with arson; and the climax confronts him with an explosive crisis that tests his moral sense as well as his maturity. The ethical questions are quite a tangle, and the outcome is not entirely satisfying; but Nick's agonized vacillations are drawn as vividly as the Fenland atmosphere, and the imaginary plot-within-the-plot is an effective caricature of the novel's real events—a colourful drama of personal attitudes, where the upright Joseph's neat moral diagrams ("maps of nowhere") are put to the test on unpredictable ground.

> *Gerald Mangan, "The Pains of Growing," in*
> The Times Literary Supplement, *No. 4469,*
> *November 25-December 1, 1988, p. 1322.*

Again, as in **Roscoe's Leap,** Cross has written a tightly plotted, highly dramatic novel exploring family relation-

ships and the meaning of responsibility; here, the fact that the people involved are otherwise ordinary lends immediacy to the extraordinary events. Spellbinding. (p. 376)

> *A review of "A Map of Nowhere," in* Kirkus
> Reviews, *Vol. LVII, No. 5, March 1, 1989, pp.*
> *375-76.*

Impeccably constructed, Cross's latest novel uses the fantasy-adventure game to explore abstract concepts, such as loyalty, trust, and courage. Her characters are ordinary working-class folk, but the conflict involves looking inward and the reconciliation of self-gratification with self-esteem. As usual Cross deals with mature, provocative topics in the guise of explosive, suspenseful, impelling stories. . . . The climax of a well wrought tale takes an unexpected but not unbelievable turn. The use of the game as a device for character delineation and for plot development is inspired, since it serves as a metaphor for the theme and as a means for engaging interest. Although sophisticated in design, the story will challenge a wide audience with its intensity.

> *Mary M. Burns, in a review of "A Map of No-*
> *where," in* The Horn Book Magazine, *Vol.*
> *LXV, No. 3, May-June, 1989, p. 375.*

[**A Map of Nowhere** is a] remarkable novel. . . . (p. 54)

If Gillian Cross is making a bid for the male readership of adolescent novels, she has certainly given boys enough to bite on. The game-playing sessions are spine-tingling. But the Ruth/Jezebel figure is the most intriguing; a girl who is shut out from other social contacts, who has already made a decision to stay with her family in the isolation and poverty which she hates. She rules the game, threatening the boys with direful consequences if they make the wrong decisions. It is her strength Nick borrows when he decides what has to be done.

In my judgement a novel like this offers a reading experience which lets teenagers examine the issues that await them in later reading. It also helps them to distinguish ambiguities that they know to be within themselves. They want to be one of the 'gang', yet they don't. The narration holds in suspense the values enunciated in the adventure game, in which Nick has had to accept the role of 'a pious twit' with virtue, faith and endurance scoring higher than strength, money or intelligence, and the 'real', dastardly, violent adventure to chase away boredom devised by the Company.

There are small, clear episodes embedded in the larger design. Nick plays 'burglars' with Joseph's little brother and tricks him into telling where the keys are kept. Later, the little brother hides the keys from his parents, causing concern more about his lying and stealing than about his treachery. Nick protests on the child's behalf that the parental treatment is 'heavy'. In effect it reveals to him the motive of his own actions.

Morality, as decisions about personal behaviour rather than ideological right thinking, is not much in fashion in books. But it is always present in our criticism of them. Gillian Cross's involvement with deep play in this novel should make its readers uneasy, for the company they keep will always, at some point, expect them, if not to break the rules of association, at least to examine them and where they come from. (p. 55)

> *Margaret Meek, in a review of "A Map of No-where," in* The Signal Selection of Children's Books, 1989, *The Thimble Press, 1989, pp. 54-5.*

Rescuing Gloria (1989)

When Leo moves to Mercy Street he finds his new surroundings hateful. By the end of the school holidays he thinks it is really great. It all started when he saved Gloria the Goat from being put down. He found a place for her in the disused garden of a house awaiting demolition. Helped by Rachel and Harjinder he branches out into chickens, ducks and bees. Soon they have built up a small business in goat's milk, eggs and fresh vegetables. Even when the lorries come to begin the demolition they find a solution with the help of the neighbours who once seemed so hateful to Leo. The Mercy Street Community Farm Project is born.

This is one of Gillian Cross' stories for younger readers of everyday affairs without recourse to fantasy or the extraordinary. Her skill with words ensures that it reads with interest and nine to ten year old children will not want to leave it until it is finished.

> *D. A. Young, in a review of "Rescuing Gloria," in* The Junior Bookshelf, *Vol. 53, No. 6, December, 1989, p. 275.*

[In **Rescuing Gloria,**] the author has worked hard to make the far-fetched believable. Leo has moved from the countryside to a block of flats in the town. Bored, lonely, and angry he encounters an old man, owner of Gloria the goat, on her way to the vet to be put down. Against all the odds, Leo rescues Gloria, smuggles her by pram into the wilderness of a garden next door to his block, and, together with Rachel and Harjinder, starts to run a small urban farm. For several weeks the children manage to conceal their animals from the local adults, until the demolition squad arrives to clear the old garden. The children manage to save all the animals and to bring the local community together as well. It's believable and heart-warming, and, more rarely in children's fiction, it manages not to patronize the working-class environment where the story is set. As a comment on green issues it shows young readers the problems involved in being a friend of the earth more sympathetically and realistically than [Judy Corbalis's] *Your Dad's a Monkey* and without sacrificing humour.

> *Carol Fox, in a review of "Rescuing Gloria," in* The Times Educational Supplement, *No. 3840, February 2, 1990, p. 28.*

Twin and Super-Twin (1990)

From the author of such incisive psychological thrillers as **Roscoe's Leap** and **A Map of Nowhere,** an unassuming story for younger readers, with more depth than is at first apparent.

David and Ben are unusually close, even for twins. When their plot to get even with the Wellington Street gang by prematurely lighting their Guy Fawkes bonfire goes awry, it also results in a magical manifestation of their unity: suddenly, Ben has the power to transform David's right arm into any object—a string of sausages, a snake to frighten the gang, even a plea for help after the gang retaliates by kidnapping Ben. Typically for Cross, what begins as a bizarre trick becomes the basis for thought-provoking action: unintended wounds and misunderstandings escalate the kids' feud until both twins begin to sympathize with their antagonists—and manage to achieve a reconciliation in which the magic arm plays an entertaining role.

Though characterization here is minimal and the effort slight compared to Cross's YA novels, the action is lively and often funny. Better than average of its kind.

> *A review of "Twin and Super-Twin," in* Kirkus Reviews. *Vol. LVIII, No. 17, September 1, 1990, p. 1248.*

Ben discovers that if he concentrates really hard, he can transform the right arm of his twin, David, into things monstrous and bizarre. When they need to fight off the neighborhood gang, Ben can make David's arm into a hissing snake. When Ben is angry at his brother, he can turn David's arm into a huge baby's rattle. When the gang kidnaps Ben, he can use his paranormal connection to send David a call for help. The action flags at times, and Cross has to keep prodding the plot along (something that never happens in her powerful thrillers for older readers, like **On the Edge.** Still, there's light entertainment in the farcical plot, the gang wars in an English city, and the magic between twins. It all takes place around Guy Fawkes Day, and the bonfires and fireworks will intrigue American readers.

> *Hazel Rochman, in a review of "Twin and Super-Twin," in* Booklist, *Vol. 87, No. 5, November 1, 1990, p. 521.*

Gillian Cross, by no means a lightweight writer, here contributes a lightweight book to Oxford's Eagle Books, a cheerful fantasy which poses some provocative ideas. . . .

The story comes out of the close affinity between identical twins, and this is explored thoughtfully. There is much interest too in the contrasted characters in both gangs, and in the city environment in which the story is set. But this is mostly a book for fun, and Ms Cross keeps up the brisk pace as crisis succeeds crisis. Easy to read, full of tension, the book deserves to be popular, but the writer, as we know, can do much better than this.

> *Marcus Crouch, in a review of "Twin and Super-Twin," in* The Junior Bookshelf, *Vol. 54, No. 6, December, 1990, p. 290.*

The Monster from Underground (1990)

Talented at football and snooker, 'Bomber' Wilson hates writing and is at a loss when he is asked to observe something each day for a week to fill a class nature-diary. Machines at the roadworks might do, though less impressive than his friend Harriet's ambitious weather chart. Unexpectedly, the plan of a night-watch on the site brings spectacular results when a huge egg hatches into a dinosaur and though it is not always visible and nobody believes Bomber's assertions, he is able to identify it from his model collection as a Diplodocus. Would photographs help to prove his case? In fact, they don't show the animal but strata revealed in the road are far more exciting and a first prize is awarded to the diary which was so reluctantly undertaken. The coloured vignettes in this 'Banana' book enforce the author's portraits of lively children and ordinary but individualised homes, in a domestic episode very flattering to the day-dreams of the young about unusual discoveries and expected diversions from school routines.

> *Margery Fisher, in a review of "The Monster from Underground," in* Growing Point, *Vol. 29, No. 6, March, 1991, p. 5491.*

Realism and fantasy are woven neatly together to create believable characters in a tale that might be a dream or might, if the reader keeps an open mind, have some substance after all. The vocabulary is challenging for the 'newly fluent readers' at whom this series is aimed, the story an absorbing incentive to keep going.

> *Elizabeth Hormann, in a review of "The Monster from Underground," in* The School Librarian, *Vol. 39, No. 2, May, 1991, p. 60.*

Wolf (1991)

Wolf is aimed at the 12-plus age range, with the plus to be interpreted liberally. Here is a teenage novel capable of entertaining adults. Its central character is 14-year-old Cassy, suddenly thrust into the land of nightmares, where reason has no place, yet they become horribly plausible. Her grandmother, precise and given to moral platitudes, sends the baffled Cassy to join her mother, partner, and his son, in a London squat. This trio, odd yet credible, comprises a theatre-in-schools company, whose current production is "Wolf". The book's mysterious opening sequence starts to make terrifying sense as Cassy's father, Mick, becomes an increasingly insidious, wolfish presence in the action.

Yet the most fascinating impact stems from the pervasive thread provided by that paradoxical species: the wolf itself. It becomes a recurring, subtly integrated source of interest as the author explores this creature's myriad facets: beautiful inhuman wails; bloodlust, but not for humans; trivia (their internal parasites); even daring verbal by-play with the name. It is ingenious, but stunningly relevant: witness their crucial role in the narrative structure and the tension from using the fairy tale of Red Riding Hood as a dream counterpoint of fearful momentum, culminating in a climax free of melodrama. The thematic issues are never contrived, most notably the introduction of the IRA ("It's war . . . the enemy runs the papers and television") whose use of semtex is vital in the story line. Lifestyle choices, moral dilemmas and priorities within the family, are unobtrusively there if the reader wishes to find them. The language is honed for pace, and driven by reiterative

descriptive verbs: shivers, shakes, screams, trembles and churns abound. Like Cassy, our skin prickles as "a pit of chaos and terror yawned at her feet". Interspersed are different flashes of imaginative power; a mirror-filled, candle-lit room in the squat becomes a magic forest whose memory lingers. *Wolf* is an outstanding achievement in its genre, true to its conventions while rising beyond them. And theatre-in-education will never be quite the same again.

> *Brian Slough, "Nightmare Rides," in* The Times Educational Supplement, *No. 3885, December 14, 1990, p. 24.*

The skilful mixture of homely domestic ingredients (food, artistic materials, dingy houses), of intricacies of personality and relationship and of a terrorism only too recognisable to today's readers, makes an electrifying and absorbing piece of fiction, bleakly topical but strong in a perception of the stresses of life for young people adjusting to unusual circumstances.

> *Margery Fisher, in a review of "Wolf," in* Growing Point, *Vol. 29, No. 5, January, 1991, p. 5449.*

At 13, Cassy's learned never to ask about her father. His name is taboo. She shuts out the questions and holds tight to her safe routine with Nan, her sensible grandmother. Even when a midnight visitor hides in Nan's back room and Cassy's sent away to live with her mother in a "squat" on the other side of London, she tries to deny that the fugitive is her father and that he's a terrorist on the run, the wolf of her nightmares. Her mother's boyfriend and his son are preparing a show about wolves, and as Cassy helps them research and perform wolf history, myth, folklore, and ecology, her view shifts and changes. She comes to see that the wolf is dangerous, seductive, cunning, vulnerable, endangered. Then finally she confronts the wolf "inside the skin of her father," as he holds her grandmother hostage in her home with a gun at her neck. As in Cross' thriller *On the Edge,* the action grabs you from the first page and builds to a stunning climax. With the suspense, Cross also makes you *think* about fear and about the walls we build to shut out the big bad wolf. Are wolves bad? They certainly care for their young better than Cassy's parents do. Can werewolves move from nightmare into the day? The wolf-as-complex-metaphor is overstated, and the squatter characters are too purposive, but the facts about wolves are as compelling as the terror. Teens will also be excited by Cross' reworking of the old "children's" stories, from *The Three Little Pigs* to *Little Red Riding Hood,* which can still reach our deepest fears. (pp. 1052-53)

> *Hazel Rochman, in a review of "Wolf," in* Booklist, *Vol. 87, No. 10, January 15, 1991, pp. 1052-53.*

This is a splendid, daring book. It hangs on, and evokes, the atavistic terrors that have silted down into what are now childhood fables: Little Red Riding Hood, The Three Little Pigs, The Big Bad Wolf, and The Boy who cried 'Wolf'. It explores mind and nature, mind in society, and approaches modern urban terrorism. It also makes a nonsense of the fact/fiction divide in narrative. Since I first admired Gillian Cross's skill in confronting, more directly than most, the ambiguity of human value judgements in *A map of nowhere,* I have been eager to see what would happen next. . . . [*Wolf* is written in a spare text that Gillian Cross has honed to nerve-tingling sharpness. This is one for that special reading list, and more.

> *Margaret Meek, in a review of "Wolf," in* The School Librarian, *Vol. 39, No. 1, February, 1991, p. 29.*

This isn't as well-constructed as some of Cross' other thrillers, with the central image of the wolf belabored artificially into the story. And while the characterizations of Goldie, Lyall, and Robert are complex and convincing, Cassy's time with them—most of the story—seems flat, lacking the incredible tension of the briefer scenes at Nan's that open and close the book. The ending is a fierce and scary shocker, and well worth waiting for. (p. 214)

> *Roger Sutton, in a review of "Wolf," in* Bulletin of the Center for Children's Books, *Vol. 44, No. 9, May, 1991, pp. 213-14.*

Chris Crutcher

1946-

American author of fiction and short stories.

Major works include *Running Loose* (1983), *Stotan!* (1986), *The Crazy Horse Electric Game* (1987), *Chinese Handcuffs* (1989).

Among the most respected writers of young adult literature to have emerged in the 1980s, Crutcher is the author of realistic novels which are considered both exciting sports stories and insightful accounts of maturation. Praised for his understanding of young people and his knowledge of sports as well as for the evocative quality of his works and his successful delineation of characterization and action, Crutcher profiles young male high school students involved in such sports as baseball, basketball, football, swimming, and track who encounter personal adversity while preparing for and participating in their games or meets. Crutcher is often acknowledged for accurately representing the thoughts and feelings of his characters, sensitive young men who face tough choices. Depicting high school sporting events as proving grounds for personal achievement, he outlines the growth of his characters, who emerge from their crises as stronger people who know themselves and their limits. The protagonists encounter sickness and death, divorce, rape and sexual abuse, alcoholism and drug abuse, suicide, discrimination, disability, AIDS, and other issues as well as pimps, prostitutes, and motorcycle and youth gangs; in addition, the dialogue in the novels includes some instances of rough language. However, Crutcher includes positive male and female friendships and romantic relationships in his works while representing the joys and pressures of competitive sports. He also underscores his books with positive messages that stress integrity, dignity, honor, courage, survival, and hope. Crutcher writes his novels in a narrative style that incorporates both first and third person; often taking a retrospective view, he also uses the format of the diary and the personal letter to structure some of his works. In addition to his novels, Crutcher is the author of *Athletic Shorts: Six Short Stories* (1991), a collection for young adults that blends the humorous with the serious and includes several of the characters from his earlier works.

Critic Christine McDonnell notes that Crutcher writes "with vitality and authority that stems from personal experience"; his novels, which are set in the Midwest, West, and Northwestern parts of the United States, areas in which Crutcher has lived, strongly reflect his background. Raised in a small Idaho logging town that is much like the one in his first novel *Running Loose,* Crutcher was involved in several school sports; his father, like Louie's in that story, was the chairman of the school committee. Crutcher's second novel, *Stotan!,* grew out of his experience as a college swimmer. After receiving a teaching credential, Crutcher taught social studies and later became the director of a nonprofit alternative school that is the

model for the one in his third novel, *The Crazy Horse Electric Game.* In 1981, he became the coordinator of the Spokane Child Protection Team, a group that deals with the most difficult cases of child abuse, and later became a therapist in the Mental Health Center. Crutcher wrote *Running Loose* during a period when he moved from California to Washington and was between jobs; he now divides his time between writing and working in the mental health field. Crutcher received mixed reviews for his fourth novel, *Chinese Handcuffs;* the story of how high school senior Dillon Hemingway tries to recover from the effects of watching his older brother commit suicide, the book is thought to include an overabundance of emotional woes. However, Crutcher is usually considered a convincing and substantial writer; critic Nancy Vasilakis calls him "a discerning reporter of the inner life of adolescent males," while reviewer Stephanie Zvirin adds that Crutcher "knows the right moves on and off the court." *Running Loose, Stotan!,* and *The Crazy Horse Electric Game* were named Best Books for Young Adults by the American Library Association in 1983, 1987, and 1989 respectively.

(See also *Something about the Author,* Vol. 52, and *Contemporary Authors,* Vol. 113.)

AUTHOR'S COMMENTARY

[The following excerpt is from an interview by Dave Jenkinson.]

Should a statue ever be erected to Chris Crutcher by his "home" town, Dayton, Ohio, and Cascade, Idaho, might both claim him as a native son. Born in Dayton on July 17, 1946, Chris explains, "My dad was in the Air Force, and my parents were just passing through. They were in Cascade before I got dry." Raised in this small Idaho logging community of some 900 people, Chris was not an outstanding student. He attributes his academic nonachievement to having an older brother who "was real bright. He was the valedictorian of the class, and I don't think he got anything under an A minus the whole time he was in high school. I got a good picture of what that was like and decided I didn't want to have anything to do with it. Along about junior high, I started letting my parents get the idea that maybe I was somewhat brain damaged." (p. 67)

Given that Chris' four YA books have all included athletics, one might assume that Chris was a school "jock." Explaining his participation in football, basketball and track, Chris says, "When your school has only 103 kids in the top four grades, you go out for sports, or they beat the hell out of you. You figured it was more fun to be beat up with a helmet on than with a helmet off. In that sense I was an athlete. I was a notorious bench sitter in basketball although that's my favorite game these days." In college, Chris became involved in swimming. "I got to be a pretty fair swimmer and qualified for small college nationals my junior and senior year. Then I got out and started doing a lot of running. My latest thing is triathalons."

Chris did do some writing during school—punishment themes. "Teachers used to like to give me 500 word themes, and I gave them lots of reasons to do it. I would get real creative doing these because there was no school structure to them." About the eighth grade, the journalism teacher saw one of Chris' themes and invited him to write for the school newspaper. From then until senior year, "I had this column called 'Chris' Crumbs.' They didn't like to let me report because I wasn't a good reporter, but I had this column where I took pot shots at everybody."

The fact that Chris is an alumnus of Eastern Washington State College is partly due to the color of its catalog. Chris admits he naively thought he could just turn up at the college of his choice on opening day and register. On learning in senior year that applications were necessary, "I ran down to the library. All the college catalogs were either black or blue, and Eastern's was red so I took it." Chris graduated in 1968 with a B.A., majoring in psychology and minoring in sociology. Chris and a good friend from high school then "did 'Route 66' for a year. We hopped in our car and flipped coins at major intersections and ended up in Dallas, Texas, pouring prestressed concrete ridge beams until we saved up a thousand dollars apiece and went to Hawaii. Then I came back and figured, 'I probably ought to do something for a career (or at least put it off a year),' and so I went back and got a teaching credential."

Not yet ready to teach, "I took off again and was a maintenance man on Mount Hood in Oregon for half a year. These hands are not made for handy work! Then a job came open in Washington's tri-cities area. For the next year and a half, I was teacher and administrator for a dropout school. When the Title money ran out, I moved into the high school and taught social studies a couple of years. And I'm a psych major! I learned a lot of government and American history that first year."

After some 3½ years of teaching in Washington, Chris moved to California's Bay Area. "I put all my stuff in my Beetle and headed down there and had to take a job as a teacher's aid in a private school." Nine years followed, first as a teacher and then as the director of a private, nonprofit school, kindergarten to high school. Chris describes the school as "the toughest place I have ever been. For a while we were in a church in a nicer part of the Oakland Hills, Then we got a chance to buy an old school building. It's the school in **Crazy Horse**, and it was in a real rough section of Oakland. The school was a place where kids who absolutely couldn't make it in the Oakland Public Schools were sent. Most of our kids were funded by the school district because they were on Title money, and the district was charged with giving them an education. It was really a good experience for me. That was an amazing place, and it was so hard to leave because every year there were kids that 'got' to me, and I'd say, 'I'll just stay and see this kid through.' "

But leave Chris finally did in 1981. Because his work in the alternative school had been so emotionally demanding, as Chris looked north, he resolved, "I just want to go some place where I don't get into these 'help' professions. I want to sell athletic shoes or work in a spa. I just want to slow things down. I wasn't in Spokane six months before I took a job as a coordinator of the Spokane Child Protection Team, a group of people who work on the toughest child abuse cases. Within a year, I was working as a therapist in the Mental Health Center, and so I guess I'm stuck."

While Chris had been doing his student teaching in Monroe, north of Seattle during 1970, he stayed with a former Eastern classmate, Terry Davis, author of *Vision quest*. Says Chris, "Terry was in the process of becoming a writer, and I got to watch him do it. When I moved down to the Bay area, Terry was a Stegner Fellow at Stanford, and we would get together once a week, run, and talk about writing. I had this **Running loose** story running around in my head then, and we talked about it. Years later, I came up to Washington on vacation, and Terry and I were on a run, and he said, 'You ought to write that story. Do it!' I went back to the Bay and, from the time I quit working in the school until I moved up to Spokane, I had about 3½ months. Because I didn't have to look for a job, I just sat down and wrote it. For whatever reason, it fell together really well in the first draft."

"I sent a copy to Terry who called me up within a week and said, 'I'm calling my agent and sending it to her.' Within another week, she'd accepted it and shortly after that it was bought. So I didn't get the runaround and the jillion rejection slips. I don't have the constitution for that.

I'd have stopped long before. There's a path there that I got on somehow that was an easier path than a lot of really good writers get on. Some luck and being in the right place at the right time were involved!" (pp. 68-9)

When writing **Running loose,** Chris did not realize he was producing a YA novel. "I didn't know there was such a thing. I'd just spent 10 years in the toughest school in Oakland, and so I wrote it in that language. My agent sent it to Susan Hirschman at Greenwillow who said, 'We'll publish this any way you want it, but you need to know that you're going to run into some difficulties in terms of sales with librarians and schools if you leave it like that.' So I took out 'two words' and shrunk it a third!"

Stotan, Chris' second novel, grew out of an experience Chris had while swimming for Eastern. "I had this 'lunatic' coach who was reading an old *Sports Illustrated.* A story about Herb Elliot, an Australian miler, basically said that Elliot was just going to kick all the Americans' butts because he was tough in ways they weren't. He was a 'stotan.' The swimming coach got the idea that we were going to have this Stotan Week, and the Stotan Week that's in the book is based on it. Actually I didn't put some of the things in because it was a tough, tough week. It was an incredible bonding thing that none of us would have done alone but nobody could stop doing as long as everybody else was doing it." . . .

Chris recalls how **Stotan**'s plot went in a direction he had not foreseen. "I had three people and needed one more character, basically to round out the relay. He was just supposed to be comic relief. I was just starting to create this Nortie Wheeler character and was writing in the morning. I went to work and got in the middle of working with this family. Their 'story' was somewhat like Nortie's story of his father's abuse of him. I had that 'story,' and I had this new character in my head at the same time, and Nortie just kind of took over." (p. 69)

In recalling the [creation of **The Crazy Horse Electric Game**], Chris says, "It's funny because I got the title before I ever had an idea. It just came by itself, and I had to figure out a way to get it into a book. Montana would be a good place for a company to be called after an Indian, such as Sitting Bull Electric. Also, I have a nephew who had some seizures when he was born and so he's got a slower left side. I had this idea that I wanted to let him see what that could look like. As well, I had a very good friend who was a football player at Eastern who had exactly the same thing. He was a center linebacker, and he just adjusted by doing what Lisa teaches Willie—find your center. And I knew I had a lot of stories coming out of the old school and some wonderful, non-preachy tough lessons for kids." (p. 70)

"**Chinese handcuffs** was going to be my first adult book, and there are those who say it is. It's run into some 'interesting' criticisms." One "criticism" took the form of the book's not being reviewed by *Booklist* though the journal devoted a half page to explaining why it could not recommend it. . . . The bottom line of this "non-review" was that **Chinese handcuffs** "is an unsuccessful book—and a disappointment—because the overloaded plot strains the novel's structure and diminishes the vital message Crutcher is trying to convey." Chris acknowledges that there "really is a lot going on in the book and, from an artistic point of view, there may be some legitimate complaints." But Chris points out that real life deals out "overloads," and others must have agreed for **Chinese handcuffs** became Chris' fourth consecutive ALA "Best Book for Young Adults."

Chris explains that, in writing a book, "I'll get a core idea or a core set of characters, and I start off. I usually have to do a lot of editing on my first chapter when I get to the end. My first few chapters take some work because I haven't gotten the direction, but I get my direction by telling the story. I like the idea that the story can tell itself and that I don't know what's going to happen. Nortie Wheeler's taking over **Stotan** was one of the magic things in my life. I had no idea of what was going to happen to **Crazy Horse**'s Willie Weaver. I didn't know whether he was going to go back home and stay or leave or what. I like the magical part, the part that says maybe I'm not in control."

"I feel that if I have a strong enough idea in the first place, then I will come up with a story. I'm a good editor, probably a better editor than I am a writer, and I really work things over. I'm comfortable just writing down any old thing and then going back and fixing and fixing. I have no compunction about putting anything down, and then I'll take it out and see how it plays, read it to people. It develops as it goes. I have an idea of what I want to say, and I'm probably going to be pretty close to that when the story's finished, but, boy, you can take some wonderful roads in between!" (pp. 70-1)

"If I never got paid a dime, I've had letters that make it worth writing some of these books because they touch kids that are hurt. A lot have said, 'This is the best book I have ever read, but you ended it wrong.' That was about **Crazy Horse** because they wanted Willie back. The books are open ended because I have this idea that my stories don't stop because I stop writing them. I like the idea that, at the last page, I present the story to you, the reader, and then you can do what you want. Willie can drive 10 miles outside of town and turn around if you want; he can do whatever he needs to do for you."

"I didn't start writing until I was 35. It's hard to imagine my life not writing. I love it. There's really a part of it that's connection. When you're watching somebody read your material and they smile and nod, you know you've found that place where your experience and their experience match, even though they aren't the same exact experience. Any time I write something and you say, 'Yah,' boy, it's a kick!" (p. 71)

Dave Jenkinson, "Portraits: Chris Crutcher," in Emergency Librarian, *Vol. 18, No. 3, January-February, 1991, pp. 67-71.*

GENERAL COMMENTARY

Christine McDonnell

Writing with vitality and authority that stems from personal experience in *Running Loose, Stotan!,* and *The Crazy Horse Electric Game,* Chris Crutcher gives readers the inside story on young men, sports, and growing up. His heroes—sensitive, reflective young men, far from stereotypic jocks—use sports as an arena to test personal limits; to prove stamina, integrity, and identity; and to experience loyalty and cooperation as well as competition.

Louie, in *Running Loose,* is no natural athlete. "I've never been all that good. Not too big, not too fast, and a lot more desire to be a football player than to play football, if you know what I mean." Walker, the swim team captain in *Stotan!,* values his team experience over his personal achievement. "I'm part of a group of really special guys—and a girl—who happen to swim. . . . It's a lot more important to me to be a part of that group of humans than it is to be in a school of fast fish." Willie, the gifted baseball player who makes his most famous move in *The Crazy Horse Electric Game,* loses his athletic gift in a boating accident and must learn both a new way of moving and a new definition for himself. For all three, winning is not the goal; doing your best, stretching your limits, is the only true measure of success.

The vitality in these books comes from the characterization, the physical action, and quick dialogue. Crutcher gives us believable glimpses of locker rooms and practice sessions, spiced with irreverent, sometimes coarse, male humor. He shows brief awkward moments of romance in contrast with the honesty, ease, and trust of male friendships. These books are overwhelmingly male, peopled with teammates, coaches, bosses, fathers, and father figures. Women do appear as mothers, girlfriends, even as a coach, and issues of sex and love surface. In *Running Loose* the death of Louie's girlfriend is a central crisis in the book. But for the most part although women are attractive, strong, and smart, they are peripheral to the action, relegated more to fantasy than to day-to-day life.

The action scenes, the training sessions, games, and meets, provide a showcase for the strongest writing in the books. In these, Crutcher's knowledge of sports and his insight into the inner lives of young men merge. He shows not only the physical details of training and practice, the laps, exercises, drills, pacing, and strategies but also the personal experience, the pain, fatigue, exhilaration, pressures, and release. In *Running Loose* and *Stotan!* the final meets rise above simple athletic competition to take on deeper meanings. Athletes compete hoping for victory but also rejoice in one another's performances. Louie runs to prove his strength and independence in a school where his idealism and honesty have isolated him; the team in *Stotan!* swims in honor of their teammate, dying from a blood disease. In both cases the characters are supported and respected by their opponents. Competition can be unifying, not divisive. Over and over again the message is stated: don't give up; give it your best; run your own race.

"I think my job in this life is to be an observer. I'm never going to be one of those guys out there on the tip of the arrow of my time, presenting new ideas or inventing ways to get more information on a smaller chip. But I think I'll learn to see pretty well." The speaker is Walker Dupree, narrator of *Stotan!* but it could be Crutcher describing himself. Speaking directly about his writing, Crutcher said, "I want to be remembered as a storyteller, and I want to tell stories that seem real so that people will recognize something in their own lives and see the connections. We are all connected. That's what I like to explore and put into stories."

The connections between Crutcher's background and the situations he describes in his novels are numerous. Taken in order, *Running Loose, Stotan!,* and *The Crazy Horse Electric Game* give a rough outline of his life. He grew up in Cascade, Idaho, a town exactly like Trout in *Running Loose,* with wilderness nearby, deer in the backyard, driving licenses for fourteen-year-olds, and a school so small that athletes participate in every sport. He played football and basketball and ran track. "There was too much snow for baseball. The high-jumpers wore wet suits and practiced on snowdrifts." Like Louie, his father was the chairman of the school committee, a thoughtful, scientific man who appreciated independence and disliked people accepting things without questioning.

In college at Eastern Washington State, . . . Chris swam competitively on a team like the one described in *Stotan!* "But the coach was even more maniacal." With his teammates he experienced a Stotan week that stretched them beyond the limits of their own endurance and forged the bonds of loyalty vividly depicted in *Stotan!*

After college Chris worked as a teacher and as director of an alternative school in Oakland, California, the model for the school described in *The Crazy Horse Electric Game.* The next stage of Chris Crutcher's life appears indirectly in his novels: fed up with waiting in lines and in traffic, he moved to Spokane where he works as a child and family therapist dealing with physical and sexual abuse cases. In Spokane he began to write seriously.

He now divides his week between his mental health work and his writing, enjoying the balance and contrast of the two. "In my work, the daily crisis of people's lives is so immediate. Time moves so fast. But the books are so permanent. They have their own life in time." Not surprisingly, he also makes time for running and basketball.

"I started writing late, when I recognized the need for a creative outlet in my life. Though I had read relatively little, I had always loved stories. So I gave it a go." While living in the Bay area, he experimented with fiction in a writing workshop. After moving to Spokane, he had time to develop his writing more fully. An author friend remembered one story that Chris had written earlier and suggested that he expand it. *Running Loose* was the result.

Chris Crutcher describes himself as being poorly read. "In high school I was less than a totally serious student. I never had a burning desire to be a writer then. In fact during my four years in high school I read one novel cover to cover: *To Kill a Mockingbird.*" He still doesn't read much, but through his work he hears stories every day. "I'm interested in relationships, in complexities, in seeing patterns in people's lives. I get information from other people's lives, and I put it into stories, expanding, adding more to make characters richer." Describing his writing process, he cites character as his primary source. "I start with character. Somewhere along the line I get plot. Plot comes last."

But inattention to plot in Crutcher's books is far overshadowed by the strength of characterization and dialogue, coupled with the detail and vitality of the sports scenes. Even when events are surprising, characters are consistently believable. Louie, Walker, and Willie, poised on the edge of manhood, measure themselves in sports and friendships and struggle with larger issues of integrity, dignity, and personal loss. Through their experiences, Chris Crutcher comments powerfully on the broader topic of growing up. At the end of **Stotan!** Walker speaks in a voice that echoes Chris Crutcher's own: "I think if I ever make it to adulthood, and if I decide to turn back and help someone grow up, either as a parent or a teacher or a coach, I'm going to spend most of my time dispelling myths, clearing up unreal expectations. . . . I think I'll learn to see pretty well. I think I'll know how things work—understand simple cause and effect—and, with any luck, be able to pass that on. And that's not such a bad thing." (pp. 332-35)

> *Christine McDonnell, "New Voices, New Visions: Chris Crutcher," in* The Horn Book Magazine, *Vol. LXIV, No. 3, May-June, 1988, pp. 332-35.*

Patricia Spencer

"Our next assignment, *No Exit,* it's not more of the same philosophy is it?" a seventeen-year-old senior queries disgustedly.

"Why do you ask?"

"I just can't get involved, but we have to read another, huh?" Lethargically, she picks up the Jean-Paul Sartre play, exiting as a second group of bright, college-bound, advanced-placement students enter.

Another discussion. Dutiful analysis. Insightful, detached comments. Probing, I search to help students find significance in an AP English unit on philosophy in literature. Instead, characters like Meursault, Marie, Estelle, Garcin, and Inez appear as alien as the philosophy of estrangement. As this class picks up copies of *No Exit,* an aloof athlete grabs a book from the shelf below, "Why don't we read something contemporary?" He holds up a copy of Chris Crutcher's **Running Loose.** Laughing, he eyes the cover kiss and does a dramatic reading of the title kicker: "For Louie the only way to make it is his way."

I pause; it's worth a try.

"Forget *No Exit* tonight. Take a copy of **Running Loose** and enjoy."

Discovering the existential elements and heroes in modern adolescent literature has been a needed addition to an advanced-placement English course. Naturally, the "classics" are not abandoned (Meursault goes on trial annually), but now the unit has the vitality of teenage existential-ists who, even in the last quarter of the twentieth century, are searching for individuality and identity, who pose questions, find conundrums, and validate insecurities casually disguised by designer jeans, lip gloss, or football jerseys.

Adolescent literature offers both novels and short stories with existential elements. The novels **The Crazy Horse Electric Game** and **Running Loose** by Chris Crutcher contain male protagonists who face personal adversity: in **Crazy Horse,** Willie Weaver, an athlete crippled in a freak water-skiing accident, struggles for physical and emotional recovery; in **Running Loose,** Louie Banks, a football player ostracized by school and community when he opposes an unethical coach, deals with the sudden death of his girlfriend. Norma Howe's *God, the Universe and Hot Fudge Sundaes* portrays Alfie, a gifted adolescent female, coping with her sister's death, parents' divorce, and her own religious doubts. All three novels illustrate various aspects of that nebulous philosophy explored by Jean-Paul Sartre:

> Man can count on no one but himself: he is alone, abandoned on earth in the midst of his infinite responsibilities, without help, with no other aim than the one he sets himself, with no other destiny than the one he forges for himself on this earth. (1964, "Sartre and Existentialism," *Life* 6 Nov.: 86-112, [87])

Sartre's words reflect basic characteristics of the literary existential world and hero.

After the accident, seemingly abandoned in his bitterness by girlfriend, parents, and teammates, Willie Weaver in **Crazy Horse** is indeed alone. The courageous bus trip from Idaho to Oakland separates him from those on whom he might depend. Physically disabled and emotionally crushed, Willie appears an alien in an unfamiliar world; the basketball court and baseball diamond no longer welcome him. His own body is foreign to him: "His gait is uneven; right side jogging, left side following—dragging. . . . Nothing about it feels athletic, nothing pleasing."

In a reading journal, a student comments, "As a wrestler, I know what it means to be in tune with my body. I feel Willie's pain; I live in fear of injury. I would lose my whole identity."

Estrangement invades the life of Louie Banks in **Running Loose** when he takes a stand against his football coach and principal. Unwilling to play dirty ball, Louie is labeled a "nigger lover" and "wussy" and loses his position on the team and the opportunity to participate in any team sports. Quick to point out a less obvious alienation, another student mentions how alone Louie is in personal mourning; surely others mourn Becky, but grief is personal, as Louie demonstrates in his outburst at the funeral. . . . Students also note the general air of individuality in Crutcher's characterization of Louie: "he doesn't follow the crowd in anything." (pp. 44-5)

"Just when I start believing I have some control, that I can take charge, instead of my parents running my life, I start to see that I really have no control," concludes one student, the day following the schoolyard slaughter in Stockton, California. In his reading-journal entry, he explores Louie Banks' situation: "The randomness of events is evident. Without reason or justification, Becky dies. Funny word: accident. Life is an accident of chance Louie must face. Me, too." Similarly, Willie Weaver in *Crazy Horse* loses his physical identity in a freak water-skiing episode, pushing himself too far, expecting superhuman powers which do not rescue him. One moment he's the baseball champion, later the crippled ex-athlete. The existential premise of a universe in chaos raises the question of external control: is there a God who allows this to happen? (p. 45)

The absurdity of death prompts brutal responses from these adolescent philosophers.

All of this would be unbearably depressing if it were not for the idea of the existential choice: to find individual meaning in this chaos. In discussion, students describe Louie's existential engagement: "Right from the start, Louie seems able to forge his own path; his principles come from within. Whether he's dealing with Boomer, Coach Lednecky, or even Becky, he's firm, striving to make his own sense of the situation." Another almost interrupts, "And take a look at how he reaches, well, pretty much the depth of despair after Becky's death. He could have continued sinking, but he attempts to put things together. I really think he finds out more of who he is when he commits to track."

Students sharing ideas on *The Crazy Horse Electric Game* are soon comparing Willie Weaver's situation to Meursault in Albert Camus' *The Stranger:* "Neither character commits until he's imprisoned: Meursault in actual confinement and Willie a prisoner in his own disabled body." Another student extends the comparison,

> Or did you notice how the scene between Willie and his father on the racquetball court parallels *No Exit?* They are torturing each other and themselves in confinement. Willie doesn't start recovery until he breaks away, takes his own path toward meaning.

An advanced-placement student devours an adolescent novel in a single evening; change of pace, ease, and interest level provide new accessibility to the difficult, cold philosophy of existentialism. Although YA novels serve as better catalysts for extensive, in-depth philosophical comparisons, young-adult short stories are viable alternatives when time or materials may be problematic. . . .

Adolescent literature in an advanced-placement classroom connects classics to the present. Even those students who read Nietzsche on their own find relevance and pleasure in sharing the lives of fellow teenagers Louie, Willie, or [Norma Howe's] Alfie. If the purpose of a unit on philosophy in literature is to ask students to think more deeply about life, death, and their place in the universe, then this succeeds: perfunctory discussions dissipate. Personal, passionate, probing exchanges vitalize literary discourse. Existential engagement in AP English . . . thanks to an unusual comparative approach. (p. 46)

> *Patricia Spencer, "YA Novels in the AP Class-room: Crutcher Meets Camus," in* English Journal, *Vol. 78, No. 7, November, 1989, pp. 44-6.*

TITLE COMMENTARY

Running Loose (1983)

Within the familiar conventions of the teen novel formula (first person narration and retrospective purge) Louie Banks tells what happened to him in his senior year in a small town Idaho high school. Besides falling in love with Becky and losing her in a senseless accident, Louie takes a stand against the coach when he sets the team up to injure a black player on an opposing team, and learns that you can't be honorable with dishonorable men. While the setting is reminiscent of Hinton, and the situation of [Robert Cormier's *The] Chocolate War,* the characterization is better than the former, and the circumstances of taking a stand less dramatic than the latter. Best of all, though, you love this kid and grieve with him when Becky dies because she is presented as a really neat person. Louie's parents and Madison, the assistant coach who argues him back into the athletic program as a runner, and Dakota, the bar owner for whom Louie works, are interesting adults who obviously care about Louie and know when and how to help him and when to leave him enough room to grow. Becky and Louie go away for a weekend together at one point and don't have sex because he is not ready, but they do make love because Becky points out that you don't have to have sex to make love.

Beside the relief this fine book offers from upper middle class New York settings, the main character is a credible, sensitive male adolescent who might possibly appeal to readers like him. The book is also a good stepping stone up from Hinton and toward titles like *Vision Quest* and *Stop Time.* Good "bridge books" are rare and first novelists this good even rarer.

> *Mary K. Chelton, in a review of "Running Loose," in* Voice of Youth Advocates, *Vol. 6, No. 1, April, 1983, p. 36.*

The turbulent, literally trying senior year of Louie Banks of Trout, Idaho, who has worked out vigorously over the summer and is rewarded with a starting place on the eight-man football team and a cheerleader girlfriend, smart and pretty newcomer Becky, who could have any guy in school but walks right up and asks Louie for a date. Then, with the Trout team aiming for its third straight state championship season, nearby Salmon Lake gets a transfer from California, a black kid named Washington who's a super athlete. Trout's coach lets his team know that "I want that Washington kid out of the game! Early!"—and that "the only way you can stop . . . those blacks . . . is to hurt 'em." So when the two teams meet, Trout's vicious Boomer slams Washington into a bench. Louie protests; the ref and the coach play dumb; and Louie quits the team. There's some fallout at school but his parents and Becky back him up and life goes on . . . until Becky is killed in a car accident and Louie, beside himself, makes another scene by lashing out at the sanctimonious imported preacher at her funeral. Louie never does surrender to the forces of hypocrisy, but his next act of resistance is better calculated, and his last impetuous outburst, embracing his father who is handing out diplomas at graduation, is a more positive one. Meanwhile he achieves some victories in a therapeutic track season: just getting him on the team takes courage and commitment from the young assistant coach, who admired Louie's earlier stand; and Louie goes on to an all-out, prodigious victory over Washington, an all-round winner who is running Louie's event, the two-mile, more-or-less on the side. Louie tells his story with strong feeling and no crap, as he might say. Perhaps the weakest element in the novel is Becky, a young man's dream of love and sweet reason. But as a dramatic, head-first confrontation with mendacity, fate's punches, and learning to cope, it's a zinger.

> *A review of "Running Loose," in* Kirkus Reviews, *Vol. LI, No. 8, April 15, 1983, p. 461.*

Louie, the narrator, is a nice guy. He wants desperately to be a good football player, but doesn't expect to be a star; he has a warm relationship with his parents that includes mutual respect; he's surprised and appreciative when one of his high school classmates, Becky, shows an interest. He comes to grief when he publicly accuses the coach of having urged the team to be rough with the black star of an opposing team. That's the end of high school football. He falls deeply in love with Becky, and is stunned by grief when she's killed in a freak accident, then adds to his reputation as a maverick when he shouts defiantly at the funeral service, resenting the platitudes of a minister who never knew her. His parents are supportive, and so is the track coach, who thinks Louie would make a good runner, and who fights the football coach and school principal to get permission to let Louie join the track team. The story ends with Louie's graduation night and his musing about all he's learned in the past year, a quiet ending for a story that is structurally controlled and capably written. Crutcher's characterization is powerful (especially in the depiction of the tyrannical and bullying football coach) and his protagonist's tender relationships are equally convincing. Above all, this is a story of honor and principles, messages that are achieved without preaching. An unusually fine first novel.

> *Zena Sutherland, in a review of "Running Loose," in* Bulletin of the Center for Children's Books, *Vol. 36, No. 9, May, 1983, p. 165.*

Louie tells his story with sensitivity, humor and outrage. His anger at the circumstances, at the God he . . . doubts and at the dishonorability and arrogance of his coach and principal is clearly understood. This is a fine young adult book with memorable minor characters as well as major ones. Even though not all readers will agree with Louie's conclusions, the book raises important issues for adolescents to consider. Unfortunately, the language, which is peppered throughout with obscenities, will be problematic to some libraries.

> *Trev Jones, in a review of "Running Loose," in* School Library Journal, *Vol. 29, No. 9, May, 1983, p. 80.*

Stotan! (1986)

Walker Dupress describes his senior year in high school in Spokane, the year in which he and his three best friends became "stotans" (a cross between a stoic and a Spartan) under the guidance of an almost mythic young swimming coach and the pressure of circumstances which tested them. Walk, the narrator/observer, describes Lion, now living as a young adolescent, Nortie, trying to free himself with his friends' help from an abusive father, and Jeff, the clown, who is dying of a rare blood disease, in whose honor the others swim an illegal three-man relay in the state finals. Similar to *Vision Quest* in theme, *Stotan!* is more similar in style and characterization to Crutcher's own *Running Loose,* depicting beautifully the joy, pain, and emotional strength of a male adolescent friendship. The novel also shows high school sports as the synonym for mastery and achievement that, with a good coach, they can be. As a lovely story and a model of the realistic adolescent novel, *Stotan!* deserves wide purchase, much booktalking, and Best Books for Young Adults recognition.

> *Mary K. Chelton, in a review of "Stotan!" in* Voice of Youth Advocates, *Vol. 9, No. 1, April, 1986, p. 29.*

Stotan! has energy and gutsiness; Crutcher gives us the flavor of the pumped-up, yet vulnerable, world of high-school sports, but fails to avoid clichéd situations or to create subtle interpersonal relationships. Macho writing, liberally spiked with routine jock humor. (p. 550)

> *A review of "Stotan!" in* Kirkus Reviews, *Vol. LIV, No. 7, April 1, 1986, pp. 549-50.*

A fine coming-of-age novel. . . . The boys are typical of many teenagers; they think a lot about sex; their language isn't always clean. They face difficult, adult situations—violence, racial prejudice, Jeff's impending death. Crutcher's novel more than moves and entertains; it teaches. It teaches young people about responsibility, about courage and heroism, and ultimately about life itself. *Stotan!* is very, very good.

> *Jerry Flack, in a review of "Stotan!" in* School Library Journal, *Vol. 32, No. 9, May, 1986, p. 100.*

The language of the story is tough, even raunchy, at times, but it seems totally appropriate to the characters as they are drawn. It is, in fact, in the realm of characterization that the book excels—each of the four is a believable young man, differentiated and distinct. *Stotan!* is part of a growing body of books, which includes Bruce Brooks's *The Moves Make the Man* and, historically, the novels of John Tunis, that use a sports setting and competition to discuss the greater issues of being young and alive.

> *Anita Silvey, in a review of "Stotan!" in* The Horn Book Magazine, *Vol. LXII, No. 5, September-October, 1986, p. 596.*

The Crazy Horse Electric Game (1987)

The title refers to the game for the Eastern Montana American Legion baseball championship, as the star pitcher, Willie Weaver, leads his team against the powerful squad from Crazy Horse Electric. But the emphasis of the novel shifts quickly away from baseball after Willie suffers a head injury in a water skiing accident. Unable to accept the loss of his athletic prowess, the pity of others, and his parents' troubled marriage, Willie runs away and ends up in the inner city of Oakland, California. After being beaten and robbed by a gang, Willie is rescued by a black bus driver/pimp, who enrolls Willie in a school for troubled youths. Thanks to the understanding staff of the school, Willie regains his mental and physical abilities and his self-confidence. He returns home to Montana, however, to learn that there is no longer a place for him in the lives of those he left. If nothing else, Crutcher manages to cram many of the most popular themes of young adult novels into this book, as Willie faces the crib death of his sister, divorce, drugs, sexual feelings, gang violence, mental handicaps, physical handicaps, prostitution, child beating, and more. Willie's present-tense narration is annoying, and does not work well for this story that covers several years. The author is best in the effective description of Willie's effort to recover from his injury. But this is the best that can be said for a novel that often seems contrived.

> *Todd Morning, in a review of "The Crazy Horse Electric Game," in* School Library Journal, *Vol. 33, No. 8, May, 1987, p. 108.*

Making a spectacular play that beats the Crazy Horse Electric baseball team for the Eastern Montana American League championship is Willie Weaver's best memory—and his worst.

At 16, Willie's athletic future looks so bright he has to wear shades, but a waterskiing accident changes all that. Partially paralyzed, his motor coordination badly impaired, he turns bitter, drives his friends away, and finally leaves home, haunted by the memory of that one play and the knowledge that he will never again be so good. He lodges at last in Oakland, where he meets Crutcher's trademark assortment of offbeat characters, and regains much of his physical and emotional balance at an alternative school for hard cases (OMLC, or "One More Last Chance" High). Two years later, he returns briefly to his startled hometown friends and now-divorced parents, but discovers that he's not yet ready to settle down there.

The broad, imaginative humor that lightened *Stotan!* struggles here beneath a weight of guilt, frustration and inner-city violence (Oakland sounds worse than the stereotypical South Bronx), and several of the character portraits are unusually amateurish—the brutal but sympathetic pimp, for instance, and the Oriental philosopher and martial artist, thinly disguised as a ribald young tai-chi teacher; nevertheless, readers will find themselves cheered by the courageous way Willie battles back, and by the way nearly everyone gets what they deserve or work for.

> *A review of "The Crazy Horse Electric Game,"*

> *in* Kirkus Reviews, *Vol. LV, No. 9, May 15, 1987, p. 793.*

As Crutcher has done before in ***Running Loose,*** and ***Stotan!,*** he does again in ***The Crazy Horse Electric Game*** with another young man being forced to dig deep for the stabilization offered by reaching one's inner strength. . . .

Crutcher writes powerfully and movingly of Willie's attempts to "become whole" again, the need to readjust his expectations of what his body can do and the means of compensating. While one can detect the physical improvement, through conversations and his improving athletic ability, it's the friendship with Sam and others that brings the mental improvement. The characterization in this book is wonderful; the reader can picture each person introduced, whether it be an amazingly bizarre schoolmate known as Telephone Man, or Dr. Hawk, a huge street dude who initially terrified Willie.

Each scene involving Willie and Jo's Boys is filled with tension; you know Willie is going to be badly beaten in his first encounter with the gang, yet you can't stop reading. Then when Willie is hiding in the OMLC school and Jo's Boys are hunting him, the scene is so realistic he practically has you shouting at Willie to offer suggestions of how to escape. Crutcher's realism doesn't stop there, however. This book could have ended "happily ever after" with Willie returning home to his girlfriend and parents, all waiting for him with open arms. But tragedies don't leave a family unscarred, and Willie's family is an especially vulnerable one. It's authors like Chris Crutcher who make our job of "selling books" that much easier.

> *Pam Spencer, in a review of "The Crazy Horse Electric Game," in* Voice of Youth Advocates, *Vol. 10, No. 2, June, 1987, p. 76.*

As in ***Stotan!*** Chris Crutcher manages to create truly believable male adolescent characters. Whether he is writing about the baseball field or the basketball court, he makes sports and the young boys who play them come alive and in the process presents the issues and problems of adolescence. Although sometimes marred by plot problems—the details about the pimp and his prostitute seem quite unnecessary—the book magnificently portrays the thoughts and feelings of a crippled athlete and is a testimony to the indomitability of the human spirit.

> *Anita Silvey, in a review of "The Crazy Horse Electric Game," in* The Horn Book Magazine, *Vol. LXIII, No. 6, November-December, 1987, p. 741.*

Chinese Handcuffs (1989)

"Human beings are connected by the ghastly as well as the glorious," the author says—and demonstrates—in this intense, painful novel.

Teen-age characters have been knocked around in Crutcher's other stories, but not to this extent: Dillon Hemingway, still trying to recover from the effects of watching his older brother Preston commit suicide, meets Jen Lawless, a classmate who's been sexually abused—first by her father, then by her stepfather. The other woman in Dillon's life is Stacy, Preston's old girlfriend, who took a long trip after Preston's suicide and now has a baby she claims is her cousin's. Threats of violence—from a motorcycle gang looking for Dillon and from Jen's twisted stepfather—underscore acts of courage: Jen finally confiding in Dillon, Stacy announcing over the school intercom that the baby is actually hers.

Told partly in long, articulate letters from Dillon to his dead brother, and partly in a third-person narrative with the point of view shifting from one character to another, the story has a patchwork quality. Stacy, Jen, and Dillon cut noble, heroic figures that, with the too-neat ending, give this an air of unreality; even so, Crutcher probes so many tender areas here that readers may end by feeling exhausted and emotionally bruised.

A review of "Chinese Handcuffs," in Kirkus Reviews, *Vol. LVII, No. 4, February 15, 1989, p. 290.*

A Chinese handcuff is one of those colored straw tubes we fooled around with as kids. Stick your index finger into the tube then try to get your finger out. Pull and the straw tightens around your knuckle. Pull harder and you're really stuck. Frustration mounts as you can't figure out how to extricate yourself. A simple gizmo that turns out to be not so simple, and until you learn its secret, is not so much fun, either.

Crutcher uses the analogy of Chinese handcuffs to delineate the character of his protagonist, Dillon Hemingway. A high school senior with a rebellious streak, Dillon is into triathlons and introspection. Shifting between third person narrative and Dillon's long letters to his dead brother, the novel depicts the maturation of Dillon.

And what a maturing process he endures. Nearly every problem that has ever been explored in a YA novel visits itself upon Dillon, his family, and/or his friends. A partial inventory of plagues includes divorce, rape, incest, alcoholism, drug abuse, and suicide. Some of these afflictions are recurrent. Throw in a Vietnam vet father (Dillon's), an adolescent widowed mother (Dillon's brother's girlfriend), a Hell's Angelish motorcycle gang, and a principal who makes the one in *Ferris Bueller's Day Off* look like Mr. Chips, and you have yourself one intense book. Perhaps even a hyperactive book.

Which brings me back to the Chinese handcuffs. To free yourself you simply release the pressure, and the thing slides right off. Dillon learns this metaphorically over the course of the novel. He is a survivor. Likewise, Crutcher draws the reader into the story and makes us have to finish, much like triathletes have to finish their races. As in his other work, Crutcher's characters think and grow, and it is through this cultivation of the inner life that we become involved with them. There may be too many harrowing incidents crammed into it, but **Chinese Handcuffs** is a rewarding novel, tough, topical, compelling, and well written. Encourage your older YAs to read it.

Randy Brough, in a review of "Chinese Hand-

cuffs," in Voice of Youth Advocates, *Vol. 12, No. 2, June, 1989, p. 98.*

Dillon Hemingway faces a lot of problems. Not only had his older brother committed suicide, he'd done it in Dillon's presence. Not only was Dillon in love with his brother's girl, but also he discovered that her parents' new baby was in fact the girl's child and his nephew. Not only did the other girl he found attractive fail to respond, but also he learned that she had been sexually abused by her father and was now being sexually abused by her stepfather. Given this plethora of woe plus the fact that the third-person narrative is interrupted (often at considerable length) by long letters to Dillon's dead brother, it's surprising that the story is as effective as it is. While all the problems don't really add up to a plot, the characterization is sound and consistent, and Crutcher's writing has both insight and fluency.

Zena Sutherland, in a review of "Chinese Handcuffs," in Bulletin of the Center for Children's Books, *Vol. 42, No. 11, July-August, 1989, p. 271.*

Chris Crutcher explores an eternally persistent theme in this many faceted tale of a contemporary family. One brother fails at life, and the other succeeds. On the face of it the major events piling up in Dillon Hemingway's last three years of high school sound like the details of a real potboiler. Drug addiction, suicide, motorcycle gangs, broken families, teenage pregnancy, unrequited love, and a brutal case of child sexual abuse cloud the lives of Dillon, his brother Preston, and friends Stacy and Jennifer. For Dillon and Jennifer, the pivotal characters in a large cast, athletic achievement is a refuge, and the book is a sports story as well as an account of personal crisis. Crutcher constructs his tangled web with intelligent insight, creating a painful, powerful story. Dillon is a wonderfully drawn, complex character; he is tough, vulnerable, and something of a loner who delights in devising ingenious schemes to outrage the high school principal. The boy's personal dilemma is the two-fold task of dealing with his guilt over Preston's death and recognizing that he, too, is marred by violence and evil within himself. Basically he is a good, imaginative, and hurt human being who gropes and grows in the face of profoundly awful circumstances. Like the issues and characters, the structure of the book is complex, the text moving back and forth through three strands of narrative. Dillon writes long letters to his dead brother as a means of unburdening himself; these are juxtaposed with flashbacks to childhood and segments of the ongoing story, all told from the omniscient view, which allows latitude for developing both teenage and adult characters. Dillon's story is intercut with that of Jennifer, whose own tragedy pulls him out of himself and forward into adulthood. In the end the story is a compelling, well-paced, and even humorous one of human failing, survival, and hope.

Margaret A. Bush, in a review of "Chinese Handcuffs," in The Horn Book Magazine, *Vol. LXV, No. 4, July-August, 1989, p. 487.*

The purpose of this column is to allow the Young Adult editorial staff to highlight book-related connections, drawing on recent teenage and adult titles that complement or counterbalance each other, indicate a trend, or speak to the perennial teenage plea for "another book just like this one." Given *Booklist's* recommended only policy, we would ordinarily not comment on Chris Crutcher's latest book; however, in addition to suggesting books for library purchase, we also feel it is important to offer opinion on some controversial titles that we do not recommend. Hence, the column in this issue focuses on Crutcher's *Chinese Handcuffs,* a recent YA novel that has turned out to be one of the season's most talked about books.

With three titles, each a Best Books for Young Adults selection, to his credit, Chris Crutcher is one of the most successful novelists writing for young adults today. It is not hard to understand why: he handles dialogue with aplomb; he evokes the inherent drama of competitive school sports with assurance; and his characters grapple with vital moral dilemmas that force their rites of passage in complicated, realistic ways. But the talent he has shown in past work is not sufficient reason to recommend *Chinese Handcuffs,* which reads more like exploitive melodrama than gritty realism or coming-of-age.

Though difficult to summarize, the novel basically concerns a teenager, caught in the aftermath of his brother's suicide, who tries to help a girl he cares about put an end to the sexual abuse she is enduring at home. Two young adults share the spotlight: Jennifer Lawless, basketball star, "A" student, abuse victim; and Dillon Hemingway, confused and angered by his brother Preston's death and by the vicious circumstances of Jen's life. A strong writer, Crutcher mines his characters' vulnerabilities in some powerful scenes. A flashback to the death of Jen's adored and adoring grandfather is exceptionally moving as five-year-old Jen, already abused secretly by her natural father and now bereft of a loving adult, first pretends Grampa is not dead, then screams at her mother, "You won't see to Grampa. Grampa's dead. Nobody ever sees to Grampa. And nobody ever sees to me!"

Managed without explicit sexual details, the depiction of Jen's further victimization by T.B., her stepfather, is one of the most chilling portrayals of sexual exploitation in teenage fiction—far more intense than Hadley Irwin's handling of the incest theme in *Abbey, My Love,* and also more brutal about the failures of social services and the legal system to protect the abused. Even a frightening-ly vivid sequence, during which Dillon and Preston bludgeon Charlie, a neighbor's cat, has meaning beyond mere violence. Recognizing that such an act can generate passion and excitement as well as horror, Crutcher makes a powerful moral point, which he continues to develop as the novel progresses: "I know we promised not to tell about Charlie," Dillon writes, "but I told Stacy—and she said it was a leak . . . a crack appears in the structure we've built to keep ourselves decent, and our own personal evil seeps out. It's one of the hard ways, she says, that we learn human beings are connected by the ghastly as well as the glorious, and we need always to walk around inside ourselves looking for those leaks. And plugging them up."

The brutality of other scenes, however, is harder to justify. While Dillon's secret videotaping of Jen's abuse by her stepfather is done to provide evidence against T.B. when all else has failed, Dillon's screening of the tape he recovers verges on voyeurism; Preston's description of a gang rape in a bar may be intended to show the final degradation that led to his suicide, but it reads too much like a mimic of recent sensational headlines; and Dillon's witnessing of Preston's self-destruction is an indulgence Crutcher easily could have passed up without compromising his theme.

Such excesses aside, the book has other weaknesses. Crutcher's authorial perspective intrudes awkwardly into the personal narratives of his characters, who, in fact, are little more than personifications of their problems. He tells us much—Dillon is funny, Jen is brilliant—but shows us far too little to make what he's revealed seem true. While supporting adult characters are essentially well drawn, it is hard to miss that they are either exceptionally wise and patient, like Jen's basketball coach and Dillon's father, or vile and manipulative, like T.B. And, for all her intuitive comments, Stacy, the mother of Preston's out-of-wedlock child, merely adds emotional junk to an already cluttered story.

Even the sports here packs less than Crutcher's usual wallop. Taken singly, the basketball sequences certainly capture the color of the court; woven between scenes about death, rape, and child abuse, however, they become lost and immaterial.

Chris Crutcher knows the right moves on and off the court. He works with teenagers and understands their problems, and he is a dynamic writer who has proved himself in the past. But *Chinese Handcuffs* is a disappointment—not because it deals straight on with difficult issues, not because it is violent or controversial, which, of course, it is. Rather, it is an unsuccessful book—and a disappointment—because the overloaded plot strains the novel's structure and diminishes the vital message Crutcher is trying to convey.

> *Stephanie Zvirin, "The YA Connection: 'Chinese Handcuffs,' by Chris Crutcher," in* Booklist, *Vol. 85, No. 22, August, 1989, p. 1966.*

Athletic Shorts: Six Short Stories   (1991)

A winning collection of stories, one of which has appeared in print before. Some of the characters from Crutcher novels pop up in these stories, often speaking in a colloquial and realistic first-person voice. As the title suggests, athletics are part of the selections; and Crutcher, as usual, is best at accurately portraying the world of high school teammates and coaches—readers can practically smell the sweat. In the first story—a monologue by a fat guy who manages to keep his dignity—the author seamlessly blends humor with more serious elements. Crutcher's fans expect almost operatic flights of emotion, and he more than delivers here. The short story format keeps the action focused and definitely packs a punch. The final entry, a gritty, no-holds-barred account of the fear surrounding AIDS, is especially effective. These *Athletic Shorts* will speak to YAs, touch them deeply, and introduce them to characters they'll want to know better.

Todd Morning, in a review of "Athletic Shorts: Six Short Stories," in School Library Journal, *Vol. 37, No. 9, September, 1991, p. 278.*

Chris Crutcher is a discerning reporter of the inner life of adolescent males. These six short stories feature some new characters and some that readers will recognize from his popular novels. Angus Bethune—fat, clumsy, and the off-spring of homosexual parents—has been chosen king of the senior ball as a joke by his classmates. At the risk of utter humiliation, he prepares stoically for the prom and a spotlighted dance with the prom queen, the girl of his dreams. His "step-dad" puts the matter to him squarely when he acknowledges the boy's vulnerability and his courage. " 'It's guys like you and me that are brave, Angus. Guys who are different and can be crushed . . . but go out there anyway.' " In other stories, the young heroes test their strengths and their limits in equally devastating situations. Johnny Rivers challenges his father to a wrestling match in order to get even for years of physical and mental abuse, only to feel empty when he vanquishes the older man. Jack Simpson—Telephone Man in **The Crazy Horse Electric Game**—questions his father's authority in a quieter but no less wrenching way. This mentally retarded boy harbors deep-seated, irrational racial prejudices instilled in him by the father he reveres. But when a young black tough rescues him from a beating, Jack begins to doubt his father's teachings. Louie Banks from **Running Loose** balances the value of his developing relationship with a young man dying of AIDS against his longstanding friendship with a fellow athlete and opts for the tougher course, even though friendship with a gay man threatens his sense of sexual identity. The characterizations in these stories are powerfully drawn, and the dialogue is quick and scorching. The issues of father-son relationships, sexuality, and the testing of personal limits—all central themes in young adult literature—are explored from an unconventional perspective in **Athletic Shorts.** One need not have read Crutcher's novels to appreciate the young men within these pages. They stand proudly on their own. (pp. 602-03)

Nancy Vasilakis, in a review of "Athletic Shorts," in The Horn Book Magazine, *September-October, 1991, pp. 602-03.*

If you do not already know Chris Crutcher's four superb novels, these six stories . . . provide a delicious introduction to his attactive, sensitive characters (like Angus Bethune and Chris Byers) and thought-provoking situations (like having homosexual parents and how do you deal with the person who has been responsible for your parents' deaths?) If you already know Louie Banks, Lionel Serbousek, Pete Shropshrire, Johnny Rivers, and the Telephone Man, you'll relish them in new situations, some that take place before and some after the settings of the novels in which they originally appeared. You do not have to be a jock to appreciate these powerful stories that provide humor and insights into teenage athletes who deal heroically with painful events and moral dilemmas. The punny title and clever dust jacket deserve a special award.

Donald R. Gallo, in a review of "Athletic Shorts," in The ALAN Review, *Vol. 19, No. 1, Fall, 1991, p. 34.*

At his best, as he is in the first story in this collection, **"A Brief Moment in the Life of Angus Bethune,"** Chris Crutcher is a nervy, energetic storyteller, not afraid to write a story about gay people—*fat* gay people—that is both real and funny. . . . **"The Pin,"** about a father-son wrestling bout, is also vintage, tough-but-tender Crutcher, but the other stories are panderingly didactic about good kids who discover how good they are, and each gives the reader (this reader, anyway) the disconcerting sense of being patted on the back just for reading it. Crutcher's introductory notes to the collection and stories are unnecessary and exacerbate the self-congratulatory tone. On the other hand, kids are often a lot more susceptible to sentimental fiction than we give them credit for, and Crutcher fans will enjoy these stories as a way to mark time until the next novel.

Roger Sutton, in a review of "Athletic Shorts: Six Short Stories," in Bulletin of the Center for Children's Books, *Vol. 45, No. 4, December, 1991, p. 87.*

Lois Ehlert

1934-

American author and illustrator of picture books.

Major works include *Growing Vegetable Soup* (1987), *Color Zoo* (1989), *Fish Eyes: A Book You Can Count On* (1990).

Ehlert is celebrated as the creator of informational picture books that introduce young children to such concepts as colors, shapes, counting, gardening, and the alphabet through their inventive design and use of stylized, brightly colored graphics. Praised for reinforcing basic concepts and presenting new information in an intriguing, often startling way, she is acknowledged as an innovative writer and artist whose works are useful as well as bold and clever. Ehlert uses fruits, vegetables, trees, animals, and fish as the subjects of her books, which are noted for their ability to inspire young readers to examine the familiar from fresh perspectives. Several of Ehlert's works have a gardening motif: her first book, *Growing Vegetable Soup,* depicts the complete process of planting and growing a vegetable garden, while its companion volume *Planting a Rainbow* (1988) addresses the raising of a flower garden. In *Eating the Alphabet: Fruits and Vegetables from A to Z* (1989), Ehlert depicts a variety of produce in the format of an alphabet book; in this work, she assembles cut shapes in assorted colors and assembles them into displays that correspond to letters of the alphabet. Ehlert is perhaps best known for *Color Zoo,* a picture book in which she uses apertures to make shapes such as the circle, square, triangle, octagon, and heart into nine animals. When young readers turn the pages of the book, they reveal another picture which forms a new animal; the shape of the last die-cut and its name appear on the reverse of each turned page. Ehlert is also the creator of *Color Farm* (1990), a companion volume which uses a similar format to depict several barnyard animals. Among her other works, Ehlert is the author and illustrator of *Fish Eyes,* a counting book which uses colorful fish to introduce the concept of simple addition, and *Feathers for Lunch* (1990), which profiles familiar birds, their food, habitats, and songs as well as flowers such as the lilac and forsythia.

An art teacher and design illustrator who is the creator of toys and games, sets for a children's theater group, and a series of basic art books, Ehlert began her career in the field of juvenile literature as the illustrator of fiction and nonfiction by such authors as Diane Wolkstein and Edward Lear; Ehlert's illustrations for Lear's *Limericks* (1965) are especially noted for their colorful, modern quality. As the illustrator of her own books, Ehlert is lauded for her use of eye-catching colors and shapes. She often coordinates her colors—which range from primary shades to hot pinks and purples—with surprising effect and characteristically employs double-page spreads for her watercolor collages. Critic Denise Wilms writes that "Ehlert's sense of color and graphic design is amazing." In several

of her works, Ehlert provides entertaining subtexts to advance her concepts: for example, in *Feathers for Lunch,* she uses verse to describe the unsuccessful attempt of a belled cat to make a meal out of the birds being profiled. Ehlert's works often include rhyming introductions, and she usually includes notes or glossaries that provide more extensive information on her subjects. *Color Zoo* was named a Caldecott Award honor book in 1990. In addition, Ehlert was the first recipient of the Addy Award in 1976 for her series of animal drawings for the Knoxville Zoo and has received several other awards for her art.

(See also *Something about the Author,* Vol. 35.)

TITLE COMMENTARY

Limericks (1965)

[*Limericks was written by Edward Lear.*]

Ultra-modern illustrations in bright colors bring Lear to a contemporary audience. Though the illustrations may be confusing to some children, they bear enough resemblance to reality for most to find them as amusing as the limericks. Since the illustrations are more readily identifiable when seen from a distance, the book will be very useful for storytelling. (pp. 142-43)

Book Review Advisory Committee, in a review of "Limericks by Lear," in School Library Journal, *Vol. 12, No. 1, September, 1965, pp. 142-43.*

The casual nonsense of Lear's limericks has been well served by the illustrator's deceptively casual looking blobs of color to represent the nonsense people and animals, with overlays of stamping and some features drawn in. The limericks have been reduced to their original four line form and one to a page with these measurements leaves an unconscionable amount of white space around the text. The facing illustrations are big, in full color and interesting in conception and execution.

A review of "Limericks by Lear," in Kirkus Reviews, *Vol. XXXIII, No. 17, September 1, 1965, p. 899.*

Growing Vegetable Soup   (1987)

A very simple text about planting and growing a vegetable garden is accompanied by psychedelically bright illustrations.

A red watering can held by a magenta hand on a green ground, a hot-orange spade against blue—these colors are painfully vivid, jumping around on the page to the point of diverting attention from any pattern or information conveyed. Information is minimal anyway—seeds are planted and grow in an unrealistic medley, and the forms are so generalized that they would be recognizable only to someone already familiar with the various plants. The book concludes with a portrait of a vegetable soup that doesn't look like something to eat (although the jacket flap provides a simple recipe a kindergarten class could make).

A plausible notion for a book, shouted down by garish illustrations.

A review of "Growing Vegetable Soup," in Kirkus Reviews, *Vol. LV, No. 2, January 15, 1987, p. 138.*

This is the boldest, brassiest garden book to hit the market, and what a delight. Intensely colored graphics capture the complete growing process from seed to cooking pot, with the focus on the plants. The unseen narrator describes the process of growing vegetable soup, from preparing the tools and digging holes for the seeds to weeding plants; picking vegetables; washing, chopping, and cooking them—and finally enjoying the homemade soup while planning to grow more next year. It's a fresh presentation of the gardening cycle with a joyful conclusion, and the added attraction of an easy and tasty recipe for vegetable soup on the flyleaf. A book to help nourish healthy readers.

Barbara Peklo Serling, in a review of "Growing Vegetable Soup," in School Library Journal, *Vol. 33, No. 7, March, 1987, p. 143.*

Growing vegetable soup. What a wonderful idea! . . . The

progression is accurate and easily followed in the simple text. The artwork is boldly colored and graphic. Unfortunately, some of the shapes of objects and vegetables are so generalized as to be confusing rather than clarifying. Background colors in several pictures are so similar to the colors of some of the items portrayed that images blend together. The best illustration is that of the soup cooking in a large stock pot. The steam wafting above the pot is white and the cut-up vegetables are vivid against this background. Granted my scientific bias, the book would have been more interesting to children if the vegetables and tools used in gardening and cooking were more true-to-life.

Susan D. Chapnick, in a review of "Growing Vegetable Soup," in Appraisal: Science Books for Young People, *Vol. 21, No. 7, Spring, 1988, p. 11.*

Planting a Rainbow   (1988)

From the artist who created last year's shoutingly vivid **Growing Vegetable Soup,** a companion volume about raising a flower garden. "Mom and I" plant bulbs (even rhizomes), choose seeds, buy seedlings, and altogether grow about 20 species. Unlike the vegetables, whose juxtaposed colors were almost painfully bright, the flowers make a splendidly gaudy array, first taken together and then interestingly grouped by color—the pages vary in size here so that colored strips down the right-hand side combine to make a broad rainbow.

Bold, stylish, and indubitably inspired by real flowers, there is still (as with its predecessor) a link missing between these illustrations with their large, solid areas of color and the real experience of a garden. The stylized forms are almost more abstractions than representations (and why is the daisy yellow?). There is also little sense of the relative times for growing and blooming—everything seems to come almost at once. Perhaps the trouble is that Ehlert has captured all the color of the garden, but not its subtle gradations or the light, the space, the air, and the continual movement and change.

A review of "Planting a Rainbow," in Kirkus Reviews, *Vol. LVI, No. 6, March 15, 1988, p. 454.*

[**Planting a Rainbow**] is a dazzling celebration of the colorful variety in a flower garden and the cyclical excitement of gardening. A young child relates in ten simple sentences the yearly cycle and process of planning, planting, and picking flowers in a garden. . . . The power of this book lies in the glowing brilliance and bold abstraction of the double-page collages. Ehlert combines simple, stylized shapes of flat, high intensity color into abstract yet readily identifiable images of plants and flowers while clearly and colorfully labeling each plant on an adjacent garden marker. Children will especially delight in the six pages of varying width depicting all the flowers of each color of the rainbow. A celebration of the garden, the power of shape and color, and the harmony of text and image in a picture book.

From Color Zoo, *written and illustrated by Lois Ehlert.*

Pamela Miller Ness, in a review of "Planting a Rainbow," in School Library Journal, *Vol. 35, No. 8, May, 1988, p. 83.*

Planting a Rainbow is a book about colour. It begins in autumn when the soil is dull and the only strong tones come from the tabs which mark where bulbs have been planted. Then in due season shoots break through the soil and flowers appear in order. Then comes the planting of summer flowers, and the rainbow grows. In a series of cut pages individual colours are isolated and identified, until a final double-spread reveals the rich tones of late summer and autumn. Lois Ehlert has a strong sense of form as well as colour, and her designs are stylized, discovering the basic shapes of everything from the wheelbarrow to the richest of summer blooms. A clever book, typically American in conception and execution; it will make parents and teachers as well as children take a fresh look at the beauty around them.

M. Crouch, in a review of "Planting a Rainbow," in The Junior Bookshelf, *Vol. 52, No. 4, August, 1988, p. 182.*

Color Zoo **(1989)**

Like Suse MacDonald's *Alphabatics,* an innovative book to stimulate the visual imagination. Ehlert uses apertures through sturdy paper to transform her boldly constructed images: a circle containing a symmetrical pattern— composed of red, orange, and green triangles and circles— believably represents a tiger's face; turning the page to remove the circular hole (labeled "circle" on the other side) reveals the same pattern with new ears, now a mouse; the next page turn (square hole) transforms mouse to fox; and at a third page turn, the three shapes used so far are col-

lected and labeled again. Two more sequences add other animals and shapes, including octagon, hexagon, heart, and oval (unfortunately, neither egg-shaped nor an ellipse but a round-ended, straight-sided figure). All the figures formed, as well as the shapes and colors used, are recapitulated on the last three pages.

Exciting use of design and color; an intriguing way to introduce or reinforce concepts of shape and color.

A review of "Color Zoo," in Kirkus Reviews, *Vol. LVII, No. 3, February 1, 1989, p. 208.*

This uniquely designed book features a series of cutouts stacked so that with each page turn, a layer is removed to reveal yet another picture. Each configuration is an animal: a tiger's face (a circle shape) and two ears disappear with a page turn to leave viewers with a square within which is a mouse. The mouse's square frame, removed, reveals a fox. There are three such series, and each ends with a small round-up of the shapes used so far. That's not all. On the reverse of the turned page is the shape cutout previously removed with the shape's printed name. While the tiger and lion are not easy to identify in their geometrically shaped components, children will readily name the seven others and will delight in identifying both animals and shapes. Boldly designed pages easily carry to the rear of the room during story hours, and brilliant juxtapositions of vibrant primary colors will make children's eyes tingle.

Susan Hepler, in a review of "Color Zoo," in School Library Journal, *Vol. 35, No. 8, April, 1989, p. 80.*

Concept and design are felicitously blended in a striking picture-concept book which introduces colors and shapes in a manner sure to intrigue preschoolers. Clever use of overlaid die-cuts allows various groupings of animals to metamorphose one into another as the pages are turned. . . . Not only an effective method for teaching basic concepts, the book is also a means for sharpening visual perception, which encourages children to see these shapes in other contexts—somewhat analogous to the activities suggested by Ed Emberley's *Wing on a Flea.* Calendered, heavy stock, brilliantly toned, gives the book instant appeal. Thoughtful production makes it more than just another handsome entry into the picture book sweepstakes, as exemplified in the conclusion. There a review of the shapes used, printed white on gray, opposes a stark white page on which all the book's colors are reproduced in logical groupings, four to a row, each carefully labeled. A sure bet for story hours, the book also promises to be indispensable for classrooms and home libraries. (pp. 471-72)

Mary M. Burns, in a review of "Color Zoo," in The Horn Book Magazine, *Vol. LXV, No. 4, July-August, 1989, pp. 471-72.*

Sturdy paper, bright colors, and the device of cut-out windows in various shapes should appeal to the very young audience for whom this triple-concept book is designed. Unfortunately, there are serious flaws that militate against the book achieving the purposes for which it is designed. This is the pattern: a purple page with a cut-out circle (caption: tiger) shows the lines and colors of other pages (the square of the next recto page: mouse) then a triangle (fox). Finally comes a page with two green dots that have served as the eyes for all three animals. First, the geometric abstractions do not look like animals; second, the book tries to do too much at once; third, the ending (3 pages that show shapes, colors, and a reprise of the 9 animals) reveals that some of the colors used in the book (purple) are missing or are misrepresented, as in a green labelled "yellow green."

> *Zena Sutherland, in a review of "Color Zoo,"*
> *in* Bulletin of the Center for Children's Books,
> *Vol. 43, No. 1, September, 1989, p. 6.*

Eating the Alphabet: Fruits and Vegetables from A to Z (1989)

Ehlert's eye-catching alphabet book splashes exuberant colors across each page. Cut shapes drenched in assorted hues are assembled into brilliant fruits and vegetables, with each page becoming an eclectic display of produce that corresponds to a letter of the alphabet. Many of the items here will be familiar, but Ehlert stretches youngsters' knowledge with some things that will be new—star fruit, for example, or xigua or quince. It's a pedagogical quibble that the words for *J, jicama* and *jalapeño,* aren't pronounced with the English sound for *J* and may thus be confusing; however, produce beginning with an English *J* is scarce, if nonexistent, and these examples can be used to expand children's understanding of the diversity of the English language. The gardening motifs of the artist's earlier books, **Growing Vegetable Soup** and **Planting a Rainbow,** are continued here with gusto. Names of fruits and vegetables are printed in both upper- and lowercase letters, and a table at the back identifies unfamiliar items. A visual feast to enjoy on several levels.

> *Denise Wilms, in a review of "Eating the Alphabet: Fruits and Vegetable from A to Z," in* Booklist, *Vol. 85, No. 14, March 15, 1989, p. 1294.*

Brilliant, vibrant watercolor collages portray fruits and vegetables that start with each letter of the alphabet. The objects depicted, shown against a white ground, are easily identifiable for the most part, and represent the more common sounds of the letter shown. (Only "J" *[jalapeño, jicama]* falls short of this criterion.) The problem letter "X" is cleverly handled with "xigua"—the Chinese name for watermelon. Both upper- and lower-case letters are printed in large, black type. A nice added touch is the glossary which includes the pronunciation and interesting facts about the origin of each fruit and vegetable, how it grows, and its uses. An exuberant, eye-catching alphabet book that's sure to be popular with parents, teachers, and youngsters.

> *Barbara B. Murphy, in a review of "Eating the Alphabet," in* School Library Journal, *Vol. 35, No. 9, May, 1989, p. 83.*

A delicious way to practise letters, identify foods, and experience colors, this picture book begins "Apple to Zucchini, / come take a look. / Start eating your way /

through this alphabet book." The illustrations and book design are tantalizing, from endpapers that feature miniature rows of fruit and vegetable icons, to a title page with a funny face made of fruits and vegetables, to spacious spreads overflowing with both the common and the unusual: "A a" shows apricots, artichokes, avocados, asparagi, and apples. Endive, fig, Indian corn, jalapeno, jicama, kiwifruit, kohlrabi, kumquat, leek, mango, papaya, persimmon, pomegranate, quince, radicchio, rutabaga, star fruit, swiss chard, ugli fruit, vegetable marrow, and xigua all make surprise appearances amidst familiar bananas, cabbages, potatoes, and strawberries. All letters and words are presented in both upper and lower case. There are a few pictures that may defy identification: the cauliflower is too stylized to be realistic, and the huckleberries look just like the blueberries, but the total aesthetic effect is so satisfying as to make these minor quibbles indeed. A glossary of fruits and vegetables in the book gives pronunciation and botanical information on each. A fabulous advertisement for natural foods as well as for appetizing words.

> *Betsy Hearne, in a review of "Eating the Alphabet: Fruits and Vegetables from A to Z," in* Bulletin of the Center for Children's Books, *Vol. 42, No. 11, July-August, 1989, p. 273.*

Fish Eyes: A Book You Can Count On (1990)

Ehlert's sense of color and graphic design is amazing. Following in the footsteps of **Color Zoo** and **Eating the Alphabet,** she makes another startling presentation that is, perhaps, her best work to date. **Fish Eyes,** a counting book, follows a familiar form, which the artist dresses with compelling color and design. A lilting rhyme prefaces the counting action and primes kids to count the fish: "If I could put on a suit of scales, / add some fins and one of these tails, / I'd close my eyes and then I'd wish / that I'd turn into a beautiful fish." An added element—cut-out eyes that peek through to the next page—adds fun, but it's the dramatic effect of the brilliant tropical colors of the fish against a polished navy background that makes the book a show stopper. All the while an exceedingly unobtrusive little fish whispers asides (printed in dark colors for effect) that ease each page into the next—another ploy to keep young eyes alert. A visual treat from start to finish.

> *Denise Wilms, in a review of "Fish Eyes: A Book You Can Count On," in* Booklist, *Vol. 86, No. 13, March 1, 1990, p. 1339.*

The slight text, occasionally in rhyme, introduces adjectives through the count, and tries to set a context of wish-fulfillment. It's a slick production, attempting several concepts at once—numbers, shapes, colors, imagining, addition to a value of one—but it doesn't quite hang together, and its result is a little breathless. MacDonald and Oakes' *Numblers* (Dial, 1988) also uses strong color and stark form to present visually the concepts of increasing quantity and transformations, but in a more thoughtful and well-integrated way, with movement inherent in the design. Another little dark fish, Lionni's *Swimmy* (Pantheon, 1963), has a more meaningful underwater exploration, incorporating the idea of changing appearances into the story.

Karen Litton, in a review of "Fish Eyes: A Book You Can Count On," in School Library Journal, *Vol. 36, No. 5, May, 1990, p. 84.*

Lois Ehlert's forte is her use of exuberant colors and simple, clean-edged shapes. The illustrator of more than a dozen children's books by other authors, as well as several of her own, Mrs. Ehlert specializes in bright picture books—books that appear much simpler than they are in both concept and execution. Her bold illustrations have the look of a Marimekko print. The images are flat, like paper cutouts, and highly stylized. The colors are tropical, electric and hot—the grape purples and sizzling pinks children tend to choose when they paint. Often she pairs complementary hues—blues and reds, greens and pinks—to startling effect, giving her illustrations a vibrant op-art feel, a visual shimmer that makes them jump off the page.

In two of her earlier books, ***Growing Vegetable Soup*** and ***Planting a Rainbow,*** Mrs. Ehlert used this eye-catching style to illustrate the cycles of gardening, from buying seeds and bulbs to planting, tending and harvesting. Yet both these books, despite the richness of their subject matter and the beauty of their execution, sometimes go over the heads of young readers. Especially for an urban child who has never cultivated a garden, the flatness of the imagery tends to be too abstract and unreal.

Happily, ***Fish Eyes*** avoids these problems without sacrificing any of the jubilance or magic of the author's sharp style. As in her earlier books, the underlying theme of ***Fish Eyes*** is progression. But here she has moved from land to cobalt-blue sea. The idea is to count, rather than to cultivate. And the lure is a passel of flip-flopping fish.

Indeed, from the first dazzling fish we meet—a languorously long, papaya-colored creature with hot pink and green spots that stretches the full length of the open book—the viewer is hooked. We are invited to "put on a suit of scales / add some fins and one of these tails," and, as we enter this elegant underwater world of cavorting fish, to count what we see: one green fish, two jumping fish, and so on. Attention is also paid to the patterns and shapes—striped, spotted, flashy—marking these lolling underwater creatures. Attention is paid to types of movements as well—jumping, darting, flipping—and to the oddities of physique: skinny, fantailed and the like. But the best bait of all comes from the cutout fish eyes on each page—holes just the size of a youngster's finger that invite him or her to touch while counting.

CURRANT currant

CORN corn

CELERY celery

CUCUMBER cucumber

From Eating the Alphabet: Fruits and Vegetables from A to Z, *written and illustrated by Lois Ehlert.*

Yet clearly Mrs. Ehlert understands that no book can hold a child's interest without an air of mystery too, for all is not as obvious as it seems. Wisely, she conceals one tiny jet-black fish somewhere on each dark blue page. Small, fugitive and hard to see, this enigmatic fish adds interest, especially for the older reader, to what might otherwise seem too predictable and plodding an exercise. Like a game of hide-and-seek it creates an element of surprise, a moment of searching, while at the same time prompting the youngster to perform simple acts of addition. "1 green fish plus me makes 2" reads the text, though most youngsters seem to call out the numbers before they are read.

Though *Fish Eyes* may be for younger children than the publisher suggests, it is a counting book with enough novelty to hold a child's interest, and enough complexity to sustain repeated readings.

> *Andrea Barnet, "Flip-Flopping Fish," in* The New York Times Book Review, *May 20, 1990, p. 40.*

Feathers for Lunch (1990)

Using the glorious color and bold technique she employed so successfully in *Eating the Alphabet,* Ehlert depicts ten familiar birds, providing drama in the form of a hungry (but belled) cat whose quest (unsuccessful except for the tokens mentioned in the title) is briefly described in verse. Though stylized, the life-size representations of the birds should serve well for identification, as will the colorful, labeled flora that also appear. Verbal approximations of birdsongs are included; illustrated notes on food, range, habitat, and song are appended. Unusual, useful, attractive, and fun.

> *A review of "Feathers for Lunch," in* Kirkus Reviews, *Vol. LVIII, No. 14, July 15, 1990, p. 1003.*

The pictures are bold collages of stylized shapes and strong, unabashed colors. A lilac bush drips purple, the better to highlight green leaves and an oriole's rich orange breast. Likewise, a pair of Rembrandt tulips offset the dark blue-blacks and hot yellow-red of a red-winged blackbirds wing. The elemental text makes a stab at rhyming, but page flow interrupts the rhythm; what really counts are the illustrations that picture not only the labeled birds, but also some colorful spring and summer greenery. Lots of fun though not to be viewed as a field guide. (pp. 56-7)

> *Denise Wilms, in a review of "Feathers for Lunch," in* Booklist, *Vol. 87, No. 1, September 1, 1990, pp. 56-7.*

From the glorious title page showing a yellow-eyed cat staring intently at a house wren, children will be drawn into this book's jaunty rhyme: "Uh-oh. / Door's left open, / just a crack. / My cat is out / and he won't / come back!" The cat is looking for a tasty bird, but because he has a bell on his collar, he can't catch anything but "feathers for lunch." Although the cat is not visible on every double-page spread, his presence nearby is always obvious since with every step his bell sounds an apt *jingle jingle.*

The book is a visual and aural treat bursting with brightly colored birds and their calls—from the repetitive *what cheer cheer cheer* of the northern cardinal to the haunting *who-o who who who* of the mourning dove—and lush flowers such as lilacs, forsythia, and geraniums, all of which are labeled. The final section, cunningly titled "The lunch that got away," offers brief facts, including size, food, habitat, and range, about the twelve birds drooled over by the cat. Ehlert has attempted many things in these pages—for instance, the birds are all drawn life-size—and has succeeded in all of them; her lavish use of bold color against generous amounts of white space is graphically appealing, and the large type, nearly one-half-inch tall, invites attempts by those just beginning to read. An engaging, entertaining, and recognizably realistic story destined to become an uncontested favorite with many children and adults.

> *Ellen Fader, in a review of "Feathers for Lunch," in* The Horn Book Magazine, *Vol. LXVI, No. 6, November-December, 1990, p. 726.*

Color Farm (1990)

Through imaginative use of cutouts, Ehlert has created two books in one. Each recto page shows a barnyard animal—cow, chicken, rooster, duck—composed almost entirely of geometric shapes. Turn the page, and the verso shows one of those shapes cut out and labeled on a contrasting background. Ehlert's characteristically electric palette and her strong, sure sense of design make this a stimulating primer of basic shapes and familiar animals. The book will also encourage awareness of and experimentation with the ways shapes combine to form—or even simply suggest—the objects in our world. (pp. 60-1)

> *A review of "Color Farm," in* Publishers Weekly, *Vol. 237, No. 41, October 12, 1990, pp. 60-1.*

"Elegant pizazz" might best describe this latest concept book of shapes and colors. Each solid-colored page displays a single cut-out shape (square, triangle, circle, oval, etc.) in its center. Around this cut-out are other printed shapes placed in a collage manner to suggest a familiar animal, which is named in bold at the bottom of the page. Depth in the design is expertly executed by means of page overlays, so that the animals' shapes build upon each other, one by one. Rooster (a square face) has been overlayed upon Duck, (octagon), which in turn has been built upon Chicken (pentagon). Verso pages label the shape that was cut out. At the end of the sequence, a single page shows, in review, the shapes and their names. Brightness, boldness, and sturdiness combine with a basic concept and unique design to inspire children to beg for some scraps of colored paper to make their own animals. Be prepared for requests from teachers to save a copy for their classroom collections or unit studies.

> *Mary Lou Budd, in a review of "Color Farm," in* School Library Journal, *Vol. 36, No. 11, November, 1990, p. 91.*

As in *Color Zoo,* Ehlert uses an array of brilliant graphics with carefully planned die-cuts to introduce geometric shapes such as squares, octagons, hexagons, ovals, and circles. In the context of this latest theme, these forms are discovered in the visages of familiar farm animals ranging from cats to cows. An introductory verse establishes the concept and concludes with an invitation to "make some more for us to see." This suggestion for audience participation adds dimension to subsequent activities for reinforcing the ideas conveyed; thus, the book can be used as an elegant teaching device without violating its aesthetic appeal. Nor are these shapes always placed in conventional positions: the heart, for example, appears on one page with the pointed end uppermost, a technique which subtly trains the eye to examine the familiar from a different perspective. In the concluding double-page spreads, the entire cast is assembled for review, bringing the book to a colorful conclusion.

Mary M. Burns, in a review of "Color Farm," in The Horn Book Magazine, *Vol. LXVII, No. 1, January-February, 1991, p. 55.*

Red Leaf, Yellow Leaf (1991)

Ehlert uses a child's voice to describe the cultivation of a sugar maple seedling as it grows and becomes a tree purchased at a garden center and planted by a father and child. The print is large, the color and composition attractive but crowded, using twigs and seeds and fabric as well as paint for double-spread collages. However, this is less effective than most of Ehlert's work because the design sometimes overwhelms the text, as with, for example, the flashy but uninformative collage accompanying the sentence "My tree was loaded onto a truck filled with other trees and delivered to the garden center." Other pictures, crowded with too many elements, lack focus. Appended information about leaves and trees is useful but seems to be aimed at an older audience than is the main text.

Zena Sutherland, in a review of "Red Leaf, Yellow Leaf," in Bulletin of the Center for Children's Books, *Vol. 45, No. 2, October, 1991, p. 36.*

Marjorie Flack

1897-1958

American author and illustrator of picture books, fiction and nonfiction.

Major works include the "Angus" series, *Taktuk, an Arctic Boy* (with Helen Lomen, 1928); *The Story about Ping* (with Kurt Wiese, 1933); *Wait for William* (1935); *Walter, the Lazy Mouse* (1937); *The Boats on the River* (1946).

Celebrated as one of the finest American creators of juvenile literature for her distinctive use of the picture book format and understanding of what appeals to young children, Flack is recognized for developing a new aspect of the genre by using her texts, illustrations, and page design to bring drama to familiar subjects. A popular author who is best known for her five picture books about Angus, an inquisitive Scottish terrier, and *The Story about Ping,* the tale of a Chinese duck, Flack is well respected for her skills as a storyteller and an artist, for accurately depicting both human and animal behavior while successfully delineating personality, for introducing children to international cultures and factual concepts in an entertaining fashion, and for the simplicity, clarity, and humor of her books, several of which are considered classics. Most of Flack's works are directed to preschoolers and readers in the early grades, although she is also the creator of several books for middle graders. She sets her works both in the United States, usually in New England, and in countries such as France and Mexico, and portrays both children and animals as protagonists. Although many of Flack's works are thoroughly realistic, she often blends fact and fantasy, especially in her informational books, which present scientific and historical information in story form. Writing in rhythmic, economical prose noted for its deftness and lively quality, Flack often addresses the feelings of young children in her works. Among her most consistent themes are the desire to belong and the need to be independent, and several of her books are about small boys and girls who are overlooked by their older siblings. In her nonfiction, Flack provides introductions to such concepts as the changing of a tadpole into a frog and the delivering of mail. Flack is especially praised for her work as an illustrator. Working in bright colors and black-and-white line, she is acknowledged for the beauty and humor of her pictures as well as for their evocation of action and space. Flack is also the illustrator of books by other authors, including the stories about Scamper the White House Bunny by Anna Eleanor Roosevelt and DuBose Heyward's *The Country Bunny and the Little Gold Shoes;* in addition, she worked with other artists on her own picture books, notably Kurt Wiese, whom she asked to illustrate *The Story about Ping* because of his knowledge of China.

Flack's interest in nature, stories, and pictures stemmed from early childhood. At the age of eighteen, she came to New York City to study at the Art Students League, where she met the artist Karl Larsson, who was her first

husband and the father of their daughter Hilma; both Karl and Hilma Larsson collaborated with Flack on several of her books as author or illustrator. Hilma Larsson married the artist Jay Hyde Barnum, who provided the pictures for two of Flack's works. Her first book, *Taktuk, an Arctic Boy* (1928), was written in collaboration with Helen Lomen, who had lived most of her life in Alaska. Lomen's stories about Eskimo children inspired Flack to create the story about ten-year-old Taktuk, the son of a seal hunter who decides that he wants to go to school to learn to read. Considered both authentic and sympathetic, *Taktuk* is underscored by Flack's depiction of the changes to Inuit life brought about by Anglo influence; she later addressed a similar theme of the acquisition of education in *Pedro,* the story of a ten-year-old Mexican boy who is rewarded for saving the life of his American friend by having the boy's father assume responsibility for his schooling. Flack's inspiration for the "Angus" books—*Angus and the Ducks* (1930), *Angus and the Cat* (1931), *Angus Lost* (1932), *Wag-Tail Bess* (1933), and *Topsy* (1935)—came from a source closer to home: she writes that *Angus and the Ducks* "is a true story about a real dog and some real ducks. The other Angus books are also based around real incidents. The cat was Hilma's cat, and she really did hide on the roof. Wag-Tail Bess was our own Airedale." In these works, Angus's inquisitiveness leads him into a series of misadventures, such as encountering a group of ducks over the other side of the fence and chasing a cat that hits him before they become friends, behavior noted for its relevance to that of young children; throughout the series, Flack introduces several new characters, such as the timid Wag-Tail Bess, whom Angus helps to overcome her shyness, and the cocker spaniel puppy Topsy. Critic May Lamberton Becker notes that Flack's "trick of making live and lovable creatures took permanent shape in the 'Angus' books; permanent, for I cannot believe that any of the series will be forgotten by children once exposed to their charms," while *Book World* adds that the "Angus" books "remain the most charming of all first picture books." When she was working on *Angus and the Ducks*, Flack became interested in the Peking ducks that terrorize Angus; after doing extensive research on life on the Yangtze River, she wrote *The Story about Ping*.

Flack describes the adventures of Ping, a baby duck who lives by night on a houseboat where his master paddles the last duck over the gangplank to encourage punctuality; afraid to go home after he stays out too late, he hides in the reeds and is captured by a family who thinks that he will make a good soup. Saved by a child, Ping finds his way back to the boat the next day just in time to go in last—and receive a spanking. Acknowledged for its charm and accuracy as well as for its appeal to the child's sense of justice, *The Story about Ping* is one of the most beloved works of children's literature; "Few books for little children," writes critic Anne Thaxter Eaton, "have the genuine artistry of this one." Flack is often noted for successfully attributing human characteristics to her animal characters; however, she received a mixed reception for *The Restless Robin* (1937), the story of a birdling who, afraid to fly after he is almost eaten by a cat in his first venture out of the nest, is helped to fly by a variety of other birds. Presenting the complete cycle of a bird's life as part of its story, *The Restless Robin* is considered questionable by some reviewers for Flack's introduction of such values as good manners and self-control into the natural world. Most observers, however, consider Flack an author and illustrator whose books are both psychologically sound and appealing to children, and would agree with critic Barbara Bader about her contributions to juvenile literature: "[what] she had was a feel for stories . . . that would tell well in words and pictures and a knack for dramatizing them: a true picturebook sense."

(See also *Yesterday's Authors of Books for Children,* Vol. 2, and *Contemporary Authors,* Vol. 112.)

GENERAL COMMENTARY

The Junior Bookshelf

Marjorie Flack has never equalled the charm of her Angus books either in text or in illustration. Her more recent volumes, though the stories all have merit, all have a crudity in their colouring. This complaint can be made of *William and his kitten,* which is a well conceived and neatly told tale of a little boy who found a stray kitten. I confess to liking *Willy Nilly* a great deal more. It is the story of a penguin "who wanted to be different." The colouring is much better with a bright blue predominating, well in keeping with the icy background of the story. It is likely to be successful.

> *A review of "William and His Kitten" and "Willy Nilly," in* The Junior Bookshelf, *Vol. 4, No. 1, October, 1939, p. 34.*

Mrs. E. G. Taylor

[The Angus books] are excellent. The dogs, the cat, the ducks are real, not sentimentalized, and their adventures are real. The illustrations are extremely good. There is no better way of learning to read than to have a beloved book read aloud so often that the child knows it by heart, and then, imitating his elders, *pretends* to read and soon finds himself reading. These Angus books have large clear print and in the last two of the series the sentences are longer. They would form an ideal "course", and should certainly find a place in the book corner of the under sevens and be enjoyed by the seven to nines. (pp. 432-33)

> *Mrs. E. G. Taylor, in a review of "Angus Lost" and others, in* The School Librarian and School Library Review, *Vol. 6, No. 6, December, 1953, pp. 432-33.*

May Massee

Marjorie Flack has perhaps more genius as author than as artist, but her unassuming drawings for the "Angus" books with their delightful stories make completely satisfying books for nursery children. And the wise Marjorie persuades other artists to illustrate her stories when she feels they are outside the field of her own experience as picture-maker. (p. 246)

> *May Massee, "Developments of the Twentieth Century," in* Illustrators of Children's Books, *1744-1945, edited by Bertha E. Mahony, Louise Payson Latimer, and Beulah Folmsbee, eds., 1947. Reprint by The Horn Book, Inc., 1970, pp. 215-46.*

Sam Leaton Sebesta and William J. Iverson

Marjorie Flack's Angus books, about a pet Scottie, have timeless appeal. First of all, these books are well plotted. Events happen *to* Angus and his reactions are expertly shown in the drawings. The first book, *Angus and the Ducks,* is a reversal story. Angus chases the ducks until they turn about and chase him. What stays in the memory are the final four pages, a sort of slow-motion sequence of Angus crawling under a sofa, his eyes turning from white alarm to blue puzzlement. *Angus Lost* has a final page worth studying: its picture synthesizes the basic elements of all three books. *Angus and the Cat* is a good example of economy in prose style, neither too terse nor too wordy. Note, too, the "body English" revealed in its drawings. In each picture of the two animals, one is reacting to the other. When the cat is asleep, Angus is skulking and curious. When she jumps in alarm to the sofa back, Angus's head and tail invite instant open communication. Angus's movements exactly complement the cat's aggression or withdrawal. (pp. 142-43)

From Taktuk, an Arctic Boy, *written by Helen Lomen and Marjorie Flack. Illustrated by Marjorie Flack.*

Sam Leaton Sebesta and William J. Iverson, "Picture Books and Folk Literature," in their Literature for Thursday's Child, *Science Research Associates, Inc., 1975, pp. 126-76.*

Barbara Bader

Marjorie Flack drew, but not very well; she wrote, but she wasn't a writer; what she had was a feel for stories—situations, for the most part—that would tell well in words and pictures and a knack for dramatizing them: a true picturebook sense.

Angus is "a very young little dog"—the words are weighed—who is "curious about many places and many things." Most of all he is curious "about a NOISE which came from the OTHER SIDE of the large green hedge at the end of the garden," and one day, the door left open, no leash attached, NOBODY around, out he goes. Angus is not wont to be silent, and having once barked and sent the ducks running, he watches them drink, and watches, and then says WOO-OO-OOF!! on the next page; but the ducks talk it over—*Quack! Quack! Quack!*—and then HISS-S-S-S-S-S-S, it is Angus who is running . . . under the green hedge, up the little path, into the house, under the sofa, where. . . .

The repetition, the emphasis, the repertoire of animal sounds are the stock in trade of oral storytelling but their delivery, like the timing, is controlled by the format and design. As a result it is virtually impossible to read **Angus and the Ducks** ineffectively. Other effects are inseparable from the format and design and are equally visual and aural: the anticipation and the pregnant pause as Angus goes under the large green hedge, the revelation and fluster when he emerges on the other side, just one instance of Flack's dramatic use of the page-turning; and the masterful conclusion, the same picture repeated on three successive pages, indicating the passage of time, while the words, perfectly paced, evenly spaced, tick out "exactly THREE minutes by the clock," minute by minute, page by page.

Angus and the Cat, which came along the next year, has a couple of comic incidents (Angus learning NOT to jump after a frog, learning that BALLOONS go—POP!) remindful of Frost, or before him Busch, and a heartwarming happy ending in dog and cat reconciled; but its centerpiece is the search of Angus for THAT CAT, that offensive cat he's been chasing futilely for three days. She runs into the bedroom, and then *pouf!* "Angus looked under the bed—no CAT was there. Angus looked out of the window". While

Angus keeps looking, more and more lonesome, children are one up on him—THAT CAT is never far off, ready to return when the time is ripe. In a rudimentary way, pictures are played against text, and the child is a co-conspirator.

Flack's strength as an illustrator, however mechanical her rendering, is that her meaning is always plain, even to a three-year-old. Looking at Angus, we can't miss the cat; looking out with him—over a vista that includes that hedge, those ducks, that watering trough from *Angus and the Ducks*—we can see clearly that "no CAT could he see ANYWHERE!" Moreover, as Dorothy White observes, "the sofa, the mantel, and the table," the places where Angus next looks, "have all been illustrated previously as haunts of the cat—the stage has been set, the background created in a substantial way before the main action takes place."

There was a third Angus story, *Angus Lost,* and equally successful with small children were *Ask Mr. Bear* and *Wait for William.* In the cumulative pattern of a Henny Penny, Danny, in *Ask Mr. Bear,* annexes one after another animal in his search for a birthday present for his mother before Mr. Bear whispers just what she'd like (shh, "a Big Birthday Bear Hug"). *Wait for William* is a before-and-after story (the 'youngest child successful' of folklore) with a resplendent middle—left-behind brother William riding down Main Street on the back of a circus elephant, the surprise of the parade.

Tim Tadpole is left behind too, and forlorn—he can't climb out to sit in the sun like Mr. Turtle, Miss Salamander and the Great Bullfrog until, after days of wiggly swimming, he finds himself kicking and he's on his way. . . . The transformation of Tim Tadpole into Tim Frog is natural science as a success story, wild life accommodated to child life (the climax: "TIM JUMPED!!"). Best is the spread pictured: the figure of Tim swinging, swimming, around the two pages, growing, changing shape, acquiring a new look, a new personality—another, different instance of Marjorie Flack's way of animating her material.

She not only begot scores of Scotties, Sealyhams and other small squat dogs, she opened up a new line of development, the almost-everyday story teased into a dramatic opus. And at the same time that she turned out others of her own, she wrote *The Story about Ping,* conceived and wrote the text for *Boats on the River,* and illustrated *The Country Bunny and the Little Gold Shoes,* each distinct and roundly satisfactory and atypical. (pp. 61-5)

> Barbara Bader, "The Dynamics and Fun of the Form," in her American Picturebooks from Noah's Ark to the Beast Within, Macmillan Publishing Co., Inc., 1976, pp. 60-72.

Book World—The Washington Post

[The "Angus" books] originally appeared in the 1930s, but they remain among the most charming of all first picture books. Angus is a Scotch terrier and, like a certain monkey named George, is very curious. In his first adventure he escapes from his house, burrows under a hedge and encounters two rather military ducks, snootily marching about. At first they flee from Angus' loud "Woo-oo-oof!!!"

but later they frighten the intruder home. Bright yellows, blues and whites alternate with pages in austere black and white, to give the story both rhythm, variety and toddler-appealing excitement.

> A review of "Angus and the Ducks," "Angus and the Cat," and "Angus Lost," in Book World—The Washington Post, May 13, 1990, p. 12.

TITLE COMMENTARY

Taktuk, an Arctic Boy (with Helen Lomen, 1928)

[*Taktuk, an Arctic Boy* and Eunice Tietjens's *Boy of the Desert*] begin to teach the boy of from six to ten years of age the fact that humanity is a unit. When he becomes a young man in the business or professional world the commercial air service will bring this fact home to him every day; for the ends of the earth, taking wings, will meet overnight at his doorstep. In judging the values of children's books to-day, we should remember that the child will be an adult in a world we have not known. Peoples we have considered foreign and very far away will be his familiars. The two fascinating little books before us, therefore, do something for the young mind besides engrossing it in charming tales. They begin its education in a worldwide neighborliness.

Taktuk's Arctic world is changing through the same forces which are changing the world of the American boy, who reads about him. The white man has begun to develop several of the rich commercial possibilities of the Far North, so long the hunting ground of Taktuk's nomadic people; and the airplane flies over it carrying mail between the white men's towns. The "Reindeer King of Alaska" can alight from a plane now on the tundra where Taktuk and his family help at the Round-up of his immense herds. And the little American boy, if he lives in one of the great cities, can eat reindeer steak.

Helen Lomen has known Alaska and the Eskimos from her childhood. She has traveled over the same trails which Taktuk follows. She has summered on the reindeer pastures and tended gate, as Taktuk does, at the Round-up. And she has observed with keen sympathy the changes which the white man's commerce has wrought in the lives of the natives. In the first chapter Taktuk, aged ten, has but one ambition; to become a seal hunter like his father. In the last, his whole desire has turned toward the school so that he may learn white men's words.

There is a wealth of Arctic detail, worked unobtrusively into the story, and adding to its charm and there is genuine tenderness and humor in the telling. The boy reader will love it and learn from it.

> Constance Lindsay Skinner, "Comrades from Strange Lands," in New York Herald Tribune Books, October 14, 1928, p. 8.

This is a book for children, marked "six to ten years," but I, who have spent more than either six or ten years in the Arctic, read it for information. It is authoritative and up to date, with one of the collaborators better informed on at least one phase of Arctic life than any Arctic explorer can well be.

Taktuk is not the story of an imaginary boy in an imaginary world, as most northern tales for children are. It is the story of an imaginary boy in a real world—the real northwest Alaska of to-day, where the Eskimos are changing in a half century from the Stone Age civilization of their hidden past to the phonograph and canned goods civilization of their problematic future.

Chiefly this is the story of the Eskimo child's relation to his new playmate and pet, the reindeer. And one of the authors is Helen Lomen, sister of that Carl Lomen who is called "Reindeer King" because the company of which he is president owns a hundred and fifty thousand reindeer that graze in larger herds over northwestern Alaska than Texas longhorns ever did over the Panhandle.

Miss Lomen has lived in Alaska among Eskimos and reindeer since she was a baby, more than twenty years. She has grown up with the reindeer change that has just come upon the Eskimos. Her boy hero's great-grandfather hunted caribou with bow and arrow, the grandfather purchased rifles from traders, and the caribou herds that might have competed forever with the weapons of the Stone Age, faded away quickly before the withering blaze of gunpowder. Taktuk's father saw no caribou in his youth, but heard of reindeer, a tame caribou, that had been brought into the country farther south by the United States Government at the suggestion of wise missionaries, especially of Sheldon Jackson. . . .

[Miss Lomen and Miss Flack] take the Eskimo as we find him to-day. Their characters still hunt polar bears and seals, just as Vermont farmers still hunt black bears and woodchucks. But the reindeer has become the chief concern of the older people and the chief romance of the young who play at whatever their elders work at.

The story is well told by the two authors and well illustrated by Miss Flack. The volume is at least as interesting as if it were the story of unreal people against an unreal background, which most Eskimo tales for children are, even the ones that have been "adapted" by educators and schools. It is the story of the Alaskan Eskimo as he is today, gradually evolving from the Stone Age "savage" of a hundred years ago to the prosperous airplane and radio civilization of 1928.

> *Vilhjalmur Stefansson, in a review of "Taktuk, an Arctic Boy," in* The Saturday Review of Literature, *Vol. V, No. 16, November 10, 1928, p. 350.*

[This story] derives its theme from the essence of life itself and the adventures of seal-hunting, rounding up reindeer and travelling by umiak make a happy life for Taktuk. The book is vigorous yet omits the stark realities and crudeness of Eskimo life in the raw. It shows the contrasting influence of white man's civilization on their thought and way of living. It is a well-told, simple tale produced suitably for the younger reader with black-and-white illustrations to match the strength of life in this country.

> *Betty Brazier, in a review of "Taktuk, an Arctic Boy," in* The School Librarian and School Library Review, *Vol. 8, No. 2, July, 1956, p. 154.*

Angus and the Ducks (1930)

Among the many indigenous picture books of this season, *Angus and the Ducks* stands out for good and sufficient reasons It is good to look at, it is delightful to read aloud, it is a convenient size for small hands to hold, and above all, it has an inner and outer harmony. Any two of the qualities would suffice to raise the book above mediocrity.

It is easy to be charmed by pictures, by brilliant color printing, but children know that this is not enough. There must be a vital thought of some kind to link the pictures, for a good text will go a long way toward making the book a constant companion instead of a momentary diversion.

There is every prospect that *Angus and the Ducks* can lay claim to a kind of permanence. The theme of the story is simple, but universal, as it should be, and the pages as you turn them portray a variety of events. From the beginning the child will sympathize with Angus, a Scottie who was "curious about many places and many things." That is the adventure element, demonstrated disastrously in most households as soon as a child can crawl. What youngster will not wriggle appreciatively and have a fellow feeling for Angus immediately?

Here are familiar scenes. Angus escapes from the house to the garden. This will seem "right" to the three-year-old: this is the kind of adventure he can appreciate. He also would like to explore beyond the garden hedge. This is all within his childworld. And then Angus meets the ducks, strange inhabitants of unfamiliar shape. There is a dreadful moment for the ducks when Angus barks at them, but their retreat is only to a safe distance where they confer solemnly, heads together. Then comes their answer, a long drawn hiss. Angus is unnerved: with unseemly haste he retires precipitately through the hedge and takes refuge under the familiar sofa. The child also will heave a sigh of relief. It is a completely satisfying adventure.

> *Margaret Jones, "The Adventure of a Scottie," in* New York Herald Tribune Books, *November 16, 1930, p. 12.*

Angus and the Cat (1931)

An amusing and attractive picture book continuing the story of Angus the Scotch terrier, who made his first appearance a year ago in *Angus and the Ducks.* Marjorie Flack's terriers are quite irresistible, and this simple little story of Angus chasing persistently and vainly the little cat that boxes his ears, takes his food and sits in his square of sunshine, until the two finally become used to one another and make friends, has an element of surprise and humor that 7 and 8 year olds thoroughly enjoy.

> *Anne T. Eaton, in a review of "Angus and the Cat," in* The New York Times Book Review, *November 8, 1931, p. 24.*

Ask Mr. Bear (1932)

While *Ask Mr. Bear* has less distinction than the author's

picture books about Angus, the Scots terrier, it will have a strong appeal to very young children because of its repetition, its use of the most familiar animals, its gay pictures and the cumulative effect of the story of the little boy who starts out to find a birthday present for his mother, asking advice of the hen, the duck, the goose, the lamb, the cow and all the rest as he meets them one after another. Marjorie Flack's pictures always give a feeling of space and motion, and children of the picture-book age will have a pleasant sense of adventure as the pages are turned. It will also be a useful book for beginners in reading.

> *Anne T. Eaton, in a review of "Ask Mr. Bear,"* in The New York Times Book Review, *January 8, 1933, p. 12.*

A very simple picture book in clear colors for the little child of two to four years of age. It is a repetition story with an original touch at the end. . . . A clever book which combines charming pictures of favorite animals with a story simple enough for the youngest listener, one he could read himself by the pictures alone.

> *Helen Neighbors, in a review of "Ask Mr. Bear,"* in Library Journal, *Vol. 58, No. 22, February 1, 1933, p. 140.*

The Story about Ping (1933)

An irresistible picture book with so much atmosphere and kindly humor that its readers of any age will unconsciously add to their understanding and appreciation of a far distant country. Marjorie Flack became interested in finding out more about the Peking ducks that figured in her first story of Angus the Scotch terrier, and the facts on which she has based **The Story About Ping** are all true. Equally true are the pictures by Kurt Wiese who has lived in China and who has created in Ping a duckling of great individuality against a background that has both accuracy and charm. Few books for little children have the genuinely artistic quality of this one.

> *Anne T. Eaton, in a review of "The Story about Ping,"* in The New York Times Book Review, *October 8, 1933, p. 11.*

I believe that when some of the proud important children's literature of the season is sitting on the shelf with dust on its head, little boys may be lugging around copies of this meek little **Story About Ping** and looking for some one to "read it again."

This opinion is based not on extensive research but on several spontaneous expressions from children of four and around eight, children not otherwise much interested in reading. They have been amused by the pictures and held by the story. Marjorie Flack proved with her first book that she had the trick not so much of "telling a story," which almost any one can do if confronted by an eager group of young listeners, as of making a telling story for very little children—brief, reaching as swiftly as possible what is to the child a dramatic climax and then rounding at once to a satisfactory conclusion. Mother Goose had this trick; Anne Stoddard used it in *A Good Little Dog* and its sequel; it made Miss Flack's picture-book, **Angus and the Ducks** strong enough to stand by itself without any pictures when it was recently reprinted in the anthology, *Told Under the Green Umbrella.* Since Angus's first adventure this chronicler has had a warm feeling for Peking ducks. Along the Yangtze they have somewhat special chances for self-development. She, therefore, put this duck story in China. Not being able to make the pictures there she asked Kurt Wiese, that eminent sinologue, to make them. A happier blend could not be reached. The colors catch children: the duckling yellow of young Ping and his many relations, the bright blue shirts and red-brown boats. The spectacle of a baby duck bobbing tail up, always irresistibly comic to a little child, leads him to bring the book to mother and listen, looking on the while, to the brief adventure of Ping who lived by night on a houseboat and by day paddled for food upon the Yellow River. The last duck up the gangplank had a spank across his back with a willow wand to discourage sloth. Ping one evening realised he would be that duck unless he played hookey. In the next twenty-four hours he is saved, by the help of a charming shave-head China baby, from forming the chief flavor of duck soup and finds his way back to the houseboat just in time (thus rounding the plot) to get the willow spank as he goes in last. There is a jolly sort of charm about the little book.

out on the OTHER SIDE.

There, directly in front of hi[m]

[w]ere two white DUCKS. [T]hey were marching forward, [o]ne-foot-up and one-foot-down.

Quack! Quack!

Quackety!

Quack!!!

From Angus and the Ducks, *written and illustrated by Marjorie Flack.*

May Lamberton Becker, in a review of "The Story about Ping," in New York Herald Tribune Books, *January 21, 1934, p. 9.*

[This] book is an outstanding example of the virtue of simplicity. The incantatory words of the text and the pure, appealing colours of Kurt Wiese's illustrations say what they have to say with perfect tact and elegance. Ping is not presented as a person; the link between animal and human behaviour is forged in the total, sincere, simple tone of the story. (p. 282)

Margery Fisher, "Who's Who in Children's Books: The Story About Ping," in her Who's Who in Children's Books: A Treasury of the Familiar Characters of Childhood, *Holt, Rinehart and Winston, 1975, pp. 281-82.*

To illustrate the difference between the commercial moralistic books and one that looks at a central dilemma of child life through the child's eyes, consider **The Story about Ping** . . . , which has been in print continuously for more than fifty years. It was . . . the first book I ever read for myself. When I picked it up again, exactly forty years later, I recognized every line in every picture so well that I could actually spot some sloppy changes and color distortions in a recent Puffin edition. . . . (p. 41)

Ping is a handsome young duck who lives, along with a flock of aunts and cousins, in a "wise-eyed" boat on the Yangtze River. Every night, as the ducks walk back up the gangplank after a day of diving and feeding on the water, their keeper lightly slaps the hindmost duck with a long switch. It's an offhand, almost benign ritual, but one so resented by Ping that he runs away. Instead of returning to the boat one evening, he hides on an island of reeds. Few readers will ever forget the wistful back view of Ping as he watches the wise-eyed boat sail into the distance. The duck is so small and stretches so yearningly for one last look against that serenely wide river vista. Kurt Wiese's softly grayed blues and yellows, and the sinuous black outline with which he highlights his simple shapes, breathe emotional life into the scene.

Ping does survive alone on the river, but not without hunger and difficulty. One of the most memorable pictures in the book is of Ping's startled encounter with a flock of cormorants: We see him back-paddle furiously in astonishment at the sight of these frightening, hook-beaked birds, with iron rings around their necks to prevent them from eating their catch. I recall my own uneasy mix of fear and compassion when I first saw those menacing, enslaved cormorants diving for their master.

Maybe I loved **The Story about Ping** because it matched my own growing complexity of perception. Family life, I was just beginning to realize, was warm, secure, the only imaginable way to exist in the threatening wide river of life. But along with the safety, one had to endure its small stings and balks. Because the child reader's sense of injustice has been deeply acknowledged through artistic representation, the moment of reconciliation, the acceptance of order at the book's finale, rings true. (pp. 41-2)

Michele Landsberg, "Books to Encourage the Beginning Reader: 'The Story about Ping',' " in

her Reading for the Love of It: Best Books for Young Readers, *revised edition, Prentice Hall Press, 1987, pp. 41-2.*

The Story about Ping has a simplicity innocent of caricature or elusive subtleties in story or pictures.

The collaboration of Marjorie Flack and Kurt Wiese is a happy one. Yet the question must arise in our minds whether Marjorie Flack's pictures for her own story might not have found an even happier expression than the interpretation of another artist. Marjorie Flack may not be one of the most distinguished of modern illustrators, yet her pictures of familiar family pets—dogs, cats, farmyard ducks and geese—have an intimate reality and a simple activity that entertain little children with their happy, instantaneous appeal. Children are fascinated by the vividness with which Marjorie Flack has caught the personality of a Scotch terrier puppy called Angus. Gay, heedless but sensitive to rebuke, he romps through the misadventures of the day in a series of episodes which have little discernible plot. The pictures are in bright bold masses of color, in which the decorative but unobtrusive background emphasizes the activity of the animal characters of the story.

In **The Story about Ping,** the story of a Chinese duck on the Yangtze River, Marjorie Flack shows a greater sense of both humor and plot than in her **Angus** books. The simplicity of her affectionate portrayal of Ping's adventures when he fails to return to the houseboat home captivates the sympathy of every child. Kurt Wiese's pictures for the story have an elementary truthfulness and an uncluttered directness that tie them closely to the text. He re-creates as a background the busy commerce of the Yangtze River with its one-eyed houseboats, curious woven baskets and ominous-looking cormorants. It is difficult to imagine that any other illustrator, even Marjorie Flack herself, could have more faithfully interpreted or more authentically pictured the scene and events of the story. (pp. 116-17)

Lillian Smith, "Picture Books," in her The Unreluctant Years: A Critical Approach to Children's Literature, *1953. Reprint by American Library Association, 1991, pp. 104-19.*

Wag-Tail Bess (1933)

Marjorie Flack's books owe their great success to their action and reality. Children enter into her stories wholeheartedly. As Angus follows the cat upstairs in futile chase a small boy shouts, "Get her, you dumb-bell, *get* her!" A better commentary on the Angus books does not exist. The new Angus book, **Wag-Tail-Bess,** seemed to me to be a little too much on the same formula as the three other books, but the children welcomed it with such joy that I have to say with them, "It's just grand to have another book about Angus!" The story is simple and well told.

Alice Dalgliesh, in a review of "Wag-Tail Bess," in The Saturday Review of Literature, *Vol. X, No. 18, November 18, 1933, p. 279.*

Tim Tadpole and the Great Bullfrog (1934)

This polliwog book is for younger children than those who read the beautiful *Wagtail* of Alice Crew Gail or the more realistic *Pollwiggle's Progress* of Wilfred Bronson. It is for an age that looks at pictures while some one reads aloud, and for that purpose the pictures are full-page scenes in color, with as little text as possible for each. In so narrow quarters Miss Flack shows her usual skill in getting to the point. A tadpole, poking about at the bottom of the pool, watches other water-creatures heading toward the sun and is very sorry for himself because he can neither sing nor jump. "What can you do?" asks the Great Bullfrog. "Swim, just swim," says Tim. "Then swim," says the bullfrog and that is that. So the wet green pictures show Tim's arms and legs sprouting one by one as he keeps on swimming, till on the last page he jumps. Simple as it can be, but a never-failing miracle.

> *May Lamberton Becker, in a review of "Tim Tadpole and the Great Bullfrog," in* New York Herald Tribune Books, *May 13, 1934, p. 7.*

In *Tim Tadpole and the Great Bullfrog* Marjorie Flack has a charming springtime book for little children, a book which has an imaginative quality, an accuracy and a feeling for out-of-doors that grown-ups as well as boys and girls will appreciate and enjoy. These are the best drawings that Mrs. Flack has yet made, and they are well reproduced in soft, harmonious colors. Her lively little tadpole has personality and so well has she drawn his surroundings that, from our first glimpse of the small pond where the tiny "peeper frogs" crowd close to the violets and the tightly curled ferns and the bullfrog sits under the Jack-in-the-pulpit, we have a real feeling of watching the progress of the season. There are delightful under-the-water pictures, when the tadpole meets the salamanders and turtles and swims after the big green bullfrog as the latter splashes into the water from the mossy bank, and children enjoy the way in which the drawings show Tim's gradual development from tadpole to frog.

It is pleasant to find the flowers changing as the season advances from the early violets and marsh marigolds of the first page to the arrowhead, the pickerel weed and the yellow water lilies that are in blossom in the last charming sunset picture, when the sun slips down behind the trees and Tim sits on a lily pad, every inch a frog, ready to jump with the best of them.

Mrs. Flack understands little children, for, while the pictures adequately tell the story, they have been kept free from an overabundance of detail. The story has the same pleasing simplicity, and both text and illustrations have a humor that 5, 6 and 7 year olds thoroughly enjoy.

> *Anne T. Eaton, in a review of "Tim Tadpole and the Great Bullfrog," in* The New York Times Book Review, *May 13, 1934, p. 11.*

Humphrey: One Hundred Years along the Wayside with a Box Turtle (1934)

Humphrey was a young turtle picked up by two children in 1834, as they were traveling with their mother by stage coach from Boston to Salem. They decide to call him Humphrey, and their Uncle Jim carves name and date on the turtle's shell. At the end of the Summer Humphrey is taken back to his home near the pond, where Thomas and Sara Ann had discovered him. That, however, is not the end of his adventures, for Humphrey lives for a hundred years and is found and carried off by many children. Sooner or later, however, he always manages to get back to his home ground in time for his Winter sleep, and in the course of his travels along the road and through the fields he sees many things happen. The "steam carriage" follows the stage coach, and it, in turn, is followed by the automobile and the motor bus. The clear and interesting pictures show typical New England scenes and, together with the very readable text, will give to 7 and 8 year olds some idea of the changes in ways of living that have taken place during the last century.

> *Anne T. Eaton, in a review of "Humphrey: One Hundred Years along the Wayside with a Box Turtle," in* The New York Times Book Review, *December 16, 1934, p. 11.*

Rachel Field's Hitty managed to span a hundred years and keep going, but she was a wooden doll and thus endowed with special resistance to time. So far as I know, *Humphrey* is the only book for children in which an animal goes on living for a century, while around it generations of children grow up amid inventions that change the face of the countryside.

Humphrey is not much impressed by all this. He keeps his poise by frequent retirement—again like Hitty, who "went into camphor" from time to time. Every winter he tucks himself away for a long and refreshing sleep. Locomotives come in; he hears the man on the engine say, "Sorry, gentlemen, but we have run short of wood," and sees the passengers cheerfully chop and chop till the iron horse is fed and puffing on its way. He makes a detour of some thirty years to the village, where mansard roofs have come in and cast-iron blackamoors stand beside the horse-blocks. He comes back to a roadside lined with telegraph poles and lives to see it sizzling with the first automobiles. He lasts indeed to watch the road changing itself completely, with gravel and rollers, with dynamite and cement mixers, to a great highway sparkling with Tea Shoppes and filling stations and resounding with long-distance buses. Humphrey is not overcome; there has always been the woodland to go to, where creatures still wear the same clothes and get about in the same ways by which they moved when Humphrey was a boy, back in 1834. Even in 1935, he confidently believes, there will be children yet too young to be modern.

> *May Lamberton Becker, in a review of "Humphrey: 100 Years along the Wayside with a Box Turtle," in* New York Herald Tribune Books, *December 30, 1934, p. 5.*

Topsy (1935)

In this picture book Marjorie Flack has added another engaging character to her gallery of lovable canine rascals.

This is the chronicle of Topsy, the cocker spaniel puppy, who lived in a store window, waiting wistfully for some one to take her to a real home, hoping especially that it might be little Judy who passed by every day.

When a nice old lady did buy her, however, the lively Topsy found life too sedate in Miss Samantha's prim Victorian mansion, especially encumbered as she was with a leash, a sweater and overshoes for bad weather. After she had disposed of these, Topsy created a good deal of havoc in the household with her experiments with feather pillows, sliding rugs and wire springs, before she ran away and met Angus and Wag-Tail Bess on the other side of the hedge. On the other side of the next hedge she found little Judy, and by that time Miss Samantha decided that a kitten would be a better pet for her, so Topsy went to live with Judy after all.

Miss Flack knows not only how to picture dogs as individual as humans, but exactly where to place the emphasis of expression in her text so as best to pique the interest and amusement of young readers. This is an appealing successor to the stories of Angus and Wag-Tail Bess.

> *Ellen Lewis Buell, in a review of "Topsy," in* The New York Times Book Review, *May 5, 1935, p. 11.*

I do not wonder that Marjorie Flack's books suit little children. I have seen her stand up before a young audience bored to apathy by preceding speeches about books, and with half a dozen strokes of charcoal produce a dog that practically begged to be taken home. The audience came up on the platform; she had scarcely crayon room. This trick of making live and lovable creatures took permanent shape in the **"Angus"** books; permanent, for I cannot believe that any of the series will be forgotten by children once exposed to their charms. They have, first of all, a good story, brief and working quickly to the point, telling something that seems to a four-year-old important. Angus's sudden about-face when meeting the Ducks, Angus's reconciliation with Cat, Angus's experiences as a little dog lost, led to the book in which he taught a worried Airdale how to be nonchalant, so that she was renamed Wag-Tail-Bess.

In this one the story apparently starts all over again with a cocker spaniel pup named Topsy, introduced in a pet-shop window looking for a home. Judy stops by every day and suggests to her mother that hers would be just the thing, but an elderly lady with a nice neat house is the one who buys the pup. What Topsy does to the house is next shown: I liked best the picture in which she discovers there are springs in the sofa—one has just come out under her sharp teeth. Shut in the coal hole, she climbs out of the chute and, running across one of the bright double-spreads in which Miss Flack excels, comes first upon Angus, then Wag-Tail-Bess, and then, of course, Judy. So Miss Littlefield buys a nice clean cat and Topsy joins the family. That's a real story, especially if you knew Angus already and the sight of him, trotting competently up to the coal-covered puppy, shows you that from now on all will be well.

> *May Lamberton Becker, in a review of*

> *"Topsy," in* New York Herald Tribune Books, *May 19, 1935, p. 9.*

Wait for William (1935)

Through the pages of **Wait for William** a circus parade rolls along with all the romance and magnificence that such a procession holds for youthful observers. In addition, a pleasant individual touch is supplied by William, the youngest of the three children whom we see starting so gayly down to Main Street, in the village of Pleasantville, to see the circus parade. William's shoe comes untied and, as we can easily guess from the pictures [by Flack and Richard A. Holberg], William, though small, boasts a personality that is both calm and determined. The shoe is tied carefully and firmly, then, as the older children have disappeared into the distance, William, still self-possessed, hears the music and takes his place on the corner to watch the parade as it comes toward him on its way to Main Street. And here, wonder of wonders, the man leading the elephant sees William standing all alone and says, "Want a ride?" Once more, entirely equal to the situation, William parades with the circus.

A jolly little story with a pleasant touch of humor, repetition that will make it easy reading for beginners, and delightful pictures, gay with color, in which we seem to see the circus move along before our eyes.

> *Anne T. Eaton, in a review of "Wait for William," in* The New York Times Book Review, *October 20, 1935, p. 12.*

Up in the Air (1935)

We all know by now that the Montgolfiers, when they sent up the first balloon in the world to carry passengers, feared to risk the lives of men and chose instead three animals, a cock, a duck and a sheep. Now Marjorie Flack, who has as good a notion of writing children's stories as of illustrating them, makes out of this historic event a legend with true folklore-fable quality.

The three animals were living on a farm in France in the days of Marie Antoinette when the call to glory came. They took it each according to his nature, even the courage of the cock and the stolidity of the duck melting at the idea of leaving home. But the sheep was of solider stuff. Through all the preparations, the grand festival at Versailles "where all the Important People at the Palace and all the Ordinary People in the Palace Yard" saw smoke rise from the fire and fill the bag "until it swelled and swelled into a great big beautiful balloon," through the terror of first flight, the sheep continued to whisper "we must all be brave together!" When they were brought safely back and the cock regained his pride, she still said stoutly, "we were all brave together." This is accompanied by many charming and trustworthy pictures [by Karl Larsson] in the spirit of old French balloon prints.

> *May Lamberton Becker, in a review of "Up in the Air," in* New York Herald Tribune Books, *November 17, 1935, p. 16.*

From The Story about Ping, *written by Marjorie Flack and Kurt Wiese. Illustrated by Kurt Wiese.*

Marjorie Flack tells the story of [the flight of the first balloon] not from the viewpoint of the assembled court of France but from that of the first living creatures to make an ascent into the air—a cock, a duck and a sheep from an unknown French farm.

The dismay, the terror and the final complacency of these celebrated animals are described very simply but effectively for children up to 6 or 7, in a style which is unobtrusively rhythmical.

> *Ellen Lewis Buell, in a review of "Up in the Air," in* The New York Times Book Review, *December 8, 1935, p. 10.*

Willy Nilly: A Children's Story for Narrator and Orchestra   (1936)

Willy Nilly was a penguin who wanted to be different; when the other penguins were parading, he went diving; when the others were diving, he went swimming. Once he even thought he would try to be a gull, and when he found he couldn't fly, he pretended to be a sea otter, which was all very well until a real sea otter nearly put an end to Willy Nilly's games.

Mrs. Flack knows children's interests and has put into the story a fun and a suspense that will charm 4 to 6 year olds. The pictures are full of humor and lively action.

> *Anne T. Eaton, in a review of "Willy Nilly," in* The New York Times Book Review, *November 15, 1936, p. 41.*

For pictures, almost pure and simple, the season offers nothing comparable to Marjorie Flack's *Willy Nilly,* which is about a rugged individualist among the penguins of Penguin Village. This is one child's book grown-ups will thoroughly enjoy . . . perhaps, indeed, more than the nursery itself. (p. 135)

> *George N. Shuster, "For the Heads of the Family," in* The Commonweal, *Vol. XV, No. 5, November 27, 1936, pp. 135-39.*

What to Do about Molly   (1936)

A gay picture book, generously illustrated [by Flack and Karl Larsson] with pictures in color and in black and white, tells the story of Molly, 5 years old, who lives in a village by the sea. That it is a New England village any one can guess from the illustrations, which have caught a real sense of that salty, bracing atmosphere. Those in black and white are more pleasing than the colored drawings, which are a trifle too gaudy to be entirely attractive.

Molly is entrusted for a morning to brother Edward's care, and there is the hitch; for Edward is going fishing and Molly is too little to go out in a boat. But Edward is ingenious, so they both go fishing: Edward in the harbor, with his friend Tom, and Molly, lashed to a post with workmanlike knots, sits on the wharf and dangles her line with true fisherman's patience. The lapping waves and the sonorous clock on the town hall lull Molly to sleep, while Tom and Edward toil manfully in the bay; but who gets the fish for the evening chowder is the author's surprise.

The little story lacks that distinctive dash of humor which we have come to associate with Marjorie Flack's books, but it is told in rhythmical prose, well calculated to tickle the ears of small listeners, and the text is skillfully spaced to hold the attention of readers.

> *Ellen Lewis Buell, in a review of "What to Do about Molly?" in* The New York Times Book Review, *January 3, 1937, p. 9.*

Walter, the Lazy Mouse   (1937)

Walter was extraordinarily lazy for so young a creature. He was even more of a sluggard than the most famous of dormice. It was not only that when he went roller-skating he could never catch up with his feet—there have been spryer youngsters in the same position—but Walter was too slow to give even the wrong answers in school. He could not keep up with his family, and since there were eleven other mice children they soon lost track of him. In fact, Walter was overlooked, left behind and lost on Spring moving day, and that was how his adventures began.

Forlornly Walter found refuge near a frog pond, where he established himself as the Mouse of Mouse Island. He roused himself to build a home and some rather impractical furniture, and made friends with the frogs, particularly with three young ones, even more witless than himself. How he gradually reformed into a busy, ambitious young mouse, how he taught his new friends some rather inaccurate rudiments of education, and how he returned to his absent-minded but welcoming family, and even distinguished himself at school, is told for 6 to 10 year olds in Miss Flack's deft, light fashion. For all her humor and fancy, however, the tale falls a little flat; the invention is not entirely convincing. Nevertheless, the idea is one with which the imaginative child will like to play in his own mind, particularly when stimulated by the author's illustrations, which are droll, imaginative and wholly charming.

> *Ellen Lewis Buell, "The Lazy Mouse," in* The New York Times Book Review, *August 22, 1937, p. 10.*

This has less of the picture book quality than Marjorie Flack's other books and is for children a little older than those who enjoy the Angus books or **Wait for William.** It tells in a most engaging manner of Walter Mouse's summer with the frogs when he lived on Mouse Island and kept a school for his friends, Lulu, Leander, and Percy Frog. As always, Miss Flack tells a convincing story keyed to the interests, imagination and humor of her young readers. The frequent illustrations with their touches of cool green are a perfect accompaniment to the story. Children in grades three and four can read the book for themselves, but it can be read to children much younger.

> *Marjorie F. Potter, in a review of "Walter, the Lazy Mouse," in* Library Journal, *Vol. 62, No. 22, October 15, 1937, p. 782.*

Lucky Little Lena   (1937)

Get this little story with big pictures into the house if there are little children in the family. Neil and Ted, who appear to be some three and five years old respectively, live in a handsome New York apartment; so does Lena, a dachshund. When the children put on their coats to go to the park, little Lena brings her little coat and heartily asks to go. They always take her. But when Neil and Ted ride—as they do on successive pages in large pictures—in a taxicab, an airplane, a bus, a train and a steamship, their four-legged friend cannot go along. "Poor little Lena," they say, "I wish she could ride," or sail or whatever, by these elegant methods. But when they go walking they take her down in the elevator (the view of her here is particularly appealing) and out in the street and into the park. "And Lena was very happy, because all the time that was where she wanted to go. Lena did not want to go riding in a taxicab, because she did not like taxicabs. Lena did not want to ride up in the air in an airplane, because she did not know about airplanes." She either did not like, or did not know, these other means of transport. "So little Lena was very happy to run on her four little legs in the park. Lucky little Lena!"

Lucky the child whose mother reads the book too, and gets from it the idea it may be unwise to create artificial needs for little children when they get so much happiness from simple, natural ones.

> *May Lamberton Becker, in a review of "Lucky Little Lena," in* New York Herald Tribune Books, *November 21, 1937, p. 9.*

The Restless Robin   (1937)

With the possible exception of the well-beloved **Ping,** one is tempted to say didactically that this is the most charming of Marjorie Flack's many and varied picture books. Here is the whole cycle of a robin's family life, beginning with Mr. Robin's migration from Georgia to New Hampshire, which, as told, emphasizes for young children the tremendous distances covered in that springtime flight taken for granted so lightly. Here is the account of the nesting in a hospitable apple tree, the hatching of eggs and finally the first venture out of the nest by the biggest and most restless of the birdlings, an injudicious move, for that villain, the cat, lurked inevitably in the bushes below. How Buffy was rescued in the nick of time; how, timorous and anxious, he sat on a lilac twig, nerving himself to fly, and how the chickadee and the flicker, the bluebird, the meadow lark and all the songsters of Spring came to encourage him is told with verve and an effective dramatic touch. The story is, moreover, a sound lesson in birdlore, complete even to the notes of the bird melodies.

The pictures in fresh pastel tones are delightful. Slim birches, sprays of apple blossoms, rosy-breasted robins and other birds in their natural colorings fill the pages with a sense of the quickening life of Spring.

> *Ellen Lewis Buell, "Bird Life," in* The New York Times Book Review, *December 26, 1937, p. 10.*

A charming story of the American robin told in text and pictures for younger children. . . . The illustrations are lovely. Every detail is given the most careful attention, and one can fairly see the trees swelling and the buds bursting as the season progresses. Although the birds are named, there is no personification and all factual material is accurate. A book for any library.

> *Eunice G. Mullan, in a review of "Restless Robin," in* Library Journal, *Vol. 63, January 15, 1938, p. 81.*

In an article published in the *School Library Journal*, Katherine Heland suggests criteria that would be useful in selecting and assessing children's books concerned with ecology. (p. 281)

The first criterion consists of the universal literary standards that apply to all books. Literary standards include not only the flow, beauty, and power of the prose, but the accuracy, format, and effectiveness of the entire book. . . . [Many nature books] provide fine examples of works that meet this criterion and combine effective prose, a beautiful format, and striking illustrations.

A second criterion cited by Heland concerns the appropriateness of ideas and concepts for the age level of the intended readership. A book can fail to meet this criterion by presenting concepts that are either too difficult for children to grasp or too simple and elementary to interest the reader. This criterion is sometimes difficult to apply for two reasons. First, children even of the same age frequently exhibit a wide range of abilities and experiences. Second, critics and authors sometimes disagree as to the appropriateness of a given idea and concept.

The difference of opinion that sometimes occurs when applying this second criterion can be seen in the reaction various individuals have to books of fantasy. For example, Marjorie Flack's **The Restless Robin** has been criticized for not fulfilling this second criterion. The book is about the life of a family of robins who exhibit an astounding array of human middle-class values. Mr. and Mrs. Robin teach their offspring—Muffy, Puffy, and Buffy—middle-class values, similar to "Robins should be seen and not heard." Good manners, self-control, and sharing feelings of pride are presented as part of the robins' daily life-style.

Some critics point out that attributing a middle-class set of values to a family of robins may confuse children. They point out that in an attempt to write an interesting fantasy, Flack is simplifying the truth and presenting ideas that will confuse, misinform, or even offend young readers. Others contend that **The Restless Robin** is only fantasy and is not meant to be an honest presentation of reality. They maintain that a precise and accurate account of a robin's existence is not called for, and may in fact detract from the effectiveness of the story.

A third point of view might also be considered. It is possible that by attributing human characteristics to robins, children may be more able to identify with, understand, and respect a robin's existence. The argument can then be made that such distortions, in the long run, may serve the useful purpose of helping young children to respect and appreciate all forms of life, and thus promote an awareness of and appreciation for our environment.

These varied assessments of **The Restless Robin** suggest the difficulty that sometimes occurs in applying this second criterion to children's books. Although some books may be difficult to evaluate in relation to this criterion, other books provide clear examples of concepts and ideas that are either too simple or too difficult for the intended readership. (pp. 281-82)

> *Myra Pollack Sadker and David Miller Sadker, "Spaceship Earth: Ecology in Children's Literature," in their* Now Upon a Time: A Contemporary View of Children's Literature, *Harper & Row, Publishers, 1977, pp. 269-85.*

William and His Kitten   (1938)

Marjorie Flack's picture-books always have a good story, which helps to explain why children like her pictures so well; they tell something in which the words have made them interested. This time four-year-old William, who has time to notice things because he does not yet have to go to school or be a father or a postman or a grocery boy, notices a lost kitten that has been trying to attract the attention of these older people but has almost given up hope. It is a nice kitten; William names it Peter and hopes nobody has left a "lost" notice at the police station that will take it away. But three people have: Peter has been successively named Minnie, May and Mouser on the days she stayed with three other citizens. They all give up their claims, however, in favor of William, and Peter lives with the little boy for a whole year (with colored pictures for each month). Then there are three kittens in the basket, of which Peter is the mother; William names them Minnie, May and Mouser, and bestows them on his cat's three previous guardians.

This may not sound much, but try it on any four-year-old child. The pictures are as gay and pretty as in the previous book where William took part in a circus procession.

> *May Lamberton Becker, in a review of "William and His Kitten," in* New York Herald Tribune Books, *December 11, 1938, p. 8.*

Pedro   (with Karl Larsson, 1940)

I thought I had reached the point where I could not read one more story about a nice little Mexican child. Fortunately, this did not stop me from starting this one, for it has the atmosphere I recall so well in the first book of this sort I ever read: *The Painted Pig*—an atmosphere not only of childhood but of warm, tender affection for children.

Pedro is ten . . . and has an enchanting, grasping five-year-old brother. When the family borrows a burro and takes father's pottery to the fiesta at Taxco, Pedro is permitted for the first time to tend the stall, sells a large pot to an American lady resident, and takes it home to her house. When her houseboy goes next day to attend his sister's wedding. Pedro's politeness gets him the job as substitute mozo for the rest of the week, and in the course of it, the extra duty of talking Spanish with Bill, an American boy of his own age. This results, as usual, in Pedro's immediately learning English: his vocabulary is comprised in Okay but it is amazing how far that one word will go. It may sound melodramatic to say that Pedro saves Bill's life in a rodeo, but this happens as naturally as that Bill's father should make himself responsible for Pedro's education. I hope it doesn't go too far. Pedro is so nice as he is.

Most of the many little pictures [by Karl Larsson] are as if drawn in red chalk, and there are some large ones in full color. Following with their aid these simple events, an American child of seven or so unconsciously takes in many details of Mexican manners and customs, together with a surrounding sense of lively domestic affection.

> *May Lamberton Becker, in a review of "Pedro," in* New York Herald Tribune Books, *April 14, 1940, p. 8.*

An attractive portrait of Pedro is in the front of this book, and Pedro lives up to it very well. He is a ten-year-old Mexican boy who becomes the mozo (house-boy) of an American lady. Through her he learns to know Bill Randolph, an American boy his own age. Their friendship, and the general background of the story, are the points on which I would recommend the book. It seems unnecessary to have brought in such an improbable occurrence as Pedro's saving Bill's life in a rodeo; the story didn't need that. If there is demand for material on Mexico, this book may be added.

> *Josephine Smith, in a review of "Pedro," in* Library Journal, *Vol. 65, No. 10, May 15, 1940, p. 454.*

Serious 10-year-old Pedro becomes real to the reader of this book from the moment when he gazes upon the lovely portrait which the artist has drawn as a frontispiece. Written for somewhat older children than Marjorie Flack's other books this story, together with Karl Larsson's pictures—there are double-spreads in full color and many drawings reproduced in a pleasing reddish brown—will make clear to children from 7 to 10 many details of the Mexican country and of the customs and ways of life of the Mexican people. . . .

The tale leaves behind it a pleasant sense of warm family affection and kindly relationships.

> *Anne T. Eaton, "In Mexico," in* The New York Times Book Review, *June 2, 1940, p. 10.*

The New Pet (1943)

In engaging pictures and a brief childlike text Marjorie Flack tells how Dick and Judy who longed for pets—a puppy dog for Dick, a kitty cat for Judy—are promised the nicest kind of a pet as a surprise. Pictures of a puppy, a kitten, a rabbit, a canary and a goldfish, indicate the children's guesses as to what their pet will be. Other drawings show the little red house in which Dick and Judy live, and the two children helping their grandmother to take care of it while their mother is away. Then comes the return of their mother from the hospital with the "new pet." The

children's slight disappointment over the fact that the baby brother takes no notice of them is soon changed to pride and pleasure as they watch him grow from day to day, agreeing by the time he takes his first step that a brother is nicer than the nicest kind of pet.

Little children are interested in babies, and boys and girls who have small brothers and sisters will enjoy the description of experiences they will recognize. Written with thorough understanding of children, *The New Pet* should help the next to the youngest in the family to adjust happily to the fact that he is no longer the baby in the house.

> *Anne T. Eaton, "A Baby Brother," in* The New York Times Book Review, *August 29, 1943, p. 7.*

Author's colorful crayon and pencil drawings of animals, children, and babies and her story circling around familiar daily experiences of children will have genuine appeal for three- to five-year-olds. In addition to its being an attractive picture book, parents will find it a psychologically sound one to use in adjusting small brothers and sisters to arrival of a new baby.

> *Margaret M. Clark, in a review of "The New Pet," in* Library Journal, *Vol. 68, September 1, 1943, p. 671.*

[In 1963, Mr. L. Leng told] the Library Association Conference: 'There are too many children's books which carefully skirt around all the facts of life, birth, work, love, marriage, age and death, anything that might arouse strong feelings other than physical courage and physical fear.' It was a librarian's job, he went on, 'to encourage children to read books that would enable them to grow.' He called on them to exclude all books which offered children a false image of human life and false ideas of the rules and values that applied in it. . . .

The New Pet concerns the arrival of a new baby boy and the reactions of his elder brother and sister. The second half of the story, showing how the children adjust themselves to the new situation and how Timmy gradually ceases to be 'it', seems to be admirable, but not all modern parents will agree with the first half. The boy wants a puppy, the girl wants a kitten, but their mother merely smiles and answers: 'Some day soon, I will have the nicest kind of a pet as a surprise for you!' Are children nowadays so often unconscious of their mother's pregnancy—and is it wise to risk their disappointment by making such coy and cryptic promises? (p. 131)

> *Geoffrey Trease, "The Family in Fiction: 'The New Pet',"* in his Tales Out of School, *second edition, Heinemann Educational Books Ltd., 1964, p. 131.*

The Boats on the River (1946)

This is a beautiful book for children of 6 to 9 who love boats, color and rhythmic writing. In this prose poem with pictures [by Jay Hyde Barnum] we see and hear how the river comes down from the mountains, then the activity on that river—the ferryboat, the river boat, the ocean

From The Restless Robin, *written and illustrated by Marjorie Flack.*

liner, the freight boat, the submarine, the warship and all the company of vessels which meet on the shores of a big city. We are told what each boat does and the sounds they make and are shown the river and its boats in the different "seasons" of the day—the bright sunshine and the mysterious fog, then the night with red, green and white lights shining from the boats. It is unusual to find a book containing factual material which has so much texture of beauty in both prose and illustration.

> *Ruth A. Gordon, in a review of "The Boats on the River," in* The New York Times Book Review, *December 8, 1946, p. 22.*

Yet [with] all the books about boats offered to little children and with all their impassioned interest in the subject, this is the first picture book I have seen that spreads before them the pageant of Hudson River craft: certainly not in such brilliant colors and with a simple narrative so flowing. Here are the ferryboats, river-boats going through the mountains, an ocean liner, a tugboat, a sailboat going with the wind and a rowboat with oars: a motorboat speeding, a freight boat bringing bananas, a submarine, a warship with its sailors spreading out all over the city. Fog comes, night comes with lights on the river, and as the stars come out the pictures close.

> *May Lamberton Becker, in a review of "The Boats on the River," in* New York Herald Tribune Weekly Book Review, *December 22, 1946, p. 9.*

The sometimes rhythmic text and illustrations, all bursting with information, create a novel approach to what is, in essence, a book of information.

Barnum's watercolor and ink paintings present an abundance of information regarding the classifications and uses of the vessels discussed, and his illustrations help move along a text that sometimes gets bogged down by its technical aspects; even though the beat and repetition in the words flow along with the illustrations, there are spots where this rhythm weakens and creates an awkwardness in the text. Barnum's compositions travel left to right across the full-page spreads, circling around the text and bringing the eye back. The moods captured during the fog scenes and the river at night recreate the still and calm of these situations.

Other than in the diversion in the text when the sailors from the warship enjoy their leave in the city, this picture book could function quite well without a text. The illustrations provide enough technical information and distinction between the vessels to generate an interesting discussion with children in which they could share their experiences without the help of a text. With the text, however, there seems little excitement or interest generated in what the words reveal, and, consequently, the strength of the illustrations becomes incidental. (pp. 268-69)

> *Linda Kauffman Peterson "The Caldecott Medal and Honor Books, 1938-1981," in* Newbery and Caldecott Medal and Honor Books: An Annotated Bibliography, *by Linda Kauffman Peterson and Marilyn Leathers Solt, G. K. Hall & Co., 1982, pp. 235-78.*

The Happy Birthday Letter   (1947)

Format like post-card packets, which can really be mailed—and content that supplies some actual facts about what happens to a letter when it pops into the mailbox at the corner. The text tells of a letter that went by train, plane and truck to Judy, and an answer that took another route back to Dicky—spanning a continent from California to Massachusetts. The tricky format and cute idea make it more of an item—merchandise-wise, than either the fairly commonplace text or undistinguished pictures by Jay Hyde Barnum would indicate.

> *A review of "The Happy Birthday Letter," in* Virginia Kirkus' Bookshop Service, *Vol. XV, June 1, 1947, p. 282.*

Minfong Ho

1951-

Southeast Asian author of fiction.

Major works include *Sing to the Dawn* (1975), *Rice without Rain* (1986), *The Clay Marble* (1991).

Ho is the author of realistic fiction for young adults and middle graders which profiles young people in her native Thailand who are involved in difficult political and social situations. Praised for providing young readers with valuable insights into an unfamiliar culture as well as for the honesty of her coverage, especially as when compared to the overly romantic accounts of some Western writers, Ho is acknowledged for writing convincing, moving dramatizations of how the conditions and injustices of her society affect the lives of her characters. Characteristically focusing on strong female protagonists who interact with their families and friends against the backdrop of real events, she is often recognized for the sensitivity and understanding with which she treats the feelings of her characters as well as for her depiction of Asian life and locale. Ho includes poverty, violence, suffering, and death in her novels as well as the corruption of government and the military and the oppression of women and the poor. However, she characteristically represents the pride and determination of her protagonists as well as their affection for their homeland and desire to improve their own lives and those of their families.

Born in Burma, Ho grew up in Singapore and Bangkok. In her childhood reading, she was concerned that the books she read about Asia presented a world of princes and emperors, "full of," as she wrote, "kites and candles and festivities at the temples. This was not the Asia I knew. . . ." Coming to the United States for her college education, Ho realized that she wanted to write about Asia in order to have an impact on the values of her changing society; homesick for Thailand while studying economics at Cornell, she wrote the short story that later became her first novel, *Sing to the Dawn*. Ho entered the story in an annual contest sponsored by the Council for Interracial Books for Children for the best manuscript by unpublished Third World Authors, and won the award for the Asian American division in 1972. *Sing to the Dawn* describes how Dawan, a schoolgirl from a rural Thai village, encounters resistance from her father and brother when she wins a scholarship to the city high school. Encouraged by her mother and grandmother as well as by a Buddhist monk, a cousin who lives in the city, and an uneducated flower girl, Dawan convinces her brother, who had placed second in the contest, and her father, who sees an educated son as their family's only hope, that she should accept the scholarship. With the proceeds from *Sing to the Dawn*, which was illustrated by her younger brother Kwoncjan, Ho set up a scholarship fund for training village girls in Thailand to become nurses. Her next novel, *Rice without Rain,* was inspired by the massacre of university students

in Bangkok by the military in 1976 and outlines how a group of students who come to a small Thai village change the lives of a drought-stricken family. Seventeen-year-old Jinda, a village girl, falls in love with the charismatic Ned, the leader of the student movement; Ned, whose group has come to the village to incite the farmers to rebel against the high taxes imposed on them by landowners, convinces the farmers to initiate a rent strike. After the death of her father, who has been jailed because of the resistance, and her witnessing of the student massacre at a Bangkok rally, Jinda separates from Ned and trades her political ideals for a belief in the land itself. In *The Clay Marble,* her first novel for middle graders, Ho describes the events in the life of twelve-year-old Dara after she leaves her Cambodian farm with her mother and older brother after the fall of the Khmer Rouge. After discovering a refugee camp at the Thai border, Dara makes friends with Jantu, a girl from the camp. When neighboring guerrilla groups force the families to flee again, Dara and Jantu become separated, and Jantu is accidentally killed by Sareen, Dara's brother, before Dara and her family return home to start a new life. Writing her books in a lyrical style that often presents information through dialogue, Ho is occasionally criticized for addressing the often horrifying events she describes with too much delicacy; however, most observers view her books as worthy additions to juvenile literature on Asia due to their unflinching treatment of both personal and collective struggle.

(See also *Something about the Author,* Vol. 15, and *Contemporary Authors,* Vols. 77-80.)

AUTHOR'S COMMENTARY

Writing, by itself, is like the sound of one hand clapping—it is incomplete, silent and with no impact. For writing to have real meaning, it must also be read. Only when the writer as the one hand, and his/her readers as the other, come together is there that clap, that spark of contact which forms the basis of communication.

During all the years that I was keeping private diaries and writing stories for myself, I ignored this basic, communicative aspect of writing, choosing instead to see it as only cathartic. It was as catharsis, therefore, and not as communication, that I wrote the short story which grew to be **Sing to the Dawn.** Written in the thick of winter in upstate New York, when sheer daily homesickness seemed too monotonous, it was about the dappled sunlight and school children of home, of Thailand. It was not written to be read, but only as a way of airing out on paper that part of me which could not find any other place in America.

At that time, I saw by chance a *Bulletin* of the Council on Interracial Books for Children, with an announcement of their annual contest in it. The Council seemed warm and friendly, vaguely cosy, and I felt an urge to join in. I sent in my just completed story and the people at the Council thus became my first readers. When I found that I had been chosen one of their winners, what excited me most was not the prize money, but the possibility of being published. That added a whole new dimension to my concept of writing.

The Council people quickly provided the links between various publishers and me . . . and before the year was out, I had signed a contract with William Morrow and Co. to put my story into book form. With that, I realized that writing could be a means of reaching outwards, and not only a self-contained device for groping inwards.

Inherent in that realization was the concept of writing as a political expression, and the Council people—through their *Bulletins,* library, discussions with me—helped underline this for me. I had never enjoyed reading stories of Asia in my own childhood, and the evaluative guidelines of the Council now helped to explain why. Children's books about Thailand, China, Burma, etc. were invariably about princes and emperors and/or their elephants, peacocks and tigers. The few about village life portrayed it as idyllic and easy-going, full of kites and candles and festivities at the temples. This was not the Asia I knew, and I had resented the writers—usually white—who out of condescension and ignorance misrepresented these countries. In pointing out and trying to correct the anachronistic attitudes of many Americans towards Asia, the Council also helped me to clarify my own stance. For the first time, I saw how "even" children's books could be effective and

have an impact in changing society's values. I knew then that I wanted to continue writing, not just for me, but for others as well. The Council, then, in a very real sense became for me "the other hand" without which that clap of communication would not have been possible. (p. 5)

When the book finally came out in early 1975, it received favorable reviews in the U.S. and in Singapore. It was also displayed at the annual book fair in Singapore, and is being sold at the local bookstores there now. . . .

Whatever impact the book has ultimately depends on how it affects the children who read it, of course, and it is perhaps rather unfortunate that I do not have much contact with children, and especially children in America. A few months ago, a good friend of mine sent me a tape of her fifth graders discussing my book. She had read it to them and in listening to her they had learnt to care about Thailand, about the brother and sister I wrote about in Thailand.

More than that, they had absorbed the basic structure of Thai society, and talked with understanding about the unequal distribution of wealth, the corruption in the bureaucracy and military, and the feudalistic values still underlying life in Thailand. Listening to them, I found that basic ideas, especially when couched in a story-form, are easy for children to grasp, and I felt very encouraged by this.

For the past year I have been back in Thailand, at first teaching at the University of Chiengmai; and now, after the military coup of Oct. 6, 1976, I am writing full time again. There are many stories to be told about the struggle which is going on, and the encouragement which the Council gave me in awarding me their prize five years ago is supporting me even now. I will try to keep on writing stories, and hope that others will keep on reading them. Only thus will the sound of hands clapping be heard. (p. 21)

> *Minfong Ho, "Writing: The Sound of One Hand Clapping," in* Interracial Books for Children Bulletin, *Vol. 8, No. 8, 1977, pp. 5, 21.*

TITLE COMMENTARY

Sing to the Dawn (1975)

Underneath the delicate lotus imagery, this small, understated story is infused with passion and determination. The Thai schoolgirl Dawan, having won a scholarship to study in the city, must fight for permission to accept it, a problem complicated by her own brother's being next in line for the honor. As Dawan desperately tries to win support for her case—from a cousin who has lived in the city, a respected Buddhist monk, her own timid mother—she hears warnings about the corruption of urban life (which, for readers here, can't help but take on a new seriousness in light of recent events). But the central issue is Dawan's inferior status as a girl, a liability she confronts again and again with rage so powerful it makes this otherwise modest narrative vibrate.

A review of "Sing to the Dawn," in Kirkus Reviews, *Vol. XLIII, No. 11, June 1, 1975, p. 604.*

There's a strong grandmother in the cast, an interesting picture of Thai life, and a convincing depiction of Dawan's family and her conflicting feelings about her brother, but the story is, although adequately written, slow-paced, and the dialogue is too often used to convey information, especially in classroom scenes.

Zena Sutherland, in a review of "Sing to the Dawn," in Bulletin of the Center for Children's Books, *Vol. 29, No. 3, November, 1975, p. 46.*

The social structure of both family and village in contemporary Thailand is insightfully conveyed as young Dawan struggles to be allowed to use the scholarship she has won to a high school in the city (an unprecedented opportunity that many feel should go to her younger brother, who placed second in the examination). Her grandmother's support plus Dawan's own determination to rid her village of the oppression and endless poverty imposed by absentee landlords lead her to withstand opposition and go off to school with her brother's ultimate blessing, though not her father's. The author's love of her native countryside is evident in her vivid descriptions, though these unfortunately slow down the story enough to make some young readers impatient. However, this provides a perspective on women's liberation far removed from and much more important than breaking into the local Little League.

Cynthia T. Seybolt, in a review of "Sing to the Dawn," in School Library Journal, *Vol. 22, No. 7, March, 1976, p. 104.*

Set in a rural Thai village, **Sing to the Dawn** is a moving account of a young girl's struggle to continue her education in the face of oppressive, feudal concepts of women's role. (p. 139)

[Dawan] receives unexpected backing from a wise and independent grandmother and from Bao, a young flower girl. Neither of these last two women, both defiant and independent, ever had an opportunity to attend any school. Yet, from Bao, Dawan learns that she must struggle to be free and, like a caged bird, seize any opportunity to fly. From grandmother, she receives the insight of the lotus bud "at first shut up tight, small and afraid, then gradually unfolding, petal by petal, understanding that without these changes, the bud would never blossom." With such wisdom and encouragement reinforcing her own determination, Dawan finally succeeds in soliciting her brother's help and convincing her father to let her go to the city school.

Although brother Kwai professes to oppose injustice he is forced by Dawan to recognize how his own selfish actions actually support the strong against the weak. This conflict between brother and sister is poignantly portrayed, showing the contradiction between their love for each other and their competition for survival. In the end, both justice and principle prevail.

This reviewer has one disagreement with the book. The author's emphasis on education as *the key* to social change has misleading implications. Education, in itself, does not cause social change. The recent history of sweeping change in Asia belies this notion. Mass movements of uneducated peasants have brought great social change which, in turn, has led to more education for the succeeding generation.

Nevertheless, **Sing to the Dawn** is exceptional reading for young people. The author's sensitive understanding of the hopes, fears and struggles of ordinary people is a refreshing change from the patronizing and romantic accounts of Asian peasants by Western writers. (pp. 139-40)

"Sing to the Dawn," in Human—And Anti-Human—Values in Children's Books: A Content Rating Instrument for Educators and Concerned Parents, *edited by the Council on Interracial Books for Children, Inc., Racism and Sexism Resource Center for Educators, 1976, pp. 139-40.*

Rice without Rain   (1986)

The author of **Sing to the Dawn** again writes about the experience of a village girl in Thailand, where she grew up.

When young intellectuals from Bangkok arrive in 17-year-old Jinda's remote village, they are greeted with suspicion as possible troublemakers; but Sri, a medical student, soon wins Jinda's friendship with her dedication to helping the sick (despite primitive conditions and local superstitions), while Jinda forms an even warmer bond with Ned, who is encouraging the hungry farmers to withhold a greater share of the rice crops given to their rapacious landlords. Reluctantly convinced, Jinda's father leads the farmers in an abortive opposition that results in his imprisonment and death. Meanwhile, Jinda visits her new friends in Bangkok; observes the brutal suppression of a peaceful, communist-led demonstration; and escapes to home, where she decides to stay with her family rather than joining Ned and the rebels—even though she and Ned are now openly in love.

Though obviously designed to illustrate the tension between rich and poor, rural and urban, and old ways and new, the story portrays Thailand vividly and with such sympathy that the contrivance is acceptable. Like Naidoo's *Chain of Fire,* this derives its strength from the dramatization of social conditions and injustice rather than from memorable characterizations; the compelling details here will be even less familiar to Americans. A valuable, memorable portrait of a little-known country.

A review of "Rice without Rain," in Kirkus Reviews, *Vol. LVIII, No. 9, May 1, 1990, p. 649.*

A foreword explains the political situation in Thailand in the mid-70's, providing a useful context for a story that succeeds dramatically on its own terms. Jinda regards herself as an ordinary village girl, in love with a revolutionary but suspicious of the visitors' slogans. "She couldn't help thinking that Maekung had just been a vacation for them. Now that the vacation was over, it was time for the good little students to go back to school." While Ned's commitment to the cause is paramount, he confesses to Jinda that "sometimes it's easier to talk like a book than a person." Their love story is inevitably fused with the political events of their country, a balance that disallows excesses of romantic melodrama or earnest didacticism. The events are painful, violent, and graphically portrayed, especially in the climactic terror of a rally in which there is a brutal massacre of students by the military. The conclusion, in which both Jinda and Ned find their futures, is sad but honest.

> *Robert Strang, in a review of "Rice without Rain," in* Bulletin of the Center for Children's Books, *Vol. 43, No. 10, June, 1990, p. 241.*

Despite its strong political subject, *Rice Without Rain* is written in such a lilting voice, and so romantically, that it's hard to believe fully. The title comes from a Thai folk song, and the language often reads as though it were translated, not composed in English. There are delicate descriptions of rice fields and flowers and a rather romantic vision of village life. Jinda is fascinated by the handsome university student who helps organize the rent strike in her village and falls in love with him.

But the novel attempts to go beyond romance. When a young revolutionary tries to make Jinda and her father symbols of gallant Thai peasantry, she resists. A practical country girl, she suspects him of wanting her father to stay in prison and remain a rallying point for the students. Jinda's wide-eyed view of the students in the movement also strikes a nice note. She finds most of them boring, preoccupied with theories that have nothing to do with her. And when Minfong Ho, who grew up and was educated in Thailand and now lives in Ithaca, N. Y., writes about the brutality of the attack on the students, the illness and death of her sister's baby and the birth of that sister's second child, she is explicit, if dainty, in her descriptions.

Ms. Ho has set herself a strange task with this book and only partly succeeds. She has tried to write a political novel about the student movement in Thailand to rally the peasants and achieve reform, but she has camouflaged it as a hybrid—part teen-age romance, part anthropological introduction to youth in a faraway land. The failure comes, I think, in the fact that young people, her contemporaries and friends, did risk everything and die in Thailand in 1976. The effort to explain them to young Americans seems to me to require a grittier effort, perhaps aimed at older teen-agers.

Although *Rice Without Rain* contains descriptions of murder and oppression it still seems to slip through the grim events without coming to grips with what happened. Young people in this country watched their contemporaries in China demonstrating for democracy and dying in Tiananmen Square in the summer of 1989. Presumably they tried, at least briefly, to imagine themselves taking such risks, caring that much about a cause. A novel about a similar time in Thailand ought to explain and amplify such stirring and frightening experiences. It ought to help American readers to understand what passions moved the young Thai people to do what they did, young people who are, after all, almost the same age as the adolescent readers

of this book. *Rice Without Rain* seems, to me, a little too lovely.

> *Linda Wertheimer, in a review of "Rice without Rain," in* The New York Times Book Review, *October 7, 1990, p. 30.*

The Clay Marble   (1991)

After the fall of the Khmer Rouge, 12-year-old Dara, her older brother Sarun, and their mother journey to the Thai border in search of food. Here they meet the remnants of another Cambodian family, one of whose members, Jantu, becomes Dara's friend; another, Nea, falls in love with Sarun. Life is going along well until infighting among neighboring guerrilla groups forces the families to flee again. In the confusion, Dara and Jantu become separated from the main group. After many incidents, they are reunited with their families, although Jantu is shot in the process and dies soon after. Sarun, once a proud farmer, wants to join the military. Dara courageously stands up to him, and convinces him to return home with the family. The title comes from Jantu's effervescence and manual dexterity, the combination of which impresses Dara as magic. She believes a clay marble, having been invested with Jantu's magic, gives her the courage to get through her ordeals. Dara and Jantu are well drawn, but the rest of the characters are not much more than pasteboard figures. Ho excels at tropical description, evoking climate and flora with skill. The contrasts of frantic activity and enervating inaction of refugee life are also vividly depicted. However, Dara's vocabulary when she thinks to herself does not ring true for her age; few 12-year-olds would consciously characterize themselves as "irritable" or others as "glib"—certainly not illiterate 12-year-olds from rural areas. Older children might find this novel of interest for its historical milieu or slice-of-life realism, albeit from a different reality.

> *John Philbrook, in a review of "The Clay Marble," in* School Library Journal, *Vol. 37, No. 10, October, 1991, p. 122.*

While the story is dramatically grounded in real events, the author's tone is instructive and the characters are idealized, displaying courage and fortitude in overcoming every hardship and setback. The only exception is Dara's older brother Sarun, who succumbs to military fervor, accidentally shooting Dara's best friend Jantu in an excess of zealous patrolling. Jantu is the chief, rather tiresome, dispenser of wisdom here, and her serene acceptance of death (" 'Sing me to sleep,' she whispered") makes *Little Women's* Beth look like a whiner. There are, however, some gritty scenes here, as when Jantu orders Dara to leave a helpless, stray child behind in a rushed escape from a bombing attack, and the friendship between the two girls makes a strong focus for a picture of a senseless, and endless, war.

> *Roger Sutton, in a review of "The Clay Marble," in* Bulletin of the Center for Children's Books, *Vol. 45, No. 4, December, 1991, p. 92.*

Jesse Jackson

1908-1983

African American author of fiction and nonfiction.

Major works include *Call Me Charley* (1945), *Tessie* (1968), *The Sickest Don't Always Die the Quickest* (1971), *Make a Joyful Noise unto the Lord! The Life of Mahalia Jackson, Queen of Gospel Singers* (1974).

Considered a pioneer in the field of children's literature for creating young adult novels that openly and realistically address racial prejudice, Jackson is praised as a skillful and sensitive writer whose thought-provoking works helped to develop the awareness of the adolescent readers of their time. He is best known as the author of *Call Me Charley,* the story of how twelve-year-old Charley Moss learns to win respect as the only black boy in a white upper-class school. Called "a breakthrough in children's literature" by critic Ruby J. Lanier, *Call Me Charley* is acknowledged as the first book to present genuine confrontations between blacks and whites and is noted as among the first books of its type to honestly discuss racism and its effects. A popular novel that is often recognized as a classic, *Call Me Charley* is the first of three works about Charley Moss; in *Anchor Man* (1947), Jackson describes how Charley, who has become an outstanding student and member of the Student Council and track team, deals with an accusation by a black transfer student that he has gone against his own people by becoming friendly with whites, while *Charley Starts from Scratch* (1958) depicts eighteen-year-old Charley's struggle to find a summer job and, in the process, become a man. Jackson is also well known for writing two books of autobiographical fiction for older teenagers, *The Sickest Don't Always Die the Quickest* and *The Fourteenth Cadillac* (1972): in these humorous books set in Ohio in the 1920s, he describes the adventures of Stonewall Jackson and his friend Steeplehead, innocent but resilient teenagers whose involvement with the world of adults exposes them to scandals, religious disputes, and other events. In his fiction, which he writes in a lively, unaffected style noted for capturing the speech of Northern blacks without dialect, Jackson considers the thoughts, feelings, and values of blacks and whites from both the lower and upper classes. In his informational books, Jackson combines individual profiles with outlines of social and cultural history: his first book of nonfiction, *Black in America: A Fight for Freedom* (with Elaine Landau, 1973) describes the black experience from slavery to the civil rights movement, and he is also the author of a biography of Mahalia Jackson that presents the singer's personal story in the context of black history.

Jackson interweaves much of his own background into his novels for young people. Born in Columbus, Ohio, he lived for several years in an area where his family were the only African Americans in their neighborhood. Most of his mother's activities centered around her Baptist church; as a boy, Jesse was closer to his Aunt Hannah, who serves

as the model for Aunt Hattie in the Stonewall Jackson books. As a young man in the 1920s, Jackson worked as a waiter and was called "Sambo," "George," and other names; later, he remembered how important being called by his own name was to him when the wrote *Call Me Charley.* Jackson became a journalist and later started a newspaper for blacks; he was also an instructor and writer in residence at the university level. In 1936, Jackson acted as a probation officer for a local juvenile center, where he decided to write books for young people: "How to write something nonreaders would want to read," he said, "became an obsession of mine and still is." Jackson received mixed reviews for some of his books, especially those written before *The Sickest Don't Always Die the Quickest.* These works were criticized for encouraging black children to want to be like whites because of their social and economic power. For example, Jackson outlines in *Tessie* how a fourteen-year-old ninth grader who is the first black student at an exclusive private school adjusts to her situation; in one notorious scene, Tessie tries to straighten her hair to appear more like her classmates. Jackson maintained that he wrote his earlier books under the supervision of white editors who required him to write as if he were a white author addressing a white audience; in his later books, Jackson felt freer to write from a black viewpoint. Some observers see Jackson's works as unrealistic and dated; however, most see his themes—such as respect, loyalty, the search for maturity, and triumph over racism—as universal ones and his protagonists as strongly profiled. He is also credited for his fearlessness in including such concepts as fair employment practices and the segregation of blacks and whites in his books, which are often thought to be appealing and well written as well as historically significant. *Call Me Charley* received the Child Study Association Award and *Anchor Man* received a commendation from the Council of Christians and Jews. *Make a Joyful Noise* was given the Carter G. Woodson Award, National Council for the Social Studies, in 1975.

(See also *Contemporary Literary Criticism,* Vol. 12; *Something about the Author,* Vols. 2, 29, 48; *Contemporary Authors New Revision Series,* Vol. 27; *Contemporary Authors,* Vols. 25-28, rev. ed., and Vol. 109 [obituary].)

GENERAL COMMENTARY

Judith Thompson and Gloria Woodard

[In *Call Me Charley*] the moral is clear. The success of black endeavor is dependent upon the magnanimity of white people. In order to receive the bestowal of this magnanimity, black children must meet certain standards set by a white-middle-class society. The index of acceptability is often marked by superficial criteria which are set even higher for blacks, whether they be manners, standards of dress, or speech patterns. It is Charley's mother who instructs her son in the ways of the white world and the role of the black boy in it. These instructions consist of platitudes that are demeaning and repressive:

> You'll have to keep out of trouble. It ain't like you were one of the other boys . . . And watch your manners, boy. Good manners go a long way to help a colored boy get along in this world. You got to keep trying. You got to work harder than anybody else.

By the end of the story, all these platitudes are realized by Charley (with the help of his friend's white liberal parents), and one more "exceptional" Negro has been accepted by the white world.

The perverse relationships that racial discrimination engenders have not been misrepresented in this book or in others with a similar theme. In a climate of prejudice, blacks *do* have to *try harder* and *be better* in order to be accepted into schools, jobs, or neighborhoods. However, by revealing the situation and only obscuring both the real solutions and the real feelings of blacks about these conditions, the various systems of institutionalized discrimination are made to appear inevitable. (p. 17)

[In the novel *Tessie*] a slightly greater sense of "black consciousness" is evinced by the younger generation—Tessie and her friends—while the idea of integration through the acceptance of individual exemplary Negroes is shown as an older-generation viewpoint. (p. 18)

Judith Thompson and Gloria Woodard,

"Black Perspective in Books for Children," in The Black American in Books for Children: Readings in Racism, *edited by Donnarae MacCann and Gloria Woodard, The Scarecrow Press, Inc., 1972, pp. 14-27.*

Ruby J. Lanier

[School] children often ask the author, Jesse Jackson, why he chose the title *Call Me Charley* for this first book. He tells the children how, as a young black man in the twenties, he worked as a table waiter in clubs, hotels, and on the Great Lake Steamers, and how important it was to him to be called by his own name. When waiting on a table, after pouring the ice water, taking the orders, and bringing the food, he always showed the members of the party his number. Usually waiters had numbers on their jackets, such as "136." He would say to the party, "Now if you need anything my number is 136 and my name is Jesse Jackson. Just holler and I'll come running." During the course of the meal, the man (usually it was the man) in the party would call out to Jesse, "George, I'd like to have another glass of water!" or "Sam (Sambo), we'd like some dessert." Never would he call, "Jesse, I'd like . . . " Young Jesse could not understand why the man refused to call him by his name; he only knew the hurt.

Therefore, in 1945 in *Call Me Charley,* when George called Charley "Sambo," Charley told George, "My name is Charles. Charles Moss." (pp. 331-33)

Concerning the title, *Call Me Charley,* Jesse Jackson further explained that

> A very small advance was asked for in using the title, *Call Me Charley* for this was in 1945, nine years before the Brown decision. Prior to this time most blacks were lost like peas in a pod under such titles as George, Sam, Sambo, Coon, Nigger . . . So with this *Call Me Charley* it was my aim to single out one black boy, to have him fight for at least the respect of being called Charles Moss. Charley had a game plan and the game plan began with recognize me as an individual and then we will go on from there and I'll try to get into the boys' club and try to win admission to the swimming pool and try to get a part in the school play.

Though asking that others call you by your name is described by Jackson as asking for a "small advance," in 1945 *Call Me Charley* was a breakthrough in children's literature. In books published before this time Negroes and whites lived separate lives. The black man was "in his place."

Jackson recalled the reaction of the public to *Call Me Charley,* by saying,

> We know these things exist. We know that black children have such experiences. We just do not write about them. We just do not talk about them. It was part of the invisible nature of the black at that time.
>
> (pp. 333-34)

Was Charley really young Jesse Jackson growing up in Ohio? Definitely some of Jesse's experiences were similar to those of Charley. Jesse Jackson was born in Columbus, Ohio in 1908 on the west side of town in a German neighborhood. His family was the only black family in this neighborhood. . . .

All this changed after the flood of the Scioto River in 1913. The family survived the flood but lost the household goods, the animals, and the beautiful flowers. Jesse, his parents, and his nine-year-old sister moved to the east side of town into a black ghetto. . . .

The family later moved . . . "to a little house in an alley just north of the street where the wealthiest people in town lived." Here Jesse and his sister were able to attend an excellent school for about three years until the school district lines were redrawn to bring about segregation. (p. 334)

Probably young Jesse was closer to his Aunt Hannah, his mother's sister, than to any other adult. She is "Aunt Hettie" in his books *The Sickest Don't Always Die the Quickest* and *The Fourteenth Cadillac*. They could always talk with each other and Hannah "completely trusted Jesse." . . .

In 1936 Jesse Jackson took a job as a probation officer for the Juvenile Court in Columbus. This was when he decided that he would try to write books for young people.

> I came to work one morning, opened the door of my office and there sat three scared-looking young boys, three of the biggest cops I'd ever seen, an assistant to the District Attorney, and a court stenographer. The three boys had killed a restaurant owner in a robbery that netted them five dollars and life terms in the Ohio pen. Investigation of their case brought out that all three boys had dropped out of school because they were ashamed to tell their teachers they could not read. Their ages ran from fourteen to sixteen when this occurred. How to write something non-readers would want to read became an obsession of mine and still is.

It was actually several years later that Jesse Jackson began to write *Call Me Charley*. (p. 335)

Charley Starts from Scratch was the third book about Charles Moss. In the preceding book, *Anchor Man*, Charley was an outstanding senior at Arlington High and a member of its winning track team. Charley had finished high school in *Charley Starts from Scratch* and against the advice of his parents and friends decided to leave home to find a summer job. He needed "to get away from people I know so I can see if I can make it alone." Charley had problems from the start but finally got a job at a Soda Palace on the Boardwalk in Atlantic City.

Of all the books Jesse Jackson has written, he recalled this book to be the most difficult one to write. He had to treat two major problems—the social separation of blacks and whites and fair employment practices. (pp. 336-37)

While waiting for a train one morning a librarian with whom Jesse happened to be talking asked him, "Why don't you do a book for girls? Girls read far more than boys." He thought about it and the suggestion jelled when he overheard a telephone conversation in which a mother complained that her daughter who was attending private

school had been asked to take the role of a maid in the school play. *Tessie* was the result. Jesse was never pleased with this book for he would have "preferred" writing a "more realistic" one, a book he "knew the editors would probably not accept."

Actually Jesse Jackson had begun writing that "more realistic" book. While completing *Tessie*, and moving on to write *Make a Joyful Noise Unto the Lord! The Life of Mahalia Jackson, Queen of the Gospel Singers* he was writing down his thoughts about Seventeenth Street in Columbus, Ohio. He gathered up this "catalog" of bits and pieces and took it to two of his writer friends and asked them to look at it. They told him he had enough material for five novels. Jesse first pulled from this material *The Sickest Don't Always Die the Quickest*. To his surprise, not only did the editor "love *The Sickest* . . ." for "its honesty," but she also asked that few changes be made, though it surely "would offend some people to death."

In *The Sickest Don't Always Die the Quickest,* Charley? Jesse? (This book is the most autobiographical of all Jesse Jackson's books.) appears again in the character of Stonewall Jackson; however, it is a new Charley. He is not concerned about trying to succeed in a white world. Stonewall is trying to define his own world. (pp. 337-38)

When questioned about this obvious change in his writing style Jesse noted

> Before doing *The Sickest Don't Always Die the Quickest* and *The Fourteenth Cadillac* I had worked closely with white editors who were anxious that my books reflect the viewpoint of a white writer writing for white readers. The difference in style between these two and my earlier works was that I told *The Sickest* . . . and *The Fourteenth Cadillac* purely from the viewpoint of a black in a black setting under the supervision of a white editor who happened to have been born in England and had less of the hangup about white being right than Americans. Miss Patricia Connelly is the name of that kind editor. . . . The difference was Miss Connelly seemed to be unafraid of violating the unwritten law in the juvenile field that all books for children must first satisfy the aunts, uncles and parents who set the tone for what children read.

Though there is a new Charley (Stonewall), children continue to read about the old Charley. *Call Me Charley* has had over a million readers.

They call him Charley—Stonewall JESSE JACKSON. (p. 339)

> *Ruby J. Lanier, "Profile: Call Me Jesse Jackson," in* Language Arts, *Vol. 54, No. 3, March, 1977, pp. 331-39.*

TITLE COMMENTARY

Call Me Charley (1945)

The race problem—in a moderate sized Ohio town—when Charley, a young Negro lad, comes with his parents to live at the home of the local doctor. They are residents—and

Charley will be the first Negro child in the school. How he and the community come to terms is the theme of the book—not an easy one. Simply and rather unpretentiously handled, the book highlights the problems of children between 11 and 18. Sympathetic family and alert members of the community make possible a comfortable resolving of the problem.

> *A review of "Call Me Charley," in* Virginia Kirkus' Bookshop Service, *Vol. XIII, No. 18, September 15, 1945, p. 423.*

There was a new boy in town—a well-to-do Mid-Western suburb—who had a good newspaper route and tended it strictly. As he passed the Hamilton house, Tom, whose mom had promised to let him carry as soon as he was thirteen, offered to help the newsboy, as "he'd got to know how." But George, whose family by moving in next door had, in the cook's opinion, lowered the tone of the neighborhood, only said, "Move on, Sambo." I have known white boys cheerfully answering to that nickname, but it's lowdown to apply it to a boy who is not white. "My name is Charles; Charles Moss," the boy replied, quietly, because his reply had become almost automatic. First colored boy in Arlington Heights, his story can be matched under like circumstances all over the United States, except that in some parts it would not work out so well as here.

Though Charley's parents work for the leading doctor, the principal won't let him attend school—till the doctor puts in a peremptory phone call. Then he is let in, on the scarcely veiled condition that at the first good pretext he'll go out. A few leading citizens are on his side, but boys don't bother with leading citizens, settling their own affairs by their own laws, in what amounts to secret proceedings. It took a school year of ups and downs before Charley was settled in the place to which by his own merits he is entitled, initiated into the club, allowed to use the pass to the amusement park that he won as a prize, and even permitted a glorious line in the school play. Even Tom—whose solid, unemotional friendship was quickened by constant proof that whenever they both got into trouble the colored boy would get the blame—was often impatient with the patience of Charley and thought him scared. Perhaps he was, but of something larger than what happened. As Tom's father says, "Charley has been hurt, again and again, in a way you know nothing about. When you feel that you are not wanted, you learn to keep your mouth shut."

A straight story of American boy-life, it is told largely in dialogue; the young author, whose ear is uncommonly sensitive, reproduces the staccato touch and distinctive turn of Negro speech without attributing dialect to educated Northern Negroes. His book is a contribution to understanding. (pp. 18, 20)

> *A review of "Call Me Charley," in* New York Herald Tribune Weekly Book Review, *November 11, 1945, pp. 18, 20.*

Call Me Charley was the first book to present anything resembling a genuine black-white confrontation. The opening scene in **Call Me Charley** has the bigot, George, saying

"Move on Sambo," and "We don't allow niggers around here." Charley responds by saying:

> "My name is Charles. . . . Sometimes I'm called Charley. Nobody calls me Sambo and gets away with it." He dropped the paper he was rolling and moved closer to George. George swung back with the stick.

The verbal exchange and the threatening gestures do not lead to physical combat either in the above scene or at any time in the book. When the white boys at school want to initiate Charley into their club, the fear of physical violence makes Charley run. It is not that Charley is a physical coward, but he knows there is a difference between fighting with the boys in his old neighborhood who belonged to his own race and fighting with white boys.

George tries very hard to make Tom Hamilton stop associating with Charley. The only time George and Charley are together is at the Hamilton house, and George usually finds a reason to go home soon after Charley arrives. George is not a likable boy. He is pampered, a victim of his parents' prejudices, and the parents are shown as not really class people: a little too loud, a little too pushy.

This idea that "class" people do not behave badly is a direct descendant of the slave attitude that masters were "quality" folk and the nonslave-owning population was "poor white trash." It is also related to the idea that "happy slaves" had good masters, while on occasion there was a bad master whose lack of good behavior caused the slaves to be unhappy. (pp. 166-67)

> *Dorothy M. Broderick, "Black-White Relationships," in her* Image of the Black in Children's Fiction, *R.R. Bowker Company, 1973, pp. 163-76.*

[This is a] realistic problem novel set in Ohio in the mid-1900s. . . . Contrived characters, situations, and dialogue combine with an earnest, instructive tone to inform young readers about prejudice against blacks. To late twentieth century readers, the book seems dated and projects a certain quaintness, the product of the era that was prologue to the big push for black rights. Very obviously written to thesis, it offers ready solutions to complex problems. (pp. 81-2)

> *Alethea K. Helbig and Agnes Regan Perkins, in a review of "Call Me Charley," in their* Dictionary of American Children's Fiction, 1859-1959: Books of Recognized Merit, *Greenwood Press, 1985, pp. 81-2.*

One of the most striking features of post-war American realistic writing for children has been a determined and continuing attempt to widen the scope of fiction to include the experience of minority groups: especially (so far) blacks. The position of the black American in a white-dominated society is of course no new theme; it goes back to *Uncle Tom's Cabin* and *Huckleberry Finn*. Among stories of the 1940s which were 'contemporary' at the time of their publication but which have now dated were John R. Tunis's

All-American (1942) and Jesse Jackson's **Call Me Charley.** The Tunis book was concerned with the admission of black (and Jewish) boys to sport teams; **Call Me Charley** with the acceptance of a black boy in a suburban community generally.

In these books the black characters bear injustice with a patience that now seems excessive. . . . Charley Moss's mother in **Call Me Charley** advises him on the last page, 'As long as you work hard and try to do right, you will always find good [white] people like Doc Cunningham or Tom and his folks marching along with you in the right path.' Actually Charley is not without spirit; when someone addresses him as Sambo he says, 'My name is Charles. Sometimes I'm called Charley. Nobody calls me Sambo and gets away with it.' Hence the book's title. Nevertheless, in the attitudes of the time there is some resemblance to the treatment of the poor by well-meaning Victorians. Just as the poor were expected to rely on and be grateful for the beneficence of the rich, so the black must rely on and be grateful for the beneficence of the white. (p. 269)

> *John Rowe Townsend, "Realism, American-Style: 'Call Me Charley'," in his* Written for Children: An Outline of English-Language Children's Literature, *third revised edition, J. B. Lippincott, 1987, pp. p. 269.*

Anchor Man   (1947)

Unfortunately an uninspired race-problem book, for although an unusual angle is offered, it doesn't build up to much feeling of reality. It centers around Clarence Duke, a Negro who spurns the acceptance of a white community, because he is too embittered against whites to live in harmony with them. A fire forces a white high school (with only one Negro boy student) to admit a group of Negroes, and Clarence, one of the "burnt out" children, is among them. He hates all whites because his brother was cheated by a white boxing manager. His precariously flashy adjustment to the white group, as a valuable team member, is upset when the prejudiced principal unfairly suspends Duke for a time, thereby proving to Duke that all white men are his enemies. He is a foil for Charley, a Negro who is happy and accepted in the white section. Eventually Duke admits that Charley has not gone against his people through his acceptance of the advantages offered by others. Since comparatively few, if any, white communities have opened their doors freely to Negroes, this book seems to dwell on a fairly theoretical aspect of the problem, especially unreal to the age level for which this book is written. In any case, not a very engaging book.

> *A review of "Anchor Man," in* Virginia Kirkus' Bookshop Service, *Vol. XV, No. 16, August 15, 1947, p. 430.*

Charley Moss of **Call Me Charley** is now an accepted member of the student body at Arlington high, on the track team, and a member of the Student council. . . . . The relations between Negro and white and between the Negroes and Charley are presented with honest realism, but the story somehow lacks vitality and the solution is unsatisfactory.

> *A review of "Anchor Man," in* The Booklist, *Vol. 44, January 1, 1948, p. 175.*

Room for Randy   (1957)

A social problem in New Jersey develops from the need to enlarge a commercial airport but suffers from a stagy dialogue and minor, unlikely happenings meant to convey drama. Randy, the hero, is the son of a caterer who still has connections with poor Tintown though he now lives in Forge Hill and has a better business. But with airport construction, the Tintown children must be sent to school in Forge Hill and Randy's old associates return to bring conflict. Through Rick, a Protestant minister's son and Randy's best friend, he makes the adjustment, but the story is too full of pronouncements and exemplary behaviour to be convincing.

> *A review of "Room for Randy," in* Virginia Kirkus' Service, *Vol. XXV, No. 4, February 15, 1957, p. 141.*

Charley Starts from Scratch   (1958)

The plight of an eighteen-year-old Negro, the only Negro boy in a snug Ohio town, could not conceivably be easy. In Charley's case it is just this handicap which fills him with a fierce determination to prove himself a man, not a child dependent on the condescending benevolence of his white neighbors. Charley's moral odyssey takes him to Atlantic City where he is confronted with a barrage of prejudice and disadvantage. Nevertheless, his integrity and his athletic prowess serve him well, and in the end he knows that he has established his manhood. A well meaning story, which may well promote greater racial understanding, but handled on a somewhat naive and superficial level which leaves one wondering what would have been Charley's fate, had he not been so unusually well endowed.

> *A review of "Charley Starts from Scratch," in* Virginia Kirkus' Service, *Vol. XXVI, No. 18, September 15, 1958, pp. 714-15.*

Tessie   (1968)

A ninth-grader from Harlem wins an ivy-clad scholarship and runs the gantlet of her first year in a mythical private school named Hobbe. Tessie Downs is challenged and sometimes confounded by the warring demands of old and new loyalties, although she has scored some tentative victories by term's end. Her conflict is so dense with implications for all of us, so absorbing in itself, that pages turn willy-nilly. All the same, the book is a barely passable effort to bridge communication gaps between the races, the generations, or the sexes.

One embarrassment is the author's (or his editors') assumption that black ritual and idiom never leak from the inner city. Few teen-agers today need to have "bread" translated into "money," whatever their address and pigmentation. The charming gesture of "giving skin," lightly palm-to-palm, has likewise been exported to the suburbs.

This is bloodless drawing-room tragicomedy, even narrower in scope than "Guess Who's Coming to Dinner." Miscegenation is dismissed at the outset as a potentiality, although Hobbe is coeducational and almost lily-white. Tessie scoffs at the thought of any love other than her soul-buddy, Jimmy, and thinks that "the question only showed how little her parents understood."

The author seems to agree with Tessie. To the pure all things are very pure indeed, and few problems so knotty that they cannot be straightened out with patience and a heated comb.

Mary Louise Birmingham, in a review of "Tessie," in The New York Times Book Review, *May 26, 1968, p. 30.*

"Have you lost your mind?" Tessie's mother asked. "Tessie going to a private school like Hobbe—where there's never been a colored girl before—can be a disaster for her and for the rest of us." It wasn't a disaster, but it was a grueling experience for Tessie, partly because she had such doubts about being accepted, and partly because her old friends in a Harlem junior high school felt alienated. She stuck it out, knowing that the pioneer has the hardest role, and she found it was possible to make new friends at Hobbe and not lose those in Harlem. Although some scenes don't ring true, others have a piercing honesty—such as the one in which Tessie, while on a weekend visit, sneaks into the kitchen at night to straighten her hair.

A review of "Tessie," in Saturday Review, *Vol. LI, No. 24, June 15, 1968, p. 33.*

Juvenile books about Harlem and its residents fall into three main categories (or traps): those that romanticize life in Harlem, those that over-simplify it, and those that portray Harlem as a place from which the lucky ones escape. *Tessie* falls partly into the second category, but mostly into the third. These attitudes are obvious from the beginning. Bright 14-year-old Tessie returns from a summer camp stay which has apparently dimmed her memories of unpleasant aspects of Harlem life and reacts as though she's returned to a minor nightmare. Tessie's escape route opens up when she wins a scholarship to Hobbe, an exclusive private school. Her father is pleased, but her mother disagrees, feeling the material and academic advantages of Hobbe by day contrasted with the realities of their Harlem home by night will confuse and embitter Tessie. But Tessie takes her scholarship, and the story chiefly concerns her resulting cross pressures: to win acceptance by Hobbe students without having her Harlem friends feel she has changed. The author handles this basic conflict in such confused and unconvincing ways that the end product is almost a hymn to the rather prevalent notion, more challenged now than ever before, that most Negroes want one thing out of life: to be white and middle-class. Tessie's addiction to white social and aesthetic values is exemplified in the entire chapter devoted to what the author calls Tessie's hair problem, which, since it is kinky, she straightens to conform to white standards of what hair should look like. Readers will inevitably be left with the unfortunate impression that Tessie, her verbal protestations to the contrary, has chosen the world of Hobbe and that it is the best of all possible worlds.

Doris Innis, in a review of "Tessie," in School Library Journal, *Vol. 15, No. 2, October, 1968, p. 169.*

The Sickest Don't Always Die the Quickest (1971)

Twelve-years old and living in Columbus, Ohio, Stonewall Jackson suspects being black is a sin, even if "people didn't come right out and say so." Thus, when the white lady clad only in long red hair and slippers hands Stoney his weekly 11 cents for delivering papers past her vicious dog, he wonders if this vision proves he's saved! With Stoney, who has a spot on one lung, the reader lives and learns. It is better (literally) to swim than sink: the sickest do not always die the quickest.

Stoney's world will be news to many of all ages, black and white. His mother's energetically schismatic congregation wants sermons that are "tearjerkers." The minister resists, "The condition of the black man in America required making blacks think not weep." His wife, proud to be among Oberlin's "first Negro graduates" wants the congregation to sing spirituals the right, white way. As the Chicago Defender shrieks "Race Riots!" Stoney laps up loving Aunt Hettie's dumplings and gravy.

While our busy hero survives more sad-funny, boy-growing up scrapes than one week (in July, 1920) and a book this size, can quite afford, *TSDADTQ* is fresh, warm, honest Americana about a real American boy. Stoney should make a lot of friends.

Betty Zoss, in a review of "The Sickest Don't Always Die the Quickest," in The New York Times Book Review, *February 14, 1971, p. 20.*

Jesse Jackson's first book, **Call Me Charlie,** published in 1945, was a landmark. It received much critical acclaim and was widely read by young people because it was the compelling story of a Black boy's defeats and triumphs as he faced the problems of being the only Black child in an upper-class community. Jackson's handling of the situation was, by far, the most honest of the few novels on the subject which were available to children at that time. Mr. Jackson's subsequent books did not compare favorably with his first and the book prior to this one, *Tessie,* seemed to have been written in rose-colored ink. It appeared to this reviewer that Mr. Jackson had lost touch with the changing times and was incapable of writing out of contemporary settings. Such may be the case, but *The Sickest Don't Always Die the Quickest* doesn't have a contemporary setting. It is historical fiction set in the Columbus, Ohio of 1920. One suspects that it is largely autobiographical.

Many adults are not going to like this book, and for a variety of reasons. Why, they will ask, is it necessary that the twelve-year-old hero bear the first name of Stonewall, that his closest friend be nick-named Steeplehead, because of his pointed skull, and that Stonewall's despised older brother carry the nickname of Pisseyes? Is it appropriate for readers to suffer with Stonewall when he is told that his favorite aunt, who is a hotel cook, is also one of the hotel whores? Should one of the major episodes of the book be built around a married minister whose congregation is trying to oust him because they suspect him of having gotten one of his young parishioners pregnant? What about Stonewall's taking his two best friends on a Peeping Tom expedition to see a nude white woman? Doesn't the author expose religion to ridicule when he so hilariously exposes the rivalry between two church factions—the Soul Savers and the Keepers of the True Faith?

Disagreement of a more fundamental nature may arise over Jackson's portrayal of the Black community. There will be some who say that the characters and situations are sketches that burlesque Black life. Others will claim that, even if Jackson's portrayal is an honest one, it is not appropriate to share it with today's young readers.

My own evaluation is that *The Sickest Don't Always Die the Quickest* is an appropriate book for teenage readers. Although it is not especially well plotted, the situations have vitality and honesty about them, basic human values are treated with sincerity and respect, and the innate decency of mankind prevails. It should also be noted that Mr. Jackson, who is Black and possesses the tools of the writer's craft, is fully qualified to write of the "Black Experience." (pp. 294-95)

> *Shelton L. Root, Jr., in a review of "The Sickest Don't Always Die the Quickest," in* Elementary English, *Vol. XLVIII, No. 4, April, 1971, pp. 294-95.*

Jesse Jackson is a very funny writer. In *The Sickest Don't Always Die the Quickest* he has created a black Tom Sawyer (Steeplehead) and a black Huckleberry Finn (Stonewall) who cavort irreverently through two weeks of hot July afternoons in 1920. Stonewall and Steeplehead are as inseparable as the bicycle they share. Steeplehead is always pumping, and Stonewall is always riding on the handlebars because he has TB and mustn't exert himself. To support Steeplehead and Stonewall, the author recreates the black society which attends Calvary Baptist Church in Columbus, Ohio. These people and the white folks who control jobs held by blacks are a microcosm reflecting the foibles of a world with which the innocent but ornery Steeplehead and Stonewall constantly collide. Lying is necessary when the truth won't suffice, bluffing is necessary when your adversary is too big to fight, amelioration is the only way to get through some hot days in life. But be quick to repent if you feel the Almighty might be angered!

Stonewall and Steeplehead are twelve and thirteen respectively. Neither is willing to shed the superstitions which adults around them practice; both boys want to be true to their own beliefs but find this difficult when threatened by adults. Jesse Jackson's adult characters often behave more like children than Stonewall and Steeplehead do. The author implies that children's honesty is warped to fit adult misconceptions. Not that a reader will believe that Stonewall and Steeplehead will be warped! These two adolescent free thinkers will survive adult misconceptions despite adult pressures!

The Sickest Don't Always Die the Quickest defies classification for a particular age group. The actions of the two major characters will be enjoyed by younger adolescents, although the implications in the story will be missed by this group. I believe older adolescents are the accepting audience for this book.

Jesse Jackson's frank language and the chapter in which Stonewall makes his weekly paper route collections may make *The Sickest Don't Always Die the Quickest* unacceptable for some readers. Read this book before recommending it to adolescents. You will enjoy it. Jesse Jackson's humor will leave a thought-provoking tingle at the end of your funny bone. (pp. 665-66)

> *John W. Connor, in a review of "The Sickest Don't Always Die the Quickest," in* English Journal, *Vol. 60, No. 5, May, 1971, pp. 665-66.*

The gutsy, hilarious and sad account of a week in the life of 12-year-old Stonewall Jackson. . . . When at last all the problems are resolved, . . . an ominous note recurs: "Awful news," they hear the newsboy shouting, "Terrible tragedy. Chicago race riots. . . ." And the book closes leaving readers with the feeling that the scenes just witnessed are about to be replayed on a more cosmic scale, with the same factors of toughness, resiliency, and faith that have kept Stonewall alive operating to help a race survive. Though endowed with greater vitality than any of the author's other books, . . . this is difficult to place. The hero is younger than those readers who could appreciate the complicated soul-searching and factional religious disputes, and the nostalgic note is definitely adult. But it seems so evidently written out of the author's own need that the story is bound to find its own audience, anywhere from age 13 and up.

> *Kay Heylman, in a review of "The Sickest Don't Always Die the Quickest," in* School Library Journal, *Vol. 17, No. 9, May, 1971, p. 75.*

The Fourteenth Cadillac (1972)

References to blacks, Afro-Americans, the hot-line, and perfume spray-bottles are familiar these days. But their use in this book is startlingly anachronistic, since the time is the mid-1920s. The story concerns a black community, in Columbus, Ohio and the effects of the death of Aunt Hettie, a wise and beloved lady. Her loss is particularly felt by her nephew, 17-year-old Stonewall Jackson. After her funeral, he tells his family that he has failed high school and is ordered to get a job and pressured to join their church. Stonewall has a bad summer but, in the end, is still his own man. He leaves town in hopes of getting a job caring for race horses. The novel is intriguing and it has some absorbing scenes but, unfortunately, it never lives up to its promise.

> *A review of "The Fourteenth Cadillac," in* Publishers Weekly, *Vol. 202, No. 20, November 13, 1972, p. 45.*

Adolescent readers who enjoyed meeting Stonewall Jackson and his pal Steeplehead in one of Jesse Jackson's previous books, *The Sickest Don't Always Die the Quickest,* will welcome the continued adventures of these two black adolescents who try to find jobs in a Southern city in 1925.

But, before Stonewall starts job-hunting in earnest, Jesse Jackson treats his readers to the laying out, the funeral, and the survivor's feast in honor of Aunt Hettie, Stonewall's favorite aunt.

Jesse Jackson has a talent for combining description and fast-paced narrative. Aunt Hettie's funeral is an elaborate affair, complete with fourteen Cadillacs to transport the mourners to her grave site; but, the funeral becomes a contest between Stonewall and the minister who is still trying to get Stonewall to join the church. During the course of his sermon the minister telephones heaven to see if Aunt Hettie has arrived. He can't get through. This communication breakdown is attributed to Stonewall who has steadfastly refused to throw in his lot with the church.

After the funeral Stonewall seems doomed to become an undertaker's helper—a job he fears because of previous spooky experiences at the undertaker's establishment. Of course Steeple intervenes, but Steeple's idea of a good job does not please Stonewall's mother.

The Fourteenth Cadillac is great fun to read. It will touch many adolescents where their weaknesses in familial relationships occur. Stonewall's younger brother is a hypocrite and a tattletale, his mother has enormous ambitions for Stonewall which are far beyond his capacities to fulfill, only Stonewall's father feels that a seventeen-year-old boy has a right to honest failure.

Adolescent readers will laugh with Stonewall and occasionally fear for him as he faces a situation for which he seems ill-prepared. But, readers know that Stonewall and Steeple will come through any situation relatively unscathed and confident of a brighter future. *The Fourteenth Cadillac* suggests that the human foibles of 1925 are much like those of 1973. Jesse Jackson, I think you are right!

> *John W. Connor, in a review of "The Fourteenth Cadillac," in* English Journal, *Vol. 62, No. 2, February, 1973, p. 307.*

Black in America: A Fight for Freedom (with Elaine Landau, 1973)

[Landau and Jackson] view the experiences of American blacks from the broadest possible perspective—beginning with a four page review of West African culture and a history of the slave trade and continuing right on through the civil rights movement. Though the text is aimed at younger readers, this is virtually the same territory covered by Goldston's *Negro Revolution* and Sterling's *Tear Down the Walls,* and the summary of the post-war era, which treats leaders from Martin Luther King and Elijah Muhammed to the Black Panthers with equal caution and approval (and follows a photo of a Panther headquarters office with one of an apparently cheery meeting between the Congressional Black Caucus and President Nixon). A new volume on Black history might be expected to devote more than two pages to events subsequent to King's assassination in 1968, and to at least attempt some sort of summary of the current socio-economic situation or political tenor of the black community; Jackson and Landau seem content to recap the highlights of the Black experience without adding any new material, style or viewpoint of their own. Redundant.

> *A review of "Black in America: A Fight for Freedom," in* Kirkus Reviews, *Vol. XLI, No. 21, November 1, 1973, p. 1207.*

A survey of black history in this country begins with background chapters about the high level of sophistication in ancient African kingdoms and about the beginnings of the slave trade in Africa. Emphasis is on the long struggle for freedom and equality. The text is adequately written and the photographs well chosen, but the book seems somewhat random in choice of material: for example, while the index shows entries for Bessie Smith, "Jelly Roll" Morton, and Joe Louis, it has no citations for Benjamin Forten, Benjamin Banneker, Robert Smalls, or George Washington Carver. There is a list of outstanding black Americans that does include some of these names. Although most of the black history books are written for slightly older readers, they are so much better written and so much more informative that a history as sketchy as this one pales in contrast. (pp. 130-31)

> *Zena Sutherland, in a review of "Black in America: A Fight for Freedom," in* Bulletin of the Center for Children's Books, *Vol. 27, No. 8, April, 1974, pp. 130-31.*

Interspersed with photographs and old prints, this is an extremely condensed and at times misleading treatment of 300 years of Afro-American history from before the arrival of slave-trading whites in West Africa through the U.S. Civil War and Reconstruction to the present. The philosophies of Booker T. Washington, W.E.B. DuBois, Marcus Garvey, Malcolm X, Martin Luther King, the Muslims, and Black Panthers are discussed, and a list of outstanding Black Americans is appended. However, analyses of complex issues such as slavery are naive and fail to incorporate the views of such recent scholars as John Blassingame and Eugene Genovese. The authors barely mention notable figures in areas other than politics, except for some already well-known jazz musicians and athletes. A more detailed and informative account of Black history can be found in Milton Meltzer's three-volume *In Their Own Words: a History of the American Negro.*

> *Norman Lederer, in a review of "Black in America: A Fight for Freedom," in* School Library Journal, *Vol. 99, No. 8, April, 1974, p. 58.*

Make a Joyful Noise unto the Lord! The Life of Mahalia Jackson, Queen of Gospel Singers (1974)

Jesse Jackson's biography of Mahalia Jackson, *Make a Joyful Noise Unto the Lord* is simply a beautiful book. . . . The story traces Mahalia's difficult childhood in New Orleans, her trip north to Chicago and her rise to success with a depth of understanding and characterization that brings her to life in these pages.

Jackson does not avoid the terrible cruelty and degradation heaped on black people by Jim Crow laws but the story is far from depressing. It is an inspiring, encouraging tale full of vivid descriptions of street life in New Orleans and Chicago, of marvelous food, and of the inner struggles of Mahalia as she rose slowly to stardom and dedicated involvement in the civil rights movement.

> *Joel Dreyfuss, "Beyond Booker T.," in* Book World—The Washington Post, *May 19, 1974, p. 4.*

Beginning with Mahalia Jackson's early childhood "in a shack with a leaky roof on Water Street" in New Orleans and continuing through her Civil Rights work in the '60's, Jesse Jackson tells the gospel singer's personal story in the context of American black experience and history. We could in fact do with a little more of the personal record—the singer's first marriage breaks up offstage, essentially unreported, a second marriage of a few years' duration is mentioned only in a parenthetical phrase, and the nature of her "very serious" illness and operation is never disclosed. There is however much color and feeling, conversation and anecdote—about her first and only voice lesson, from a cultured black concert singer who berated her for singing "in a way that makes the Negro race ashamed of you," about her famous vow never to sing in a place that served liquor, which she made in 1934 when her grandfather seemed near death and kept, as he recovered, for the rest of her life—all of which goes a long way toward projecting the subject's own strength and vitality.

> *A review of "Make a Joyful Noise unto the Lord: The Life of Mahalia Jackson, Queen of Gospel Singers," in* Kirkus Reviews, *Vol. XLII, No. 11, June 1, 1974, p. 590.*

Anyone who ever heard the magnificent voice of gospel singer Mahalia Jackson knows what an inspiring artist she was. Although she died in 1972, at the age of 60, Miss Jackson has left us with her message still alive on her recordings. This biography details the course of her life from her early years in New Orleans, where she first impressed people with her singing at age 5, through her triumphs all over the world and her brave participation in the civil rights movement.

The same woman whose voice touched the hearts of 250,000 people at the famous March on Washington during the summer of 1963 had two unsuccessful marriages, suffered through the degradation of segregation and, worst of all, the subtle discrimination of those who outwardly praised her artistry. But Jesse Jackson makes it clear that she lived and breathed to spread the word of peace and love through gospel music.

Jesse Jackson tells the story well—explaining vividly why Miss Jackson stuck with gospel rather than singing the blues and how she was willing to do the toughest kind of housework for white people so that she could sing. There are times when the author tries to convey in the narrative what Miss Jackson was thinking. I'm a little suspicious of this, and it makes no sense in view of the disclaimer which appears in the acknowledgments: "The author regrets not having space for more of the wonderful things Mahalia said about her life, her music, the black experience, religion, and God." I would have preferred more of Mahalia Jackson, less of Jesse Jackson.

The book lacks a discography, rather a serious omission in a biography of a singer. But on the whole it will induce young readers to listen to some of Mahalia Jackson's recordings and to discover for themselves what made her gift so special.

> *Loraine Alterman, in a review of "Make a Joyful Noise unto the Lord! The Life of Mahalia Jackson, Queen of the Gospel Singers," in* The New York Times Book Review, *June 16, 1974, p. 8.*

Here is a moving biography. . . . The life, music, and times of Mahalia Jackson are related in a sincere and unaffected manner. The reader becomes acquainted with a character possessing a strong and forceful personality, but who is also extremely humble. More meaningful to older children.

> *Jo Hudson, in a review of "Make a Joyful Noise unto the Lord! The Life of Mahalia Jackson, Queen of Gospel Singers," in* Children's Book Review Service, *Vol. 2, No. 11, July, 1974, p. 104.*

Ursula K(roeber) Le Guin

1929-

American author of fiction and picture books.

Major works include the Earthsea Quartet: *A Wizard of Earthsea* (1968), *The Tombs of Atuan* (1971), *The Farthest Shore* (1972), *Tehanu: The Last Book of Earthsea* (1990); *Very Far Away from Anywhere Else* (1976), *The Beginning Place* (1980), *Catwings* (1989).

The following entry presents criticism of the Earthsea Quartet.

Often considered the best contemporary writer of fantasy for children and young adults, Le Guin is lauded as a brilliant and original author whose works have expanded the scope of the genre by using the fantasy format to successfully explore essential themes. Although she has written realistic fiction and picture books as well as other works of fantasy, Le Guin is best known as the creator of the four novels for readers in the upper elementary grades through high school that form the Earthsea Quartet. These books, which delineate the life of their main protagonist, the wizard Ged, from youth to old age, are set on various locations in Earthsea, a rural archipelago complete with its own anthropology, geology, and language. A world that is both like and unlike our own, Earthsea is a land of forests, islands, and bodies of water that incorporates a variety of nations and customs; although Earthsea is governed by secular rulers, its real laws are made by a hierarchy of wizards, men whose inborn affinity for magic is augmented by disciplined study that teaches them to know, and to be able to name, the essence of each person or thing in the world. The basis of the magic of Earthsea is thus in language: in knowing the true name of someone or something, one has power and control; true names, then, are given only to the trusted. The mages of Earthsea are also responsible for keeping the balance or equilibrium of the world: since order is not imposed by a deity, the wizards and other powerful humans act or refrain from acting based on their insights into both the world and themselves. Thus, individual responsibility and the acceptance of oneself as both good and evil are pivotal qualities in maintaining the balance of Earthsea. Le Guin depicts her wizards as artists, poets and shamans who devote themselves to retaining an integrated universe, a world in which light and darkness, life and death are equally acknowledged and revered. Throughout her quartet, Le Guin stresses the importance of self-knowledge through each stage of life, especially as it relates to the world: in the first three novels, Ged overcomes pride and fear and learns to accept himself and his own mortality as well as to love and trust others; as Archmage of Earthsea, he succeeds in laying the groundwork for a society based in justice and peace through his selfless and profoundly dangerous acts of will. In the fourth novel, Le Guin suggests that the responsibility for maintaining the equilibrium of the world has shifted

from male wizards such as Ged, whose final act as Archmage causes his loss of power, to women.

The daughter of the anthropologist Alfred Louis Kroeber and the writer Theodora Kroeber, Le Guin was raised in a home that embraced both literature and science. Influenced by Celtic and Teutonic lore as well as by authors such as Hans Christian Andersen, Lord Dunsany, Padraic Colum, and her main inspiration J. R. R. Tolkien, a writer to whom she is often favorably compared, Le Guin was also inspired by the anthropological views of Sir James Frazer, whose *The Golden Bough* first thrilled her as a child when she discovered a juvenile adaptation written by his wife, and Bronislaw Malinowski. The Earthsea Quartet also reflects Le Guin's integration of Eastern philosophy, especially Taoism; use of Jungian archetypes; and interest in cultures as diverse as medieval European and Native American. Before writing the Earthsea stories, Le Guin developed a reputation as a major artist for creating science fiction and fantasy novels and short stories that share several of the themes she was later to address in the quartet: liberation of the sexes, ecology, and humanity's potential to retain balance in the universe. Critic Harold Bloom calls Le Guin "the best contemporary writer of literary fantasy," and Meredith Tax has dubbed her "a prophet unhonored in her own country." Le Guin introduced the world of Earthsea in the short stories "The Word of Unbinding" and "The Rule of Names" that were published in *Fantastic Magazine* in 1964; in these stories "I discovered Earthsea," she has written. In 1967, the publisher of Parnassus Press asked her to write a book for children; the result was *A Wizard of Earthsea.*

In *A Wizard of Earthsea,* which is considered a classic story of coming of age and is often considered the most popular book of the series, Le Guin describes how young Ged, a richly gifted but impetuous student, unleashes an evil shadow through hubris; when Ged confronts the shadow, they call each other by the same name, and the shadow and Ged become one. Ged nearly loses his life again when he searches for the broken half of an ancient silver ring in *The Tombs of Atuan.* Lost in a maze of catacombs within a decaying temple, he is near death when he is discovered by Tenar, a fifteen-year-old priestess. Part of an evil ritualistic female cult, Tenar is exploring the dark city as part of her initiation, and she holds the second half of the powerful ring that Ged wishes to bring to light. Tenar pities Ged and saves his life; in return, he convinces her to renounce the darkness and to choose freedom and liberation. Le Guin ends *The Tombs of Atuan* with the hope that Earthsea might be united under its true king; in *The Farthest Shore,* Ged guides teenage Arren, the future king of Earthsea, on a quest to discover the source of the evil which is demoralizing the archipelago. The wizard and the prince journey to an island peopled by the walking, silent dead where a former classmate of Ged's has achieved a macabre immortality; in order to restore death to its rightful place in the universe, Ged heals the crack in the fabric of the world caused by the crazed wizard but uses all of his mage power in the process. Through his apprenticeship with Ged, Arren comes to understand his role in keeping the balance of the universe and accepts his position as Earthsea's governor, thus fulfilling the prophecy of the coming of a great king who restores peace to Earthsea. Nearly twenty years after the publication of *The Farthest Shore,* Le Guin returned again to Earthsea with *Tehanu:* beginning twenty-five years after the ending of *The Farthest Shore,* the novel describes how the powerless Ged is joined once again with Tenar, the heroine of *The Tombs of Atuan.* Now a middle-aged widow, Tenar has chosen to forego her own powers and to live anonymously. Le Guin introduces a new and pivotal character in *Tehanu,* the abused child Therru, a six-year-old girl who is found by Tenar after she has been raped and beaten by her father and uncle and left to die in a fire. Therru, who begins to heal emotionally through her relationships with Tenar and Ged, saves them from the last of the wizards who have chosen to defy death when she discovers her power to call dragons. Receiving the name "Tehanu" from the eldest of the dragons, the child fulfills the prophecy that "a woman on [the island of] Gont" will be Ged's successor. Thus, the power on Earthsea and the responsibility to keep its balance has passed from men to women, and the patriarchal system is replaced by female magic.

Praised for creating a believable, consistent three-dimensional world with Earthsea, Le Guin is often ac-knowledged for the success of her vision in the series as well as for the beauty and clarity of her writing. The Earthsea books are usually considered Le Guin's finest achievements both as children's literature and as adult fiction, and she is often celebrated for her skill as a storyteller; for her characterizations, especially that of Ged; and for the compelling nature and emotional force of her books. Although the Earthsea series is sophisticated and demanding for young readers due to the complexity of its subjects, the stories are usually regarded as accessible due to the plainness of their narratives, their sensitivity, and their humor as well as the appeal to adolescents of such themes as self-discovery and the attaining of maturity. Le Guin has received some less than favorable comments on the recent direction of her series; however, most observers regard the quartet among the greatest of all contributions to fantasy literature. Critic Michael Dirda has written, "Perhaps no modern work of fantasy has been honored and loved more. . . . Though marketed as young adult novels, [the books] are as deeply imagined, as fiercely wrought, as grown-up as any fiction of our time. They deserve that highest of all accolades: Everyone should read them." The first three volumes of the Earthsea Quartet were published in omnibus volumes in both the United States and Great Britain. *A Wizard of Earthsea* received the *Boston Globe-Horn Book* Award in 1969 and the Lewis Carroll Shelf Award in 1979. *The Tombs of Atuan* was named a Newbery honor book and was a finalist for the National Book Award in 1972, while *The Farthest Shore* received the National Book Award the next year. *Tehanu* received the Nebula Award in 1990. Le Guin is also the recipient of several awards for her adult works and has received a number of honorary degrees from national universities.

(See also *CLR,* Vol. 3; *Contemporary Literary Criticism,* Vols. 8, 13, 22, 45; *Something about the Author,* Vols. 4, 52; *Contemporary Authors New Revision Series,* Vols. 9, 32; *Contemporary Authors,* Vols. 2-22, rev. ed.; *Dictionary of Literary Biography,* Vols. 8, 52; and *Concise Dictionary of Literary Biography,* 1968-1988.)

AUTHOR'S COMMENTARY

[The following excerpt is from an essay that originally appeared in Algol #21, *November, 1973; a portion of the essay also appeared in* CLR, *Vol. 3.]*

Andy Porter called from New York earlier this year to try and tell me what he hoped I'd write for *Algol.* The conversation was pleasant, though disarranged by a bad connection, several explosive intrusions by a person at this end who wanted some cookies and attention, and a slight degree of misunderstanding. Andy kept saying things like, "Tell the readers about yourself," and I kept saying things like, "How? Why?" (p. 5)

Where Andy and I temporarily misunderstood each other was at this point: Wanting me to write about the Earthsea trilogy, the background of it, he said (excuse me, Andy, for misquoting) something like, "People would be interested in knowing things like how you planned the Earthsea world, and how you developed the languages, and how you keep lists of places and characters and so on." To which I returned some kind of garble-garble, of which I recall only one sentence, "But I didn't plan anything, I found it."

Andy (not unnaturally): "Where?"

Me: "In my subconscious."

Now as I think about it, perhaps this is worth talking about a little. Andy and I surprised each other because we had different, unexamined notions of how writing is done; and they were so different that their collision produced a slight shock. Both of them are completely valid; they're just different methodologies. As mine is the one not talked about in writers' manuals, however, perhaps it needs some explanation.

All my life I have written, and all my life I have (without conscious decision) avoided reading How-to-write things. The Shorter Oxford Dictionary and Follett's and Fowler's manuals of usage are my entire arsenal of tools. However in reading and teaching and talking with other writers one does arrive at a certain consciousness of technique. The most different technique to my own, the one that starts from the point farthest removed, is just this one of preliminary plans and lists and descriptions. The technique of keeping a notebook and describing all the characters in it before the story is begun: how much William weighs and where he went to school and how his hair is cut and what his dominant traits are . . .

I do have notebooks, in which I worry at plot ideas as if they were old bones, growling and snarling and frequently burying them and digging them up again. Also, during the writing of a piece, I often make notes concerning a character, particularly if it's a novel. (pp. 5-6)

But I don't write out descriptions beforehand, and would indeed feel ridiculous, even ashamed, to do so. If the character isn't so clear to me *that* I know all that about him, what am I doing writing about him? What right have I to describe what William did when Helen bit his knee, if I don't even know what he looks like, and his past, and his psyche, inside and out, as well as I know myself? Because after all he is myself. Part of myself.

If William is a character worthy of being written about, then he exists. He exists, inside my head to be sure, but in his own right, with his own vitality. All I have to do is look at him. I don't plan him, compose him of bits and pieces, inventory him. I find him.

There he is, and Helen is biting his knee, and he says with a little cough, "I really don't think this is relevant, Helen." What else, being William, could he say?

This attitude towards action, creation, is evidently a basic one, the same root from which the interest in the *I Ching* and Taoist philosophy evident in most of my books arises. The Taoist world is orderly, not chaotic, but its order is not one imposed by man or by a personal or humane deity. The true laws—ethical and aesthetic, as surely as scientific—are not imposed from above by any authority, but exist in things and are to be found—discovered.

To return circuitously to Earthsea: this anti-ideological,

pragmatic technique applies to places, as well as people. I did not deliberately invent Earthsea. I did not think "Hey wow—islands are archetypes and archipelagoes are super-archetypes and let's build us an archipelago!" I am not an engineer, but an explorer. I discovered Earthsea. (pp. 6-7)

The history of the discovery of Earthsea is something like this:

In 1964 I wrote a story called **"The Word of Unbinding"** about a wizard. Cele Goldsmith Lalli bought it for *Fantastic*. . . . I don't recall now whether the fact is made much of in the story, but it was perfectly clear in my mind that it took place on an island, one among many islands. I did not give much attention to the setting, as it was (as William would say) not relevant; and developed only such rules-of-magic as were germane to the very small point the very minor story made.

Soon after, I wrote a story, **"The Rule of Names,"** in which both the islands and the rules of magic were considerably more developed. . . . This story was light-hearted (the other one was glum), and I had fun playing around a bit with the scenery, and with the old island ladies drinking rushwash tea, and so on. It was set on an island called Sattins, which I knew to be one of an outlying group East of the main archipelago. The main character, a dragon known first as Mr. Underhill and then, when his nature is revealed, by his true name Yevaud, came from a westerly isle called Pendor. (pp. 7-8)

Along in 1965 or 66 I wrote a longish story about a prince who travels down through the archipelago from its central island, Havnor, in search of the Ultimate. He goes southwest out into the open sea, beyond all islands, and finds there a people who live on rafts all their lives long. He ties his boat to a raft and settles down with them, content with this as the Ultimate, until he realizes that out past the farthest journey of the drifting raft-colony there are sea-people, living in the sea itself. He joins them. I think the implication was that (not being a merman) he'll wear out eventually, and sink, and find the ultimate Ultimate. This story wasn't submitted for publication as it never worked itself out at all well; but I felt strongly that the basic image—the raft-colony—was a lulu, and would find itself its home somewhere eventually. It did, in the last of the Earthsea books, *The Farthest Shore.*

I explored Earthsea no further until 1967, when the publisher of Parnassus Press, Herman Schein, asked me if I'd like to try writing a book for him. He wanted something for older kids; till then Parnassus had been mainly a young-juvenile publisher, putting out the handsomest and best-made picture books in America. He gave me complete freedom as to subject and approach. Nobody until then had ever asked me to write anything; I had just done so, relentlessly. To be asked to do it was a great boon. The exhilaration carried me over my apprehensions about writing 'for young people,' something I had never seriously tried. For some weeks or months I let my imagination go groping around in search of what was wanted, in the dark. It stumbled over the Islands, and the magic employed there. Serious consideration of magic, and of writing for kids, combined to make me wonder about wizards. Wizards are usually elderly or ageless Gandalfs, quite rightly and archetypically. But what were they before they had white beards? How did they learn what is obviously an erudite and dangerous art? Are there colleges for young wizards? . . . And so on.

The story of the book is essentially a voyage, a pattern in the form of a long spiral. I began to see the places where the young wizard would go. Eventually I drew a map. Now that I knew where everything was, now was the time for cartography. Of course a great deal of it only appeared above water, as it were, in drawing the map.

Three small islands are named for my children, their baby-names; one gets a little jovial and irresponsible, given the freedom to create a world out of nothing at all. (Power corrupts.) None of the other names 'mean' anything that I know of, though their sound is more or less meaningful to me.

People often ask how I think of names in fantasies, and again I have to answer that I find them, that I hear them. This is an important subject in this context. From that first story on, *naming* has been the essence of the art-magic as practiced in Earthsea. For me, as for the wizards, to know the name of an island or a character is to know the island or the person. Usually the name comes of itself, but sometimes one must be very careful: as I was with the protagonist, whose true name is Ged. I worked (in collaboration with a wizard named Ogion) for a long time trying to 'listen for' his name, and making certain it really was his name. This all sounds very mystical and indeed there are aspects of it I do not understand, but it is a pragmatic business too, since if the name had been wrong the character would have been wrong—misbegotten, misunderstood.

A man who read the ms. for Parnassus thought 'Ged' was meant to suggest 'God.' That shook me badly. I considered changing the name in case there were other such ingenious minds waiting to pounce. But I couldn't do so. The fellow's name was Ged and no two ways about it.

It isn't pronounced Jed, by the way. That sounds like a mountain moonshiner to me. I thought the analogy with 'get' would make it clear, but a lot of people have asked. One place I do exert deliberate control in name-inventing is in the area of pronounceability. I try to spell them so they don't look too formidable (unless, like Kurremkarmerruk, they're meant to look formidable), and they can be pronounced either with the English or the Italian vowels. I don't care which.

Much the same holds for the bits of invented languages in the text of the trilogy.

There are words like rushwash tea, for which I can offer no explanation. They simply drink rushwash tea there; that's what it's called, like lapsang soochong or Brisk Lipton's here. Rushwash is a Hardic word, of course. If you press me, I will explain that it comes from the rushwash bush, which grows both wild and cultivated everywhere south of Enlad, and bears a small round leaf which when dried and steeped yields a pleasant brownish tea. I did not know this before I wrote the foregoing sentence. Or did

I know it, and simply never thought about it?—What's in a name? A lot, that's what.

There are more formal examples of foreign languages in the trilogy; in *The Farthest Shore* there are several whole sentences in the Language of the Making, as dragons will not speak anything else. These arrived, spelling (formidable) and all, and I wrote them down without question. No use trying to make a lexicon of Hardic or of the True Speech; there's not enough in the books. It's not like Tolkien, who in one sense wrote *The Lord of the Rings* to give his invented languages somebody to speak them. That is lovely, that is the Creator Spirit working absolutely unhindered—making the word flesh. But Tolkien is a languist, as well as a great creator. (pp. 8-10)

I said that to know the true name is to know the thing, for me, and for the wizards. This implies a good deal about the 'meaning' of the trilogy, and about me. The trilogy is, in one aspect, about the artist. The artist as magician. The Trickster. Prospero. That is the only truly allegorical aspect it has of which I am conscious. If there are other allegories in it please don't tell me: I hate allegories. A is 'really' B, and a hawk is 'really' a handsaw—bah. Humbug. Any creation, primary or secondary, with any vitality to it, can 'really' be a dozen mutually exclusive things at once, before breakfast.

Wizardry is artistry. The trilogy is then, in this sense, about art, the creative experience, the creative process. There is always this circularity in fantasy. The snake devours its tail. Dreams must explain themselves.

It was interesting, trying to write for children (i.e., people over twelve years old). It was hard. What I wanted to send Andy Porter was a long passionate article about the status of 'children's books.' He wanted something more personal. But believe me, I take the matter personally. (pp. 10-11)

Though I'd like to strike a blow here for the women's movement, I don't really know where to aim it. I know of no circumstance where, as a writer, I have been treated unfairly or suspiciously or patronizingly on account of my sex. . . . But as an SF writer I resent being low-paid in comparison to dreck-writers: and if SF writers think they're low-paid, they should look at writers for children. I am not complaining personally. . . . What is wrong is the whole scale—all the publishers' budgets for their children's books. There is seldom big quick money in kiddylit, but a successful kid's book has an unusually long life. It sells to schools, to libraries, and to gift-giving adults, and it goes on selling, and making money, for years and years and years. This is not reflected in the advances or the royalties. It is a very badly paid field, in general.

But the economic discrimination is only an element, as usual, of the real problem: a reflection of a prejudice. The real trouble isn't the money, it's the adult chauvinist piggery.

"You're a juvenile writer, aren't you?"

Yeth, mummy.

"I love your books—the real ones, I mean, I haven't read the ones for children, of course!"

Of courthe not, daddy.

"It must be relaxing to write *simple* things for a change."

Sure it's simple, writing for kids. Just as simple as bringing them up.

All you do is take all the sex out, and use little short words, and little dumb ideas, and don't be too scary, and be sure there's a happy ending. Right? Nothing to it. Write down. Right on.

If you do all that, you might even write *Jonathan Livingston Seagull* and make twenty billion dollars and have every adult in America reading your book!

But you won't have every kid in America reading your book. They will look at it, and they will see straight through it, with their clear, cold, beady little eyes, and they will put it down, and they will go away. Kids will devour vast amounts of garbage (and it is good for them) but they are not like adults: they have not yet learned to eat plastic. (pp. 11-12)

The most childish thing about *A Wizard of Earthsea,* I expect, is its subject: coming of age.

Coming of age is a process that took me many years; I finished it, so far as I ever will, at about age 31; and so I feel rather deeply about it. So do most adolescents. It's their main occupation, in fact.

The subject of *The Tombs of Atuan* is, if I had to put it in one word, sex. There's a lot of symbolism in the book, most of which I did not, of course, analyse consciously while writing; the symbols can all be read as sexual. More exactly, you could call it a feminine coming of age. Birth, rebirth, destruction, freedom are the themes.

The Farthest Shore is about death. That's why it is a less well-built, less sound and complete book than the others. They were about things I had already lived through and survived. *The Farthest Shore* is about the thing you do not live through and survive. It seemed an absolutely suitable subject to me for young readers, since in a way one can say that the hour when a child realizes, not that that death exists—children are intensely aware of death—but that he/she, personally, is mortal, will die, is the hour when childhood ends, and the new life begins. Coming of age again, but in a larger context.

In any case I had little choice about the subject. Ged, who was always very strong-minded, always saying things that surprised me and doing things he wasn't supposed to do, took over completely in this book. He was determined to show me how his life must end, and why. I tried to keep up with him, but he was always ahead. I rewrote the book more times than I want to remember, trying to keep him under some kind of control. I thought it was all done when it was printed here, but the English edition differs in three long passages from the earlier American one: my editor at Gollancz said, "Ged is talking too much," and she was quite right, and I shut him up three times, much to the improvement of the whole. If you insist upon discovering in-

stead of planning, this kind of trouble is inevitable. It is a most uneconomical way to write. The book is still the most imperfect of the three, but it is the one I like best. It is the end of the trilogy, but it is the dream I have not stopped dreaming. (pp. 12-13)

Ursula K. Le Guin, "Dreams Must Explain Themselves," in her Dreams Must Explain Themselves, *Algol Press, 1975, pp. 4-13.*

Ruth Hill Viguers

Sparrowhawk, the son of a bronzesmith, was born on Gont, famous for wizards who had gone forth to serve in cities throughout the Archipelago, seeking adventure, working magic from isle to isle of all Earthsea. At first Sparrowhawk studied with the great mage of Gont who gave him his true name, Ged, and, when he went to far-away Roke to the School for Wizards, the message to the Archmage read, "I send you one who will be the greatest of the Wizards of Gont if the wind blow true." But Ged, goaded by pride and jealousy, displayed his powers before he had learned the importance of "Balance and Pattern which the true wizard knows and serves and which keep him from using his spells unless real need demands." The result, almost costing him his life, loosed an evil shadow that pursued him. Once he fled over wild seas in what "was in truth no boat but a thing more than half charm and sorcery and the rest of it mere planks and driftwood which, if he let slack the shaping-spells and the binding-spell upon them, would soon enough lapse and scatter and go drifting off as a little flotsam on the waves." He took shelter on strange islands, fought with dragons, was lured into the cold towers of a sorcerer, and escaped from the creatures set upon him. Only when Ged turned from his flight to become hunter instead of hunted, did his power against the evil shadow increase. The book will probably be compared with classic hero stories and with various fantasies in which a complete world has been created, but it bears little resemblance to them. It is wholly original, but it has the conviction of a tale told by a writer whose roots are deep in great literature of many kinds, including traditional lore and fantasy. She is at home in the ancient world of rites and runes and "true names," the knowledge of which gives supernatural power; of mage, wizard, and sorcerer; of feats of illusion and spells of changing. Her way with words results in prose beautiful to read and to listen to. Every word is important; fascinating unfamiliar ones (like "rushwash tea") are often introduced, their obscurity sparking the imagination and never detracting from the clarity of the style. Older people may dismiss the book as merely another allegory, but not if they push aside their usual preoccupations and read it with a free mind. Unusual allegory or exciting quest, it is an unforgettable and a distinguished book. (pp. 59-60)

Ruth Hill Viguers, in a review of "A Wizard of Earthsea," in The Horn Book Magazine, *Vol. XLV, No. 1, February, 1969, pp. 59-60.*

Theodore Sturgeon

Writing is surely the area in which women least need liberating, yet it is surprising how often one hears expressions of amazement when a woman produces a creditable work outside the areas of love-romance, whodunits or, latterly, sex. . . . Swords-and-sorcery, it happens, has never been one of my favorite categories, yet along comes Ursula K. Le Guin to demonstrate forcefully that I just might have been missing something. . . . Mrs. Le Guin knows how to spin a strong and stirring yarn.

A Wizard of Earthsea is that increasingly rare delight, a "journey" story, which ever since Homer sang the Odyssey (and probably before) has had its own special magic. Take me to a strange country and lead me over the mountains and across the seas, never knowing what monsters, what men, what adventures I might encounter, and you have me well hooked. The planet Earthsea is a strange country indeed, where real magic, with harsh disciplines and real self-consistency, exists and operates, and where the trained sorcerer (who must be gifted before he can be trained) is treated with respect, for he has vital functions. Here again is the one impossible thing you are asked to believe, and the author makes you believe it. And in addition to being a simple journey story, *Wizard* is a fable—that is to say, an analogy with a moral you can comprehend and use. When the young wizard's pride is stung, he makes a terrible mistake—terrible in its truest, terror-full, terrifying sense; and for that he has to pay off. How he does it, and the nature and name of the dreadful force he must confront and overcome, is the story and its high moral. (pp. 39, 41)

The author makes you give a damn about her people; you feel you know them, or have known them, or could if you saw more of them; and her description of the various ways in which a scattered and defeated humanity organizes itself is inventive, credible and often surprising. I carp at only one practice of this author, and even there I suppose I compliment her: I could wish that, having given me subsidiary characters to become interested in, she would fully round out her narrative and let me know what became of them. Otherwise, hers are competent hands, and you may feel secure in them and certain of a good evening of wonders. (p. 41)

Theodore Sturgeon, "Memento Mori—Et Seq.," in National Review, *New York, Vol. XXIII, January 12, 1971, pp. 39, 41.*

The Times Literary Supplement

Any quick list of the outstanding books for the young of the past forty years or so will reveal that almost all have drawn on the extra dimension of magic or fantasy—Tolkien, White, Lewis, Pearce, Garner, Hoban and the rest. The numbers are not so many, though. It should also be remembered that most of the vast mass of quickly forgotten tales have been rashly drawn from the same dangerous sources, by authors not realizing the limitations and subtleties as well as the obvious pantomime powers of the supernatural. To find one novel a year to join the first group noted above is as much or more than one may expect, but there seems little doubt that *A Wizard of Earthsea* is the likeliest candidate that we have had for some time: if a book as remarkable as this turns up in the next twelve months we shall be fortunate indeed. . . .

The notable section on the work of the College of Roke may owe something in impetus to *The Sword in the Stone;* but it is doubtful if a more convincing and comprehensive account of a sorcerer's training exists anywhere in fiction outside the *Earthsea* chapters. The boding journey through the vast bleak snowfilled empty plain to the Castle of the Terrenon Stone—most ancient and most evil—may recall, in a quick flicker of the mind, Childe Roland's journey to Browning's nameless Tower. The *gebbeth* itself, appearing on this very plain, or, no less horribly, in Ged's boat on a lonely sea, may be a cousin to the shapeless creature in Edwin Muir's poem "The Combat"—or, even, to Stevenson's Mr. Hyde.

Yet these may as well be parallels as borrowings. And what comes out of them all is a new quest-story, an original allegory. Curiously, while there is almost nothing local or datable in its machinery, yet every piece of mage-advice seems immediate and topical. (Most learning, skills and crafts that come our way are, after all, a form of wizardry.) One finds in *Earthsea* none of the private and scratchy hates and theological quiddities that even a marvellous yarn cannot cover over in the stories of C. S. Lewis. The matter of the true and secret Name which every creature and thing possesses goes back into the furthest reaches of myth. . . . But it is as valid today as ever it was; need one point to its uses in the fields of advertising and politics? The advice to change the role of pursuer and pursued: to look for the fear instead of running away from it, is again wholly sound. Nor is the warning against using magic needlessly, and without considering its results (which may disturb the world's Equilibrium), a dictum merely for fairy tales.

There are many memorable passages—not only the great midsummer scene when Ged raises the *gebbeth,* nor the final engagement, with its brilliant resolution, on the fixed waves of the sea. Ged's defeat of the great dragon of Pendor, not by butchery but by counter-moves of power, should be added to every dragon-anthology. And there are lighter passages, such as the riddling interviews with the Master Doorkeeper, when the boy arrives, and later, when he leaves. But the book is more than a sum of its parts. An image used by Ged himself about a boat he takes on one of his expeditions comes to mind. Was it "illusion" that made it watertight? he was asked. Partly (he replies),

> because I am uneasy seeing the sea through great holes in my boat, so I patched them for the looks of the thing. But the strength of the boat was not illusion . . . but made with another kind of art, a binding spell. The wood was bound as one whole, one entire thing, a boat.

The book has this kind of wholeness.

"The Making of a Mage," in The Times Literary Supplement, *No. 3605, April 2, 1971, p. 383.*

Virginia Haviland

[*The Tombs of Atuan*] is the allegorical sequel to *A Wizard of Earthsea,* in which the powers of darkness play their role in the blackest of scenes. Over labyrinthine desert tombs reigns Arha, who had been born on the day the previous head priestess had died and at the age of five had become imprisoned there in boredom and horror. But, with the saving appearance of Ged from Earthsea and the joining of two parts of the Ring of Erreth-Akbe, she who has "cried for the waste of her years in bondage" makes a necessary decision and begins to learn "the weight of liberty." Scenes and events are economically etched and ideas tautly conveyed. Children who love the strange will indeed revel in the drama of Ged's unlikely survival and the awesome aspects of the vast underworld—and will find them unforgettable.

> *Virginia Haviland, "A Magical Tour," in* Book World—The Washington Post, *November 7, 1971, p. 4.*

The Times Literary Supplement

A book as formidable as *A Wizard of Earthsea* might well raise doubts about any work that follows. Could the feat be managed a second time, without pastiche or self-imitation? But Earthsea has many regions and, indeed, *The Tombs of Atuan* . . . again has its own completeness. Though it keeps to a more restricted theme, it is very clearly out of the same imagination; its value comes from the same qualities. One is a total realization of place, time, customs, laws of behaviour, of magic too; the Atuan detail is as unerring as that of the youthful Brontës' imaginary countries. And though, in the areas of the supernatural, the author's eerie force is hard to match, her human creatures—and even wizards and priestesses are mortals first and last—hold the foreground interest; they change and grow, and this change directs the plot.

Ritual and responsibility are the opposing poles of the new book. . . .

The girl Tenar is marked out as an infant to be High Priestess of the Nameless Ones. It was her chance to be born when the last one died; the age-old rule of appointment, though many village mothers (like Tenar's) would try to conceal the birth. We see her, at the age of six, perfectly trained, go through the rites that turn her into Arha, the Eaten One (her soul being eaten by her Masters) and follow her through austere years of duties, ceremonials, and a special education; she must re-learn, as it were, what she knew "before she died". At 15, haughty, bored, but still unquestioning, she comes into her full powers; she must impose the ultimate dreadful penalties (for treason and sacrilege); hers alone are the mysterious keys to all the unknown doors: only she may explore the great dark city that lies underneath the tombs, with its dust and dread, and evil prisons, and rooms of untold treasure, and the vast frightful labyrinth. This underworld, where all paths must be learnt by number and touch, for no light is allowed, becomes her refuge; the only kind of journey that she knows.

From A Wizard of Earthsea, *written by Ursula K. Le Guin. Illustrated by Ruth Robbins.*

But someone does enter the unenterable: the wizard Ged, seeking the utmost treasure, the broken half of an ancient silver ring. . . .

For the girl's first sense of outrage has given way to an unwonted pity; as his strength, and magic, ebb, and he lies near death, lost in the maze, she brings him her own meagre food, and hides him (by a route so secret and so terrible that even she has never dared to use it) in the room where the ultimate treasures are supposed to lie. But by contravening the laws by which she lives, she destroys all that she owns, her authority. The old powers are not dead, the wizard tells her, in the magnificent escape chapter, but they are not for humans to worship. She must take on the greater burden of freedom, which is heavier than the old one of belief. "It is not a gift given, but a choice made, and the choice may be a hard one. The road goes upwards towards the light; but the laden traveller may never reach the end of it." If the book could flag it is here, as they make their troubled way through the hills and dunes, but there is a solution and a path: it satisfies, and it is not commonplace.

"Earthsea Revisited," in The Times Literary Supplement, *No. 3661, April 28, 1972, p. 284.*

Wendy Jago

I think it significant that [*A Wizard of Earthsea*] has been written for children. I suspect it would have been difficult indeed to write of the same themes for adults without having to make choices of mode and presentation—between myth, philosophy, religion, psychological 'inscape'. Maybe, since we have lost long ago our tribal singers and poets, we can now write myth only for children. If our reality is fantasy, the myth which is the measure of our reality can only find a home as 'fiction'—and children's fiction at that. (pp. 25-6)

One can look at the book in many ways and on different levels. It is a compelling story, as adventure and as the embodiment of a created world with its geography, its nomenclature, its peoples and beasts, all livingly and livelily differentiated and characterized. It is about growing up, with the rivalries, friendships and arrogance—and the humility, responsibility and loyalty—which are felt so strongly in adolescence. It is about apprenticeship, the learning of crafts and skills and the acceptance of tasks. It is about the painful acquisition of knowledge of oneself and others. It does not shy away from death, or the deathlike and deathseeking impulses in people. It is not afraid of dealing with those crises of individual development which Erikson has pinpointed. In more strictly psychological terms, it turns on the repression and then the recognition and acceptance of that which is felt to be bad in the self. It is full of the poetry of rhythm, the evocativeness of strange names, the timeless significance of gnomic phrases. As quotations will show, the web of language does not simply convey the author's meaning: it is the meaning.

The book is concerned with morality, and with the enactment of morality in choice. One of its major themes is the use and abuses of the nature of things and people. (p. 26)

The word 'shadow' is one of the recurring themes of the book: the shadow is nebulous—an evil glimpsed but out of the corner of one's eye—but it is also precise—the name given in the absence of name to the Power of unlife Ged has released. It follows him like a shadow, before he in turn shadows it, and it is in the end recognized to be just that—an image of himself, an alter ego which only acquires substance as he and it embrace. (p. 27)

[It] is on the sea beyond all known seas, which yet supports Ged like sand, where the separation Ged had allowed is finally made whole. The ageless theme of dark and light, evil and good, is woven through the mists and clarities of this book just as it is through the grand monochromed fabric of *Paradise Lost*.

Naming and recognition . . . are of central importance in the book. At one level there is the need to know others and be known by them, to trust and be trusted. Ged's first test on the wizards' island of Roke is to find the password at the door; this is to give himself into the power of his teachers by telling his true name; his final test is to name the same Master Doorkeeper by his proper name, which he can only do through being humble enough to admit that for all his wizardry he cannot do it unless he is freely told it. This humble recognition of the other's otherness, and willingness to entrust oneself into his power, lies also behind a moving interchange between Ged and his friend Vetch. Ged is damaged and isolated by his act of folly, and Vetch, as he is leaving to take up his first post, says:

And if you ever need me, send for me, call on me by my name Estarriol.
At that Ged lifted his scarred face, meeting his friend's eyes.
'Estarriol,' he said, 'My name is Ged.'

No man knows a man's true name but himself and his namer. He may choose at length to tell it to his brother, or his wife, or his friend, yet even those few will never use it where any third person may hear it . . . If plain men hide their true name from all but a few they love and trust utterly, so much more must wizardly men, being more dangerous, and more endangered. Who knows a man's true name, holds that man's life in his keeping. Thus to Ged who had lost faith in himself, Vetch had given the gift only a friend can give, the proof of unshaken, unshakable trust.

And it is the power and recognition of naming which, while providing the dramatic climax to the action of the book, is its central symbol. After long searching into realms eventually unknown, Ged sees 'at the faint outermost edge of the light a shadow that came towards him over the sand . . .

At that Ged lifted up the staff high, and the radiance of it brightened intolerably, burning with so white and great a light that it compelled and harrowed even that ancient darkness. In that light all form of man sloughed off the thing that came towards Ged . . . As they came right together it became utterly black in the white mageradiance that burned about it, and it heaved itself upright. In silence, man and shadow met face to face, and stopped.

> Aloud and clearly, breaking that old silence, Ged spoke the shadow's name, and in the same moment the shadow spoke without lips or tongue, saying the same word: 'Ged.' And the two voices were one . . .

> . . . Now when [Vetch] saw his friend and heard him speak, his doubt vanished. And he began to see the truth, that Ged had neither lost nor won, but, naming the shadow of his death with his own name, had made himself whole: a man: who knowing his whole true self, cannot be used or possessed by any power other than by himself, and whose life therefore is lived for life's sake and never in the service of ruin, or pain, or hatred, or the dark.

This powerful resolution is reached through choice: Ged chooses wrongly in evoking the spirit from the dead, and chooses wrongly in his initial flight from the shadow. This double error is balanced and redeemed by the choice to accept his master Ogion's parabolic advice to turn and seek the shadow out: Ged's recognition that it bears his name and no other and his acceptance of that can be seen in moral, Christian, mythic or psychological terms.

There is much honest reality in the book, too—indeed the moral qualities would be cold and abstract if they were not deeply inwoven with the characteristics of different folk, the concern for patient craftsmanship, whether in magery or in boatbuilding, and the sense of warm human relationships. Security and even cosiness are there, but seen in relation and sometimes contrast to the necessities arising from actions and obligations. They do not provide an escape.

Bruner points out that 'externalization makes possible the containment of terror and impulse by the decorum of art and symbolism' and that 'the economical function of myth is to represent in livable form the structures of the complexities through which we must find our way.' *A Wizard of Earthsea* seems to me significant because it is concerned with the individual as a potent agent in a complex world of pressures and choices. To those who complain that literature, especially children's literature, does not adequately reflect the complexities of a rapidly changing world in which the individual is dwarfed by society, institutions and technological change, it asserts both that being involves choice and that our freedom to be fully human is not compromised unless we allow it. Like all poetry (and I would follow Sidney in the wider use of this word) it is not *about* these things: its themes and patterns are often implicit, as they are in the piece of poetry which prefaces it and recurs at its climax:

> Only in silence the word,
> only in dark the light,
> only in dying life:
> bright the hawk's flight
> on the empty sky.

> (pp. 27-9)

Wendy Jago, " 'A Wizard of Earthsea' and the Charge of Escapism," in Children's literature in education, *No. 8, July, 1972, pp. 21-9.*

Aidan Warlow

In *A Wizard of Earthsea,* Ursula Le Guin created for us a mysterious and original legendary world in which magic ritual and intercourse with the supernatural assumed a serious meaning for the reader. [*The Tombs of Atuan*] is the sequel—an equally strange and frightening book. . . .

It is a cold, colourless, humourless novel whose rather formal style and slowly unfolding plot make considerable demands on the young reader. But, for those who can manage it, this is very powerful stuff. Our belief in the reality of Earthsea is total, our concern for the solitary heroine runs deep and, as an account of religious experience, the book has exceptional interest.

> *Aidan Warlow, in a review of "The Tombs of Atuan," in* The School Librarian, *Vol. 20, No. 3, September, 1972, p. 258.*

Shirley Toulson

It is tempting to read Ursula Le Guin's *The Farthest Shore* as a socio-political myth. This is Mrs Le Guin's concluding book in her trilogy about Earthsea, a rural archipelago set up and held in balance by a hierarchy of benevolent magicians. When the people turn away from the old rites, spells and traditions, and grab at a security and immortality of their own making, the equilibrium is shaken. Arren, a young prince from one of the largest islands, sets out with Sparrowhawk, one of the magicians, to discover the source of the evil that is blighting the world. They journey to an island in the far west where the walking, silent dead spin out their sham existence, and where the sluice-gates of the world must be closed again before all the real life is drained through them. On their way they encounter a community debilitated by drug-taking, who have been lulled into supposing that magic lies in hallucinations, and a group of former craftsmen absorbed in the apathetic production and feverish marketing of nondescript trash. Only the sea people, who live and work on rafts, are exempt from the general malaise. They alone accept inevitable danger and death. This is a book for older children, and adults too, and will no doubt give rise to a sizeable student cult. There is all the necessary paraphernalia: an involved and metaphysical cartography, a mass of names of varying degrees of potency, and a syntax leaning heavily on incantation. It may seem grudging to suggest that stripped of these trimmings a pretty run-of-the-mill parable would emerge. (p. 780)

> *Shirley Toulson, "Childhood Haunts," in* New Statesman, *Vol. 85, No. 2201, May 25, 1973, pp. 780, 782.*

Margery Fisher

Though there are hints of further journeys for the magician Ged, this new adventure [*The Farthest Shore*] takes place in his advanced years and has at least a temporary finality about it, for the argument resolved by his victory over evil concerns the one-ness of Life and Death. A onetime fellow student of Ged's has through dangerous experiments achieved a grim immortality by denying the joyousness of life. His magic is demoralising the archipelago, island by island, and Ged, now Archmage of Roke, receiving disturbing reports of accidia and the cessation of magic arts, travels through the South Reach with young Arren, heir apparent to the kingdom of Havnor, who serves as his apprentice and increases his stature as he helps, even saves Ged in the various encounters which culminate in a final contest of emotional and physical endurance on and over the very frontier of Death. Through Arren the story is seen as a completion of *The Tombs of Atuan,* in which the ring of Havnor was restored to light; as regards Ged, the story is a striking stage in his search for the Good. This book seems to me the most impressive of the three so far written. It is rich in words, images and events and has an extraordinary precision in the creation of believable worlds which win credence through geographical association (for example, the Children of the Sea are recognisably Polynesian) but have their own magic reality as well. In her imaginative embodying of the archipelago Ursula Le Guin has shown herself to be the only writer at present able to challenge Tolkien on his own ground.

> *Margery Fisher, in a review of "The Farthest Shore," in* Growing Point, *Vol. 12, No. 2, July, 1973, p. 2200.*

Peter Nicholls

The saga of Ged the Magician is ostensibly for children. It began with an epic, *A Wizard of Earthsea.* It continued with a romance (in the old sense), *The Tombs of Atuan.* And now it is ended with *The Farthest Shore,* which begins as a quest, and shades into a lament, and finishes appropriately, not as a paean, but as a muted triumph, a quiet lyric. Ursula Le Guin is not a writer to rework earlier successes it will be seen. Certainly not within the scope of a single trilogy. It is amazingly varied in tone, even though in theme the three books knit into a single, integrated work.

The last fifteen years, which have seen the decline of the traditional novel growing ever more marked, have been fortunate years for the children's book. The art has never been more healthy. In my own order of priorities, I would put Ursula Le Guin in the first rank, along with Alan Garner, and perhaps T. H. White from an earlier generation. (p. 71)

The *Earthsea* trilogy tells of the growth and adult power of a magician, Sparrowhawk. His secret name is Ged, but this is only revealed to a few, for a man who possesses the secret name of another knows his essence, and consequently has power over him. In our own world, laughingly known as the "real" world, the theory of secret names is very ancient, both in traditional magic and traditional religion. Mrs. Le Guin can nowhere be faulted in her anthropology, by me at least. . . . (p. 72)

Being a magician is no easy matter. One may be born with an aptitude, but his power over the world of matter is possible only if he has a full knowledge of the nature of that world, and this knowledge is gained only by patience and hard work. The secret name theory, which is so prominent in the trilogy, seems to me a sort of shorthand for the understanding of essences—what Gerard Manley Hopkins

used to call the "inscape"of things. In this respect the magicians of these stories are the same as the scientists of today. . . . In all the essentials [Mrs Le Guin's] magicians are indeed scientists. She never uses magic as a narrative gimmick, a cheap and easy way of working the impossible and allowing the reader the mild *frisson* of identifying with the superhuman. Indeed, she is at pains to show how difficult it is to upset the natural balance, the equilibrium of the created world, by magical or any other means. Only the greatest of magicians are shown as being able to harness real natural forces, and that at the cost of a sapping of energy. Most magic is of appearances only. A magnificent feast may be conjured up, but the illusion of nourishment will last only as long as the spell is maintained. It has no permanent effect. Protein is not conjured up where no protein was before.

Acclaim for *A Wizard of Earthsea* was just about universal, but that book set up expectations in its readers which were not always fulfilled by the second, *The Tombs of Atuan.* In the latter book, our field of vision is narrower and more concentrated, the tone more sombre. The sphere of action has shrunk from that of a whole world to the walled-in darkness of the catacombs where an adolescent girl, perverted by her training, is using her new-found powers of womanhood to celebrate the old powers of earth and darkness. (In each of the three books a voyage into darkness is central). The patience and understanding of the magician, Ged, now grown into a mature man, finally release the girl priestess from the bondage of her training and the warping of her own budding sexuality. We see all this through the eyes of the heroine, a girl who understands little of what she sees. Ged is seen from the outside, and takes on a kind of bulky strangeness, a little alarming for readers who have identified strongly with him in the first book of the trilogy. The sense of an oppressive spiritual danger, rendered with frightening immediacy and narrowly averted, is strong in this book. The book was deliberately different in kind from its predecessor, I would guess, but this confused many of the critics. Where the earlier book seemed expansive, this concentrates all of its power into one single, massive metaphor.

The Farthest Shore is different again. It is barely possible to summarize the nature of this complex book in only a few paragraphs. Its subjects—maturity, death, ambition, balance, corruption, the significance of meaning itself— are so big. Far bigger than one has any right to expect in a book for children, and some might think too big to cope with, for writer as well as reader. Most of the themes, it's worth noting, are also present in Tolkien's *The Lord of the Rings;* they are, after all, the epic themes. Individual similarities with the Tolkien book are many. In both trilogies we find the traditional quest pattern for instance, where the external voyage becomes the mirror of an internal movement towards maturity, acceptance, self-knowledge, and finally the ability to come to terms with one's own imagined death. Both writers, to take a more trivial example, are fascinated with dragons as symbols of ancient knowledge and power, although here Mrs Le Guin clearly has the better of it. Her dragons are more dignified than Tolkien's. Incidentally, unlike Tolkien, Mrs Le Guin makes almost no use (apart from dragons) of beasts and monsters. No wargs or orcs or balrogs here, only people, rarely seen in the morally absolute blacks and whites that Tolkien uses.

The important differences are these: where Tolkien is expansive, Ursula Le Guin is condensed; where he has a tendency to approach his wonders through allusiveness and indirection, she renders them with clarity and precision. I admire Tolkien very much, but I believe Mrs Le Guin has deeper resources of language than Tolkien possessed. (pp. 73-4)

[Both] writers have a taste for the incantatory and poetic, and here the danger of over-writing is the strongest. Tolkien used regularly to succumb to a rather hollow "high" style, jerry-built from a number of medieval sources, sometimes looking as if they had been filtered through William Morris. It comes out with the elves, the men of Gondor, and the Rohirrim, and sometimes, too, with Gandalf. . . . Both Tolkien and Le Guin have a tendency to archaize, to claim a dignity of expression by evoking rhythms and word orders which themselves recall the great books of the past. Even Mrs Le Guin does it too much for my taste ("quiet were their faces", "there was in their shadowed eyes no hope") but she is a very mild offender when compared with Tolkien. She does have in common with Dante a telling precision of imagery. . . . Her language does not attain the ease or naturalness of Dante's, but she does understand, as he did, that the strongest emotional resonances are achieved through accuracy, by capturing the individuality of a particular situation or character. (pp. 74-5)

There are times when one wishes that some of the adjectives, the ones that don't work hard enough, had been blue-pencilled. These are the moments that most remind me of Tolkien, usually in his graver mood—words like "strange", "dim", "vast", "fierce", "sad", "lean", "cold", "noble". The writing is never simply mechanical, but it is tauter and more attentive in some places than others. However, the reader is seldom given the chance to become impatient. Every few paragraphs a phrase here, a word there, astounds by its freshness and directness of vision.

Mrs Le Guin is a metaphysician. Her ultimate belief, at least as expressed in this series of books, is that dualities are mutually necessary, that only death gives meaning to life, that joy cannot exist in the total absence of its opposite. It is said that she has been much influenced in her writing by the Tao, and this may be. Certainly the philosophy seems more Chinese than, say, Indian, but I would have thought it more Western than either, in its emphasis on dualism. The still, intuitive centre that she so finely implies in Ged may seem Eastern, but his readiness to act seems alien to Taoism, which I take to be an essentially passive belief, but here I am aware of displaying a possibly massive ignorance.

Certainly, whatever the source of the beliefs expressed in her books, I am in profound agreement with them. I would guess that Mrs Le Guin (to continue evoking possibly grandiose comparisons) is a reader of Yeats and of Donne. Tricks of thought and phraseology often recall those two poets whose concerns were so close to Mrs Le

Guin's own. There are temperamental affinities too. Mrs Le Guin's trilogy is by no means as sombre as I may seem to be suggesting, with its constant awareness of death and pain, but as with Donne and Yeats happiness is rarely unalloyed.

The theme runs through all three books of the trilogy. It is expressed on page one of **A Wizard of Earthsea,** where the epigraph is a small poem:

> Only in silence the word,
> only in dark the light,
> only in dying life:
> bright the hawk's flight
> on the empty sky.

It is no coincidence that Ged is usually known as Sparrowhawk.

In **The Tombs of Atuan** the final knowledge is *not* that darkness is evil, but rather, that it gives meaning to light. (Ursula Le Guin is always careful not to see darkness and death as evil *per se*—that is part of the point of her books. Her dualism is not of that Zoroastrian variety that was later imported into Christianity, where the light simplistically signifies good, and the darkness, evil. She is not, I would think, a *moral* dualist.)

The plot of **The Farthest Shore** is based on the discovery by a warped magician that there is a way to ensure partial immortality. The whole balance of nature and being in Earthsea is upset by his actions, for if death is rendered meaningless, then life too, by a natural balancing out, is drained of meaning and desire. And if life is drained of meaning, then magic, which relies on the knowledge of meanings and the names of things, can no longer operate. Ged and his assistant, the young prince Arren, have ultimately to journey into Death themselves, not to attack it, but paradoxically, to renew its power. Death cannot be conquered by making it go away. The sense of oppression built up in the book by a profound misuse of power lingers even through the final triumph . . . a literary triumph too, in its finely rendered realization that even good men acting on the side of right cannot expect to get something for nothing. Ged is able to keep the natural powers alive and available for the use of men, but only at the cost of exhausting and losing his own powers—powers through which he had moved like a hawk through the sky, at home in his element. This summary of the theme of **The Farthest Shore** shows it, I hope, to be a wholly natural, even inevitable climax to the trilogy, though I am sure that many critics will once again accuse Mrs Le Guin of having changed direction.

The theme is not new. So well worn is it, in fact, that it may not even be supposed important. On the other hand, a theme that has endured some thousands of years may be allowed to have intrinsic staying power, and to many children it will be new. I hope that they make sense of the often beautiful but sometimes cryptic metaphors Mrs. Le Guin uses to make her point, as where Ged explains to Arren:

> There is no safety. There is no end. The word
> must be heard in silence. There must be darkness

to see the stars. The dance is always danced
above the hollow place, above the terrible abyss.

Again, there, just a touch of over-writing. I would have
preferred "abyss" to have been unqualified by "terrible",
but all in all, it is a moving and true statement. Again, too,
we see that precision of metaphor, in this case given by the
context, where two pages later, on midsummer eve, a
dance is performed on a great raft, floating above the hollow of the deep, open ocean, giving life retrospectively to
what may have seemed a rather notional image.

All three books, incidentally, are quite deeply un-
Christian, though not anti-Christian. The abode of the
dead that Mrs Le Guin invents is neither heaven nor hell,
but much closer to the Greek Hades. When she speaks of
"only in dying life" she does not speak of a life after death.
She means, I think, that the keenness of living is kept
sharp by the imminence of death, and that is a very different point. The trilogy is certainly religious, and she speaks
of "creation", but there is no sense of any Jehovah figure
brooding over it, let alone ever interceding. . . . Ursula
Le Guin's "philosophy" values *this* world highly, and one
feels that the Eastern Nirvana and the Christian Heaven
would be equally distasteful to her, as representing states
which turn the spirit away from what it can make of itself
in the here and now. For Mrs Le Guin's other great theme
is the growth of the spirit—the "self", if a less loaded
word is preferred—towards understanding its own nature,
and the best way to bring that nature into inter-action with
the world it inhabits. (Yes, I know that Christians and
Buddhists too encourage the growth of the spirit, but my
own biases lead me to see the emphasis and purpose of this
as being rather different from what I take Mrs Le Guin
to be writing about.)

All of the above, no doubt, has the misleading effect of
making the three books sound like heavy going, but in fact
the brisk sweep of the narrative, with much sparkle and
wit along the way, makes the stories compulsively readable, though always too intelligent to make for totally *easy*
reading. I would like to know how much they appeal to
children, and would be interested to read Mrs Le Guin's
fan mail. It seems to me that they should appeal, but it is
difficult for an adult to recapture the sort of thing that
touched him most deeply as a child.

The *Earthsea* trilogy is Mrs Le Guin's finest achievement
to date, I believe, but the themes are very similar to those
we find in her recent science fiction—in **The Lathe of
Heaven,** and notably in **The Left Hand of Darkness.** Mrs
Le Guin herself . . . distinguishes between her fantasies
and her science fiction, but it seems to me that the similarities are more essential than the differences. In both genres
she uses metaphor to speak about what most matters to
people in the real world.

It is tempting to over-praise her, and perhaps I have done
so. The sensitivity and accuracy of her writing are so far
beyond what we expect in adult fantasy, let alone children's, that by those standards she is made to seem
amongst the greatest. She combines intelligence with feeling in a genre normally preoccupied with the most simplistic feelings to the near exclusion of thought. It is this that
we value her for, and yet I feel that the honesty and depth

of her feelings, and the transparently subtle intellect, have
not yet found their wholly adequate form. In the *Earthsea*
trilogy, and occasionally in **The Left Hand of Darkness,**
the quality of feeling drifts sometimes towards the plan-
gent, and minor characters especially seem a little sentimentalized. I think of Vetch in **A Wizard of Earthsea,**
whose rough sincerity and kindly solidity seem a bit too
much like Horatio to Ged's Hamlet. But these faults, if
such they are, are superficial matters of writerly control.
For me, the inner impulse of the books is as lucid as crystal. I look forward to her next with genuine excitement.
(pp. 76-80)

*Peter Nicholls, "Showing Children the Value
of Death," in* Foundation, *No. 5, January,
1974, pp. 71-80.*

The Economist

The real life of man is epic. His existential condition not-
withstanding, man sees his own life in terms of possibilities, of aspirations, of ordeals heroically surmounted or
stoically succumbed to. No man is venal in his own imagination. Fortunately there remains a class of reader in full
understanding of these truisms: uncorrupted by critical
fashion, confident in the reliability of its own judgment
about what is important, it will demand the satisfaction
of that epic dimension and will not be gainsaid. Children
at least are not content to see their own unfree existences
reflected in social-realist tales of trouble at t'launderette,
or welfare-clinic gossip or of wet days on the housing es-
tate.

It is increasingly through this permissibly epic-conscious
audience that writers of unconfined imagination are seeking to articulate their own response to the deep springs of
our literature. "Through" rather than "to" this audience
because surreptitiously (or blatantly, for the cult of Tolkien is hardly *sub rosa*) adults are stealing much of this literature for themselves. Nobody would pretend that such
transference is a new phenomenon—most parents have
found themselves at some time engrossed in a child's book
begun at a bedtime reading—but the seriousness of the
themes handled is new, and so is the serious way in which
the writers have handled them, not to mention the serious
reception they enjoy in heavy literary company. There
must be a strong suspicion that this transfer audience is
in fact the target one.

The suspicion is hardly diminished by learning that the
two books in which this line of thought has germinated—
Richard Adams's *Watership Down* and Russell Hoban's
The Mouse and his Child—were respectively seven and
three years in the making. This is not the kind of invest-
ment that Miss Enid Blyton would put into a book—nor
Miss Margaret Drabble. But it is, for example, the kind
of timescale in which Mr William Golding works; and
there are indeed instructive comparisons to be drawn between certain of his books, *The Inheritors* particularly,
and the best of this new children's literature.

It is possible to distinguish (after no very deliberate selection from one child's bookshelves) two manifestations of
this epic mode. In the first, humans or surrogate humans
(Hobbits, for example) are set to work out their picaresque

sagas in imaginary but comprehensively-defined lands within a framework of invented but totally consistent physical, magical and linguistic laws as inescapable as those of the place we inhabit. These are certainly traceable as far back as "Sir Gawain and the Green Knight"; but the modern progenitors of the line are J. R. R. Tolkien and C. S. Lewis. Both "The Lord of the Rings" and the Chronicles of Narnia are familiar enough and popular enough as objects of rather inflated analysis to need little extra attention. But there are powerful newcomers to the genre, the most substantial and satisfying of them perhaps being Ursula Le Guin's Earthsea trilogy. Earthsea is as fully realised as Middle Earth, the story itself less self-indulgent than Tolkien's, the metaphorical charge more powerful than the specifically religious parables of C. S. Lewis. The saga of Ged discusses, behind its screen of heroic action, the question of equilibrium—the fusion and balancing of passion and rationalism against a background of technology (magic or "magecraft") proposed as the permissible complement to, rather than the all-destroyer of, nature. Written in a heightened and uncolloquial, rather Bunyanesque English of great aptness and felicity, this is a true saga of serious purpose, worth taking seriously.

A review of "Earthsea," in The Economist, *Vol. 251, No. 6816, April 13, 1974, p. 70.*

George Edgar Slusser

The *Earthsea Trilogy* has generally been ignored by commentators on Le Guin. Some may have been deterred by the silly publishing classification which designates the books as "children's literature." More likely, though, the trilogy has simply seemed a world apart, self-contained, obeying the laws of the high fantasy genre, and having little in common with the Hainish "mainstream." Such logic may apply to writers whose world view is incoherent or inconsistent, but not to Le Guin. *Earthsea* does stand apart to the extent that it forms a carefully balanced whole. But, more essentially, it creates a universe which is parallel to that of the Hainish novels, one in which major themes are not simply mirrored or reflected, but carried forward and developed in new ways. The problems of individual responsibility, of folly, evil and the search for selfhood, are examined throughout these books in all their purity. (p. 31)

[The] Earthsea books prove the value of positive individual action. The three novels celebrate the ability of one man, Ged, to overcome his pride and fear, and defeat an adversary who has succumbed to both, and then, from the base of his heroic combat, to project a new society of peace and justice to replace the old world of disunity and violence. (p. 33)

Earthsea is a work of high style and imagination. **The Farthest Shore** is a work of genuine epic vision.

Ged is a fully developed hero, and interestingly, one of a new sort. Le Guin's earlier heroes were scientists or statesmen. Ged is a "mage." In her essay, **"Dreams Must Explain Themselves"**, Le Guin tells us her mage is an artist—the trilogy is an artist-novel. Traditionally, the artist is the most private of heroes; the struggle to create is primarily a struggle with self, with one's own powers and the need

to control them and their consequences. The scientists and "observers" of earlier novels occupy an intermediate position between men of action and the artist. But in Le Guin the pull is always toward action. Both Rocannon and Genly Ai are drawn into an active role through contact with a man of action. Ged is a loner. *Wizard* tells the story of a private battle; the two books which follow show the hero moving toward companionship and collaboration. The quest in *Farthest Shore,* though undertaken in the same secretive, unassuming spirit as always, has profound public implications. The artist no longer travels alone; and the one he takes with him is not another mage, but a young prince, trained not in the arts, but with the sword. . . . Ged learns that, although the magician is safe on Roke, the wizard's school, real creation begins only when he has left the ivory tower and gone forth into life. (p. 34)

[*Farthest*] is the hero's last and greatest adventure. First an apprentice, then a master, Ged-grown-old now takes a new apprentice with him, thus completing the epic chain. The adventure is also, in a way, a return. Young Ged became a man by accepting and absorbing the shadow of his own death. Now he goes to fight a man who has refused death, who has been possessed by his shadow.

The central theme of all these novels is the nature of human evil. The exploration takes place within the same limits as always: the universe is still a creative, dynamic balance, Yin and Yang, not a Manichean contention between light as good and darkness as evil. Evil is still explicable as a misunderstanding of the dynamics of life. What has become awesome, however, is the power one man, each man, wields, potentially and actually, to disrupt the balance. The setting in *Left Hand* is realistic; here it can only be called allegorical. Ged is both an ideal hero in an idealized world order, and an everyman. His powers seem exceptional, and yet he wins his greatest battles with means we all possess. *Earthsea,* in its sharp, limited vision, explores in depth the question of individual responsibility. To deny death is to turn from life. But worse still is to project an anti-shadow, abstracting personal fear into a general virtue, and making fear of death into a quest for eternal life.

The image of the shadow dominates *Wizard,* as it does *Left Hand.* Like all of Le Guin's heroes, Ged is an alien, an orphan in the spiritual sense, ignored by his insensitive parent. Like the odd ones of myth and fairy tale, this child of innate gifts is sired by ordinary people. The "mage born" is adopted by the wizard Ogion and made his apprentice. But in his god-given gift lie the dangers of pride and ambition, and to these Ged succumbs. His attempt to raise the dead, to prove his power through an unnatural act, looses the terrible shadow upon him. He had been warned by Ogion that danger surrounds power as shadow surrounds light. Like all men, Ged must learn his limitations the hard way, and bear the consequences of his act. These consequences, fortunately, also have their limits; if it were not so, the balance would have long since failed. Young Ged is foolish, not wicked; but he releases a force which nonetheless seeks to possess him, to turn him into an instrument of evil. The novel narrates his struggle with the shadow—first his attempts to flee, then his resolve to hunt it down, and finally his confrontation and victory.

But what is the nature of Ged's struggle? The enemy is a shadow, part of the hero himself, something from within. And, yet, Ged moves in a world where things seem to be working against him, leading him to ruin. He is pursued by a hostile destiny. It is the young witch girl on Gont who, daring Ged, first suggests raising the dead. This leads him to read the fatal runes in Ogion's book. Jasper again dares him—and this time he raises the dead, and releases the shadow with it. Then there is the mysterious messenger who directs him to Osskil, where the shadow nearly takes his life. These figures exist—we see and hear them. But as "antagonists," they too are shadows, of Ged's own mind. He comes close at one point to believing in fate. This is more than illusion; Ged is fooling himself. For in seeking "causes" outside of himself, he avoids the look within. His own pride and fear have invested neutral shapes with purpose and hostile will in an attempt to cast the weight of responsibility onto something beyond him. In the final episode on the open sea, the man is alone with his shadow. Before he finally absorbs it, it changes shape. What passes before him is his own life. One of the shapes is Jasper; but he also sees his father, and Pechvarry his friend. The shadow is formed of his own acts and choices, and in accepting it, he accepts responsibility for them. For he, not Jasper or any other man or force, must bear the blame for what he does.

At first reading, the mood cast by *Wizard* is strange and dream-like; we seem to fluctuate between objective reality and the hero's mind. The shadow is loosed into a very real world—an Archmage dies sealing the breach—but is gradually drawn back towards Ged. The hero's adversaries are sometimes phantoms of his own creation, and sometimes real powers, like the dragons and the Lord of Terrenon. Behind this fluctuation lies a carefully controlled pattern. The traditional novel of apprenticeship shows the hero first learning, then doing. But Ged is the sorcerer's apprentice—he does before he learns, and his first deed is misbegotten. For this mistake he is not sequestered; instead he becomes a mage, and is sent forth, master of his craft, but still ignorant of its implications. Again and again, life forces him to act first and learn later. Confronting the problem of action, he comes to see a deeper truth: to do great deeds, one must be whole oneself. And one is whole only by knowing one's limits.

Ged learns that what is done counts less than the spirit in which it is done. Tired of waiting in fear on the archipelago where he has become mage, Ged goes recklessly forward to brave the dragon, hoping to force the shadow into the open. But along with these private motives goes a public duty—he goes to prevent the dragons from invading his islands. Though he defeats the worm, it comes close to defeating him in turn. He has won the right to one mastery, one only. The dragon tempts him by offering the name of the thing that pursues him. Ged does not fail the archipelago, but the choice is painful. Self has gotten in the way of the deed, and the gift cannot be given freely. The Stone of Terrenon tempts him too in the same way, with that illusive name. To know something's true name is to have

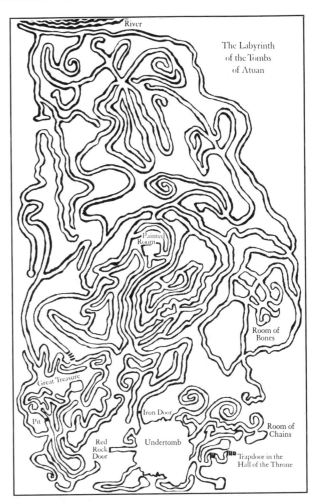

From The Tombs of Atuan, *written by Ursula K. Le Guin. Illustrated by Gail Garraty.*

power over it. Ged realizes that one can act freely, without reservations, only when such temptation is put aside. To do so, he must accept in himself the thing whose name he seeks—death. The hardest task for Ged is not the heroic deed; it is the act of mind which necessarily denies his exceptional nature, and places him on a level with all the rest—the acceptance of his common mortality. What he has begun, all men begin and finish—their lives.

But what is the nature of evil in *Wizard*? What does the symbolism of darkness signify? Earthsea contains many "dark powers"—the Stone of Terrenon, the dragons. But these are primeval, inhuman powers; beside them and over them man has built up civilization. The use of the Old Speech, for instance, binds a man to truth, but dragons can twist true words to false ends, because this language is theirs. These true-namers are fundamentally indifferent to man, they are unman. In order to exist, man must strike a balance with them. They cannot be conquered, but they must be contained: Ged names and fixes the dragon, and the stone is sealed in the fortress. They must not be served, because, in seeking to rule these forces, man enslaves himself to them—he consents to darkness. In the same way,

Ged, wishing to rule over death by his conjuring, consents to it, and so becomes its prey.

But just what is this "shadow" he releases? Does it represent Death, a figure that walks among us; or is it a figure of his mind, the "shadow of his own death"? Ged flees the shadow, and it nearly claims him. Is he the victim of his own fears? The Otak dies to remind us that the struggle is not entirely in the mind. Ged pursues the shadow, and runs aground, nearly perishing. Finally, he stops running or searching; he knows that neither can escape their fate. When they have finally come to the time and the place destined for their last meeting, then they will meet. This other is Death, but the hero does not meet it here. But what does he encounter on the sand inside the ocean? The place is nowhere if not in the mind. And the act is inconclusive in terms of conquest or defeat: Ged neither loses nor wins, but in naming the shadow of his death with his own name, he makes himself whole again as a man. The evil here is neither death nor the darkness; it is rather Ged's refusal to grant these things their rightful place in the balance of nature. Only the whole man, who has accepted death, is free to serve the powers of life. Yet for all of this, Le Guin does not intend death to lose its sting or its reality. The ambiguity of the shadow is purposeful, for it reminds us that the mind is not everything. Death is, as Ged affirms in a moment of gloom, more than fear or a misunderstanding of life. It is a power as well, perhaps the only one that has any real hold on man.

It is significant that the struggle with the shadow is not mentioned in the epic poem celebrating the mage's life, whereas the journey to the tombs is. The first merely lays the foundation for deeds, the second is the true public act. In *Tombs,* Ged goes to the Kargad lands, home of the savage blond barbarians who raid Gont in the earlier novel, to recover the lost half of the ring of Erreth-Akbe from the tombs. As long as the ring remains divided, Earthsea will know neither unity nor peace.

Ged goes seeking neither fame nor fortune. His goal is a quest for knowledge. The two halves of the ring joined together form the "lost rune." To know the "true name" of a thing in Earthsea is to know its essence; so it is here. The true nature of unity is no longer understood because its sign is lost. This loss occurred long ago, when the attempts of the mage Erreth-Akbe to unify the world were defeated, and Earthsea slipped back into faction and darkness. This is no Christian fall which will end in a redemption. Ged follows Erreth as another man of wisdom and moral courage who attempts to bring harmony to a world. The tension between making and unmaking is constant and ongoing; man's continuing responsibility is to oppose the forces of disorder. The task is neverending, and utterly necessary. Against the permanence of chaos, mankind forms chains: the task passes from Estraven to Ai, from Erreth to Ged. In *Left Hand,* these forces of unmaking were collective bodies; in *Tombs,* their locus is an opposite sort—the tomb, the void. Yet significantly, this heart of darkness supports temples erected to a "god-king," maintained by a new political tyranny of "divine rights," and an oppressive priesthood.

The ring has been broken in two; one half was scattered to the winds, the other buried in the tombs. The world seems permanently in the grip of fear and greed. A false unity has been imposed on men by laws and priests. True harmony, in Le Guin, comes only from the gift freely given. The half of the ring in the world was thought buried at the ends of the earth—on a nameless sandbar along with the pair of royal siblings—and yet it returns. Ged is accidentally shipwrecked on the island in *Wizard.* Though rendered a near-savage from isolation, the woman nonetheless reaches out to mankind, and gives Ged the fragment. A chain of gifts begins which leads the hero to Selidor in the extreme west, where the dragon reveals to him the meaning of the object, then back to Atuan in the farthest east where, in the bowels of the tombs, the priestess Tenar gives him with the other half of the ring his greatest gift—his life.

At the heart of the public deed, we find a very private experience. The real drama is not Ged's, but Tenar's. She is faced with the same ordeal that Ged faced in *Wizard*—the coming of age. But she has no Ogion to guide her, and no school of wizardry to teach her. Her world is one that has sunk into ignorance and perversion. The proper balance of light and darkness, death and life, has been upset. Tenar is a person of great natural strength and imagination, but the priestesses guide her to darkness and denial of life. All feelings are repressed; her mind has nothing open to it but the dark labyrinth beneath the tombs. Ged's initiation began with water to life and a name. Tenar's name is taken from her in a grotesque ceremony in which the proper relationship between life and death is willfully inverted. A figure in white wields the sword of sacrifice, while one in black stays the hand at the last minute, and claims Tenar for the darkness. Thus, ironically, she becomes "the reborn"—her name is replaced by that of the "immortal" priestess Ahra. But this is eternal death, not life; the living are entombed, "eaten," swallowed by darkness: the dead become their master. In the case of the young child Tenar, it is Blake's "marriage hearse," the corruption of life at its source.

Ged is taken prisoner in the tombs. Tenar, the master of prisoners, holds him, and yet is fascinated by the presence of life in her dark domain. She will not yield him up to the God-King's priestess and death. Through their mutual contacts she comes, gradually, to see she is the one imprisoned, and not Ged. This mage shows her the marvels of the wide world beyond, but she claims superiority over him in the knowledge of her domain: "You know everything, wizard. But I know one thing—the one true thing!" Tenar is an intrepid explorer. She has gone farther than anyone else in the labyrinth, and now she pursues Ged with the same intellectual passion—she would know. It is only because her mind is great that she can make the breakthrough. Suddenly, she realizes Ged has gone farther than she even in her own realm of darkness. Seeing the scars on his face, she sees that "he knew death better than she did, even death." Their relationship is not only inverted, it changes levels as well. What was prisoner and jailer now becomes pupil and teacher. Ged knows one more thing—her name—and he gives it back to her. Only now, in accepting this gift, is she truly reborn. It is fruit from the tree of knowledge, for with her name the undying one must accept her mortality. The burden of life, she will discover, is a heavy one.

Once more, freedom comes only through acceptance of limitation. This is symbolized by the ring itself. Unlike the chains of the tombs, this "ring" is an armband which, in being joined and bound together, will free mankind. Tenar calls Ged a thief when she first meets him. But, just as the first half of the ring was freely given, this one must be too. It is Tenar who ultimately gives Ged both the ring and his freedom. In the tombs, literally, there is freedom only in joining. Tenar is surprised that Ged's magic seems powerless there. He must use it to keep from succumbing to darkness. But fighting the inner battle, he has not the strength to take the ring and return. Neither person alone, in fact, has the power to return to the light. Their only hope lies in the bond of mutual trust. The Ged who had lost faith in himself in *Wizard* was saved by a friend's kindness. Now Ged gives Tenar her name and life; in return, she gives him back water and life: "It was not the water alone that saved me. It was the strength of the hands that gave it." The union of these two is that of minds reaching out across the void. The result is a flood of light: from Ged's staff and hands a "white radiance" shows the walls of the great vault to be diamonds. Their opposite (the image runs through this novel and the next) is the spider, self-sufficient, weaving his futile web out of himself in dry, dark places.

Once again, darkness is emptiness, a negative thing with the power neither to make nor unmake. The tomb merely contains Ged and Tenar; it collapses of its own accord when they leave. Evil occurs only when men serve this darkness, and there are many degrees of evil in *Tombs.* When Tenar escapes into the world she feels a need to entomb herself again for the evil she has done. Ged tells her she was but "the vessel of evil"—it is now poured out: "You were never made for cruelty and darkness; you were made to hold light, as a lamp burning holds and gives its light. I found the lamp unlit . . ." More evil is the force that misuses this gift for life. But perversion is no absolute either; the priestess Kossil has corrupted herself. Her evilness can no longer be poured out, for she has taken the vessel within, and made of her mind a labyrinth. Her fear causes her to deny even the darkness, negating the order of things she has served all these years. The other servants of darkness have only wasted their lives: Thar's dignity, Manan's love, could find nothing to fulfill them. Kossil serves the destructive God-Kings, who have replaced the natural order with expediency and venality. Light is forbidden in the tomb, yet Kossil brings her feeble candle. She is no spider. The tomb collapses on her, digging by candlelight at empty graves, "like a great fat rat."

In a sense the last Earthsea novel, *Farthest Shore,* again plays out the struggle of *Wizard,* but this time on a different level, and in what appears a much more perilous and imperilled universe. Through the earlier novel there runs a deeper faith in the balance of things—it will right itself eventually, no matter what. Even if Ged had succumbed, and become an instrument of darkness, Vetch was still there to sink the boat. Ged had no intention of going to Iffish, his friend's home; a fortunate "chance" simply took

him there. In *FS,* however, such checks and balances seem to have failed. A great wizard has yielded to the darkness, and his actions menace the equilibrium in Earthsea. To some extent, this wizard is again Ged's shadow, since Ged is largely responsible for the man's actions. Out of anger and vanity, Ged had once challenged a renegade mage named Cob, who had debased the summoning of the dead to a carnival trick, and dragged him to the wall that separates the land of the living from that of the dead. "Oh, a lesson you taught me, indeed," Cob later tells Ged, "but not the one you meant to teach! There I said to myself: 'I have seen death now, and I will not accept it.' "

Cob begins turning people from the natural rhythm of things by offering them eternal life. Against this irrational lure, knowledge is impotent—there must be power as well. The rune of peace has been procured, but the world remains divided. Without a central authority, a king on the throne, men and islands fall easy prey to him who would be Anti-King. The new leader will be young prince Arren, who comes to Roke and agrees to go with Ged to seek out the source of this evil.

Their journey takes them south, then west to land's end. At first, the object of their search is vague: it is a "break," a "breech." They seek a place, then a person, and eventually realize that what they are looking for is ultimately in themselves. Evil, in *Farthest Shore,* is more than ever "a web we men weave." The Anti-King is present in each man's mind, and their journey is that of each man to his death. But at the same time, it is also a journey through a series of real lands, people, and things; ultimately, it is a journey to Cob—an evildoer is destroyed, the breach in the universe is healed. The devastation is not only in their minds; real people are ravaged, leaders turn aside from duty, their lands fall to waste. More purposefully than ever, allegory functions here on several levels; the result is almost Dantesque. Symbolic levels are not only beautifully woven together, but firmly rooted in a concrete world which at every moment claims a reality of its own.

Ged soon realizes that he is not leading but following. Young Arren, although he accompanies the mage, is going his own way—to kingship, to the center of things. The path is, as usual, a circuitous and unexpected one. It takes him less to heroic deeds (his sword remains sheathed until the final adventure) than to out-of-the-way places: it is a true odyssey. To achieve their goal, both must cross the dry land of death. But this is a crossing Ged is ill-prepared for; the old man is at the end of his possibilities, and has already accepted death in the sunlight. Arren, however, is young; gradually he discovers his fear of death, and his desire for life. "It is your fear, your pain I follow," Ged tells him. But Arren in turn needs Ged and his wisdom of life. The task accomplished only through a bond of trust and love: "I use your love as a man burns a candle."

The physical journey may be read as a projection of Arren's fears, doubts and hopes. The trip south ends in a deadpoint—a slack sail and a paralyzed will. All along there is, significantly, little wind from Ged's magic. Arren in fact begins to doubt his power: what use is it? What can an old man and a boy do alone? *Farthest Shore* reflects Le Guin's interest in dreams. Arren dreams again and again—always visions of promise which end in chaos and darkness. The silk fields of Lorbanery become entangling spider webs. He hears the call to "come" during the seance with the drugged wizard Hare, and plunges deep into darkness. Later Roke itself falls victim to the same blight: students and masters begin to doubt their magic, recourse to crystal balls yield visions of unmaking, the Master Summoner loses himself in darkness. Arren becomes totally twisted around: he believes Ged is seeking death, and allies himself with the madman Sopli in the boat, whose madness is fear of death, water, and life itself. After the attack by the savages which wounds Ged, he himself is caught in the web of inaction; reality becomes a dream: "I could think of nothing, except that there was a way of not dying for me, if I could find it." Yet he cannot move, and life flows from him as from a broken scab.

The turning point is their rescue by the raft people, who beyond all land have built life and community over the abyss of the sea. Arren first believes this world a dream; but it is real, and the Long Dance is danced here as in all other lands of Earthsea; its people know joy and death. Here the young man learns that to refuse death is to refuse life—their relation is easy to see on the rafts, but is the same everywhere. More importantly, Ged shows him that no one is immune to this evil: "What is a good man . . . one who has no darkness in him? Look a little farther. Look into yourself! Did you not hear a voice say 'Come'? Did you not follow?" Arren is now freed to act; when the singers fail at the Long Dance, he can complete the song. But for him there is more to achieving selfhood than there was for young Ged. He is to be the king; the evil must be rooted out of the kingdom before he can rule. All nature comes to his aid, as helpful now as it was recalcitrant before. The dragon flies before them as their guide, and magewind fills the sails. The ancient powers join with men to combat the ultimate perversion. As with the tombs of Atuan, but on a vaster scale, the land of the dead is part of the balance. Cob has violated it.

The last pages of **Farthest Shore** are filled with a series of unforgetable images. Arren sees the dragons flying, and experiences a burst of joy in life. . . . The "fierce willed concord" of the dragons' patterned flight, the beauty formed of a triad of "terrible strength, utter wildness and grace of reason," is the essence of life, to be gloried in. Orm Embar, the great dragon, dies impaled on the enemy's staff, like Mogien diving selflessly, and gives his life to save balance itself. Here, on the very spot where his ancestor Orm died fighting against man, he now dies fighting alongside him. More moving, however, is the confrontation with Cob at the heart of dryness. Under Ged's questions, his powers melt away, revealing the utter desolation of one who has traded the supreme gift, life, for nothing. He is withered, ugly, a spider of dust; he is blind when even the shades of the dead see, nameless when even they have names: when my body dies, Ged tells him, "I will be here, but only in name . . . in shadow . . . Do you not understand?" Death does not diminish life. It is *there.* "Here is nothing, dust and shadows." Cob is between, in limbo. And when he finally cries out for life, he sees that he has already forfeited it. Cob's tragedy, as with the Shing, is one of profound error; his "eternal life" is a colos-

sal lie, and he is the first to be duped by it. This lie comes close to destroying mankind. It is not, however, an alien lure; it is man's deepest temptation.

Wisdom can heal the breach, but physical strength alone can make the return journey—Ged must rely on Arren to help him cross the Mountains of Pain and return to life. The young man, who failed Ged once before, now sets his will, and they escape back to the ocean shore, to water and life. To refuse death was to refuse life; in **Wizard,** here, the acceptance of death becomes a thirst for life. In his final voyage to the underworld, Arren, like the young Ged before him, learns what it is to be a man: "Only to man is given the gift of knowing he will die . . . Would you have the sea grow still and the tides cease to save one wave, yourself ?"

The thrust of this epic is not simply "pre-Christian"; it is quite un-Christian, un-Western, in its naturalism, its reverence for the balance of life, and its refusal of transcendental values. The story is Arren's—his deed, like Ged's, is the acceptance of his own limits, his achievement of selfhood. He meets victory for the first time standing "alone, unpraised, at the end of the world." His victory is the act of closing his hand over a piece of dark stone from the Mountains of Pain. He thus accepts pain, and yet encapsulates it, enclosing it in warm life. Neither Ged nor Arren retreat from life in order to find it. Ged's "making" is the control of natural powers. More significantly, his successor is not a mage, but a king; the sword he wields may only be in the service of life, but it is nonetheless a sword. Power has become more and more necessary to the world of Earthsea. In this shift of focus from artist to ruler, Le Guin affirms the primacy of the social realm. (pp. 35-46)

George Edgar Slusser, in his The Farthest Shores of Ursula K. Le Guin, *R. Reginald, The Borgo Press, 1976, 60 p.*

Margery Fisher

The three stages in the life of the mage of Earthsea—as the apprentice Sparrowhawk in **A Wizard of Earthsea,** as a mysterious unknown in **The Tombs of Atuan** and as Archmage of the Inner Lands in **The Farthest Shore**—are each complete and self-contained, yet to read the three books in sequence [in **Earthsea**] rather than spaced over eight years or so is to see how consequent one book is upon another and how naturally and consistently the character of Ged is developed. It becomes evident, too, that although each story takes place in a different (and ethnically distinct) part of the archipelago, the enormous world which Ursula Le Guin has realised with such imaginative force depends mainly upon two cultures—for setting and atmosphere on a Mediterranean pattern, with Greece foremost, but for the elements of behaviour, ritual and magery as much on American Indian stoicism as on fluctuating elements of Eastern, Celtic and medieval mysticism sensed in the impersonal grandeur and hilarity of dragons, the wind-spells and disputations of the Masters at Roke.

As we read, though, we are not aware of any one dominant influence. Rather, we are drawn into a world alien yet recognisable, mysterious yet as familiar as bread, a world of long quests and dangers which suggest but do not represent our own emotional perplexities. If there are meanings to be found in the Earthsea trilogy they are meanings that reach us through imagery, suggestively, and not by challenging statements. Ged's occasional gnomic utterances ("The Balance is not a stillness. It is movement—an eternal becoming") are the immediate concern of the fiction. They are not read for any prescription for *our* behaviour. We read the fantasy for a sensuous and aesthetic experience.

We receive this experience from the inventive power which has made a world complete in itself but with significant possibilities of extension into the Open Sea and with a history, evidenced in references to old myths and legendary heroes, of which Ged's life is a part only, a world whose topography, civilisations and races are precisely described. Young people would do well to read this trilogy of heroic adventure before *Lord of the Rings,* not because it belongs to a lesser order of literature but because it is more accessible, being simpler, more pictorial, plainer in narrative and technique. There is oratory at the author's command but she uses it rarely, at critical moments when action and thought fuse, and similarly she employs archaism (the bane of science fiction and fantasy writers) sparingly and with few embarrassing moments of banality. Her prose changes constantly to suit the occasion but it has a consistent rhythm that compels attention.

There is, perhaps, one way in which we can relate this other-world adventure intellectually to ourselves. *Earthsea* is about learning, about teachers communicating their wisdom and about one man learning to become a teacher of himself and of others. Ged shows Arha the Eaten, caught in the null darkness of her priesthood, how to become Tenar and to live free in the light. He shows Arren the virtues he will need to rule the kingdom of Havnor—virtues of loyalty, responsibility and courage which the youth finds in himself as he learns to trust his master and friend. Ged has learned from his own grim mistake to discipline his pride, but the instinct to teach, to reach out in kindness and share his experience and knowledge with others, seems an innate, not an acquired part of his character. Reading right through the three books, it is this element of loving pedagogy, of a human desire to instruct and strengthen, that has struck me most forcibly. Other people will read the books in other ways. For a fantasy as bold and generous as *Earthsea* need not abide by one or indeed by many interpretations; it is a living book. (pp. 3118-19)

> *Margery Fisher, in a review of "Earthsea," in* Growing Point, *Vol. 16, No. 1, May, 1977, pp. 3118-19.*

T. A. Shippey

Magic is a difficult business for writers nowadays. Nobody believes in it, except in a selfconsciously provocative way, and yet there is a charm in the shrewd, solid, consistent fantasies of past ages which is not to be denied and can rarely be matched by mere individual inventions. How do you get dragons and spells and sorcerers through the barriers of scepticism which we all learn now as part of our language? Most writers solve the problem with a little fuzziness, mysterious lack of explanation. It is Ursula Le

Guin's distinction to have tackled it head-on, giving us in the *Earthsea* trilogy (printed now for the first time in one volume) not just a story and not just an argument, but the two together, enriched on the one hand by all the archetypes of antiquity and on the other by the equally powerful rationalization-myths of our fathers and grandfathers.

In the past century, for instance, there have been two dominant theories about magic: Sir James Frazer's *Golden Bough* thesis, that it was an analogue of science, opposed to religion and practised by people who thought the universe ran on law; and Bronislaw Malinowski's, that it was a "cathartic" operation resorted to when men were afraid. The "Sorcerer's Apprenticeship" which is the backbone of *A Wizard of Earthsea* starts, typically, by clearing both opinions out of the way. The hero Ged's first self-disclosure comes when he uses his witch-aunt's charm for summoning a goat—and *all* the goats come, crowding and huddling round him as if under compression, so that he starts to cry. Magic is *not* like science, then, because it all depends on who does it; the talent makes the difference. But it does not work "like magic" either, as we realize a little later when Ged, facing a Kargish pirate-raid, rummages in his memory for some blasting stroke or spell—and finds nothing, for "need alone is not enough to set power free: there must be knowledge". The magic of Earthsea is too disciplined to be just "cathartic". It is in fact outside our normal set of ideas on the supernatural, and just to make the point from the start, Mrs Le Guin is scrupulous to avoid the common but tainted word "magician". Ged is a "mage", his art is "magery".

The core of his education is likewise familiar but rethought. It is the "Rumpelstiltzkin" theory, that to control something you need to know its name—an ancient opinion which has been completely quashed by the insistence of all scientists since Francis Bacon that things are much more important than words. That is an exploitative attitude, suggests Mrs Le Guin, connected with a fundamental disrespect for individuality. But she makes the point covertly and positively by taking us through Ged's training in what he can do, and even more in what he cannot. For at the heart of Earthsea lies the myth of *Aeneid* Book VI, the descent into the Shadowland—except that Ged is not given a "golden bough".

His temptation, continually, is necromancy. Three times he tries to bring back the dead, following one of them, his friend's little son Ioeth, deep into the gloomy, passionless imitation of life that is Earthsea's Erebus (or Hell, or Heaven, or happy hunting grounds), only to have a last glimpse of him running uncatchably downhill into the dark—a striking and pathetic image, lonelier, less cruel, but more fearful than Virgil's Styx. One might think that it would take a brave child to read such things and understand them, but Earthsea is full of courage and magnanimity, its people perched on the brink of the ocean as of the Shadowland, yet unperturbed as well as clear-sighted. They are people any child (or adult) would want to emulate. So the balancing of life and death, of magic, science, and religion, which the trilogy expounds, is not just a bitter pill inside the jam of pseudo-medieval fantasy, but something integral to the fable: to follow the Archmage's story you have to grow with him in understanding.

Each of the second and third books of the trilogy then takes a bold step away from what has gone before. *The Tombs of Atuan* opens with a new heroine, a priestess of the Kargs, people who have appeared so far only as nameless Vikings, but who turn out to be more like us than the other inhabitants of Earthsea—white-skinned, imperialistic, religious, well organized, and corrosively sceptical. Ged appears only half-way through, and then as a nameless robber. His liberation of Arha the priestess, the Eaten One, dramatizes the distinction between the *lacrimae rerum* of the universe and the institutionalized cruelty of ritual which men invent to try to palliate it—a strong theme that again hovers on the edge of sadness, embodied this time in the wretched, kindly, terrified maroons who lurk on the fringes of the Kargish Empire.

And in *The Farthest Shore* the magic runs out and the spiders come in: spiders of doubt and fear with a wish to live for ever that must arise, surely, from Svidrigaylov's horrible picture of eternity in *Crime and Punishment*, "just a little room, something like a village bath-house, grimy and spiders in every corner, and that's all eternity is". This time it is Ged's task to go down into the Shadowland with his new assistant, the boy Arren, to fight the antimage Cob (the great spider, as in "cob-web"), and in a sense to Harrow Hell—only his intention is not to let the souls out but to keep them in, to maintain the barrier between living and dead and save his world from the vain hope of immortality that is rotting it with fear. A bold and gloomy theme, once more. But once more the beauty of Earthsea is so strong and its relation to our world sufficiently oblique that only its positive aspects take hold.

Earthsea deserves praise over and above what it has earned as "breathtaking fantasy". It is not an allegory and not a myth, both literary forms now firmly relegated to antiquity. But it *does* challenge comparison with Virgil or Dante or James Frazer, exploring themes which can perhaps now only be treated outside realistic fiction, but doing so with the severity and power of modern rationalism. Mrs Le Guin is the daughter of famous anthropologists . . . and the achievements of that science are embodied in her work. She is an iconoclastic writer at least as much as a "mythopoeic" one; but if ever myths were to come again, they would come from creations like her name-magery, her Shadowland.

> *T. A. Shippey, "Archmage and Antimage," in* The Times Literary Supplement, *No. 3931, July 15, 1977, p. 863.*

Richard Erlich

Ursula K. Le Guin's Earthsea trilogy is something fairly unusual: tightly constructed heroic fantasy. Moreover, it is heroic fantasy that incorporates into its "fable" (in the Elizabethan sense) intelligent considerations of doing and being in a godless world, a world in which magic is a science and in which powerful human beings act or refrain from acting guided only by their insight into the Equilibrium, the Balance. . . .

In these three books, . . . Le Guin traces the development of her hero from youth to old age, showing his heroic restorations of himself, his society, and the cosmos. She deals with the atheistic existentialist themes of finding values in a godless world, of learning to trust the always-alien Other, of coming to terms with the finality of death. Before she had ever read Jung, she deals with the Jungian pattern of the development of the individual and with such "Jungian" archetypes as the Shadow, the anima, and the Old Man. She deals with power and the limits of power, with ontology and ecology, and with the Taoist concept of the Yin-Yang nature of all things.

And all this she does in books that can be read and understood by children.

Why do I like the Earthsea trilogy? Partly because I like fantasy, and I like tightly-constructed fictions. Mostly because my major field is Shakespeare and the tragic drama, and I know that the highest art is that which can entertain and instruct an entire culture. Le Guin's trilogy meets that criterion for the highest art. If it is "kiddie lit," well, "The Tempest" is the world's greatest kids' show.

> *Richard Erlich, "Why I Like the Earthsea Trilogy," in* English Journal, *Vol. 66, No. 7, October, 1977, pp. 90-3.*

Dennis J. O'Brien

The Earthsea Trilogy presents a world of realized magic. It is easy enough to wheel in the mechanisms of magic—charms and spells, sorcerers and dragons—it is another thing to make us believe in such a world. Ursula Le Guin's special gift is making magic real and important. The archmage Sparrowhawk's power rests on a world view that we still dimly perceive and would wish to validate. The secret of magic in Earthsea lies in names. Dragons who speak in the old tongues know the true names of things, and the art of the mage lies in the names which give power. The world view of Earthsea is pre-modern, a world in which the powers of the earth could be *summoned*. To name a thing is only sensible if there lies deep down a core of spirit that can be called upon as we summon the person by invoking a proper name. In archaic and even classical cultures the world was full of gods, spirits, daimons, muses who dwelt in sea and air, in sex and science. The arts and commerce both high and low lived in and through the invocation of these spirits. The world was there to be summoned by a name.

The journey to modernity can be seen as the loss of names, the inability to summon any spirit at the core of the things and events. The old *powers* are still there, but they are now regarded as nameless, impersonal forces which master us and resist being called by name. In the second (and to my mind, best) of the volumes in the Trilogy, *The Tombs of Atuan,* the basic conflict is between the mage and the priestess of The Nameless Ones who dwell in eternal darkness. The strength of Ursula Le Guin's writing is to make us feel the spiritual struggle between a world to be summoned and a world of nameless power. In that dimension it is more than fairy tale and fantasy.

> *Dennis J. O'Brien, in a review of "The Earth-*

sea Trilogy," in Commonweal, *Vol. CIV, No. 25, December 9, 1977, p. 797.*

Francis J. Molson

Ursula K. Le Guin in her public statements has yet to be completely reconciled to the fact that in the United States the Earthsea trilogy has been classified as children's literature. . . . Le Guin's irritation is understandable once it is perceived as deriving not from any dissatisfaction with children's literature . . . but from her impatience and frustration over readers, commentators, and critics who, manifesting [in her words] "adult chauvinist piggery" in one form or another, tend to denigrate the trilogy. . . .

However, for anyone who cares for the quality of reading available to children and, at the same time, respects their intelligence and taste, labeling a work as children's literature is a culmination of the critical process and is meant to be laudatory. Indeed, the Earthsea trilogy *is* children's literature which ranks among the best written in recent times.

As the author of the Earthsea trilogy, Ursula K. Le Guin belongs to a group of authors—prominent among whom are C. S. Lewis, Lloyd Alexander, Madeleine L'Engle, Susan Cooper, and, possibly, J. R. R. Tolkien—who have written outstanding fantasy of a kind whose special appropriateness for the contemporary child is becoming increasingly manifest. Sometimes this kind of fantasy is termed heroic fantasy or romance because it utilizes traditional heroic or mythic conventions and material. . . . At other times this fantasy is called high fantasy, perhaps because its makers are not content just to refashion traditional material in order to update old stories that may still be interesting, but design them for a purpose "higher" than entertainment. (pp. 128-29)

Despite the currency of the terms "heroic fantasy" and "high fantasy," this essay proposes the term "ethical fantasy" to designate the kind of fantasy Le Guin and the other authors, mentioned above, have written. Like the other two terms, "ethical fantasy" recognizes that fantasy for children is purposeful; but, unlike the former terms, "ethical fantasy" refuses to restrict itself to traditional notions of heroism and eschews any possible invidious comparisons between so-called "high" or "low" purposes. Moreover, "ethical" fantasy specifies more openly than either "heroic" or "high" fantasy the fundamental purpose of this kind of fantasy: to teach and instruct as well as to please. In other words, "ethical fantasy" acknowledges that for most readers a book's capacity to "teach" and the kind of "message" it delivers continue to be, as they have been from the origin of children's literature, important criteria (although often unexpressed or unavowed) for evaluating its merits as a children's book. Finally, because its own phraseology avoids the connotation of tedious moralizing and simplistic thinking often associated with the word "didactic," "ethical fantasy" is, by far, preferable to yet a fourth possible designation, "didactic fantasy."

Ethical fantasy, as it has emerged in contemporary children's literature, dramatizes several interrelated propositions whose continuing validity is taken for granted: making ethical choices, whether deliberate or not, is central in the lives of young people; actions do bear consequences not only for oneself but for society, and sometimes apparently insignificant actions can bring about momentous consequences; maturity involves accepting responsibility for one's actions; and character bespeaks destiny. Ethical fantasy, moreover, is a symbolization of these propositions which does not usually endorse or reflect explicitly any particular religion, sect, or ideology. At the same time, generally speaking, ethical fantasy presupposes a world either enmeshed in a vast struggle between Right and Wrong, Good and Evil, or grievously periled by an unexpected shift in equilibrium between Light and Dark, Balance and Imbalance. (pp. 129-30)

Ethical fantasy, then, is didactic but not exclusively or simplistically so: it does not moralize. The fantasies of the authors mentioned above, in addition to being didactic, are also exemplary literary entertainment because the authors are skilled fabulists who never allow theme or subject matter to overwhelm or distort other narrative elements—plot, characterization, pace, and so on. (pp. 130-31)

As an alternative to, if not a substitute for, much traditional didactic literature, ethical fantasy has a lot to offer. On account of its tendency to espouse no one religion or ideology, ethical fantasy has considerable potential for engaging young readers who may be indifferent to or repelled by overt references to a particular sect or group. With its stress on the centrality of ethical choice in the lives of youth and the interrelation of accepting responsibility and maturing, moreover, ethical fantasy champions a morality similar to that which contemporary cognitive, developmental, and humanistically oriented approaches to ethical growth argue for. Traditional literature, on the other hand, has championed, by and large, an absolute code of morality buttressed by originally supernatural sanctions. Finally, because it is contemporary, ethical fantasy cannot help but reflect or incorporate psychoanalytic understanding of human consciousness. (pp. 132)

Interpreting the Earthsea trilogy as ethical fantasy does not exhaust the meaning of the work. Indeed, other interpretations can be presented and themes distinguished; but of these only one directly relates to a reading of the trilogy as ethical fantasy. This is the trilogy's investigation of the nature of the hero; in particular, the mage as hero. Wizards have been heroes before; consider Merlin and Gandalf, whose deeds are stupendous and conventionally heroic. Ged, as celebrated hero, is a bit unusual. He too can perform conventionally heroic deeds such as conquering the dragons of Pendor Island, and traveling into the Kingdom of the Dead and coming out alive. But the deeds Le Guin singles out for extended treatment are anything but traditionally heroic. Accepting oneself as a finite creature made up of good and evil, and assisting a fifteen-year-old adolescent girl to shed an unnatural lifestyle and opt for genuine freedom are not the actions usually celebrated in heroic romance. That Le Guin chooses to stress this side of her hero underscores her intent to point out to her readers that coming of age is important for youngsters and that it consists mainly of accepting responsibility for oneself, one's actions, and one's relationship with others. (p. 138)

Le Guin's handling of the summoning [of a spirit from the dead in *A Wizard of Earthsea*] is most provocative. Imagery of brightness and darkness, sometimes in balance, more often contrasting or blended harmoniously or wildly, suggests the inextricability of good and evil motives in Sparrowhawk and the consequent moral ambiguity of his actions. For instance, as Ged speaks the rune of summoning, he falls forward on the earth and rises holding something dark and heavy in his arms. The dark mass splits apart, and light, the form of Elfarran, emerges from between his arms. Then a breech in the "fabric of the world" opens and a "terrible brightness" appears; out of it springs a "clot of black shadow." The tantalizing, submerged metaphor of violent birth hints, further, Ged's aborting of the opportunity to complete his rite of passage. Ironically, instead of the integrated personality that accompanies maturity, he has produced a monstrous symbol of the childishness he persists in. (Subsequently, as the shadow-monster and Ged engage in their pursuit-flight ritual, the former will grow considerably—paralleling a growth in Ged's ethical character).

Moreover, it is fitting that the shadow leap upon Sparrowhawk, seeking to cleave to him, and then, meeting resistance from "Ged," viciously claw his face and wound him almost fatally before taking off into the darkness. For the shadow, embodying arrogance and immaturity, wishes to return to what it assumes is its origin and master, Sparrowhawk. When it encounters resistance, however, it senses the presence of Ged and not "Sparrowhawk" and attempts to destroy its enemy. Unsuccessful, the shadow is forced to retreat, but not before it leaves on Ged's face a mark of their close kinship and enmity.

Two other points must be made. Obviously, the shadow is an intrinsic part of Ged since it knows his true name. This point, incidentally, Ged does not begin to grasp until Ogion will ask why it is that the shadow in the form of Skiorh spoke to him his true name. The second point concerns a further role of the shadow. As has been remarked, the shadow represents the "Sparrowhawk" within Ged. At the same time, the shadow also constitutes the best evidence that Ged may be the greatest of all mages inasmuch as he did successfully summon Elfarran from the dead. If this is so, then the shadow must be joined ultimately to Ged both to signal the young man's full acceptance of his responsibility for doing wrong and to seal his status as a great wizard.

Surviving the shadow's attack, Ged determines to stay at Roke and undo the evil he has perpetrated. Daunted by what he perceives as a formidable task, he begins to lose faith in himself and his capabilities: his survival as Ged becomes problematic. What restores his faith is Vetch's unexpected revelation of his true name to Ged. This offering of friendship and trust so moves him that immediately Ged divulges his true name to Vetch. This action, because it involves a willingness to entrust one's survival to a second party, is convincing evidence that at last "Ged" has attained dominance over "Sparrowhawk." Hence, the action marks the real beginning of Ged's coming of age. Le Guin underscores the importance of the exchange of true names by having it take place on the anniversary of Ged's

public Passage four years earlier when Ogion bestowed upon him his true name:

> He had not thought of these things for a long time. Now they came back to him, on this night he was seventeen years old. All the years and places of his brief broken life came within mind's reach and made a whole again. He knew once more, at last, after this long, bitter, wasted time, who he was and where he was.

"Ged," the young man realizes, is his true name while "Sparrowhawk" is only a use name. From this point in the narrative, then, Ged's destiny involves finding out and accepting all that is implied in his true name. (pp. 137-38)

A bit more than half of *WOE* is given over to Ged's adventures as a wizard and his several confrontations with the shadow. Roughly half the adventures have Ged fleeing the shadow; the other half, Ged playing Sparrowhawk and aggressively pursuing the shadow. Interesting as the adventures are, their real purpose is to reveal the permanence of the changes within Ged. His unsuccessful attempt to save the life of Pechvarry's son indicates a generous, caring person. His rejection of Yevaud's offer to divulge the name of the shadow in return for allowing the dragons to continue raiding signifies a man who will not swerve from his duty. His immunity to Serret's sexual blandishments reveals a young man who can control his emotions. Exhausted by the ordeal of escaping from Terrenon, Ged returns to Gont and home. There Ogion heals the young man's physical hurt and attempts to do the same for his soul by reminding Ged that the shadow knows his true name. Hinting at the final outcome, he recommends that Ged become, as his use name indicates, a hunter. The fact that "Sparrowhawk" is a use name does not preclude Ged's ever again being aggressive or resourceful. At the same time, however, adopting one or two of the characteristics of "Sparrowhawk" need not entail internalizing all the latter represents, in particular, "Sparrowhawk's" self-sufficiency. Nevertheless, Ged does not yet understand this and sets out alone to track down the shadow. Not unexpectedly, failure dogs his endeavors, and the only success he enjoys is to comprehend, belatedly, the true nature of his quest: "never . . . to undo what he had done, but to finish what he had begun".

The final chase and confrontation chapters are rich in thematic implications. His quest, for instance, takes Ged beyond the farthest island in the East Reach where there is no land or sea, only earthsea. Here, in the uttermost east, the mythic place of origins and beginnings, he learns all he is and what he is capable of. Also appropriate is that this breakthrough occurs after days spent in silence; in this way Ged comes to appreciate the very first lesson Ogion ever gave him: "To hear, one must be silent". Except for the last, the various forms the shadow takes as Ged approaches it—his father, Pechvarry, Jasper, Skiorh—are of people who contributed in one way or another to his ethical development. However, the shadow's final form is unknown, even unrecognizable, neither human nor monster—perhaps suggesting the potential for good or evil which still exists within Ged. Undaunted, Ged lifts up his staff and in view of its brilliance "all form of man sloughed off the thing . . . ". That is, when the young mage irre-

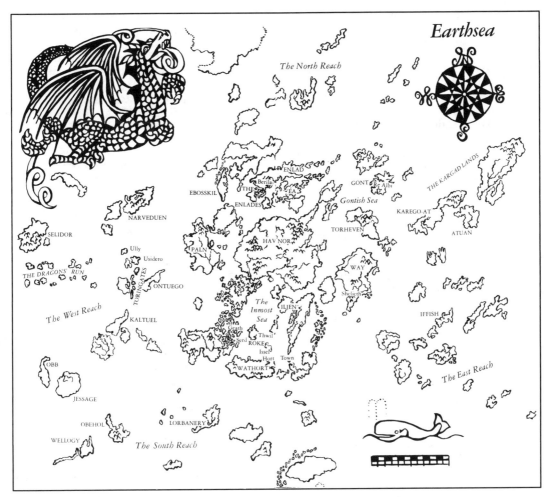

From The Farthest Shore, *written by Ursula K. Le Guin. Illustrated by Gail Garraty.*

versibly determines to be Ged, the shadow is revealed not as an independent entity but as the ugliness each person is capable of doing and can control only when both its evil and its source are acknowledged and accepted. Finally, the shadow can do nothing but return to its origin. Face to face, they call each other the same name, embrace, and become one. At this moment Ged becomes whole, of age, and free—free of the tyranny of impulse and external force, free to choose to act or not. (pp. 139-40)

By dividing her focus between Arha and Ged [in *The Tombs of Atuan*], Le Guin underscores what she may believe is too often overlooked: girls, as well as boys, come of age, make ethical choices, and become free. In designing the plot of *TOA* around two protagonists whose survival depends upon each other, moreover, Le Guin again intends to dramatize for her young readers both the inadequacy of the solitary, self-sufficient hero as a model, and the necessity of social interdependence.

TOA opens with a prologue that introduces little Tenar as a healthy, normal girl whose parents respond differently to the knowlege that their daughter will soon be taken from them so that she can become priestess of the Tombs. Her mother wants to hug and love her as much as she can,

pretending that nothing has really happened. Her father is bitter, feeling that for all practical purposes she is already buried and dead to them. Thus, at the very beginning is sounded the dominant note of the novel—the disruption of the natural, organic development of a girl and its deleterious effects upon her maturation. (pp. 140-41)

Perhaps more than anything else, it is Arha's wanting contact with some human other than the stunted priestesses and half-men around her that continues [her] revitalization and brings about the eventual restoration of balance and orderly development in her life.

The importance Le Guin attaches to Arha's wanting human contact can be inferred from the fact that she devotes nearly half of *TOA* to depicting painstakingly and with a heavy reliance on dialogue the relationship between Arha and Ged. Some readers may consider this part of the novel too long, too slow, and too talky, especially for young readers. Even granting that some of the latter might be turned off, still Le Guin's decision to spend so much time on the trust that developed between Arha and Ged is sound.

Arha's hesitation over what to do with Ged reflects her keen awareness that her decision involves more than summary judgment and punishment: her own life, as well as the interloper's, is in jeopardy. To kill the latter would be, for all practical purposes, to make permanent her acquiescence in the rites of the Masters, thus sealing her own psychological and moral death. On the other hand, not to kill Ged represents an opportunity, at the least, to defy Kossil and, at the most, to claim independence of action with the promise of more in the future. In short, Arha's decision is fraught with ethical implications. To make Arha's decision convincing, then, Le Guin must take sufficient time and space to show all that went into her making it: her defense of her vocation; her faith in the Masters and their power; her panic that there will be nothing to replace her faith if she abandons it; her wanting to believe Ged, who knows her real name; her eagerness to learn more about the world above; and Ged's argument that the Nameless Ones are real and deserving of her respect but not worship.

The longer Arha speaks with Ged, the more likely it is that she will not have him killed. What this also means is that the more she speaks with Ged, the less likely it is that "Arha" is her true name. Thus, the probability that what "Tenar" represents will become dominant depends upon the length of the exchanges between Ged and Arha. To put it still another way, the lengthy conversations in toto constitute a verbal matrix within which a valid naming ceremony can take place. Gradually divesting herself of her use name, the young priestess is more and more ready either to receive a true name or to regain her real name. Ged, sensing what is happening and hoping to assist the young woman in her struggle, decides to reveal her real name. It is true that Ged's revelation of Arha's real name may not be totally disinterested; obviously, he knows that as long as the priestess thinks of herself as Arha his chances of living are slim. . . . The lengthy dialogue is, then, necessary since it shows Ged broadening his concerns to include Tenar as he maneuvers and pleads to save the young woman's soul from evil. In this way Le Guin demonstrates the characteristic behavior of the ethical hero.

The heavy emphasis on dialogue serves one other important function: it is essential for the development of an authentic human relationship between Arha and Ged. Unable to see each other clearly in the dark, and physically separated from one another, the two have just one means of relating—speech. The extensive dialogue leaves Arha the option to break off whenever she wants to. It also allows her to mask the shock of discovering the intruder and learning that he is not as wizards have been described. Indirect, slow, and tentative talking also enables Arha to begin establishing the grounds for friendship and trust, whereas direct, immediate, and physical contact might prove harmful to a young woman who is repressed and knows no other relationship with a male than that of mistress toward a slave. For his part, Ged realizes that the young priestess needs gentle and sympathetic handling; and his role vis-à-vis Arha becomes that of an older brother. (Such a role, incidentally, precludes any romantic or sexual involvement between Tenar and Ged. Further, the absence of any hint of such an involvement in the section describing Tenar's unfolding self-awareness as a female is a sign of Le Guin's tact and sensitivity.) Like a brother,

Ged suspects Tenar may need a parent. Since he knows of no better surrogate parent than Ogion, who has been like a father to him, he determines to take Tenar to Gont and Ogion. His performing the role of an older brother watching over a young and inexperienced sister accounts, in part, for the touching relationship that ensues after the two young people escape from the tombs. It also gives context to the last sentence of the novel: "Gravely she walked beside him up the white streets of Havnor, holding his hand, like a child coming home". (pp. 143-44)

Regardless of her age, Tenar is not yet a woman. Her decision to escape is clearly ethical and admirable, granted; but it has been fundamentally a decision not to be Arha. What she is to become, whether she is really Tenar, or whether she is to have another name, her true name, are questions only the future holds answers to. This is even more reason why at the end of the novel Tenar has become a child eager for real living, eager to begin anew the process of coming of age.

What *TFS* directly says concerning coming of age involves young Arren. When first introduced, he is clearly of princely rank; as a prince, he suffers no identity crisis. He is generous, blessed with good fortune, inexperienced, and untried. As soon as he meets Ged, boyishly, enthusiastically he loves the great mage and thereby takes his "first step out of childhood". Subsequent steps—in fact, Arren's entire rite of passage—are also a test of the depth and permanence of his devotion to Ged. These steps comprise an ordeal of pain—the heartfelt pain of suspecting that Ged is not his hero and is unworthy of love, the intellectual pain of doubting whether Ged knows what their goal is, and the physical and spiritual pain of the journey through the Kingdom of the Dead—which Arren must undergo to reach the glorious end that has been prophesied for him, King of All the Isles. Furthermore, the very last steps out of childhood are the arduous ones Arren forces himself to take back to the beach where the initial journey into death's kingdom commenced. In successfully traversing the underworld Arren wins through to his adulthood and enjoys the keen sense of victory and accomplishment each youngster, regardless of circumstances, requires and is too often denied or has postponed needlessly. . . .

Arren's coming of age, unlike Ged's and Tenar's which necessitated a fundamental rebirth before their passage could be completed, is more traditional in that it stresses what the boy is to become in the end. That is, Arren's end is contained within him: character bespeaks destiny. (p. 145)

What *TFS* indirectly says concerning coming of age is part of the novel's overarching concern for death. Surely, the sense of accomplishment and victory Arren savors on the beach encompasses the realization that he has conquered fear of his own dying, not by denying its actuality and taking refuge in the childish sense of being immortal, but by facing death courageously and honestly. Because he has internalized at last what hitherto had been only Earthsea gnome—one must do only what one must do—Arren perceives the truth of what Ged had pointed out to him earlier: "You enter your manhood at the gate of death". Moreover, Arren's acceptance of death is neither stoic nor existentialist, for he does not just endure life until its inevitable end. On the contrary, he is prepared to live to the fullest since he has ample reason to assume the validity of the other insights into death's meaning and value Ged (here also spokesman for Le Guin's acceptance of Taoism) has shared with him. (p. 146)

Ged's preoccupation with death and dying is not just a concomitant of a plot built around a journey into the world of the dead but also an essential trait of his character. His insights into the meaning of death are the fruits of his silences and meditations in which he has pondered, among other things, whether his life and career have moved in the right direction. Early in their relationship Ged remarks to Arren:

> Try to choose carefully, Arren, when the great choices must be made. When I was young, I had to choose between the life of being and the life of doing. And I leapt at the latter like a trout to a fly. But each deed you do, each act, binds you to itself and to its consequences, and makes you act again and yet again. Then very seldom do you come upon a space, a time like this, between act and act, when you may stop and simply be. Or wonder who, after all, you are.

Arren is puzzled by Ged's self-doubts, believing that such are proper to adolescents like himself. But Arren is, obviously, in no position to know that what Ged is experiencing is the doubt that often attacks the successful person at the height of his career. To put it another way, what Ged is undergoing is the onset of the process of individuation which, Jung hypothesized, occurs around middle age. (p. 147)

A good part of *TFS* reveals a Ged who has become dissatisfied with his public role. Gnawing away at his self-assurance is the deepening realization that doing, even doing magic, in spite of the good its practice can bring about, is not the entire purpose of living. Perhaps Ged even suspects that his original commitment to a life of action, although readily justified ethically and psychologically, was unduly influenced by youth's conviction that virtually all options and possibilities are available to it. But the imminence of death drastically narrows these and forces a reconsideration of what a person must do. Ged says as much to Arren.

> You are young, you stand on the borders of possibility, on the shadowland, in the realm of dream, and you hear the voice saying *Come*. But I, who am old, who have done what I must do, who stand in the daylight facing my own death, the end of all possibility, I know that there is only one power that is real and worth the having. And that is the power, not to take, but to accept.

The power to accept is attainable not by seizing at it or aggressively pursuing it but by not doing anything except to stand quiet in the presence of life. Thus, as he approaches the shore of Selidor and the confrontation with Cob, Ged looks forward to what he senses may be the final and most important phase of his life: "There is no kingdom like the forests. It is time I went there, went in silence, went alone.

And maybe there I would learn at last what no act or art or power can teach me, what I have never learned".

After Ged's quest is completed—paradoxically using every bit of his magic—and he is "done with doing," a new integration of inner resources will take place, and a new "self," a new Ged will develop. Like coming of age, coming of old age marks the end of one period of life and the beginning of another, momentous and challenging. Of this new self, this new Ged, nothing is known except for the provocative remark of King Lebannen: "He rules a greater kingdom than I do".

Old age and death are subjects not often found in children's literature. . . . The excellence of the Earthsea trilogy as ethical fantasy stems, in large part, from the fact that Le Guin has not been afraid to confront the fact of human mortality. Her lack of fear amounts to more than just the fortitude not to back off from a distasteful subject. Rather, Le Guin is positive, insistent, celebratory: growing old is as natural, necessary, and good as leaving behind youth and becoming adult. Maturation, moreover, implies a constant coming of age; and admitting responsibility for one's actions involves meeting the challenges old age entails.

This does not mean that Le Guin believes that growing old is any easier or less troublesome than maturing and becoming adult. *TFS* testifies to both the inevitability of the aging process and the difficulty of accepting and adjusting oneself to that inevitability. The novel also testifies that old age may be the best portion of life in that it allows an individual, provided he or she sloughs off a frenzy for doing and getting, to contemplate, to open himself or herself to the ultimate potentiality of being human and alive. Unfortunately, this last testimony is—rather, *must be*—more exhortative than definitive, as Le Guin herself intimates. The difference between exhortation and statement, furthermore, affects the narrative quality of the trilogy. The first two novels, compared with the last, are lean and economically written—the result of speculation annealed by experience. The third is lengthy, filled with *sententiae*, and bordering on verbosity—as if its author, trying to convince herself of the validity of what her protagonist says, needs to repeat, coax, and underline. Nonetheless, what seems weakness may be, paradoxically, a source of strength whereby the trilogy becomes outstanding ethical fantasy. For the weakness, as regrettable as it may be, is the unavoidable result of Le Guin's attempt to render more honestly and courageously than any other writer of juvenile fantasy what constitutes the process of coming of age. (pp. 147-49)

> *Francis J. Molson, "The Earthsea Trilogy: Ethical Fantasy for Children," in* Ursula K. Le Guin: Voyager to Inner Lands and to Outer Space, *edited by Joe De Bolt, Kennikat Press, 1979, pp. 128-49.*

Susan Wood

By 1975, Ursula Le Guin was acknowledged as a leader of the science fiction field. . . . It seems fitting, however, that the major work of this mature writer, who is bringing a new adult concern with the living of life to science fiction, should be a work nominally for children: the Earthsea trilogy. . . . This work, which has won praise and professional honours, reconfirms the importance of fantasy as a timeless vehicle for examining basic human concerns: growth, maturity, and death. (pp. 157-58)

Le Guin's best work, the Earthsea trilogy, derives its great strength from the direct translation of ideas into shared experience. Fantasy is, as Le Guin recognizes, "a journey into the subconscious." The truth found there can be communicated directly, without the intervening barriers of social and philosophical constructs; but first the writer must find an appropriate style, one exhibiting the "permanent virtues" of clarity and simplicity. The Earthsea novels clearly exemplify this ideal.

The patterning of the Earthsea trilogy is that of a human life: growth, the acceptance of power, mature action, the abdication of power, death. Within this circle of experience, each book presents another pattern: a quest through death's realm to adult knowledge and power. Like the magic of Earthsea itself, the books draw their strength from the specific knowledge of individual things. The life they present, while universal in its implications, is always particular: that of the mage Sparrowhawk, whose true name is Ged.

Though *A Wizard of Earthsea* opens in the context of legend, it moves quickly from the evocation of the shadowy figure "who in his day became both dragonlord and Archmage", to the daily life of the goatherd boy of Gont as he discovers his power to call down hawks and to shape the fog. The complementary patterns of *The Tombs of Atuan* and *The Farthest Shore,* too, are firmly rooted in the individual stories of Tenar, Priestess of the Nameless Ones who becomes White Lady of Gont, and Arren, prince of Enlad who becomes King of All the Isles. Ged, in these books, is presented from the outside as a mature and somewhat enigmatic figure of power, performing actions whose significance the young protagonists can only half comprehend. Yet he remains a sharply-realized individual: the Sparrowhawk indeed, with his "reddish-dark" face, "hawk-nosed, seamed on one cheek with old scars," and his "bright and fierce" eyes. He and his companions eat dry bread, and suffer hunger; they sail the world's seas and are parched by its sun; they act rashly and, when they must call on magic to restore the balance they have upset, they suffer exhaustion and pain. Their actions have the inevitable rightness of myth, always supported by the credibility of human feeling.

Earthsea, too, like Gethen and Anarres [in Le Guin's adult fiction], is a fully-realized world. From the actuality of its wave-washed islands comes its strength as metaphor. An archipelago, Earthsea stretches some 2,000 miles from the cold North Reach south to the warm waters of the raft-people, the Children of the Sea; and another 2,000 miles from Selidor where the skull of Erreth-Akbe lies amid the bones of the dragon Orm, east to the semibarbaric Kargad Lands. These islands hold many kingdoms and several races; the trilogy presents each particular of life—fisherman and sorceress, goat and dragon, appletree and sparkweed—in all its richness. Yet Earthsea is a finite world. The Children of the Sea still dance the midsummer Long Dance, "one dance, one music binding together the sea-divided lands". Yet they move on fragile rafts above, and upon, a waste of limitless ocean, in celebration of the human spirit whose dance of life always moves "above the hollow place, above the terrible abyss". Ged sails Earthsea from edge to inhabited edge, seeking beyond the world for the shores of death's realm. Thus the physical islands of Earthsea exist in a delicate balance with the sea; the known human world lies surrounded by the unknown; and all life exists defined by death. This balance is central to the magic, and the meaning, of Earthsea.

Though secular rulers, kings, and lords govern the people of Earthsea, true power rests with the mages: men whose inborn power is augmented by long study to know the essence of each created thing, the "true name" by which it can be controlled. Though they can summon and use "the immense fathomless energies of the universe," the most important aspect of their art is the recognition of its natural limits, of "the Balance of the Pattern which the true wizard knows and serves".

Magic is an art which must be learned, patiently. *A Wizard of Earthsea* and *The Farthest Shore* show gifted apprentices at school on Roke Island, learning to weave spells with gestures, unseen powers, and the words of the Old Speech now spoken only by wizards and dragons. Le Guin's wit, and a gift of humor rare in fantasy, find full scope in the School of the Island of the Wise, as Gamble teases Prince Arren with tales of enchanted dinners, and Ged shoots arrows made of breadcrumbs and spells after Vetch's chickenbone owls.

Magic must not be used lightly, however; for evil, in Earthsea, is a "web we men weave" by the misuse of power. In *A Wizard of Earthsea,* Ged, who believes that a mage is "one who can do anything," must, like Le Guin's other protagonists, learn painfully that "as a man's real power grows and his knowledge widens, ever the way he can follow grows narrower; until at last he chooses nothing, but does only and wholly what he *must* do . . . ". In pride and anger, he summons a spirit of the dead; and so he lets a dark spirit of unlife enter the world. To name, to control that Shadow, he must journey over the oceans of Earthsea, into his own spirit, to confront and accept his "black self". His companion Vetch, watching, understands that Ged:

> by naming the shadow of his death with his own name, had made himself whole: a man: who, knowing his whole true self, cannot be used or possessed by any power other than himself, and whose life therefore is lived for life's sake and never in the service of ruin, or pain, or hatred, or the dark.

In the later books of the trilogy, Ged's power is founded in abnegation; he has learned to " 'desire nothing beyond my art,' " and to do only "what is needful"—even to relinquish that art.

In contrast to the heroic sweep of *A Wizard of Earthsea,* with its sparkle of sun on waves and roar of dragons, *The Tombs of Atuan* offers the narrow, intense focus of psychomyth: Le Guin's own term for her explorations in the timeless regions of the human mind. With its single action, setting, and central character, the novel powerfully suggets the claustrophobia of its controlling metaphor: the dark labyrinth beneath the Tombs, the dark passages of the human spirit inhabited by the " 'powers of the dark, of ruin, of madness" '.

The narrative opens with a symbolic death as the child Tenar becomes Arha, "the Eaten One," priestess of the Nameless Ones. The impersonal ritual of her sacrifice effectively suggests the denial of human life in the world of the Tombs. Tenar exists behind stone walls in a barren desert, her life and sexuality expressed only in ritual dances before the Empty Throne: celebrating death as the Long Dance celebrates life. Her only freedom is to wander her labyrinth, "the very home of darkness, the inmost center of the night," a place of corrupted power suggesting the fear, hatred, and utter loneliness which imprison her spirit. Her only right is to kill the men imprisoned there—and then live with her terrible nightmares of guilt.

Ged comes to the labyrinth seeking the Ring of Erreth-Akbe with its lost Rune of Peace, bringing the gift of "life in the place of death". Just as the light of his wizard's staff reveals beauty in the dark caverns, so his wizard's knowledge reveals Tenar's true name. When he, in turn, shares his true name with her, the gift of human trust is complete: a treasure more potent than the restored Ring. By its power, Tenar can choose freedom for them both. The novel ends with rebirth, as she walks from the crumbling Tomb into "the huge silent glory of light", accompanying Ged into the human world "like a child coming home".

The Farthest Shore completes the trilogy with Ged's third and final journey through the realm of death, accompanied by Prince Arren who thus fulfils the prophesy of Maharion: *"He shall inherit my throne who has crossed the dark and living and come to the far shores of the day".* Its action is a sombre, ironic balance to that of *A Wizard of Earthsea.* Just as the Archmage Nemmerle gave his life to close the door which Ged, by his rash act, opened between life and death, so Ged gives his power to close the door which the wizard Cob opens in his attempt to escape death. Death is not, in itself, evil; rather, it is necessary, "the price we pay for our life, and for all life. Cob's denial of death, however, has evil consequences, for he denies life and thus destroys the essential balance of creation.

Le Guin suggests the evil effects of Cob's action in vivid, specific terms: Hort Town's foul disorder; the former wizard Hare's drugged ramblings; and especially the creeping mistrust, the numbing despair, which slowly dim Arren's shining devotion to Ged. Enduring these symptoms of imbalance, Ged and Arren come to their cause: the open door through which the light and joy of the living world flow into the lands of death. Again, the controlling images are resonant archetypes, evoking the sterility of denial and despair: the Dry River where only night flows, the Dry Land filled with "dust and cold and silence". Yet though even "the springs of wizardry have run dry", the human love and faith which are "the springs of being" do not fail. Arren, by his courage and devotion, leads Ged over the Mountains of Pain; and both regain life once more. The trilogy ends, not with triumph as Arren is crowned, but

in a more appropriate mood of serenity. Ged, dragon-borne, vanishes from the world of action; and his story returns, full circle, to the timeless cadences of legend.

Peter Nicholls, in common with many critics, has praised Le Guin for her "telling precision of imagery," her ability to achieve "the strongest emotional reasonances . . . by capturing the individuality of a particular situation or character," as in the account of Arren's descent among the dead:

> All those whom they saw—not many for the dead are many, but that land is large—stood still, or moved slowly and with no purpose . . . They were whole and healed. They were healed of pain, and of life. They were not loathesome as Arren had feared they would be, not frightening in the way he had thought they would be. Quiet were their faces, freed from anger and desire, and there was in their shadowed eyes no hope.

> Instead of fear, then, great pity rose up in Arren, and if fear underlay it, it was not for himself, but for all people. For he saw the mother and child who had died together, and they were in the dark land together; but the child did not run, nor did it cry, and the mother did not hold it or ever look at it. And those who had died for love passed each other in the streets.

Yet it is not just the details—the mother not looking at her child—which make this section moving. The simplicity of the language, its directness, and the sonorous cadencing of phrase and sentence into a timeless lament all combine with the specific images to make the passage unforgettable.

In Le Guin's work, even lamentation becomes a celebration of life, of the human spirit's power and desire to express its uniqueness.

> 'I must go where I am bound to go, and turn my back on the bright shores. I was in too much haste, and now have no time left. I traded all the sunlight and the cities and the distant lands for a handful of power, for a shadow, for the dark.' So, as the mageborn will, Ged made his fear and regret into a song, a brief lament, half-sung, that was not for himself alone . . .

Like the mageborn, Ursula K. Le Guin also finds words of power, and weaves them into complex evocative patterns of human truth. In the limitless imaginative world of science fiction and fantasy, she finds:

> precise and profound metaphors of the human condition . . . the fantasist, whether he used the ancient archetypes of myth and legend or the younger ones of science and technology, may be talking as seriously as any sociologist—and a good deal more directly—about human life as it is lived, and as it might be lived, and as it ought to be lived.

This seriousness of purpose, combined with rare skill and a determination to continue "pushing out toward the limits—my own and those of the medium" have established Le Guin as a major artist, exploring a unique vision of human life. (pp. 175-79)

Susan Wood, "Discovering Worlds: The Fiction of Ursula K. Le Guin," in Voices for the Future: Essays on Major Science Writers, Vol. 2, edited by Thomas D. Clareson, Bowling Green University Popular Press, 1979, pp. 154-79.

Richard F. Patteson

[*The following excerpt is from an essay originally presented at the International Conference on the Fantastic in Literature and Film in 1980.*]

Hardly any aspect of life in Ursula Le Guin's Earthsea archipelago is untouched by belief in the essential wholeness or interrelatedness of the universe. This philosophical undercurrent, with its obvious ecological implications, has made the trilogy popular with adults. Robert Scholes remarked that Le Guin's metaphysic "is entirely responsible to modern conditions of being." It is, he continued, characterized by "a reverence for the universe as a self-regulating structure." This sort of cosmology in turn is akin not only to oriental religions but to the view of the universe being developed by modern physics. Yet despite these interesting complexities, the Earthsea trilogy remains primarily a tale for children, and the real key to its popularity must be sought in its attraction to younger readers. Le Guin's strategy is to fuse elements of the fairy tale and the epic romance into a narrative design of great emotional force. Narrative patterns often convey meaning directly, without the mediation of discursive explanation. Bruno Bettelheim demonstrated how this process works in fairy tales, and I follow his example here. The Earthsea trilogy is a carefully fabricated fantasy, not a true folk tale, but by judiciously selecting particular fairy tale and romance motifs to shape that fantasy, Le Guin fashioned a story with profound psychological reverberations as well as esthetic and intellectual appeal. (p. 239)

Like traditional fairy tales, [Le Guin's fantasy of Earthsea] speaks directly to children and adults in a symbolic language of archetype and plot. Translating this language involves both exposure of the trilogy's narrative design and a discussion of the design's psychological import.

The romance structure of the Earthsea trilogy should not be distinguished too sharply from fairy-tale features, since the fairy tale itself is essentially romance. But the general contours of romance, as defined by Northrop Frye and his legion of followers, provide a convenient framework for examining the larger, overall plot of the trilogy. Everyone who has read Frye's work knows that romance narratives can be divided into three parts: preliminary adventures (the testing and maturation of the hero), conflict (frequently including the hero's apparent defeat), and triumph over adversity. Frye argued that the romance pattern is fundamental, because it articulates the way we visualize human life: "Romance is the structural core of all fiction: being directly descended from folktale, it brings us closer than any other aspect of literature to . . . man's vision of his life as a quest." If human life is the paradigm for romance narrative, the three parts of romance can be seen as roughly corresponding to three periods in life itself—youth, maturity, and old age. The first phase of romance focuses on youthful adventures; the second, on major achievement; and the third, on wisdom.

Most romances are anchored in one or two of these phases. A few, such as the Earthsea trilogy, fully exploit the resources of all three. Although each volume of the trilogy is self-contained and has its own romance plot, each is also an extended episode in the epic of the whole. As a single great tale, the Earthsea trilogy concerns the role of the hero Ged in reuniting a kingdom long divided and ushering in a new golden age of peace among men and harmony with nature. *A Wizard of Earthsea* chronicles Ged's youth (the first phase of romance) and details preliminary adventures and crises. The Shadow that Ged looses on the world in this volume prepares the reader for greater, although similar, evils later in the story. The fragment of the Ring he obtains makes him eager to find the other half, for without the joining of this talisman the archipelago itself, long fragmented, can never be rejoined. *The Tombs of Atuan* provides the trilogy with both a major struggle and a glimpse of Ged at the height of his powers. Here Ged descends into the underground realm of the dark forces (a common motif in romance), rescues the young girl Tenar, and retrieves the other half of the Ring of Erreth-Akbe. In the context of the whole epic this last action is the crucial one that makes possible the trilogy's happy conclusion. *The Farthest Shore*, a fine example of "third-phase" romance, reveals Ged as Archmage of all of the islands, ripe with wisdom, once again doing battle with evil. In this volume the overall plot is brought to a successful (and for the young reader, satisfying) conclusion when Ged's protegé, the youthful Prince Arren, is crowned king, restoring the political harmony that must correspond to the balance in nature.

The first volume of the trilogy, then, tells the story of Ged's youth—his preparation for great deeds; the second brings to life one of those deeds—the struggle on which everything in Ged's world depends; and the third highlights Ged's ultimate triumph. All three phases of romance, and all segments of the romance structure, are represented. But within this larger design, other patterns can be detected. Each volume contains its own smaller romance plot. In *A Wizard of Earthsea,* for instance, Ged's life on his home island, his coming to Roke, and his loosing of the Shadow constitute the preliminary adventures, the testing of the hero. His long battle with the Shadow is the major conflict, and his defeat of it by giving it his own name (recognizing evil as a part of himself) is his victory. In *The Tombs of Atuan* Ged and Tenar undergo a simultaneous but different set of adventures; they join to do battle with a wicked priestess named Kossil (who is allied with the dark forces), and together they win out. A similar configuration characterizes the third volume, in which Ged and Arren set out to discover why wizardry is declining, undergo a series of trials, find the source of the problem in a mage who uses his powers for evil, and finally defeat him.

This pattern, which shapes both the trilogy and the individual volumes, must be especially meaningful to a child. Finding himself in a world not yet familiar, much less secure, the young reader can clearly identify with a hero who faces a seemingly unending series of obstacles or crises. In the major struggle all opposing forces symbolically coalesce and are defeated by Ged, who by this time has discovered within himself sufficient resources to confront life's larger conflicts. The final stage, celebration of Ged's victory, is somewhat foreshortened in all three volumes, but it is still important. This is particularly true at the trilogy's conclusion, when the kingdom is reunited with young Arren on the throne. The equilibrium both in nature and in the body politic has been put right. Attainment of a kingdom is a key feature of fairy-tale literature, as Bettelheim pointed out. The child, through the character with whom he identifies (in this case Arren), comes into his own at last. Even more important, however, is Ged's restoration of the natural balance, since from this point on the external world can be seen not as enemy territory but as a home in which it is possible to live.

One central theme of romance narratives has a more particular psychological significance. The hero's adventures frequently constitute an initiation rite in which he learns, specifically, how to develop and exercise power both over himself and over the world without. It is through these powers that the hero discovers his identity. The adaptability of themes like this to children's literature should not be underestimated. They strike such a responsive chord in children because they are, as Frye said, so basic to human experience.

If the romance pattern in general appeals to the child's imagination, the particular features of the fairy tale do so even more forcefully. Bettelheim, in his *Enchantment,* argued persuasively that fairy tales, "unlike any other form of literature, direct the child to discover his identity and calling, and they also suggest what experiences are needed to develop his character further". They hint "that a rewarding, good life is within one's reach despite adversity—but only if one does not shy away from the hazardous struggles without which one can never achieve true identity". This is precisely the lesson that Ged and the other child-heroes (Tenar, Arren) learn in the Earthsea trilogy. Le Guin's work, in fact, contains a number of the distinctively fairy-tale elements discussed in detail by Bettelheim.

A Wizard of Earthsea is the closest to "pure" fairy tale of the three volumes. On the most basic level it is the story of a boy who rises to become Archmage of Earthsea. Since the islands have been without a king or central government for centuries, the Archmage is, in effect, the archipelago's highest-ranking personage. Le Guin carefully filled in Ged's background with details calculated to make him more recognizable, and his story therefore more pertinent, to the ordinary child. His family situation, which corresponds closely to that of many fairy-tale heroes, is extremely important. Bettelheim observed that parental figures often come in pairs—good and bad—in which the child can see reflected ambivalent feelings toward his own parents. Sometimes the "bad" parent is merely absent—the mother or father who is not there when needed. Frequently, though, that figure is present but negligent or even hostile. In Ged's case both factors are evident. His mother "died before he was a year old," and his father "was a grim unspeaking man" who "made him work as

a smith's boy, at a high cost in blows and whippings." Ged's fairy godmother, his mother surrogate, is an aunt who teaches him the rudiments of the wizardry that will eventually make him strong and powerful. This obviously reinforces the child's confidence in the efficacy and dependability of his mother's nurturing. Similarly, Ged is provided with a father figure—Ogion the Silent, the Mage of Re Albi—whose teachings are a continuation of the aunt's. Ogion further instructs Ged, preparing him for the day when he will leave his home island and sail to Roke for formal schooling in wizardry. Despite an inadequate family situation, Ged finds both the mother and the father that he (and every child) needs to help him grow and mature.

Other aspects of Ged's early life also conform to fairy-tale patterns. Like a number of folklore heroes, Ged finds he has special talents that set him apart from the rest of the children. He is eager to develop these abilities, in part to compete with his peers, over whom he otherwise would have no advantage. More relevant to his gradual discovery of himself, however, is Ged's learning his true name. In the world of Earthsea, "the Old Speech" is "that language in which things are named with their true names". Magic consists in "the true naming of a thing," for to know that is to know its being, its real nature beyond all illusory appearances. Ged cannot know himself without knowing his own true name. As an infant he is called Duny by his mother, and that remains his "use-name" until he begins to be called Sparrowhawk by other children. The name change also has its parallel in fairy-tale tradition. Bettelheim remarked that the young hero is "often called simpleton" by parents who "do not think well enough of him". In one fairy tale ("The Three Feathers") the boy is called Dummy. Not much of an imaginative leap is required to get from "Duny" to "Dunce" or "Dummy," particularly since Duny's father calls him "fool". It may be only a linguistic coincidence that Duny's true name, Ged, is only a vowel away from "God"; if so, the coincidence is a happy one. The neglected, abused Duny (a character in whom most readers cannot fail to recognize parts of themselves) becomes after a long period of difficult ordeals Ged, the Archmage with almost godlike powers.

The trials Ged must undergo begin even before he leaves his home island, when he inadvertently calls out the Shadow that will later hunt him to the ends of the Earth. Ogion dispels the Shadow, but it gives Ged a foretaste of the dangers to come. When his studies with Ogion are completed, Ged sets out toward Roke, the Isle of the Wise, to continue his pursuit of knowledge. Ged realizes that neither Gont, the island of his birth, nor Roke can ever be called home. He is the quintessential fairy-tale youth—cast adrift, homeless, in search of a place in life to call his own.

One more fairy-tale element in *A Wizard of Earthsea* is worth mentioning. While studying on Roke Ged acquires an animal companion, a small mammal called an "otak." The otak remains with Ged at all times, providing companionship and occasionally assistance of a more tangible sort. This faithful animal may be connected symbolically with the figure of the mother. At one point, after a nearly fatal visit to the underworld, Ged lies close to death. The otak licks his temple: "Later, when Ged thought back upon that night, he knew that had none touched him when he lay thus spirit-lost, had none called him back in some way, he might have been lost for good". Here, as in the tales cited by Bettelheim, the animal performs a nurturing function; it does the kind of thing a child would normally expect a mother to do.

Although Ged—now grown to young manhood—is still the "hero" in *The Tombs of Atuan,* the primary subject of the trilogy's second volume is a girl's search for her identity. Once again, a character's true name is central to the question of identity. Tenar, at the age of six, is taken from her real parents, renamed Arha, and made high priestess of the dark powers of the Earth. These powers, like the forces of light, are necessary to the universal balance, but they are not meant to be worshipped, as Tenar later learns. Her awakening occurs slowly, however. Only when she recalls her true name, Tenar, is she able to reject the dark powers of Atuan and go forth with Ged into the world of men and women.

Tenar's family background, like Ged's, is significant. She barely remembers her real parents, but she strongly feels their absence. For Tenar the maternal relationship is particularly important; in the Atuan temple complex she has two surrogate mothers—the gentle, wise Thar and the sinister, jealous Kossil. We have already seen that this pattern is common in fairy tales. Bettelheim interpreted the two figures as "the all-good mother of infancy and the all-bad mother of the oedipal crisis". True to this scheme, Le Guin contrived for Thar to die first, leaving Tenar in the clutches of Kossil. But the teachings of Thar protect Tenar (just as the teachings of his aunt protected Ged) until she is strong and resourceful enough to gain her independence.

At this point Ged enters the story in search of the other half of the Ring of Erreth-Akbe, which is presumably hidden beneath the Tombs of Atuan. Tenar has mixed feelings about her role as priestess of the Tombs, but until Ged's arrival she has been unable to think seriously of escape. The plot here assumes the damsel-in-distress configuration so familiar in fairy tales, but Le Guin's lesson is not only that a woman needs a man's help to survive; they need each other. Their escape from the Tombs is a joint venture; indeed, without Tenar's aid Ged could never have retrieved the missing fragment of the Ring. Far from being an unfortunate example of sexism, this episode is a vivid model of part of the growth process. It begins, as Bettelheim put it in his *Enchantment,* "with the resistance against the parents and fear of growing up, and ends when youth has truly found itself, achieved psychological independence and moral maturity, and no longer views the other sex as threatening or demonic, but is able to relate positively to it". This is exactly what happens to Tenar. Her learning to trust Ged (whom she at first feared) is an essential part of her maturation—her evolution from a helpless child dependent upon elders to a young woman capable of functioning in a wider world.

The Farthest Shore follows much the same formula as *A Wizard of Earthsea.* As in the earlier volume a young boy sets out to prove himself, endures a series of tests, and fi-

From Tehanu: The Last Book of Earthsea, *written by Ursula K. Le Guin. Illustrated by Margaret Chodos-Irvine.*

nally achieves a brilliant triumph. Arren, like Ged before him, seeks his identity, and as much as Ged he needs support from parental figures. This time the real parents are neither dead nor hostile, but they are far away, and Arren looks to Ged, now Archmage, for encouragement and instruction. Also like Ged, Arren possesses special talents—in this case the courage and wisdom necessary to rule—although he long remains unaware of these qualities. Arren considers himself ordinary, and he stands in awe of the great Archmage. But Ged recognizes in Arren the king whom the archipelago has awaited for centuries. Once more a youth finds that he has become an adult. The dominant psychological thrust of fairy tales, from Bettelheim's point of view, is the movement from chaos and danger to order and safety. Children find in stories like this a dramatization of their progress beyond a world in which others protect (or fail to protect) them to a world in which they can take care of themselves. That is why the motif of inheriting a kingdom looms so large in children's literature. At the end of *The Farthest Shore* Arren, instead of returning to the security of his father's house (for which he has longed), goes to Havnor, ancient capital of Earthsea, to assume his adult responsibilities and be crowned King of All the Isles.

The Earthsea trilogy, both in its epic entirety and in each of its parts, contains the features we usually associate with romance plots—testing of the hero through preliminary adventures, descents into an underworld, a major climactic conflict, and victory over a powerful enemy. These elements by themselves can easily be seen as a model of a child's struggle for security and a sense of identity. But aspects of the trilogy that relate specifically to the fairy-tale tradition speak even more directly to the child's imagination. Moreover, Le Guin managed to present these ideas in different contexts: a neglected boy who attains high spiritual rank, a girl who learns how to grow up and live in the world, and a prince who comes into a magnificent inheritance. Each volume of the trilogy has a young person for its protagonist, but the hero of the work as a whole is Ged alone. Consequently, children who read the trilogy can identify not only with the youthful characters but also with a hero they see grow up and grow old.

The Earthsea trilogy's appeal to children cannot be divorced from its interest to adults. The philosophy of Earthsea, with its emphasis on an integrated universe, an ecological and social balance, is closely related to our infantile perceptions of the world in which we live. Northrop Frye contended that the dragon killing typical of chivalric romance "suggests a civilizing force gradually increasing its control over a turbulent natural order. The myth of Eden, similarly, suggests a final reconciliation with nature as something to be attained after the human community has been reordered." In the Earthsea trilogy, significantly, dragons are dangerous, and their ways are not the ways of humans, but they can be dealt with. Although Ged kills several in *A Wizard of Earthsea,* he quickly becomes a "Dragonlord" (one who can speak to the dragons in the original "Language of the Making") and strikes bargains with them. By the last volume human and dragon cooperate in defeating the evil mage who has upset the world's balance. Le Guin's dragons seem to stand not so much for the hostility of nature as for a nature in which savagery is a necessary part of the whole—something to be respected more than feared. Like so much else in Le Guin's trilogy, her dragons are probably of oriental lineage. In a recently published book on dragons [*Dragons,* 1979], Peter Hogarth and Val Clery remarked that "Chinese dragons, perhaps reflecting the humane simplicity and unaggressiveness of China's prevailing religion, generally preserved a unique benevolence toward mankind not found in either the chaos-born dragons of Near Eastern myth or in the malevolent creatures who were to terrorize medieval Europe." This different conception of the dragon is emblematic of deeper philosophical differences between oriental civilizations and what Le Guin called the "ecology-breaking" cultures that separate humans from nature. The restoration of balance—with the help of dragons—at the end of the trilogy corresponds to Frye's description of the Eden myth in other romance narratives. Everything in Le Guin's fantasy world is ultimately related, everything reconciled. Very young children, Bettelheim observed, have a view of the world similar to this. They believe that inanimate objects are alive, and that all things are related in some way to themselves. To the child, so recently out of the womb, the world is much more of a piece than it is to an adult. Le Guin's achievement in the Earthsea trilogy is that she encouraged children to grow and develop in the ways we have seen,

while reminding them that their youthful perceptions of the universe are not completely wrong. In this respect the Earthsea trilogy differs from traditional fairy tales, and herein also lies one major source of its popularity with older readers nostalgic for the holistic perspective of childhood. (pp. 240-46)

Richard F. Patteson, "Le Guin's Earthsea Trilogy: The Psychology of Fantasy," in The Scope of the Fantastic—Culture, Biography, Themes, Children's Literature, *edited by Robert A. Collins and Howard D. Pearce, Greenwood Press, 1985, pp. 239-47.*

Brian Attebery

What kinds of meanings are expressed in the stories of Earthsea? What questions are asked—and answered—by Ged's adventures? The questions are big, familiar ones. Who am I? in the first book. What is evil? in the second, and, alongside it, What is love? In the third book: What is death, and What does my life mean in relation to it? These questions are unanswerable in that there are so many answers to them that we can accept none as final or wholly satisfactory. But a work of fiction, especially a work of fantasy, can posit trial answers and, by eliminating certain of the confusions of actual existence, construct a world in which those answers seem complete, like a simulation game for philosophy. Then it is the reader's job to compare the simplified world with the world he knows and judge how accurately the abstraction represents reality.

The answer to the question, Who am I? is: I am Ged. Speaker, observer, maker of patterns, unleasher of evil, binder of evil—that is, man, in Earthsea at any rate. Because both question and answer are couched in story form they become personal and concrete. It is a matter of life and death to Ged to know what he is. And because the story is a fantasy we actually see the elements that make up Ged as they start to grow and connect with one another. One part is the witch-aunt who mumbles spells to call goats or influence the weather. Another part is the girl who wants to know about shape-changing and summoning the dead. Anther is the Zen-like master whose teaching is his own way of life. Another is the wily, fierce dragon, so much a part of nature that magic is its native tongue. Yet another is the fragile, graceful sailboat *Lookfar,* with eyes painted on its prow. And the fountain at Roke. And the small trusting otak on Ged's shoulder. And the falcon in whose shape he flees from Terrenon. And most of all the shadow, like a shapeless black beast, that he tames with his own name.

The answers in Le Guin's fantasy are coherent and cumulative. Once Ged knows who he is, he is able to explore the world around him and to sort it out into light, dark, loved, unloved, good, and evil. That is the adventure in *The Tombs of Atuan:* to accept the whole of existence and yet to align oneself with the better part of it. Again the issue is concretely symbolized: empty throne, dark labyrinth, prisoners starved to death, on the one hand; rune-covered ring, glowing wizard's staff, Tenar bringing water to unconscious Ged, on the other.

Armed with that knowledge of good and evil, knowing that both are human responses to the natural order, Ged is prepared in *The Farthest Shore* to make his own ultimate response. He pledges himself to maintaining the Balance, which is a metaphysical rendering of a concept more familiar to Americans from science. We know it as ecology—the sense that all things are related in a closed, finite system. It is a concept rather alien to most of Western philosophy: to our linear or progressive idea of history, to our notion of manifest destiny, to our image of an unbounded God, and to our man-centered system of values. The ecological concept has come to us primarily from scientific observation, and thus in a colorless and mechanistic form, but there are other cultural systems to which ecological theory would come as verification of a whole way of looking at and living in the world. Zen Buddhism offers one approach to an ecological viewpoint in its interlocking yin and yang, light and dark. Native American religion, based on circles of time and space, offers another. Primitive magic, which treats the universe as a living, powerful entity, offers a third. In *The Farthest Shore,* those world views are joined with a scientific understanding of natural cycles and interrelationships to produce a new literary myth, or myth-imitation if you prefer. The book is an attempt to express the emotional side of an intellectual truth, and, conversely, to validate a set of old beliefs with the stamp of scientific approval.

Le Guin does not just talk about Balance; she has Ged pledge his life to it. The old myths were not only pictures of the universe, but guides for living as well. Any successful world view must also provide for personal fulfillment. We can see the pleasure Ged takes in understanding the Balance and watching it at work, but at the end of the story, when he shouts the spell that may kill him but will heal the world, he achieves more than satisfaction. It is a moment of absolute commitment, beyond joy or sorrow, a moment of knowing without doubt the worth of his own life.

I have compared Le Guin's waste land to T. S. Eliot's, and her manipulation of symbolic action to that of Theodore Roethke. I might also compare her Americanization of Oriental philosophy to Gary Snyder's Zen-inspired poetry, and her way of drawing strength from the idea of death to Walt Whitman's. It is in poetry that we are used to finding such ideas tested against the immediacies of sensation and emotion. Le Guin's fantasies do, indeed, operate on a level of meaning that almost demands to be called poetic. Without falling into a mannered kind of prose poetry, she matches the orphic, prophetic quality distinctive to much of the best American poetry. She establishes patterns of metaphor and paradox that lead, of their own accord, to new insights into significant experience. And she is pursuing the same lines of inquiry that occupy most modern American poets. (pp. 180-82)

> *Brian Attebery, "After Tolkien," in his* The Fantasy Tradition in American Literature: From Irving to Le Guin, *Indiana University Press, 1980, pp. 154-86.*

Fred Inglis

Ursula Le Guin's way out of the arbitrary parallelism of

Now and Then is to make up a new world. It is the device of the science-fiction writer she is also, and *Earthsea,* though archaic and picturesque in a Yeatsian sort of way—'cold Clare rock and Galway rock and thorn'—is a science-fiction archipelago, a bleak, vivid reminiscence of Seattle and the Orkneys. . . . [Her] book both meets C. S. Lewis's test—adults may enjoy it as well as children—and convincingly holds together the ideal and the real world. That subject-matter includes far more than the fixed fight between the ideal and the real. Indeed, she gives children a way of acknowledging the uncertainty of both categories, and of understanding that the most universal of human gifts, language, is also the most wonderful.

She does so, at times, in a dauntingly high-minded tone:

> He looked for a spell of self-transformation, but being slow to read the runes yet and understanding little of what he read, he could not find what he sought. These books were very ancient, Ogion having them from his own master Heleth Farseer, and Heleth from his master the Mage of Perregal, and so back into the times of myth. Small and strange was the writing, overwritten and interlined by many hands, and all those hands were dust now. (*A Wizard of Earthsea,* p. 61)

The hand is the hand of Mrs Le Guin, but the voice is her master's voice, the familiar compound ghost who speaks through and for Alan Garner, Susan Cooper, Judy Allen, Rosemary Harris, and all. Ursula Le Guin speaks to a wide audience. . . . She speaks to her audience, I think, on behalf of intelligence, and its struggle to command, however precariously, the surging and unquenchable magic of language itself. She is, after all, an anthropologist and the daughter of anthropologists, concerned with the human science above all. She makes language, as it always was and is for·Magi, the special preoccupation of her hero-intellectual. She sends him to university—the island of Roke—and she makes his access to learning the slow, difficult initiation by rite and discipline which for an intellectual it must be. She makes thought a rare vocation, which it is, although she fails to add that those so called to the vocation take the thought in trust for others (the phrase tells); a proper wizard is a man of the people who look up to him, *and* he serves the human mind and its unique responsibility towards the 'living principle' which is given form and regulation in language.

Her books are spare and stark, consciously wrought and shaped. They smell, sometimes intolerably (as [Alan] Garner's books do), of the study and the library stack; like their fellows they lack not only colour and eventfulness, but also a depth of characterization in which the author is hardly interested, but which it is simply unimaginative and therefore morally unsympathetic to suppose her audience does not count on. With Yeats, she wants to make a 'great magic book of the people', to simplify landscape to cold stone and thorn, character to hawk-like and sinewy purpose, eschatology to the self, pitching in the huge swell of empty seas. Time and again, her brief, rapid, striking tale gets onto the stilts of the epic movie—'the great oars shot out . . . the rowers bent their strong backs'—and a Goodies pastiche—'I do not understand.' 'That is because my lord Benderesk has not been wholly frank with you. I will be frank. Come sit by me here'. Never mind. The best events in these books—the first and last splits Ged causes in the universe, the last defeat of the dragons, the two passages through the valley of the shadow of death, the rescue of the mistress of Atuan—these are set pieces of grand storytelling.

The larger moral climate they move in is abstract and austere. Ursula Le Guin rescues Idealism and its magic grammar from its role in children's novels as a measure of the dreariness of the present day, and restores it to its importance at the heart of intellectual life. She leaves children out of it, gives the action back to the Shaman-Magus, and simply assumes that the children will follow such a man—he starts out a boy—wherever he goes. Her ideal world of Earthsea is, for all its archaism, a recognizable and real world—it has its Cities of the Plain, its plague, treason, and debauchery, as well as the lean, brown, long-striding wizard. (pp. 245-47)

> Fred Inglis, "Rumours of Angels and Spells in the Suburbs," in his The Promise of Happiness: Value and Meaning in Children's Fiction, *Cambridge University Press, 1981, pp. 232-50.*

Barbara J. Bucknall

[Taoism] is something really essential to Le Guin's view of life, and it recurs throughout her work. Journeys and marvels are quite consistent with Taoism. Legend has it that Lao Tse disappeared from sight, at the end of his life, while on a mysterious journey, and later Taoists were alchemists and magicians. But it is not Taoist magic, which was largely sexual and concerned with obtaining long life, that Le Guin describes in the Earthsea trilogy. Searching in her unconscious and relying on impressions of magic received from her reading in childhood, she comes up with a type of magic more consistent with the teachings of Lao Tse than the Taoist magic actually was. (p. 36)

These stories are ageless because they deal with problems that confront us at any age. They are about attaining maturity and self-knowledge, a theme for which we are never too old. (p. 37)

[The] battle between light and darkness . . . recurs throughout the Earthsea trilogy. Here, light and darkness stand for good and evil, as they do traditionally. They also represent the polarities of life and death, knowledge and ignorance, wisdom and stupidity, the power to act and the impotence of possession. What they do *not* stand for is God and the devil, concepts that are absent from the Earthsea trilogy. . . .

The Earthsea trilogy is an atheistic fairy tale. But the struggle between the powers of the light and of the dark is taken with quite as much seriousness as if Le Guin were a Christian. (p. 41)

[At the end of the trilogy,] Ged has faced his shadow, his anima (or feminine archetype), and death in turn. In Jungian terms Ged performs the deeds that every man has to perform in the course of his life if he wishes to be whole.

This is also a very Taoist, as well as a Jungian, conclusion. (pp. 61-2)

In the last part of his life, having lost the magical power that was all he desired, Ged becomes a true Taoist sage, living only for contemplation. Completely reconciled to life and death, he disappears into the unknown, beyond the ken of all who knew him, like Lao Tse. The Earthsea trilogy is the work in which Le Guin has expressed her Taoism most artistically. It is also her greatest achievement, because the philosophical message is perfectly expressed in poetic metaphors that do not have to be recognized as metaphors by the reader but can be accepted simply as part of an exciting story. This means that someone who is reading purely for pleasure, without any thought of learning from a book, takes in her message almost unconsciously. In no other work of Le Guin's are form and content so completely inseparable. (p. 62)

> Barbara J. Bucknall, in her Ursula K. Le Guin, *Frederick Ungar Publishing Co., 1981, 175 p.*

Sue Jenkins

Two of the most important strands in Ursula Le Guin's ideology are the Jungian concept of universal archetypes and the Taoist idea of balance or equilibrium between complementary forces throughout creation. These are interwoven in complex and subtle ways that condition both the structures and themes of her fiction. The Earthsea Trilogy in particular embodies her peculiar vision or awareness of the processes of human maturation in terms derived from these two systems of thought.

The Earthsea Trilogy is High Fantasy; that is, the actions depicted in the stories take place in a secondary world of the author's invention, and involve an irreducible element of the "impossible" or "unreal." Causality in Earthsea is magical causality, and the most powerful and important members of that society, in the absence of an heir to the throne, are those who wield the Art Magic. LeGuin asserts the importance of the Equilibrium at an early stage in the trilogy; she is concerned with re-emphasising it in the closing stages:

> The world is in balance, in Equilibrium. A wizard's power of Changing and of Summoning can shake the balance of the world. It is dangerous, that power. It is most perilous. It must follow knowledge and serve need.

> The word must be heard in silence. There must be darkness to see the stars. The dance is always danced above the hollow place, above the terrible abyss.

The similarities and differences between these two quotations are important both thematically and structurally in the Earthsea stories. Insofar as they both assert the same philosophy, the idea of balance, they state the underlying philosophical or moral background against which the development of the individual protagonists is worked out. The first statement is made *to* the young Ged, when, in his teens, he is too impetuous and self-willed to accept or fully to understand what he sees as a restriction on individuality and self-fulfillment. The second is made *by* him many years later, for the instruction of the younger Arren and as an expression of how completely the reality of the Equilibrium and its imperatives have become part of his personal growth and awareness. To this extent, the two quotations show how thoroughly bound up with each other are the two concepts of maturity of the individual and the maintenance or sustaining of the Equilibrium of Creation, in Le Guin's imagined world. There is a profound sense in which the identification of oneself as on the side of, as a supporter of, "good" or Light and, through these, of Equilibrium, is equivalent to growing up, becoming mature, autonomous, responsible. Although it seems to the immature and arrogant Ged that he is merely being asked to fit his individual abilities and potential into a pre-existing system without consideration for his personal need, the mature Ged, the Archmage, can see the free-will decision to fit into that system as a valid way into maturity and freedom. He is able to embrace and contain the paradoxes inherent in that notion. Superficially it may seem that he has only consented to "behave well" according to a preconceived and conventional system of belief. But in fact both the value system and the individual are validated and revitalised by this meeting, within Ged, of identity and morality. Each individual's insight and realisation changes the system; the system provides the measure and sounding-board for the emerging individual. There is a close parallel and an unbreakable link between the two decisions which Le Guin sees the emerging individual consciousness making. In the outer, social sphere, the maturing person has to decide on his or her commitment to the Light, and through that to the sustaining of the Equilibrium. This, like the choices of the folk-tale or epic hero, will involve a denial of self-interest and a dedication to some quest or task of importance to others, possibly to the whole society. In the inner or psychic dimension too, the themes of light and darkness emerge. (pp. 21-2)

[Within] the individual there must also be an Equilibrium; the dark, or in Jungian terms the shadow side of the individual, must be in an active and constructive balance with the light or conscious side. According to Fred Inglis, "identity and morality cross"; successful integration with society, positive response to the moral or social imperatives outside oneself, cannot be reached without integration between the apparently opposed elements within the self. The story of Earthsea is the story of the acquisition of that balance and integration by three different individuals. It also shows, in the personal stories and in the wider adventures and descriptions of society, how the balance may be threatened or disturbed and what the consequences of that disturbance might be.

Le Guin was expressly asked to write for younger readers when she produced the Earthsea books. She records in the essay **"Dreams Must Explain Themselves"** her own view of what the trilogy is about and why its themes are important for older adolescent readers. She feels that the dominant theme of the first novel, *A Wizard of Earthsea,* is that of coming of age, growing up. In *The Tombs of Atuan* the theme is more specifically the adolescent's need to come to terms with sexuality. The third book, *The Farthest Shore,* deals with acceptance of death. These themes are undeniably important; but in another sense all three nov-

els are about coming-of-age. The growth to self-awareness, inner integration, and commitment to "something outside itself, beyond itself, bigger than itself," is delineated three times; once in the story of Ged's struggle with his shadow, once in Tenar's fight to regain her true self, and again in the story of Arren's quest to the dark land where he grows sufficiently in stature to fit the throne he is heir to. In each case there is an imbalance or lack of awareness in the protagonist that reflects or threatens to contribute to an imbalance in the outer world. In each case the protagonist must take positive steps to correct both the outer and inner imbalances; by going on a quest, by making a new commitment, by broadening his or her awareness. (p. 23)

Ged's quest for his shadow teaches him the futility of over-violent action and self-assertion. He learns to accept the dark side of himself, the destructive possibilities that can only be effectively controlled by humble acceptance of them and by their integration into the total personality. In the wider sphere of relationships with the rest of creation, he learns the value of restraint and of balancing the needs and desires and rights of others with one's own impulses. Clearly Le Guin feels that this is a vital step toward self-awareness for the adolescent. The first stirrings of a real sense of the individual self, of its potential power for effective action in society, join with the energy and enthusiasm of youth to plunge young people into what may be violent, aggressive, and rebellious activity. There is frequently a rejection of the values associated with tradition, such as Ged directs towards his teachers. Le Guin tries to express for the young reader the senses in which true maturity involves establishing a sense of proportion, and in which discipline and self-control are not self-repressive, but self-developing. Awareness of and sensitivity to the lives of others, the attitudes of others, is a vital part of this. The loyal friendship of Vetch and the way in which Ged grows up sufficiently to allow himself to lean on that friendship, gives moving expression to that idea. Le Guin shows deep compassion for the suffering of Ged, but makes it clear that he brings it on himself by his refusal to cultivate these qualities of awareness and responsiveness. She evidently feels that youth cannot be allowed to go on being an excuse for the willful abuse of power in a way that brings harm to the young individual himself and threatens harm to the rest of society. The Archmage Gensher sternly tells Ged that he is in danger of being possessed by the Shadow—of becoming a servant of evil. So Ged learns that power—adulthood—carries with it responsibility and duty, and that freedom itself is shaped by the necessary limitations each must impose upon his or her actions. The Master Summoner puts this into words for him:

> " . . . the truth is that as a man's real power
> grows and his knowledge widens, ever the way
> he can follow grows narrower and narrower;
> until at last he chooses nothing, but does only
> and wholly what he *must* do . . . "

Ged is still only nineteen years old at the end of *A Wizard of Earthsea;* but he has won the battle for identity and integration:

> . . . Ged had neither lost nor won but, naming
> the shadow of his death with his own name, had
> made himself whole; a man; who, knowing his

> whole true self, cannot be used or possessed by any power other than himself, and whose life therefore is lived for life's sake and never in the service of ruin, or pain, or hatred, or the dark.

The story of *The Tombs of Atuan* is the story of Tenar's escape from the service of the dark. Tenar is priestess of the Nameless Ones, believed to be the reincarnation of the One Priestess who has served these dark forces for thousands of years. Her willing service to this cause, which subsumes her to such an extent that she loses her individual name and identity, becoming Arha, the Eaten One, shows that the imbalance in her nature is the opposite of Ged's. There is too great a dominance of the dark, the negative, the passive. She is, like the fairy-tale protagonists described by Bruno Bettelheim, in an enchanted sleep of paralysis of the will and loss of purpose. She is Sleeping Beauty or Snow White. Applying Bettelheim's schema, Tenar and Ged can be seen as embodying the two characteristic features of adolescent experience, ". . . periods of utter passivity and lethargy alternating with frantic activity. . . ." Her journey to adulthood is a journey towards the light and towards accepting the necessity of integrating the light with the dark; the mirror image of Ged's progress. In Taoist terms, he is *yin* and she is *yang;* he is the active, light, forward-reaching principle traditionally regarded as masculine, but present within both male and female. She is the dark, passive, conserving force traditionally regarded as female, but also present within both female and male. The balance of these two forces *is* the Equilibrium. Tenar lacks all confidence in herself, all true sense of her own identity, and hides in the darkness and apparent security of the only place she knows. Ged, who has never known these lacks in his own psyche, breaks into her private world and literally takes her out of herself, out of the dark, out of the Place of the Tombs, to experience the fuller possibilities of life. So she has help that Ged did not have; he is the only one of the three Earthsea protagonists who is forced to learn through the bitter pain of his own mistakes—which is, perhaps, what gives him the authority and the strength to help in turn at the emergence to adulthood of Tenar and Arren.

The imbalance within Tenar is linked with an imbalance in society, the existence of which brings Ged to Atuan and motivates the story. In Tenar's keeping in the Treasury of the Tombs is one half of the Ring of Erreth-Akbe. This arm-ring, missing for many years, is broken in such a way that the Lost Rune, the Rune of Peace, is also broken where it is engraved on the ring. Ged, having retrieved the first half in a side-adventure during the Quest of the Shadow, comes to try to retrieve the second half and bring peace to the lands of Earthsea. So at the climactic point where Tenar willingly surrenders her half of the ring to Ged and helps him to rejoin the Rune, there are many levels of symbolism coming into play. Ged's words have many applications; "It is whole now as if it had never been broken."

On an obvious, surface level this refers to the physical mending of the ring itself; in terms of the wider society, it is peace that has been restored to wholeness; but in terms of the personal maturation of Tenar, it is her identity that has been mended, restored, healed. Although Le

Guin does not describe or hint at any physical relationship between Tenar and Ged, it is presumably the sense in which Tenar's healing is dependent upon her response to Ged that leads the author to assert that the novel is "about" sexuality. It is essential that Tenar trust Ged, that she respond warmly and positively to him, if they are to escape from the Tombs and really give Tenar the chance of a new life and the ring a chance to function properly as a force for peace and Equilibrium. She cannot imagine any other possibilities for herself; all hinges on her being moved by her personal response to Ged, as Sleeping Beauty is moved by the Prince's kiss. In the person of Ged, Tenar confronts everything that is outside herself, bigger than herself, more important than herself. It does not seem appropriate to speak of her as "falling in love" with Ged. Nevertheless there is deep significance in their relationship in terms of her personal growth to maturity. A turning point comes shortly before they escape from Atuan in Ged's boat *Lookfar.* Tenar is assailed by misgivings and fear and, in a temporary revulsion against Ged, prepares to kill him as he meditates. This negative reaction to her new freedom is psychologically accurate according [to Erich Neumann in *The Great Mother*]:

> In reality we are dealing with the existential fact that the ego and individual that emerge from a phase of containment, whether in a gradual and imperceptible process of development or in sudden "birth," experience the situation as rejection. Consequently we find a subjective experience of distress, suffering and helplessness in every crucial transition to a new sphere of existence.

Tenar is momentarily aware only that she has lost the security of the familiar world of her childhood, and she turns on the person whom she sees as the instrument of that loss. Her next step is to learn the double nature of freedom and maturity—the burden of responsibility for the self.

> A dark hand had let go its lifelong hold upon her heart. But she did not feel joy. . . . She put her head down in her arms and cried. . . . She cried for the waste of her years in bondage to a useless evil. She wept in pain, because she was free.

> What she had begun to learn was the weight of liberty. Freedom is a heavy load, a great and strange burden for the spirit to undertake. It is not easy. It is not a gift given, *but a choice made,* and the choice may be a hard one. The road goes upward towards the light; but the laden traveller may never reach the end of it. (Italics added.)

"A choice made"; a choice in which morality and identity cross; a choice in which Tenar, by committing herself to another person, and through him to the supra-personal cause that he serves, forges another link in the chain of her developing self, takes another step along the road to maturity.

In *The Farthest Shore,* Arren's story is not one of the correction of an imbalance; at the beginning of the book he is a pleasant and attractive adolescent, warm and impulsive—he is moved to swear fealty to Ged during their first conversation—open and sociable:

Arren was an active boy, delighting in games, taking pride and pleasure in the skills of body and mind, apt at his duties of ceremony and governing, which were neither light nor simple. *Yet he had never given himself entirely to anything.* (Italics added.)

The story of Arren's growth is to be the story of dormant potential released and developed. At the end the boy becomes, as Ged in his wisdom foresees, the King. This is significant on two levels. In order to restore lasting peace on the outer or social level, there must be a king to fill the throne that has been empty for eight hundred years. Identity and duty cross; in order to fill the throne adequately, Arren must grow up—must give himself. On the inner, or psychic level, the business of becoming a king in a fairy-tale or fantasy stands for becoming adult, integrated, for fulfilling one's potential. Bettelheim says: "There are so many kings and queens in fairy tales because their rank signifies absolute power, such as the parent seems to hold over his child."

Arren is at first content to think of himself as a servant or assistant to Ged in his quest to restore the disturbed Equilibrium that threatens the existence of Earthsea. He has, naturally, no awareness of the deeper implications of the quest for himself in terms of personal growth; and he remains delightfully unaware of his public destiny until the closing scenes of the story, when Ged kneels to him before the people. The reader is given an early clue when a student at the school for Wizards on Roke quotes the prophecy of Maharion, the last King; "*He shall inherit my throne who has crossed the dark land living and come to the far shores of the day.*" Le Guin packs into the story of the crossing of the land of the dead, both the meanings of her tale. To cross the dark land living is to come to terms with the knowledge of one's own mortality. To inherit the throne is to achieve maturity as well as to become king in the literal, political sense. Balance is restored to Earthsea by the same series of acts that establish for Arren his understanding of the balance between life and death and his own role in the unending cyclical pattern of growth and decay.

This series of events, the story of the novel, serves to carry forward both tales at once. On one level, Le Guin traces Ged's quest to reestablish the balance that the evil mage Cob has destroyed. This theme in itself is a complex one and reveals how far from simplistic is Le Guin's understanding of psychology. For within this strand of the story, Ged himself is seen to be still learning, still failing, still striving towards the elusive maturity and growth that Arren assumes so great a man must have achieved long ago. In fact, the imbalance in the Equilibrium must be said to be Ged's responsibility. It was he who, in a fit of resurgence of the arrogant pride that in his youth released the Shadow, punished Cob for summoning the spirits of the dead by driving him into the place of the dead. Cob's resultant terror of death is what leads him to open the gap between the lands of the living and dead in his desperate search for immortality. So it is Ged's personal quest to restore the imbalance Cob has created.

For Arren, as for Tenar, growth is stimulated and devel-

oped in terms of a deep personal response to Ged. Indeed, all three young protagonists could be said to grow through love for Ged. Ged learns, in subsuming his negative shadow into himself, the vital importance of self-acceptance, of self-love. Tenar is initially attracted more to Ged himself than to the idea of freedom from her enclosed life in the dark. Arren passionately devotes himself to Ged; and the story of the evolving love he feels for the mage, of *its* maturing, is the story of his own developing awareness.

There are several stages in this love story. Arren, like Tenar, goes through a period of disillusionment, during which he rejects Ged and feels let down or cheated by him. He has to face up to the human limitations of his hero and learn to accept him as he is. This rejection episode is much more strongly developed than is the corresponding one in Tenar's story. Arren's misery and sense of loss are very deep. In both episodes Ged is lying helpless, at risk because of his companion's hostile attitude. Whereas Tenar almost stabs Ged while he is in meditation, Arren leaves him unattended and feverishly ill from a wound sustained in the course of the quest. This is an example of Le Guin's use of the folktale technique of externalising aspects of one personality in various characters. She blends this with the realistic novelist's method of representing distinctive individual characters, but at times the externalising is obvious. Ged's helplessness while the two young people go through their periods of darkness and despair strongly suggests that Ged here stands for the positive and growth-seeking principle within them which is paralysed by fear of the unexpected turn of events that has laid on them the awful duty of taking responsibility for themselves.

There are three key moments in Arren's relationship with Ged that express clearly his growth and development. The first is when he first swears allegiance to Ged on Roke:

> But now the depths of him were wakened, not by a game or a dream, but by honour, danger, wisdom, by a scarred face and a quiet voice and a dark hand holding, careless of its power, the staff of yew that bore near the grip, in silver set in black wood, the Lost Rune of the Kings.

This is genuine emotional response, but along with the fervour of adolescence it displays the idealisation, the loading onto the individual person of all kinds of symbols of impersonal concepts like honour and wisdom, that typify hero-worship. Ged is a great man; but at this stage he seems to Arren to be greatness embodied, to be perfection. To follow him will be enough. Arren has to unlearn this and the process is painful. . . . (pp. 24-30)

But there comes a third time when Arren looks at his friend, and this time he sees a good deal:

> He stopped, but in his eyes as he looked at Arren and at the sunlit hills there was a great, wordless, grieving love. And Arren saw that, and seeing it saw him, saw him for the first time whole, as he was.
>
> "I cannot say what I mean," Ged said unhappily.
>
> But Arren thought of that first hour in the Fountain Court, of the man who had knelt by the run-

ning water of the fountain; and joy, as clear as that remembered water, welled up in him. He looked at his companion and said, "I have given my love to what is worthy of love. Is that not the kingdom, and the unperishing spring?"

Arren's new understanding of his friend, like his eventual accession to the throne, is seen as a restoration; he recalls the first moment of his love for Ged, and feels again what he felt then. But now he is more self-aware, and his love is more balanced. He feels for Ged as he really is, not for the idealised Ged he first saw. And the whole of this moment of insight is charged with Arren's new awareness, learned from Ged, of the inevitability of death, of its part in the Equilibrium as the opposite pole to life. Learning that the two can only exist in and through each other, he learns to transcend them, moving beyond despair at the thought of mortality to an informed and conscious alignment of himself with optimism and growth. He has learned to give himself to something, and in so doing has achieved self-knowledge and self-control.

The path to maturity is not represented by Le Guin as easy; but the ultimately triumphant note of the trilogy sets it forth as inspiring and attractive, and for some adolescents may provide encouragement during a turbulent period of life; ". . . Ged had neither lost nor won but, naming the shadow of his death with his own name had made himself whole . . ." (pp. 30-1)

> Sue Jenkins, "Growing up in Earthsea," in Children's literature in education, *Vol. 16, No. 1, Spring, 1985, pp. 21-31.*

Lois R. Kuznets

Stated as tersely as possible, the "Arthurian myth of male development" belongs not to the mythic but to the romance mode as defined by Northrop Frye. It depicts an adolescent rite of passage in terms of the quest of an unacknowledged son for the phallic sword and or uterine cauldron or grail. These objects, and particularly the sword, will establish his true identity, enabling him to restore order and fertility (symbolized by the cauldron) or purity (symbolized by the grail) to a domain grown chaotic and fallow under the rule of his aging and enfeebled father. . . . This concept, stated thus baldly, is controversial, but, I think valid for [this discussion]. (p. 27)

[Le Guin's] relationship to the Arthurian myth of male development is even more complex [than that of Susan Cooper and Lloyd Alexander]. First I want to contrast the first and third books in the [Earthsea] Trilogy, *A Wizard of Earthsea* and *The Farthest Shore,* and then return to the second, *The Tombs of Atuan.* The first book is not about the development of a new king, but about his helper and prophet, the magician or wizard—in this case, Ged. This topic is not generally treated in Arthurian material, although there are a few legends about Merlin extant. Le Guin is clearly not using that material, but she approaches Ged's development in a manner that is, nevertheless, not new to fantasy. Like a number of nineteenth-century fantasists, Mary Shelley among them, Le Guin explores in Ged's development the concept of the *Doppelgänger,* the double, the other self. In doing so, Le Guin acknowledges

the influence of Jungian ideas; this is perhaps one of the reasons why she differs from these nineteenth-century fantasists in several essential ways. They traditionally tell a tale in which the protagonist somehow lets loose upon the world his dark self and, in recognizing it, is either destroyed or totally alienated from the community. Le Guin, in Ged's development, adds to the drama of separation and recognition of the "dark side" a kind of therapeutic re-integration of dark and light which also means re-integration of Ged into the community. The story of the *Doppelgänger* in Le Guin's hands is thus neither a story of personal disintegration nor of rebellion against society's strictures against self-expression—as it tends to be in some earlier non-Jungian versions—but an ameliorative identity crisis from which Ged emerges a sadder but a better man.

In the third book of the Trilogy, *The Farthest Shore,* Ged becomes the Merlin-like figure who aids the young prince Arren to find his own identity as the high king of the Earthsea archipelago. There is no mystery about Arren; he is already aware that he is a king's son; yet, although the sword he wields turns out not to work against the living-deadman Cob, the Arthurian myth still lingers in the sense of testing and pre-destination. Arren will become the redeemer of a fallow land. Arren's crisis is not the deeper identity crisis of Ged, who must unite in himself the dark and the light, nor even the uncertain groping of Taran for his true calling [in Alexander's Prydain Chronicles]. Rather, like Bran's [in Cooper's "The Dark Is Rising" series], it is finally a test of physical endurance under mental stress—while Arren tries not to be seduced by the idea of

Le Guin at her desk.

179

eternal life which Cob holds out. In Arren's opting for mortality and for the hard job of governing, we have an ameliorative ending to a story of development which is quite orthodox in its use of the romance-quest. Ged's development is not. Unlike Alexander, Le Guin does not seem particularly American in her handling of the traditional material.

It often passes unnoticed that most of the sympathetic characters in *Wizard of Earthsea* are not white, including Ged, whose skin is a kind of coppery red-brown color. In race-conscious America, this casualness in coloring is, in itself, an important statement. Protagonists of the next two novels are, however, the white Tenar and the rather golden Arren and, in relation to them, Ged becomes not only the traditional magus but the good dark guide, a not-so-uncommon figure in American literature. Incidentally, accompanying this slipping back into a certain kind of color stereotyping is a really insidious commercial subversion of Le Guin's intention in that the latest illustrations in the Bantam editions show Ged as white.

If I am anything other than eclectic in my critical stance, I am a feminist. This means that I cannot let this topic of Arthurian male development pass without commenting on the effect it has on the depiction of female development. Both Cooper and Alexander create girl characters who have some potential for development that is for the most part ignored, even though the young women participate to some extent in the action of these stories. (pp. 30-1)

This failure to deal with female development is, of course, not particularly surprising: patriarchal myth becomes patriarchal romance which, in turn, becomes patriarchal fantasy. As Joseph Campbell points out about the great archetypal plots: they are all concerned with the struggles of "the hero with a thousand faces" for "the mastery of the universe," and of the heroine with a thousand faces, "to be the mastered world"—clearly not equivalent developmental roles. Yet, although the symbol of the belligerently masculine sword is often predominant, the symbol of the life-giving cauldron, before it became the *eternal* life-giving grail, left some place in the romance-quest for the female principle at least, and gives hints of the earlier importance of fertility goddesses. Recent scholars are working more insistently with the idea that there are still other universal plots which involve female goddesses and female development, stories that were suppressed at some time in human history. . . . Cooper's *Greenwitch*, which depicts a female fertility rite, and Le Guin's *The Tombs of Atuan* are quite fascinating in that they both incorporate powerful female nature deities of the type that are featured in those suggestive fragments of female myths that remain to us.

Neither book, however, really uses the potential in these plots to make new roles for the young women. *The Tombs of Atuan* is especially disappointing since in telling Tenar-Arha's story it actually depicts the suppression of a female cult. But it devolves into the typical rescue story of the maiden in distress—and compounds the anti-feminism by having her rescued from female captors in a uterine cave rather than from the traditional male captor in the phallic tower. Ged helps Tenar destroy her own cult, leaving in-

tact the rival male cult which is in conflict with it. He also convinces her that the earth spirits that she worships (here not identified as female as they usually are) are evil and she should abandon them. The all-female community (except for eunuchs) in *The Tombs of Atuan* is endowed with a menace not at all evident in the all male school for wizards that Ged attends. Women do not automatically write feminist books, especially when they are using mainly the traditional materials of a patriarchal culture. (pp. 31-2)

> *Lois R. Kuznets, " 'High Fantasy' in America: A Study of Lloyd Alexander, Ursula Le Guin, and Susan Cooper," in* The Lion and the Unicorn, *Vol. 9, 1985, pp. 19-35.*

Jane Yolen

Ursula Le Guin's *Earthsea* trilogy concerns a young wizard Sparrowhawk who overplays his magic and loses his shadow on the land. It takes him three books and many adventures to reintegrate himself and thus save his world from the destructive force he has set in motion. Described that way, the trilogy sounds like a dry parody of Jung crossed with the Tao. Yet Le Guin, one of the genre's finest prose stylists . . . sweeps the reader along with her gnomic prose and her anthropologist's eye for detail. A masterful storyteller, she might be describing her own writing when one of the great mages tells Sparrowhawk: "To light a candle is to cast a shadow."

> *Jane Yolen, in a review of "The Earthsea Trilogy," in* Book World—The Washington Post, *December 7, 1986, p. 7.*

Michele Landsberg

The publication of *A Wizard of Earthsea* in 1968 immediately established Ursula Le Guin as the leading writer of fantasy in North America; her invention of a "secondary world" is second only to Tolkien's (if that) in richness, detail, consistency, and fascination. (p. 177)

A fantasy writer, in creating an wholly fabricated world, spins a web of imagination that is easily torn. A clumsy word, an anachronism, an accent of "Poughkeepsie," and our eager belief is fatally torn. Le Guin, however, never puts a word wrong. Her prose is vigorous, precise, clear, and sturdy enough to sustain a whole archipelago; even at her most incantatory (" . . . this was the way he was to follow all his life, the way of magery, the way that led him at last to hunt a shadow over land and sea to the lightless coasts of death's kingdom . . . ") she does not embarrass her readers with a falsely exalted tone. Her mages speak with the kind of runic simplicity that delights young readers while it illuminates her mode of thought: When Sparrowhawk, impatient for more dazzling feats of magical power, asks Ogion, "When will my apprenticeship begin, sir?" Ogion answers, "It has begun." "But I haven't learned anything yet!" "Because you haven't found out what I am teaching."

What Ogion is teaching is restraint and moderation, the search for the innate Balance and Pattern in all creation. But Sparrowhawk wants more, and rashly uses a spell to raise the dead. "Looking over his shoulder, he saw that something was crouching beside the closed door, a shapeless clot of shadow darker than darkness." Ogion rescues him from the nameless nightmare that Sparrowhawk has summoned, but deeply reproves him: Danger surrounds power as shadow does light, Ogion tells him, and he sends his headstrong pupil at last to the school of wizardry at Roke to learn the High Art.

A school of wizardry offers almost unlimited scope to a gifted writer, and Le Guin makes the most of it; we are shown in fascinating detail what Sparrowhawk learns, and it is the densely realized detail that is enchanting: the lessons in shape changing, the spells over wind and weather taught by Master Windkey, the long hours in the Isolate Tower under the stern tutelage of the Master Namer, who teaches them the thousands of true and hidden names of things in which real magic inheres.

Unlike most fantasy writers, however, Le Guin does not equip her hero with nifty weapons and send him out to defeat evil in one great clanging battle. Sparrowhawk-Ged's true battle is with himself. Time and again, arrogance and ego lead him to rash acts of excess. His enemy is the dark thing, "the shadow," the Archmage tells him, "of your ignorance, the shadow that you cast." (pp. 177-78)

One reason the fantasy never loses its grip on our attention is Le Guin's power to create intensely attractive male heroes. Ged's potency is admirable rather than bellicose and repellent. His maturity is not that of a warrior or conqueror, but the maturity of a man who recognizes and leashes his aggression. His tenderness is the movingly gentle gesture of a man of great power and self-knowledge.

The second story in the trilogy is equally compelling and even more tautly written. In *The Tombs of Atuan,* the scene shifts to a distant, dusty island of the archipelago where an order of priestesses presides over ancient rituals in the place of ancient tombs. Images of ruin, dryness, and emptiness predominate in LeGuin's evocation of this grim place. As usual, details of food, work, materials, and crops, herbs, and songs appear naturally, unforcedly, in the narrative. And this is a convincingly three-dimensional world, in which all these details accord. You always know, with Le Guin, that if the local people eat corn porridge, there will be cornfields, workers who must draw water for the fields, a ritual and a pattern for the watering and harvesting, and a sharp feel for the taste of the thing.

Tenar, the peasant girl chosen in infancy to be Arha, the Eaten One, the high priestess of the Tombs with their dark gods, is the heroine of the story. By the time she reaches the age of fifteen, we know her fierceness, her somber resolution, and the deeply buried gleam of defiance in her character that will lead her, with Ged's help, to shatter the ancient maze of underground tombs and find her freedom. The clutch of a fearful religion on a young soul is shown this powerfully in only one other children's book that I know of: *The Blue Hawk,* by Peter Dickinson, in which a boy, Tron, is doomed to priesthood in an equally baleful ancient order. Like Tenar, he, too, is freed at last with the help of his own questioning mind and of a young man on a quest of his own.

But as a story of a young womanhood bursting the bonds

of repression, *The Tombs of Atuan* is unique, reverberating with archetypal echoes that Le Guin herself recognized as Jungian only some years after writing the book. And though Ged is at his prime in this book—gentle, knowing, profoundly resigned—it is friendship, not sexual love, which he offers the struggling Tenar. All his magic is placed at the service of her emergence from the suffocating, impersonal dark. "You told me to show you something worth seeing," says Ged, imprisoned in the tombs by the priestesses, and ordered by a hostile Tenar to create a magical illusion. "I show you yourself." Later, when the two have escaped, Tenar wakes outside the temple compound on a hillside, filled with sweetness and pleasure. "Living, being in the world, was a much greater and stranger thing than she had ever dreamed." Though Tenar naturally is drawn romantically to her rescuer, Ged, the impulse is unexpressed except for one sentence ("What was in her heart as she looked at him in the firelight she could never say"). This reserve deepens the impact of the story, mirroring a truth in the lives of young girls and leaving Tenar as the center of energy and action in a story that is open-ended.

The last book in the trilogy, *The Farthest Shore,* is the most complex and least satisfying; perhaps that is inevitable, since its subject is the confrontation of the aging Ged, now Archmage, with death itself. The sense of confusion in the philosophical underpinnings of the story is reflected in the first falterings of Le Guin's pristine language: There are more "Aye, lad" slips into strained dialogue, and the overwhelming aura of moral disorder and decay is disheartening. But the book is distinguished by the most original and magnificent dragons in literature, ancient and thunderously immense creatures whose eyes glitter with a remote and ironic amusement at the doings of men. (pp. 178-79)

Michele Landsberg, "Fantasy," in her Reading for the Love of It: Best Books for Young Readers, *Prentice Hall Press, 1987, pp. 157-82.*

Michael Dirda

Perhaps no modern work of fantasy has been more honored and loved than Ursula Le Guin's Earthsea trilogy. Though marketed as young-adult novels, *A Wizard of Earthsea, The Tombs of Atuan* and *The Farthest Shore* are as deeply imagined, as finely wrought, as grown-up as any fiction of our time. They deserve that highest of all accolades: Everyone should read them. *Tehanu: The Last Book of Earthsea* unexpectedly turns the trilogy into a tetralogy; though less sheerly exciting than the earlier books, it may be the most moving of them all.

The earlier novels describe the life of Sparrowhawk, whose secret name is Ged, from youth to maturity, each installment in the sequence focusing on a particular moment of crisis. In *A Wizard of Earthsea,* for instance, young Ged must master his dark half, so as to pass from childhood to maturity. The other two books deal with—what else?—sex and death. Archetypal imagery predominates—light and dark, labyrinths, night journeys. The prose is grave and elevated, a style of moral seriousness to match these soundings into the soul's journey through life, the voice that of the chronicler or mythmaker: "But in the Deed of Ged nothing is told of that voyage nor of Ged's meeting with the shadow, before ever he sailed the Dragon's Run unscathed, or brought back the Ring of Erreth-Akbe from the Tombs of Atuan to Havnor, or came at last to Roke once more, as Archmage of all the islands of the world."

At the conclusion of *The Farthest Shore,* Ged journeys to the land of the dead, battles his greatest enemy and heals a crack in the world's fabric. In so doing, he uses up all his mage-power. He returns to the wizards' stronghold at Roke clinging to the back of the ancient dragon Kalessin, bestows a blessing on the young companion who will become king, and then vanishes into the mists of legend.

Or does he? This is where *Tehanu* begins. A mage no longer, Ged is a broken, emptied vessel, another poor guy who's lost his job after 30 years and doesn't know what to do with himself or what remains of his life. All he can think to do is go back to his childhood home on the island of Gont. But what becomes of a hero, a superman once he's grown old and lost his power?

In Tennyson's poem the old Ulysses sails off into the sunset, to certain death, proclaiming heroic verse: "To strive, to seek, to find, and not to yield." But Ged feels nothing of this, only shame and fearfulness. His particular powerlessness Le Guin naturally associates with the general condition of women. As a result, *Tehanu* enlarges its focus to take up again the story of Tenar, once priestess of the Tombs of Atuan, but now a middle-aged farmer's widow who has put all magery behind her and chosen the classic path to happiness: To live unknown.

An artist who has lost his power, a woman who has refused any: Together they shape *Tehanu* into a study of two people coming to terms with age, weakness, mortality. (pp. 1, 9)

Throughout the earlier *Earthsea* books Le Guin emphasized the importance of balance, of integrating shadow and self, of trust; she examined the nature of power and how it shapes us, seducing us to its own ends. These same themes reappear in *Tehanu,* but with a darker, more realistic edge. We are done with journeying and boys' adventures. This is a woman's world, a realm of socially imposed weakness and of male stupidity, of child abuse and evil with a human face. It is also a tale, not of an individual hero, battling to save himself or his realm, but of a family in the making, trying to live quietly, coming to terms with what abides after much is taken. It is consequently meditative, somber, even talky.

As such, *Tehanu* may be a little too autumnal for many young people. It is in fact a kind of pastoral, almost a woman's novel like *Cranford,* where most of the characters are women: the naughty old witch Aunty Moss (right out of Frost's "Witch of Coos"), the kind-hearted Lark, the bright as a button Apple, the envious crone Ivy. All, though, are finally "good" where most of the men prove wanting at best and usually actively malevolent. And for all its quietness, *Tehanu* builds to a climax of almost pornographic horror, nearly too shocking for its supposedly young adult pages.

Yet, maybe because it is a fantasy, all comes right in the end. Therru turns out to be much more than a burned little girl: As Ogion said on his deathbed, "They will fear her." But then sharp readers will have suspected as much, those who remember that Odin paid for wisdom with an eye, that dragons, the wisest of beasts, live in fire, and that wholeness embodies a balance of light and dark. The least shall be made great.

Some critics feel that in recent books Le Guin's writing has grown windy and soft, too feminist, too mythic, too preachy. Certainly this book is pointedly feminist and the motivation of its male villains a little fuzzy. But make no mistake. Le Guin can still stand your hair on end with her sentences. At one point Ged and Tenar balance on the edge of a stony cliff high above the sea, awaiting almost certain death. Made mute by a spell, Tenar unexpectedly points up to the sky. Her enemies mumble something about an albatross. Then Tenar "laughed aloud."

"In the gulfs of light, from the doorway of the sky, the dragon flew, fire trailing behind the coiling, mailed body. Tenar spoke then."

" 'Kalessin!' she cried, and then turned, seizing Ged's arm, pulling him down on the rock, as the roar of fire went over them, the rattle of mail and the hiss of wind in upraised wings, the clash of the talons like scytheblades on the rock."

At the end of *Tehanu* a new world seems dawning, and there is obviously much more to tell, especially of Therru. But we can guess her future, as well as Ged's and Tenar's. Still, it would be wonderful if this were not in fact our last visit to Earthsea. (p. 9)

> *Michael Dirda, "The Twilight of an Age of Magic," in* Book World—The Washington Post, *February 25, 1990, pp. 1, 9.*

Robin McKinley

[*Tehanu: The Last Book of Earthsea*] is a story of loss, of the unfairness of fate and of people's carelessness and cruelty to one another and to their world. And yet it is also a story of joy, of finding brightness behind the shadow, of learning to look.

Tehanu is a major novel by a major novelist. It is deceptively short, and written in a deceptively simple style. It is also another tale of Earthsea, the realm made famous by Ursula K. Le Guin's early trilogy . . . [The prizes won by those works] explain why the new novel is being published as a children's book. . . . But this label, and the publicity sheet that came with the book, declaring that *Tehanu* addresses "issues of aging, feminism and child abuse," are doing the novel no favors. Ursula Le Guin is an important figure in American letters, so *Tehanu* has a much better chance of finding its audience than a similar one by a lesser-known, or more genre-bound, author. But the excellence it contains transcends the glib, false packaging of "children's book" or "sociological novel."

It isn't that *Tehanu* is not about aging, feminism and child abuse; it is just that saying this is like saying that *Bleak House* is about judicial corruption and *Tess of the*

D'Urbervilles is about postal error. *Tehanu* is a novel rich in the ways of humanity. Some of that richness works within the genre of fantasy, for here there be dragons, and Ms. Le Guin's dragons are some of the best in literature.

But the characters here are not on fire with the grand, world-threatening passions that we are accustomed to in much traditional fantasy. By those standards *Tehanu* is unbearably sad. It requires a certain quietness of mind—a quietness the wizard Ogion would approve of—to recognize and appreciate the subtler world-threatening passion here.

As *Tehanu* begins, Tenar, the middle-aged widow of a farmer, receives a message that Ogion, her old mentor, is dying and has called for her. She sets off to visit him, taking with her Therru, the abused child she has rescued. As Tenar sits beside him Ogion dies, speaking his last words about Therru's fate. His death leaves his house empty, so Tenar decides to stay in it.

The wizard had hoped that his favorite student, the one called Sparrowhawk, might also return to him once more, and Tenar believes she might ease Sparrowhawk's grief by telling him of Ogion's death herself. When she was a young priestess trapped in the Tombs of Atuan, she had known Sparrowhawk as Ged, the wizard of Earthsea, the Archmage of Roke.

Ged does return, magnificently, on the back of a dragon. But he tumbles unconscious from his terrifying perch. As Tenar nurses him back to health, he clings to some unnamed sorrow more bitter than the loss of Ogion.

The very best thing about this novel is its sense of growth, of distance traveled as well as time passed. The Earthsea trilogy is deservedly considered a classic. Ursula Le Guin shows courage in writing a sequel to an accomplished series that demonstrated the full but traditional intellectual and magical gifts of wizards who were always male. The astonishing clearsightedness of *Tehanu* is in its recognition of the necessary and life-giving contributions of female magic—sometimes disguised as domesticity. This book would be admirable and evocative by itself, but it has the advantage of the resonance it gains from the three that went before, and our memories of them. *Tehanu* isn't a children's book. Young readers of the Earthsea trilogy should be obliged to wait a decade or two before they read it. Adults may read the quartet as a finished work.

> *Robin McKinley, "The Woman Wizards's Triumph," in* The New York Times Book Review, *May 20, 1990, p. 38.*

Meredith Tax

Therru, a little girl crippled by the sadism of her father and his friends, is the center of [*Tehanu: The Last Book of Earthsea*] One of Therru's eyes is blind, one hand has been burned into a claw, and half her face is a hard mask of scars. "They raped her and beat her and burned her; these things happen, my lord," says Tenar, who takes care of her. "These things happen to children." It could be a story from Child Abuse Hotel or Crack House Street. It could be the story of Lisa Steinberg.

But it isn't. Because, suddenly, there are dragons. And they make all the difference. *Tehanu: The Last Book of Earthsea* is about child abuse, but it is also about the common heritage and uncertain borderline between humans and dragons. It is about power: male power and what happens when it's lost; female power and how no one knows what it is; and the mysterious, fragile power of Therru, the burnt child.

And it is a children's book. People in this country are rather strict about the boundary between children's and adult's literature, but I have never felt completely at home on either side of that divide. I read most kinds of novels, classic, modernist, realistic, science fiction, "young adult," detective stories, depending on my mood. Why eat a steak if what you really want is a peach? When I feel anxious, sad, or needy, when I long for a world simpler and cleaner than my own, where the individual's ability to affect events is a given, responsibility is clear, and morality is more important than success, then I read fantasy. These qualities are, of course, found in religious literature as well; the end of *Tehanu,* in fact, reminds me of that moment in Milton's *Samson Agonistes* when the hero's torment turns suddenly, out of all reason, to power and transcendence.

Milton? Aren't we getting a bit grand for "kiddielit," as it is called in the trade?

Don't be fooled by marketing categories. The *Earthsea* books are children's literature like the *Odyssey* and *Beowulf* are children's literature. Composed sparely, shaped by narratives so basic they must be inscribed upon our cells, they read as if they were not written but found, dug out like jewels from rock.

Each tale in the *Earthsea* trilogy is an extended metaphor. *A Wizard of Earthsea,* concerning young Ged's flight from, then pursuit of the Shadow he has arrogantly called up from the netherworld, is about overcoming childish grandiosity, accepting one's mortality along with one's strength. *The Tombs of Atuan* tells of Ged's rescue of Tenar, and her efforts to escape the dark goddesses she has been raised to serve—the struggle to emerge from the darkness of childhood fears and irrationality, to learn to think clearly, to find the light of civilization and friendship. *The Farthest Shore* is the tale of Ged's fight against a monstrous, immensely powerful egoist willing to send everyone in the world to death that he might live forever.

The battle is so grueling Ged loses his own powers in winning it, but he also finds and tests the young king who will bring order to the world.

The Farthest Shore, published in 1972, was supposed to be the end of the series. Now there's *Tehanu,* which takes up where the last book left off, but is a different kettle of fish entirely. The first Earthsea books are linear, gestural, full of action; this one is talky and abrupt, doubling back on itself, full of unresolved menace, without closure. Its heroes wait, hide, and flee; they have no power to fight. The first three books lay out the answer to the problem of evil with some confidence (lack of balance); this one asks, like Gertrude Stein on her deathbed, "What is the question?"

The answer to the missing question has already been revealed. Since Ged has lost his powers, the wizards who keep balance in the universe need a new Archmage. One of them has a vision, "a woman on Gont," the small island where Tenar and Therru live. But what does the vision mean? A woman cannot be Archmage; this would be a contradiction in terms. What can the question be to which the answer is a woman?

Tehanu is a feminist deconstruction of heroic fantasy, Le Guin's critique of a younger, simpler self, who, as she told me recently, took as her model Tolkien, the great breakthrough writer who legitimized the form, "though he was heir to a long, purely male tradition of heroic adventure fantasy. My Earthsea trilogy is part of this male tradition—that is why I had to write this fourth volume. Because I changed. I had to show the other side."

Feminism has made heroic fantasy—and a number of other classical literary modes, not to mention social relations—impossible, without developing alternative modes to put in their place. Like the worker in Brecht's poem who asked, "Who built the seven gates of Thebes?" Le Guin asks, by implication, who did the dishes for all those feasts in Tolkien? And how can any of us—even men who share housework—be heroes when we have to spend so much time caring for house and children? And without heroes, how can evil be defeated?

So many questions. Some feminist writers try to substitute female knights in armor for male, but that doesn't work for me. What works is books that ask questions of myth, like Christa Wolf's *Cassandra,* Leslie Marmon Silko's *Ceremony,* and the fiction of Ursula Le Guin. Le Guin is a prophet unhonored in her own country. Oh, she is honored (one Horn Book Award, one Newbery Medal, three Hugos, one National Book Award for Children's Literature), but as a writer of genre books—the ones you find under "Science Fiction" or "Children" instead of "Literature."

Le Guin disdains such boundaries. "I am always trying to break down walls," she says. She writes science fiction, fantasy, *New Yorker* stories, young adult books, poetry, and essays. Almost all her work is political. This fact has not been noticed too much by the people in charge of standards—you know, the guys who set the value of books, the literary equivalent of the Federal Reserve system. Of course, they think the political novel is dead anyhow, and they aren't about to recognize one that pops up in the wrong part of the bookstore. They expect political writing to be set in the real world, and Le Guin's is set in a universe of possibility. . . .

[In *Tehanu*] one has the sense of an evil growing stronger, of a good barely able to defeat it. Who is there to stand against the dark but Ged, a wizard who has lost his power, and Tenar, a woman who gave hers up to marry and have kids? It is no accident that the central symbol of *Tehanu* is a burned, abused child.

But this is fantasy, so there are dragons. And in Le Guin's dragons, as in Tolkien's, lies much of the satisfaction of her universe. There is also the homespun American purity

of her language. For, as she says in one of her essays, in fantasy, style is everything:

> There is no borrowed reality of history, or current events, or just plain folks at home in Peyton Place. There is no comfortable matrix of the commonplace to substitute for the imagination, to provide ready-made emotional response, and to disguise flaws and failures of creation. There is only a construct built in a void, with every joint and seam and nail exposed. . . . Where the act of speech is the act of creation. The only voice that speaks there is the creator's voice. And every word counts.

Kid stuff? Sure, if all adults need are stories of mundane cleverness and failure, small loves and missed connections. Children's literature, sure, if children are the only ones who need stories that remind us of the firelight flickering on the walls of the cave.

Meredith Tax, "Fantasy Island," in The Village Voice, *Vol. XXXV, No. 44, October 30, 1990, p. 75.*

John Clute

[*A Wizard of Earthsea*] which traced the life of the Archmage Ged from birth to early manhood, seemed from the first as polished and word-perfect a tale for older children as could be imagined. Nor did its sequels, *The Tomb of Atuan* and *The Farthest Shore,* diminish in the slightest one's sense of Le Guin's achievement.

Nor, again, did it seem, after she moved on to other things, that she had left the Earthsea trilogy incomplete. Like any "High Fantasy" saga of more than sensational interest—like, for instance, Tolkien's *Lord of the Rings,* which Le Guin's sequence emulates in small—the Earthsea books are at heart tales of ontology, quests for the true meaning of the roots of the world. In language almost any child over ten will comprehend, the three tales also work as a song of praise.

Ged the Sparrowhawk's progress from wild boy to Archmage of all Earthsea is an epic of contemplation, a progress from uncontrolled action to the immobility of the sage. In the first volume, Ged learns that his every act jostles the Equilibrium which governs the plenitude of Earthsea, whose archipelagos and sheltering seas are a ravishing dream of the Earthly paradise. In the second, he and a young girl, Tenar of Atuan, re-forge a ring whose wholeness will enable the kingdoms of the world themselves to re-unite after aeons, in imitation of the Long Dance of Being. In the third, some final and profoundly unChristian lessons are taught: that time is a cycle, that death is inevitable, and that the Long Dance, which occurs at the shortest day of the year, is performed over the abyss. In the end, having given up his power, Ged retires to his home island, to contemplate (we guess) things in themselves.

None of this seems undeliberate, or lacking in wholeness, and *Tehanu: The last book of Earthsea* comes therefore as a kind of shock. This is clearly deliberate. The first half of *Tehanu* is a forcible—and at times decidedly bad-tempered—deconstruction of its predecessors. It is a statement that the wholeness of the trilogy is an artefact and an imposition, because the order which expresses that wholeness is inherently male. That the centre of the world no longer holds is evident enough, and social dissolution threatens; but for Tenar of Atuan, now middle-aged and a widow, as a "mere" woman, there is nothing new in a world gone blind and deaf. Earthsea has always been a man's world, as defined in the harsh, abstractly rational cadences of the father's tongue; and has always been blind and deaf to the weave and shuttle of women's talk. So Tenar must dodge and hide; she must protect her ward, Therru, whom men have ravaged. Ged (who is nothing like the Ged of the trilogy) sulks because he is powerless, but comes at last to Tenar's bed, where she teaches him what wizards cannot know. We now learn that the absence of females of power from the trilogy derives, not from conventions of storytelling to which Le Guin adhered and which the reader therefore did not notice, but from the fact that wizards cannot have sex. Finally, young Therru, whose scarred face has seemed from the first dragon-like, saves Tenar and Ged from the last of the death-denying wizards, and herself turns out to be the new shaper of Earthsea.

Tehanu ends, therefore, in a sudden flush of the old magic. But most of it, told deliberately in the chuntering rhythms of the disfranchised women of Gont, has a slightly sour effect on the reader. It is not that Le Guin is wrong in her analysis of power, of the "dance of masks" which makes up man's world, or that it is inappropriate to create tales in which women live whole. But in the end one resents the corrosiveness of *Tehanu,* for in telling this particular tale Le Guin has chosen to punish her own readers for having loved other books she herself wrote.

> John Clute, "Deconstructing Paradise," in The Times Literary Supplement, *No. 4578, December 28, 1990, p. 1409.*

Elizabeth Cummins

The coming-of-age experiences depicted in each of the Earthsea novels represent journeys that are both physical and psychological. The crucial encounter for each of the three protagonists is with the temptations of the powers of darkness. The adolescents in each of the three novels are aided by wise men who teach them that part of becoming an adult is learning that they are an integral part of the network of existence which they must learn to respect by coming to know not merely the use of each thing but also its essence, its uniqueness.

The reader who completes Le Guin's fantasy trilogy returns from the journey through the text with a heightened awareness of the nature of the coming-of-age experience, of the interdependency of person and place, and of the significance of language. If the coming-of-age experience is thought of as a hero's quest, then the reader wrestles with a new aspect of the hero, the ability to know when not to act. Further, the reader has a new model to consider for the quest. It is not a single, adventurous journey but rather a lifelong journey from adolescence to old age through a series of changes. In addition to questioning the coming-of-age experience, the reader also reexamines the human relationship with the environment and the human ability to know and affect that reality. Le Guin's Earthsea em-

phasizes the interdependency among all existing things, certainly an ongoing concern for this planet and its advanced technological societies which make holes in the ozone layer, create radioactive fallout, oil slicks, and endangered species. Her world also emphasizes language, the human tool for learning about and affecting the environment as well as each other. The wizard's power of naming, the reader realizes, symbolizes the power of language to make reality; it is a tool by which humans participate in, cooperate with, or control reality. (pp. 10-11)

Each volume of the Earthsea trilogy tells a different story about the coming-of-age process. When viewed together, the completed trilogy provides Ged's life history, which is both a story of the epic hero who successfully deals with the forces that threaten the Equilibrium and the kingdom and a story of the epic hero as creative artist.

Each of the novels recounts a quest at a different stage in Ged's life. As a youth he hunted down the shadow which he released into the world; as a mature wizard he searched for the missing half of the Ring of Erreth-Akbe whose Bond-Rune ensures the king's successful reign; and as an old man he tracked Cob, who opened a hole in the world and returned from the dead. (p. 56)

Le Guin has emphasized the psychological qualities of the story in her selection of the key events of Ged's life to narrate. The reader learns, for example, that Ged's most famous deeds are not featured in the three novels. Instead of focusing on the public deeds, the deeds that ensured his sociopolitical role in external society, Le Guin examines the deeds which show Ged's inner struggles and psychological growth. After all, as Ged tells Arren in *The Farthest Shore,* heroes are "the ones who seek to be themselves".

As the life story of a wizard, the trilogy is also a story of the efficacy of art. In **"Dreams Must Explain Themselves,"** Le Guin discusses this meaning:

> I said that to know the true name is to know the thing, for me, and for the wizards. This implies a good deal about the "meaning" of the trilogy, and about me. The trilogy is, in one aspect, about the artist. The artist as magician. The Trickster. Prospero. That is the only truly allegorical aspect it has of which I am conscious. . . .
>
> Wizardry is artistry. The trilogy is then, in this sense, about art, the creative experience, the creative process. There is always this circularity in fantasy. The snake devours its tail. Dreams must explain themselves.

Ged should not be regarded as a disguised Le Guin; he is more like a muse for her, a model for the artist to aspire to. Le Guin has called him her guide in Earthsea. The magic of Earthsea, sometimes called "artmagic," depends, as does fiction, on the user's genius and knowledge of language. Like the work of art, the magic transforms reality. Patricia Dooley summarized the correspondences among magic, art, and the world: "Magic becomes a sophisticated metaphor for the ability of art to influence the experiential world through the insubstantial medium of the imagination." The magician, trickster, and Prospero are all creator-destroyers who shock and delight and edify.

Just as the life of the epic hero is developed in stages from youth to old age, so the trilogy also depicts the life of the artist-wizard progressively from youth to maturity. In *A Wizard of Earthsea* Ged becomes aware of his innate power and learns from his masters, as an artist learns from mentors, how to discipline it. Discipline of the imagination, Le Guin has written, "does not mean to repress it, but to train it—to encourage it to grow, and act, and be fruitful." Like Ged, the artist must have a fully developed knowledge of the self and will, in fact, find the journey into the self a creative connection between the conscious and the collective unconscious. Le Guin writes: "To reach the others, the artist goes into himself. Using reason, he deliberately enters the irrational. The farther he goes into himself, the closer he comes to the other." Ged learns to resist the easy roads to knowledge and power, the route of a Faustus or a formula novelist who barters away power or talent.

The artist-wizard, once sure of his talent, begins a lifelong search for names, the "right words," by which he exercises his power. "For me," Le Guin wrote, "as for the wizards, to know the name of an island or a character is to know the island or the person. Usually the name comes of itself, but sometimes one must be very careful: as I was with the protagonist, whose true name is Ged." In general, the power of language for the writer comes from the idea that if a thing can be named (be it an object, a theory, a tool, a psychological trait), then its existence can be dealt with, can be made a part of the reader's experience. The threat of the dragons of Pendor is solved when Ged can call Yevaud by its name; the threat of the shadow, of all that Ged fears and represses, is absolved into an acknowledged part of himself when he can name it, Ged. More specifically, in Le Guin's philosophy of life, the power of naming also lies in its ability to honor the thing which is being named. As T. A. Shippey has argued, Le Guin's emphasis on the word "is bound up with an attitude of respect for all parts of creation (even rocks), and a wary reluctance to operate on any of them without a total awareness of their distinct and individual nature." Shippey asserts that Le Guin thus critiques the modern attitudes of materialism and industrialization, which are anthropocentric. Shippey states that Le Guin puts the word above the thing, but it is more accurate to say that Le Guin regards them as equal.

A Wizard of Earthsea can be regarded as depicting the artist in apprenticeship, and *The Tombs of Atuan* depicts the mature artist confronting a hostile audience and gradually transforming that person's perception of reality. What Ged tells Tenar about the world outside the Place and the Kargad Empire is, to her, fiction in the sense that it is a very different world and one which she has never experienced. Her hostility toward his art is based on her false education and on fear. She is a disbeliever and sneers at his art as mere illusion. Le Guin wrote of such a hostile audience in **"Why Are Americans Afraid of Dragons?"** where she identified the "hardworking, over-thirty American male" in business as one who dismisses fiction, especially fantasy, because he has learned to repress his imagination. Ged assists Tenar by showing her beauty, joy, and light; he assists her by the words which reveal a larger, more humane world and by the word for her other self, Tenar.

The Farthest Shore depicts the artist toward the end of his life, assisting an entire country in dealing with a crisis of language. His action for the prince, the kingborn, is the same as that for Tenar; he gives assistance, offers stories of another kind of existence and a different system of values, and then allows the young prince to choose. All of Earthsea is threatened by the disbelief in artmagic; wizards are forgetting the true names of things and are losing their own true names, dragons lose the power of speech. The artist in his old age is the only one who can reestablish balance because, as Ged says of himself, "I desire nothing beyond my art". He is not vulnerable to temptation.

Ged's belief that there is no escape from death is carried to its logical extension when he retires at the end of *The Farthest Shore.* Powerful as artistry is, it cannot provide a permanent escape to another world. Artist and reader alike must also deal with the consensus reality which surrounds them and with the limits of time and power. No artist's power is permanent, and one who is tempted to believe that it is goes the way of Cob or Faustus. No artist's role as aesthetic and moral guide for the people is permanent. An artist, Le Guin suggests in this novel, may uphold the standards when the ruling powers are deficient, but such is not the permanent role of the artist. Le Guin is conscious of her own lapses into didacticism, i.e., when the message overpowers the story, when the artist begins "to preach" rather than allowing people the freedom they need to be transformed. So the trilogy ends with news of the coronation of Arren as King of Earthsea, and the reader's attention is focused on the social realm. Ged retires, satisfied and fulfilled. Given the difficulty with which he has learned the lesson of turning clear around, of always seeking to connect with his roots in his actions, the ending is—like all of his quest journeys—an open circle. He returns to his beginning, to Roke and to the life of contemplation which he had rejected as a young man. But he returns as a changed man. The creative process has also transformed the artist. (pp. 57-62)

Elizabeth Cummins, in her Understanding Ursula K. Le Guin, *University of South Carolina Press, 1990, 206 p.*

Ann Welton

Taken as a whole, the [three Earthsea] books sing. There is poetry in the literal sense, in the portions from "The Creation of Ea." There is also the deeper poetry of the truth being spoken with beauty, clarity, and economy.

With the memory of the first three books fresh, I approached *Tehanu* cautiously. How could it complete something already whole in itself? The answer is, quite simply, that it cannot. Le Guin's style is as pellucid as ever, and her plotting as strong, but *Tehanu* owes its parentage not so much to Earthsea, but to the short fiction and essays of the last fourteen years.

Le Guin says, ". . . until the mid-seventies I wrote my fiction about heroic adventures, high-tech futures, men in the halls of power, men—men were the central characters, the women were peripheral, secondary." What *Tehanu* provides is a working through, a statement, of issues of women's rights, the male power structure, and what Le Guin perceives as an imbalance in the yin/yang of current civilization. In a recent essay she states that, "Our civilization is now so intensely yang that any imagination of bettering its injustices or eluding its self-destructiveness must involve a reversal." True for planet Earth, but, even given fantasy as a creative form of addressing real world problems, these concerns slop over uneasily into Earthsea. A thought-provoking and necessary book in its own right, *Tehanu* differs markedly from the three previous books in tone and direction. . . . In *Tehanu,* women's power comes out of the closet. (p. 15)

The images of Earthsea, stumped in their inability to find an archmage to succeed Ged, had only the words of the Master Patterner to go on: "A woman on Gont." Therru is obviously that woman—and obviously, as far as the author is concerned, it is time for the power on Earthsea to pass from the men to the women.

The problem with all this is that though it follows from the other three books, it is entirely unlike in temperament and sweep. Tied by plot, characters, and intellectual issues, it is not linked in spirit with its predecessors. The fit is at best uneasy, and at worst unnatural, much like one of those grafted roses which shows so poor a match between root stock and blossom. The question of power and its use is certainly very much in evidence, is in fact debated and discussed much more openly in *Tehanu* than it is in *Earthsea.* But while the debate encompasses both the general employment of power and its proper use, at its center are the issues of male power over women, differences in male and female power, gender fear. (p. 16)

The center of the vortex in this novel, the person around whom all the action turns, is the burned child, Therru. Her character development is dark and minimal, stated but little shown. Yet she provides a powerful and pivotal symbol: a raped, abused female child, crippled physically and emotionally to the point that recovery seems a slim hope at best. Despite this, she has a latent and indominable power.

There are at least two levels to this symbolism. The first and most obvious lies in the identification that many adult and young adult readers of both genders, but generally female, will feel regarding both the sexual and physical abuse. A depressing percentage of our children, both girls and boys, will have experienced some form of sexual abuse by the age 18. Addressing this issue and naming it, and in the form of a fantasy in which the bibliotherapeutic element is unobtrusive, will speak to these young adults.

However, it is on the broad, analogistic level that Therru's state is best interpreted. The burned, abused child represents Everyone in the state in which she has been held by men. She has been made to be afraid, as Lark observes, because of men's fear of her. She has been made to think little of her power compared to that of men. Indeed, she has

been told that she is powerless. The entire thrust of the book indicates that the author believes that it is past time for both the oppression and the suppression to end. Ged himself, stripped of power and now a man among other men, recognizes and names the power that he sees in Tenar. "Lifegiver," he calls her, and indeed the female generative ability is part of the fear Western man has traditionally felt for women.

Jamake Highwater discusses in depth in *Myth & Sexuality* the mythic roots of women's loss of power in Western Civilization in what he terms "nothing less than a mythological conspiracy." Women can give life, can apparently create life out of their wombs, something that men cannot do. ". . . the Greeks worshiped the universal fecundity of the Great Mother at the same time that they reviled women. This love-hate attitude about women—the awe of their creative powers and the fear of their influence upon the young—gave enormous energy to the Greeks' leadership and religious authority." That this state of affairs has continued to exist, augmented by the teachings of the Christian church, to the present day is reflected in much of our common given "wisdom"—women emotional, men rational; women fickle, men trustworthy, etc. The polarization has been a tremendous source of loss, a failure to integrate the best each gender has to offer, and a missed opportunity, missed countless times, to find common, human ground.

So on Earthsea, it is time for the women to become not the mages, but what they are; for little Therru, the "woman on Gont" that the Master Patterner has seen in his vision, to take the reigns of power from the men, and to do with it something they cannot—affirm life rather than deny it. As such, Therru's lack of character development is comprehensible. She is not a person but a symbol.

As in the first three books, there is truth here. There is also an argument for the kind of equality of treatment and respect we'd all like to see, and for the end of the dichotomy of male power/female submission. What, then, makes the book basically unsuccessful? This: that it is not sufficiently of a piece with the trilogy to which it is attached. If the characters and *mise-en-scene* are borrowed almost entirely from Earthsea, the message comes from someplace else, and the effect is deleterious to both the *Earthsea Trilogy* and to *Tehanu.* It dilutes the strength and force of the former, while reducing the message of the latter to a form of axe-grinding. It is all too easy for the reader, eager to enter back into the world created in *A Wizard of Earthsea* or *The Tombs of Atuan,* to feel manipulated, tricked into reading something that is not what it purports to be. *Tehanu,* static in its plotting, and insistent on its message, is a largely philosophical work. What it says needs saying. It bears repeating. It is true. But it needs to stand on its own merits, not to be bound to a former successful work. While Earthsea is about men, *Tehanu*'s strength lies in the fact of its being a woman's book—about women, their lives, their concerns. These are the concerns, the "ordinary fears" that Tenar expresses to the Master Windkey. The large sweep is there, but on a domestic scale. It is a forum in which men may not find themselves at home, but one that women will identify with viscerally.

Prominent in the construction of *Tehanu* is the concept of polarization, binary opposition—man/woman; good/evil; life/death. The *Earthsea Trilogy* takes a less Western and more Oriental stand on these issues. Good and evil are not opposites, but complements, parts of a whole, and their constant interaction both creates tensions and leads to their resolutions. Similarly, a more productive view of the differences between men's and women's powers would be to see them as parts of a complementary whole, that neither is complete in itself. Men may, as Highwater comments, fear women's reproductive powers. Those powers, however, are only potential without a man to give his semen. And all the semen in the world would amount to just one large, sticky mess without the woman to provide ovum and womb. Obviously, we are again dealing with complements, and not just in the reproductive arena. The nurturing powers of women, the female connection to the earth, should receive respect equal to that of the more force-driven male power. And somehow these could, in some ideal world, be combined to form a human world view, a human power. *Tehanu* presents a yin view of Earthsea in an attempt to balance out the "men in the halls of power" yang of the trilogy. And yet, standing on its own, the *Earthsea Trilogy* did provide a balanced world. This attempt to balance something already in harmony results in a serious weakening of both works.

In an earlier book, *The Left Hand of Darkness,* Le Guin created a world and a race in which one was neither male nor female but, during a certain period called "kemmer" became one sex or the other. The sexual orientation was not determinable before hand. An ambassador from Earth is sent to this place. In his time there, Genly Ai becomes accustomed to the genderlessness of the inhabitants. His initial revulsion changes to understanding until, upon dealing with his own people, he finds that he yearns for " . . . not a man's face and not a woman's, a human face . . . familiar, right . . ." Le Guin herself says, "I eliminated gender to find out what was left. Whatever was left would be, presumably simply human. It would define the area that is shared by men and women alike." Let us hope that in her concern for the rights of women, Ursula Le Guin has not lost sight of that human face. (pp. 16, 18)

> *Ann Welton, "Earthsea Revisited: Tehanu and Feminism," in* Voice of Youth Advocates, *Vol. 14, No. 1, April, 1991, pp. 14-16, 18.*

Margaret Miles

[For] me, *Tehanu* brought completion instead of disappointment, I would like to give some views in contrast to those of Ann Welton in "Earthsea Revisited: Tehanu and Feminism" (*VOYA* April 1991). (p. 301)

It's ironic, perhaps, how well the structure of the completed four books of Earthsea agrees with inner themes and events of the stories. In *The Tombs of Atuan* Ged comes to the Place of the Tombs trying to reunite the broken Ring of Erreth-Akbe and restore the split Lost Rune of Peace. Moreover, the Equilibrium is the essential philosophic factor in Earthsea's magic—the Equilibrium was what the trilogy had lacked all along. There were two books of Ged, the first and the third—men's books, if you

want to call them so, though in their dominantly thoughtful rather than active tone they are to me a man's story told very much in a woman's way. Then there had been just one book of Tenar. While *A Wizard of Earthsea* and *The Farthest Shore* established a balance in their treatment of Ged's youth and then his maturity, the tale of Tenar's youth had been without its balance. *Tehanu,* in which Tenar is the dominant force in thought and events, provides the missing elements. Now the "shape" of the series is complete: what had been an uneasy, unbalanced triangle as a "trilogy" now reveals itself as a completed cycle of interlinked smaller circles. The missing parts of the ring have been found and joined in *Tehanu,* and Tenar and Ged both can now be at peace together. Equilibrium has been restored.

The finished pattern is equally satisfying when viewed in other ways. For instance, all four books can be seen as books about education in the most basic sense: about how and what you are taught brings you to the point of learning to define who and what you are. From this angle, in the first two books Ged and Tenar respectively are the students; in the second pair of books they become the teachers, who go on learning as they in turn teach the young Lebannen and Therru who will shape the powers of the world to come. Just as the *Wizard/Shore* and *Tombs/Tehanu* pairs link together and make complete cycles, so from this perspective can *Wizard/Tombs* and *Shore/Tehanu* pairings complete circles and link together. In either pair of pairings, the Equilibrium remains.

And that, obviously, is the point at which Welton and I disagree. For her, *Tehanu* goes past pairing to polarity, becoming a book that argues instead of acts. Partly because all of the other Earthsea books had been more important to me because of philosophy and character than because of action, I am delighted with *Tehanu* precisely because it is a book which takes the time for thought which is necessary to conclude the previous age of Earthsea and truly make ready for the new.

There was one thing about *Tehanu* that did frustrate me for some time, though: why didn't such a superlative book receive more awards and honors? Of course, I was perfectly able to answer myself that many excellent books just never do. I also knew perfectly well that *Tehanu* was by the most generous definitions at the very very upper limit of the age range for the "children's" awards—though that didn't stop me from spending the last nine months of 1990 proclaiming sardonically to most of my reading acquaintance that *Tehanu* was by far the best book of the year but was probably too good to win the Newbery. (pp. 301-02)

[Neither] *Tehanu* nor the other Earthsea books are books for boys and girls. Rather, all four are books for men and women, but for young men and women as well as older ones—and as such are books that YAs, men and women in process, ought not to miss. (p. 302)

> *Margaret Miles, " 'Earthsea Revisited' Revisited," in* Voice of Youth Advocates, *Vol. 14, No. 5, December, 1991, pp. 301-02.*

Uriel Ofek

1926-

(Born Uriel Popik) Israeli author of fiction, nonfiction, poetry, and plays; reteller; editor; and translator.

Major works include *The Dog That Flew: And Other Favorite Stories from Israel* (1969); *My Shalom, My Peace: Paintings and Poems by Jewish and Arab Children* (edited by Jacob Zim, 1975); *Smoke over Golan* (1979).

One of Israel's leading authors for children as well as an internationally known scholar of children's literature, Ofek is best known in the English-speaking world as the author of *Smoke over Golan,* a story for middle graders that describes how a ten-year-old Israeli farm boy becomes involved in the Yom Kippur War of 1973. Both in this work and *My Shalom, My Peace,* a collection of poetry and art by Jewish and Arabic Israeli children that he selected, Ofek promotes understanding of people of different cultures and beliefs. *Smoke over Golan* describes how young Eitan, who lives with his parents on a farm near the Syrian border and is left alone when war is declared, spends three action-filled days surrounded by fighting. Eitan, who is the only Israeli child in the area, has made friends both with the soldiers and with the Syrian boy Saleem who lives across the border; before the end of his ordeal, Eitan cares for a wounded Israeli soldier and helps to capture a prisoner who turns out to be a Syrian intelligence chief. At the conclusion of the novel, which was published in Hebrew as *Ashan kissa et ha-Golan* in 1975, Eitan goes to find Saleem so that they can build a new world together. Praised for the excitement and interest of his story as well as for his characterization of Eitan and evocation of Israeli life, Ofek focuses on the humanity of his characters more than on the effects of war or the philosophy behind it; throughout the book, both Israelis and Syrians act with dignity and nobility towards each other. Ofek's only other English-language work is *The Dog that Flew,* a collection of retellings centering on childhood and life in Israel.

Ofek served as a sergeant in the Plamch Har'el and was a member of the Israel Reserve Defence Forces for over twenty years. As a soldier, he participated in three wars; in 1948, he was a prisoner of war in Trans-Jordan, where he learned to understand the Jordanian soldiers and to like many of them. After returning home from prison, he began to write stories for children which have friendship and the joyfulness of life as their themes. During the October War, he was ill in the hospital; unable to fight, he began to imagine what would happen if he was in the war as a small boy and later wrote most of *Smoke over Golan* while lying in bed. Ofek began his work in the field of juvenile literature as the editor of a weekly newspaper for children in Tel-Aviv. As an author, he has published many books in Hebrew in a variety of genres and has also written best-selling fiction and poetry for adults as well as textbooks on children's literature. In addition, Ofek is well

known for translating the works of such authors as Mark Twain, Lewis Carroll, E. Nesbit, Rudyard Kipling, Kenneth Grahame, Joel Chandler Harris, and Tove Jansson into Hebrew. Ofek is the founder and president of the Israeli national section of the International Board of Books for Young People (IBBY) and has lectured on children's literature in the United States and Canada. In 1978, he was asked to present the May Hill Arbuthnot Honor Lecture by the Association for Library Services to Children. Ofek has received several awards for his works, such as the Ze'ev Preis from the Israeli Ministry of Culture and Education for *Ein sodot ba-shekhuna* (*No Secrets in the Neighborhood*) in 1974 and a certificate of honor from the Hans Christian Andersen Awards committee for *Smoke over Golan* in 1976.

(See also *Something about the Author,* Vol. 36; *Contemporary Authors New Revised Edition,* Vol. 18; and *Contemporary Authors,* Vol. 101.)

AUTHOR'S COMMENTARY

In spite of its title, **Ashan Kissa et Hagolan (Smoke over Golan),** it is not only a war story, but first of all a book about peace and friendship. During my not-so-long lifetime I have found myself taking active part in three wars. I saw some of my best friends being killed or wounded around me; and I still cannot understand why and how I survived to be able to stand here before you today. In 1948 I was a prisoner of war in Trans-Jordan; and there, in the prison camp, I learned to understand the Arab-Jordanian soldiers and even to like many of them. They were really nice people, young men not unlike my friends and I, who also longed to return to their homes and families. After returning home from prison I started to write stories for boys and girls, stories whose main themes were friendship and the joys of life.

And now to come back to my book *Smoke over Golan.*

When the October War broke out—three years ago this week—I was in hospital. I lay there sick, not knowing that the doctors had informed my wife that she was going to be a widow. . . . My first desire upon hearing the news of the new war was to run away from the hospital and join my friends who were fighting on the Golan Heights. But since I could not really do so, I did it in my imagination: I saw myself on the Golan Heights, but this time not as a soldier but as a boy—the 10-year-old Eitan, who lives alone with his father in the small farm by the Syrian border, and whose only friend is Salim, the Arab boy across the border.

So I wrote most of this book in hospital, identifying myself with Eitan, who suddenly found himself on a terrible battlefield, and who went to find his friend Salim after the war, so that they might be able to build a new world together, a world of peace and friendship. (pp. 6-7)

> *Uriel Ofek, "Acceptance Speech on Behalf of the Authors and Illustrators on the 1976 Andersen Honor List," in* Bookbird, *Vol. XIV, No. 4, December 15, 1976, pp. 6-7.*

TITLE COMMENTARY

My Shalom, My Peace: Paintings and Poems by Jewish and Arab Children   (1975)

[My Shalom, My Peace *was edited and designed by Jacob Zim. The poems were selected by Uriel Ofek.*]

"I had a paintbox . . . I sat down and painted peace." That's just what these Israeli schoolchildren (a few are Arab) did and the result is a rainbow of visions, everything from multicolored doves and tanks shooting flowers to one darkly menacing painting of soldiers embracing on a bloody battlefield. The poems, perhaps because they too often dwell on PEACE as an abstract concept, rather than on the warfare these children know firsthand, carry considerably less impact. Literary values aside, a dramatically designed good will gesture.

> *A review of "My Shalom, My Peace: Paintings and Poems by Jewish and Arab Children," in* Kirkus Reviews, *Vol. XLIII, No. 17, September 1, 1975, p. 1002.*

The longing for peace permeates every page of this haunting compilation of poems and pictures by Jewish and Arab Israeli children. The offerings, submitted in a contest for Israeli schoolchildren, make up a unique, contemporary collection which is valuable for its expression of a current world situation through the eyes of children directly involved.

> *Judith S. Kronick, in a review of "My Shalom, My Peace: Painting and Poems by Jewish and Arab Children," in* School Library Journal, *Vol. 22, No. 6, February, 1976, p. 50.*

These are the works of youngsters who were invited in their schools to set down their vision of what it would be like to live in peace. Some of the youngsters who are less than ten years old are already veterans of two wars, and the way in which they dream and yearn for peace is very touching. What makes the book especially impressive is that the poems come from both Jewish and Arab children. It is the kind of document that we wish could find its way onto the desks and into the hearts of the leaders of the nations for truly here out of the mouths of babes has come real wisdom.

> *Jack Riemer, in a review of "My Shalom, My Peace," in* Commonweal, *Vol. CIII, No. 5, February 27, 1976, p. 156.*

Smoke over Golan   (1979)

Finally, a novel about Israel by an Israeli, as opposed to a visiting American. There is such relief in not being told what sabras are and what they eat for breakfast that one can hardly help liking the book immediately. On top of this, Ofek has defined his characters and setting with vivid clarity and put them through the paces of a plot involving the Yom Kippur War of 1973. The book seems to fall into two parts: the establishment of a border farm (including a one-pupil school) by young Eitan and his parents, which is developed to an interesting depth; and the Syrian attack, which, conveying more exciting action than grim reality, finds Eitan alone with his dog and later with a wounded Israeli soldier and an Arab prisoner. Eitan's friendship with an Arab village boy is believably low key; the whole story favors human detail over nationalist philosophizing. Let's hope for more translations as smooth as this.

> *Betsy Hearne, in a review of "Smoke over Golan," in* Booklist, *Vol. 76, No. 1, September 1, 1979, p. 45.*

On a farm in Israel near the Syrian border, Eitan attends "the smallest school in the world," in a storeroom where a "girl soldier" who is also a certified teacher has been assigned just to him. Through his teacher Eitan meets the soldiers on a nearby base, and on his own he becomes friendly with a Syrian boy who has crossed the border in pursuit of a wandering skin-and-bones donkey. Then, with Eitan's mother off to town to have a baby, the Yom Kippur War breaks out; his army major father is called up; the evacuation bus fails to appear; and Eitan finds himself surrounded by fighting. From there, the story of Eitan's rising to the occasion is bound to progress from coping to heroism: Eitan deals with a burst water main, does his best to keep up with the farm chores, cares for wounded soldier friend Asher'ke and, with Asher'ke, takes a prisoner who turns out to be a Syrian intelligence chief loaded with top secrets. But despite this last, Ofek doesn't play the events for wartime heroics. If anything, this is too gentle a view of war: all concerned are so humane and unprejudiced toward the enemy that readers might wonder how they came to be fighting at all; and [translator Israel I.] Taslitt's outmoded American slang furthers a bland, watered-down impression. Nevertheless there is honesty and appeal in Ofek's sympathetic portrayal of Eitan as a vulnerable ten-year-old, the same child we met tame and happy in the "smallest school," now doing his best in a situation he recognizes as too much for him. (pp. 67-8)

> *A review of "Smoke over Golan," in* Kirkus Reviews, *Vol. XLVIII, No. 2, January 15, 1980, pp. 67-8.*

The Three Day War on the Golan Heights took place in 1973 and this story in Hebrew was written in 1974. . . . The participants on both sides act with the degree of nobility expected in a war story written for small boys. It belongs to the age when soldiering and patriotism go hand in hand and must have been popular amongst young readers in Israel. As a straightforward adventure story it transfers easily to another scene where boys have grown tired of what they read in comics and are ready for something more meaty and more demanding upon their reading ability.

> *D. A. Young, in a review of "Smoke over Golan," in* The Junior Bookshelf, *Vol. 45, No. 5, October, 1981, p. 215.*

Smoke Over Golan is an action-filled description of the Yom Kippur War in 1973. It is told by a ten-year-old Israeli farm boy who lived near the Syrian border on the Golan heights. Readers ten to twelve will probably find this first person narrative quite interesting and exciting. They see the tension and danger the boy experienced during the war and they also get a very comprehensive view of what life is like for the Israeli people during time of peace. It is a nicely crafted here-and-now story of a significant historical event.

> *Patricia J. Cianciolo, in a review of "Smoke over Golan," in* Bookbird, *No. 1, March 15, 1984, p. 10.*

Stéphane Poulin

1961-

Canadian author and illustrator of picture books.

Major works include *Have You Seen Josephine?* (1986); *Benjamin and the Pillow Saga* (1986); *My Mother's Loves: Stories and Lies from My Childhood* (1990).

Regarded as one of the most outstanding recent contributors to Canadian literature for children, Poulin is lauded for creating droll, witty picture books that are set in and around his home in Montreal and often reflect his personal background. He is also praised as an illustrator whose distinctive style beautifully combines a childlike vision with sophisticated design, characterization, and use of perspective. In his works, Poulin blends reality, fantasy, and humor to introduce children both to Quebec and to elements of his own childhood; in addition, he often includes details in his pictures to extend his plots and further amuse young readers. For example, in his trio of books about Josephine, a cream-colored cat who leads her young master Daniel on chases through Montreal, his school, and the farm belonging to his aunt and uncle, Poulin provides his audience with such images as Josephine hiding in the school taxidermist's office, where she blends in with the stuffed animals, and a country wheat field, where her head and tail are barely visible among the stalks. Poulin is often acknowledged for his vivid depictions of the Canadian landscape: his first work, *Ah! Belle cité!/A Beautiful City ABC* (1985), a bilingual alphabet book that represents each letter with words in French and English, highlights the various districts of urban Montreal, as does *Have You Seen Josephine?*, Poulin's first story about the feline escape artist, which is set in Montreal's east end. *Could You Stop Josephine?* (1988), a story said by Poulin to be his final work in the Josephine series, is set in the Quebec countryside where he spent ten of his boyhood years. Poulin puts a whimsical spin on his childhood recollections for the popular *My Mother's Loves* and its companion volume *Travels for Two: Stories and Lies from My Childhood* (1991), tall tales that stress both action and personality. In the first book, a prose variation on the nursery rhyme of the old woman who lived in a shoe, Poulin describes how his mother, who lives with her "loves"—her nine children—in a tiny house, marries the local garbageman and joins her family with his, while in the second story the family is stranded on a desert island and encounters pirates after winning a vacation to the tropics. Poulin is also the author and illustrator of *Benjamin and the Pillow Saga,* the story of a talented singer who works in a pillow factory whose humming gives his pillows magical powers, and is the illustrator of Louise Beaudin's *Animals in Winter* (1991), an informational picture book about the winter activities of Canadian animals.

As an illustrator, Poulin characteristically invests his works with colorful oil paintings and pencil sketches that

reflect the humor of his simple, lyrical texts. He is particularly noted for juxtaposing naturalistic scenes with stylized figures whose features include short, squat bodies, long necks, and masklike faces with protruding eyes. As with the subjects of his books, Poulin's illustrations also reflect his personal history. For example, Poulin includes a picture of a small boy with glasses, drawing, on the dedication page of *My Mother's Loves,* while in the last illustration he portrays the boy balancing an ornate picture frame from which he looks out at the reader; critic Sarah Ellis calls this "a portrait of the artist as a young man." Reviewer Peter Carver writes of Poulin that his "pictures are coloured with the brilliance of the child's vision of the world. At the same time, Poulin's work belies his youth: totally in charge of his medium, in each book he reveals new dimensions of his considerable artistic talent." Poulin received the Canada Council Prize for illustration of a French language book for *As-tu vu Josephine?* (*Have You Seen Josephine?*) in 1987 and the Governor General's Award for illustration for *Benjamin and the Pillow Saga* in 1990; he also won the international Quebec/Wallonie Bruxelles Children's Book Award in 1990 as well as the Vicky Metcalf Award in the same year for his body of work.

TITLE COMMENTARY

Ah! Belle cité!/A Beautiful City ABC (1985)

Children's literature, in the past decade or two, has come to be viewed as an area worthy of academic study, with picture-books forming a valid part of the curriculum. But outside the walls of Academe, the picture-book is still too often regarded as suitable only for the very young—and the alphabet book for the even younger.

Along comes *Ah! belle cité! A Beautiful City ABC*—a book that is hit with the double whammy of being both a picture-book and an alphabet-book. But don't write this one off too quickly.

Illustrated and compiled by Stéphane Poulin, a young Montreal artist, the book is truly bilingual, illustrating each letter of the alphabet with a word that starts with that letter in both French and English. Then, in illustrations depicting Montreal scenes, Poulin has included images that also start with the letter in question—but which differ in the two languages (for example, A is *antiquaire*/antique dealer but the painting also shows *arbre, automne,* awning, and arms). A list provided at the back of the book challenges readers to find their own words. At least one 10 year old triumphantly noted the tiny apple painted on a child's backpack and the angel on a sign pointing to the antique-shop door. Published by Tundra, this Montreal ABC is the third in a series presented by the publisher—the first being Ted Harrison's *A Northern Alphabet* and the second, Allan Moak's *A Big City ABC,* about Toronto.

Poulin's contribution to the series is a delight. The paintings are evocative and full of humour: **N** is *nombril* or navel; **B,** for *balcon*/balcony, includes a shop window streaked with pigeon poop. The artist displays a sense of fun that gives the paintings appeal for both young and old. And the bilingual nature of this book adds a whole new dimension—one that should help it break out of the niche usually reserved for alphabet picture-books to reach a wider audience.

> *Bernie Goedhart, "Picture-Books: Some Succeed, Others Better Read Than Seen," in* Quill and Quire, *Vol. 51, No. 12, December, 1985, p. 24.*

Although unique in concept—an alphabet book whose vibrant illustrations acquaint children not only with words but also with the places and life of a city—this book is not totally successful. Each page is given over to a full-color painting that illustrates some aspect of Montreal and one word (in both French and English). The paintings are in a primitive style, making use of broad areas of flat color, with a wealth of detail in each picture, sometimes quite humorous. While these paintings are of typical places in Montreal, Poulin's portrayal of people is rather curious. They are either long of neck or short and squat, their complexions range from pinky-white, to blue to a bilious green, and most all have lively expressions which add an enigmatic note to each setting. But this would not detract from the attractive colorfulness of the artwork and the unique quality of a "city ABC" if children were acquainted with the caption-like narrations for each letter given *at the end of the book* and thereby easily overlooked. It is un-

fortunate that these paragraphs (in both French and English) are not on the same or the opposite page of each illustration. As it is, the book does not make a cohesive whole out of its separate parts. Although visually attractive, this book does not work as either an alphabet book or a tour of a city.

> *Patricia Homer, in a review of "Ah! Belle cité!/A Beautiful City ABC," in* School Library Journal, *Vol. 32, No. 8, April, 1986, p. 78.*

Ah! Belle cité!/A Beautiful City ABC is the third in the series of children's books Tundra is producing on Canadian districts and cities. . . . Each book is illustrated by an artist who is familiar with, and a lover of, the area he paints. These books are not alphabet books in the sense of teaching small children the letters of the alphabet. They reveal the charm of certain districts of Canada and can encourage a child to look around and "alphabetize" favourite surroundings.

Stéphane Poulin was only twenty-two years old when he began writing and illustrating *Ah! Belle cité!/A Beautiful City ABC.* By that time he had already won two awards for children's book illustration. To create a true flavour of Mont Montreal, the author travelled miles on his bicycle, through the streets of the city, sketching, photographing, and taking notes on places he loved as a child. Poulin used only four colours from his palette for all the paintings in the book, yet each painting is alive with colour, feeling, action, and realism.

This is a book to be shared by children and adults. Each page is a complete story. The reader (or readers) may spend hours discovering each area of Montreal that is visited in this little tourist's guide to the city. " 'M' is for marché or market" says one page. The detail is so complete in this picture, one can almost hear what is happening and is tempted to help oneself to a jar of jam or large orange pumpkin from the shelf.

It is fun to share the discoveries each new page brings. This book is perfect for reading aloud, for children sharing the discovery with other children or with an adult. Children are being widely encouraged to adopt two official languages and this book makes it fun to learn French and compare the word to the English equivalent. A book for everyone.

> *Barbara Egerer Walker, in a review of "Ah! Belle cité!/A Beautiful City ABC," in* CM: A Reviewing Journal of Canadian Materials for Young People, *Vol. XIV, No. 3, May, 1986, p. 137.*

Have You Seen Josephine? (1986)

This Canadian publication . . . depicts the journey its young hero takes in search of his cat.

Josephine is a loving, home-abiding cat—except on Saturdays. One Saturday, Daniel decides to find out where she goes. His search takes the reader on a sightseeing tour of East Montreal, where the vistas are sometimes cosmopolitan, sometimes bohemian, sometimes just seedy. Finally, Josephine is found—next door at the home of Mr. and Mrs. Gagnon, retired restauranteurs, who have a party for the neighborhood cats every weekend.

Poulin is the 26-year-old author/illustrator of the well-received *Ah! Belle Cité/A Beautiful City,* an ABC book about his Montreal home. He brings the same mordant attention to realistic detail and extensive use of bright colors contrasted with almost gloomy shadows to this book, so that most illustrations look cheerful and sinister at the same time. The use of strange perspectives and the solemn atmosphere lend an air of sophistication to a simple, reassuring story. A picture book for readers who enjoy using their eyes to extend the bounds of the plot.

A review of "Have You Seen Josephine?" in Kirkus Reviews, *Vol. LIV, No. 20, October 15, 1986, p. 1580.*

Stéphane Poulin's first book, an ABC of Montreal, entitled *Ah! belle cité/A Beautiful City!,* was greeted with much enthusiasm. His newest book, *Have You Seen Josephine?,* while ostensibly a small, charming tale about the meanderings of Daniel's cat Josephine, is in fact also a pictorial tour of that *belle cité,* Montreal, and more specifical-

ly, a loving look at an east-end Montreal neighbourhood. . . .

Poulin's humans are bizarre creatures, considerably less than human. Daniel, for instance, is a small, wild-looking boy with blank eyes staring out of a mask-like face. His characters walk like puppets through a landscape where cats and alley-ways are the main events. This is an intriguing book and a harbinger, one hopes, of more good things to come.

Susan Perren, "Picture-Book Plums for Christmas Gift-Giving," in Quill and Quire, *Vol. 52, No. 12, December, 1986, p. 16.*

Poulin's large full-page color paintings should immediately attract children's attention. Poulin shows a working-class Montreal neighborhood in vivid detail. . . . The story is slight, but the paintings invite a second look. The variety of scenes and the barely visible cat hold readers' interest and create suspense. Pencil sketches beside the simple text elaborate the story further. Older preschoolers through primary graders will have fun looking for Josephine.

Nancy Kewish, in a review of "Have You Seen

From Ah! Belle cité!/A Beautiful City ABC, *written and illustrated by Stéphane Poulin.*

Josephine?" in School Library Journal, *Vol. 33, No. 11, August, 1987, p. 74.*

The colourful and detailed illustrations in this book are wonderful. They catch the atmosphere of Montreal's east end, where the 26-year-old author/artist lives. It's a friendly old urban neighbourhood, which looks both seedy and quaint. The pictures are very realistic as far as building, street scenes, cats, and adults are concerned—but the child's face is sometimes odd and unesthetic. He looks different in different pictures—sometimes he seems like a strawman/boy, othertimes like a bug-eyed dwarf, and once like a ghoul-child. (It seems that many Canadian children's illustrators have trouble drawing children's features). Otherwise, Poulin's pictures are altogether charming and rich in detail. Supporting the pictures is a text which will intrigue children and cat-loving adults alike—where does Josephine the cat go on Saturdays when she slips out? Daniel and his father follow her through the city to find out and there's a sense of mischievous feline trickery as she eludes them again and again—but the reader gets a capital tour of the Saturday sights of old Montreal in the process, and the warmth of the area comes through in people's responses to the little boy's question "Have you seen my cat?"

Mary Rubio, in a review of "Have You Seen Josephine?" in Canadian Children's Literature, *No. 46, 1987, p. 108.*

Can You Catch Josephine? (1987)

In the further adventures of the cat Josephine, as recorded in *Can You Catch Josephine?,* Poulin shows how masterful he is at setting a droll story in a droll landscape, yet combining story and picture so that each melts into the other. *Can You Catch Josephine?* is a charming, flawless performance by cat and author-illustrator.

Fleeting glimpses were all one got of Josephine in *Have You Seen Josephine?* In *Can You Catch Josephine?* she is almost as elusive. We see her tail poking out of Daniel's school-bag as he walks to school and her paw emerging from the vestigial ink-well in Daniel's school desk. Mr. Martin, Daniel's teacher, catches sight of the paw, yells "CATCH THAT CAT", and the chase is on. We see Josephine perched on the third-floor window-ledge, in the library on the shelf marked J-K-L, and a flash of her as she careens through the locker-room. We see only her eyes poking out of the janitor's bucket in the washroom, and we mistake her for just another product of the taxidermist's art in the scariest room in the school, the science room. We see more of Josephine as she races, pursued by Daniel, through the gym and up the stairs. We finally catch up with Daniel and Josephine in the principal's office, where a pleasant surprise awaits cat and boy.

If *Have You Seen Josephine?* was an excuse to travel through the lively streets of east-end Montreal, then *Can You Catch Josephine?* is another excuse: an opportunity to travel to school and through school, ending up in that holiest of holy places, the principal's office. *En route* we see the bright yellow school bus; the dyspeptic Mr Martin with his fleur-de-lys and maple-leaf flags and his large map

of Quebec, Canada Est; small feet in rows in the toilet stalls; and the pompadoured librarian with her carmine lips and nails amidst the library stacks. These scenes are wonderful, but what makes Poulin's work so special are the characters that populate his books. Daniel and his classmates are small ghouls with truncated bodies, ochre skin, and enormous protruding eyes. This weird little world of Poulin's illustrations—which the reader enters so eagerly—coupled with his minimal, poetic prose style, makes his books distinctive and rewarding for readers of all ages. (pp. 18-19)

Susan Perren, "Annabel and Goldie Go to the Sea, Josephine Goes to School," in Books for Young People, *Vol. 1, No. 5, October, 1987, pp. 18-19.*

This has more universal appeal than its predecessor, which seemed at times to be a dark exploration of some of the bleaker back alleys of Montreal. Here, while the same design of full, brightly colored right-hand pages facing text embellished with black-and-white details is used, the school might be any urban elementary school; the grotesque visage of the grown-ups is typical of any child's-eye view; and the occasional distortions of perspective lend an antic rather than an eerie quality. A delightful choice for the older picture-book set.

A review of "Can You Catch Josephine?" in Kirkus Reviews, *Vol. LV, No. 20, October 15, 1987, p. 1520.*

For the third year in a row, Montreal author/illustrator Stéphane Poulin has produced one of the season's finest picture books. . . . [In] *Can You Catch Josephine?* Daniel unwittingly brings his pudgy, wilful pet to school in his knapsack. . . . The book's great strength is its artwork. While many children's book illustrations suffer from an excess of pastel cuteness, Poulin uses overcast colors to paint figures with expressive faces. His artwork has an unconventional beauty—and considerable wit. In one classroom picture, Josephine is easy to miss at first glance. But a closer look reveals a furry paw poking through a desk's inkwell holder. (p. 54)

Pamela Young with Celina Bell and others, "Joys for Young Readers," in Maclean's Magazine, *Vol. 100, No. 49, December 7, 1987, pp. 54, 56.*

Could You Stop Josephine? (1988)

A third book . . . about the elusive cat Josephine, from an illustrator who presents his Canadian milieu with unusual dexterity: when Daniel visits his country relatives, Josephine unexpectedly hitches a ride in the family car. At the farm, she's chased by both a dog and another cat, thus visiting the farm animals and fields during an eventful tour that's sure to amuse small listeners; the three make friends in time to share the remnants of Daniel's birthday picnic. Poulin's bright paintings have a childlike appeal; their uncompromising lack of sentimentality, flair for design, and creative use of points of view will also interest adults. This could be used as an easy reader.

A review of "Could You Stop Josephine?" in Kirkus Reviews, *Vol. LVI, No. 21, November 1, 1988, p. 1609.*

Children have found the Quebec style fresh, idiosyncratic, witty, imaginative—and above all *fun* to play with and respond to. . . .

Poulin's work is typical of what's come out of Quebec in the 1980s. The illustrator is boyishly disarming personally, and his pictures are coloured with the brilliance of a child's vision of the world. At the same time, Poulin's work belies his youth: totally in charge of his medium, in each book he reveals new dimensions of his considerable artistic talent. In **Could You Stop Josephine?**—his third book based on the adventures of Josephine, the deft and elusive cat—young Daniel goes to the country with his family and, he thinks, *without* Josephine. But of course his pet isn't so easily left behind and before long is leading Daniel and his cousin Norman on a wonderful chase through the pigpens, pastures, barns, and fields of the Quebec countryside—where Poulin himself spent 10 years of his boyhood.

Poulin's young characters have the delightfully messy appearance of children totally absorbed in their own pursuits. The rich colours, the child's-eye and bird's-eye perspectives of the oil paintings—along with the innocent charm of the story—make this just as entertaining as Josephine's previous romps and a fittingly upbeat finish to the Josephine series.

Peter Carver, "Quebec Illustrators' Welcome Invasion," in Books for Young People, *Vol. 2, No. 6, December, 1988, p. 8.*

Young readers will enjoy the usual breathless chase (kids against Josephine and her animal friends), and especially the game of spotting Josephine on every page. (Poulin's triumph is the wheatfield, where my daughter delighted in detecting the animals by the ears, tail and face barely peeping out over the top of the ripening grain.)

For adults, the interest lies in the book's mock-serious tone. With their unsmiling, strangely-rounded, sallow faces, Poulin's people evoke the haunting, bleak figures in the works of Canadian Miller Brittain, or American Reginald Marsh. Yet the story is essentially comic, as Daniel frantically pursues his elusive cat—over fences, into barns, under tractors, along cliffs—confronting threatening bulls and stampeding piglets along the way. The ominous quality of the full-page oils (the greens deepen into black with the approaching storm) meshes perfectly with the text, for Daniel's panic is deadly serious:

Rain came down. Thunder roared. Lightning flashed. It was a very big storm.

"Josephine is scared in storms," I told him. "ALL animals are scared in storms," Norman said.

"Josephine doesn't like to get wet," I said. "NO animal likes to get wet," Norman said.

"DUCKS like to get wet," I said. "Ducks aren't animals," Norman said.

With a flash of lightning illuminating the two boys in the barn (Daniel hunched over in despair, Norman frowning and resigned), and the two cats in the gloom of the rafters, the illustration captures this mood perfectly.

Poulin's small pencil drawings on the left-hand pages intensify the humour; my favourite is a rear view of the two cats, heads touching and tails linked for security during the storm.

I'm not sure how much farther afield Daniel can pursue Josephine—to Paris? to Tokyo?—without running out of steam, but I'm looking forward to more exotic fare from Poulin's fertile pen and brush. (pp. 106-07)

Marjorie Gann, in a review of "Could You Stop Josephine?" in Canadian Children's Literature, *Nos. 57-58, 1990, pp. 106-07.*

Benjamin and the Pillow Saga (1989)

Author-illustrator Stéphane Poulin has once again created what is sure to become a favourite picture-book for children. The hero of this book is Benjamin, a shy, happy man who is always humming. Benjamin lives with his parents and, in the evenings, he enjoys making music with them. [One] illustration pictures Benjamin contentedly humming in the bathtub while his mother, perched on the sink, plays the tuba and his father, seated on the toilet, strums his harp.

Like most people in his village, Benjamin works in the local pillow factory. The reader soon learns that these aren't ordinary pillows; they're extraordinary because they always give people a deep, delicious sleep.

The story of the magic pillows spreads far and wide and soon people from distant lands are buying up the pillows to sell in their own countries. While the factory owner is showing one of many groups around his factory, an Italian visitor hears Benjamin quietly humming as he sews and promptly invites him to hum at her opera house. Benjamin and his parents are off to Italy!

Soon the family trio become world celebrities. In the meantime, back at the village, the magic pillows have lost their magic and customers are beginning to complain. The factory owner in his frustration tears a pillow apart and as the feathers float out, the room is filled with the sweet, soft music of Benjamin's humming coming from inside the pillow. From then on, people are encouraged to bring their pillows to the concerts as Benjamin and his parents tour around the world. That way, they can open them up so that Benjamin's voice will flow into them and they can become magic pillows once more.

This book is balanced with text on one page and a full-colour illustration on the facing page. The detail in each picture makes the reader want to linger and therefore this is an excellent choice for individual reading. On the other hand, because of the large size of the full-page illustrations, this is also an effective choice for reading aloud.

Highly recommended for a Kindergarten to grade 6 collection, especially for the primary grades. (pp. 14-15)

Patricia Fry, in a review of "Benjamin and the Pillow Saga," in CM: A Reviewing Journal of Canadian Materials for Young People, *Vol. XVIII, No. 1, January, 1990, pp. 14-15.*

Poulin alternates left-hand pages of text, presenting a subtle story of shy Benjamin and his ancient musical parents, a harpist father and a tuba-playing mother, with self-framing right hand paintings in oil on canvas. The story in words and pictures is evocative of old Europe, in a time when even the world of commerce cared about making people happy. Poulin's paintings are cut to interesting shapes—a romanesque arch, cut-away corners, a great variety of shapes set on white into which an occasional figure strays (as a loop of telephone cord, a car wheel). Only once is the format prominently changed, when in the middle of the book, in the middle of the story, at a critical point when the strangers arrive, Poulin's art spills across the divide onto the left-hand page, and the visual silently announces its marriage to the text. (p. 98)

Allan Sheldon, "Secret Marriages: Unified Text and Visuals," in Canadian Children's Literature, *No. 61, 1990, pp. 96-9.*

My Mother's Loves: Stories and Lies from My Childhood (1990)

The childhood recollections of the author-illustrator form the basis of this often rollicking modern tale. "Lies" (tall tales) from the author's childhood are really extensions of real life. For instance, the family house "had only one room so it was impossible to fit both the furniture and my family in at the same time."

Full-page illustrations brimming with exaggerated humour, imagination and warmth show how the family, made up of the mother and her nine children, managed to have a lot of fun together in their tiny house and narrow yard. The mother and her nine loves played baseball in summer, tobogganed off the roof in winter, and took in Tuba the elephant who had escaped from the zoo.

When the mother meets and falls in love with a man and soon afterwards marries him, the children from both sides of the marriage are seen playing leapfrog together, having themselves a jolly good time.

Here's a picture-book that begins with a happy family and ends with a happy, albeit changed, family. This book will evoke a response from young and old. Unfortunately, the text is somewhat disjointed and the story-line too sparse. It's the superb illustrations with their richness of detail that carry this story.

Ellen Pauls, in a review of "My Mother's Loves: Stories and Lies from My Childhood," in CM: A Reviewing Journal of Canadian Materials for Young People, *Vol. XIX, No. 1, January, 1991, p. 30.*

This tall tale involves a large family and a small house. With nine children, one mother, and a dog, there is no room for both the family and the furniture in the house. When the family is inside, the furniture has to be moved to the yard. Sometimes the furniture even has to be moved to the roof so that family members can play baseball or escape an encroaching flood.

Stéphane Poulin has a well-deserved reputation as one of the finest illustrators of children's books, and his work in this book is up to his usual high standards. The pictures are lovely, with plenty of detail, action, and humour to entertain young children. The texture of the canvas shows through the paint and adds a physical dimension to the art. Each picture evokes a different feeling and mood, and every character has a unique personality. Children will return again and again to look at these illustrations.

The story is not quite as satisfying as the illustrations. The main plot involves the mother chasing after a garbage man who has mistakenly collected the furniture from the yard. They fall in love and marry, and he brings along many children of his own to swell the numbers filling the happy, tiny house. The richness of the illustrations complements this simple, joyful story. Unfortunately, an episode in the middle of the book, in which the family befriends an elephant who eventually becomes homesick and returns to the zoo, is intrusive and disturbs the flow of the story.

Despite the elephant, this book deserves a place on everyone's shelf.

Fred Boer, in a review of "My Mother's Loves: Stories and Lies from My Childhood," in Quill and Quire, *Vol. 57, No. 2, February, 1991, p. 22.*

Stories and Lies from My Childhood, the subtitle of **My Mother's Loves,** . . . accurately suggests the blend of nostalgia and whimsy that characterizes this variation on the story of the old woman who lived in a shoe. Poulin's *famille nombreuse,* headed by a spunky single mother, is depicted in various fantastical vignettes that culminate in *Maman*'s unexpected marriage to the garbage collector, after which the whole gang lives happily ever after. As my tolerance for whimsy is notoriously low, I found **My Mother's Loves** resistable, feeling that it veers, in both text and pictures, over the edge of cuteness. It's possible, though, that the book's rather self-conscious charm may appeal to other parents and young readers.

Anne Denoon, in a review of "My Mother's Loves: Stories and Lies from My Childhood," in Books in Canada, *Vol. XX, No. 3, April, 1991, p. 37.*

The cover of Stéphane Poulin's **My Mother's Loves: Stories and Lies from My Childhood** gives us a broad hint as to its tone. The title is printed in a clear, dignified, sans-serif typeface; the subtitle in the wiggly printing of a child. Throughout this warm and extravagant book these two points of view—child and adult—interact.

Part memoir, part tall tale, this family album tells of a huge family growing up in a tiny house in the country. There is no linear plot, no real problem to be solved. Instead we are treated to a series of anecdotes. The first two

From Have you seen Josephine?, *written and illustrated by Stéphane Poulin.*

pictures, in Poulin's characteristic painterly style, are tidy and organized. The first is a view, from the distance, of the tiny house between two cabbage patches. The second is a composition of the single mother and her nine squat, homely children, neatly arranged, as for a photograph, staring out at us. The sober, first-person narrative seems to promise a sort of documentary.

But chaos soon erupts as Poulin, in words and pictures, describes moving the furniture in and out of a house that is so small that it can contain people or possessions, but not both. The personality of the mother is captured absolutely in a family baseball scene in which she plays catcher, equipped with an oven mitt on her hand and a kitchen sieve across her face. The action becomes more outrageous as an escaped elephant moves in, attracted by the smell of the mother's cabbage soup. The whole thing ends on a note of comedic joy as the mother falls in love with the garbage collector and they marry, mingling their families and settling down happily in the tiny house.

Poulin's previous books have included a series featuring Josephine the cat. In these books the challenge is to spot Josephine in the busy scenes Poulin creates. There is a game element in *My Mother's Loves* as well. The back end of the family dog is somewhere in every picture, as is a child who is always dozing. But there is even a more subtle subplot. On the dedication page one child is pictured, a bespectacled middle-sized boy, lying on his stomach, drawing. Surely this is the young Stéphane Poulin. Always, in subsequent pictures, he is observing, storing up images. And he is the bookish one. In an illustration where the whole family is crowded on the roof of their house, surrounded by flood waters, Stéphane's nose is buried in a book, the story of Noah.

Little Stéphane's final triumph is portrayed on the back cover illustration. He is shown balancing a heavy, ornate picture frame, through which he looks out at us. It is a portrait of the artist as a young man, as is, indeed, the whole book. (pp. 632-33)

Sarah Ellis, in a review of "My Mother's Loves:

Stories and Lies from My Childhood," in The Horn Book Magazine, *Vol. LXVII, No. 5, September-October, 1991, pp. 632-33.*

Animals in Winter (1991)

[Animals in Winter *was written by Louise Beaudin.*]

[Stéphane Poulin] has a real winner once more.

This charming book about the winter activities of Canadian animals is directed towards a young audience. The introduction shows Mr. Click and his camera having returned from another photo safari. We are told that this book is his souvenir album, which will answer the question of what animals do in the winter.

The outstanding illustrations, along with only a few direct comments on each double-page spread, tell the story and impart the necessary facts about animals in winter. Each animal has been clearly and realistically painted with touches of humour sprinkled throughout. It will take more than one reading to catch all of Poulin's clever details; young readers will appreciate the polar bear clutching his pillow during his dormancy period and the groundhogs and bats with matching hats during hibernation.

A simply written text with more detailed information follows in two pages at the back of the book. Seven- or eight-year-olds will be able to read and understand this themselves and young children can have the information read aloud to them. This book gives all readers an insight into the animals' winter activities and will no doubt leave them anticipating Mr. Click's next animal safari.

Although this talented Québécois illustrator/author has not previously published non-fiction about animals (to my knowledge), the facts are presented accurately and this book will be a welcome addition to the science area for young students. (pp. 76-7)

Ann Fagan, in a review of "Animals in Winter," in CM: A Reviewing Journal of Canadian Materials for Young People, *Vol. XX, No. 2, March, 1992, pp. 76-7.*

Travels for Two: Stories and Lies from My Childhood (1991)

Following last year's *My Mother's Loves,* Stéphane Poulin has created another fanciful story described by the author as "stories and lies from my childhood." *Travels for Two* is a quick-paced tale that includes all the elements of a great adventure story. After winning a vacation for two to cruise the tropics, our narrator and his family find themselves parachuting from an airplane, marooned on a desert island, captured by pirates, and, finally, rescued on the high sea.

The humour of the story is infectious, and is carried through in the illustrations. The jubilant children, the harried mother and the wickedly funny pirates all contribute to the sense of fun and adventure.

Highly recommended for adventurous spirits.

> *Rebecca Raven, in a review of "Travels for Two: Stories and Lies from My Childhood," in* CM: A Reviewing Journal of Canadian Materials for Young People, *Vol. XX, No. 2, March, 1992, p. 84.*

Louis Sachar

1954-

American author of fiction and short stories.

Major works include *Sideways Stories from Wayside School* (1978), *Someday Angeline* (1983), *There's a Boy in the Girl's Bathroom* (1987), *Wayside School Is Falling Down* (1989).

A popular author of humorous realistic fiction for middle graders and junior high school students that is praised for appealing to young readers while deftly exploring their relationships and feelings, Sachar is often acknowledged for his understanding of his audience and of what appeals to them. Noted for investing his works with both hilarity and poignancy, he is also celebrated as a talented creator of character, dialogue, and situation. A former teacher's aide at a California elementary school, Sachar often writes books with classroom settings that focus on such character types as the class genius, the class bully, and the class clown. The protagonists of his books, who are both male and female and are often labeled as outcasts by their schoolmates, learn about themselves from their relationships with other children or adults; through their experiences, which often reflect the anxieties of home and school life, the characters begin to discover their own talents and to be accepted by their peers. Critic Carolyn Phelan writes, "[Children] will recognize Sachar as a writer who knows their territory and entertains them well."

Sachar is perhaps best known as the author of *There's a Boy in the Girl's Bathroom,* a story about the transformation of fifth grade terror Bradley Chalkers. The oldest boy in his class, Bradley is loathed by his classmates for his bullying behavior. Through his relationships with the school counselor and a new boy who refuses to be intimidated by him, Bradley learns to see himself in a more positive light; the story ends with Bradley's victorious attendance at a birthday party, the first social event to which he has been invited in three years. Sachar is also well known as the creator of the zany fantasies about Wayside School, an elementary school thirty stories high in which the classrooms—one on each floor—are stacked on top of each other. In the short story collection *Sideways Stories from Wayside School* and its sequel *Wayside School Is Falling Down,* Sachar depicts a gallery of familiar characters, both teachers and students, in a variety of amusing situations. The stories include examples of puns, jokes, and broad humor as well as dialogue along the lines of popular teacher Mrs. Jewls's statement, "If you want to be great and important, you have to wear expensive underpants"; Sachar is also the author of *Sideways Arithmetic from Wayside School,* a story in which transfer student Sue learns the Wayside approach to mathematics. Among Sachar's works of realistic fiction, which contain funny moments as well as more serious themes, is the well-received story *Someday Angeline,* in which an eight-year-old genius, who is placed in the sixth grade because of her

intelligence but ostracized because she is different, learns to become comfortable with herself through the friendship of a teacher and another loner, Gary "Goon" Boone, a jokester who disguises his feelings through humor. In *Dogs Don't Tell Jokes* (1991), Gary becomes successful at a school talent show and learns to communicate in a more straightforward manner. Sachar has received several child-selected awards for his books.

(See also *Something about the Author,* Vols. 50, 63; *Contemporary Authors New Revision Series,* Vols. 15, 33; and *Contemporary Authors,* Vol. 81-84.)

TITLE COMMENTARY

Sideways Stories from Wayside School (1978)

I had great hopes for these thirty short stories. They have the broad humor that children love and are set in a mixed-up school. Yet I was vaguely dissatisfied. They were not as funny as they could have been and were unreal to the point of silliness. The writing is simply not comparable to Roald Dahl or Joan Aiken, masters of the art of fanciful humor. On the other hand, slow readers might enjoy their brevity and easy vocabulary.

Jennifer Brown, in a review of "Sideways Stories from Wayside School," in Children's Book Review Service, *Vol. 6, No. 14, August, 1978, p. 136.*

The Wayside School is 30 stories high with a classroom on each floor. This is about the teachers and children on the top floor. Mrs. Gorf, the mean teacher, gets herself turned into an apple and is eaten by Louis, the playground teacher. Absent-minded Mrs. Jewls' system is to send children home at noon on the kindergarten bus for three infractions of discipline on any one morning. On the other hand, she dispenses liberally from a coffee can full of Tootsie Roll pops. The children form a recognizable class: the poor athlete, the bully, the good kid, and so on. The vignettes about each of them are deadpan nonsense, echoing faintly some of Carl Sandburg's *Rootabaga Pigeons* but with none of his grace and sweetness. Some of the anecdotes are macabre—chilling, but not deliciously so. Eventually, even the nonsense palls. In the end, it is revealed that Louis, the playground teacher, wrote the book. The classroom of children are seen from an adult's point of view and, while the book has something oblique to say about teaching, there is no story and no particular focus. (pp. 147-48)

Matilda Kornfeld, in a review of "Sideways Stories from Wayside School," in School Library Journal, *Vol. 25, No. 1, September, 1978, pp. 147-48.*

Johnny's in the Basement (1981)

No wonder Johnny Laxatayl is in the basement. He has just turned 11, and he looks like a dog; his parents and five-year-old sister mock him and take advantage of him. Johnny's claim to fame is his bottle-cap collection, which takes up his whole cellar. But not for long. After his birthday party, his parents force him to give up the caps to a junk metal dealer. His mother also makes Johnny take dancing lessons, a birthday present from his aunt. At his first lesson, he meets Valerie Plum, who takes a liking to him because he reminds her of her dog. (Readers who haven't figured out what Johnny's last name means are treated to Valerie's explanation—"he looks like a dog, but lacks-a-tail.") Finally, the bottle caps are hauled away, and Johnny, Valerie and another friend use the $86.33 "blood money" to buy "junk" (meaningless consumer items), a preadolescent way to show contempt for adults' exploitation of him. Then it's back to the basement, now empty, except that Valerie's with him. Johnny's grown up—he's graduated from bottle caps to puppy love. Easy to read, but hard to take, the story is a meaningless string of unrelated episodes, told in short, *Catch-22*-like seminonsense dialogue. Its characters and plot (what little there is) are there as putty for the gaps in the mostly unhumorous dialogue.

Jack Forman, in a review of "Johnny's in the Basement," in School Library Journal, *Vol. 28, No. 4, December, 1981, p. 68.*

This is an odd, jumpy, episodic story, full of sly humour, and while it won't be everybody's favourite, a few readers will really enjoy its peculiar flavour.

Joan McGrath, in a review of "Johnny's in the Basement," in Emergency Librarian, *Vol. 9, No. 5, May-June, 1982, p. 30.*

[*The following excerpt is from a review of the paperback edition published in 1983.*]

Another corker by the author of **Someday Angeline,** this story appeals to kids' sense of justice and humor. Johnny Laxatayl (Sachar likes punning names; the boy's friends think he looks just like a handsome dog, only "lacks a tail") rejoices in owning the biggest bottle-cap collection in the world. The things cover the entire basement of his house and excite the admiration of everyone, especially his pals Valerie Plum and Donald Duckworth. But when Johnny's 11th birthday arrives, so do responsibilities that, in sum, persuade him that staying a child is preferable. The worst blow is his parents' plan to dispose of the great collection. It's sold to cheats, owners of Metal Press, for $86.33. What Johnny, Valerie and Donald do with that money is the core of the plot, a sharply satiric view of today's values. All the many characters in the story are superbly realized, particularly Johnny's eldritch little sister.

A review of "Johnny's in the Basement," in Publishers Weekly, *Vol. 224, No. 7, August 12, 1983, p. 67.*

Someday Angeline (1983)

Sachar's unaffected humor and linguistic art invest the story of Angeline Persopolis with pure magic. Angeline, eight, is a genius and an outsider. At school, the students call her Freak; her nasty teacher rejoices in putting her down. Angeline's mother is dead; her loving father Abel, in awe of the child, fumbles his attempts to talk with her. Luckily, another loner, Gary Boone (known as Goon), and another teacher, Miss Turbone (Mr. Bone), become Angeline's friends and treat her like a person, not something special. Along with Abel's friend Gus and other kind people, Goon and Mr. Bone gladden Angeline's days and see her through a fearful crisis in a novel readers will want to go on and on.

A review of "Someday Angeline," in Publishers Weekly, *Vol. 224, No. 5, July 29, 1983, p. 71.*

A charming offbeat story about an eight-year-old with a high IQ, who has trouble fitting in with the rest of the world. . . . Angeline's age makes this a good fit for middle-graders though some of the author's allusions and maverick philosophy may be too obscure for that age group. What children will like is the sense of fun that pervades the story and the feeling of hope that comes shining through. Suggested for gifted children.

Ilene Cooper, in a review of "Someday Angeline," in Booklist, *Vol. 80, No. 1, September 1, 1983, p. 91.*

Eight-year-old Angeline Persopolis swims to the beat of

a different drummer. She is attuned to life under water: her first spoken word was *octopus,* her favorite beverage is salt water, her most desired outing would be to the ocean—but she flounders on dry ground relationships because of others' reactions to her extraordinary intelligence. Her insensitive teacher taunts her, her well-meaning widowed father is unable to relate to this genius. Enter the unlikely hero, Boone, a fifth-grade version of Henny Youngman, whose penchant for incessant jokes hooks Angeline's heart and Mr. Bone (Miss Turbone), who teaches more than just the fifth grade. Young readers, gifted and not, will sympathize with Angeline's trials, wonder at her talents and grin at Boone's groaners.

> *Marilyn Payne Phillips, in a review of "Someday Angeline," in* School Library Journal, *Vol. 30, No. 3, November, 1983, p. 82.*

There's a Boy in the Girl's Bathroom (1987)

The fall and rise of Bradley Chalkers, class bully, are chronicled in this humorous, immensely appealing story.

Bradley, 11, known alternatively as Chicken Chalkers and a "monster," is hated and feared by his fifth-grade classmates and teacher, teased unmercifully by his older sister, and treated warily by his well-meaning but ineffectual parents. He derives a modicum of comfort from playing with his only friends—a motley collection of little glass and brass animals. When Jeff, a new kid, arrives in class and offers friendship, a confused Bradley first demands a dollar or he'll spit on the newcomer; he later exchanges the dollar for Jeff's friendship. It's a shaky alliance at best, considering the state of Bradley's psyche and the fact that, as Jeff grows more comfortable, he begins to prefer his more well-adjusted classmates. Then, into Bradley's life comes Carla Davis, newly-hired school counselor. This lovely, caring young woman is a model of therapeutic wisdom, and it is their slow-to-grow, but eventually solid, relationship that helps Bradley to see himself as a worthy and capable individual, deserving of friendship, gold stars, and an invitation to a girl's birthday party. His transformation is beautiful to see, though, of course, there are mishaps, failures, and disappointments, as well as triumphs, some of which are quite moving, others highly comical.

Even the happiest of children feel like misfits from time to time; most have also encountered bullies like Bradley. As the story moves along, readers will begin to sympathize with Bradley; they'll root for him, hoping he'll exchange his misfit status for reasonable contentment. Happily, readers are also likely to come away from the story with the sense that they've been rooting for themselves, too.

> *A review of "There's a Boy in the Girl's Bathroom," in* Kirkus Reviews, *Vol. LV, No. 3, February 1, 1987, p. 224.*

Bradley Chalkers is the quintessential class outcast, and he makes sure that no one gets near enough to change his status; when he's sure of failure, there's no risk of being unable to succeed. Then a new boy arrives who weathers Bradley's obnoxious front, and a school counselor breaks the rejection cycle by convincing him that she finds him interesting and intelligent. Slowly Bradley works his way toward normal—if individualistic—behavior, which is almost immediately threatened by the counselor's leaving. This is a funny book, not in the flip way implied by the title, but in the slightly sad sense that touches all true comedy. Neither Bradley's family nor the school authorities are cast into a villainous role; they are simply unable to deal with a boy who is his own worst enemy. Bradley's retreat into friendship with his ceramic animals is touching, as are many of the scenes of his mishaps and misdemeanors. Readers will cheer during his triumphant attendance of a girl's birthday party (he is in fifth grade and has not been invited to a party since he sat on someone's birthday cake several years ago) because the author has managed to show both Bradley's point of view and the reasons for his classmates' low expectations of him. Sachar has also imbued everyday details of school life, such as a book report, with the kind of weight they carry for children. The personality of the counselor is occasionally overdrawn, along with a few parent reactions against her in a farcical example of PTA-type meetings; but those notes of exaggeration fit in with the absurdist, catch-22 tone of the whole book.

> *Betsy Hearne, in a review of "There's a Boy in the Girl's Bathroom," in* Bulletin of the Center for Children's Books, *Vol. 40, No. 8, April, 1987, p. 155.*

An unlikely protagonist, Bradley Chalkers is a friendless, lying, insecure bully who is the oldest boy in his fifth-grade class. In this humorous novel that tells of Bradley's learning to like himself and to make friends, Sachar ably captures both middle-grade angst and joy. Bradley's triumph comes through the friendship of a new boy at school and the help of the new school counselor. Readers, like the astute counselor, can see the strengths that Bradley has, and will cheer at his minor victories and cringe at his setbacks along the way. The story is unusual, witty, and satisfying, if not always believable: a few incidents just do not work. For instance, even though Bradley has not been doing his homework, his complete ignorance of it is unlikely ("He hadn't realized . . . he would need to bring his book home"), and his total unfamiliarity with birthday parties is too extreme for a ten year old, even one who hadn't been to a party in three years. Yet Bradley's need for acceptance even as he holds back from classmates who might mock or hurt him is genuine, and his eventual success will gratify readers.

> *David Gale, in a review of "There's a Boy in the Girls' Bathroom," in* School Library Journal, *Vol. 33, No. 7, April, 1987, p. 103.*

There's a Boy in the Girls' Bathroom might, by its title, be another anecdotal book about how funny it is to be a 5th grader, misery and all. But Bradley Chalkers doesn't fit. He's an island, an alien, as isolate as a werewolf. How he got that way isn't clear, but there he is, and you'd know him. He sits in the back row, corner seat, with no one else nearby. He scribbles on paper and desk, chuckling when the pencil breaks, and he spits. He cuts his language test (marked F) into little squares and feeds the pieces to his talking toy animals at home. *They* like him but no one else does. And Bradley hates everybody. That way, he can't be harmed.

The world seems divided among those who insist that the Bradleys in our midst snap out of it, those who would surround them with therapy to get them to adjust and conform, and those who step around the Bradleys and look the other way. In this book a new boy, Jeff, doesn't fit these categories—he's something of an alien himself and he views Bradley with uneasy recognition, but he doesn't turn away. The new counselor, Carla, doesn't turn away either, even when the Concerned Parents Organization wants her out of her job.

It seems to me that books like this often go awry. Authors start out with a big problem and a planned solution, a kind of hidden agenda, a didactic. But *this* author struggles right along with his characters. Bradley, he seems to say, is just too important to be a case study. Would you want Hamlet to be just a case study? So Bradley, thanks to Louis Sachar, is real, worrisome, and funny and this book, sometimes sacrificing control for resourcefulness, is a triumph.

> *Sam Leaton Sebesta, in a review of "There's a Boy in the Girls' Bathroom," in* The Reading Teacher, *Vol. 42, No. 1, October, 1988, p. 83.*

Sixth Grade Secrets (1987)

The author of **There's a Boy in the Girls' Bathroom** shows how easy it is for one secret to become a catacomb of secrets—some harmless, some harmful—even when no one has intended them to go so far. Laura has hair down to *there* that is the envy of the sixth grade girls and admired by one boy—Gabriel. She starts a club called Pig City; members offer their own secrets as "insurance" against their telling anyone else of the club's existence. A rival club springs up—Monkey Town—and soon there are so many secrets that it looks as if their teacher, Mr. Doyle, will have to take drastic measures. Sachar has created a bunch of kids and worries that are quite real; his witty, well-paced story shows off his impeccable ear for classroom banter.

> *A review of "Sixth Grade Secrets," in* Publishers Weekly, *Vol. 232, No. 9, August 28, 1987, p. 80.*

Laura's below-the-waist hair and her spirited personality have earned her a leadership role among classmates and the secret worship of Gabriel. She starts a secret club called "Pig City" and begins a covert chalkboard writing campaign featuring "pig" words. In an effort to win Laura's attention, Gabriel sends a note, which jealous Sheila intercepts and changes. When Laura reads the now insulting letter, the battle begins. Eventually a rival club, Monkey Town, is formed. Warfare begins with silly pranks but soon escalates into ugly and destructive acts, culminating when Sheila and a friend sabotage Laura and cut her hair. The sheared Laura sees how foolish they've been, and the truth of Gabriel's affection comes to light. Laura's instant maturity may be a bit too rapid, given her stubbornness and intense pride, but overall, characters

and their actions are realistic, uncomfortably so. The plot is predictable, and the writing style is just adequate, but the situations presented are on-target. The humor, frequent dialogue, and brief chapters make this suitable for reluctant readers.

> *Heide Piehler, in a review of "Sixth Grade Secrets," in* School Library Journal, *Vol. 34, No. 1, September, 1987, p. 182.*

Sachar has done an excellent job of plotting with twists and turns that will hold readers' attentions. However, there is a mean spiritedness among the rival factions that, while probably realistic, leaves an uncomfortable feeling, especially when it leads to physical confrontations— Laura, for instance, gets her waist-length hair cut off. This unpleasantness is partially negated by the story's sassy humor and the on-target happenings, in which kids will see their own lives reflected.

> *Ilene Cooper, in a review of "Sixth Grade Secrets," in* Booklist, *Vol. 84, No. 5, November 1, 1987, p. 484.*

Wayside School Is Falling Down (1989)

Thirty rib-tickling tales of Wayside School, where the classrooms are stacked one atop the other, dead rats live in the basement, and there's no 19th floor—usually.

It's a long haul from the playground to the 30th floor, past the principal's office (lair of Mr. Kidswatter), past the lunchroom, where Miss Mush makes her Mushroom Surprise, past Miss Zarves' class on the 19th floor that isn't there; but the children don't mind, for Mrs. Jewls—their favorite teacher—is waiting for them. Wayside School is never dull; if Mrs. Jewls isn't demonstrating gravity by dropping the new computer out the window or delivering words of wisdom ("It doesn't matter what you wear on the outside. It's what's underneath that counts. If you want to be great and important, you have to wear expensive underpants"), her students liven things up: among other startling events, Sharie brings in a hobo for show-and-tell; Calvin shows off his birthday tattoo; and the ghost of dreaded former teacher Mrs. Gorf animates Miss Mush's potato salad. Each short episode is prefaced with a simple, evocative line drawing [by Joel Schick]. Sachar has a gift for having fun without poking it too sharply, and beneath all the frivolity there very often lurks some idea or observation worth pondering.

A sure-to-please sequel to **Sideways Stories from Wayside School.** (pp. 127-28)

> *A review of "Wayside School Is Falling Down," in* Kirkus Reviews, *Vol. LVII, No. 2, January 15, 1989, pp. 127-28.*

Each of the 30 stories in this collection features an unusual vignette or character sketch. The stories are only loosely tied together, and many have a shaggy dog quality. While adult readers may be left quizzical, children who relish the ridiculous will enjoy themselves tremendously. With bad puns, extended jokes, and an irreverent attitude, Sachar keeps his readers amused.

Anne Connor, in a review of "Wayside School Is Falling Down," in School Library Journal, *Vol. 35, No. 9, May, 1989, p. 111.*

A sequel to Sachar's *Sideways Stories from Wayside School,* this offers 30 more episodes about the children whose classroom is on the thirtieth floor of the world's wackiest elementary school. As the popularity of the earlier book attests, Sachar's humor is right on target for middle-grade readers. Add an element of fantasy and a playfulness with literary conventions and readers will have a series of connected stories to happily devour. Few could resist reading the chapter entitled **"Mush,"** which begins with an expressive line drawing of school cook Miss Mush and the following advice: "Warning: Do not read this story right after eating. In fact, don't read it right before eating, either. In fact, just to be safe, don't read this story if you're ever planning to eat again." Another unforgettable incident is when Miss Jewls, the teacher, drops a computer out the window to demonstrate gravity. While adults may not be charmed by the baser elements of schoolyard humor that surface occasionally, children will recognize Sachar as a writer who knows their territory and entertains them well.

Carolyn Phelan, in a review of "Wayside School Is Falling Down," in Booklist, *Vol. 85, No. 17, May 1, 1989, p. 1553.*

Humorous is the best way to describe Louis Sachar's **Wayside School Is Falling Down.** This zany novel will be cheered by young readers who have read Sachar's earlier novel about Wayside School. It will also be enjoyed by those who haven't had that pleasure. The improbable humor is fresh and delightful and the chapters are just right for oral reading.

Lee Galda, in a review of "Wayside School Is Falling Down," in The Reading Teacher, *Vol. 43, No. 9, May, 1990, p. 671.*

The Boy Who Lost His Face (1989)

Ever since his best friend Scott dropped him to join a popular group, David feels certain he's been cursed. He follows along when the group harasses kind, old Mrs. Bayfield, but afterward he is overcome with guilt. And that's when the curse strikes: David insults his mother, cracks a window and embarrasses himself in class. It's bad enough that Scott's group excludes and taunts David, but the worst moment is when Tori, a girl he likes, sees his pants fall down. Two new friends help David to stand up to Scott's devious friends, rid himself of the curse and find the courage to ask Tori out. The story culminates with a hilarious rumble and a poignant realization. Sachar captures awkward junior high school experiences with humor and sensitivity. Readers will empathize with David's troubles and cheer his triumphs in this delightful, funny book.

A review of "The Boy Who Lost His Face," in Publishers Weekly, *Vol. 239, No. 2, July 14, 1989, p. 79.*

A wry, uneven story in which a junior-high-schooler has

his fling with the "in" crowd but ultimately finds more rewarding friends. . . .

Like **There's a Boy in the Girls' Bathroom,** this features plenty of wildly funny moments and deftly depicted social interaction; but once again Sachar keeps underestimating readers, halting the action to explain points he wants to make. Meanwhile, the final scenes, including a bibliotherapeutic epilogue set 150 years hence, are contrived and awkwardly handled.

A review of "The Boy Who Lost His Face," in Kirkus Reviews, *Vol. LVII, No. 19, October 1, 1989, p. 1480.*

While Sachar's plot tantalizingly suggests that David really is cursed, the story's resolution grounds everything firmly in reality, to the point of psychological analysis that suggests David's embarrassing moments were subconsciously self-inflicted out of guilt for his actions. This seems a labored way to justify plot contrivances; moreover, a tacked-on finish that reveals David went on to international fame doesn't fit. The story's strength is the truth of its characterization of David as a passive boy who finally realizes the importance of standing up for himself. Some insulting language appears in scenes of confrontation, but it's entirely in keeping with the characters at hand.

Denise Wilms, in a review of "The Boy Who Lost His Face," in Booklist, *Vol. 86, No. 6, November 15, 1989, p. 675.*

Sideways Arithmetic from Wayside School (1989)

Devotees of Sachar's other Wayside School titles will delight in the new math that Sue must learn when she transfers to Wayside, where "elf + elf = fool" and "dog $\times$ ad = agog." Dreaded story problems take on a new meaning: "How many meals will Miss Mush, the lunch teacher, have to cook for the food to taste as bad as it smells?" Logic and laughter combine as Sachar schools the reader in wacky Wayside brainteasers.

A review of "Sideways Arithmetic from Wayside School," in Booklist, *Vol. 86, No. 8, December 15, 1989, p. 840.*

Dogs Don't Tell Jokes (1991)

Gary "Goon" Boone tells jokes instead of having conversations; almost everyone—parents, teachers, schoolmates—is tired of him. When a talent show with a $100 prize is announced at school, Gary decides to make his stand-up debut memorable. His parents promise him another $100 if he stops telling jokes for three weeks. For Gary this is a minor struggle; he tries to understand why other boys his age collect baseball cards, and he gains gradual acceptance in their friendly football games. Their practical joke on Gary does help launch his career as a comedian, but it is his hard work and practice that lead to his overwhelming success at the show.

Readers themselves may feel benumbed by the endless litany of bad jokes; even Sachar's talent for creating humorous situations (***There's a Boy in the Girls' Bathroom,*** 1987; ***Sideways Stories from Wayside School,*** 1985—which gets a plug in this book) can't shine through the too-familiar riddles. Still, Gary is a likable, completely good-hearted boy who turns out to be refreshingly frank about his own shortcomings. (pp. 934-35)

> *A review of "Dogs Don't Tell Jokes," in* Kirkus Reviews, *Vol. LIX, No. 14, July 15, 1991, pp. 934-35.*

Seventh-grader Gary Boone, popularly (or, rather, unpopularly) known as Goon, is a jokester. "Gary never cried," Sachar explains rather baldly. "He laughed. The more it hurt, the more he laughed." Goon's angst-ridden preparation for a stand-up comic routine in the school talent show becomes an identity crisis in which he must sort out his real gift from a habit of comically camouflaging his feelings. This aspect of the book is well developed, but the non-stop jokes become wearing, and the actual appearance of one of Gary's fictitious characters, Mrs. Snitzberry, seems too abrupt a break from realism to fantasy—or, if it's a symptom of nervous breakdown, unconvincing. The balance between action and character dynamics in ***There's***

a Boy in the Girls' Bathroom is missing here, but the tension between humor and poignancy is delicately maintained. Readers who enjoyed *Class Clown* by Johanna Hurwitz will find a more complex, if sometimes frustrating, treatment of the same prototype here.

> *Betsy Hearne, in a review of "Dogs Don't Tell Jokes," in* Bulletin of the Center for Children's Books, *Vol. 45, No. 2, October, 1991, p. 47.*

This story would make a wonderful read-aloud as the chapters are short (3-5 pages), and the talent show monologue is certain to be a favorite of readers. As in the case of Sachar's previous works, especially ***There's a Boy in the Girl's Bathroom,*** this book deals with the emotions, thoughts, and feelings of adolescents who find themselves labeled as different by their peers. ***Dogs Don't Tell Jokes*** entertains while it explores the dangerous terrain of middle school/junior high relationships and friendships.

> *Teri S. Lesesne, in a review of "Dogs Don't Tell Jokes," in* The ALAN Review, *Vol. 19, No. 2, Winter, 1992, p. 21.*

CUMULATIVE INDEX TO AUTHORS

This index lists all author entries in *Children's Literature Review* and includes cross-references to them in other Gale sources. References in the index are identified as follows:

AAYA: *Authors & Artists for Young Adults* Volumes 1-8
CA: *Contemporary Authors* (original series), Volumes 1-136
CAAS: *Contemporary Authors Autobiography Series,* Volumes 1-15
CABS: *Contemporary Authors Bibliographical Series,* Volumes 1-3
CANR: *Contemporary Authors New Revision Series,* Volumes 1-37
CAP: *Contemporary Authors Permanent Series,* Volumes 1-2
CA-R: *Contemporary Authors* (first revision), Volumes 1-44
CDALB: *Concise Dictionary of American Literary Biography,* Volumes 1-6
CLC: *Contemporary Literary Criticism,* Volumes 1-70
CLR: *Children's Literature Review,* Volumes 1-28
CMLC: *Classical and Medieval Literature Criticism,* Volumes 1-8
DC: *Drama Criticism,* Volumes 1-2
DLB: *Dictionary of Literary Biography,* Volumes 1-114
DLB-DS: *Dictionary of Literary Biography Documentary Series,* Volumes 1-9
DLB-Y: *Dictionary of Literary Biography Yearbook,* Volumes 1980-1990
LC: *Literature Criticism from 1400 to 1800,* Volumes 1-19
NCLC: *Nineteenth-Century Literature Criticism,* Volumes 1-34
PC: *Poetry Criticism,* Volumes 1-4
SAAS: *Something about the Author Autobiography Series,* Volumes 1-14
SATA: *Something about the Author,* Volumes 1-68
SSC: *Short Story Criticism,* Volumes 1-9
TCLC: *Twentieth-Century Literary Criticism,* Volumes 1-44
YABC: *Yesterday's Authors of Books for Children,* Volumes 1-2

Author Index

CUMULATIVE INDEX TO NATIONALITIES

Nationality Index

CUMULATIVE INDEX TO TITLES

Title Index

Title Index

Title Index

Title Index

Title Index

Title Index

Title Index

Title Index

ISBN 0-8103-5701-1

90000